MPI Studies on Intellectual Property and Competition Law

Volume 31

Edited by

Josef Drexl

Reto M. Hilty

Joseph Straus

Heiko Richter
Editor

Competition and Intellectual Property Law in Ukraine

Springer

Editor
Heiko Richter
Max-Planck Institute for Innovation
and Competition
Munich, Germany

ISSN 2191-5822 ISSN 2191-5830 (electronic)
MPI Studies on Intellectual Property and Competition Law
ISBN 978-3-662-66100-0 ISBN 978-3-662-66101-7 (eBook)
https://doi.org/10.1007/978-3-662-66101-7

This Springer imprint is published by the registered company Springer-Verlag GmbH, DE, part of Springer Nature.
The registered company address is: Heidelberger Platz 3, 14197 Berlin, Germany

Acknowledgements

This book would not exist without the support of colleagues and friends to whom I am sincerely indebted: Moritz M. Sutterer for inspiration and continuous encouragement for this endeavor; Sophia Sorg for her devoted and skillful commitment that made this project possible and always kept it going; Daria Kim for her invaluable expertise and cordial support throughout the project; Claudia Dalmau Gomez for numerous hours of diligent editing and effective correspondence; Allison Felmy and Charles Heard with his team for their meticulous language review; Reto M. Hilty for supporting the enterprise with his trust and his approval of funding; Liubov Maidanyk, Nataliia Mazaraki, and Yuriy Kapitsa for their heartfelt offer of support and knowledge, which eventually enabled the finalization of this book.

When we discussed our draft chapters in autumn 2021 in Kyiv, no one could foresee how drastically the world would change in the winter. From one day to the next, the authors found themselves in a stage of existence beyond our imagination. The Russian invasion of Ukraine on February 24, 2022 completely changed our realities and beliefs. This volume came about in a time when all the authors had accomplished in their lives was at stake. Words cannot express my personal admiration and my gratitude for every author's dedication, persistence, and faith in completing this work under such arduous circumstances. I am convinced that Ukraine's journey, while certainly challenging, will ultimately be successful. Also, I sincerely hope that this volume is not the end of a project, but that it will ignite prosperous cooperation and exchange in future, not least among the next generation of scholars.

Munich, Germany
Summer 2022

Heiko Richter

Contents

List of Authors

Oles Andriychuk (Олесь Андрійчук) Ph.D. in Law; Professor, Newcastle University Law School, UK; Visiting Senior Researcher, Vytautas Magnus University, Kaunas, Lithuania; Director of Digital Markets Research Hub. e-mail: oles.andriychuk@newcastle.ac.uk

Olga Bakalinska (Ольга Бакалінська) Doctor of Legal Sciences, Ph.D. in Law; Professor at The Academician F. H. Burchak Scientific-Research Institute of Private Law and Entrepreneurship of the National Academy of Legal Sciences of Ukraine, Kyiv, Ukraine; Member of the Scientific and Expert Council of the Antimonopoly Committee of Ukraine. e-mail: bakalinskaya@ukr.net

Anzhelika Gerasymenko (Анжеліка Герасименко) Doctor of Economic Sciences; Ph.D. in Economics; Professor and Head of the Economic Theory and Competition Policy Department of the State University of Trade and Economics, Kyiv, Ukraine. e-mail: a.gerasymenko@knute.edu.ua

Olga Gurgula (Ольга Гургула) Ph.D. in Law (London); Senior Lecturer in Intellectual Property Law at Brunel Law School, Brunel University London, UK. e-mail: Olga.Gurgula@brunel.ac.uk

Yuriy Kapitsa (Юрій Капіца) Doctor of Legal Sciences; Ph.D. in Law; Director of the Centre for Intellectual Property Studies and Technology Transfer of the National Academy of Sciences of Ukraine, Kyiv, Ukraine. e-mail: kapitsa@nas.gov.ua

Oksana Kashyntseva (Оксана Кашинцева) Ph.D. in Law; Head of the Department of Intellectual Property Rights and Human Rights in Healthcare of the Intellectual Property Scientific Research Institute of the National Academy of Legal Sciences of Ukraine, Kyiv, Ukraine; Associate Professor at the Intellectual Property and Information Law Department of the Educational and Scientific Institute of Law at Taras Shevchenko National University of Kyiv, Ukraine. e-mail: kashyntseva@ukr.net

Tetyana Komarova (Тетяна Комарова) Doctor of Legal Sciences; Ph.D. in Law; Professor of the Department of European Union Law at the Yaroslav Mudryi National Law University, Kharkiv, Ukraine. e-mail: t.v.komarova@nlu.edu.ua

Olha Kronda (Ольга Кронда) Ph.D. in Law; Associate Professor at the Intellectual Property and Information Law Department of the Educational and Scientific Institute of Law at Taras Shevchenko National University of Kyiv, Ukraine. e-mail: OlgaKronda@knu.ua

Anastasiia Kyrylenko (Анастасія Кириленко) Researcher at the Global Innovation Law and Policy, University of Alicante, Spain. e-mail: anastasiia.kyrylenko@ua.es

Liubov Maidanyk (Любов Майданик) Ph.D. in Law; Associate Professor at the Intellectual Property and Information Law Department of the Educational and Scientific Institute of Law at Taras Shevchenko National University of Kyiv, Ukraine. e-mail: Liubov_maidanyk@knu.ua

Nataliia Mazaraki (Наталія Мазаракі) Doctor of Legal Sciences; Ph.D. in Law; Professor and Head of the International, Civil and Commercial Law Department of the State University of Trade and Economics, Kyiv, Ukraine. e-mail: n.mazaraki@knute.edu.ua

Kateryna Militsyna (Катерина Міліцина) Ph.D. Student in International Law at the Private International Law Department of the Educational and Scientific Institute of International Relations at Taras Shevchenko National University of Kyiv, Ukraine. e-mail: mpp.militsyna@clouds.iir.edu.ua

Zvenyslava Opeida (Звенислава Опейда) Doctor of Legal Sciences; SJD in Law; LL.M. (Illinois); Associate Professor of International Trade Law at the National University of Kyiv-Mohyla Academy, Kyiv, Ukraine. e-mail: z.opeida@ukma.edu.ua

Olena Orliuk (Олена Орлюк) Professor; Doctor of Legal Sciences; Ph.D. in Law; Director of the State Organisation "Ukrainian National Office for Intellectual Property and Innovations", Kyiv, Ukraine. e-mail: olena.orliuk@knu.ua

Roman Petrov (Роман Петров) Doctor of Legal Sciences; Ph.D. in Law (London); LL.M. (Durham); Professor and Head of the International and European Law Department at the National University of Kyiv-Mohyla Academy, Kyiv, Ukraine. e-mail: roman.petrov@ukma.edu.ua

Oleg Podtserkovnyi (Олег Подцерковний) Doctor of Legal Sciences; Ph.D. in Law; Professor and Head of the Economic Law and Procedure Department at the National University 'Odesa Law Academy', Odesa, Ukraine; Corresponding

Member of the National Academy of Legal Sciences of Ukraine. e-mail: opp@ukr.net

Heiko Richter (Хайко Ріхтер) Ph.D. in Law; LL.M. (Columbia); Senior Research Fellow at the Max Planck Institute for Innovation and Competition, Munich, Germany. e-mail: Heiko.Richter@ip.mpg.de

Anna Shtefan (Анна Штефан) Doctor of Legal Sciences; Ph.D. in Law; Associate Professor and the Head of the Copyright and Related Rights Department of the Intellectual Property Scientific Research Institute of the National Academy of Legal Sciences of Ukraine, Kyiv, Ukraine. e-mail: anna_shtefan@ukr.net

Kseniia Smyrnova (Ксенія Смирнова) Doctor of Legal Sciences; Ph.D. in Law; Professor of the Comparative and European Law Department of the Taras Shevchenko National University of Kyiv, Ukraine; Vice-Rector for International Cooperation of the Taras Shevchenko National University of Kyiv, Ukraine. e-mail: kseniia.smyrnova@knu.ua

Hanna Stakheyeva (Ганна Стахєєва) Ph.D. in Law; Assistant Professor at the Bogazici University, Department of International Trade, Istanbul, Turkey. e-mail: hanna.stakheyeva@boun.edu.tr

Leonid Tarasenko (Леонід Тарасенко) Ph.D. in Law; Associate Professor at the Intellectual Property, Information and Corporate Law Department of the Ivan Franko National University of Lviv, Ukraine. e-mail: leonid.tarasenko@lnu.edu.ua

Kostiantyn Zerov (Костянтин Зеров) Ph.D. in Law; Assistant Professor at the Intellectual Property and Information Law Department of the Educational and Scientific Institute of Law at Taras Shevchenko National University of Kyiv, Ukraine; Senior Research Fellow at the Intellectual Property Scientific Research Institute of the National Academy of Legal Sciences of Ukraine, Kyiv, Ukraine. e-mail: zerov@knu.ua

Competition and Intellectual Property Law in Ukraine: Navigating the Landscape

Heiko Richter

Contents

Abstract This introduction to the volume "Competition and Intellectual Property Law in Ukraine" outlines the goal of the book while providing further factual background. It invites the reader into Ukraine's legal landscape by briefly outlining the country's governance and politics. The chapter then offers seven possible "tours" that may guide through the book and help the reader to grasp competition and intellectual property law in Ukraine from different perspectives, namely by legal areas, EU approximation, Ukrainian features of laws, Ukrainian institutions, special interests, methodology and interdisciplinarity, and public policy. The chapter concludes with future considerations.

H. Richter (✉)
Max Planck Institute for Innovation and Competition, Munich, Germany
e-mail: Heiko.Richter@ip.mpg.de

H. Richter (ed.), *Competition and Intellectual Property Law in Ukraine*,
MPI Studies on Intellectual Property and Competition Law 31,
https://doi.org/10.1007/978-3-662-66101-7_1

1 Background and Goal

This volume provides the most comprehensive contemporary academic writing on Ukrainian competition and intellectual property (IP) law in English. It is the result of a two-year process of conceptualization, drafting, and editing—accompanied by an online workshop, an in-person workshop in Kyiv, and numerous discussions. The publication is addressed to a wide range of international scholars, practitioners, and policy makers. It aims to make the state-of-the-art in Ukrainian legal scholarship visible and accessible to the international research community and to stimulate global debates in academia and politics. The publication's substance may be of interest and use to anyone who is interested in IP and competition law, and/or in Ukraine.

Yet—as Sec. 3 of this introduction will reveal—the following few hundred pages reach far beyond this subject matter. Rather than being a mere collection of unrelated pieces, this book follows an overarching composition. It covers a broad range of different topics, and the chapters share a forward-looking perspective and minimize thematic overlaps. Also, the chapters cross-refer to each other where suitable to effectively navigate the reader through the book. Often, the chapters start by outlining the basic background that is necessary to understand the context of the issue discussed, especially with regards to the legal system of Ukraine. This allows especially those readers who are not yet familiar with Ukrainian law or Ukraine to better grasp the context and relevance of the discussed issues. Also, references to basic literature allow the reader to delve into further sources if needed, so that a chapter can be used as a "gateway" to the topics discussed.

This introduction serves as a starting point for different readers by providing guidance through the book. It starts by presenting the very basics on governance and politics of Ukraine (Sec. 2). It then provides the reader with possible tours they may take through the book, according to interest and perspective (Sec. 3), before concluding with an outlook for the future (Sec. 4).

2 Governance and Politics of Ukraine in a Nutshell

2.1 Basic Information

A brief overview on the governance and politics of Ukraine can serve as a starting point, while the following 22 chapters will further elaborate on several aspects. On 24 August 1991, Ukraine gained independence from the Soviet Union. The current Constitution of Ukraine was adopted on 28 June 1996. Ukraine is divided into

24 regions (oblasts),[1] two municipalities with oblast status,[2] and the Autonomous Republic of Crimea. Ukraine's capital Kyiv is the country's largest city, followed by Kharkiv and Odesa. The area of Ukraine totals 603,550 km^2, making it the second largest country in Europe. In 2021, Ukraine had a population of around 44 million.[3]

Ukraine joined the World Intellectual Property Organization in 1970 as "Ukrainian Soviet Socialist Republic", has been a member of the Council of Europe since 1995 and became a member of the World Trade Organization in 2008. The EU–Ukraine Association Agreement (AA) started to be initialized on 30 March 2012 and was fully signed on 27 June 2014. The provisions formally came into force on 1 September 2017.[4] On 7 February 2019, the Constitution of Ukraine was amended to state the country's strategic objectives to join the EU and NATO. After Ukraine was invaded by Russia on 24 February 2022, Ukraine applied for membership of the EU on 28 February 2022. On 23 June 2022, the European Council granted Ukraine the status of a candidate for accession to the EU.

2.2 *Executive, Legislative, and Judicial Branch*

As for the political system, Ukraine can be classified as "semi-presidential", meaning that the president as the head of state exists alongside a prime minister and a cabinet. The president is directly elected by absolute majority popular vote. According to the Constitution, the president is allowed to serve a maximum of two five-year terms. The president proposes the Prime Minister of Ukraine to the Parliament of Ukraine (Verkhovna Rada). The Cabinet of Ministers is nominated by the prime minister and approved by Verkhovna Rada, except for the Minister of Defense and the Minister of Foreign Affairs, which are proposed by the president. The president has the power to dismiss the prime minister and the cabinet. To date, Ukraine has had seven presidents: Leonid Kravchuk, the first president, from 1991 to 1994; Leonid Kuchma, who took office following Kravchuk's resignation and was president for two terms from 1994 to 2005; Viktor Yushchenko, from 2005 to 2010, who took office following the "Orange Revolution" (see below); Viktor Yanukovych, from 2010 to 2014, who fled the country and was removed from office in February 2014 following the Maidan Revolution (see below); Petro Poroshenko, from June 2014 to 2019, who was elected in June 2014 after Oleksandr Turchynov had temporarily assumed office as acting president in February 2014; and Volodymyr Zelenskyy, who was elected in May 2019 and currently holds the office.

---

[1] Cherkasy, Chernihiv, Chernivtsi, Dnipropetrovsk, Donetsk, Ivano-Frankivsk, Kharkiv, Kherson, Khmelnytskyi, Kyiv, Kirovohrad, Luhansk, Lviv, Mykolaiv, Odesa, Poltava, Ryvne, Sumy, Ternopil, Vinnytsia, Volyn, Zakarpattia, Zaporizhia, and Zhytomyr; each divided into districts (raions).

[2] Kyiv and Sevastopol.

[3] Comparing to 52 million in 1991, see 'Data Bank – World Development Indicators' *The World Bank* https://databank.worldbank.org/source/world-development-indicators accessed 27 July 2022.

[4] Provisional application of Titles III, V, VI, and VII to the extent it is EU competence, of 1 November 2014, and provisional application of Title IV, to the extent it is EU competence, of 1 January 2016.

Ukraine's legislative power is vested in its unicameral Parliament—the Verkhovna Rada. In total, it consists of 450 seats. One half of these (225 members) are directly elected in single-seat constituencies by simple majority vote; the other half are directly elected in a single nationwide constituency by closed, party-list proportional representation vote.

The established system of law in Ukraine is civil law. As for the judicial branch, the Supreme Court is the highest judicial body of Ukraine with general jurisdiction. It consists of approximately 100 judges, and it is organized into the Grand Chamber of the Supreme Court, the Administrative Court of Cassation, the Commercial Court of Cassation, the Criminal Court of Cassation, and the Civil Court of Cassation. The Constitutional Court is composed of 18 judges, which are appointed in equal shares by the president, Verkhovna Rada, and the Congress of Judges. They are appointed for non-renewable terms of nine years.

2.3 Major Political Events

Ukraine has had a turbulent recent political past and present. Being aware of that is important in order to understand its legal developments, not least in the areas of competition and IP law. Three significant events are to be mentioned in this regard: the "Orange Revolution' in 2004–2005, the "Maidan Revolution" in 2014, and the Russian invasion of Ukraine in 2022.

The peaceful "Orange Revolution" was triggered by the presidential runoff elections in Ukraine on 21 November 2004, which were overshadowed by allegations of election manipulation and fraud. Although forecasts and exit polls had predicted a victory for Viktor Yushchenko, Viktor Yanukovych officially won the election. Subsequently, hundreds of thousands of people in Ukraine took to the streets to demand fair elections and more democracy, wearing orange, the color of Viktor Yushchenko's election campaign. The protesters camped out on Kyiv's central Independence Square, "Maidan Nezalezhnosti", for several weeks. Finally, the Supreme Court of Ukraine declared the election invalid and ordered a repeat of the runoff election for 26 December 2004. Under the close watch of international election observers, Viktor Yushchenko won the election with 52%.

The 2014 movement known as the "Maidan Revolution" or "Euromaidan" had its roots in late November 2013, when then-prime minister Mykola Azarov surprisingly announced the intention of the Ukrainian government not to sign an association agreement with the EU, but instead to choose closer ties to Russia and the Eurasian Economic Union, which was in the process of formation back then. Ukrainians took to the streets in peaceful mass protest, especially on Kyiv's Independence Square. In December 2013, the government began dispersing demonstrators with violence. Eventually, the protests resulted in more than 100 deaths, occurring mostly between 18 and 20 February 2014. The revolution led to the dismissal of President Yanukovich on 22 February 2014 by impeachment vote of Verkhovna Rada on the grounds that he was unable to fulfill his duties.[5] Subsequently, Petro Poroshenko was elected on 25 May 2014 as the new president, who eventually signed the EU–Ukraine Association Agreement. The Maidan Revolution also led to Russian violation of Ukraine's territorial integrity. In March 2014, Russia occupied and annexed Crimea. Only a few countries and international organizations recognize the legality or legitimacy of this move.[6] 2014 also witnessed the beginning of war in Donbas: Between 2014 and 2022, Ukrainian forces fought Russian-backed separatists for control over the two regions of Donetsk and Luhansk. Between September 2014 and February 2015, Russia, Ukraine, France, and Germany signed the "Minsk I" and "Minsk II" Protocols, which sought to end the war in Donbas. But these agreements were never fully implemented, due to different interpretations of its provisions, and while the forward movement of the separatists was stopped, the fighting transformed into a trench war.

On 24 February 2022, Russia began a full-scale invasion, attacking Ukraine on several fronts. On the same day, Ukraine's president declared martial law. On 13 April 2022, the Law "On the Protection of Rights of Intellectual Property Subjects during Martial Law in Connection with Military Aggression of the Russian Federation Against Ukraine"[7] entered into force. Amongst other, it provides for the suspension of deadlines and extensions of protection terms for the duration of the martial law period. Already on 2 March 2022, the UN General Assembly adopted a resolution demanding that Russia immediately end its military operations in Ukraine. 141 of the 193 member states voted for the resolution, 35 abstained, and five[8] voted against. As of July 2022, more than 5.5 million refugees from Ukraine were recorded across Europe.[9] At the time of finalization of this volume, the war is still ongoing.

3 Navigating the Competition and IP Law Landscape—Seven Tours

3.1 Overview

Different readers have distinct expectations and tastes. As the title of this volume suggests, it deals with competition and IP law in Ukraine, and this naturally sets the common denominator of interest. However, the pages that follow contain a much

---

[5] Decree on self-removal of the President of Ukraine from the exercise of constitutional powers and appointment of extraordinary elections of the President of Ukraine, Verkhovna Rada of Ukraine https://zakon.rada.gov.ua/laws/show/757-18#Text accessed 27 July 2022.

[6] Afghanistan, Armenia, Belarus, Bolivia, Burundi, Cambodia, Cuba, Laos, Myanmar, Nicaragua, North Korea, Sudan, Syria, Venezuela, and Zimbabwe.

[7] Ukrainian Law on the Protection of Rights of Intellectual Property Subjects during Martial Law in Connection with Military Aggression of the Russian Federation Against Ukraine 2022, 2174-IX.

[8] Belarus, Eritrea, North Korea, Russia, and Syria.

[9] 'Operational Data Portal – Ukrainian Refugee Situation' UN Refugee Agency (26 July 2022) https://data.unhcr.org/en/situations/ukraine accessed 27 July 2022.

richer variety of topics, so that it may be worthwhile to provide detailed signposts at the front gate. Like a travel guide, this section highlights some possible "tours" that the reader may take according to individual preference.

The intuitive and classic order is by legal areas (Sec. 3.2). Yet, EU approximation crosscuts several topics (Sec. 3.3) as well as the Ukrainian features of policies and laws (Sec. 3.4), and the view on the Ukrainian institutions in particular (Sec. 3.5). Some readers might follow special interests, such as life sciences or the digital economy (Sec. 3.6), and a particular methodology and interdisciplinarity may appeal to other readers (Sec. 3.7). Finally, the public policy dimension is omnipresent and provides another, certainly important theme for a tour through this volume (Sec. 3.8).

3.2 *The Classic Tour: Legal Areas*

Legal areas classically provide the primary orientation for legal scholars, and they set up the general structure of the volume accordingly. Part II deals with competition law, subdivided into antitrust law on the one hand (see the chapters of Kseniia Smyrnova—who also includes state aid, Hanna Stakheyeva, Anzhelika Gerasymenko and Nataliia Mazaraki, Oles Andriychuk, and Olga Gurgula) and the law of unfair competition on the other hand (see the chapters of Olga Bakalinska and Olha Kronda).

Part III deals with IP policies and law, and it contains: three general chapters dealing with EU approximation (Yuriy Kapitsa), IP strategy (Olena Orliuk) and the IP court system (Anna Shtefan and Olga Gurgula); five chapters on industrial property, including patents, utility models, designs, and geographical indications (Leonid Tarasenko, Oksana Kashyntseva, Tetyana Komarova, and Anastasiia Kyrylenko); four chapters on copyright and related rights, including collecting societies (Anna Shtefan, Kostiantyn Zerov, Kateryna Militsyna, and Liubov Maidanyk). As for subareas of—arguably—IP, there are some hidden trails that are not obvious from the chapters' titles, but that are worth mentioning: commercial/trade secrets are addressed by Olga Bakalinska as well as Olha Kronda, who also elaborates on trademarks in the context of unfair competition.

To commence, Part I draws the bigger picture by putting the legal framework of Ukrainian competition and IP law into perspective. For this purpose, it elaborates on laws and policies beyond competition and IP and addresses the general interplay between international and domestic order of economic law in particular. Translated into legal areas, Roman Petrov's introduction into the EU–Ukraine Association Agreement deals with international law, but also with Ukrainian constitutional law. Zvenyslava Opeida inquires into the general significance and domestic application of international trade law (law of the WTO). Oleg Podtserkovnyi sheds light on Ukrainian economic policies and laws, which crosscut a wide array of public and private laws.

3.3 The Tour d'Europe: EU Approximation

The impact of EU law on Ukrainian competition and IP law should not be underestimated. After it was finally signed, the EU–Ukraine AA of 2014 set the track: it has made approximation to EU rules an international obligation for the Ukrainian legislature. It does not come as a surprise that a great deal of legislative reforms of the last years revolve around the issue of "EU approximation". Roman Petrov's chapter outlines the genesis, essence, and domestic reception of the AA. Moreover, Kseniia Smyrnova delves into the "Europeanization" of modern Ukrainian competition law, while Yuriy Kapitsa inquires into the significance of the AA and associated problems that arise for approximating IP legislation of Ukraine with the EU *acquis*. In the same vein, Anastasiia Kyrylenko not only inquires into design law in substance, but takes the recent Ukrainian design law reform as an occasion to discuss the much more general question of the fruits and perils of EU Trade Agreements.[10]

Almost every chapter in Parts II and III discusses the approximation of concrete legal regimes of the EU *acquis* in Ukrainian legislation or takes at least a side glance at EU rules, be it on competition, patent, or copyright law. The fact that so many individual authors consider this topic needful of discussion suggests how authoritative EU law has become for Ukraine in recent years and how challenging it is to make it work. Kateryna Militsyna ventures even further, discussing the legislative proposal for *sui generis* protection on AI-generated output, a vigorously debated issue in WIPO and across jurisdictions but without any laws enacted elsewhere so far.

Some authors cross the boundaries of legal areas, a prime example being Olga Gurgula, whose chapter on pharmaceuticals in Ukraine offers inspiration to generally improve competition law enforcement in the field of IP. Also, Olha Kronda elaborates on the interface of IP and unfair competition.

3.4 The Ukrainian Tour: An Emphasis on Ukraine's Policies and History

While certainly EU approximation is a *leitmotiv* and EU law sometimes appears inseparable from Ukrainian law, the chapters are much wider in scope. As this volume is about Ukrainian law, naturally every chapter deals with Ukraine. Yet, some chapters provide more systematic information on the embeddedness of rules and policies in the Ukrainian system. A good example is Olena Orliuk's chapter, which discusses how IP strategy is conceptualized and made workable, including the institutional processes and the interplay between international and domestic policy making and academic expertise in Ukraine. Yuriy Kapitsa describes the actual law-making process in Ukraine throughout different periods, and Leonid Tarasenko's

[10] For further reading, see Josef Drexl et al., *EU Bilateral Trade Agreements and Intellectual Property: For Better or Worse?* (Springer 2016).

chapter on patent law also travels through time, starting with the 1990s, and outlines crucial developments and reforms in Ukraine during the last three decades. Moreover, Olga Bakalinska reaches back into the 1990s to explain the current developments of the regulation of unfair competition in Ukraine.

The Soviet heritage of Ukraine has considerably influenced its legal system. This becomes clear when looking at the chapter by Olga Bakalinska, who describes the evolvement of competition theory in Soviet times, and it also becomes clear when reading Oleg Podtserkovniy's chapter, which discusses the broader lines of economic policy and the according legal and social transformation: from the Soviet planning economy and the economic transformation periods after Ukraine gained independence. Anastasiia Kyrylenko travels even further back into Soviet history to determine why so few geographical indications are registered in Ukraine and delivers a powerful legal and socio-economic explanation.

3.5 The Institutional Tour: Enforcing the Law

Lawyers seek to comprehend a system not only by familiarizing themselves with the substantive law, but also by getting acquainted with enforcement and the relevant institutions—namely, courts and authorities. As their central object of examination, Anna Shtefan and Olga Gurgula discuss the creation of the new IP Court in Ukraine while also outlining the substantial judicative reforms necessary to its establishment and discussing the Ukrainian court system and the relationship between the new IP Court and the civil courts.

With regards to relevant authorities, Olena Orliuk's and Leonid Tarasenko's chapters comprehensively outline the relevant public bodies and the recent establishment of the National Intellectual Property Authority. As for the enforcement of competition law, the Anti-Monopoly Commission of Ukraine (AMCU) is in charge. Kseniia Smyrnova discusses its role regarding general aspects of competition law enforcement in Ukraine, including mergers and vertical exemptions, but also the relevance of issuing decisions and giving guidance to affected stakeholders. Olga Gurgula specifically discusses enforcement by AMCU in the field of competition law and IP, and Hanna Stakheyeva does the same with respect to vertical restraints. Complementarily, Olga Bakalinska elaborates on the AMCU's role on the enforcement of unfair competition, while Olha Kronda delves into the specific differences between administrative enforcement, through the AMCU, and judicial enforcement, through administrative and civil courts, in Ukraine.

The picture becomes more complete when reading the contribution by Liubov Maidanyk, who looks beyond state actors in her chapter on collective management organizations. She embeds them into the wider institutional questions of private negotiations, state oversight, and dispute settlement mechanisms.

3.6 The Special Interest Tour: Life Sciences, Digital Markets, and Beyond

Many readers with special or sectoral interests may also find something of interest in this volume. While Oleg Podtserkovnyi touches on security issues, there is an emphasis on life sciences. Here, Olga Gurgula and Oksana Kashyntseva focus on the pharmaceutical sector, the first from a competition law perspective, the latter with particular view on IP and TRIPS. Also in this category, Tetyana Komarova comprehensively discusses the regulation of biotechnological inventions in Ukraine.

Another focus lies on the digital economy and e-commerce. From a competition law point of view, these sectors are the subject of inquiry of Anzhelika Gerasymenko's and Nataliia Mazaraki's joined chapter, which also provides insights on the status quo of Ukrainian digital platform markets. Oles Andriychuk discusses the relevance of digital gatekeeper regulation for Ukraine, and Hanna Stakheyeva discusses the relevance of vertical restraints for e-commerce. On the side of IP, Kostiantyn Zerov discusses the reform of Ukrainian copyright in the context of the internet.

3.7 The Methodological Tour: Between Legal Doctrine, Economics, and Sociology

For readers who are interested in methodology, the chapters certainly contain a fair amount of legal doctrine. The chapters of Olga Bakalinska, Olha Kronda, and Leonid Tarasenko provide some enlightening examples for readers who would like to know about Ukrainian doctrine and case analysis.

Yuriy Kapitsa develops a methodology of approximation of IP legislation in Ukraine and more generally for associated and PCA countries to that in the EU. In doing so, he develops a theory of general relevance which can be applied to different jurisdictions.

Competition law and IP deal with property and competition—conceptual pillars of a market economy. It does not come as a surprise that several chapters combine economic reasoning with the law, or even apply economic theory. Resale price maintenance is a topic that Hanna Stakheyeva discusses with a particular view of its underlying economic reasoning. The chapter on the platform economy and challenges for modern competition law is co-authored by an economist (Anzhelika Gerasymenko) and a lawyer (Nataliia Mazaraki) and, accordingly, provides a comprehensive theoretical economic background of the legal conclusions derived. They also provide empirical evidence and market information, as does Olga Gurgula in her chapter on pharmaceutical markets. More philosophically, Oles Andriychuk looks at different economic paradigms and inquires into the "legacy of the USSR-style planned economy and the remedy of reductionist non-interventionism of the Chicago School".

Moreover, Anastasiia Kyrylenko combines the legal, political, and socio-economic perspectives to generate new valuable insights in her chapter on geographical indications.

3.8 The Policy Tour: On Policy and Possible Reforms

Finally, this book not only addresses academics and practitioners. It should also appeal to policy makers, who can gain general insights and find suggestions for reform in many chapters—sometimes rather specific, sometimes far-reaching. The book has been deliberately conceptualized in a forward-looking manner, meaning that implications for future law-making and application can be drawn from the past and the present and are spelled out where possible.

A prime example is Olena Orliuk's chapter on the Ukrainian IP Strategy, which is forward-looking by definition. Also, Leonid Tarasenko's chapter takes a policy perspective when outlining the conditions of the patent reform of 2020. Oleg Podtserkovniy's chapter can be generally classified as elaborating on economic policies and the state's role, as he discusses ways and directions of legal stimulation of investments, including innovations and competition protection in the state economic policy of Ukraine. Other chapters propose reforms and therefore legislative "works in progress", such as Anna Shtefan's and Kateryna Militsyna's chapters in the area of copyright. Moreover, Zvenyslava Opeida makes very concrete reform suggestions when proposing "to introduce competition considerations into the trade defense policy of Ukraine by strengthening one of the elements of trade remedy investigations, namely the public interest requirement".

4 Outlook

This book presents the essence of three decades of the development of Ukraine's legal order in the areas of competition and IP law, policies, and scholarship. Especially over the last few years, these areas have been in considerable flux, a main driver being the EU–Ukraine AA. Ukrainian legal scholarship has played a significant role in preparing many recent reforms and will certainly play a vital part in the years to come. While the circumstances that have led to granting Ukraine the status of a candidate for accession to the EU are dreadful, the candidate status provides the country with a unique chance to lay down tracks for future individual professional exchange on the micro level, institutional cooperation on the meso level, and an advancement of the Ukrainian legal order on a macro level. Much can be found in this volume that prepares the ground, and for this very reason, the authors and the editor anticipate the reader's reception of this volume's rich content with curiosity and confidence.

References

'Data Bank—World Development Indicators' *The World Bank* (26 July 2022) https://databank.worldbank.org/source/world-development-indicators

Josef Drexl, Henning Grosse Ruse-Khan and Souheir Nadde-Phlix, *EU Bilateral Trade Agreements and Intellectual Property: For Better or Worse?* (Springer 2016)

'Operational Data Portal—Ukrainian Refugee Situation' UN Refugee Agency (26 July 2022) https://data.unhcr.org/en/situations/ukraine

Putting the Legal Framework in Perspective

The EU–Ukraine Association Agreement as a General Framework of Contemporary EU–Ukraine Relations

Roman Petrov

Contents

Abstract This chapter looks at the objectives, scope, implementation, and application of the EU–Ukraine Association Agreement (AA), which triggered unprecedented political, economic, and legal reforms in Ukraine. In particular, the chapter focuses on the constitutional challenges that have arisen while the AA is being embedded within Ukraine's legal system. There are two issues which the chapter considers. The first is the effective implementation and application of the AA within the Ukrainian legal order in line with the "common values" and "market access"

R. Petrov (✉)
International and European Law Department, National University of Kyiv-Mohyla Academy, Kyiv, Ukraine
e-mail: roman.petrov@ukma.edu.ua

H. Richter (ed.), *Competition and Intellectual Property Law in Ukraine*, MPI Studies on Intellectual Property and Competition Law 31,
https://doi.org/10.1007/978-3-662-66101-7_2

conditionality tools provided by the EU. The second issue is the compatibility of the AA with the Constitution of Ukraine. The latest political and legal developments in Ukraine are analysed through the prism of effective implementation of the EU–Ukraine Association Agreement and promotion of EU common values. In conclusion the EU–Ukraine AA is evaluated against the background of Ukraine's application for EU membership on 28 February 2022. It is argued that the EU–Ukraine AA still remains the main contractual tool to lead Ukraine through the turbulent path of EU accession and considerably contributes to the adaptability of the national constitutional order to the future EU membership and EU common values.

1 Introduction

Ukraine's road towards the signature and entry into force of the EU–Ukraine Association Agreement (the Association Agreement, AA) was highly dramatic.[1] Following unprecedented economic and political pressure from Russia, on 21 November 2013 the government of Ukraine decided to suspend the process of preparation for signature of the Association Agreement.[2] Further events led to the "Maidan" revolution, which claimed more than 100 lives and led to the dismissal of President Viktor Yanukovich on 22 February 2014, the annexation of Crimea by Russia in March 2014, and bloody military conflict in the Donbass area. However, the Association Agreement instigated far-reaching economic, political, and constitutional reforms in Ukraine which will determine its future geopolitical orientation and economic stability.

The formal triggering of Art. 49 TEU by Ukraine in February 2022 was a surprise. Very few people expected President Zelenskiy and his government to even think about EU membership amidst the avalanching invasion of the Russian army on a scale comparable to that of Operation "Barbarossa" in 1941. President Zelenskiy proudly signed the formal application to the EU while Russian army troops were only about 20 kms from his office in Kyiv. The long-cherished dream of the Ukrainian nation to apply for EU membership suddenly took place in the most critical and mortal moment of its history. This historic moment also changed the role of the EU–Ukraine AA as a core pillar of the EU–Ukraine relations. Henceforth, the EU–Ukraine AA has been transformed into a major pre-accession tool that can consolidate Ukraine's efforts to meet the Copenhagen criteria and to successfully negotiate all the chapters of the EU "pre-accession" acquis.

Taking the above as a starting point, the aim of this chapter is to highlight the constitutional challenges that have arisen for Ukraine on the road of the implementation of the Association Agreement into its legal system. The chapter focuses on

---

[1] Association Agreement between the European Union and its Member States, of the one part, and Ukraine, of the other part (2014) OJ L161/1 (EU–Ukraine Association Agreement); Roman Petrov et al., 'The EU-Ukraine Association Agreement: A New Legal Instrument of Integration Without Membership?' (2015) Kyiv-Mohyla Law and Politics Journal 1 (1–19).

[2] Ukrainian Cabinet of Ministers, Decision No. 905-p (2013) http://zakon0.rada.gov.ua/laws/show/905-2013-%D1%80 accessed 26 October 2022.

two major features of this intricate process. The first is effective implementation and application of the Association Agreement within the Ukrainian legal order, and the second is the compatibility between the Association Agreement and the Ukrainian Constitution.

2 Impact of the EU–Ukraine Association Agreement on the Ukrainian Legal System

2.1 Scope of the EU–Ukraine Association Agreement

The AA is the most voluminous and ambitious of all the EU's association agreements with third countries (7 titles, 28 chapters, 486 articles and 44 annexes, on about 2,000 pages). This is a comprehensive mixed agreement based on Art. 217 of the Treaty on the Functioning of the European Union (TFEU) (association agreements) and Arts. 31(1) and 37 of the Treaty on European Union (TEU) (EU action in area of Common Foreign and Security Policy). There are many novelties here, the most prominent of them being a strong emphasis on comprehensive regulatory convergence between the parties, and the possibility for the application of the vast scope of the EU *acquis* within the Ukrainian, Moldovan, and Georgian legal orders. A significant feature of the AA is the ambition to set up a "deep and comprehensive free trade area" (DCFTA), leading to gradual and partial integration of Ukraine into the EU Internal Market. Accordingly, the AA belongs to the selected group of "integration-oriented agreements", i.e. agreements that include principles, concepts and provisions which are to be interpreted and applied as if the third country is part of the EU. It is argued that the AA is unique in many respects and provides a new model of integration without membership.

2.2 Objectives and Specific Features of the Association Agreement with Ukraine

In opinion of Van Elsuwege the EU–Ukraine AA is characterised by three specific features: *comprehensiveness*, *complexity,* and *conditionality*. The AA is a *comprehensive framework agreement* which embraces the whole spectrum of EU activities from setting DCFTAs to cooperation and convergence in the field of foreign and security policy, as well as cooperation in the "area of freedom, security and justice" (AFSJ).[3]

---

[3] Peter Van Elsuwege et al., 'The EU–Ukraine Association Agreement: Assessment of an Innovative Legal Instrument' (2014) EUI Working Paper LAW 2014/09.

The *complexity* of the AA reflects a high level of ambition on the part of Ukraine to economically integrate with the EU Internal Market through the establishment of the DCFTAs, and to share the principles of the EU's common policies. This objective requires comprehensive legislative and regulatory approximation including advanced mechanisms to secure the uniform interpretation and effective implementation of relevant EU legislation into the national legal order of Ukraine. To achieve this objective, the AA includes several specific provisions on legislative and regulatory approximation including detailed annexes specifying the procedure and pace of the approximation process for different policy areas. These are laid out in more than 40 annexes and are based on specific commitments and mechanisms identified in both the annexes and specific titles to the agreement.

Furthermore, the AA is founded on a strict *conditionality* approach which links the third country's performance and the deepening of its integration with the EU. In addition to the standard reference to democratic principles and fundamental freedoms as defined by international legal instruments,[4] the AA contains common values that go beyond classical human rights to include very strong security elements, such as the "promotion of respect for the principles of sovereignty and territorial integrity, inviolability of borders and independence, as well as countering the proliferation of weapons of mass destruction, related materials and their means of delivery" (Art. 2 EU–Ukraine AA).

2.2.1 Enhanced Conditionality in the Association Agreement with Ukraine

Conditionality is one of the key strategic tools of the ENP and the EaP and it is, therefore, no surprise that this instrument also occupies a prominent place in the AA. Two different forms of conditionality can be distinguished in these agreements. The AA includes several provisions related to Ukraine's commitment to the common European values of democracy, rule of law and respect for human rights and fundamental freedoms ("common values" conditionality). On the other hand, the EU–Ukraine DCFTA is based on an explicit "market access" conditionality implying that Ukraine will only be granted additional access to a section of the EU Internal Market if the EU decides, after a strict monitoring procedure, that the country has successfully implemented its legislative approximation commitments. Both forms of conditionality bear some revolutionary features when compared with other external agreements concluded between the EU and third countries.[5]

---

[4] For instance, art 2 EU–Ukraine AA refers to Helsinki Final Act, the Charter of Paris for a New Europe, the UN Universal Declaration on Human Rights and the European Convention on Human Rights and Fundamental Freedoms.

[5] Roman Petrov, 'Implementation of Association Agreements between the EU and Ukraine, Moldova and Georgia: Legal and Constitutional Challenges' in Tanel Kerikmäe and Archil Chochia (eds), *Political and Legal Perspectives of the EU Eastern Partnership Policy* (Springer 2016) 153 (153–165).

2.2.2 "Common Values" Conditionality

International agreements concluded on behalf of the EU include standard conditionality clauses. In general, an "essential element clause" defining the core common values of the relationship is combined with a "suspension" clause with a procedure to suspend the agreement in case of violation of those essential elements. Such a mechanism is also included in the AA (Art. 2 in conjunction with Art. 478 EU–Ukraine AA). First, in addition to the standard reference to democratic principles, human rights and fundamental freedoms as defined by international legal instruments (Helsinki Final Act, the Charter of Paris for a New Europe, the UN Universal Declaration on Human Rights, and the European Convention on Human Rights and Fundamental Freedoms), a specific reference to human rights and fundamental freedoms is included in the AA's provisions on "dialogue and cooperation on domestic reform" and in the AA's provisions dealing with EU cooperation with Ukraine on justice, freedom and security (Art. 7 EU–Ukraine AA). Second, the essential elements of the AA also cover the issue of the territorial integrity of Ukraine (i.e. the "promotion of respect for the principles of sovereignty and territorial integrity, inviolability of borders and independence"). Third, "the principles of free market economy," along with a list of other issues such as "rule of law, the fight against corruption, the fight against the different forms of trans-national organised crime and terrorism, the promotion of sustainable development and effective multilateralism" are not included in the definition of essential elements. Rather, they are considered to "underpin" the relationship between the parties and are "central to enhancing" this relationship. In other words, the AA makes a clear distinction between hard core common values related to fundamental rights and security, and a range of other general principles that are deemed crucial for developing closer relations but which cannot trigger the suspension of the entire agreement (Art. 478 EU–Ukraine AA).

2.2.3 "Market Access" Conditionality

Apart from the more general "common values" conditionality, the AA contains a specific form of "market access" conditionality, which is explicitly linked to the process of legislative approximation. Hence, it is one of the specific mechanisms introduced to tackle the challenges of integration without membership.[6] Of significance here is a far-reaching monitoring of Ukraine's efforts to approximate national legislation to EU law, including aspects of implementation and enforcement (Art. 475(2) EU–Ukraine AA). To facilitate the assessment process, the government of Ukraine is obliged to provide reports to the EU in line with approximation deadlines specified in the Agreements. In addition to the drafting of progress reports, which is

---

[6] Tanja A Börzel and Frank Schimmelfennig, 'Coming Together or Drifting Apart? The EU's Political Integration Capacity in Eastern Europe' (2016) (24) Journal of European Public Policy (278–296); Alexander Duleba et al., *Integration without Membership: Potential and limits of Ukraine's Association* (Research Center of the Slovak Foreign Policy Association 2017).

a common practice within the EU's pre-accession strategy and the European Neighbourhood Policy (ENP) and the Eastern Partnership (EaP), the monitoring procedure may include "on-the-spot missions, with the participation of EU institutions, bodies and agencies, non-governmental bodies, supervisory authorities, independent experts and others as needed" (Art. 475(3) EU–Ukraine AA). Arguably, the latter option is a new and far-reaching instrument introduced precisely to guarantee that legislative approximation goes beyond a formal adaptation of national legislation.[7]

2.2.4 Protection of EU Values in the Association Agreement with Ukraine via EU's Sanctions Towards Third Countries

The principles of sovereignty and territorial integrity, inviolability of borders, and independence are considered to be core values of the AA which must be shared and respected by the EU and Ukraine.[8] Furthermore (particularly in the case of the EU–Ukraine AA), these principles constitute essential elements of the agreement.

The overall security situation in the EU's neighbouring countries for the last decade has gradually deteriorated. Moldova has a prolonged continuing conflict with its breakaway region Transnistria (the so-called "Pridenstrovian Moldovan Republic"). This territory is not recognised by any of the UN's members and formally constitutes part of the Republic of Moldova (Transnistria autonomous territorial unit with special legal status). However, Transnistria is de facto an independent state bolstered with a strong presence of Russian troops. The EU is engaged in solving the Transnistrian conflict via the European Border Assistance Mission to Moldova and Ukraine (EUBAM). This structure, as part of the EU Common Security and Defence Policy, helps to control traffic on the borders between Moldova and Ukraine around Transnistria in order to prevent illegal movements of people and goods from and to Transnistria.[9]

Georgia went through a military conflict with Russia over the breakaway areas of Abkhazia and South Ossetia. The conflict took place August 2008 and led to many casualties and the loss of Georgian control of Abkhazia and South Ossetia. Russian military forces are currently stationed in Abkhazia and South Ossetia and de facto control those territories.[10]

---

[7] Guillaume Van der Loo et al., 'The EU–Ukraine Association Agreement: A New Legal Instrument of Integration Without Membership?' (2015) Kyiv-Mohyla Law and Politics Journal 1 (1–19).

[8] Preamble to the EU–Ukraine Association Agreement reads "Committed to Promoting the Independence, Sovereignty, Territorial Integrity and Inviolability of Borders" of the Parties.

[9] Xymena Kurowska and Benjamin Tallis, 'Border Assistance Mission: Beyond Border Monitoring?' (2009) 14(1) European Foreign Affairs Review (47–64).

[10] Roman Petrov et al., 'Constitutional Orders of Non-Recognized Entities in Georgia and Ukraine. Can Façade Constitutions Ensure Adequate Protection of Human Rights?' (2020) 45(1) Review of Central and East European Law (92–125).

The EU played quite a modest role in settling the conflict in the Caucasus allowing some EU Member States to lead the peace process in the region, but no sanctions were applied by the EU in the aftermath of the Georgian-Russian conflict.[11]

However, Ukraine was faced with the next security challenge, and that compelled the EU to apply its full arsenal of sanctions against the Russian Federation. This happened after the self-proclaimed authorities in the Autonomous Republic of Crimea held an unrecognised referendum under the shadow of a Russian military presence in March 2014. As a result, an integral part of Ukraine—the Autonomous Republic of Crimea and the city of Sevastopol—was annexed by the Russian Federation on March 21, 2014. The fact of annexation is not recognised by Ukraine and the United Nations UN (General Assembly Resolution 68/262 (2014)) and is universally considered to be a blatant violation of international public law by the Russian Federation.[12]

Following turbulent events in Crimea the EU decided to apply wide scale sanctions against Russia. The EU sanctions led to a complete halt in EU–Russia relations (including the suspension of bilateral talks on visa matters and on a new EU–Russia agreement, and the cancellation of the EU-Russia summit). Measures were imposed against "certain persons responsible for actions which undermine or threaten the territorial integrity, sovereignty and independence of Ukraine." These included travel bans and asset freezes.[13] The list of these persons is constantly increasing and covers leading Ukrainian, Russian and Crimean politicians who played some part in the annexation of the Crimea. The EU had to extend the scope of sanctions against Russia after the security situation in Ukraine drastically deteriorated at the end of the summer of 2014. The world was shocked when Malaysia Airline flight MH17 was shot down above the part of Eastern Ukraine controlled by pro-Russian separatists. This incident led to the loss of 298 lives and a drastic deterioration of the security situation in the region and for the EU. A bloody conflict between Ukraine and the armies of the self-proclaimed "peoples' republics" of Donetsk and Lugansk led to several thousand

[11] Syuzanna Vasilyan, 'The External Legitimacy of the EU in the South Caucasus' (2011) 16(3) European Foreign Affairs Review (243–261).

[12] Christian Marxsen, 'The Crimea Crisis – An International Law Perspective' (2014) 74(2) Heidelberg Journal of International Law (367–391).

[13] Council Regulation 269/2014 of 17 March 2014 concerning restrictive measures in respect of actions undermining or threatening the territorial integrity, sovereignty and independence of Ukraine (2014) OJ L78 amended by Council Regulation 476/2014 of 12 May 2014 (2014) OJ L137; Council Regulation 783/2014 of 18 July 2014 (2014) OJ L214/2; Council Regulations 810/2014 and 811/2014 of 25 July 2014 (2014) OJ L221; Council Regulation 959/2014 of 8 September 2014 (2014) OJ L271; Council Implementing Regulation 961/2014 of 12 May 2014 (2014) OJ L271/8; Council Decision 2014/145/CFSP concerning restrictive measures in respect of actions undermining or threatening the territorial integrity, sovereignty and independence of Ukraine (2014) OJ L78 amended by Council Decision 2014/265/CFSP of 12 May 2014 (2014) OJ L137; Council Decision 2014/119/CFSP concerning restrictive measures directed against certain persons, entities and bodies in view of the situation in Ukraine (2014) OJ L66; Council Regulation 883/2014 of 31 July 2014 concerning restrictive measures in view of Russia's actions destabilising the situation in Ukraine (2014) OJ L229 amended by Council Regulation 960/2014 of 8 September 2014 (2014) OJ L271/2.

casualties, and about a million refugees fled from the East of Ukraine (UN Report on the human rights situation in Ukraine in 2021).[14] The EU Member States had to speak with one voice in order to show their solidarity against direct Russian involvement in civil conflict in Ukraine. As a result, the EU Member States agreed on a new level of sanctions against Russian and Ukrainian officials and nationals involved in supporting the separatists' movement in the Donbass region of Ukraine. The EU's sanctions against Russia concerned the following: diplomatic measures (cancellation of the EU-Russia political dialogue and dismantling of G8); restrictive measures (asset freezes and visa bans of persons and entities responsible for actions against Ukraine's territorial integrity); restrictions for Crimea and Sevastopol; and "economic" sanctions against Russia (prohibition of exports of arms, energy and military related technologies and dual use goods, freezing economic cooperation).[15]

The EU sanctions were issued upon a unanimous decision of all the EU Member States based on Art. 215 TFEU as part of the Common Foreign and Security Policy (CFSP). This was a demonstration of solidarity by all EU Member States in the face of a violation of the territorial integrity of one of the EU's nearest neighbours which was about to enter into association relations with the EU.

3 Constitutional Amendments Caused by the Implementation of the EU–Ukraine Association Agreement

3.1 Constitutional Amendments of 2016

One of the first "post-Maidan" constitutional amendments took place in June 2016 when the *Verkhovna Rada* adopted the "Law on amending the Ukrainian Constitution (as to justice)".[16] These constitutional amendments were proposed by President Poroshenko in light of the fight against corruption and the independence of the judiciary in Ukraine. The constitutional amendments sparked considerable public debate in Ukraine and beyond. Externally, the European Commission for Democracy through Law (Venice Commission) twice scrutinized the draft amendments for their compliance with European standards and issued several important reservations.[17] Internally the draft amendments were criticized for giving extended powers

[14] Annual UN Human Rights Reports on Ukraine are available at https://www.ohchr.org/en/countries/enacaregion/pages/uareports.aspx accessed 26 October 2022.

[15] More information on the EU's restrictive measures in response to the crisis in Ukraine is available at https://www.consilium.europa.eu/en/policies/sanctions/ukraine-crisis/ accessed 26 October 2022.

[16] Ukrainian Law on Amending the Constitution of Ukraine 2016, 1401-VIII, No. 2.

[17] The reservations mainly concerned the scope of judges' immunity and preserving the balance of power in the procedure for appointing judges and prosecutors (election of the Supreme Law Council, which is responsible for appointing judges (qualified majority voting) and the right of the

to the President of Ukraine to influence the appointment of judges, narrowing the scope of judges' immunity, and for keeping a complicated system of specialized courts in Ukraine. The President of Ukraine's position was that the constitutional amendments were crucial to achieve the objectives of the Association Agreement in terms of sharing common values, fighting corruption, and improving access to the judiciary. In particular, the constitutional amendments ensured that Ukraine observed the essential elements of the Association Agreement, such as respect for the principle of the rule of law,[18] and met the objectives of Title III of the Association Agreement on justice, freedom and security. These call on Ukraine to consolidate the rule of law, to improve the efficiency of the judiciary, to safeguard the independence and impartiality of the judiciary, and to combat corruption.[19]

The official position of the EU institutions regarding constitutional reform in Ukraine was rather supportive. The annual report on progress in implementing the Association Agreement hailed the constitutional amendments of 2016 as legislation that "strengthens judicial independence and [reorganizes] the court system, by streamlining the judicial instances (from four to three) and by subjecting the sitting judges to examinations and mandatory electronic asset declarations".[20] Furthermore, it should be acknowledged that the most recognized impact of the Association Agreement[21] on constitutional reform in Ukraine can be seen in revised Art. 124 of the Constitution, wherein it is stated that "Ukraine may recognize the jurisdiction of the International Criminal Court (ICC) as provided for by the Rome Statute of the International Criminal Court". This amendment overruled a decision of the Ukrainian Constitutional Court in 2001 which explicitly considered recognition of the jurisdiction of the ICC as incompatible with the national Constitution, thus ruling out ratification of the former by the Ukrainian Parliament.[22] The wording of revised Art. 124 of the Ukrainian Constitution opens a possibility for the Ukrainian Parliament to ratify the Rome Statute in the near future. However, ratification of the Rome Statute is likely to be postponed until the eventual implementation of the "Minsk

---

Ukrainian Parliament to veto the appointment and removal of Ukraine's General Prosecutor); Venice Commission of the Council of Europe, 'Opinion on the Amendments to the Constitution of Ukraine Regarding the Judiciary as Proposed by the Working Groups of the Constitutional Commission in July 2015' (Opinion) 803/2015 (2015).

[18] EU–Ukraine Association Agreement, Preamble art 1(2)(e) and art 2.

[19] EU–Ukraine Association Agreement, art 14.

[20] Council of the European Union, 'Association Implementation Report on Ukraine' SWD(2016) 446 final.

[21] EU–Ukraine Association Agreement, art 8.

[22] Ukrainian Constitutional Court on the Statute of the International Criminal Court, Decision Case No. 1–35/2001 (2001), where the Ukrainian Constitutional Court stated that in accordance with the Rome Statute the International Criminal Court complements the system of national judiciaries. For example, the International Criminal Court may exercise its jurisdiction on the territory of States Parties to the Rome Statute. This contradicts Title VIII "Judiciary" of the Ukrainian Constitution, under which (art 124) "delegation of the competences of the national judiciary is not permitted.".

II Agreement"[23] regarding the military conflict in Eastern Ukraine (Donbass area) which directly or indirectly involves multiple actors. Those involved in the conflict must ensure an effective ceasefire, effective control by Ukraine of its eastern border with Russia and guarantee an amnesty for illegally armed belligerents. These actions must take place before the ratification of the Rome Statute by Ukraine.[24]

3.2 Education Law of 2017 and Its Impact on the EU–Ukraine AA

Another test of Ukraine's devotion to common EU values as enshrined in the Association Agreement took place in September 2017, when the *Verkhovna Rada* adopted a new education law. This legislation foresees a reduction in the scope of instruction in the mother tongue of a national minority at secondary education level. According to the new education law, only primary school education can be given in the mother tongue of a national minority in Ukraine. Secondary and higher education must be offered only in the official language (Ukrainian) with the possibility to study the mother tongue as one of the courses. This immediately sparked a protests by representatives of national minorities (mainly the Hungarian community) in Ukraine.[25] The Hungarian government fiercely protested against the new educational law on the ground that it violates the rights of the Hungarian minority in Ukraine.[26] Furthermore, the Hungarian government asserted that the Ukrainian education law is in conflict with the objectives and human rights commitments by Ukraine in the Association Agreement.[27] In order to prevent the escalation of tension with some EU Member States, the Ukrainian authorities submitted Art. 7 of the education law for assessment by the Venice Commission. In its assessment issued on 11 December 2017, the Venice Commission noted the vague nature of the relevant provisions of the national education law and recognized the narrowing of access by national minorities to obtaining secondary education in their mother tongue. The Venice Commission

[23] More information on Minsk II Agreement is available at https://www.chathamhouse.org/2020/05/minsk-conundrum-western-policy-and-russias-war-eastern-ukraine-0/minsk-2-agreement accessed 26 October 2022.

[24] Briefing of the European Parliament "Ukraine and the Minsk II Agreement: On a Frozen Path to Peace?", available at http://www.europarl.europa.eu/RegData/etudes/BRIE/2016/573951/EPRS_BRI(2016)573951_EN.pdf accessed 26 October 2022.

[25] Ukrainian Law on Education 2017, 2145-VIII, No 38–39.

[26] EU Observer, 'Hungary Threatens to Block Ukraine's EU Approach', *EU Observer* (27 September 2017) https://euobserver.com/tickers/139173 accessed 8 December 2021; Lyliya Hrynevych, 'Ukraine Education Law Does Not Harm Minorities', *EU Observer* (20 October 2017) https://euobserver.com/opinion/139550 accessed 8 December 2021.

[27] 'Hungary Seeks to Recognize Ukraine Violator of Association Agreement over Educational Law' *Unian* (16 October 2017) https://www.unian.info/politics/2190089-hungarian-foreign-minister-to-put-ukraines-education-law-on-agenda-of-ua-eu-association-councils-meeting.html accessed 8 December 2021.

recommended adopting further implementing legislation to ensure a sufficient level of teaching in languages of the EU Member States in Ukraine. However, the Venice Commission recognized discrimination against the languages of national minorities that are not official languages of the EU (Russian) and called on Ukraine not to endanger "the preservation of the minorities' cultural heritage and the continuity of minority language education in traditional schools".[28] Ukrainian law on State Language of 2019 sparked further protests from the Hungarian and Russian minorities that expressed concerns about the impact of this law on the language rights of the respective national minorities. Again, the Venice Commission was asked to issue an opinion on this law in 2019. On this occasion the Venice Commission considered that the State Language Law of Ukraine "fails to strike a balance between strengthening Ukrainian and safeguarding minorities' linguistic rights" and, therefore, recommended that the application of the State Language Law should be postponed until the adoption of the National Minorities Law.[29] The Ukrainian government welcomed the findings of the Venice Commission and agreed to follow most of them in the course of drafting and adopting further legislation relating to education and national minorities, and to ensure a transitional period for implementation of the education law until 2023.[30] Meanwhile, the EU's reaction to the language issue in the education and state language laws and their compatibility with the objectives of the Association Agreement remains neutral.[31] However, it is possible that the Venice Commission's recommendations may be taken on further by EU institutions and become part of the EU conditionality requirements towards Ukraine in the process of further implementation and application of the Association Agreement in area of protection of human rights.

3.3 *Constitutional Amendments "European Integration Clauses" of 2019*

One of the most significant constitutional developments caused by the implementation of the EU–Ukraine Association Agreement is the introduction of so-called "European integration clauses" in February 2019.[32] These clauses were amended to the preamble and provisions of the Ukrainian Constitution on the competences of

[28] Venice Commission of the Council of Europe, 'Ukraine: Opinion on the Provisions of the Law on Education of 5 September 2017 '(Opinion) 902/2017 (2017).

[29] See https://go.coe.int/acBTf accessed 8 December 2021.

[30] Council of the European Union, 'Association Implementation Report on Ukraine' SWD(2019) 433 final (n 20).

[31] Ibid (n 20).

[32] Ukrainian Law on Amendment to the Constitution of Ukraine Regarding Strategic Course of the State Towards the Acquisition of the Full Membership in the EU and NATO 2019, 2680-VIII. The amended relevant provision of the preamble of the Constitution of Ukraine reads as "strengthening civil accord on the Ukrainian soil and confirming the European identity of the Ukrainian peoples and irrevocability of the European and Euroatlantic course of Ukraine".

the President of Ukraine, the *Verkhovna Rada* and Cabinet of Ministers of Ukraine. The aim of the "European integration clauses" is twofold. Firstly, they formalize the irrevocability of the strategic course of Ukraine and its legislature, executive and judiciary towards the full membership in the EU and NATO, and they may encourage and legitimize the pro-European activism of the Ukrainian judiciary that implies application of the relevant case law of the Court of Justice of the European Union (CJEU). Secondly, the "European integration clauses" were adopted on the eve of the presidential and parliamentary elections in Ukraine in March 2019 that saw a political newcomer—former comedian Volodymyr Zelenskiy—elected president. These clauses were introduced as a constitutional guarantee with a purpose to prevent a possible change of course of Ukrainian foreign and domestic policies caused by potential change resulting the presidential and parliamentary elections in 2019. In fact, there was actually no need to trigger the "European integration clauses" in the Constitutions of Ukraine since the government of President Zelenskiy and—dominated by his party "Servant of People"—the *Verkhovna Rada of Ukraine* continued the democratic reforms envisaged in the EU–Ukraine AA. For instance, further legislative and executive measures were taken to reinvigorate public administration reform, including the promotion of e-governance and administrative services delivery in line with the highest EU standards.[33] The promotion of EU common values in the fields of justice, freedom and security in Ukraine were accelerated via the long-awaited launch of the High Anti-Corruption Court of Ukraine in 2019 and National Anti-Corruption Bureau of Ukraine, although many legislative and procedural impediments of these reforms are still in place.[34]

4 Application and Direct Effect of the EU–Ukraine Association Agreement in the Ukrainian Legal Order

The effectiveness of the implementation and application of the EU–Ukraine AA rests not only on the approximation of the Ukrainian legislation with the relevant EU *acquis* but also on the application of the ECJ case law by the Ukrainian judiciary. In fact, it had already occasionally referred to the fundamental principles of EU law and some elements of the EU *acquis* as well as to CJEU case law before the Association Agreement was signed.[35] A combination of external and internal factors may explain this. First, since 2004 Ukraine's pro-European foreign policy has been underpinned by binding national law. "On the All State Program on the adaptation of Ukrainian

[33] Ukrainian Law on Civil Service 2015, 889-VIII.

[34] Ukrainian Law on High Anti-Corruption Court 2018, 2447-VIII and Ukrainian Law on National Anti-Corruption Agency 2014, 1698-VII.

[35] Roman Petrov, 'Regulatory Convergence and Application of EU Law in Ukraine' in Peter van Elsuwege and Roman Petrov (eds), *Legislative Approximation and Application of EU Law in the Eastern Neighbourhood of the European Union: Towards a Common Regulatory Space?* (Routledge Press, Oxford 2014) (137–158).

legislation to EU laws" of 2004 encouraged the Ukrainian judiciary to use the EU *acquis* as an important source of reference.[36] This law, which has already become outdated, envisages export of the whole "accession *acquis*" into Ukraine's legal system.[37] This has served as vital encouragement for the few Ukrainian judges with expertise in EU law to refer to the relevant EU *acquis* in their decisions. Second, the EU has been offering result-oriented, technical, and financial support to the Ukrainian judiciary. This support has resulted in significant internal institutional reforms within the Ukrainian judiciary, such as the establishment of a system of administrative courts. According to the case law of the Ukrainian courts, mostly administrative judges have been inclined to pioneer application of the EU *acquis* within the Ukrainian judiciary.[38] A third factor is the increased transparency of the Ukrainian judiciary. A national registry of Ukrainian case law (an online resource open for public use) was launched in 2006 and drew positive feedback from the Ukrainian legal community. National judges and lawyers are regularly informed about developments in EU law via workshops and courses in Ukrainian higher legal education institutions and EU-funded educational projects.[39]

The Ukrainian judiciary (including the Ukrainian Constitutional Court) has a log track record of applying the EU *acquis* as a persuasive source of law. For example, the Ukrainian courts recognized the priority of the Association Agreement's predecessor (the EU–Ukraine PCA) over conflicting provisions of national law.[40] Furthermore, in cases related to state liability, the Ukrainian administrative courts imported the concept of legal certainty, previously unknown to the Ukrainian legal system, from the EU legal system. For example, in the *Person v Kyiv City Centre for Social Assistance* case,[41] the Kyiv District Administrative Court held that the rights of the disabled to claim social and financial assistance from the state flow from the principle of legal certainty. This means that a state cannot justify its failure to guarantee constitutional rights by the absence of a specific national law. For this purpose, the Kyiv District

---

[36] Ukrainian Supreme Court Law on the All-State Programme of Adaptation of Ukrainian Legislation to that of the EU 2004, 1629-IV, No. 29.

[37] The main objective of this law is "alignment of the Ukrainian legislation with the *acquis communautaire*, taking into consideration criteria specified by the EU towards countries willing to join the EU".

[38] Roman Petrov and Paul Kalinichenko, 'The Europeanization of Third Country Judiciaries through the Application of the EU Acquis: The Cases of Russia and Ukraine' (2011) 60(2) International and Comparative Law Quarterly (325–353).

[39] For example, see "Association4U" https://www.facebook.com/association4u.ua and "Pravo-Justice" https://www.pravojustice.eu projects accessed 26 October 2022.

[40] Ukrainian High Commercial Court, Judgment No. 12/267 (2005); Also Ukrainian High Commercial Court, Judgment No. 7/299 *Closed Stock Company 'Chumak' v Kherson Custom Office* (2005); Also Ukrainian High Commercial Court, Judgment No. 18/303 *'Odek' LTD v Ryvne Custom Office* (2005).

[41] Kyiv District Administrative Court, Judgment No. 2/416 (2008). Apparently, this judgment became a pattern for subsequent decisions by Ukrainian administrative judges; see Kyiv District Administrative Court, Judgment No. 5/503 (2008); Kyiv District Administrative Court, Judgment No. 5/451 (2008); Kyiv District Administrative Court, Judgment No. 5/435 (2008).

Administrative Court referred to the CJEU judgment in *van Duyn v the Home Office*,[42] wherein it was held that nationals may rely on the state's obligations, even in cases when those obligations are contained in a law without direct effect. Furthermore, the Ukrainian courts developed the principle of legitimate expectations in the case of *Person v Darnitsa District of Kyiv Center for Social Assistance*[43] concerning the right to benefits of those who took part in the liquidation operation during the Chernobyl catastrophe. The Kyiv District Administrative Court held that the principle of state liability to offer compensation to those involved in the liquidation of the Chernobyl disaster also flows from the same CJEU case *van Duyn v Home Office*. Therein, the Kyiv District Administrative Court found that if the state formally acknowledged its commitment to offer compensation to those involved in the Chernobyl disaster, it could not refer to its own failure to fulfil its commitments to avoid liability, which would also violate the legitimate expectations of Ukrainian nationals.

Such bold judicial activism of administrative judges, previously unknown for a post-Soviet legal system, was not welcomed by all representatives of the Ukrainian establishment. In response to a growing number of similar decisions by the administrative courts, the Ukrainian government under President Yanukovich went to the Ukrainian Constitutional Court to question the compensation-related case law of the administrative courts concerning those involved in liquidation of the Chernobyl disaster. In its judgment of 25 January 2012 the Constitutional Court overruled the established case law of the administrative courts on the ground that social support for Ukrainian nationals guaranteed by the Ukrainian Constitution must be provided in line with the financial capacities of the state in accordance with the principles of proportionality and justice.[44] The Constitutional Court did not consider the relevance of the principle of legal certainty at all but referred to selected decisions of the ECtHR in justifying its own position. This controversial decision by the Constitutional Court was widely criticized—by the expert community in Ukraine and even by some Constitutional Court judges in their special opinions—for lack of reasoning, a pro-governmental position and misleading references to ECtHR case law.[45] The situation became even worse when the Supreme Disciplinary Body for judges in Ukraine opened a disciplinary procedure against those administrative judges who referred to CJEU case law in their compensation-related decisions concerning those involved in the Chernobyl disaster.[46]

Further dramatic political events in Ukraine, including the Maidan Revolution in 2013–2014—which led to signature of the Association Agreement in June 2014—reinvigorated the debate on application of the CJEU case law by the Ukrainian judiciary. At the end of 2014, the Ukrainian High Administrative Court decided to

[42] ECJ C-41/74 *Van Duyn v Home Office* (1974) EU:C:1974:133 (on free movement of workers between EU Member States and direct effect of EU Directives).

[43] Kyiv District Administrative Court, Judgment No. 4/337 (2008).

[44] Ukrainian Constitutional Court, Decision No. 1–11/2012 (2012).

[45] For example, see Special Opinion of Constitutional Court Judge Viktor Shyshkin in Ukrainian Constitutional Court, Decision No. 1–11/2012 (2012).

[46] For instance, see https://court.gov.ua/archive/975679 accessed 26 October 2022.

intervene and to fill this gap in a way that is now traditional for post-Soviet courts—to issue an information letter to all administrative judges in Ukraine,[47] in which the Ukrainian High Administrative Court stated that the EU founding treaties do not bind Ukraine and that EU law and the case law of the CJEU therefore cannot be considered as part of the Ukrainian legal system. Additionally, the Ukrainian High Administrative Court confirmed that "legal positions as they are formalized in decisions of the CJEU can be taken into consideration by administrative courts as argumentation, reflection regarding harmonious interpretation of Ukrainian legislation in line with established standards of the EU legal system, but not as a legal foundation (source of law) of a situation that caused a legal dispute".

This statement by the Ukrainian High Administrative Court played a dubious role. It repudiated any formal grounds for Ukrainian judges to apply various sources of the EU *acquis* in their decisions while giving a green light for Ukrainian judges to refer to general principles, doctrines, and case law of the CJEU as a persuasive source of interpretation in their decisions. Unfortunately, the Ukrainian High Administrative Court kept silent on the issues of application of the EU *acquis* referred to in the text of the Agreement and of binding decisions of the EU–Ukraine Association Council. Ironically, new constitutional amendments of 2016 abolished the entire system of high specialized courts in Ukraine. Consequently, the issue of legal value of the statement of the Ukrainian High Administrative Court to the Ukrainian judiciary on the application of the EU *acquis* by Ukrainian courts remains open. Nevertheless, current judicial practice of the Supreme Court of Ukraine confirms that it approves references to decisions of the CJEU "because legal positions [of the CJEU] can be considered by the [Ukrainian] courts as argumentation regarding the interpretation of national legislation in line with established standards of the legal system of the EU".[48]

Beyond all expectations this clarification by the Ukrainian High Administrative Court on applying CJEU case law found wide support among judges of common and administrative courts in Ukraine. In the period 2015–2016, Ukrainian general, specialized, and high courts referred to the Agreement and case law of the CJEU in dozens of decisions.[49] In most cases, Ukrainian judges who already possess considerable experience and knowledge in applying the ECHR and ECtHR-related case law strengthened their argumentation with frequent references to the EU *acquis* and the

---

[47] Informational Letter of the Ukrainian High Administrative Court on 18 November 2014, No. 1601/11/10/14-14.

[48] Supreme Court of Ukraine, Judgment No. 9901/636/18 (2019); Also see Kyiv Commercial Court, Judgment No. 910/13209/18 (2019).

[49] Detailed information on the case law of the Ukrainian judiciary is available at http://www.reyestr.court.gov.ua accessed 26 October 2022. For example, analysis of decisions by the Ukrainian courts issued in 2014 and 2016 indicates a significant rise in references to the Association Agreement and various sources of the EU *acquis* (e.g. fundamental principles, secondary acts, case law of the CJEU). For more detailed analysis see Roman Petrov, 'The Impact of the ECJ on the Legal System of Ukraine', in Arie Reich and Hans-W Micklitz (eds), *The Impact of the European Court of Justice on Neighbouring Countries* (OUP, Oxford, 2020) 173 (n(173–198).

Association Agreement (particularly in decisions concerning protection of fundamental human rights in Ukraine). For instance, since 2015 most decisions by administrative courts on rights of pensioners provide a standard statement that the court applies the principle of rule of law in line with ECtHR and CJEU case law. In these cases, Ukrainian judges cited the above-mentioned Statement of the Ukrainian High Administrative Court on taking into account CJEU case law as a source of argumentation concerning harmonious interpretation of Ukrainian law with the EU *acquis*.[50] Judges of the Supreme Court unequivocally confirmed the primacy of provisions of the EU-Ukraine Association Agreement over conflicting provisions of national legislation in *Zentiva* case.[51] Some judges went even further and considered the entry into force of the Association Agreement in Ukraine as an obligation to apply EU common values in Ukraine.[52] References to the Association Agreement and relevant EU *acquis* found application in cases regarding Ukrainian natural persons and companies that claimed direct effect of these provisions in cases concerning the payment of customs duties when crossing the Ukrainian border[53]; supply and trade of natural gas[54]; defining the origin of goods (honey)[55]; or the legality of legislative drafts by the Ukrainian president.[56] Furthermore, the Ukrainian courts have already started recognizing the direct effect of provisions of the EU–Ukraine Association Agreement in their decisions. The first decisions on this matter related to the field of protection of intellectual property rights. In the *Kanzhut* judgment of 2019 Supreme Court of Ukraine explicitly recognized the direct effect of Art. 198 of the EU-Ukraine AA "since [Art. 198] establishes new standards of protection of intellectual property rights" in Ukraine.[57] It was without doubt one of most straightforward acceptances of direct effect of provisions of EU external agreements by judiciaries of third countries. The issue of direct effect of provisions of the EU–Ukraine AA requires further clarification by the Ukrainian judiciary. Furthermore, it should find relevance in the case of possible litigation on the correspondence of Ukrainian laws and other legal acts with the objectives, principles and "essential elements" of the Association Agreement before the Constitutional Court and general courts. Among the most recent examples are the Executive Order of the President of Ukraine on banning Russian social

---

[50] For example, Chernigyv District Court, Judgment No. 750/5197/16-a (2016).

[51] Ukrainian Supreme Court (Commercial Chamber), Judgment No. 910/14972/17 (2018).

[52] For example, the Kolomya City Court, Judgment No. 346/3499/16-c (2016) contains a rather emotional passage "The Court notes that after the signing of the Association Agreement with the European Union by the President of our country, and after the ratification by the supreme legislative body (Verkhovna Rada Ukraine – author), Ukraine, as a state aspiring to full membership in the EU, must respect the private property rights of every person as a basic tenet and a cornerstone of European values and inviolable foundation of the EU, which must by complied with by all Member States and by associated countries" (Translation by the author).

[53] Lviv Regional Appellate Court, Judgment No. 33/783/241/16 (2016).

[54] Kyiv District Administrative Court, Judgment No. 826/594/16 (2016).

[55] Tsyrypinsk District Court, Judgment No. 664/906/16-c (2016).

[56] Ukrainian High Administrative Court, Judgment No. 800/251/16 (2016).

[57] Ukrainian Supreme Court (Commercial Chamber), Judgment No. 910/4947/18 (2019).

networks (in the matter of national security and sanctions against the Russian Federation caused by the annexation of Crimea in 2014 and military intervention in eastern Ukraine)[58] and the Law of Ukraine on banning the St. George (Guards') Ribbon. These were widely used by paramilitary separatist groups and Russian army units in the Donbass area and during the annexation of Crimea and thus may be considered as propaganda for Russian military intervention in Ukraine.[59] However, these legislative acts raise some concerns regarding their compliance with the objectives of the Association Agreement in general, and freedom of expression and the principle of proportionality (as applied and interpreted within the ECHR and the EU Charter of Fundamental Rights) in particular.[60] It is argued that one of the possible solutions to ensure the direct effect of provisions of the EU–Ukraine AA in the Ukrainian legal order is to mention this option in the specialised law on the application of the AA to be issued by the Ukrainian Parliament. Such law may pursue the objective of clarification of political importance and legal significance of the EU–Ukraine AA for the Ukrainian political and legal systems and elaborate on the meaning and scope of fundamental principles of EU law, importance of the CJEU case law in the process of the application and implementation of the EU–Ukraine AA. Furthermore, this law can foresee direct effect of some provisions of the EU–Ukraine AA conditional on the exercise of the requirement of direct effect as provided in the CJEU case law.

During implementation of the EU–Ukraine AA the Ukrainian judiciary increased references to the relevant CJEU decisions within the scope of the EU–Ukraine sectoral cooperation. Most of such references are in the field of competition law.[61] For instance, the Supreme Commercial Court of Ukraine and Appellate Commercial Courts referred to the Case C-8/08 (*T-Mobile Netherlands BV and Others v Raad*)[62] with the purpose of applying the concept of "concerted practice" (i.e. a causal connection between concerted action and the market conduct of undertakings in competition law). Furthermore, Ukrainian administrative courts (regional appellate level) made numerous references to the CJEU case C-255/02 *Halifax plc and Others v Commissioners of Customs & Excise*.[63] These references concerned the application of the doctrine of "business purpose" in the course of exemption from paying the VAT.

58 Executive Order (*Ukaz*) of the President of Ukraine of 15 May 2017, No. 133/2017.

59 Law of Ukraine on Amending the Administrative Code Regarding the Ban on Production and Propaganda of the St. George (Guards') Ribbon 2017, 2031-VIII, No. 26.

60 Peter van Elsuwege, 'Ukraine's Ban on Russian Social Media: On the Edge Between National Security and Freedom of Expression' *Verfassungsblog (2 June* 2017) http://verfassungsblog.de/ukraines-ban-on-russian-social-media-on-the-edge-between-national-security-and-freedom-of-expression accessed 8 December 2021.

61 See Kseniia Smyrnova, 'The "Europeanization" of Competition Law in Ukraine' in this Volume.

62 ECR C-8/08 T-*Mobile Netherlands BV and Others v Raad* (2009) I-4529.

63 ECR C-255/02 *Halifax plc and Others v Commissioners* of Customs & Excise (2006) I-1609.

5 Application of Decisions of the EU–Ukraine Common Institutions

The Association Agreement established a specific institutional framework (the Association Council, the Association Committee, and the Parliamentary Assembly) characterized by the competence to issue decisions and legal acts of a binding nature. The prime objective of the Association Council is to supervise and monitor the Association Agreement within the "framework of regular meetings between the representatives of the Parties."[64] For this purpose, the Association Council has the power to take decisions which are binding upon the parties. This power can be delegated to the Association Committee which assists Ukraine in achieving the results of the association.[65]

The binding force of decisions and acts by joint EU–Ukraine institutions is new for the Ukrainian legal system, so that their legal effect has not yet been clarified. Neither the EU–Ukraine Association Council nor other common institutions have so far issued any decisions of a binding nature, so there has been no reason for the Ukrainian judiciary to clarify their position on this complicated issue. In the meantime, the Ukrainian Parliament and the government are working on a draft law to regulate all legal issues related to implementation and application of the Association Agreement. Unfortunately, this draft law has not yet been proposed for even a first reading in the Ukrainian Parliament. According to the draft law, decisions by common EU–Ukraine institutions will not be directly applicable but will be enforced in the same way as international agreements. In particular, the draft law considers binding decisions by common EU–Ukraine institutions either as international agreements,[66] or as national laws, or as secondary acts—depending on their content. In the former two cases, binding decisions of common EU–Ukraine institutions must be regarded as part of the national legal system, which takes precedence over conflicting national legislation but not over the Constitution. In the latter case, it will be regarded as a secondary legal source for the Ukrainian legal system. The draft law obliges the Ukrainian judiciary to apply these decisions as sources of law. Non-binding recommendations by common EU–Ukraine institutions can be used as a source for interpreting Ukrainian legislation and Ukraine's international obligations.

---

[64] EU–Ukraine Association Agreement, art 463(1), 2014, OJ L161/1.

[65] EU–Ukraine Association Agreement, art 465(2), 2014, OJ L161/1.

[66] Within the issues related to politics, territory, human rights, participation in international unions and organizations, collective security, usage of Ukrainian territory and natural resources, military assistance, and deployment of Ukrainian troops abroad (Ukrainian Law on International Treaties 2004, 1906/IV, art 3(2).

6 Conclusion

The objective of effective implementation of the Association Agreement was to enhance the adaptability of the national constitutional order to the European integration project and European common values. Internally, Ukraine went through a dramatic transformation from a country which pursued a multi-vector foreign policy aimed at appeasing two conflicting integration projects (European and Eurasian) to a country with a firm pro-European policy as cemented in the Association Agreement. Externally, Ukraine committed itself to demanding the conditionality and monitoring processes envisaged in the Association Agreement in return for better access to the EU internal market, establishing a Deep and Comprehensive Free Trade Area and a so called "industrial visa regime" with the EU.

The Association Agreement established a sustainable institutional and legal framework for application of the EU *acquis* including CJEU case law and comprehensive legislative approximation between Ukrainian and EU law. However, the institutional reforms that have already taken place cannot be regarded as sufficient. The Ukrainian Parliament has failed to establish substantive and procedural foundations for applying and implementing the Association Agreement in the Ukrainian legal order. This gap is being partially filled by a surprising judicial activism in Ukraine. The Ukrainian judiciary has already started referring to the Association Agreement and relevant parts of the EU *acquis*, thereby laying a foundation for regular application of general principles of EU law in applying the provisions of the Association Agreement. Furthermore, the Ukrainian judiciary recognised the direct effect of some provisions of the AA within its legal order. This is undoubtedly a great challenge for the Ukrainian legal system. A significant role in this process is expected from the Ukrainian judiciary, particularly from the Constitutional Court and the Supreme Court (which must eventually clarify the status of the Association Agreement within the Ukrainian legal order), and the newly formed Ukrainian Supreme Court, which has recruited EU-minded judges and academics.

Furthermore, the Ukrainian Constitution has already been amended to encompass specific requirements of the Association Agreement (such as ratification of the Rome Statute and access to the judiciary). Further amendments related to implementing the Association Agreement may also be expected, such as strengthening the role of international law within the Ukrainian legal system, reference to common EU values—languages of national minorities in the new education law—along with acknowledging and formalizing the potential transfer of some of Ukraine's sovereign powers to supranational international organizations.

Blatant invasion of Ukraine by the Russian Federation on 24 February 2022 unintentionally triggered the formal application of the Ukrainian government for the EU formal membership on 28 February 2022. Despite all tragedy of the moment this political act was warmly received by the EU institutions and the EU Member States and considered as a necessary toll to support the war effort of the Ukrainian people. With unprecedented speed the European Commission issued a positive report on the membership application of Ukraine (as well as Moldova and Georgia) on 17 June

2022.[67] Soon after the European Council formally endorsed the candidate status for Ukraine (as well as for Moldova and potentially for Georgia).[68] The candidate status of Ukraine inevitably refocuses the role of the EU–Ukraine AA from being a key tool of political, economic and legal rapprochement of Ukraine with the EU to becoming a key tool of the EU pre-accession process, as happened with the countries of Central and Eastern Europe before their membership in the EU in the period of 2005–2007.

Looking more widely at the pattern of adaptability of the Ukrainian constitutional order to the EU accession project, we may conclude that external factors—such as the aims of EU–Ukraine relations, including the membership in the EU—play a catalytic role for constitutional change in Ukraine. Furthermore, the external factors of the AA are inextricably linked to the enhancement of its internal factors. For example, it is hoped that the procedure of political dialogue and institutional framework of the AA can and will be effectively used to protect the principles of sovereignty and territorial integrity, inviolability of borders and independence considered as core values of the AA and will be an effective toolbox for Ukraine's project of accession to the EU.

References

Tanja A Börzel and Frank Schimmelfennig, 'Coming Together or Drifting Apart? The EU's Political Integration Capacity in Eastern Europe' (2016) (24) Journal of European Public Policy 278

Council of the European Union, 'Association Implementation Report on Ukraine' SWD(2016) 446 final

Alexander Duleba, Martin Lačný, Vladimír Bilčík, Oleksandr Sushko and Yaroslav Zhalilo, *Integration without Membership: Potential and limits of Ukraine's Association* (Research Center of the Slovak Foreign Policy Association 2017)

Peter Van Elsuwege, '*Ukraine's Ban on Russian Social Media: On The Edge Between National Security and Freedom of Expression' Verfassungsblog (2 June* 2017) http://verfassungsblog.de/ukraines-ban-on-russian-social-media-on-the-edge-between-national-security-and-freedom-of-expression

Peter Van Elsuwege, Guillaume Van der Loo and Roman Petrov, 'The EU–Ukraine Association Agreement: A New Legal Instrument of Integration Without Membership?' (2015) Kyiv-Mohyla Law and Politics Journal 1–19

Peter Van Elsuwege, Guillaume Van der Loo and Roman Petrov, 'The EU–Ukraine Association Agreement: Assessment of an Innovative Legal Instrument' (2014) EUI Working Paper LAW 2014/09

EU Observer, 'Hungary Threatens to Block Ukraine's EU Approach', *EU Observer* (27 September 2017) https://euobserver.com/tickers/139173

Guy Harpaz, 'The European Union's Conflict-Resolution Policy in Georgia: The Way Forward' (2018) 23(2) European Foreign Affairs Review 243

Liliya Hrynevych, 'Ukraine Education Law does not Harm Minorities' *EUObserver* (20 October 2017) https://euobserver.com/opinion/139550

[67] European Commission, 'Commision Opinion on Ukraine's Application for Membership of the European Union' (Communication) COM(2022) 407 final, 2022.

[68] European Council, 'European Council Meeting (23–24 June 2022) – Conclusions' EUCO 24/22, 2022.

'Hungary Seeks to Recognize Ukraine Violator of Association Agreement over Educational Law' *Unian* (16 October 2017) https://www.unian.info/politics/2190089-hungarian-foreign-minister-to-put-ukraines-education-law-on-agenda-of-ua-eu-association-councils-meeting.html

Xymena Kurowska and Benjamin Tallis, 'Border Assistance Mission: Beyond Border Monitoring?' (2009) 14(1) European Foreign Affairs Review 47

Guillaume Van der Loo, *The EU-Ukraine Association Agreement and Deep and Comprehensive Free Trade Area (*Brill | Nijhoff 2016)

Christian Marxsen, 'The Crimea Crisis – An International Law Perspective' (2014) 74(2) Heidelberg Journal of International Law

Roman Petrov, 'The Impact of the ECJ on the Legal System of Ukraine', in Arie Reich and Hans-W. Micklitz (eds), *The Impact of the European Court of Justice on Neighbouring Countries* (OUP, Oxford, 2020) 173

Roman Petrov, Gaga Gabrichidze and Paul Kalinichenko, 'Constitutional Orders of Non-Recognized Entities in Georgia and Ukraine. Can Façade Constitutions Ensure Adequate Protection of Human Rights?' (2020) 45(1) Review of Central and East European Law 92

Roman Petrov, 'Implementation of Association Agreements between the EU and Ukraine, Moldova and Georgia: Legal and Constitutional Challenges' in Tanel Kerikmäe and Archil Chochia (eds), *Political and Legal Perspectives of the EU Eastern Partnership Policy* (Springer 2016) 153

Roman Petrov, 'Regulatory Convergence and Application of EU Law in Ukraine' in Peter van Elsuwege and Roman Petrov (eds), *Legislative Approximation and Application of EU Law in the Eastern Neighbourhood of the European Union: Towards a Common Regulatory Space?* (Routledge Press, Oxford 2014) 137

Roman Petrov and Paul Kalinichenko, 'The Europeanization of Third Country Judiciaries through the Application of the EU Acquis: The Cases of Russia and Ukraine' (2011) 60(2) International and Comparative Law Quarterly 325

Syuzanna Vasilyan, 'The External Legitimacy of the EU in the South Caucasus' (2011) 16(3) European Foreign Affairs Review 341

Venice Commission of the Council of Europe, 'Ukraine: Opinion on the Provisions of the Law on Education of 5 September 2017'(Opinion) 902/2017 (2017)

Competition and International Trade: Complementing Trade Defense Policy with Effective Competition Policy in Ukraine

Zvenyslava Opeida

Contents

Abstract This chapter focuses on the relationship between competition and international trade. Competition policy is aimed at achieving the most efficient allocation of resources and thereby the maximization of national welfare. The primary goal of trade defense policy, on the other hand, is to assist domestic producers in recovering from the injury caused by imports. In other words, whereas the focus of competition policy is on preserving *competition* rather than protecting competitors, the main purpose of trade remedies is protecting *domestic competitors*. The latter often generates negative effects on competition. The chapter looks at the origin of such inconsistency in objectives, which could be found in both World Trade Organization (WTO) and Ukrainian law, and argues that both policies can nevertheless be complementary. To

Z. Opeida (✉)
National University of Kyiv-Mohyla Academy, Kyiv, Ukraine
e-mail: z.opeida@ukma.edu.ua

H. Richter (ed.), *Competition and Intellectual Property Law in Ukraine*, MPI Studies on Intellectual Property and Competition Law 31,
https://doi.org/10.1007/978-3-662-66101-7_3

reconcile the conflicting objectives, it is proposed to introduce competition considerations into the trade defense policy of Ukraine by strengthening one of the elements of trade remedy investigations, namely the public interest requirement.

1 Introduction

Ukraine is a country with an open economy that has made substantial progress in reducing barriers to trade. Ukraine acceded to the WTO in 2008, with wide-ranging commitments on market access and the average bound tariff rate of 6.1%. Further integration of Ukraine into international markets was achieved by joining regional and bilateral trade agreements. To date, Ukraine has concluded 18 free trade agreements with such trading partners as the European Union, the United Kingdom, Canada and Israel.

To mitigate the adverse impact of imports on domestic industries, Ukraine adopted trade remedy law in 1998. Although originally not especially popular, trade remedies have become a frequently used instrument as the market has become increasingly open. Given that the law is primarily designed to protect domestic producers from competing imported products, this chapter is concerned with a potential anti-competitive effect of trade remedies in the Ukrainian market in situations where less efficient Ukrainian producers get protected at the expense of more efficient foreign producers, downstream Ukrainian industries producing more value-added goods and final consumers.

This chapter proceeds as follows. Section 2 examines the origin and evolution of the trade remedy regime in the WTO and provides a brief overview of trade remedy law in Ukraine (namely, law on anti-dumping, on subsidies and countervailing measures and on safeguards). Since Ukrainian law was designed to ensure consistency with WTO rules, the underlying objectives, key characteristics as well as deficiencies of Ukrainian law cannot be fully appreciated without understanding the WTO's approach to this issue and the reasons behind it. Section 3 addresses conflicting objectives of trade remedy rules and competition policy. It demonstrates in more detail how WTO law on trade remedies (and, as a consequence, Ukrainian law) is inconsistent with basic objectives of competition law. Finally, Sec. 4 argues that trade remedy use could still be disciplined so that the amended Ukrainian law is consistent with both the current WTO rules and the objectives underlying competition policy. To that end, it is proposed to strengthen the public interest requirement by introducing a set of rules aimed at: (1) defining economic factors to consider in the course of investigation and providing explanations as to how these factors are assessed; (2) clarifying the sources of evidence and data to be used; (3) expanding the list of possible outcomes of the finding that the measure will negatively affect the Ukrainian economy; and (4) enhancing the transparency of the process by making the conclusions (including those regarding public interest) publicly available.

2 The Basics of WTO and Ukrainian Trade Remedy Law

2.1 Origin and Evolution of Trade Remedy Regime in the WTO

The WTO was created first and foremost to facilitate free trade, which had a profound impact on the way WTO trade remedy law was designed. According to the Preamble for the Marrakesh Agreement Establishing the World Trade Organization, the ultimate objectives of the WTO are rather broad and include an increase in standards of living, the attainment of full employment, the growth of real income and the expansion of production of, and trade in, goods and services. At the same time, the principal means to achieve these objectives are limited to (1) the reduction of trade barriers and (2) the elimination of discriminatory treatment in international trade.[1]

When the General Agreement on Tariffs and Trade (GATT) was negotiated in 1947, the main purpose was to impose limitations on the use of the trade barriers most often used at the time: tariffs and quotas. Rules on market access are therefore at the core of WTO law. Article II GATT requires WTO Members to limit their tariffs to a certain maximum specified in their tariff commitments or "bindings".[2] Furthermore, Art. XI prohibits quotas, import and export licenses and any other measures that prohibit or restrict trade other than duties, taxes and other charges. To secure fair conditions of trade, WTO law imposes two main non-discrimination obligations. A most-favored-nation treatment obligation prohibits a country from discriminating between other countries (Art. I GATT). According to a national treatment obligation, imported and locally produced products should be treated equally (Art. III GATT).

Nevertheless, WTO Members are allowed to unilaterally impose trade remedies to protect domestic industry from injury caused by unfair trading practices (by introducing anti-dumping (AD) and anti-subsidy measures) or by unforeseen surges in imports (by introducing safeguard measures). One of the rationales behind the unfair trade rules is "a desire to create a level playing field where the producers of the world all have an equal chance to compete".[3] Safeguard measures, on the other hand, allow fairly traded imports to be restricted. Given "the importance of structural adjustment",[4] the basic idea behind this rule is to provide a "breathing space"

---

[1] Marrakesh Agreement Establishing the World Trade Organization 1994, No. 31874.

[2] General Agreement on Tariffs and Trade 1947, 61 Stat. A-11, 55 UNTS 194 (GATT), art II.

[3] John Howard Jackson et al., *Legal Problems of International Economic Relations: Cases, Materials and Text on the National and International Regulation of Transnational Economic Relations* (West Academic 6th ed. 2013) 831; see also Peter Van der Bossche and Werner Zdouc, *The Law and Policy of the World Trade Organization: Texts, Cases and Materials* (Cambridge University Press 4th ed. 2017) 1625.

[4] Marrakesh Agreement Establishing the World Trade Organization 1994, No. 31874, annex 1A Preamble for the Agreement on Safeguards.

during which the domestic industry which suffered serious harm from imports and trade concessions can take the action necessary to improve its competitiveness.[5]

The original rules regarding trade remedies contained in the GATT 1947 were rather limited. First, Art. VI(1) GATT provides that "dumping [...] is to be condemned" if it "causes or threatens material injury to an established industry in the territory of a contracting party or materially retards the establishment of a domestic industry". It also permits WTO Members to take certain actions against dumping in order to limit its impact. Under Art. VI(2), "[i]n order to offset or prevent dumping, a Member may levy on any dumped product an anti-dumping duty not greater in amount than the margin of dumping in respect of such product". Second, with regard to subsidies, Art. XVI contains a general obligation to notify subsidies and to discuss, upon request, the possibility of limiting them, and distinguishes export subsidies on non-primary products that are totally prohibited from export subsidies on primary products that, in many cases, are permitted. Article VI authorizes Contracting Parties to countervail against subsidies by imposing countervailing duties (CVDs), which may not be levied "in excess of an amount equal to the estimated bounty or subsidy determined to have been granted, directly or indirectly, on the manufacture, production or export of such product in the country of origin or exportation". Finally, safeguard measures are governed by Art. XIX—often referred to as the escape clause—which allows WTO Members to escape from their WTO obligations by imposing safeguard measures. Such measures can only be applied when "as a result of unforeseen developments and of the effect of obligations incurred" under the GATT, increased imports "cause or threaten serious injury to domestic producers".

These rules, however, were brief, vague, and provided no specific guidelines with respect to the essential questions of the application of trade remedies. The primary concern was that countries were applying trade remedy law in a manner that raised additional barriers to trade.[6]

The existing deficiencies made it difficult to challenge the imposed measures, which were applied rather arbitrary and often in violation of the GATT provisions. For instance, U.S. anti-dumping law allowed the imposition of provisional measures without a preliminary finding of injury to domestic industry caused by dumped imports.[7] Canada did not require a finding of injury before applying AD measures.[8] Similarly, in the area of subsidies, in the United States—the only country that actively used CVDs—these measures could be imposed merely upon determination of a

[5] Mitsuo Matsushita et al., *The World Trade Organization: Law, Practice, and Policy* (Oxford University Press 2nd ed. 2006) 438–439; Simon Lester et al., *World Trade Law: Text, Materials and Commentary* (Hart Publishing 2nd ed. 2012) 537.

[6] John Howard Jackson, *The World Trading System: Law and Policy of International Economic Relations* (MIT Press 2nd ed. 1997) 256.

[7] Kenneth Dum, *The GATT: Law and Economic Organization* (University of Chicago Press 1970) 177.

[8] Ibid 174.

subsidy, without assessing the injury to the domestic industry caused by the subsidized imports.[9] Such provisions continued to exist in the domestic law of certain GATT signatory parties despite the fact that Art. VI(6)(a) GATT explicitly provides that anti-dumping and CVDs can only be imposed after the determination of material injury to the domestic industry caused by dumped or subsidized imports. This became possible because under the Protocol of Provisional Application—through which the GATT 1947 was applied until 1995—a GATT contracting party was entitled to maintain legislation that was in force on accession to the GATT even though it was inconsistent with Part II GATT (so-called grandfather rights).[10] Furthermore, with regard to CVDs, since there was no general definition of the term "subsidy" in the GATT, the precise scope of Arts. VI and XVI GATT was not entirely clear. As a result, a country could impose CVDs even if the granting of the subsidy involved was authorized by the provisions of Art. XVI.[11]

Many countries considered it necessary to redress these problems by setting more detailed standards for the application of trade remedies. After some unsuccessful attempts to tighten up the rules through a series of codes concluded at the Kennedy and Tokyo rounds of negotiations, significant progress in this area came with concluding three WTO agreements: Agreement on the Implementation of Art. VI GATT (hereinafter "Anti-Dumping Agreement"), Agreement on Subsidies and Countervailing Measures (hereinafter "SCM Agreement") and Agreement on Safeguards, which entered into force in 1995.

The three Agreements amplify and supplement the provisions on trade remedies contained in the GATT; they also substantially strengthen the requirements for their application. Therefore, today, the Agreements, together with Arts. VI, XVI and XIX GATT, contain the substantive rules and procedures on the application of AD, CVDs and safeguard measures. Crucially, unlike the GATT 1947, these Agreements became equally binding on all WTO Members (Art. II:2 WTO Agreement). Each WTO Member thus must "ensure the conformity of its laws, regulation and administrative procedures with its obligations as provided in the [...] Agreements" (Art. XVI:4 WTO Agreement). This had a profound effect on the domestic legislation of WTO Members, including that of Ukraine.

---

[9] Robert O'Brien, *Subsidy Regulation and State Transformation in North America, the GATT and the EU* (Palgrave Macmillan 1997) 107 (noting that "[t]hey successfully argued that since their law predated the GATT and did not contain an injury measure, the GATT provisions were not applicable").

[10] Protocol of the Provisional Application of the 1947 GATT (U.N.T.S. 308, BISD IV/77, TIAS 1700) (Part II of the GATT applied only "to the fullest extent not inconsistent with existing legislation").

[11] Contracting Parties to the General Agreement on Tariffs and Trade, 'On Antidumping and Countervailing Duties' (Second Report of the Group of Experts) L/1141, 1960, para 32. See also John James Barceló III, 'A History of GATT Unfair Trade Remedy Law: Confusion of Purposes' (1991) 517 Cornell Law Faculty Publications 311 (324) ("GATT's failure to link countervailing duties to the direct regulation of subsidies in Article XVI compounds the unboundedness of the Article VI language").

2.2 *Brief Overview of Trade Remedy Law in Ukraine*

The existing legal framework for trade remedies in Ukraine is set out in the Law of Ukraine on Protection of National Producer against Dumped Imports (hereinafter "the Law on AD"), the Law of Ukraine on Protection of National Producer against Subsidized Imports (hereinafter "the Law on CVD") and the Law of Ukraine on Application of Safeguard Measures against Imports to Ukraine (hereinafter "the Law on Safeguards"). The Laws contain the substantive and procedural rules on the application of trade remedies.

Adopted in 1998, the Laws have been substantially amended since then, in particular in order to bring them in line with the WTO remedial regime.[12] As a result, the provisions of the Laws largely correspond to those of the WTO.

2.2.1 Anti-Dumping

In order to impose AD measures against dumped imports, three elements need to be established during the course of investigation: (1) there is dumping; (2) the domestic industry producing the like product in Ukraine is being injured; and (3) there is a causal link between the dumping and the injury.[13]

With regard to the determination of dumping, the Law on AD follows the language of the Anti-Dumping Agreement. Under Art. 1(5) Law on AD, dumping is "the importation of products […] at prices lower than the comparable price of the like product in the exporting country". Dumping therefore exists where the "normal value" of the product exceeds the "export price" (Arts. 1(6) and 9 Law on AD).[14] Determinations regarding the "normal value" of a product are guided by Arts. 1(17) and 7, which state that the "normal value" of a product is the price in the ordinary course of trade in the exporting country, whereas "the export price" is the transaction price at which the product is sold from the country of export to the importing country (Arts. 1(1) and 8 Law on AD).

[12] Ukraine became a WTO Member on 16 May 2008. See Ukrainian Law on Ratification of the Protocol on Accession of Ukraine to the World Trade Organization 2008, 250-VI.

[13] Ukrainian Law on Protection of National Producer against Dumped Imports 1999, 330-XIV, arts 7–10; World Trade Organization Agreement on Implementation of art VI of the General Agreement on Tariffs and Trade 1994 (Anti-Dumping Agreement), 1868 U.N.T.S. 201, arts 2, 3; General Agreement on Tariffs and Trade 1994 (GATT 1994), 1867 U.N.T.S. 187, art VI:6(a) ("[n]o contracting party shall levy any anti-dumping […] duty on the importation of any product of the territory of another contracting party unless it determines that the effect of the dumping […], as the case may be, is such as to cause or threaten material injury to an established domestic industry, or is such as to retard materially the establishment of a domestic industry").

[14] Similarly, according to art 2(1) Anti-Dumping Agreement the product is "dumped, i.e. introduced into the commerce of another country at less than its normal value, if the export price of the product exported from one country to another is less than the comparable price, in the ordinary course of trade, for the like product when destined for consumption in the exporting country".

An affirmative determination of injury to the domestic industry is a precondition for the imposition of AD measures. Articles 1(8) and 10(1) Law on AD largely mirror the language of Art. 6 GATT and footnote 9 Anti-Dumping Agreement, indicating that the term "injury" means either: (1) material injury to a domestic industry; (2) threat of material injury to a domestic industry; or (3) material retardation of the establishment or expansion of production of like products by a domestic industry. The third form of injury seems to be somewhat broader in Ukrainian law, though, since it covers the retardation of both establishment and expansion of production, whereas both Art. 6 GATT and footnote 9 Anti-Dumping Agreement limit this form of injury to the material retardation of the "establishment of a domestic industry" only.

Article 10(2) Law on AD—exactly mirroring the language of Art. 3(1) Anti-Dumping Agreement—provides the basic guiding principles of an injury determination, stating that a determination of injury must be based on positive evidence and involve an objective examination of (1) the volume of the dumped imports and the effect of the dumped imports on prices in the domestic market for like products, and (2) the consequent impact of these imports on the domestic producer.

Finally, Art. 10(6) Law on AD requires that a causal link between the dumped imports and the injury to the domestic industry must be established. Like the provisions of Art. 3(5) Anti-Dumping Agreement, Art. 10(7) Law on AD contains a "non-attributable requirement" under which the investigating authority may examine other known factors that are injuring the domestic industry at the same time, and the injury caused by such other factors must not be attributed to dumped imports. The list of such factors includes: the volume and prices of imports not sold at dumping prices; contraction in demand or changes in the patterns of consumption; trade restrictive practices of and competition between the foreign and domestic producers; developments in technology; the export performance and productivity of the domestic industry (Art. 10(7) Law on AD, Art. 3(5) Anti-Dumping Agreement).

Consistent with WTO law,[15] the Law on AD provides for two types of relief in AD proceedings: (1) the imposition of AD duties (provisional and definitive duties); or (2) a price undertaking.

The Law on AD follows the language of Art. 7(1) Anti-Dumping Agreement in providing that the investigating authorities may apply provisional measures only after making a preliminary affirmative determination of dumping and consequent injury to a domestic industry (Art. 14(1)(5) Law on AD). Moreover, under Art. 14(1)(6) Law on AD, provisional measures may be applied only after it is established that the national interests require their application in order to prevent injury being caused during the investigation. In accordance with Art. 7(4) Anti-Dumping Agreement, Art. 14(13) Law on AD states that provisional measures may be applied for no more than four months. This period can be extended for up to six months upon request by exporters representing a significant percentage of the trade involved.

When an affirmative final determination of dumping and injury is made by the investigating authorities, definitive AD measures are applied (Art. 16(5)(1) Law on

[15] World Trade Organization, Anti-Dumping Agreement (n 13) arts 7, 8, 9.

AD). Like Art. 9(3) Anti-Dumping Agreement, Art. 16(5)(3) Law on AD requires that the amount of AD duty cannot exceed the margin of dumping. Regarding the duration of AD duties, Arts. 18(1), (2) Law on AD mirror the language of Arts. 11(1) and 11(3) Anti-Dumping Agreement. AD duties remain in force as long as and to the extent necessary to counteract the dumping which is causing injury.[16] Yet the duty must be terminated on a date not later than five years from its imposition or from the date of the most recent review unless the authorities determine that the expiry of the duty would be likely to lead to continuation or recurrence of dumping and injury.[17]

Finally, as an alternative to imposing AD duties, Art. 15 Law on AD (consistent with the provisions of Art. 8 Anti-Dumping Agreement) permits a "price undertaking", i.e. voluntary undertakings from exporters to revise their price or to cease exports at dumped prices.

2.2.2 Subsidies and Countervailing Duties

In order to impose CVDs against subsidized imports, three elements need to be established during the course of the investigation: (1) the imports concerned are benefiting from the countervailable subsidy; (2) the domestic industry producing the like product in Ukraine is suffering injury; and (3) there is a causal link between the subsidized imports and the injury.[18]

With regard to its definition of a subsidy, the Law on CVD closely follows the language of Arts. 1 and 2 SCM Agreement. For a measure to constitute a subsidy, two cumulative conditions must be met: (1) there must be a financial contribution by a government or any form of income or price support; and (2) there must be a benefit conferred thereby (Arts. 1(20) and 6(1) Law on CVD).

Pursuant to Art. 7(1) Law on CVD, subsidies shall be subject to countervailing measures only if they are specific. In other words, "specificity" is a condition for imposing CVDs. In accordance with the provisions of Art. 2(1) SCM Agreement, Art. 8 Law on CVD states that a subsidy is specific when it has been provided to a certain enterprise or industry or a group of enterprises or industries. Like in the WTO, while export subsidies (i.e. subsidies contingent upon export performance) and import substitution subsides (i.e. subsidies contingent upon the use of domestic

---

[16] Ukrainian Law on Protection of National Producer against Dumped Imports 1999, 330-XIV, art 18(1).

[17] Ibid art 18(2).

[18] Ukrainian Law on Protection of National Producer Against Subsidized Imports 1999, 331-XIV, arts 6–14; World Trade Organization Agreement on Subsidies and Countervailing Measures (SCM Agreement) 1869 U.N.T.S. 14, arts 1, 2, 15; General Agreement on Tariffs and Trade 1994 (GATT 1994), 1867 U.N.T.S. 187, art VI:6(a) ("[N]o contracting party shall levy any […] countervailing duty on the importation of any product of the territory of another contracting party unless it determines that the effect of the […] subsidization, as the case may be, is such as to cause or threaten material injury to an established domestic industry, or is such as to retard materially the establishment of a domestic industry").

over imported goods) are automatically considered as specific and therefore countervailable, other subsidies must be specific in order to be countervailable (Art. 8(3) Law on CVD).

The determination of injury to the domestic industry and a causal link between the subsidized imports and the injury are governed by Arts. 13 and 14 Law on CVD, which largely correspond to their equivalent in Arts. 15 and 16 SCM Agreement. Apart from the references to dumping or subsidization, they are almost identical to the rules described above regarding the determination of injury and a causal link in AD procedures.

Likewise, the Law on CVD provides for two types of relief in CVD proceedings: (1) the imposition of CVD (provisional and definitive duties); or (2) a price undertaking. The rules regarding remedies are contained in Arts. 17–19 Law on CVD; they largely follow the language of Arts. 17–21 SCM Agreement. Consistent with Art. 19(4) SCM Agreement, Art. 19(6)(3) Law on CVD provides that definitive CVD may not exceed the total amount of countervailable subsidies established. The rules on the application of remedies in CVD proceedings are mostly identical to the ones in AD proceedings provided above.

2.2.3 Safeguards

Safeguard measures may only be applied when three requirements are met: (1) there is an increase in imports; (2) the domestic industry producing the like product in Ukraine is suffering injury; and (3) there is a causal link between the increased imports and the injury.[19]

The language of Art. 16(1) Law on Safeguards closely resembles the language of GATT Art. XIX:1(a) and Art. 2(1) Agreement on Safeguards, requiring that there must be an increase of imports "in such increased quantities" as to cause or threaten to cause injury to a domestic industry. Similarly, Art. 13(2)(1) Law on Safeguards follows the language of Art. 2(1) Agreement on Safeguards and states that the increase in imports can be "absolute or relative to domestic production".

The determination of injury to a domestic industry and a causal link between the increased imports and the injury are governed by Art. 13 Law on Safeguards, which is largely consistent with the provisions of Art. 4 Agreement on Safeguards. These rules are also very similar to the rules for AD and CVD investigations described above, but

[19] Ukrainian Law on Application of Safeguard Measures against Imports to Ukraine 1999, 332-XIV, arts 10(3) and 16(1); World Trade Organization Agreement on Safeguard 1869 U.N.T.S. 154, art 2(1); General Agreement on Tariffs and Trade 1994 (GATT 1994), 1867 U.N.T.S. 187, art XIX:1(a) ("[i]f, as a result of unforeseen developments and of the effect of the obligations incurred by a contracting party under this Agreement, including tariff concessions, any product is being imported into the territory of that contracting party in such increased quantities and under such conditions as to cause or threaten serious injury to domestic producers in that territory of like or directly competitive products, the contracting party shall be free, in respect of such product, and to the extent and for such time as may be necessary to prevent or remedy such injury, to suspend the obligation in whole or in part or to withdraw or modify the concession").

with one notable difference. Unlike AD and CVD proceedings, where under WTO law the term "injury" must be taken to mean "material injury" (footnote 9 Anti-Dumping Agreement and footnote 45 SCM Agreement), the injury in safeguard proceedings should be greater because safeguard measures counteract imports that are not unfair. Accordingly, Art. 4.1 Agreement on Safeguards provides for "serious injury", which is defined to mean a "significant overall impairment in the position of a domestic industry". Likewise, Ukrainian law distinguishes between the "material injury" for AD and CVD investigations (Art. 1(8) Law on AD and Art. 1(6) Law on CVD) and the "serious injury" for safeguards investigations (Art. 1(5) Law on Safeguards).

Finally, pursuant to GATT Art. XIX:1, when an affirmative determination of the increased imports, the injury and the causal link is made, a WTO Member is permitted to "suspend the obligation in whole or in part or to withdraw or modify the concession". Article 11 Law on Safeguards closely mirrors the language of Art. 6 Agreement on Safeguards. It allows the application of provisional safeguard measures in the form of tariff increases "where delay would cause damage which would be difficult to repair", and provides that provisional measures may only be applied for a maximum of 200 days.

Article 16 Law on Safeguards governs the application of definitive safeguard measures. Consistent with WTO law, definitive safeguard measures can take the form of tariff increases or quantitative restrictions (Art. 16(3) and 16(3) Law on Safeguards). Under Art. 18 Law on Safeguards (in accordance with the provisions of Art. 7 Agreement on Safeguards), safeguard measures may be applied for up to four years, unless the extension is warranted, in which case the total period of application of safeguard measures, including any provisional measure and period of extension, must not exceed eight years.

3 Conflicting Objectives of Trade Defense and Competition Policy

Concluding the three WTO Agreements and subsequent changes made in the national laws of WTO Members to bring them in line with WTO rules substantially strengthened the requirements for their application and made it more difficult to WTO Members to use them for protectionist purposes. Nevertheless, the current legal framework continues to be inadequate to address the disturbing anti-competitive effect of trade remedies. Having been designed to protect national producers from competing imported products rather than protecting competition itself, they often generate negative net effects on the economy.

The main goal of trade remedy law is to assist a domestic producer in recovering from the injury caused by imports. Their effect, however, is not limited exclusively to domestic producers. They also affect the economy of an importing country as a whole. Accordingly, by imposing costs on other economic sectors and on consumers which are not outweighed by the benefits to the industry receiving protection from imports, trade remedies may result in reducing economic welfare.[20]

Indeed, the effect of trade remedies has a broader impact. First, the imposition of duties generally does not benefit consumers, since prices will increase and the product range available to the consumer may also be reduced. Second, since trade remedies often target raw materials and intermediate goods, which are further used by domestic industries for processing purposes, the imposition of duties may result in an increase of production costs for other products. This, in turn, may impact the ability of downstream industry to compete both on domestic and export markets. In Ukraine, of 33 trade remedies that are currently in force, 27 are imposed on intermediate goods such as cement, polymeric materials, thermal insulation materials, aerated concrete blocks, steel fasteners and urea-formaldehyde resin.[21] This potentially has a far-reaching effect on a number of other sectors of the Ukrainian economy and overall economic welfare. For example, when in 2019 the Commission of International Trade initiated a safeguard investigation against imports of fertilizers to Ukraine,[22] the Kyiv School of Economics conducted research on possible effects of introducing such measures and concluded that whereas domestic fertilizers producers might benefit up to 238 million USD, the losses of Ukrainian farmers due to higher fertilizer prices would be up to 509 million USD (with small farmers bearing the larger costs).[23] The overall conclusion was that the total effect of the potential introduction of trade remedies on imports of fertilizers would be negative and would in fact reduce the country's overall welfare from an estimated 100 million USD to 238 million USD.[24]

Finally, trade remedies might lead to a reduction of competition and even to a domestic producer monopoly. For example, in April of 2019, upon the Ukrainian

[20] See eg Marco Bronckers, 'Private Remedies Against Foreign Subsidization: A European View' in Jacques Bourgeois (ed), *Subsidies and International Trade: A European Lawyers' Perspective* (Kluwer Law International 1991) 187 (192); Sungjoon Cho, 'Anticompetitive Trade Remedies: How Antidumping Measures Obstruct Market Competition' (2009) 87 North Carolina Law Review 357 (360) (arguing that "[w]hile internal competition is highly protected in the domestic market, external competition from foreign producers has been largely neglected and, thus, has avoided antitrust scrutiny. In fact, the government, through its trade policies, often hampers foreign competition, protecting domestic producers at the expense of all the benefits that foreign competition might bring to the economy").

[21] See the list of all current trade remedy measures at the official website of the Department of Foreign Economic Activity and Trade Defense at the Ministry of Economy of Ukraine https://td.me.gov.ua/en/zaxodyzovn/ accessed 19 January 2022.

[22] Interdepartmental Commission of International Trade, Notice on Initiating and Conducting a Safeguard Investigation on Imports of Some Nitrogen Fertilizers to Ukraine Regardless of a Country of Origin and Export, No. СП-425/2019/4411–03, 21 August 2019.

[23] 'Ukraine's Economy May Lose up to $238 Million from the Introduction of Quotas on Imports of Mineral Fertilizers' *Kyiv School of Economics* https://kse.ua/ua/about-the-school/news/ekonomika-ukrayini-mozhe-vtratiti-do-238-mln-dol-ssha-vid-zaprovadzhennya-kvot-na-import-mineralnih-dobriv/ accessed 19 January 2022; See also Natalia Datskevych, 'Dangerous Quotas: Limiting Fertilizer Imports Might Kill Competition, Benefit Oligarchs' *Kyiv Post* (11 July 2020) https://www.kyivpost.com/business/dangerous-quotas-limiting-fertilizer-imports-might-kill-competition-benefit-oligarchs.html accessed 19 January 2022.

[24] Ibid.

cement producers' petition, the Ukrainian government introduced anti-dumping duties on cement from the Russian Federation, Belarus and Moldova[25] and a month later an embargo on cement from the Russian Federation.[26] That year, the Ukrainian cement producers that initiated the investigation controlled over 90% of the domestic market; the imported cement constituted the only competition to their products and its market share did not exceed 8% (90% of imported cement was coming from the Russian Federation, Belarus and Moldova).[27] The imports from those countries ceased with the entry into force of anti-dumping measures and an embargo and was replaced by imports from Turkey. In September of 2020, upon request from the same domestic producers, another anti-dumping investigation was initiated, this time against the imports of cement from Turkey.[28] In April of 2021, the Antimonopoly Committee of Ukraine (AMCU) observed that Ukrainian cement producers were substantially raising the prices before the end of both investigations despite the absence of any "objective factors" for such an increase.[29] The AMCU emphasized that such "iterative behavior of producers who raised prices in anticipation of the Commission's anti-dumping measures" can be viewed "as anti-competitive concerted actions in the cement market".[30] Nevertheless, the anti-dumping duties on cement from Turkey were also introduced,[31] leaving the entire market to the domestic producers.

These kinds of examples, when the possible effects of trade remedies on other industries and competition are not taken into account during the investigation, are not only typical to Ukraine but are rather part of a larger problem rooted in WTO trade remedy law itself.

Despite quite elaborated rules contained in the WTO Agreements, there is no clear answer to the question: what is the ultimate purpose of the regime the Agreements establish? Of all WTO Agreements, only the Anti-Dumping Agreement and the SCM Agreement do not contain a preamble, which usually provides some indication of the object and purpose of a treaty. This is to a large extent because the WTO trade remedy discipline embodies a difficult compromise between the differing views

---

[25] Interdepartmental Commission of International Trade, Notice on Application of Definitive Anti-dumping Measures on Imports of Cement from the Russian Federation, the Republic of Belarus and the Republic of Moldova to Ukraine, 28 May 2019.

[26] Decree of the Cabinet of Ministers of Ukraine on a Ban on Imports into the Customs Territory of Ukraine of the Goods Originating from the Russian Federation, 30 December 2015, No. 1147.

[27] Antimonopoly Committee of Ukraine, Recommendation to Domestic Cement Producers Not to Raise Prices, 13 April 2021.

[28] Interdepartmental Commission of International Trade, Notice on Initiating and Conducting an Antidumping Investigation on Imports of Cement Originated from the Republic of Turkey to Ukraine, АД-463/2020/4411–03, 2 September 2020.

[29] Antimonopoly Committee of Ukraine, Recommendation to Domestic Cement Producers Not to Raise Prices, 13 April 2021 (n 27).

[30] Ibid.

[31] Interdepartmental Commission of International Trade, Notice on Application of Definitive Anti-dumping Measures (n 25).

on many systemic issues.[32] For example, as explained by Michel Cartland, Gerard Depayre and Jan Woznowski—members of the Uruguay Round Negotiating Group on Subsidies and Countervailing Measures—the SCM Agreement does not contain an "explicit/implicit indication of its object and purpose because the drafters specifically decided that it would be impossible to agree on these matters".[33]

Nevertheless, it is commonly understood that one of the main goals was to constrain the unilateral use of trade remedies in order to avoid widespread abuse of such measures, which would frustrate the market access expectations created by the reciprocal tariff concessions of GATT.[34] Although a number of constraints indeed have been imposed, the underlying idea remained unchanged: WTO Members are allowed to impose trade remedies on dumped, subsidized or increased imports that injure their domestic industry. The Agreements make no reference to consumer welfare, to market structure or to labor-market conditions. To the contrary, the injury to domestic industry is the only element that must be established in order to impose trade remedies; their effect on consumers and downstream industries in an importing country is not relevant. The discipline, therefore, is aimed at promoting producers' interests only. In other words, its main purpose is to protect domestic competitors rather than the process of competition as such.

The objectives underlying trade remedy law contrast starkly with those of competition law. The main objective of competition policy is to achieve the most efficient allocation of resources and thereby the maximization of national welfare. Thus, from a competition perspective, dumped or subsidized imports affect competition only when they allow inefficient companies to survive artificially to the detriment of more efficient competitors. Put differently, in order to be compatible with competition objectives, trade remedy discipline should not be concerned with any harm to competitors but only harm to competitors that are more, or at least equally, efficient.[35] The existing legal framework, however, does not serve this purpose. To the contrary, as Nobel economist Joseph Stiglitz points out, "[p]erpetuating unfair trade laws that are themselves unfair thus imposes substantial burdens on our consumers and on

---

[32] Matsushita et al. (n 5) 335; Lester et al. (n 5) 477–478.

[33] Michael Cartland et al., 'Is Something Going Wrong in the WTO Dispute Settlement?' (2012) 46 Journal of World Trade: Law, Economic Policy, Public Policy 979 (992).

[34] Se e.g. John Howard Jackson, *World Trade and the Law of GATT* (Bobbs-Merrill Co. 1969), Chap. 16.

[35] Alan Sykes and Richard Cooper, 'Antidumping and Antitrust: What Problems Does Each Address?' in Robert Zachary Lawrence (ed), *Brookings Trade Forum* (Brookings Institution Press 1998) 1 (25–27) (arguing that "the injury test was crafted to permit duties in any case of actual or threatened "injury" to an industry and was in no way limited to circumstances in which foreign competitors were in a position to extinguish domestic competition and acquire monopoly power"); see also Luka Rubini, *The Definition of Subsidy and State Aid: WTO and EC Law in Comparative Perspective* (Oxford University Press 2009) 382–385; Gene Grossman and Petros Mavroidis, 'Here Today, Gone Tomorrow? Privatization and the Injury Caused by Non-Recurring Subsidies' in Henrik Horn and Petros Mavroidis (eds), *The WTO Case Law of 2001* (Cambridge University Press 2003) 170 (180–186); Sungjoon Cho (n 20) 357 (370–371).

our most efficient exporters while protecting our least-efficient import-competing firms".[36]

For applying anti-dumping duties, which are by far the most frequently used measures globally and in Ukraine,[37] the existence of dumping must be established. Article VI GATT and the Anti-Dumping Agreement define dumping extremely broadly so as to encompass a wide spectrum of behavior that may be motivated by factors other than anti-competitive intent.

It is worth noting that early national anti-dumping laws derived from competition concerns rather than from the protection of domestic industries; only later did the two areas of law diverge. In particular, the U.S. Anti-Dumping Act of 1916 was aimed specifically at predatory dumping; in other words, it required evidence of intent on the part of exporters to injure a domestic producer and/or to achieve a monopoly position in the relevant domestic market. Moreover, dumping was narrowly defined as international price discrimination only, i.e. setting an export price below the price charged for the same product in the exporter's home market. In 1921, however, the scope of the U.S. anti-dumping law had widened to allow the introduction of anti-dumping measures without establishing predatory intent. Furthermore, in the 1970s the law was amended to require that not only price discrimination but also sales below the cost of production be considered dumping.[38] Consequently, under the new rule, national investigating authorities may disregard a sale of the product in the domestic market if such sale is below the cost of production. Since dumping exists where the value of the product in the domestic market of the exporting country exceeds the "export price", such exclusion of below-cost sales made it easier to find dumping.

To a large extent, the U.S. law provided a basis for GATT Art. VI, which set forth the basic principles to be followed by WTO Members when dealing with dumping issues.[39] As a result, WTO law (and subsequently domestic laws of WTO Members such as Ukraine) shares the same characteristics that eventually marked the divergence of anti-dumping law from competition law. Anti-dumping law in its current form does not protect competition from predation. On the contrary, it is typically applied in the situations where the necessary conditions for successful predation are not satisfied. For instance, in a study of anti-dumping cases in the European Union, it was concluded that of the 461 cases initiated between 1980 and 1997, only 12 (around 2%) met the requirements necessary for predatory behavior.[40] A similar

---

[36] Joseph Stiglitz, 'Dumping on Free Trade: The U.S. Import Trade Laws' (1997) 64(2) Southern Economic Journal 402 (418).

[37] Of 33 trade remedy measures which are currently in force in Ukraine, 29 are anti-dumping measures https://td.me.gov.ua/en/zaxodyzovn/ accessed 19 January 2022.

[38] For more historical context see Alan Sykes and Richard Cooper, 'Antidumping and Antitrust: What Problems Does Each Address?' in Lawrence (n 35) 1 (17–18); Sungjoon Cho (n 20) 357 (364–367); Chad Bown and Rachel McCulloch, 'Antidumping and Market Competition: Implications for Emerging Economies', 2015 European University Institute Working Papers 1 (2–4).

[39] The World Bank, 'The Origin and Evolution of Antidumping Regulation', (Working Papers) WPS 783, 1991, 1 (24–25).

[40] Jacques Bourgeois and Patrick Messerlin, 'The European Community's Experience' in Robert Zachary Lawrence (ed), *Brookings Trade Forum* (Brookings Institution Press 1998) 127 (133–144).

study of U.S. anti-dumping cases for the period 1980 through 1989 concludes that the domestic market-concentration criterion for successful predatory dumping was satisfied in only 39 of 282 cases (less than 14%).[41]

The definition of dumping—which includes price discrimination and sales below cost—is clearly too broad, so that practices that are not necessarily anti-competitive may be regarded as dumping. For example, sales below cost may occur during intense competition or a decline in demand due to a recession. Similarly, international price discrimination may exist when there are differences in elasticity of demand between the exporting and importing countries.[42]

Consequently, due to quite loose standards for determining dumping and injury—the central elements of an anti-dumping investigation—anti-dumping law, which originally was intended to protect competition, became an instrument of "the protection of domestic industry from international competition".[43]

Finally, Art. 9(3) Anti-Dumping Agreement requires that the amount of duty cannot exceed the margin of dumping. Similarly, Arts. 14 and 19 SCM Agreement require that the maximum amount of CVDs be the amount of the subsidy found to exist. This can only be understood as an attempt to restore the status quo prior to the injury to the domestic industry rather than to restore competition on the relevant market.

The current approach adopted by the WTO Agreements is to a large extent the result of viewing trade remedies from a trade perspective, focusing on market access. This means that the emphasis is on the protection of the relevant tariff commitments and trade expectations of WTO Members. It is useful to recall that the U.S. CVD law—one of the first national CVD laws—originally only applied to dutiable imports, and no injury test was required.[44] This suggests that, at that time, the main goal of trade remedy law was to preserve the level of protection established by existing tariffs. Even though trade laws have undergone significant changes since those nineteenth-century provisions, the fact that the WTO Agreements cap the level of anti-dumping duties and CVDs at the level of the margin of dumping or a subsidy rather than the actual injury suggests that the primarily goal of imposing trade remedies is not to remedy injurious effects caused by dumping or a subsidy, but instead to simply restore the status quo prior to the injury or, put differently, to "re-establish" the balance of concessions between the parties.[45]

In conclusion, the existing Ukrainian law on trade remedies, as discussed in the previous section, is mostly consistent with WTO law. Accordingly, it shares the same philosophy and important features which in turn make it inconsistent with the

[41] Hyun Ja Shin, 'Possible Instances of Predatory Pricing in Recent U.S. Antidumping Cases' in Robert Zachary Lawrence (ed), *Brookings Trade Forum* (Brookings Institution Press 1998) 81 (87–94).

[42] Matsushita et al. (n 5) 396–399.

[43] Dum (n 7) 168.

[44] Tariff Act 1897, (Dingley Tariff) ch. 11, § 5, 30 stat 151, 205.

[45] David Palmeter and Stanimir Alexandrov, 'Inducing Compliance in WTO Dispute Settlement' in Daniel Kennedy and James Southwick (eds), *The Political Economy of International Trade Law: Essays in Honor of Robert E. Hudec* (Cambridge University Press 2002) 646 (646–647).

underlying objectives of competition policy. In its current form, Ukrainian law and the practice of its implementation raise serious concerns about its possible abuse for anti-competitive purposes when less efficient Ukrainian producers get protected at the expense of more efficient foreign producers, downstream Ukrainian industries producing more value-added goods, and final consumers.

4 Potential Solutions for the Problem

The most straightforward way to address this problem would be repealing the national law on trade remedies and replacing it with measures developed in competition law. Some scholars have advocated this solution, arguing that existing laws have no convincing efficiency rationale, neither from a national nor from an international perspective.[46] I do not suggest such a radical solution, as trade remedies continue to be an important protection tool in some situations and the law could be beneficial if crafted and implemented accordingly.

It is important to note that by virtue of Art. XVI:4 WTO Agreement Ukraine is under an obligation to keep its national law consistent with the WTO Agreements. Consequently, the most important and principal changes that are necessary in order to introduce competition policy considerations into the trade remedy regime can only be made in Ukrainian law after the respective changes are made in the WTO Agreements.

Although competition policy rules are not included in the GATT, there is a growing recognition among WTO Members and scholars that they must be incorporated into the WTO regime.[47] There are significant differences between international trade and international competition law: whereas the WTO is based on a trade approach, focusing primarily on market access and the relevant tariff commitments, competition law is more concerned with the possible distortions of competition. These differences are particularly evident in the current trade remedy regime, which is designed mostly with trade considerations in mind. Introducing competition policy considerations, however, does not suggest that the competition approach will replace the trade approach; rather, they will be suitably reconciled. Indeed, despite the differences between these two bodies of law, they can be complementary.[48] Yet in light of the current crisis in the WTO, the adoption of such changes, although highly desirable, is highly unlikely.

---

[46] John James Barceló III, 'The Antidumping Law: Repeal It or Revise It' (1979) Michigan Journal of International Law 53 (54–57); Bernard Hoekman and Petros Mavroidis, 'Dumping, Antidumping and Antitrust' (1996) 30(1) Journal of World Trade 27; Alan Sykes, 'Countervailing Duty Law: An Economic Perspective' (1989) 89 Columbia Law Review 199 (199–263).

[47] Paragraph 20 of the Singapore Ministerial Declaration established a Working Group on Trade and Competition Policy.

[48] See e.g. Martyn Taylor, *International Competition Law: A New Dimension for the WTO?* (Cambridge University Press 2006) 177.

Therefore, the amendment of the national law of Ukraine is the only possible option at the moment. Since the law must remain consistent with the existing WTO Agreements, it would be impossible to introduce the major changes necessary to make the application of trade remedy entirely compatible with competition objectives. It is argued, however, that trade remedy use still could be disciplined so that the amended law is consistent with both the current WTO rules and the objectives underlying competition policy. To that end, it is proposed to strengthen the public interest requirement, which is already embodied in Ukrainian law.

4.1 Strengthening the Public Interest Requirement

Trade remedies assist a domestic producer in recovering from the injury caused by dumped, subsidized or increased imports. However, as discussed in the previous section, their effect is not limited exclusively to domestic producers. Accordingly, by imposing costs on other economic sectors and on consumers which are not outweighed by the benefits to the industry receiving protection from imports, trade remedies may result in reducing economic welfare. To address these concerns, and to strike a balance between the various competing interests, some WTO Members have introduced a "public interest" provision. Although the precise scope of this clause differs in different countries, it generally requires that before duties are imposed, investigating authorities examine the impact this would have on the users of the imports subject to investigation and on the consumers of the final products embodying imported intermediate goods.

A public interest clause is incorporated into the domestic laws of Argentina, Brazil, Canada, China, the EU, the UK and some other countries. Some WTO Members such as the EU and the UK consider public interest a substantial element (together with dumped/subsidized/increased imports, injury to a domestic industry and causal link); the investigating authorities, therefore, must give consideration to the public interest before imposing trade remedies. In other jurisdictions a public interest inquiry is not a mandatory part of an investigation. In Canada, for example, after having established that imports have caused injury to the domestic producer, the investigative authority may initiate a public interest inquiry either on its own initiative or on the request of an interested party.[49]

Ukrainian law has contained a public interest clause (called a "national interests" requirement) since 1998, when trade remedy laws were adopted for the first time. Under Art. 36 (1) Law on AD: "The conclusion as to whether national interests require antidumping measures should be based on an assessment of all interests, including those of the national producer and consumer, the impact of imports subject to investigation on employment, the national producer and consumer's investment, and international economic interests of the importing country [...] Anti-dumping measures may not be applied if the Commission, based on the submission from

[49] Special Import Measures Act R.S.C., 1985 c. S-15, art 45.1.

the Ministry and taking into account all the information received, concludes that imposition of such measures contradicts national interests."[50]

Although the language is rather vague as to whether a public interest assessment is in fact mandatory, the Commission does conduct it and the final reports normally contain a separate conclusion regarding the public interest. While until 2020 most investigations were concluded by introducing the measure, this major trend has recently started to change. For example, in 2021 ten investigations have been concluded; in four of those cases a negative determination was made. In two out of the four negative determinations, the decision not to impose trade remedies was made because they were not in the public interest.

One of those two cases is of particular interest. In September 2021, the Commission published its decision on imposing definitive safeguard measures on imports of cable,[51] only to announce that it would be reviewing this decision ten days later.[52] The review was launched at the request of the Ministry of Digital Transformation of Ukraine. The Ministry argued that the imposition of such measures would reduce the pace of internet deployment in the country. In particular, it could seriously jeopardize the budget-funded program aimed at connecting more than 3,000 villages to internet.[53] Just two weeks after launching the review of its decision (in which it was explicitly stated that such measures would not be against the public interest) the Commission announced the decision not to impose safeguard measures on imports of cable because they would be against the public interest.[54]

Apart from the obvious concerns regarding transparency in this particular case, it also reveals the lack of a systemic and consistent approach in assessing public interest by the Ukrainian investigating authorities. Indeed, evidence from many jurisdictions demonstrates that vaguely defined public interest clauses have little impact, while introducing a more specifically defined public interest requirement and a detailed guidance on its application generate more legal certainty and make this tool more suitable for its purpose.[55]

On 21 September 2020 three new draft laws regarding trade remedies were registered in the Ukrainian parliament: Draft Law on Protection against Dumped

[50] Provisions with the exact same language can be also found in art 35(1) Law on CVD and art 17(1) Law on Safeguards.

[51] Interdepartmental Commission of International Trade, Notice on Application of Safeguard Measures on Imports of Cable to Ukraine Regardless of a Country of Origin and Export, 23 April 2021.

[52] Interdepartmental Commission of International Trade, Notice on Review of the Decision of Commission on Application of Safeguard Measures on Imports of Cable to Ukraine Regardless of a Country of Origin and Export, 24 September 2021.

[53] Ministry and Committee of Digital Transformation of Ukraine, Imposition of Duties on Imports of Cable May Result in Increasing Costs for Internet Connection for Ukrainians, 27 April 2021.

[54] Interdepartmental Commission of International Trade, Notice on Reversal of the Decision of Commission on Application of Safeguard Measures on Imports of Cable to Ukraine Regardless of a Country of Origin and Export, 11 October 2021.

[55] WPS 783 (n 39), 1 (23); Simone Maciel Cuiabano, 'When Anti-dumping Meets Antitrust: Brazil's Innovative Experience Analyzing Public Interest in Commercial Defense Investigations' (2020) 21 Journal of International Law and Trade Policy 41 (45–49).

Imports,[56] Draft Law on Protection against Subsidized Imports[57] and Draft Law on Safeguards.[58] The draft laws propose a number of changes, including some to a public interest requirement.

Most importantly, the draft laws clearly stipulate that trade remedies "cannot be applied or continued without conducting assessment and determining their compliance with national interest".[59] The suggested language leaves no ambiguity as to whether a public interest assessment is a mandatory part of an investigation. Likewise, it makes it clear that such an assessment should be taken into account in the framework of a review investigation too. This is an important development which demonstrates a growing understanding of the importance of considering interests other than those of the domestic industry that initiated the complain when imposing trade remedies.

Nevertheless, these changes, if adopted, will unlikely make a decisive difference for the outcome of investigations. One of the chief problems with such investigations in Ukraine is the absence of any methodological guidance defining the parameters of the public interest test and specifying how all the factors to be considered are assessed. Indeed, the main goal of public interest analysis is to answer the question whether the benefits to the industry receiving protection outweigh negative effects to other affected industries, consumers and the competition environment. Achieving this goal requires an in-depth and evidence-based analysis based on a consistent and systemic approach which is clearly understandable for an investigating authority and all the parties involved.

The current practice shows the lack of such an approach. Although final reports normally include the section on public interest (containing conclusions regarding possible effects of the proposed measure on domestic producers, consumers, employment and competition), these conclusions are very general, often without presenting any specific data that has been considered and without clarification of the reasoning behind the decision. As a result, the public interest test in its current form does not serve its purpose and could instead easily become an instrument for abuse. Similarly, the minor changes regarding the public interest assessment proposed in the draft laws will not solve the problem.

To address this issue, it is proposed to strengthen the public interest requirement by introducing a set of rules aimed at: (1) defining economic factors to consider and providing explanations as to how these factors are assessed; (2) clarifying sources of evidence and data to be used; (3) defining possible outcomes of the finding that the measure will negatively affect the Ukrainian economy; and (4) enhancing the transparency of the process by making the conclusions regarding public interest publicly available.

---

[56] Draft Law on Protection Against Dumped Imports 2020.

[57] Draft Law on Protection Against Subsidized Imports 2020.

[58] Draft Law on Safeguards 2020.

[59] Draft Law on Protection Against Dumped Imports 2020, art 23(1), Draft Law on Protection Against Subsidized Imports 2020, art 18(1), Draft Law on Safeguards 2020, art 12(1).

4.1.1 Economic Factors to Be Considered in the Course of the Public Interest Inquiry

The parameters of the public interest inquiry must be clearly outlined. The law, however, poorly identifies the economic factors that must be considered when assessing the public interest. Crucially, neither the existing law nor the draft law distinguishes likely consequences for competition as a separate factor to examine. It is proposed to amend the law by including the following factors, which an investigating authority is required to assess: injury caused to a Ukrainian industry by dumped/subsidized/increased imports; possible impact on affected industries and consumers and their economic significance to the Ukrainian economy; possible consequences for the state of competition and for the structure of markets for goods in Ukraine. It should also be in the discretion of an investigating authority to assess any other matters that it considers relevant. Likewise, it is important to have guidelines for assessing each of those factors. The law provides a very detailed instruction as to which factors and indicators must be considered to determine the existence of dumping, subsidy, increased imports, as well as injury to a domestic industry. Neither the existing law nor the draft law does that with regard to assessing the public interest, and therefore it is proposed to amend the law to this effect.

Regarding injury to a domestic industry, since the existence of such injury has already been established in the previous stage of an investigation, the main purpose at this stage is to ascertain whether a proposed measure might affect the injury caused to a domestic industry. Furthermore, for the purpose of the public interest assessment a domestic industry must be defined more broadly than for the purposes of injury determination and, thus, must include all Ukrainian producers of the product under investigation, regardless of whether a certain producer is also an importer or has some association with a foreign exporter.

Assessing the possible impact on affected industries and consumers would first require identifying such industries and assessing their economic significance in terms of employment, production volumes (including for export), market share, market structure (by identifying the downstream and upstream industries in Ukraine and their relationship to the companies that initiated the investigation) and value added by these industries at different stages of the supply chain. The introduced measure will increase the price of the imported products and most likely domestically produced like products, which in turn will increase costs to downstream industries. It is necessary, therefore, to assess the impact of such an increase in costs on the downstream industry, considering such indicators as the size of the expected price increase; availability and price of substitute goods; ability to switch suppliers; ability of a domestic industry to meet demand from the downstream industry; expected price response of the downstream industry; and expected impact on their sales, production and employment. It is also necessary to separately assess the likely impact on other affected industries such as importers, suppliers and distributors in terms of sales, production and employment. As for the final consumers that could be affected by a proposed measure, they first must be identified, including their characteristics that might be relevant (for example, income or age). In assessing the impact of the price increase on consumers, the factors to be considered may include the size of the expected price increase, the ability of consumers to absorb this price increase based on their income, availability of substitutes and the extent to which these products are necessities.

To ensure that competition is not adversely affected by the proposed measure, the investigating authority must assess the existing market structure and state of competition in the relevant market, paying particular attention to such factors as market concentration, pricing behavior of companies, level of innovation, range of goods and their quality. Any discovered practices that harm competition (for example, high level of market concentration, coordination between producers or predatory behavior) must be given serious consideration. The main goal at this stage is to assess how the proposed measure may affect competition in the market by looking at the long-term viability of Ukrainian industry if the measure is not introduced, at whether it will affect market concentration by excluding imports subject to investigation from the market as well as at the ability of new Ukrainian producers and other imports to enter the market after the imposition of such measures.

4.1.2 Sources of Information to Be Used

With regard to the sources of information which an investigating authority will be using, most of such information is not publicly available and can only be collected from the relevant market participants. Interested parties of investigation, which include the domestic producers, foreign producers, exporters and importers of the product under investigation, are therefore important for this purpose. Today in Ukraine, on average ten interested parties actively participate in an investigation. In the high-profile case of a safeguard investigation on fertilizer imports, more than 50 interested parties were registered.[60] That said, interested parties represent a valuable source of information. Yet only national producers and importers obtain deep knowledge about the Ukrainian market. Likewise, under the existing law, the right to provide comments and evidence regarding public interest is limited to such interested parties as domestic industry and importers (Art. 36(2) Law on AD, Art. 35(2) Law on CVD and Art. 17(2) Law on Safeguard). For that reason, only questionnaires issued to domestic industry and importers contain questions regarding public interest.

However, to get a more detailed understanding of the supply chain for the products under investigation, it is necessary to gather information from a wide range of market participants, including those that cannot be registered as interested parties (in particular, downstream user industries, upstream supplier industries, consumer associations). They could be identified in two ways: by asking the interested parties

[60] Anzhela Makhinova, 'Export Markets are Closing, so Ukrainian Companies Must be Ready to Defend Their Place under the Sun' *Yurydychna Hazeta* (26 August 2020) https://yur-gazeta.com/interview/eksportni-rinki-zakrivayutsya-tomu-ukrayinski-kompaniyi-mayut-buti-gotovi-vidstoyuvati-svoe-misce-pi.html accessed 1 June 2022.

to identify these groups in their questionnaire and by allowing them to identify themselves by registering for the purpose of participation in the public interest assessment stage only. Upon identification, they should also receive questionnaires tailored specifically for that purpose.

The investigating authority should also be proactive in gathering further data and evidence from publicly available sources and collected by other state agencies. The effective information exchange cooperation with the Antimonopoly Committee of Ukraine, which conducts its own market research, might be particularly useful.

4.1.3 Possible Outcomes of the Finding

With regard to the legal consequences of the finding that the negative impacts to the Ukrainian economy would be greater than the benefits to the injured domestic industry, the existing law only provides for one possible outcome—the decision not to impose the measure (Art. 36(1) Law on AD, Art. 35(1) Law on CVD and Art. 17(1) Law on Safeguard). Quite often, however, the investigation is conducted with respect to several goods, which, especially in the case of intermediate goods, could be a part of different supply chains. For such situations, it is suggested to stipulate another possible option: not to impose the proposed measure on the specific goods subject to investigation that did not meet the public interest test.

4.1.4 Making Findings Publicly Available

To ensure transparency and legal certainty, the final reports of an investigating authority, containing a clear reference to the data and evidence it considered and reasoning in reaching its decision, must be available to the public.

Under Art. 3(1) WTO Agreement on Safeguards, an investigating authority must "publish a report setting forth their findings and reasoned conclusions reached on all pertinent issues of fact and law". In *US—Steal Safeguards*, the WTO Appellate Body expressly stated that the Member imposing a safeguard measure must demonstrate in its "published report" through "a reasoned and adequate explanation" and "a reasoned conclusion" that the requirements for the imposition of such measures are met.[61] The Ukrainian law on safeguards, on the other hand, does not specifically stipulate the obligation of an investigating authority to publish a final report. Article 16(11) Law on Safeguards only requires publication of a notice on imposing the measure, instead of an entire report, without specifying the contents of the notice.

As a result, in practice, a final report (the Key Findings) containing analysis and conclusions is only circulated among the interested parties as well the representatives of the affected exporting countries in order to comply with Arts. 3, 4 and 12 Agreement on Safeguards. In fact, in some instances even the interested parties

[61] World Trade Organization, 'United States – Definitive Safeguard Measures on Imports of Certain Steel Products' (Dispute Settlement Report) DS248(2003) para 273, 289–291.

were refused access to the safeguard investigation Key Findings and could only get it through court order.[62] In *Ukraine—Passenger Cars*, the panel already concluded that the Key Findings do not constitute the kind of published report required by Art. 3.1 Agreement on Safeguards.[63] The document that is publicly available is the notice on imposing or not imposing a measure, which is published in the official newspaper *Uryadovyi Kuryer*. This notice, however, only contains a rather short summary of a final report, without providing much data or an explanation of how the decision was reached. For example, the part of the notice regarding public interest analysis usually includes one sentence merely stating that the national interests of Ukraine require or do not require imposition of the measure.

Likewise, under WTO law on AD and CVD (Art. 12(2)(2) Anti-Dumping Agreement and Art. 22(5) SCM Agreement),

> [A] public notice of conclusion or suspension of an investigation [...] shall contain, or otherwise make available through a separate report, all relevant information on all on the matters of fact and law and reasons which have led to the imposition of final measure [...] [i]n particular, the notice or report shall contain [...] the reason for the acceptance or rejection of relevant arguments or claims made by the exporters and importers.

Unlike in the case of safeguard investigations, for AD and CVD investigations WTO law does not require publishing exclusively a report, giving an investigating authority the option to publish either a notice or report. Nevertheless, the language makes it clear that it is still required "to explain their final determination, providing sufficient background and reasons for that determination, such as its reasons for concluding as it did can be discerned and are understood".[64] Yet Ukrainian law only stipulates that a notice must contain "a summary of facts and main conclusions regarding the existence of dumping/unlawful subsidy and injury" (Art. 28(2) Law on AD and Art. 27(2) Law on CVD). The existing law, therefore, requires the authorities neither to explain the reasons for their determination nor provide a summary of facts and conclusions with regard to a public interest inquiry in a public notice.

Draft laws, although they put it slightly differently, do not propose any substantive changes: "official notices must contain all public information which was considered in the course of preparing decisions or conclusions" (Art. 37(3) Draft Law on Protection against Dumped Imports, Art. 33(3) Draft Law on Protection against Subsidized

---

[62] Anzhela Makhinova, 'Trade Defense Remedies: The Most Frequently Used Protectionist Measures of 2020' (11 August 2021) https://sk.ua/publications/trade-defense-remedies-the-most-frequently-used-protectionist-measures-of-2020/ accessed 1 June 2022.

[63] World Trade Organization, 'Ukraine – Definitive Safeguard Measures on Certain Passenger Cars' (Panel Report) WT/DS468/R, 2015, para 7.36 (it is important to note, however, that the panel made this conclusion for the purpose of establishing which documents comprise the competent authorities' "published report" within the meaning of art 3(1) only. Exercising judicial economy, the panel decided against making a finding regarding whether Ukraine acted inconsistently with art 3(1) by failing to provide a reasoned and adequate explanation as to how the facts support the findings).

[64] World Trade Organization, 'European Union – Anti-Dumping Measures on Certain Footwear from China', (Panel Report) WT/DS405/R, 2012, para 7.844.

Imports and Art. 24(3) Draft Law on Safeguards). Consequently, the final conclusions will continue to be published in the form of a notice rather than a report and no reasoning for reaching the decisions will be required.

Therefore, the existing Ukrainian law (just as the proposed draft laws) and the subsequent practice are inconsistent with the WTO obligations of Ukraine, firstly, to include in its published final determinations adequate and sufficient findings on all pertinent issues of fact and law and reasons that led to imposition of the measure and, secondly, to publish final determinations in safeguard investigations in the form of a report instead of a notice. It is important to note, however, that since the scope of the WTO public notice obligation only covers substantive requirements for the imposition of trade remedies set forth in the WTO Agreements (i.e. dumped/subsidized/increased imports, injury and causal link), not including findings or reasoning concerning a public interest inquiry in the notice will likely not constitute a breach of WTO law, because such inquiry is not required by the relevant WTO Agreements.[65]

Even irrespective of the issue of consistency with WTO law, it is crucial that the final determinations regarding the imposition of trade remedies become publicly available. The practitioners have voiced their concern over transparency and limited access to the materials in trade remedy investigations in Ukraine.[66] Indeed, a final determination must be perceived by the interested parties and by society as being the result of a transparent procedure, of proper factual evaluation and of a correct application of legal rules. Proper reasoning is an imperative necessity which not only makes the decision easier for the parties to understand and be accepted but also becomes a safeguard against arbitrariness. Yet the Key Findings often lack clear reasoning and analysis and are not publicly available to other industries and consumers which might be affected by the introduced measure and to society in general.

There is no sound justification for this practice to continue. In *Ukraine—Passenger Cars*, the Ukrainian government itself admitted that even though notices are published in the official newspaper *Uryadovyi Kuryer*, because it is reserved only for notices about the Commission decisions, publication in this newspaper is not the only legally accepted method of publication provided by law.[67] Indeed, today court decisions and decisions of other governmental agencies such as the Antimonopoly Committee of Ukraine are freely accessible online. In November 2021, the Ministry of Economy launched the trade defense website, which in addition to consolidating all information concerning the current investigations, the introduced measures, relevant legal acts and guidelines will also be serving as a platform for electronic submission of the

---

[65] World Trade Organization, 'China – Countervailing and Anti-Dumping Duties on Grain Oriented Flatt-Rolled Electrical Steel from the United States' (Appellate Body Report) WT/DS414/AB/R, 2012, paras 256–257.

[66] Oleksiy Pustovit, 'Tariffs Behind the Shadow: What is Wrong with Trade Defense in Ukraine' *Ekonomichna Pravda* (8 October 2021) https://www.epravda.com.ua/columns/2021/10/8/678549/ accessed 1 June 2022.

[67] World Trade Organization, 'Ukraine – Definitive Safeguard Measures on Certain Passenger Cars' (n 63) para 6.11.

materials by interested parties.[68] This certainly could be an appropriate platform for providing public access to the Key Findings.

It is proposed, therefore, to amend the law so that it specifically requires that final reports (1) contain all relevant information on all issues of fact and law (including that of public interest) and reasoned and adequate explanation in support of the determination and (2) be publicly available through an appropriate platform.

In conclusion, the changes proposed in this section will substantially enhance the role of competition policy in trade remedy investigations and to some extent reconcile the conflicting objectives of trade defense and competition.

5 Conclusion

The increase in the use of trade remedies that we have recently witnessed in Ukraine raises serious concerns over negative effects they might have on the economy by increasing production costs for downstream industries and the price for final consumers as well as by reducing competition.

A closer look at the law on trade remedies reveals that it is inadequate to address this issue and is mostly concerned with promoting the interests of domestic producers harmed by competing imports. It is the injury to domestic industry that must be established in order to impose trade remedies, while their adverse effect on the economy is not considered. Likewise, a very broad definition of dumping covers practices that are not necessarily anti-competitive, and as a result the law does not specifically target predatory behavior. Finally, the fact that the law caps the level of anti-dumping and countervailing duties at the level of the margin of dumping or a subsidy rather than the actual injury suggests that the primarily goal of imposing trade remedies is not to remedy injurious effects caused by dumping or a subsidy, but instead to simply restore the status quo prior to the injury.

This inconsistency with the competition objective, which we can find in Ukrainian law, was largely inherited from WTO law. The latter was developed with trade concerns in mind, focusing primarily on market access and the relevant tariff commitments. Although WTO law on trade remedies has undergone substantial changes, the main purpose of such changes was to prevent abuses when imposing trade remedies and thus protect the market access expectations. In other words, the main concern was negative effects on imports coming to the country imposing the measure rather than potential distortion of competition in the internal market of this country.

Since Ukrainian law must remain consistent with the existing WTO rules, the most important changes that are necessary in order to introduce competition policy considerations into the trade remedy regime can only be made in Ukrainian law after the respective changes are made in the WTO Agreements. Nevertheless, it is argued that trade remedy use could still be disciplined so that the amended law is

[68] Official website of the Department of Foreign Economic Activity and Trade Defense at the Ministry of Economy of Ukraine https://td.me.gov.ua/ accessed 1 February 2022.

both consistent with the current WTO rules and more in line with the objectives underlying competition policy. To that end, it is proposed to strengthen one of the requirements for introducing trade remedies, namely the public interest requirement.

The public interest requirement requires that before duties are imposed, investigating authorities must examine the impact this would have on the users, final consumers and the economy in general. While not envisaged by WTO law, this requirement is incorporated into the domestic law of some countries, including Ukraine. Yet the poorly defined public interest clause does not serve its purpose and could instead easily become an instrument for abuse. To address this issue, it is proposed to strengthen such requirement by introducing a set of rules aimed at: (1) defining economic factors to consider in the course of investigation and providing explanations as to how these factors are assessed; (2) clarifying the sources of evidence and data to be used; (3) expanding the list of possible outcomes of the finding that the measure will negatively affect the Ukrainian economy; and (4) enhancing the transparency of the process by making the conclusions (including those regarding public interest) publicly available. The proposed rules will substantially increase the role of competition considerations in trade investigations and will become safeguards against abuse and arbitrariness in the authorities' application of the public interest test.

References

Jacques Bourgeois and Patrick Messerlin, 'The European Community's Experience' in Robert Zachary Lawrence (ed), *Brookings Trade Forum* (Brookings Institution Press 1998) 127

Chad Bown and Rachel McCulloch, 'Antidumping and Market Competition: Implications for Emerging Economies', 2015 European University Institute Working Papers

Marco Bronckers, 'Private Remedies Against Foreign Subsidization: A European View' in Jacques Bourgeois (ed), *Subsidies and International Trade: A European Lawyers' Perspective* (Kluwer Law International 1991) 187

Michael Cartland, Gérard Depayre and Jan Woznowski, 'Is Something Going Wrong in the WTO Dispute Settlement?' (2012) 46 Journal of World Trade: Law, Economic Policy, Public Policy 979

Sungjoon Cho, 'Anticompetitive Trade Remedies: How Antidumping Measures Obstruct Market Competition' (2009) 87 North Carolina Law Review 357

Natalia Datskevych, 'Dangerous Quotas: Limiting Fertilizer Imports Might Kill Competition, Benefit Oligarchs' *Kyiv Post* (11 July 2020) https://www.kyivpost.com/business/dangerous-quotas-limiting-fertilizer-imports-might-kill-competition-benefit-oligarchs.html

Kenneth Dum, *The GATT: Law and Economic Organization* (University of Chicago Press 1977)

Gene Grossman and Petros Mavroidis, 'Here Today, Gone Tomorrow? Privatization and the Injury Caused by Non-Recurring Subsidies' in Henrik Horn and Petros Mavroidis (eds), *The WTO Case Law of 2001* (Cambridge University Press 2003) 170

Bernard Hoekman and Petros Mavroidis, 'Dumping, Antidumping and Antitrust' (1996) 30(1) Journal of World Trade 27

John Howard Jackson, William Davey and Alan Sykes, *Legal Problems of International Economic Relations: Cases, Materials and Text on the National and International Regulation of Transnational Economic Relations* (West Academic 6th ed. 2013)

John Howard Jackson, *The World Trading System: Law and Policy of International Economic Relations* (MIT Press 2nd ed.1997)
John Howard Jackson, *World Trade and the Law of GATT* (Bobbs-Merrill Co. 1969)
Hyun Ja Shin, 'Possible Instances of Predatory Pricing in Recent U.S. Antidumping Cases' in Robert Zachary Lawrence (ed), *Brookings Trade Forum* (Brookings Institution Press 1998) 81
John James Barceló III, 'A History of GATT Unfair Trade Remedy Law: Confusion of Purposes' (1991) 517 Cornell Law Faculty Publications 311
John James Barceló III, 'The Antidumping Law: Repeal It or Revise It' (1979) Michigan Journal of International Law 53
Simon Lester, Bryan Mercurio and Arwel Davies, *World Trade Law: Text, Materials and Commentary* (Hart Publishing 2nd ed. 2012)
Simone Maciel Cuiabano, 'When Anti-dumping Meets Antitrust: Brazil's Innovative Experience Analyzing Public Interest in Commercial Defense Investigations' (2020) 21 Journal of International Law and Trade Policy 41
Anzhela Makhinova, 'Trade Defense Remedies: The Most Frequently Used Protectionist Measures of 2020' *Sayenko Kharenko* (11 August 2021) https://sk.ua/publications/trade-defense-remedies-the-most-frequently-used-protectionist-measures-of-2020/
Anzhela Makhinova, 'Export Markets are Closing, so Ukrainian Companies Must be Ready to Defend Their Place under the Sun' *Yurydychna Hazeta* (26 August 2020) https://yur-gazeta.com/interview/eksportni-rinki-zakrivayutsya-tomu-ukrayinski-kompaniyi-mayut-buti-gotovi-vidstoyuvati-svoe-misce-pi.html [Анжела Махінова, 'Експортні ринки закриваються, тому українські компанії мають бути готові відстоювати своє місце під сонцем' *Юридична газета* (26 серпня 2020)]
Mitsuo Matsushita, Thomas Schoenbaum and Petros Mavroidis, *The World Trade Organization: Law, Practice, and Policy* (Oxford University Press 2nd ed. 2006)
Robert O'Brien, *Subsidy Regulation and State Transformation in North America, the GATT and the EU* (Palgrave Macmillan 1997)
David Palmeter and Stanimir Alexandrov, 'Inducing Compliance in WTO Dispute Settlement' in Daniel Kennedy and James Southwick (eds) *The Political Economy of International Trade Law: Essays in Honor of Robert E. Hudec* (Cambridge University Press 2002) 646
Oleksiy Pustovit, 'Tariffs Behind the Shadow: What is Wrong with Trade Defense in Ukraine' *Ekonomichna Pravda* (8 October 2021) https://www.epravda.com.ua/columns/2021/10/8/678549/ [Олексій Пустовіт, 'Мита за темною завісою: що не так з торговельним захистом в Україні' *Економічна правда* (8 жовтня 2021)]
Luka Rubini, *The Definition of Subsidy and State Aid: WTO and EC Law in Comparative Perspective* (Oxford University Press 2009)
Joseph Stiglitz, 'Dumping on Free Trade: The U.S. Import Trade Laws' (1997) 64(2) Southern Economic Journal 402
Alan Sykes and Richard Cooper, 'Antidumping and Antitrust: What Problems Does Each Address?' in Robert Zachary Lawrence (ed), *Brookings Trade Forum* (Brookings Institution Press 1998)
Alan Sykes, 'Countervailing Duty Law: An Economic Perspective' (1989) 89 Columbia Law Review 199
Martyn Taylor, *International Competition Law: A New Dimension for the WTO?* (Cambridge University Press 2006)
The World Bank, 'Antitrust-Based Remedies and Dumping in International Trade' (Policy Research Working Paper) WPS 1347, 1994
The World Bank, 'The Origin and Evolution of Antidumping Regulation', (Working Paper) WPS 783, 1991
Peter Van der Bossche and Werner Zdouc, *The Law and Policy of the World Trade Organization: Texts, Cases and Materials* (Cambridge University Press, 4th ed. 2017)

Legal Support of State Economic Policies of Ukraine in the Context of Investment Development and Protection of Competition

Oleg Podtserkovnyi

Contents

Abstract This chapter examines the general legal framework of Ukrainian state economic policies in the sphere of investment and competition development. It presents the descriptions of the tools and role of state economic policy in solving the challenges of today, the main features of the legal framework of Ukrainian state economic policy, the directions of the legal stimulation of investments, including innovations and competition protection in the state economic policy of Ukraine, and the general perspectives of the implementation of successful foreign experience. The material is aimed at suggesting ways of improving the legislative quality of state economic policy of Ukraine in the context of developing the efficiency of law

O. Podtserkovnyi (✉)
Economic Law and Procedure Department, National University 'Odesa Law Academy', Odesa, Ukraine
e-mail: opp@ukr.net

H. Richter (ed.), *Competition and Intellectual Property Law in Ukraine*,
MPI Studies on Intellectual Property and Competition Law 31,
https://doi.org/10.1007/978-3-662-66101-7_4

enforcement, transparency and consistency of managerial decisions, sufficiency of incentives and guarantees, anti-corruption effectiveness, access to capital, protection of corporate rights and stability of legal regulation of the economy, ensuring the balance of private and public interests.

1 Introduction and Problem Statement

This chapter explores the main components of state influence in the area of investments and innovations, based on a comprehensive analysis and critical examination of the methods and forms of the state regulation of the economy in Ukraine. An attempt will be made to assess the extent and limit of state impact on these relations, as well as to identify economic and legal problems facing the state and society in overcoming Soviet management traditions and implementing the best global experience in investment development. The state's economic policy can stimulate or conversely inhibit development in this area, encourage or deter competition amongst businesses, creative professions and innovation projects. But precisely private activity is the most productive source of innovations so that it should not be enslaved by public power. Therefore, it will be shown that state power aims at economic and legal regulation to balance the interests of both private business and public authority.

Given that the state of research in Ukraine in early 2022 has changed radically due to the Russian invasion and the destruction of the entire principles of social life, certain conclusions of this work are oriented on martial law and the prospects for the restoration of economic relations in the postwar period.

The general idea of this chapter is to present public economic policy as a set of legal, organizational, informational, managerial, and other means of state impact that should be combined and consistent with economic, political, security and other factors of society in order to develop and to introduce a promising model of investment and economic legislation of Ukraine in general. The chapter argues that commercial legislation should ensure innovative development in Ukraine and the involvement of citizens and businesses in cross-border innovation processes based on the protection of intellectual property and the promotion of creative activity as elements of a free and democratic world.

2 The Regulatory Role of the State in a Market Economy: From Negation to Recognition and Meaningful Discussion

2.1 *The Regulatory Role of the State in the Economic Sphere*

In modern society, almost any economic process is subject to state regulation. This applies to investment, innovation, and the turnover of intellectual property rights. The modern state not only carries out the legal regulation of economic relations and protects property rights as has been the case for recent centuries, but also becomes a direct participant through its special authorities, enterprises, and organizations.

As a regulator, the state tries to act as a bearer of public economic interests, which are based on considering the interests of the whole of the people. But the development and implementation of this policy is influenced by competition between the public interest and the private interest of every citizen in the context of objective economic laws and the challenges of social life. This statement is especially true for democracies, whose power is formed under the influence of voters who oblige the state to take care not only of the common good, but also of human rights and fundamental freedoms. After all, it is almost consensual for society that "depending on the efficiency of the political process, social welfare either increases or decreases".[1]

There are many definitions by economists and lawyers of state regulation of the economy in the literature. For example, it is noted that "regulation in general is a form of government intervention in economic activity and interference with the working of the free-market system",[2] or "regulation is state intervention in the private domain, which is a byproduct of our imperfect reality and human limitations".[3] State regulation of the market economy is determined by a set of standard measures of a legislative, executive and control nature, which are carried out by competent state institutions and public organizations to stabilize and adapt the existing socio-economic system to changing conditions.[4]

The term "state management of the economy" is also used in Ukrainian legal and other literature. In particular, O. Vinnyk notes that management (as a legal form of state management of the economy) means the adoption by the competent authority of legally significant decisions for business entities on operational issues of economic life (state registration of business entities, certain types of contracts and property; issue of licenses, patents and other permits; establishment of quotas; approval of standards and certification of products; setting limits on the use of natural resources,

---

[1] Johan den Hertog, 'Review of Economic Theories of Regulation' (2010) 10–18 Tjalling C Koopmans Research Institute Discussion Paper 1.

[2] Imad A Moosa, 'Good Regulation, Bad Regulation: The Anatomy of Financial Regulation' in Philip Molyneux (ed), *Palgrave Macmillan Studies in Banking and Financial Institutions* (Springer 2015).

[3] Barak Orbach, 'What Is Regulation?' (2012) 30 Yale Journal on Regulation Online 1, 10.

[4] Anatolii Pelikh, *Fundamentals of Entrepreneurship* (Gardarika 1996).

etc.).[5] The competent state bodies perform the full range of necessary management functions. According to O. Ryabchenko, state management of the economy is a special part of the management of social development, which is carried out by authorized bodies of state power and local self-government, the action of which is aimed at implementing the constitutionally enshrined provisions on the social orientation of the economy. State management of the economy has a powerful, organizational and executive nature.[6]

For legal research, the concept of regulation has to be narrowed down to the measures of state influence on the behavior of subjects of market relations reflected in the law. It is no coincidence that authors insert provisos that "regulation will be taken to mean the employment of legal instruments for the implementation of social-economic policy objectives".[7]

The answer to the question of what the regulatory role of the state in the economic sphere should be depends on many factors. They are not the same for countries of different legal culture and traditions, the level of productive forces achieved, the political regime, location, economic potential, the level of corruption and the criminalization (shadowing) of economic relations. Finally, it depends on conditions of external security, stability of the financial and economic system and social standards. These factors are well known to economists and managers, but there are no ready-made recipes for an effective set of tools and forms of state impact to stimulate economic development for a particular country in a given historical period.

The general problem lies in the collision of theories of economic regulation, while the preference for one or another theory, in fact, is based not only on considerations of objective market failures and potential government efficiency but on trust in the state authority and its political institutions at the present level of social development.

> Free marketeers dislike regulation because they do not like any form of government intervention and prefer to feel the full power of the market. However, those who believe that government intervention may be necessary (even a necessary evil), and that people should not be exposed to the full tyranny of the market, find regulation to be tolerable, even desirable.[8]

Regulation elicits a very diverse reaction amongst economists, "[b]ut this difference has narrowed considerably, because economists now understand that regulation and tariffs share a common political susceptibility to the influence of organized interests".[9] The need to uphold high social standards and economic freedoms, European integration, and the above-mentioned circumstances of renewed military aggression,

[5] Oksana Vinnyk, *Commercial Law: A Course of Lectures* (Atika 2004) (456–457).

[6] Olena Riabchenko, 'State Management of the Economy of Ukraine, Administrative Legal Aspect' (2000) University of Internal Affairs.

[7] Johan den Hertog, 'Review of Economic Theories of Regulation' (2010) 10–18 Tjalling C. Koopmans Research Institute Discussion Paper 1, 1.

[8] Imad A Moosa, 'Good Regulation, Bad Regulation: The Anatomy of Financial Regulation' in Molyneux (ed) (n 2), 1.

[9] Sam Peltzman, 'George Stigler's Contribution to the Economic Analysis of Regulation' (1993) 101(5) Journal of Political Economy, 818.

global health problems and environmental threats leave the state's efforts to develop a common economic policy in the public interest without alternative.

State economic policy embodies an authentic set of measures, methods, tools, and forms of regulating influence of the state on socio-economic processes in different socio-economic situations. To a large extent, it also depends on the accumulated experience of state intervention in a particular sector of the economy. As for technology and innovation, the mentioned policy largely focuses on the idea that

> the future economy is going to be driven by knowledge and the tools that access, direct, and use this knowledge are going to be key to any state's economic future. Technology, talent, and capital will be the issues that states need to address.[10]

Certain directions of modern state economic policy reflect the public demand for economic development as a prerequisite (a) for solutions to basic social, security, demographic and other society issues; and (b) for the fulfillment of the international obligations undertaken by the state according to its international economic and political purposes. Due to these prerequisites, the state is forced not only to create legal conditions for economic freedom, but also to support economically weak entities, eliminate risks of economic instability and ensure public interests, protect human rights and open world values, invest in human development, education and science, maintain economic competition. This is reflected in the legal enshrinement of forms and methods of supporting economic and intellectual activity, protection of the economic order and combating the shadow economy.

The state plays an active role in the mechanism of economic regulation through certain methods of impact, the purpose of which is to create and ensure economic conditions in accordance with national economic policy and ideas to stimulate economic development.

> Regulations at all levels of government attempt to promote economic welfare primarily by correcting imperfections in private markets, such as monopolistic and oligopolistic practices, negative externalities generated in both production and consumption, imperfect information, and fraud.[11]

There are no ready-made recipes for combining different methods of influencing one or another branch of the economy. Institutional complexity is also attested to by "the institutional diversity of capitalism," that is, by the various forms of articulation between the state, the market, and other institutions. Historically, the absence of a general rule or pattern is shown by the various forms of political mediation.[12] In fact, the existence of numerous theories of economic regulation (public good theory, capture theory, and special interest theory, etc.[13]), most of which are based

---

[10] Walter H Plosila, 'State Science-and Technology-Based Economic Development Policy: History, Trends and Developments, and Future Directions' (2004) 18(2) Economic Development Quarterly, 113 (125).

[11] Robert Tannenwald, 'State Regulatory Policy and Economic Development' (1997) New England Economic Review, 83 (83–108).

[12] José Reis, 'The State and the Market: An Institutionalist and Relational Take' (2012) 4 RCCS Annual Review, 86 (433 – §21).

[13] Richard A Posner, 'Theories of Economic Regulation' (1974) w0041 NBER Working Paper, 1.

on different assessments of the direction and effectiveness of state regulation of the economy, proves the inexhaustibility of the relevant topics. Its dynamics are conditioned by the unpredictability of social life. There seems to be a fairly "intermediate strategy", according to which the private enforcement of public rules may emerge as an efficient strategy of the social control of markets.[14]

The problems facing the world after the full-scale invasion of Ukraine by the Russian Federation have led to radical changes in approaches to state intervention in the economy. After all, the military economy, as world history shows, is always characterized by state intervention in even those areas where the traditional is a private way of business. This leads to many restrictions on human activities and freedom, including conscription, resource mobilization, limitation in non-military research investment, severance of industrial, scientific and other ties, restrictions on freedom of speech, mobility and subordination of human behavior to military governance, etc. Although this military issue in the context of state regulation of the economy and investments requires a separate study, we can already try to predict that the modern world will never return to the state of openness, freedom and creative cooperation which existed until 24 February 2022. Warnings about security, protection of democracy and universal freedoms from such forms of external influence as tyranny, contempt for human life and national sovereignty, imperial ideology and propaganda, war of aggression will require the formation of the economy and its legal support on a new basis, the achievements of civilization and investments to prepare for the destruction of other countries, the conquest of peoples and the forcible imposition of foreign values. This is clearly demonstrated by the impressive statement of Joe Biden:

> Things are changing so rapidly that the next 10 years will be the decisive decade of this century, because they're going to shape what our world looks like and the values that will guide it not just for the immediate future, but for generations to come.[15]

Due to these issues, as well as related to deadly pandemics and the accelerating climate crisis, the sphere of innovations and investment, creative achievements and technology will objectively need new measures of protection and defense, and renewed direction for state support and financing.

In the legal analysis of economic regulation, the political will of the legislator comes to the fore, which has acquired a static dimension in legislative acts. The legislation actually fixes the chosen model of regulation of economic relations. Of course, beyond the formal reflection of measures of state influence remain a number of political, executive, psychological, informational, security, moral and cultural factors that distort the overall picture of the legal influence of the state on economies. But it is the legal form of state economic policy that is the core of appropriate regulation,

[14] Andrei Shleifer, 'Understanding Regulation' (2005) 11(4) European Financial Management, 439 (445–450).

[15] 'Remarks by President Joe Biden at the United States Naval Academy's Class of 2022 Graduation and Commissioning Ceremony' The Whitehouse (27 May 2022) https://www.whitehouse.gov/briefing-room/statements-releases/2022/05/27/remarks-by-president-biden-at-the-united-states-naval-academys-class-of-2022-graduation-and-commissioning-ceremony/ accessed 26 October 2022.

the criterion for its evaluation in terms of efficiency, sufficiency or redundancy. That is why the legal provision of state economic policy is the object of primary attention in this aspect.

2.2 *The Ukrainian State and the Regulation of the Economy*

In Ukraine, for a long time, the approach to the state role in the economy ranged from nothing private to nothing public,[16] which corresponded to the transition from the Soviet economic system to the market situation at the end of the twentieth century. In the early 1990s, Ukraine found itself with declarations of a market economy but with the state leadership completely unable to ensure honest business practices, and a paternalistic approach was accompanied by a lack of laws that could effectively protect private property and investment, and counter corruption. The main obstacle to normal business was the constant change of laws and regulations, as well as the lack of a clear division of functions between government agencies.[17] In fact, it was a time of a messy legal infrastructure of market relations. This naturally led to the illegal redistribution of property, the formation of monopolistic and oligarchic groups, the liquidation of many enterprises, chaos in public administration and the crisis of investment in research. This period was called the period of wild capitalism and clearly demonstrated that the free market was unable to overcome the shortcomings of economic abuses and negative stereotypes of citizens concerning the perception of private property.

Nowadays, under the pressure of realizing the risks of economic chaos provoked by the state's exclusion from the economy, the need to protect individuals not only from state arbitrariness but also from abuses of monopolies, according to the awareness of the harm of shadow business and market imbalances, there has been a revolution in the socio-political sense about the role of the state in the mechanism of economic development. This is due to the presumption that the state acts in the interests of business and society as a whole, and not of individual economic groups.[18]

The awareness of the value of state regulation is largely explained by the wide penetration of Western approaches into Ukraine with regard to the organization of the economic sphere, support for investment and innovation, combating monopoly and corruption. In particular, China, the USA and some models of the European states have demonstrated that innovations cannot be massive and programmable without direct state funding and other state support: "The government makes these incentives through two ways: either tax breaks while decreasing government incomes

[16] Volodymyr Gaivoronskyi, 'Civil Legislation: From "Nothing Private" to "Nothing Public"?' (1997) 4 Bulletin of the Academy of Legal Sciences of Ukraine (91), 96.

[17] Volodymyr Lytvyn et al., 'Economic History of Ukraine: Historical and Economic Research' (2011) 2(1) Nika-Center, 526.

[18] Dmytro Zadykhailo, 'State Regulation of Market Relations as an Actual Legal Problem' (2005) 6 Ukrainian Commercial Law, 18 (18–22).

without spending or issuing grants raising spending without decreasing any direct income."[19] Also, strong investment in the country's economy does not require formal liberalization, but the creation of an attractive investment climate that will guarantee entrepreneurs profitability and investment protection. In addition, excellent Western examples of the correlation between high technology, innovation development and public welfare have clearly shown that investment needs to be innovative, expressed by the statement: "Innovation is a major driver of economic transformation and development".[20]

Nowadays it is widely believed that technological change has become the main goal to reach. That is why

> the role of the state goes far beyond fixing market failures. Investing in risky but potentially profitable economic activity, incurring high costs of uncertain research increases the attractiveness of new technologies, that without 'sunk costs' covered by public funds would have never come up to the market. It means that state by de-risking of some fields of scientific interest points out 'the winners'—new industry branches. It means that state's role goes beyond innovation support. It also crowds-in private investment, dynamizes-in innovation and growth, creates the vision, mission and the plan.[21]

The successful experience of developed countries and Eastern European democracies that were able to shift the economy from the Soviet economic system to a market economy without losing the scientific potential of its development, forces Ukrainian scholarship to pay attention to the relevant basis of state intervention in the economy.

The main directions of Ukraine's economic policy during the period of independence were first declared by Resolution 1698a-X of Verkhovna Rada of Ukraine dated 25 October 1991. The act provided for the creation of "reliable economic guarantees of sovereignty". That stood the test of time. Later, this policy took on a more internal dimension, but changed with each change of government, and turned into "permanent reforms". As a result, economic relations were destabilized and investor confidence in Ukraine's economic and legal climate were disrupted. The latest document "on approval of the National Economic Strategy for the period up to 2030" was adopted by Cabinet of Ministers of Ukraine Decree on 3 March 2021 No. 179. The Strategy outlines the primary aim as being "the formation of competitive conditions for business and investment, as well as the restoration of trust in state institutions."[22]

The full-scale war started by Russia against Ukraine markedly changed society's demands for state economic policy, and led to the expectation of giant peace-time

---

[19] Farahim Huseynzade, 'Role of the State Budget and Venture Capital in the Boom of Start-ups and Innovations' Lawels (26 October 2019) https://lawels.com/en/2019/10/26/role-of-the-state-budget-and-venture-capital-in-the-boom-of-start-ups-and-innovations-2/ accessed 26 October 2022.

[20] United Nations, UNCTAD, 'Investing in Innovation for Development' TD/B/C.II/21, 2013 (3).

[21] Elżbieta Pohulak-Żołędowska and Arkadiusz Żabiński, 'The State's Role in Creating Innovation-driven Economic Growth' (2015) 214 Scientific Journals Wroclaw University of Economics, 201 (212–213).

[22] Ludmyla Denisova, '"Cannot be Supported": Commissioner for Human Righton the Anti-oligarchic Law' *Epravda* (7 September 2021) https://www.epravda.com.ua/news/2021/09/7/677548/ accessed 27 July 2022.

reforms. It is not just about the priorities of ensuring security, the needs of the Armed Forces of Ukraine and the adjustment of market mechanisms to the needs of the martial law and further defense capabilities. This is also about the prospects of the restoration of the economy of Ukraine and membership of the European Union, regarding which a decision was adopted by the European Commission and the Council, which puts before the state of Ukraine new tasks of adaptation of legislation to EU law, review of regulatory and law enforcement principles of the protection of investors' rights, demonopolization (deoligarchization) of the economy, anti-corruption and institutional reforms.

3 Measures and Forms of Regulating Influence of the State on Economic Activity: The Search for Economic and Legal Content

In previous sections of this chapter, we described the general problems of understanding state economic policy and its current condition in Ukraine. This section will be devoted to the analysis of the legislative reflection of the forms and methods of state regulation of the economy in Ukraine because these provisions will shape the investor's ideas about the boundaries of such policy and guaranteed economic freedoms.

3.1 Terminological Basis of Legal Regulation of State Intervention in the Economy

The legal regime of the measures of state intervention in economic relations is determined most often in the laws fixing the discretionary powers of state bodies that carry out functions of state economic regulation. Although we cannot wait until the state adopts the laws with the entire content of administrative measures—state management requires a discretionary field for operational decision-making—we can determine a general list of measures of state intervention in economic relations and rules of their application that conform to the rule of law, and are beneficial to both society and economic entities.

The measures of regulating the state's influence on economic relations can be understood as a set of instruments of state impact on the economic activity of economic entities in order to create and ensure conditions for economic development in accordance with national economic policy.

A distinction should be made between the methods of legal regulation of economic activity and the way the state impacts the economy. The first is a purely legal concept, which provides a set of methods and techniques by which the legal norms affect economic relations. For example, V. Shcherbyna understands it comprehensively as a set of methods of autonomous decisions (approval, permission), mandatory orders (orders, prohibitions) and recommendations.[23] G. Znamenskyi singles out the unifying method of economic and legal regulation—equal subordination of subjects to the public economic order.[24] In contrast, the method of the state's economic impact (regulation) has a purely managerial meaning, as it allows the content of state economic policy to be undertaken for the purposes of further legal consolidation (formalization).

The form of state impact on economic activity is an external expression of the state bodies' actions directed to the realization of their special tasks and functions in the course of application of the chosen method of impact on the economy.[25] One and the same method of state impact on economic relations might be characterized by various forms of its implementation.

By analogy with the forms of management (regulation, organization, control, supervision, etc.) we should talk about the forms of state impact on the economy. In particular, in Ukraine the legalization of economic activity is reflected in such forms as regulation (e.g. laws of Ukraine "On State Registration of Legal Entities, Individuals—Entrepreneurs and Public Associations", "On Licensing of Types of Economic Activities" etc., Resolution of the Cabinet of Ministers of Ukraine from 24 March 2021 No. 365 "On Approval of Licensing Conditions for Educational Activities"), individual regulation (issue of a specific certificate or license, patent), management (multifunctional activities of licensing authorities), control (set of measures of registration authorities, licensing, tax and other bodies to monitor compliance with the registration procedure, licensing conditions), etc.

For legal research, it is extremely important to consider that forms and measures of regulating state influence should be distinguished in the sense that economic solutions to economic problems cannot be replaced by purely formal management tools. As a result of incorrect delimitation of the content and form of state regulation of the economy, there are overvalued expectations of the improvement of domestic legislation to stimulate investment and innovation.

Ukraine's negative experience in implementing and abolishing guarantees for foreign investors in the early 1990s, empty benefits for innovation projects, technology parks and special economic zones at the beginning of the twenty-first century, the failed attempt to implement the concept of "innovation enterprise" and many other legislative projects that remain a dead legislative field have clearly demonstrated the importance of understanding the following point: legal novelties alone, without economic preconditions and deep justification, are not able to promote economic development. In other words, reforms cannot be linked to a change in governance and the adoption of new laws without government worrying about the economic course it will pursue.

---

[23] Valentyn Shcherbyna, *Textbook on Economic Law (*Yurincim Inter 2001), 18.

[24] Valentin Mamutov, *Textbook of Economic Law* (Yurincom Inter 2002), 31.

[25] Oleg Podtserkovniy and Olena Lomakina, 'Problems of Determining the Methods and Forms of State Regulation of Economic Relations' (2002) 8 Entrepreneurship, Economy and Law, 3 (3–6).

It is noteworthy that the category of the method of state impact on the economy is reflected in many ways in the legislation. In particular, the Commercial Code of Ukraine, Arts. 12–18, applies the concept of measures of state regulation of the economy, understanding them as public procurement, licensing, regulation of prices and tariffs, and so on.

In this context, we can say that the methods of regulating state influence on the economy consist of a set of tools. In particular, the legalization of economic activity includes such measures as registration of an intellectual property rights object in the customs register adopted recently, licensing of educational activities, issuing different permits (for example, for the development of mineral deposits, or for the import of products containing genetically modified organisms for research). And the means of financial support such as accounting policy, insurance of venture investments, subsidizing research programs, etc. provide another tool. In many respects, the methods (measures) of state regulation of the economy derive their power from the functions of the state.

3.2 *Legislative Detailing of State Intervention in the Economy*

The enshrining of forms and measures to regulate economic relations in the laws of Ukraine is carried out throughout the hierarchy of legislative acts, but preference is given to laws. This multiplicity creates practical problems of the application of legislative regulation and has been called in scholarship "inflation of laws".[26]

The Constitution of Ukraine, Art. 13, contains a provision on the duty of the state to protect the rights of all economic entities and ensure the social orientation of the economy. This necessitated the consolidation of the basic principles of state regulation of the economy in the codified act.

The Commercial Code of Ukraine has taken an important step to limit the state within the legal framework. The provisions are set forth in Section 2 Code "Main directions and forms of participation of the state and local governments in the sphere of economic activity". Articles 12–18 Commercial Code of Ukraine first classified, and only then revealed the main measures of regulating state influence on business activities: state order; licensing, patenting, public tenders; certification and standardization; applying standards and limits; regulation of prices and tariffs; providing investment, tax and other benefits; providing grants, compensations, target innovations and subsidies. Specific forms of implementation of state regulation of the economy are also provided for in special legal acts.[27]

---

[26] Yurii Oborotov, 'Inflation of Power and Rights as an Indicator of a Weak State' (2010) 9 Scientific Works of the Odessa National Law Academy, 89 (89–97).

[27] E.g. Ukrainian Laws on the Main Principles of State Supervision (Oversight) in the Area of Economic Activity; on Principles of the State Regulatory Policy in the Sphere of Economic Activity;

Although state economic policy generally remains largely dependent on the managerial skills, knowledge and professionalism of the political establishment that prevails in the country, the legal framework of this policy established in national legislation at institutional level affects the content of such policy and the directions of its implementation. In Ukraine, such principles are enshrined in many legislative acts, among which stand out constitutional norms that enshrine a number of powers of public authorities in the field of economic regulation, as well as the procedure for these bodies to perform control, incentive, protective and other functions, e.g. Arts. 13, 42, 85, 92, 98–100, 106, 116 and 119.

These provisions are further developed, for example, in Art. 11 Commercial Code, which establishes that the use of certain measures of state regulation of economic activity is determined not only by the laws of Ukraine, but also by specific programs and plans for the economic and social development of the state.

The fairly common division of the measures of state regulation into economic and administrative tools[28] examined seems erroneous, because any kind of economic regulation is powerless without elements of administration and management. Therefore, any state measures that regulate influence on the economy are public and administrative. This approach allows for systematic research of measures of state interference in economic relations, opposing them to measures of market self-regulation, but not mixing with each other.

The division into direct and indirect state measures of influencing market relations obviously has the greatest practical benefit among these classifications. It allows a division in legislation of the measures of compulsion and stimulation. The specifics of the direct methods of state influence on the business sector can be seen in the fact that they are characterized by direct force on the business entity or investor to act in a certain way in the business environment (for example, to disclose the ultimate beneficial owner of the capital). However, indirect methods of state influence on the economy do not involve such forcing. Indirect methods are those regulators of the economic environment that stimulate efficient management, investment and make certain behavior economically profitable, desirable for society and the state (for example, VAT on imports does not directly force domestic businesses to produce similar products in Ukraine, but makes domestic production economically feasible).

---

on Sanctions; on the Permit System in the Field of Economic Activity; on Standardization; on Securities and the Stock Market; on Government Aid for Business Entities; on Protection of Rights to Marks for Goods and Services; on Investment Activity; on the Use of Registrars of Payment Transactions in the Sphere of Trade, Public Catering, and Services; on Circulation of Bills of Exchange in Ukraine; on Assessment of Property, Property Rights, and Professional Assessor Activity in Ukraine; on Distribution of Copies of Audiovisual Works, Soundtracks, Videos, Computer Programs and Databases; on Securing the Claims of Creditors and Registration of Encumbrances; on Certified Warehouses and Simple and Double Warehouse Certificates; on Measures Aimed at Sustainable Functioning of the Fuel and Energy Sector Companies; on Securities and Stock Market; on Motor Transport; on Joint Stock Companies; on Government Procurement, and many others.

[28] E.g. Ivan Mykhasiuk et al. '*Textbook of State Regulation of the Economy*' (Attika, Elgan 2nd ed. 2000), 6–7.

The application of certain measures of regulating state influence on economic relations depends on the condition of the economy, emergencies, social policy, international obligations of the state, as well as economic tactics and strategies stated in Art. 9 Commercial Code of Ukraine.

There are many areas of the economy in which it is difficult to manage market relations without direct methods of regulating influence. This statement is true for control over monopolistic entities; ensuring environmental safety and conservation of non-renewable natural resources, health care, safe living and working conditions (minimum wage, social benefits and assistance); protection of national economic interests, ensuring economic security.

Areas of intellectual and innovative activity, on the contrary, can correlate with those areas where indirect methods are most effective, because it is quite difficult to ensure intellectual activity by compulsion. In this regard, "[d]irect government intervention in the market acquisition of intellectual property in support of innovation is relatively rare. It is, in principle, a second important channel by which technology policy could shape the rate and direction of innovation."[29]

An example of such a policy can be demonstrated in cases where the state issues security documents on objects of industrial property rights. But applying for a patent for an invention, utility model or industrial design is not mandatory, so only a protection document entitles the person to have exclusive rights to manufacture or use the product.

Measures of direct state intervention usually carry the risk of violating the freedom of economic competition, as they can create advantages or obstacles in the business conduct of some entities over others. Particularly, the EU–Ukraine Association Agreement defines the general principles which should be adhered to by Ukraine in the formation of state economic policy:

> Any aid granted by Ukraine or the Member States of the European Union through state resources which distorts or threatens to distort competition by favouring certain undertakings or the production of certain goods is incompatible with the proper functioning of this Agreement insofar as it may affect trade between the Parties.[30]

It can be noted that among the relevant exceptions the Association Agreement defines "aid to make good the damage caused by natural disasters or exceptional occurrences" and "aid to promote the economic development of areas where the standard of living is abnormally low or where there is serious underemployment". Obviously, the post-war period of Ukraine restoration, which will inevitably come, will allow a spread of the corresponding exclusions to the investment and innovation sphere in Ukraine.

---

[29] Edward W Steinmueller, 'Economics of Technology Policy' in Bronwyn H Hall and Nathan Rosenberg (eds), *Handbook of the Economics of Innovation Volume 2* (MIT Press 2010), 1181 (1181–1218).

[30] Assosiation Agreement between the European Union and its Member States, of the one part, and Ukraine, of the other part 2(014) OJ L161; for the general aspects, see Roman Petrov, 'The EU–Ukraine Association Agreement as a General Framework of contemporary EU–Ukraine Relations' in this Volume. On specific aspects on competition law and state aid, see Kseniia Smyrnova, 'The "Europeanization" of Competition Law in Ukraine' in this Volume.

Ukraine has also undertaken to regulate the support measures in accordance with WTO rules in order to limit the anti-competitive measures systematically. This is because WTO terminology in general identifies subsidies as "boxes" which are given the colors of traffic lights: green (permitted), amber (slow down—i.e. need to be reduced), red (forbidden).[31]

In order to arrange the direct state support of the economy in Ukraine, the Law "On State Aid to Economic Entities" was adopted. This law establishes rules for the application by the state of various measures of aid to economic entities, some of which may directly relate to investments and innovations such as: provision of subsidies and grants; granting tax benefits, deferral of or payment by installment of taxes, fees or other mandatory payments. The general caution made in many studies on this issue is that legislative provisions of state support should provide national enterprises with competitive opportunities that are not less than foreign entities have in their own countries,[32] including "just to adapt to the current global innovation trends".[33]

In summary, it can be concluded that the legislative regulation of the means of state economic policy is carried out not only considering economic and managerial objectivity, but also taking into account the obligations undertaken by Ukraine within its international treaties. Legislation is more focused on limiting measures of direct support of business entities because they can affect the competitive environment. At the same time, we should talk about the economic content of state support measures for certain spheres and the real state of legal protection, and not only the presence of programs, strategies, laws or other formal acts in the economic sphere.

4 Issues of Economic Security and Protection of Economic Competition in the Trends of State Regulation of the Economy

The Russian aggression, which began in 2014 and took the character of a full-scale invasion by Russian troops of the territory of Ukraine on 24 February 2022, radically changed the state's approach to economic security. It has motivated Ukrainian

[31] Domestic support in agriculture: WTO, 'Domestic Support in Agriculture: The Boxes' WTO https://www.wto.org/english/tratop_e/agric_e/agboxes_e.htm accessed 26 October 2022. See Zvenyslava Opeida, 'Competition and International Trade: Complementing Trade Defense Policy with Effective Competition Policy in Ukraine' in this Volume.

[32] E.g.: Oleh Zahnitko, 'Economic and Legal Protection of the Domestic Product Producer – Comparative Legal Study' (IEPD 1999), 2; Oleg Podtserkovnyi and Valentyna Chaikovska, 'State Regulation of Foreign Economic Activity under Globalization and Financial Crisis', (2009) 2 Custom Business 75 (75–80); Denys Chernikov, 'Modernization of the System of State Support of Business Entities in Ukraine' (2013) National Institute of Strategic Studies.

[33] Anna Zausková et al. 'How Cthe State Support the Innovations to Build Sustainable Competitive Advantage of the Country' (2013) 8(2) Serbian Journal of Management 255 (265).

legislators to set numerous prohibitions on investing in the economy by Russian investors.

Since 2014, legislation on privatization, on investments, on public procurement has been amended, imposing corresponding restrictions for the "aggressor country."[34] The law "On sanctions" No. 1644-VII, which defined the scope of special economic and restrictive measures that the state could take in order to protect the national interests, national security, sovereignty and territorial integrity of Ukraine", was adopted on 14 August 2014. Initially, the sanctions concerned mainly the defense industry and the public sector. Following the full-scale Russian invasion and the declaration of martial law in Ukraine, the legislation adopted the approach of a complete termination of economic relations with persons of private or public law connected with this country.

First of all, the Law of Ukraine "On the Main Principles of Forced Withdrawal in Ukraine of the Property Rights of the Russian Federation and its Residents" No. 2116-IX adopted on 3 March 2022, has defined the legal principles of forced seizure on the grounds of social necessity (including cases in which this is urgently required by military necessity) of objects owned by the Russian Federation as a state that began a war against Ukraine and its residents. No less important is the Resolution of the Cabinet of Ministers of Ukraine "On Protection of the National Interests of Ukraine in Future Claims related to the Military Aggression of the Russian Federation" No. 187, dated 3 March 2022, which introduces a moratorium on the performance of obligations to Russia and its residents. Moreover, the Resolution of the Cabinet of Ministers of Ukraine "On Application of Ban on Import of Goods from the Russian Federation" No. 426 dated 9 April 2022 prohibited the import of goods from the Russian Federation. Other ongoing legislative measures may also be mentioned.[35] It is obvious that regardless of the results of the war and the future settlement, investments and other relations between the economic entities of Ukraine and the Russian Federation will be the exception rather than the general rule.

The European Commission has also taken the unprecedented step of singling out two hostile investor countries (Russian Federation and Republic of Belarus) for Member States to consider in applying foreign direct investment screening laws.[36]

---

[34] See e.g. Ukrainian Law on the Privatization of State and Communal Property 2018, No. 2269-VIII, art 8, provided that buyers of privatization objects cannot be "buyers originating from an aggressor state", "a state recognized by the Verkhovna Rada of Ukraine as an aggressor state, as well as legal entities in which such a state has a stake, and persons, which are under the control of such legal entities", "legal entities, beneficial owners of 10 percent or more of the shares (parts) of which are residents of the aggressor state", "natural persons - citizens and/or residents of a state recognized by the Verkhovna Rada of Ukraine as an aggressor state".

[35] See e.g.: Ukrainian Law on the Approval of the Decree of the President of Ukraine; on the Decision of the National Security and Defense Council of Ukraine 2022; on the Forced Seizure in Ukraine of Objects of Property Rights of the Russian Federation and its Residents 2022, 2249-IX; on Amendments to Certain Legislative Acts of Ukraine Regarding Increasing the Effectiveness of Sanctions Related to the Assets of Individuals. 2022, 2257-IX, etc.

[36] Commission Guidance to the Member States concerning foreign direct investment from Russia and Belarus in view of the military aggression against Ukraine and the restrictive measures laid down in recent Council Regulations on sanctions (2022) OJ C151 I/01.

This is a remarkable step for EU policies. Historically, FDI regimes have been drafted somewhat diplomatically, restricting investments from certain bodies without expressly listing who they are.[37] This policy was the implementation of comprehensive sanctions imposed by the EU, the USA and many other countries against Russia and Belarus due to the aggression in Ukraine.

In this respect, it is important to answer questions about the safety of foreign investment in general. In addition to the problem of the Russian aggression, Ukraine has also faced a global trend over the past decade to evaluate risky investment projects.

In the early 2000s there was an optimistic global view of cross-border investment, when it was believed that foreign direct investment held important potential benefits for the national economy and that "the maintenance of strong competition policy frameworks ensures that the benefits of foreign market entry are brought to bear while guarding the host economy from undesirable degrees of market concentration".[38] But the growing threats to the sovereignty of states objectively forced people to pay more attention to assessing the security of foreign investment. Recipient countries have been made aware of the fact that "foreign investments can potentially endanger entire economic areas and jeopardise their independence."[39] Awareness of this fact led to the idea of adopting legal provisions on the screening of foreign investment to protect national security and the strategic objects of the state. The American equivalent of investment screening is the Foreign Investment Risk Review Modernization Act (FIRRMA)[40] adopted in 2018. This document arose in response to the growing risks of Chinese investment in US corporations. In the EU, the Foreign Direct Investment Screening Regulation (FDIR)[41] officially entered into force on 10 April 2019.

The aim is to establish criteria for ensuring stability in economic relations, because quite often investments are "hostile" when they are aimed at the elimination of competitors, destroying economic ties, industrial espionage and so on. A clear example of the negative impact of foreign direct investment on the national economy of Ukraine is the acquisition of the Zaporizhia Aluminum Plant, which in 2004 came under the control of the Russian group SUAL (since 2007—RusAl): the ultimate purpose of this acquisition was the destruction of the competitor.[42]

---

[37] Tobias Caspary et al., 'EU Singles Out FDI "Hostile Investors" For the First Time: Russia and Belarus' *Fried Frank* (5 May 2022) https://www.friedfrank.com/siteFiles/Publications/FFITIECCommunicationsArticle05022022.pdf accessed 27 October 2022.

[38] Stephen Thomsen, 'Economic and Other Impacts of Foreign Corporate Takeovers in OECD Countries' in OECD, *'International Investment Perspectives: Freedom of Investment in a Changing World'* (OECD 2007).

[39] Catharine Titi, 'Public Actors in International Investment Law' in Marc Bungenberg et al., (eds), *European Yearbook of International Economic Law* (Springer 2021), 180.

[40] Foreign Investment Risk Review Modernization Act 2018, H.R.5841.

[41] Regulation (EU) 2019/452 of the European Parliament and of the Council of 19 March 2019 establishing a framework for the screening of foreign direct investments into the Union (2019) LI 79/1.

[42] Yuliia Korneeva, 'Does Ukraine need Investment Screening? How to Check Foreign Investors and Not Crete Additional Barriers for the flow of Capital to Ukraine' *Epravda* (7 April 2021) https://www.epravda.com.ua/rus/columns/2021/04/7/672759/ accessed 27 July 2022.

This has inspired the general idea of investment screening behind the Law of 3 March 2021 No. 5011 "On Foreign Investment in Economic Entities of Strategic Importance for the National Security of Ukraine", which provides for state control of investment in strategic sectors of the economy, which seems to be correct and reasonable. At the same time, the legislative regulation should overcome the problematic risks, which are summarized by experts as "possibly weak institutional capacity and inefficient procedures": "an additional bureaucratic", "corruption risks", arbitration disputes under "bilateral investment treaties" and the system can serve the interests of "oligarchs" and "limit competition".[43]

In addition to addressing these issues, it is equally important to clearly define the scope of the relevant precautions considering the experience of EU legislation. Attention should be paid to sensitive areas of foreign investment such as the following:

- critical infrastructure (energy, transport, water, health, communications, media, data processing and storage, aerospace, defense, election, or financial infrastructure);
- critical technologies (artificial intelligence, robotics, semiconductors, cybersecurity, aerospace, defense, energy-saving technologies, as well as quantum, nuclear, nano- and biotechnologies);
- supply of critical resources (energy, raw materials, food security);
- access to confidential information (protection of personal data, media freedom and pluralism).

This list illustrates that the issues of investment monitoring and the steps taken by modern states to restrict investments that distort economic freedom and harm state security are largely related to the field of new technologies and innovations. Such restrictions do not hinder investment if they are fair and friendly. But unfair and "hostile" investment cannot by their very nature benefit society.

The category of investment security, of course, has many components, not limited to the origin of such investment. Above all, investment screening should also include an analysis of the investment impact on economic competition as a whole, because in terms of obstacles to economic development in Ukraine, this problem is on a par with economic security.

Thus, the European Commission has remarked in its Opinion on Ukraine's application for membership of the European Union that "[p]ersistent major weaknesses in the business environment are the main cause for the lack of investment. In 2019, Ukraine ranked 85th in the global competitiveness index of the World Economic Forum, primarily due to weak institutions, the high prevalence of market dominance and an ineffective anti-monopoly policy".[44]

---

[43] Dmytro Goriunov, 'FDI Screening in Ukraine' (2021) Centre for Economic Strategy.

[44] European Commission, 'Commission Opinion on Ukraine's application for membership of the European Union' (Communication) COM(2022) 407 final, 2022.

If we summarize the practice on this issue, it turns out that the Antimonopoly Committee acts effectively only in relation to state-owned enterprises, such as Ukrzaliznytsia, or small and medium-sized enterprises. As for large monopolistic entities, the results of enforcement are very modest: Big business monopolies "traditionally avoid punishment by the AMCU",[45] but "the level of market concentration is growing".[46]

"Deoligarchization" has been chosen as one of the ways to overcome the negative phenomena in this sphere in Ukraine. The new trend is the anti-oligarchic movement. The Ukrainian Parliament adopted in 2021 the Law "On the Prevention of Threats to National Security Related to the Excessive Influence of Persons who have Significant Economic or Political Weight in Public Life (Oligarchs)". But this Law actually carries a political rather than an economic burden. Not coincidentally, it has provoked numerous negative comments from lawyers, including the Ukrainian Parliament Commissioner for Human Rights.[47] Therefore, the above-mentioned Opinion of the European Commission is considered necessary to "implement the Anti-Oligarch law to limit the excessive influence of oligarchs in economic, political, and public life; this should be done in a legally sound manner, taking into account the forthcoming opinion of the Venice Commission on the relevant legislation". It should be borne in mind that the very concept of oligarchy is mostly journalistic and not significant for practice. From a legal point of view, it is difficult if at all possible to identify oligarchs. An attempt to qualify the term "oligarch" on the basis of exclusive legal features and properties encounters the difficulty of including in the law the evaluative relations of political influence, the social authority of the individual, and the separation of economic and political power. Probably this is why there is no ue of the term "oligarchy" in the legislation of civilized countries. Effective legislation on the protection of economic competition completely closes the issue of the centralization of economic power. Otherwise, there is a risk of transferring state economic policy to manual control, fighting political opponents, destroying large financial and industrial complexes in the country without a chance to somehow influence foreign TNCs, which in the global economy gain non-competitive advantages over domestic economic entities.

The problem of overcoming the influence of the oligarchy on the economy should not be solved by creating certain "lists" of individuals—oligarchs by authorities' resolutions—but primarily by demonopolizing the economy, fighting corruption, and preventing any influence on judges in decision-making. These measures should be brought to the level of practical implementation by promoting the development of SMEs. Thus, it is not enough to establish certain measures in the law, it is necessary

[45] Agia Zagrybelska, 'Kolomoisky Fuel Cartel: Will the Antimonopoly Committee be able to Punish the Oligarch?' ZN,UA (30 March 2021).

[46] Oksana Tkachenko, 'The AMCU's Performance Indicator is the Level of Competition in the Markets, not Fines' FBC (28 September 2021) https://fbc.ua/news/ekonomika-uk/pokaznik-roboti-amku-tse-riven-konkurentsiyi-na-rinkah-a-ne-shtrafi-ekspert/ accessed 27 July 2022.

[47] Ludmyla Denisova, '"Cannot be Supported": Commissioner for Human Righton the Anti-oligarchic Law' Epravda (7 September 2021) https://www.epravda.com.ua/news/2021/09/7/677548/ accessed 27 July 2022.

to link these provisions with the real mechanisms of law enforcement and managerial potential.

5 Stimulation of Innovations in the Context of the State Economic Policy

The previous paragraph examined the security factor, which is fundamental for state regulation of investment activities in Ukraine these days. This section will consider the problems of improving the effectiveness of government measures to support innovation as a key area of investment and the basis for the development of the modern economy.

5.1 Support of Innovations as a Direction of State Economic Policy

The concept of innovation is ambiguous. Innovation can have different meanings depending on the context.[48] The Law of Ukraine "On Innovation Activity" notes that "innovations" shall mean newly created (applied) and (or) improved competitive technologies, products or services, as well as organizational and technical solutions of a production, administrative, commercial or other nature, which significantly improve the structure and quality of production and (or) social sphere. This definition can be taken as a starting point for further discussion.

It is no exaggeration to say that the thesis of the need for innovative reorientation of the economy is the most reasonable hope for accelerating socio-economic reforms. According to the OECD, 85% of all economic growth in the US economy is a result of innovation. So it is taken as axiomatic that innovative activity has been the single most important component of long-term economic growth.[49] Unfortunately, the connection with investment development is observed in the fact that "innovation" is "investing innovations".[50]

State stimulation of innovation can be considered one of the most difficult areas of state economic policy. This is due to the riskiness of innovation: "an innovation

[48] Anneli Stenberg, 'What Does Innovation Mean – A Term Without a Clear Definition' (2017) University of Halmstad 2017.

[49] Nathan Rosenberg, 'Innovation and Economic Grow' in OECD (ed), *Innovation and Growth in Tourism* (OECD 2004).

[50] Valentin Mamutov, 'Development of Economic Legislation and Economic and Legal Thought in Sovereign Ukraine' (2004) Institute of Economic and Legal Studies of the National Academy of Sciences of Ukraine, 14.

project acts as an investment, but with greater cost, duration, complexity, the degree of uncertainty of parameters and results, as well as riskiness”.[51]

Building an innovative model of the economy requires complex government measures. They usually lie in the planning of effective economic policy of the state, macroeconomic stability, and so on. There is a need to solve problems of intellectual property protection, to plan (program) scientific and technical developments, to achieve gradual intersectoral structural changes, improve the social position of scientists and, finally, to ensure the effectiveness of the protection of investors’ rights. However, it seems that such elements of a complex system of building an innovative economic model as the public provision of conditions for raising funds for the development of mechanical engineering and technology, direct public funding of research projects and tax incentives for innovation are of paramount importance. It is on these relations, of a monetary nature, that as a result the main components of the innovation process will be brought together.

An example is EU legislation that applies an insurance guarantee mechanism to investors.[52] Relevant procedures require budget funding, but without considering the content of insurance relations based on private law, the relevant public-law measures may not be effective.

From the point of view of innovative development, such an approach means (a) a clear identification of the sphere of development of the nation’s intellectual potential, in which the state does not interfere, and (b) the establishment of dispositive regulation that stimulates private initiative and protects economic competition, that will also exclude encroachments of the state and local self-government.

After gaining independence, Ukraine had to create new policies to support innovation. Soviet legislation, which used the terminology of “stimulating scientific and technological progress”, established a command-and-control system of economic management, which was based on the systematic development of the public sector of the economy without recruiting private initiative. The introduction of scientific and technical achievements was not the basis for the implementation of production programs.[53] Many advanced technical innovations, the significant advantages of which were obvious, have not been used in industry for years.[54] Only in the 1970–1980s did they begin to talk about creating “incentives” for the introduction of new advances in science and technology.[55] But that call did not have large-scale

---

[51] Cergii Prylypko et al., ‘Draft Innovation Code of Ukraine as a New Stage in the Development of Norm-making in the Innovation Sphere’ National Academy of Legal Sciences of Ukraine (FINN 2011); National Law Academy of Ukraine named after Yaroslav Mudry, Research Institute of Intellectual Property of the Academy of Legal Sciences of Ukraine, FINN, 2008, 271.

[52] Kathryn Gordon, ‘Investment Guarantees and Political Risk Insurance: Institutions, Incentives and Development’ (2008) OECD Investment Policy Perspectives, 91.

[53] Opanas Pidoprygora, ‘Problems of Legal Regulation of Scientific and Technological Progress in the USSR’ (Higher School 1985), 170.

[54] Georgii Sofonov, ‘Creative Activity of Inventors and Innovators – The Most Important Lever for Improving Production Efficiency’ (1979) 2 Issues of Invention, 9 (11).

[55] See e.g.: Victor Dozortsev, *Legislation and Scientific and Technological Progress* (Juridicheskaya Literatura 1978), 32–37; Evgeny Artemiev and Leonid Kravets, *Inventions, New Technique, Control*

prospects, given the lack of economic interest of enterprises in innovation and the narrow object of the implementation of research results.

Extensive privatization and the development of private ownership of the means of production have opened new opportunities for innovative projects in Ukraine. However, there was little incentive to innovate during the 1990s, and public funding for research was sharply reduced. Gradual awareness of purposeful steps of the state to support innovations was first legalized in the Concept of Scientific, Technical and Innovative Development, approved by the resolution of the Verkhovna Rada of Ukraine on 13 July 1999. It was clearly stated in the Strategy of Economic and Social Development for 2000–2004: "The basis of the new strategic course, its defining priority should be the development and implementation of state policy aimed at restructuring industry and developing an innovative model of economic growth, the establishment of Ukraine as a high-tech state."

In 2002, the above-mentioned specialized law "On Innovation" was adopted, which was aimed at supporting not only public but also private innovation investments. The difficulty of choosing the forms of state stimulation of innovative activity is evidenced by the fact that Ukraine's parliament overcame the President's veto three times, and the legislative process took three years. For example, the President's Proposals to the draft law state that "the Law provides for the provision of state support to innovation entities for the implementation of innovative projects [...]. The sources of such costs are not provided by law, [...] while solving the issue of preferential taxation it is necessary to take into account the real state of the financial system of the state and the possibilities of state and local budgets, the funds of which are not enough even to solve urgent social problems."[56] But despite these comments, not all problems were solved. The problem of the inconsistency of the legal declaration with the economic content of support measures remains a central shortcoming of the state innovation policy.

In 2011, scientists from the National Academy of Legal Sciences of Ukraine proposed a draft Innovation Code.[57] But these plans have remained on paper, given the frequent changes in government approaches to economic development and the presence of a large number of budget priorities, which have put the issue of stimulating innovation in the background.

In the context of the full-scale Russian aggression in Ukraine, the issues of support for innovative development by the state are objectively postponed, which requires companies to focus on innovative development according to the general investment model defined by the legislation of Ukraine.

(Economica 1974), 103–104; Mikhail Ring, *Self-sustaining System for the Creation and Implementation of New Technology: Legal Problems* (Nauka 1982), 335; Vitaly Rassokhin, 'Organizational and Legal Problems of Introducing Fundamentally New Achievements of Science and Technology into Production' (1987) Institute of State and Law, 5–6.

[56] Proposals of the President of Ukraine to the Ukrainian Law on Innovative Activity 2022.

[57] S M Prylypko et al., 'The Draft Innovation Code of Ukraine as a New Stage in the Development of Norm-making in the Innovation Sphere' (2011) Scientific and Practical Materials, 381.

5.2 The Current Legislative Measures to Support Innovation

The central goal of state innovation policy is defined in Art. 3 Law of Ukraine "On Innovation Activity": creating socio-economic, organizational and legal conditions for effective reproduction, development and use of scientific and technical potential of the country, ensuring the introduction of modern clean, safe, energy and resource efficient technologies, production and sale of new types of competitive products. In accordance with this goal, the law enshrines the basic principles of state innovation policy, among which the most important are: "focus on the innovative path of development of the Ukrainian economy"; "ensuring the interaction of science, education, production, financial and credit sphere in the development of innovations"; "implementation of measures to support international scientific and technical cooperation, technology transfer, protection of domestic products in the domestic market and their promotion on the foreign market"; "financial support, implementation of favorable credit, tax and customs policies in the field of innovation; promoting the development of innovation infrastructure".

At the same time, if we try to compare the set of such principles and relevant powers of state bodies, it will become clear that the normative enshrinement of these powers is not fully detailed, but that there is a lot of room for free interpretation and ignoring.

The principles of the state stimulation of innovative development will only become a tool for the public to regulate influence on innovative development, when in practice a way will be found to fill the gaps in the content of state economic policy in the chosen field that will serve as a basis for the direct application of the law. But this is possible only under the condition of a strong and independent judiciary, above all free from the dictates of the government's practice of "telephone law". Unfortunately, expectations of such an independent organizing influence of legal provisions on the state of innovation development are not justified in Ukraine yet. And it is not only a matter of endless judicial reform, which takes place with each change of power in the state, but also due to the general underdevelopment of the political and legal spheres, the prevalence of normativism over natural law and other problems of the legal system of the developing state.

Under these circumstances, only clear legal permits, obligations and prohibitions that establish certain parameters of public funding for innovation projects and innovation structures, tax benefits and incentives, indirect measures that motivate intellectual work and create organizational and technical benefits of private investment in innovation products become instruments of real state innovation policy.

Unfortunately, even those types of financial support for innovation activities that are enshrined in the Law "On Innovation Activity" lose all force due to the lack of budget, and of banking and tax mechanisms for their implementation.

For example, Art. 17 of the Law stipulates: (a) full interest-free crediting of priority innovation projects at the expense of budgets funds; (b) partial (up to 50%) interest-free crediting of priority innovation projects at the expense of budgets provided that the other funds necessary for project financing were invested by the project agent and (or) other subjects of innovation activity; (c) reimbursement (at the expense of budgets funds) of interest paid by the subjects of innovation activity to commercial banks and other financial crediting establishments for financing innovation projects; (d) granting of state guarantees to commercial banks which finance priority innovation projects; and (e) property insurance for the implementation of innovation projects by the insurers in compliance with the Law of Ukraine "On Insurance".

But the importance of all financial support measures has been weakened by the provisions of the Law itself: "Financial support for innovation from the State Budget of Ukraine, the budget of the Autonomous Republic of Crimea, local budgets is provided within the funds provided by the respective budgets." As a result, any support measures are reviewed every year and innovation actors have no prospects for the long-term planning of their activities. But innovation activity has been counted on just for the long term. After all, only as a result of long-term efforts of an intellectual nature can systemic and equal results be achieved in science and technology. New knowledge emerges as a result of consistent intellectual action, as a rule, not as a result of leaps in innovation activity.

At first sight, this problem is partially solved through the use of "protected articles" of the State Budget. The category of protected budget expenditures was introduced in Ukraine in 1998 as a result of the need to indicate expenditures that are not subject to change in budget execution, even in the event of an increase in the deficit, which will inevitably reduce expenditures approved in the state or local budget.[58] Article 55 Budget Code of Ukraine states that protected budget expenditures are expenditures of the general budget fund, the amount of which may not change when reducing the approved budget allocations. Expenditures on "scientific and scientific-technical activities" are included in the protected budget items. But "protection" in this case applies only to the implementation of budget expenditures for the current year. Recipients of public funding have no guarantee that funding for innovation programs will not be reduced for each subsequent year.

As a result, the urgent problem is the need for budget planning for three years instead of one year. And the first step for such changes has been taken by the Ukrainian authorities. On 15 July 2021, the Verkhovna Rada of Ukraine adopted a budget declaration for three years. Some steps have been taken to support innovation. In particular, the Cabinet of Ministers of Ukraine is obliged during the preparation of the draft Law of Ukraine on the State Budget of Ukraine for 2022 and the drafting of the Budget Declaration for 2023–2025 to develop and take measures to address issues "on the creation of industrial parks with tax incentives for new production and research enterprises". This is clearly not enough for the projected development of new technologies and the stimulation of intellectual work in the field of innovation. The very general nature of the provisions of the budget resolution in this part is declarative. But the very logic of the long-term planning of public finances in this area should be considered a positive example of the legal regulation of public economic policy.

---

[58] Mamutov, 'Development of Economic Legislation and Eonomic and Legal Thought in Sovereign Ukraine' (n 50); Yuliia Atamanova, *Economic and Legal Support Innovative State Policy* (FINN 2008), 271; Vira Stoian et al., *Textbook of Treasury System* (TSUL 3rd. ed. 2014), 113.

Incidentally, the current state support is isolated and does not allow the systematic raising of funds to finance innovative developments by economic entities.

In general, the expectation of the economic effect, which is actually implemented today in the legislation on public financing of innovation, is unnaturally designed for its risk-free nature and the inevitable profitability of the results of innovation. Such contradiction should be removed especially for the public investment in innovation sphere.[59]

5.3 Problems of Taxation of Innovative Projects

The problem of incentives to conduct research and innovation in the Tax Code of Ukraine 2010 are based on the lack of increased depreciation rates, and the problem of allocating costs for fundamental and applied research to the cost of production.

Operations related to scientific and technical activities receive certain tax benefits defined in the Tax Code. For example, Art. 197.1.22 indicates that fundamental research, research and development, and development and design is reimbursed by the person immediately collecting the funds from the account of the authority responsible for treasury servicing of budget funds.

Unfortunately, such benefits are not provided for funds received from other sources, in particular in the implementation of developments at the expense of economic entities that act as their customers.

In addition, the Tax Code of Ukraine creates benefits for certain sectors of the economy, which introduces an imbalance in the innovative direction of the entire economic activity.

For example, tax-exemption is allowed for transactions for import into the customs territory of Ukraine: of renewable energy equipment, energy conservation equipment and materials, means for measuring, control and management of expenses for fuel and power resources, equipment and materials for alternative fuel manufacture and for renewable energy generation (Art. 197.16.1 Tax Code of Ukraine). Accordingly, the interest of business entities in carrying out their own innovative developments in the manufacture of such equipment instead of importing finished equipment begins to fall. An adequate reaction in this case would be state subsidies for the production of similar equipment in Ukraine. But this is not happening.

Other taxation problems that hinder the commercialization of innovations are noted in the literature. In particular, in order to increase the effectiveness of the tax policy to stimulate innovation and investment activities, it is proposed to amend the Tax Code and introduce an investment tax credit, including a list of taxes, which may be excise duties, value added tax and tax on the extraction of minerals, while setting the terms of this tax credit, which would correspond to the payback period of the investment project on the basis of relevant agreements with tax authorities, as

[59] Oleg Podtserkovnyi, 'Legal Problems of Innovative Projects Funding' (2006) 4 Entrepreneurship, Economy and Law, 63 (63–65).

well as to use the experience of Western countries to allow companies to establish tax-free reserves for innovative investment.[60]

5.4 Promising Steps to Support Innovation

Ukrainian experts and scholars have drawn up numerous recommendations for strengthening the effectiveness of state support for innovation as an element of economic development. If we try to group the relevant proposals, they can be divided into three major groups: (1) proposals for the expansion of direct state aid (including preferential taxation, insurance and lending) and financing of innovative projects[61]; (2) proposals for infrastructural support of innovation activities (including by expanding access to venture capital[62] and access to cross-border scientific and technical programs,[63] support for innovative public procurement and innovative exports[64]); and (3) proposals to improve the overall investment climate in Ukraine.[65]

The latter direction is fundamental in a context that provides the basic ability of the economy to accumulate resources for innovation and the corresponding budget allocations. The first issue is solving the problem of economic competition protection which is discussed separately in this volume.[66] In addition this direction is covered by

---

60 Andrii Podlevskyi and M Yu Perevyazki 'Tax Incentives for Investment and Innovation in Ukraine' (2011) 18(4) Problems of Rational use of Socio-economic and Natural Resource Potential of the Region: Financial Policy and Investment, 48 (48–55).

61 See e.g.: Olga Tkachuk and Natalia Germanjuk, 'Modern Improvement of Innovative Activity of the Enterprise' (2020) 4(40) Economics and Organization of Management, 91 (97); Anna Puchko, 'System of State Financing of Innovative Activities' (2015) 19 Investments: Practice and Expereince 64 (67); Nina Ischenko, 'The Current State of Innovative Activity at Ukrainian Enterprises and Its Financing' (2020) 4 (46) The Problems of Economy, 320, 323.

62 Roman Tarnavskyi, *Economic and Legal Incentives for Venture Investment in Ukraine (*NU "OLA" 2017), 146 177.

63 See e.g.: Viacheslav Lyashenko, Olga Prokopenko and Vitaliy Omelianenko, 'Institutional Model of Innovative Economy' (Institute of Industrial Economics 2019), 74–97.

64 See e.g. Natalia Sedovolosa 'Economic and Legal Support for the Export of Innovative Products by Ukrainian Business Entities' (2015) Yaroslav Mudryi National Law University 2015, 19; Kyiv International Economic Forum, 'Eight State Incentives for Innovation Development – Global Experience' *Forumkyiv* (23 April 2018).

65 See e.g.: Yuliya Olvinskaya et al., 'Current State and Trends of Development of Innovative Activity in Ukraine' (2021) 4 Economy and State, 64 (64–71); Iaroslav Petrunenko and Oleg Podtserkovnyi, 'Transformation of the Strategy of State Economic Policy in Modern Conditions' (2020) 6(3) Baltic Journal of Economic Studies, 107 (107–113); Kateryna Sutormina and Yevhen Osadchiy, 'Effectiveness of Finding Innovations: International Experience' (2016) Effective Economy.

66 See Kseniia Smyrnova, 'The "Europeanization" of Competition Law in Ukraine' in this Volume; Oles Andriychuk, 'Towards a New Digital Competition Policy of Ukraine: The EU Matrix' in this Volume; Olga Gurgula, 'The Intersection Between Intellectual Property and Competition Laws in the Pharmaceutical Sector: A Ukrainian Perspective' in this Volume; Anzhelika Gerasymenko and Nataliia Mazaraki, 'The "New Normal" in Competition – Filling the Gaps of Ukrainian Competition Law in the Digital Economy Age' in this Volume.

both purely legal and administrative, managerial, financial and other actions of state power. The proportionality and effectiveness of these measures can be assessed in terms of national legal tradition, Ukraine's international obligations and modern foreign regulatory experience. Here, the issues of a proper legal framework are combined with issues of law enforcement efficiency, transparency and consistency of management decisions, adequacy of incentives and guarantees, effectiveness of anti-corruption, access to capital, protection of corporate rights and stability of the legal regulation of the economy.

Among other things, the mechanism for raising funds for innovative projects needs to be changed. For example, good prospects of attracting funds of venture investors will be enjoyed by those means that ease the burden of permitting procedures for the implementation of innovative projects, when these are offered by state and self-government bodies for cooperation and/or financing, accompanied by the insurance of relevant risks. This will create procedural and other organizational preferences for those who are trying to invest in the development of public-connected innovation. After all, today's situation, when officials do not see it as their duty to create conditions for private innovations, when the state and utilities consider the only proper distribution of public funds, the amount of which is extremely insufficient, is the wrong practice. It provokes corruption and contempt of officials for the problems of investors. This not only creates obstacles in the way of the latest technologies, because advanced technology is not always accompanied by adequate support from managers and promoters, but also actually leads to the deprivation of innovative projects of any investment attractiveness.

Therefore, it is appropriate to reorient the sources of state funding for innovation activities from the financing of ready-made investment projects to the financing of research and development activity and bringing the projects to the stage of direct implementation, which should be accompanied by a full set of legal permissions.

Summarizing this section, it can be noted that there may be many recipes for improving the state regulation of innovation, but their effectiveness depends not only on the amount of public funding for innovation projects and the transparency of its distribution mechanism, the perfection of expert evaluation of innovation projects and other factors that require effective public management. We must also focus on creating the legal and infrastructural conditions for private innovation, among which the security and stability of the investment environment is a priority for the state, which can hardly be fully ensured in Ukraine without ending the war and Ukraine's full membership in Euro–Atlantic structures.

6 Requirements for Balancing State Regulation of Investment Relations

Measures of state economic policy will always intrude on the freedom of entrepreneurial activity and investment activity. In this section, we address the question of whether it is possible to create a frame for appropriate interference given the presence of private interest.

Economic freedom, which is the basis of innovation and investment activity, is in many cases limited by law in the interests of the state and society. Finding a just limit to this freedom, including economic freedom, is a non-trivial task, as thinkers of all times and peoples have debated the issue. Here mention can be made of the economic doctrines of mercantilism, classical political economy, Keynesianism, neoliberalism, institutionalism, dirigisme and many others, each of which differently perceives the limit of economic freedom as a criterion of social development.

Without resorting to controversial issues, it is appropriate to focus on the postulate proven by Ukraine's experience that excessive and inefficient government intervention can destroy the economic interest of entrepreneurs and provoke them into investing abroad, which is becoming even easier in the digital and global economy. Ukrainian economists have come to understand that state regulation requires an implementation that provides for market mechanisms "in addition in those places and cases, in those time parameters when the activities of the latter are not effective enough."[67] This is why public regulation needs constant adjustment to avoid unproductive restrictions on economic freedom by interfering in the economy. From this position, the science of commercial law in Ukraine distinguishes the concept of "finding a balance of private and public interests."[68] In this context, there are several constitutional and international legal provisions that shape the agenda in this field. The provisions of Art. 13 Constitution of Ukraine that "the state ensures the social orientation of the economy" is probably the first reference point for the economic model. This model is not accidental. It was substantiated by the creator of

---

[67] Anatolii Galchinskyi, 'Economic Science: Problems of Methodological Renewal' (2007) 3 Economy of Ukraine, 4 (4–13).

[68] Olena Belianevich, *Economic Contract Law of Ukraine (Theoretical Aspects)* (Yurincim Inter 2006), 342–372; Heorhii Znamenskii, *Economic Legislation of Ukraine: Formation and Development Prospects* (Naukova Dumka 1996), 50–54; Oleg Podtserkovnyi, 'The Economic Code is an Important Means of Harmonizing Private and Public Interests' (2000) 3 Market Economy: Modern Management Theory and Practice, 263 (263–268); Oksana Vinnyk, 'Private and Public Interests, their Role and Reflection in Economic Law' (2001) 5 Entrepreneurship, Economy and Law, 11, 12; Valentyn Shcherbyna, 'Public and Private Interests in Economic Relations' (2014) 13 Private Law and Entrepreneurship, 28, 28–31; Iryna Lukach, 'The Paradigm of Public and Private Norms in the Regulation of Economic Relations (2006) 8 Entrepreneurship, Economy and Law, 43 (43–46).

the German economic "miracle" Ludwig Erhard in his book "Prosperity for All".[69] This economic model is recognized in many other European countries.[70]

Current recommendations for finding a compromise between economic freedom (private interest) and economic policy of the state (public interest) include the UN Sustainable Development Goals,[71] as well as the principles of proportionality[72] set out in EU law, and a number of other legal guidelines.

However, it should be borne in mind that legal instruments are not able to provide the right balance, in contrast to current economic policy, considering that "[t]he welfare state is not the implementation of the model enshrined in the constitution, but the result of a political idea."[73] The democratic formula of "government by discussion" rather than "government by law" seems to allow us to find this balance on the basis of human nature[74] in the most effective way. The task of law is to develop general principles for an appropriate compromise between the measure of economic freedom on the one hand, and international, social security and other aspirations of society on the other hand. Interference should not be excessive and in violation of the law. But it is important that it addresses issues of social development and stability of the legal order.[75]

Very often the balance between private and public is so difficult to grasp that it becomes very complicated to describe it in law. But this complexity does not abolish the need to enshrine such link in law. This can be fully demonstrated in the statement:

> In general, 'balance between public interests and private property' is an artificial definition, which can be accepted in a certain way, in a certain time, not absolute. Like the law, 'balance' is an ideal state, which governments want to make perfect but it can never be done. Life is changing; it requires a different element for different circumstances.[76]

---

[69] Ludwig Erhard, *Wohlstand für Alle* (Econ-Verlag 1957).

[70] See e.g.: Otto Wiesheu, 'Social Market Economy – Economic Order with Values and Rules' (2017) Bavarian Chemical Associations https://www.bayerische-chemieverbaende.de/wp-content/uploads/sites/4/2018/02/rede_dr_wiesheu_web.pdf accessed 26 October 2022,12.

[71] United Nations, 'Transforming our World: The 2030 Agenda for Sustainable Development' (UN General Assembly) A/RES/70/1, 2015; Iryna Sotnyk, Valeriia Havrylova and Yevhen Kovalenko, 'Social Entrepreneurship as a Tool for Implementing Global Sustainable Development Goals' (2018) 2 Actual Problems of Economy, 62 (62–73).

[72] Takis Tridimas, *The General Principles of EU Law* (Oxford University Press 2nd ed. 2007), 591; Oleh Zahnitko, 'Economic and Legal Protection of the Domestic Product Producer – Comparative Legal Study' (IEPD 1999); Stanislav Pohrebniak, 'The Principle of Proportionality in Ukrainian Legal Practice and the Practice of the ECtHR' (2012) in Serhii Kivalov (ed) Conference paper *Legal Provision of Effective Execution of Decisions and Application of the Practice of the European Court of Human Rights*, 294 (294–310).

[73] Hans-Jürgen Papier, 'Wirtschaftsordnung und Grundgesetz' *Bundeszentrale für Politische Bildung* (19 March 2007) https://www.bpb.de/shop/zeitschriften/apuz/30557/wirtschaftsordnung-und-grundgesetz/ accessed 26 October 2022.

[74] Andrew Farrant, *Hayek, Mill and the Liberal* Tradition (Routledge 2011), 70–73.

[75] Valentin Mamutov, 'On the Combination of State Regulation and Market Self-regulation' (2006) 1 Economy of Ukraine 59.

[76] Tania Salerno 'Striking the Right Balance Between the Public and Private Interests in Compulsory Acquisition of Land in Vietnam' in Phan Trung Hien (ed) *Conference Paper No. 39 – Land Grabbing,*

Therefore, "striking the right balance between public and private interests" is the strategic objective of state economic and law policy.

An example of such a task is the rule of paragraph 5 of Art. 11 Commercial Code of Ukraine: "business entities that do not take into account social interests, reflected in program documents of economic and social development, may not be granted the law-established benefits and privileges in carrying out business activity".

This problem has become particularly relevant for patent law in the context of the COVID-19 pandemic. Patent law should reconcile different interests: On the one hand, it should reward inventors to encourage them to make new innovations, while ensuring on the other hand that the general public and not only a few privileged individuals benefit from the inventions. Outside times of crisis, the patent system has proved its worth and has always provided for an appropriate balance between the various interests. However, this assessment will require adjustments for the coronavirus crisis. Governments in different countries apply provisions that set limits to the exclusive right of the patent holder in the interest of the public.[77]

During martial law, the need to ensure a balance of public and private interests in state regulation of the economy recedes into the background, because the state restricts civil rights and freedoms in the interests of winning the war. This is evidenced by the powers of military administrations to "impose conscription", "forcibly alienate property in private or communal ownership", "use the capacity and labor resources of enterprises, institutions and organizations of all forms of ownership for defense", provided by the Law "on martial law". In this case, compliance with the legal procedures of wartime, which eliminates the unjustified deprivation of property, prevention of arbitrariness and inaction in the performance of state bodies assigned to them in the economy becomes a promising indicator of the state's ability to maintain economic order. This is the criterion which can be correlated with the European Commission's statement when processing Ukraine's application for EU membership: "Membership requires: that the candidate country has achieved stability of institutions guaranteeing democracy, the rule of law, human rights and respect for and protection of minorities."[78] In fact, regardless of the predominance of public or private interest in regulating the economy, maintaining order in the economy becomes a constant, without which any investment activity and economic policy loses its meaning.

Conflict and Agrarian-environmental Transformations: Perspectives from East and Southeast Asia (BRICS, MOSAIC, LDPI, RCSD, Transnational Institute 2015).

[77] Claudia Milbradt and Florian Reiling, 'Patent Law: Appropriate Balance Between Private and Public Health Interests in Times of Coronavirus Crisis' Clifford Chance (April 2020). https://www.cliffordchance.com/content/dam/cliffordchance/briefings/2020/04/patent-law-appropriate-balance-between-private-and-public-health-interests-in-times-of-coronavirus-crisis.pdf accessed 26 October 2022.

[78] European Commission, 'Commission Opinion on Ukraine's application for membership of the European Union' (Communication) COM(2022) 407 final, 2022.

7 Conclusion

Economic and legal reforms in Ukraine have demonstrated that public economic policy must be systematic and consistent.

In 2022, Ukraine faced unprecedented challenges to its own sovereignty and independence due to the full-scale and unprovoked aggression of the Russian Federation. A full-scale war disrupted the normal functioning of the economy and forced power to reconsider its approaches to state regulation, including the security of economic cooperation with Russia and its satellite countries. However, it also provoked processes of reassessment of the experience of state intervention in the economy and brought Ukraine together with the civilized world. The countries of the European Union have sent a strong signal of support to Ukraine and its people not only in the form of military-political and economic support for our country, but also in granting Ukraine the status of a candidate for EU membership and assuring its post-war recovery. These factors open up new opportunities for building an investment-attractive economy of Ukraine in the near future.

In any case, the state will not avoid active interference in economic relations due to national security needs, which in a broad sense means control of investment in critical sectors of the economy and infrastructure enterprises, eliminating the impact of large monopolistic business on competition, overcoming corruption in licensing procedures and state financing of investment projects, increasing the efficiency of the law enforcement system. Constitutional social guarantees and the need to overcome market "failures" in accordance with the experience of the world's leading countries will serve as a constant motivator of state intervention in the economy. This intervention should be proportionate, which will determine investor confidence in public economic policy.

Legislative support for methods of intervening in market relations from year to year in Ukraine acquires a clearer framework of legal procedures enshrined in the powers of public authorities. The need to overcome the political and oligarchic influence on state decision-making processes in the economic sphere, which reduces the effectiveness of state regulation and provokes a destructive discourse on the feasibility of state regulation of the economy, remains a topical issue.

An important condition for improving the effectiveness of measures to support investment activities and innovation continues to be the elimination of differences between declarative and legal support measures and their real financial and economic content. This relates to the state financing of investment projects, long-term budget processes, stability of tax benefits and organizational advantages for innovation and investment activities, the pursuit of antitrust and competition policies based on equal treatment of large and small businesses, as well as public control over the proper state support to serve the economy and its individual subjects.

References

Evgeny Artemiev and Leonid Kravets, *Inventions, New Technique, Control* (Economica 1974) [Евгений Артемьев и Леонид Кравец, *Изобретения. Новая техника. Управление* (Экономика 1974)]

Yuliia Atamanova, *Economic and Legal Support Innovative State Policy* (FINN 2008) [Юлія Атаманова, *Господарсько-правове забезпечення інноваційної політики держави* (ФІНН 2008)]

Olena Belianevich, *Economic Contract Law of Ukraine (Theoretical Aspects)* (Yurincim Inter 2006) [Олена Беляневич, *Господарське Договірне Право України (теоретичні аспекти)* (Юрінком Інтер 2006)]

Tobias Caspary, Neda Moussavi and Romain Girard 'EU Singles Out FDI "Hostile Investors" For the First Time: Russia and Belarus' *Fried Frank* (5 May 2022) https://www.friedfrank.com/siteFiles/Publications/FFITIECCommunicationsArticle05022022.pdf

Denys Chernikov, 'Modernization of the System of State Support of Business Entities in Ukraine' (2013) National Intitute of Strategic Studies [Деніс Черніков, 'Модернізація Системи Державної Підтримки Суб'єктів Господарювання в Україні' (2013) Національний Інститут Стратегічних Досліджень]

European Commission, 'Commission Opinion on Ukraine's application for membership of the European Union' (Communication) COM(2022) 407 final

Commission Guidance to the Member States concerning foreign direct investment from Russia and Belarus in view of the military aggression against Ukraine and the restrictive measures laid down in recent Council Regulations on sanctions (2022) OJ C151 I/01

Ludmyla Denisova, '"Cannot be supported": Commissioner for Human Righton the Anti-oligarchic Law' *Epravda* (7 September 2021) https://www.epravda.com.ua/news/2021/09/7/677548/ [Людмила Денисова '"Не може бути підтриманим": Уповноважена з Прав Людини про Антиолігархічний Законопроект *Еправда* (7 вересня 2021)]

Victor Dozortsev, *Legislation and Scientific and Technological Progress* (Juridicheskaya Literatura 1978) [Віктор Дозорцев, *Законодательство и научно-технический прогресс* (Юридическая литература 1978)]

Ludwig Erhard, *Wohlstand für Alle* (Econ-Verlag 1957)

Andrew Farrant, *Hayek, Mill, and the Liberal Tradition* (Routledge 2011)

Volodymyr Gaivoronskyi, 'Civil Legislation: From "Nothing Private" to "Nothing Public"?' (1997) 4 Bulletin of the Academy of Legal Sciences of Ukraine 91 [Володимир Гайворонський, 'Цивільне Законодавство: від "Нічого Приватного" до "Нічого Публічного"?' (1997) 4 Вісник Академії Правових Наук України 91]

Anatolii Galchinskyi, 'Economic Science: Problems of Methodological Renewal' (2007) 3 Economy of Ukraine 4 [Анатолій Гальчинський, 'Економічна Наука: Проблеми Методологічного Оновлення' (2007) 3 Економіка України 4]

Kathryn Gordon, 'Investment Guarantees and Political Risk Insurance: Institutions, Incentives and Development' (2008) OECD Investment Policy Perspectives 91

Dmytro Goriunov, 'FDI Screening in Ukraine' (2021) Centre for Economic Strategy

Johan den Hertog, 'Review of Economic Theories of Regulation' (2010) 10–18 Tjalling C. Koopmans Research Institute Discussion Paper 1

Farahim Huseynzade, 'Role of the State Budget and Venture Capital in the Boom of Start-ups and Innovations' *Lawels* (26 October 2019) https://lawels.com/en/2019/10/26/role-of-the-state-budget-and-venture-capital-in-the-boom-of-start-ups-and-innovations-2/

Nina Ischenko, 'The Current State of Innovative Activity at Ukrainian Enterprises and Its Financing' (2020) 4(46) the Problems of Economy 320 [Ніна Іщенко, 'Сучасний Стан та Фінансування Інноваційної Діяльності Підприємств в Україні' (2020) 4(46) Проблеми Економіки 320]

Yuliia Korneeva, 'Does Ukraine need Investment Screening? How to Check Foreign Investors and Not Crete Additional Barriers for the flow of Capital to Ukraine' *Epravda* (7 April 2021) https://www.epravda.com.ua/rus/columns/2021/04/7/672759/

Oleg Kravchuk, *Planning and Regulation of Business Development* (Lviv Polytechnic 2000) [Олег Кравчук, *Планування та Регулювання Розвитку Підприємницької Діяльності* (Львівська Політехніка 2000)]

Kyiv International Economic Forum, 'Eight State Incentives for Innovation Development – Global Experience' *Forumkyiv* (23 April 2018) https://forumkyiv.org/uk/analytics/visim-derzhavnih-stimuliv-dlya-rozvitku-innovacij-svitovij-dosvid [Київський Міжнародний Економічний Форум, 'Вісім Державних Стимулів для Інновацій – Глобальний Досвід' *Forumkyiv* (23 квітня 2018)]

Iryna Lukach, 'The Paradigm of Public and Private Norms in the Regulation of Economic Relations (2006) 8 Entrepreneurship, Economy and Law 43 [Ірина Лукач, 'Парадигма Публічних та Приватних Норм у Регулюванні Господарських Відносин (2006) 8 Підприємництво, Господарство, Право 43]

Viacheslav Lyashenko, Olga Prokopenko and Vitaliy Omelianenko, *Institutional Model of Innovative Economy* (Institute of Industrial Economics 2019) [Вячеслав Ляшенко, Ольга Прокопенко та Віталій Омельяненко, *Інституціональна Модель Інноваційної Економіки* (Інститут Економіки Промсловості НАН України 2019)]

Volodymyr Lytvyn, H. Borjak and others, 'Economic History of Ukraine: Historical and Economic Research' (2011) 2(1) Nika-Center [Володимир Литвин, Г. Боряк та інші, 'Економічна Історія України : Історико-економічне Дослідження' (2011) 2(1) Ніка-Центр]

Valentin Mamutov, 'On the Combination of State Regulation and Market Self-regulation' (2006) 1 Economy of Ukraine 59 [Валентин Мамутов, 'О Сочетании Госрегулирования и Рыночной Саморегуляции' (2006) 1 Экономика Украины 59]

Valentin Mamutov, 'Development of Economic Legislation and Eonomic and Legal Thought in Sovereign Ukraine' (2004) Institute of Economic and Legal Studies of the National Academy of Sciences of Ukraine [Валентин Мамутов, 'Развитие Хозяйственного Законодательства и Хозяйственно-правовой Мысли в Суверенной Украине' (2004) Институт Экономико-правовых Исследовании НАН Украины]

Valentin Mamutov, *Textbook of Economic Law* (Yurincom Inter 2002) [Валентин Мамутов, *Хозяйственное право: Учебник* (Юринком Интер 2002)]

Claudia Milbradt, Florian Reiling, 'Patent Law: Appropriate Balance Between Private and Public Health Interests in Times of Coronavirus Crisis' *Clifford Chance* (April 2020)https://www.cliffordchance.com/content/dam/cliffordchance/briefings/2020/04/patent-law-appropriate-balance-between-private-and-public-health-interests-in-times-of-coronavirus-crisis.pdf

Imad A Moosa, 'Good Regulation, Bad Regulation: The Anatomy of Financial Regulation' in Philip Molyneux (ed), *Palgrave Macmillan Studies in Banking and Financial Institutions* (Springer 2015)

Ivan Mykhasiuk, Alla Melnyk, Mykhailo Krupka and Zinovia Zaloha, *Textbook of State Regulation of the Economy* (Attika 2000) [Іван Михасюк, Алла Мельник, Михайло Крупка та Зіновія Залога, *Державне Регулювання Економіки: Підручник* (Атіка 2000)]

Yurii Oborotov, 'Inflation of Power and Rights as an Indicator of a Weak State' (2010) 9 Scientific Works of the Odessa National Law Academy 89 [Юрий Оборотов, 'Инфляция Власти и Права как Индикатор Слабого Государства' (2010) 9 Наукові Праці Одеської Національної Юридичної Академії 89]

Yuliya Olvinskaya, Elena Samotoenkova and Ekateryna Vitkovskja, 'Current State and Trends of Development of Innjovative Activity in Ukraine' (2021) 4 Economy and State 64 [Юлія Ольвінська, Олена Самотоєнкова, Катерина Вітковська, 'Сучасний Стан та Тенденції Розвитку Інноваційної Діяльності в Україні' (2021) 4 Економіка та держава 64]

Barak Orbach, 'What Is Regulation?' (2012) 30 Yale Journal on Regulation Online 1

Hans-Jürgen Papier, 'Wirtschaftsordnung und Grundgesetz' *Bundeszentrale für Politische Bildung* (19 March 2007) https://www.bpb.de/shop/zeitschriften/apuz/30557/wirtschaftsordnung-und-grundgesetz/

Anatolii Pelikh, 'Fundamentals of Entrepreneurship' (Gardarika 1996) [Анатолий Пелих, 'Основы предпринимательства' (Гардарика 1996)]

Sam Peltzman, 'George Stigler's Contribution to the Economic Analysis of Regulation' (1993) 101(5) Journal of Political Economy 818

Iaroslav Petrunenko and Oleg Podtserkovnyi, 'Transformation of the Strategy of State Economic Policy in Modern Conditions' (2020) 6(3) Baltic Journal of Economic Studies 107

Opanas Pidoprygora, *Problems of Legal Regulation of Scientific and Technological Progress in the USSR* (Higher School 1985) [Апанас Подопригора, *Проблемы Правового Регулирования Научно-технического Прогресса в СССР* (Вища школа 1985)]

Walter H Plosila, 'State Science- and Technology-Based Economic Development Policy: History, Trends and Developments, and Future Directions' (2004) 18(2) Economic Development Quarterly 113

Andrii Podlevskyi and M. Perevyazki, 'Tax Incentives for Investment and Innovation in Ukraine' (2011) 18(4) Problems of Rational use of Socio-economic and Natural Resource Potential of the Region: Financial Policy and Investment 48 [Андрій Подлевський та М. Перев'язко, 'Податкове Стимулювання Інвестиційно-інноваційної Діяльності в Україні' (2011) 18(4) Проблеми Раціонального Використання Соціально-економічного та Природно-ресурсного Потенціалу Регіону: Фінансова Політика та Інвестиції 48]

Oleg Podtserkovnyi, 'Legal Problems of Innovative Projects Funding' (2006) 4 Entrepreneurship, Economy and Law 63 [Олег Подцерковний, 'Правові Проблеми Фінансування Інноваційних Проектів' (2006) 4 Підприємництво, Господарство і Право 63]

Oleg Podtserkovnyi, 'The Economic Code is an Important Means of Harmonizing Private and Public Interests' (2000) 3 Market Economy: Modern Management Theory and Practice 263 [Олег Подцерковный, 'Хозяйственный Кодекс – Важное Средство Согласования Частных и Публичных Интересов' (2000) 3 Ринкова Економіка: Теорія та Практика Управління 263]

Oleg Podtserkovnyi and Valentyna Chaikovska, 'State Regulation of Foreign Economic Activity under Globalization and Financial Crisis', (2009) 2 Mytna sprava 75 [Олег Подцерковний та Валентина Чайковська, 'Державне Регулювання Зовнішньоекономічної Діяльності в Умовах Глобалізації та Фінансової Кризи' (2009) 2 Митна Справа 75]

Oleg Podtserkovniy and Olena Lomakina, 'Problems of Determining the Methods and Forms of State Regulation of Economic Relations' (2002) 8 Entrepreneurship, Economy and Law 3 [Олег Подцерковний та Олена Ломакіна, 'Проблеми Визначення Методів та Форм Державного Регулювання Господарських Відносин' (2002) 8 Підприємництво, Господарство і Право

Stanislav Pohrebniak, 'The principle of Proportionality in Ukrainian Legal Practice and the Practice of the ECtHR' (2012) in Serhii Kivalov (ed) Conference paper *Legal Provision of Effective Execution of Decisions and Application of the Practice of the European Court of Human Rights*, 294 [Станіслав Погребняк, 'Принцип Пропорційності в Українській Юридичній Практиці та Практиці ЄСПЛ' (2012) у Сергій Ківалов (ред) зб. конф. *Правове Забезпечення Ефективного Виконання Рішень і Застосування Практики Європейського Суду з Прав Людини*, 294]

Elżbieta Pohulak-Żołędowska and Arkadiusz Żabiński, 'The State's Role in Creating Innovation-driven Economic Growth' (2015) 214 Economic Studies. Scientific Journals of the University of Economics in Katowice 201

Richard A Posner, 'Theories of Economic Regulation' (1974) w0041 NBER Working Paper 1

Cergii Prylypko, Yuliia Atamanova and Dmytro Zadykhailo, *Draft Innovation Code of Ukraine as a New Stage in the Development of Norm-making in the Innovation Sphere' National Academy of Legal Sciences of Ukraine* (FINN 2011) [Сергій Прилипко, Юлія Атаманова та Дмитро Задихайло, *Проект Інноваційного Кодексу України як Новий Етап Розвитку Нормотворення в Інноваційній Сфері* (ФІНН 2011)]

President of Ukraine, Proposals to the Ukrainian Law on Innovative Activity 2002, 40-IV

Anna Puchko, 'System of State Financing of Innovative Activities' (2015) 19 Investments: Practice and Expereince 64 [Анна Пучко, 'Система Державного Фінансування Інноваційної Діяльності' (2015) 19 Інвестиції: Практика та Досвід 64]

Vitaly Rassokhin, 'Organizational and Legal Problems of Introducing Fundamentally New Achievements of Science and Technology into Production' (1987) Institute of State and Law

[Виталий Рассохин, 'Организационно-Правовые Проблемы Внедрения в Производство Принципиально Новых Достижений Науки и Техники' (1987) Институт Государства и Права]

José Reis, 'The State and the Market: An Institutionalist and Relational Take' (2012) 4 RCCS Annual Review 86

'Remarks by President Joe Biden at the United States Naval Academy's Class of 2022 Graduation and Commissioning Ceremony' *The Whitehouse* (27 May 2022) https://www.whitehouse.gov/briefing-room/statements-releases/2022/05/27/remarks-by-president-biden-at-the-united-states-naval-academys-class-of-2022-graduation-and-commissioning-ceremony/

Olena Riabchenko, 'State Management of the Economy of Ukraine, Administrative Legal Aspect' (2000) University of Internal Affairs [Олена Рябченко 'Державне Управління Економікою України (АдміністративноПравовий Аспект)' (2000) Університет Внутрішніх Справ МВС України]

Mikhail Ring, *Self-sustaining System for the Creation and Implementation of New Technology: Legal Problems* (Nauka 1982) [Михаил Ринг, *Хозрасчетная Система Создания и Внедрения Новой Техники: Правовые Проблемы* (Наука 1982)]

Nathan Rosenberg, 'Innovation and Economic Grow' in OECD (ed), *Innovation and Growth in Tourism* (OECD 2004)

Tania Salerno, 'Striking the Right Balance Between the Public and Private Interests in Compulsory Acquisition of Land in Vietnam' in Phan Trung Hien (ed) Conference Paper No. 39 – *Land Grabbing, Conflict and Agrarian-environmental Transformations: Perspectives from East and Southeast Asia* (BRICS, MOSAIC, LDPI, RCSD, Transnational Institute 2015)

Natalia Sedovolosa, 'Economic and Legal Support for the Export of Innovative Products by Ukrainian Business Entities' (2015) Yaroslav Mudryi National Law University [Наталія Сєдоволоса, 'Господарсько-Правове Забезпечення Експорту Інноваційної Продукції Суб'єктами Господарювання України' (2015) НЮУ ім. Ярослава Мудрого]

Valentyn Shcherbyna, 'Public and Private Interests in Economic Relations' (2014) 13 Private Law and Entrepreneurship 28 [Валентин Щербина, 'Публічні й Приватні Інтереси у Господарських Відносинах' (2014) 13 Приватне Право і Підприємництво 28

Valentyn Shcherbyna, *Textbook on Economic Law* (Yurincim Inter 2001) [Валентин Щербина, *Господарське право: Навчальний посібник* (Юринком Інтер 2001)]

Andrei Shleifer, 'Understanding Regulation' (2005) 11(4) European Financial Management 439

Georgii Sofonov, 'Creative Activity of Inventors and Innovators – The Most Important Lever for Improving Production Efficiency' (1979) 2 Issues of Invention 9 [Георгий Софонов, 'Творческая Активность Изобретателей и Рационализаторов - Важнейший Рычаг Повышения Эффективности Производства' (1979) 2 Вопросы Изобретательства 9]

Iryna Sotnyk, Valeriia Havrylova and Yevhen Kovalenko, 'Social Entrepreneurship as a Tool for Implementing Global Sustainable Development Goals' (2018) 2 Actual Problems of Economy 62 [Ірина Сотник, Валерія Гаврилова та Євген Коваленко, 'Соціальне Підприємництво як Інструмент Реалізації Глобальних Цілей Сталого Розвитку' (2018) 2 Актуальні Проблеми Економіки 62]

Edward W Steinmueller, 'Economics of Technology Policy' in Bronwyn H Hall and Nathan Rosenberg (eds), *Handbook of the Economics of Innovation* (MIT Press 2010) 1181

Anneli Stenberg, 'What Does Innovation Mean – A Term Without a Clear Definition' (2017) University of Halmstad 2017

Vira Stoian, Oleksandr Danevich and Myhailo Mats, *Textbook of Treasury System* (TSUL 2014) [Віра Стоян, Олександр Даневич та Михайло Мац, *Казначейська Система: Підручник* (ЦУЛ 2014)]

Kateryna Sutormina and Yevhen Osadchiy, 'Effectiveness of Finding Innovations: International Experience' (2016) 11 Effective Economy [Катерина Суторміна та Євген Осадчий, 'Ефективність Фінансування Інновацій: Міжнародний Досвід' (2016) 11 Ефективна Економіка]

Robert Tannenwald, 'State Regulatory Policy and Economic Development' (1997) New England Economic Review 83

Roman Tarnavskyi, *Economic and Legal Incentives for Venture Investment in Ukraine* (NU "OLA" 2017) [Роман Тарнавський, *Господарсько-Правове Стимулювання Венчурного Інвестування в Україні* (НУ "ОЮА" 2017)]

Stephen Thomsen, 'Economic and Other Impacts of Foreign Corporate Takeovers in OECD Countries' in OECD (ed), *International Investment Perspectives: Freedom of Investment in a Changing World* (OECD 2007)

Catharine Titi, 'Public Actors in International Investment Law' in Marc Bungenberg, Markus Krajewski, Christian J Tams, Jörg P Terhechte and Andreas R Ziegler (eds), *European Yearbook of International Economic Law* (Springer 2021)

Oksana Tkachenko, 'The AMCU's Performance Indicator is the Level of Competition in the Markets, not Fines' *FBC* (28 September 2021) https://fbc.ua/news/ekonomika-uk/pokaznik-roboti-amku-tse-riven-konkurentsiyi-na-rinkah-a-ne-shtrafi-ekspert/ [Оксана Ткаченко 'Показник Роботи АМКУ – це Рівень Конкуренції на Ринках, а не Штрафи' *FBC* (28 вересня 2021)]

Olga Tkachuk and Natalia Germanjuk, 'Modern Improvement of Innovative Activity of the Enterprise' (2020) 4(40) Economics and Organization of Management 91 [Ольга Ткачук та Наталія Германюк, 'Сучасне Удосконалення Інноваційної Діяльності Підприємства' (2020) 4(40) Економіка і Організація Управління 91

Takis Tridimas, *The General Principles of EU Law* (Oxford University Press 2007)

Oksana Vinnyk, 'Private and Public Interests, their Role and Reflection in Economic Law' (2001) 5 Entrepreneurship, Economy and Law 11 [Оксана Вінник, 'Приватні та Публічні Інтереси, їх Роль і Відображення в Господарському Праві' (2001) 5 Підприємництво, Господарство і Право 11]

Oksana Vinnyk, 'Commercial Law: A course of Lectures' (Atika 2004) [Оксана Вінник, 'Господарське Право: Курс Лекцій' (Атіка 2004)

Otto Wiesheu, 'Social Market Economy – Economic Order with Values and Rules' (2017) Bavarian Chemical Associations https://www.bayerische-chemieverbaende.de/wp-content/uploads/sites/4/2018/02/rede_dr_wiesheu_web.pdf

WTO, 'Domestic Support in Agriculture: The Boxes' *WTO* https://www.wto.org/english/tratop_e/agric_e/agboxes_e.htm

United Nations, 'Transforming our World: The 2030 Agenda for Sustainable Development' (UN General Assembly) A/RES/70/1, 2015

United Nations, UNCTAD, 'Investing in Innovation for Development' TD/B/C.II/21, 2013

Dmytro Zadykhailo, 'State Regulation of Market Relations as an Actual Legal Problem' (2005) 6 Ukrainian Commercial Law 18 [Дмитро Задихайло, 'Державне Регулювання Ринкових Відносин як Актуальна Юридична Проблема' (2005) 6 Українське Комерційне Право 18]

Agia Zagrybelska, 'Kolomoisky Fuel Cartel: Will the Antimonopoly Committee be able to Punish the Oligarch?' ZN,UA (30 March 2021) https://zn.ua/ukr/energy_market/palivnij-kartel-kolomojskoho.html [Агія Загрибельська, 'Паливний Картель Коломойського: чи Зможе Антимонопольний Комітет Покарати Олігарха?' ZN,UA (30 березня 2021)]

Oleh Zahnitko, *Economic and Legal Protection of the Domestic Product Producer – Comparative Legal Study* (IEPD 1999) [Олег Загнітко, *Господарсько-Правове Забезпечення Захисту Вітчизняного Товаровиробника (Порівняльно-Правове Дослідження)* (ІЕПД 1999)]

Anna Zausková, Artur Bobovnicky and Adam Madleňák, 'How the State Supports Innovations to Build a Sustainable Competitive Advantage of the Country' (2013) 8(2) Serbian Journal of Management 255

Heorhii Znamenskii, *Economic Legislation of Ukraine: Formation and Development Prospects* (Naukova Dumka 1996) [Георій Знаменский, *Хозяйственное Законодательство Украины: Формирование и Перспективы Развития* (Наукова думка 1996]

Competition Law

The "Europeanization" of Competition Law in Ukraine

Kseniia Smyrnova

Contents

Abstract The EU–Ukraine Association Agreement (the EU–Ukraine AA) significantly affects the particular application of national competition rules. Due to including strict and specific provisions on competition rules within the EU–Ukraine AA, we can observe a tendency towards the "Europeanization" of competition law due to the transposition of commitments on the implementation of competition

This article has been prepared with the support of the Erasmus+ Programme of the European Union within the Jean Monnet Centre of Excellence Project No. 611625-EPP-1-2019-1-UA-EPPJMO-CoE "Advancing European Studies in Ukraine: Interdisciplinary Approach".

K. Smyrnova (✉)
Comparative and European Law Department, Taras Shevchenko National University of Kyiv, Kyiv, Ukraine
e-mail: kseniia.smyrnova@knu.ua

H. Richter (ed.), *Competition and Intellectual Property Law in Ukraine*,
MPI Studies on Intellectual Property and Competition Law 31,
https://doi.org/10.1007/978-3-662-66101-7_5

acquis into Ukrainian legal order. The competition chapter of the EU–Ukraine AA is lengthy and divided in two sections: anti-trust and mergers; and state aid. This chapter analyzes the main achievements of Ukrainian competition law from the perspective of the transposition of substantial norms (merger regulation, vertical restraints and exemptions) and the implementation of procedural principles. Particular attention is paid to the practice of the Anti-monopoly Committee of Ukraine (the AMCU), including the grounding of decisions and the adoption of specific by-laws. This chapter also analyzes current judicial practice of Ukrainian courts with strict reference to the provisions and commitments of the EU–Ukraine AA, and it examines the norms of the obligatory approximation of substantial norms, as well as the necessity of their enforcement to the system. Particular attention is also paid to state aid and the current enforcement practice of the AMCU, as well as judicial practice, including two current Ukrainian Supreme Court decisions in the field of state aid.

1 The Preliminary Process of Transposing EU Competition Law Standards into Ukrainian Competition Law

Ukraine created a national system of competition law during the period of global interest in and rapid growth of developing national competition regimes. In the early 1990s, only about twenty countries had competition laws and enforcement mechanisms in place. Today more than 130 jurisdictions around the world have introduced systems of competition law.[1] After moving away from a planned economy, Ukraine started developing its competition rules by using the European model of competition for its domestic legal regime. When comparing with other countries with competition protection systems, the United Nations Conference on Trade and Development (UNCTAD) noted that Ukraine has begun the process of introducing competition law and the formation of its implementation policy under very difficult initial conditions. The economic and political circumstances in Ukraine, as well as in other former Soviet republics, were particularly challenging. Ukraine introduced its competition law system at the beginning of a period of rapid growth around the world in the number of jurisdictions with competition laws. UNCTAD experts stressed that the journey towards an effective competition policy system in Ukraine has been arduous.[2]

The first Ukrainian law on competition was introduced in 1992, the Law of Ukraine "On Restriction of Monopoly and Prevention of Unfair Competition in Entrepreneurial Activity", which was aimed at the "elimination of monopolization".

From 2000 the emphasis of anti-trust and competition policy shifted from restricting monopoly power in the economy to the development and protection of

---

[1] See Alison Jones and Christopher Townley, 'Competition Law' in Catherine Barnard and Steve Peers (eds), *European Union Law* (Oxford University Press 3rd ed. 2020) 149, 544.

[2] See the United Nations Conference on Trade and Development, Voluntary Peer Review of Competition Law and Policy: Ukraine Overview', UNCTAD/DITC/CLP/2013/3, 2013.

real competition. The Law of Ukraine "On the Protection of Economic Competition" (the LPEC)[3] entered into force in 2002 and was based on the principles of EU competition law. Such provisions as leniency policy (Art. 6(5) LPEC) and liability (Art. 52 LPEC) were taken from EU law. Nevertheless, domestic competition policy continues to focus on measures to liberalize economic sectors that are in a state of natural monopoly, by improving legal mechanisms for regulating the activities of natural monopolies and introducing mechanisms to protect real and potential competition. The LPEC has been constantly amended to improve the system of control over compliance with competition rules. All these changes were adopted to comply with the European model, adopting the practices of EU institutions. In relation to regulating cartels, the EU and US leniency programs were also introduced (Art. 6(5) LPEC, 2012 AMCU order[4]).

Due to Ukraine's integration policy, its accession to the WTO in 2008,[5] the entering into force of the free trade agreement with EFTA countries in 2012,[6] and the signing and ratification of the Association Agreement[7] with the EU, the free trade areas opened their doors for Ukraine. Due to that the most important issue related to liberalized trade is competition rules, which are becoming increasingly crucial for Ukraine.

2 The 2014 EU–Ukraine Association Agreement as an Accelerator of the Europeanization of Competition Law and Enforcement in Ukraine

Ratified in September 2014, the EU–Ukraine Association Agreement (AA)[8] specifies in its preamble that the signing of the AA contributes to the gradual economic integration and deepening of the political association between the parties. Upon its

[3] The Ukrainian Law on the Protection of Economic Competition 2001, 2210-III.

[4] The Antimonopoly Committee of Ukraine, Order 399-r on the Establishing of the Order of Release from Responsibility 2012, No. 1553/21865.

[5] The Ukrainian Law on the Ratification of the Protocol of Ukraine's Accession to the World Trade Organisation 2008, 250-VI.

[6] The Ukrainian Law on Ratification of the Agreement on free trade between Ukraine and Member States of EFTA 2011, 4091-VI.

[7] The Association Agreement between the European Union and its Member States, on the one part, and Ukraine, on the other (2014) OJ L161/3 (EU–Ukraine Association Agreement), 3–2137.

[8] European Commission, 'Council Decision on the Union position within the Association Council stablished by the Association Agreement between the European Union, the European Atomic Energy Community and its Member States, of the one part and Ukraine, of the other part with regard to the adoption of a Recommendation on the implementation of the EU–Ukraine Association Agenda' JOIN(2015) 4 final, 2015. For details on the AA, see also Roman Petrov, 'The EU–Ukraine Association Agreement as a General Framework of Contemporary EU–Ukraine Relations' in this Volume.

entry into force the AA is considered to be a part of national legislation[9] and in case of conflict with the norms of current legislation is subject to priority application.[10] The preamble stresses the leading role of a mechanism for approximation of laws that is needed to create a comprehensive and deep free trade area between Ukraine and the EU. It is noteworthy that the term "harmonisation" is not used widely in the text of the AA. Various notions are used instead, such as "adaptation", "legal convergence", "recognition of international standards", "transposition", etc. However, the vast majority of researchers use the term "harmonization" as an umbrella term in this context.[11]

Comparing the AA with Ukraine with analogue acts signed by the EU with other countries, it can be said that this is a "fourth generation agreement". It is the first of a new generation of association agreements between the EU and the countries of the Eastern Partnership that covers a deep and comprehensive free trade area (a DCFTA). Considering the "deep" and "comprehensive" character of a free trade agreement (an FTA), the EU–Ukraine DCFTA is the first of a new generation of FTAs concluded by the EU which will, once in force, gradually and partially integrate the Ukraine's economy into the EU's Internal Market. However, this integration will take place only if Ukraine approximates its legislation to the EU acquis. For this purpose, the DCFTA contains numerous legislative approximation clauses according to which Ukraine must approximate its domestic legislation or standards to the EU acquis. Title IV of the EU–Ukraine AA shows that the AA not only covers traditional FTA areas, such as market access for goods, but also includes public procurement, intellectual property rights, competition, energy, etc.

Articles 253–267 EU–Ukraine AA provide for the ensuring of an effective competitive environment within the established free-trade area and reproduce EU law, with provisions referring to EU regulations.[12] Such provisions on competition (known as a "competition clause") are included in a Chapter 10 of the AA (Arts. 253–267 AA), which consists of two sections: (1) Anti-trust and Mergers; (2) State Aid. This replicates the same division found in EU law. Attached to the AA is a special Annex 23

[9] Chapter 1, art 9 Ukrainian Constitution of 1996 states that: "International treaties in force, consented by the Verkhovna Rada of Ukraine (Ukrainian Parliament) as binding, shall be an integral part of the national legislation of Ukraine. Conclusion of international treaties, contravening the Constitution of Ukraine, shall be possible only after introducing relevant amendments to the Constitution of Ukraine".

[10] See Ch. 2, art 19, the Ukrainian Law on International Agreements of Ukraine 2004.

[11] For example, Viktor Muravyov, 'Legal Approximation: Evidence from Ukraine' in Marise Cremona and Gabriella Meloni (eds), *The European Neighbourhood Policy: A Framework for Modernisation?—EUI Working Papers LAW 2007/21* (European University Institute Law Department 2007) 129–136; Cristophe Hillion, 'A New Framework for the Relation Between the Union and its East-European Neighbours' in Marise Cremona and Gabriella Meloni (eds), *The European Neighbourhood Policy: A Framework for Modernisation?—EUI Working Papers LAW 2007/21* (European University Institute Law Department 2007) 147–154; Roman Petrov and Peter van Elsuwege, 'Article 8 TEU: Towards a New Generation of Agreements with the Neighbouring Countries of the European Union?' (2011) 36(5) European Law Review 688–703.

[12] Kseniia Smyrnova, 'The Implementation of the Competition Provisions in the Association Agreement Between Ukraine and the European Union' (2015) 8 Law of Ukraine 75–82.

which contains a glossary of basic definitions relating to competition matters, such as "public undertakings", "exclusive rights", "services of general economic interest (SGEI)", "state monopoly of commercial character", and "important project in the common European interest or in the common interest of the Parties". This glossary is not legally binding and is used exclusively for interpretation of the provisions of the AA.

An important feature of the EU-Ukraine AA is that none of the parties thereto may resort to dispute settlement procedures with regard to the questions referred to the field of competition (Art. 261 AA). The only obligation that may be subject to dispute settlement procedures relates to the terms of the harmonization of Ukrainian legislation in accordance with Art. 256 AA. This means that the substantive provisions of the EU–Ukraine AA that regulate the main principles and rules of free competition in the market, such as prohibition of anti-competitive practices in the form of concerted action or agreements, abuse of dominance and the principle of control of concentrations, are not subject to dispute settlement.

The EU-Ukraine AA identifies the key practices and economic transactions that could potentially adversely affect the functioning of markets and undermine the benefits of trade liberalization established between the parties. Those anti-competitive practices include: (a) agreements and concerted practices between undertakings which have the purpose or effect of impeding, restricting, distorting or substantially lessening competition in the territory of either party; (b) the abuse by one or more undertakings of a dominant position in the territory of either party; and (c) concentrations between undertakings which result in monopolization or a substantial restriction of competition in the market in the territory of either party.[13]

Generally, Ukrainian legislation encompasses the fundamental principles of fair competition and prohibits the foregoing acts that are clearly enshrined in Art. 42(3) Constitution of Ukraine, which ensures the protection of competition in entrepreneurial activity. Types and limits of monopolies are also determined by applicable law. In other words, the substantial matter of Art. 254 AA is reflected in current Ukrainian legislation and regulations issued by the AMCU.

3 Substantial Changes in Ukrainian Competition Law

The AA emphasizes the existence of some gaps in the harmonization process, and it clearly defines the requirements that must be incorporated into Ukrainian law and the terms of their performance. A special provision of the AA is devoted to the substantial aspects of the approximation of Ukraine legislation to European competition law and the timing of its implementation into the national legal system.[14] Conventionally, these substantial requirements can be grouped according to the areas to which they relate, i.e. procedural aspects of competition law enforcement, the legal regime on

[13] EU–Ukraine Association Agreement, art 254.

[14] Ibid art 256.

concerted actions, control of concentrations, the activity of state monopolies and state aid. The following sections of this chapter take a closer look at merger regulation (Sec. 3.1) and vertical restraints of competition (Sec. 3.2).

3.1 Merger Regulation

3.1.1 Amendments to Applicable Law

The AA contains requirements for the improvement of existing national laws on concentrations. In particular, Art. 256(2) AA requires Art. 1, Art. 5(1) and Art. 5(2) of Regulation 139/2004[15] to be implemented into Ukrainian legislation within three years of the AA entering into force.

One should note that the thresholds and procedures established under Ukrainian competition law in the early 2000s are outdated. They do not meet the needs of the current conditions of ensuring an effective balance between the need for prior control of economic concentrations to prevent restrictions on competition and the monopolization of commodity markets and administrative costs. As a consequence, the harmonization of the merger control regime is primarily aimed at reducing the number of notifications, allowing the AMCU to focus on transactions that can significantly change the market structure in the long run.

The Ukrainian reform regarding mergers began in 2016. The legislator amended the LPEC by increasing the financial thresholds for notification of concentrations. From the one side it follows from the EU–Ukraine AA (Art. 256(2)) that the financial criteria should be increased to the EU dimension (as is stipulated in the EU Merger Regulation). But, from another side, the financial calculation for the Ukrainian market differs from the EU internal market. In fact, a middle way was found, and the new financial criteria on merger notifications was adopted due to the amendments to Art. 24 LPEC. Pursuant to Art. 24 LPEC, such criteria are: Ukrainian turnover or assets for each of at least two parties that exceed 4 million EUR, and combined worldwide turnover or assets of all parties that exceed 30 million EUR; *or* Ukrainian turnover or assets of at least one party that exceed 8 million EUR and worldwide turnover of at least one other party that exceeds 150 million EUR. At the same time, some of the notification thresholds remained unchanged, i.e. those regarding: mergers of undertakings, or the taking over of one undertaking by another; the establishing of a newly formed full-function joint venture performing on a lasting basis the functions of an autonomous economic entity; and the acquisition of control by way of the appointment to certain management positions persons who already occupy similar position(s) in other undertakings.

Moreover, the reform introduced a fast-track 25-day procedure for transactions raising no competition concerns. This would include, for example, cases where only

[15] Council Regulation (EC) 139/2004 of 20 January 2004 on the control of concentrations between undertakings (the EU Merger Regulation) (2004) OJ L24/1, 1–22.

one party is active in Ukraine or the parties' combined market shares do not exceed certain thresholds. Alongside these reforms the use of formal consultations with the AMCU during the review of the merger notifications was introduced, as well as an increase in the filing fee (between 600 EUR and 1,300 EUR).

The reform also implemented another essential legislative act: the Law of Sanctions. This law states that when merger is prohibited thereby, the AMCU will reject notifications or drop its review.[16] The AMCU clarified that these rules would apply if any of the parties to a merger (or any individuals or entities connected to them by a relationship of control) are on the Ukrainian sanctions list; and a particular type of sanction applies to a given individual or entity, for e.g. the prohibition on the disposal of assets or equity.[17] The new rules may apply on group-wide grounds, for example when a party is not on the sanctions list but is part of a group controlled by, or controlling, sanctioned individuals or undertakings.

Several by-laws that apply to merger regulation were also updated. The AMCU adopted the Guidelines on the Assessment of Horizontal Mergers in December 2016[18] and the Guidelines on the Assessment of Non-horizontal Mergers in March 2018.[19] Those guidelines provide rules and the procedure for reviewing different types of concentrations and identify issues to focus on. The AMCU has also adopted the Guidelines on the Definition of Control,[20] which provide guidance on when the AMCU will impact different structures of the transaction and defines rules relevant to specific deals. In general, the guidelines provide a concept of control which is similar to EU competition law and strictly follows the European Commission's Consolidated Jurisdictional Notice under Council Regulation (EC) No. 139/2004 EU. The AMCU tends to follow EU practice where a case is uncertain or where Ukrainian law does not regulate the relevant issue. Finally, in September 2019 the AMCU issued important guidelines on the consideration and clearance of mergers leading to the establishing of joint ventures (JVs). Those guidelines were inspired by the European Commission's Consolidated Jurisdictional Notice under Council Regulation (EC) No. 139/2004 on the control of concentrations between undertakings. They set out the elements for the creation of a JV to fall under the notion of concentration and significantly ease the burden for many foreign parties to transactions who are unfamiliar with the peculiarities of the AMCU's approach towards JVs.

---

[16] The Ukrainian Law on Sanctions 2012, 1644-VII.

[17] Igor Svechkar and Alexey Pustovit, 'Merger Control 2021' Chambers and Partners (7 July 2021) https://practiceguides.chambers.com/practice-guides/merger-control-2021/ukraine/trends-and-developments accessed 17 February 2022.

[18] The Antimonopoly Committee of Ukraine, Guidelines on Providing Recommendations on the Procedure for Applying Part One of art 25 Law of Ukraine on Protection of Economic Competition (on the Assessment of Horizontal Concentrations) 2016, No. 49-rr, 226–16.

[19] The Antimonopoly Committee of Ukraine, Guidelines on Providing Recommendation Clarifications on the Procedure for Applying Part One of art 25 Law of Ukraine On Protection of Economic Competition (on the Assessment of Non-horizontal Concentrations) 2018, No. 13-rr.

[20] The Antimonopoly Committee of Ukraine, Guidelines on the Application of the Concept of Control, 1 November 2018 https://amcu.gov.ua/storage/app/sites/1/imported_content/5d69108d71592.pdf accessed 26 October 2022.

3.1.2 Merger Practice in Ukraine

In 2020, the AMC reviewed 13% more notifications than it had in 2019 (602 notifications) and issued 477 clearances.[21] In 2020, more than 37% (i.e. 223) of notifications came from foreign investors or companies in which foreign investors participated, which is an increase of 3% compared with 2019.[22] The number of decisions taken by the AMCU in 2020 to consider an application under the simplified procedure increased by 22% (i.e. 184 cases) compared with 2019 (151 cases).[23]

The sectors most commonly applying for the AMCU's approval were the industrial, agricultural, fuel and energy, and housing and utility sectors. The AMCU focused on in-depth investigations in the markets for the fuel and energy, agricultural products, pharmaceutical products, and healthcare.[24]

In 2019, the AMCU imposed two record fines for merger control violations. The first fine, of 1.8 million EUR, was imposed on the TAS Group (controlled by a former member of the Ukrainian Parliament, Sergei Tygipko) for the acquisition of control over Dniprometyz, a subsidiary of Severstal.[25] This development is notable, not only because of the amount of the fine, which is three and a half times higher than the previous highest fine,[26] but also because the AMC did not clear the transaction due to the sanctions imposed on Severstal, a Russian steel and mining company controlled by Alexei Mordashov.

The second fine (2 million EUR) was imposed on DCH Group, which is controlled by Oleksandr Yaroslavsky, another former member of the Ukrainian Parliament, for the acquisition of control over Dnipropetrovsk Metallurgical Plant, a subsidiary of Evraz.[27] In contrast to the Dniprometyz case, the AMCU approved the acquisition of control over the Dnipropetrovsk Metallurgical Plant by the DCH Group following a review of the case.

These precedents show the intention of the AMCU to increase the level of fines for merger control violations Fines for closing transactions that technically meet the filing thresholds but have no effect in Ukraine have been gradually increasing over the last few years but remain reasonably low, reaching the level of 20,000 EUR. While the AMCU does not specifically target purely technical violations, it pursues every failure to obtain approval for any notifiable transaction that appears on its radar.

---

[21] The Antimonopoly Committee of Ukraine, 'Annual Report on Providing State Aid to Undertakings in Ukraine in 2020' (Annual Report), 2020, 101.

[22] Ibid 103.

[23] Ibid 104.

[24] Ibid.

[25] The Antimonopoly Committee of Ukraine, Decision (2019) No. 284-r.

[26] The previous highest fine was approximately 500,000 EUR, for the acquisition of control over a Ukrainian bank.

[27] The Antimonopoly Committee of Ukraine, Decision (2019) No. 286-r.

3.1.3 Future Reforms

On 28 October 2020, the AMCU submitted to the Ukrainian Parliament proposed amendments to the draft law introducing new merger filing thresholds in Ukraine. The amendments were developed by the AMCU in co-operation with competition law experts from the EU and the US. The draft was registered with the Parliament in 2021.[28] Two of the aims of the reform are attracting foreign investors and making a positive impact on economic development.

Two major changes are proposed by the AMCU. First, the turnover of a controlling seller would be excluded after calculating the target's notification thresholds (currently, the turnover of the seller controlling the target is taken into account when calculating the merger thresholds of the target and a filing may be technically triggered based on a seller only). Second, the local threshold for a target would be decreased, from 4 million EUR to 2 million EUR.[29] Moreover, the proposal aims to strengthen the AMC's powers with regard to collecting evidence in cases of breach of competition law (primarily cartels and abuses of dominance); in future the AMCU will co-operate closely with the national police. Thus the draft law tackles some essential problems in Ukraine's merger control regime.[30]

3.2 *Vertical Restraints and the Exemptional System*

A number of requirements exist regarding the approximation of Ukrainian legislation to EU law with respect to the mandatory implementation of rules concerning exemptions from prohibited anti-competitive conduct for vertical agreements. The current text of Art. 10 LPEC only contains general requirements for exemptions regarding prohibited concerted practices.[31] At the same time, a detailed procedure

---

[28] The Ukrainian Draft Law on Amendments to Certain Legislative Acts of Ukraine on Improving the Activities of the Antimonopoly Committee of Ukraine 2021, 5431-1.

[29] Anastasia Usova and Denys Medvediev, 'New Merger Control Thresholds in Ukraine and Other News From the AMC' *Kluwer Competition Law Blog* (27 October 2020) http://competitionlawblog.kluwercompetitionlaw.com/2020/10/27/new-merger-control-thresholds-in-ukraine-and-other-news-from-the-amc/ accessed 16 February 2022.

[30] Igor Svechkar and Alexey Pustovit, 'Merger Control 2021' Chambers and Partners (7 July 2021) https://practiceguides.chambers.com/practice-guides/merger-control-2021/ukraine/trends-and-developments accessed 16 February 2022.

[31] The Ukrainian Law on Protection of Economic Competition, art 10: "Concerted Actions which May be Authorized

(1) The concerted actions, provided for by Article 6 of this law, may be authorized by the appropriate bodies of the Antimonopoly Committee of Ukraine, if their participants prove, that these actions promote:
    the improvement production, procurement or sale of goods;
    technical, technological and economic development;
    the development of small and medium enterprises;
    the optimization of export or import of goods;

for the granting of prior authorization for concerted actions is set out in a special act on the Procedure Applicable to Submissions of Applications for Authorization for Concerted Practices of Economic Entities[32] of 2002 (the Procedure for Concerted Practices).

To comply with the EU–Ukraine AA, the AMCU adopted a Vertical Block Exemption Regulation, effective from 5 December 2017. The Exemption explains and codifies the approach of the AMCU in the assessment of agreements on the supply, distribution, and use of products.

Vertical agreements containing vertical restraints (supplier–customer level) are exempted from the prohibition of anti-competitive agreements and do not require the prior approval of the AMC, provided that the market share of each of the parties does not exceed 30% on the markets where they, respectively, buy and sell relevant goods or services.

Exemption from AMCU approval also applies to vertical concerted actions related to a buyer's use of intellectual property rights and certain vertical concerted actions between a contractor and a subcontractor.

The exemption does not cover a number of situation in which prior individual approval must be obtained from the AMCU, i.e.:

- vertical agreements between competing undertakings (except for non-reciprocal agreements);
- vertical agreements which contain "hard-core" vertical restraints

    (1) on resale prices (except for provisions regarding maximum or recommended prices),

---

the development and application of the uniform specifications or standards for goods;
the rationalization of production.

(2) The concerted actions, provided for in paragraph one of this Article, may not be authorized by the bodies of the Antimonopoly Committee of Ukraine, if the competition is significantly restricted on the whole market or in its significant part.

(3) The Cabinet of Ministers of Ukraine may authorize concerted actions, which have not been authorized by the Antimonopoly Committee of Ukraine pursuant to paragraph two of this Article, if participants of concerted actions prove that the positive effect for public interests prevails over adverse consequences of competition restriction.

(4) The authorization provided for in paragraph three of this Article may not be given if:
participants of concerted actions apply restrictions which are not required for the implementation of the concerted actions;
the restriction of competition constitutes a threat to the system of market economy.

(5) It shall be prohibited to take concerted actions, provided for in this Article, until authorization has been granted by bodies of the Antimonopoly Committee of Ukraine or the Cabinet of Ministers of Ukraine".

[32] The Regulation on the Procedure for Applying to the Antimonopoly Committee of Ukraine for Granting Permission for Concerted Actions of Undertakings (Regulation on Concerted Actions) 2002, No. 26-p, No. 11, 253.

(2) territorial restrictions and customer restrictions (except for some restrictions on active sales under exclusive distribution arrangements and on sales to unauthorized distributors under selective distribution arrangements),
(3) restrictions on cross-supplies between members of a selective distribution system, and
(4) restrictions on selling product components as spare parts to consumers and repairers;

- non-compete clauses the duration of which is indefinite or exceeds five years, subject to some exceptions;
- obligations of a buyer not to manufacture, purchase, sell or resell goods/services after the termination of the agreement; and
- obligations of a member of a selective distribution system not to sell brands of a particular competitor.

If undertakings are in doubt as to whether a vertical agreement contains any provisions which may be an anti-competitive vertical restraint, they may apply to the AMCU for guidance.

The aforementioned block exemption classifies the fixing of minimum or fixed prices for the resale of goods or the prohibition of the sale of goods in certain territories or to groups (categories) of consumers, with certain exceptions, as "hard core" restrictions. At the same time, such common practices in the Ukrainian market as the introduction of exclusive and selective distribution systems do not generally fall under the prohibited categories, subject to the fulfilment of certain criteria.

This document was adopted due to the implementation of the EU–Ukraine AA commitment to incorporate provisions of the General Block Exemption Regulation (Regulation 330/2010) in Ukraine. And it is worth stressing that the introduced rules are close to the EU Regulation, as the Ukrainian resolution incorporates all the titles and notions thereof.

4 Procedural Aspects of Competition Law Enforcement in Ukraine

4.1 The Principle of Transparency and Appropriate Decision-Making Processes for the AMCU

The principle of transparency of and appropriate decision-making processes for the AMCU has attracted the attention of the courts. The EU–Ukraine AA imposes a commitment to introduce to national Ukrainian law a strict legal basis for publishing AMCU decisions in cases of an infringement of national competition rules, as well as concentration control cases, within three years from the date of the AA entering into force.[33] Pursuant to this commitment the decisions of the AMCU are now published on its official website.[34] This commitment derives from Art. 256(1) AA, which clearly specifies the rule to be implemented into the Ukrainian legal system, i.e. Art. 30 EU Regulation No 1/2003.[35] On 12 November 2015, the Ukrainian Parliament adopted amendments to the laws of Ukraine, committing the AMCU to publish its decisions on its website within ten working days of the date on which such decisions are taken. These transparency measures are intended to make the AMCU's work clearer, to make analysis of decisions possible and to enable stakeholders to understand the approach of the AMCU.

Decisions published on the official website of the AMCU include decisions on mergers or concerted actions (e.g. a decision granting merger clearance) and decisions relating to violation of the laws regarding unfair competition. In addition, the AMCU is required to publish its internal orders upon acceptance of an application for approval of concentration(s) or concerted action(s). However, this involves only the company name and type of concentration or concerted action affected.

4.2 The Principles in the Setting of Any Pecuniary Sanctions Imposed for Infringements of Competition Law

The EU–Ukraine AA also lays down, in Art. 255(5) thereof, a strict obligation for the AMCU to adopt and publish a document explaining the principles to be used in the setting of any pecuniary sanctions imposed for infringements of competition law. Pursuant to Art. 255(6) thereof the AMCU has to publish a similar document explaining the principles used by the Ukrainian competition authority in the assessment of horizontal mergers.

The AMCU uses and introduces guidelines, which are not binding, but are mentioned in the AA, to understand and to interpret the current legislation. One such guideline is that on the calculation of fines,[36] which provides the methodology for calculating the necessary level of fines for infringement of competition law, including cases involving mergers. Leniency policy in Ukraine is regulated by the Act on Immunity from Fines (2012).[37] Those companies that are the first to inform

---

[33] The EU–Ukraine Association Agreement, art 256(1); Council Regulation (EC) No 1/2003 of 16 December 2002 on the implementation of the rules on competition laid down in Articles 81 and 82 of the Treaty, OJ 2003 L 1/1 (Implementation of the Rules on Competition Directive), art 30.

[34] AMCU, Search for official documents https://amcu.gov.ua/npasearch?&category=12 accessed 26 October 2022.

[35] Implementation of the Rules on Competition Directive, (n 33) 1–25.

[36] The Antimonopoly Committee of Ukraine, Guidelines on Recommendations for the Application of the Provisions on Ukrainian Law on the Protection of Economic Competition 2001, art 52(2)(5), and on Ukrainian Law on Protecting Against Unfair Competition 1996, art 21(1)(2) No. v1 6, 226–15, 15 September 2015, No. 16-rr.

[37] Antimonopoly Committee of Ukraine on the Procedure for Exemption from Liability 2012, No. 399-r; Official Journal of Ukraine 2012, No. 73, 206.

the AMCU about an undetected cartel, or other anti-competitive concerted practices, should benefit from a reduction of the fines to be imposed if they provide significant evidence to the AMCU. Leniency has been underused in Ukraine, because currently only the first applicant may benefit. There are also plans to introduce a comprehensive settlement procedure.

The AMCU has been criticized for the lack of transparency in the way it sets fines, resulting in appeals to the courts for clarification. In the past the courts have rejected complaints, arguing that the guidelines are non-binding and their application by the AMCU is not reviewable.[38] However, on 21 January 2021, the Ukrainian Supreme Court annulled one of the highest fines imposed by the AMCU,[39] (1.9 million EUR), which was imposed in 2019 on a Ukrainian group subsidiary DCH for the acquisition of a local metallurgical plant by way of a share-purchase agreement without obtaining prior clearance (i.e. gun-jumping).[40] Fines were also imposed on other subsidiaries. Although the fine was formally addressed to DCH, it had been calculated based on the total turnover of the group. The Supreme Court, agreeing with the lower court, found that the AMCU had erred in law by applying the group-wide turnover as the basis of the fine. The AMCU argued that it had made a technical error, which could be seen as an "excusable error" defense, in the manner it had calculated the fine. Under applicable law the fine should have been based on the turnover for the year immediately preceding the year in which the fine was imposed, which would have been for 2018. But the AMCU had used the group-wide turnover for 2017 as the basis for the fine. The AMCU argued that the lower court should not have annulled the decision in its entirety because it was a "non-decisive procedural error". The Supreme Court rejected the argument, finding that the DCH merely managed corporate rights of controlled entities and had no turnover from the sale of goods or provision of services. Therefore, the AMCU should have imposed a nominal fine of 6,000 EUR. The AMCU had committed a decisive error by applying the group-wide turnover to calculate the fine.

The Supreme Court decision is an important development. The Supreme Court rejected the AMCU's argument that the guidelines for the imposition of fines were not reviewable. The AMCU had relied on the fining guidelines in its statement of defense and had relied on aggravating factors, mentioned only in the guidelines, and not in the applicable law, in that another subsidiary of the DCH group also had been fined.

---

[38] For example, Poltava Regional Commercial Court, Decision (2016) 917/2711/15, does not take into account the clarifications of the Guidelines, noting that this document has not been registered with the Ministry of Justice and is of a recommendatory nature; In cases No. 13/200-06-7383 and No. 13/199-06-7382 the Ukrainian Commercial Court of Cassation of the Supreme Court stated that the legislation does not refer to the powers of commercial courts to decide on the reduction of the fine.

[39] Ukrainian Commercial Court of Cassation of the Supreme Court, Decision (2021) 910/10017/19.

[40] See Sergiy Glushcenko and Ivan Yaremchuk, 'Ukrainian Supreme Court Annulled One of the Highest Fines for Gun-jumping' *Kluwer Competition Law Blog* (19 March 2021) http://competitionlawblog.kluwercompetitionlaw.com/2021/03/19/ukranian-supreme-court-annulled-one-of-the-highest-fines-for-gun-jumping/ accessed 16 February 2022.

The Supreme Court also ruled on the concept of an undertaking in relation to fines. It held that the concept of an "undertaking" for the purpose of fines is not synonymous with the concept in its wider meaning of "single economic unit". Therefore, when calculating the fine the total turnover of all entities should not be used. This is different to the situation where a single economic unit concept is deployed to administer the merger thresholds. As a consequence, the AMCU had a way to amend the law that so that it was clear that only when a parent company has decisive influence over a subsidiary which is the direct infringer of competition law should the parent company and the subsidiary, which is a direct acquirer, should be jointly and severally liable for payment of the fine.[41]

Despite these changes, there is still work to be done on up-dating and improving the older laws on competition. For example, on 29 December 2017, the AMCU launched a public discussion on the draft Methodology of Market Definition. Currently, the AMCU uses a law dating back to 2002.[42] In order to avoid double regulation of market definition, the AMCU plans to approve a new version of the Rules on Monopoly Methodology and the Methodology of Market Definition. Also, after analyzing the responses received during public consultations, the AMCU is likely to approve the Non-Horizontal Merger Guidelines alongside the Methodology of Market Definition.

Finally, there is scope for draft laws amending procedural rules governing investigations, increasing the list of cases for the simplified procedure for obtaining merger clearance and providing for the removal of the seller from the calculation of turnover and assets value in the case of a merger. Several drafts were not passed through the voting procedure in the Parliament.[43] Detailed procedures for carrying out competition investigations are governed by the Rules for the Consideration of Cases on Violation of the Legislation on the Protection of Economic Competition.[44] These were adopted in the mid-1990s on a temporary basis. These rules describe the stages and competence of the AMCU but need to be improved to fill gaps in the procedural processes.

[41] See footnote 28: The AMCU has published draft amendments to the law that, inter alia, allows addressing the fine to the parent based on the argument that the parent has decisive influence over the direct infringer. In such cases, the parent and subsidiaries (direct acquirers) will be jointly and severally liable for payment of the fine. This amendment seeks to bring the Ukrainian laws closer to the EU *acquis*.

[42] Methodology for the establishment of the monopoly (dominant) market position of undertakings, approved by the Antimonopoly Committee of Ukraine, Order (2002) No. 49-p.

[43] Such as Ukrainian Draft Law 2431, 2015, concerning the implementation of principles of imposing fines wasn't supported by the Parliament.

[44] Approved by the Antimonopoly Committee of Ukraine, Resolution (1994) No. 5, registered with the Ministry of Justice of Ukraine on 6 May 1994 after No. 90/299.

5 Regulation of State Aid in Ukraine: New Legislative Enforcement and Judicial Practice

5.1 Legal Standards for State Aid in Ukraine

One of the aspects of the "Europeanization" of competition law in Ukraine regards state aid.[45] The main precondition of transposition of EU state aid rules was the EU-Ukraine AA. It is worth noting that before this new system of norms there was a huge gap in regulating state resourcing. The EU–Ukraine AA pays particular attention to state aid, which is still unregulated in Ukraine. Article 262 AA states that "any aid granted by Ukraine or the Member States of the European Union through state resources which distorts or threatens to distort competition by favoring certain undertakings or the production of certain goods is incompatible with the proper functioning of this Agreement insofar as it may affect trade between the Parties". Article 262 AA imposes upon Ukraine the strict obligation to adopt a special act governing the system of monitoring and control of state aid schemes under Art. 107 TFEU with all implementing regulations in the field of state aid.

Following analogy of the EU law, the EU–Ukraine AA contains conditions under which state aid can be acceptable and can be recognized as valid. One example of such is state aid granted in order to provide consumers with socially important goods, on the condition that such assistance is not discriminatory in relation to the place of origin of these goods, and aid given to victims of man-made emergencies and natural disasters. The above two types of state aid are considered acceptable according to Art. 262(2) AA. The second category of exceptions permits the following types of state measures: aid intended to promote economic and social development of geographic regions in which the standard of living is abnormally low and the unemployment rate high; aid to promote the execution of national programs and/or the solving of social and economic problems of a national character; aid to facilitate the development of certain economic activities or of certain economic areas where such aid does not adversely affect trading conditions contrary to the interests of the EU and/or Ukraine; and aid to promote culture and heritage conservation where such aid does not adversely affect trading conditions contrary to the interests of the EU and/or Ukraine (Art. 262(3) AA). In line with EU practice, the second group of exemptions is different from the first insofar that for their admissibility it is necessary not only to submit a relevant notification, but to receive approval from the European Commission, which has exclusive authority to decide on this issue.

The AA also emphasizes the need to introduce rules on *de minimis* state aid which does not, *a priori*, make a significant impact on trade between the parties. Article 263 AA states that notification does not need to be made with regard to any aid below the threshold of 200,000 EUR per undertaking over three years.

---

[45] See also Kseniia Smyrnova and Natalia Fokina, 'The 'Europeanization' of Competition Law of Ukraine' (2022) 71(1) GRUR International 1 (1–2).

It is worth stressing that the state aid rules contained in the AA are to be applied in light using as sources of interpretation the criteria arising from the application of Arts. 106, 107 and 93 TFEU, including the relevant jurisprudence of the CJEU, as well as relevant secondary legislation, frameworks, guidelines and other administrative acts in force in the EU.

5.2 *Implementation of State Aid Rules in Ukraine and Enforcement Thereof*

Special attention has to be paid to the mechanism of implementation of state aid in Ukraine, which has led to the adoption of the Law "on State Aid to Undertakings", which entered into force on 2 August 2017.[46] Since then, the AMCU has been overwhelmed by notifications regarding state aid. The AMCU's 2020 Report states that there were 2,061 notifications regarding state aid during 2017–2020. There has been an increase in findings of incompatible state aid: 2 decisions in 2018, 13 decisions in 2019 and 19 decisions in 2020. The AMCU recognizes that it needs to create guidelines and educate local authorities about the acceptable forms of state aid, especially de minimis aid, in order to free up its time to focus on the larger and more problematic cases. Several AMCU by-laws on procedural issues have been adopted.[47] Under the Law on State Aid relevant by-laws were envisaged, specifying the criteria on the compatibility of State Aid in different spheres. These were adopted by the Cabinet of Ministers of Ukraine between 2018 and 2021.[48]

The Administrative Courts are the main forum for state aid issues. The AMCU may refer a case to the Administrative Court in Kyiv. The Administrative Courts handle the review of AMCU decisions. To date, the Supreme Court has rendered one decision on state aid, as part of the panel of judges of the Administrative Court of Cassation.[49] The Court of First Instance had concluded that the plaintiff's assertion that the AMCU had misused the sources of EU law when adopting a decision was false, groundless, unsubstantiated and contrary to applicable law and the case file. The

---

[46] Kseniia Smyrnova and Erika Szyszczak, 'Modern Approaches to State Aid: Ukraine' (2020) 19(1) European State Aid Law Quarterly (8–18).

[47] For example, Antimonopoly Committee of Ukraine Order (2015) No. 43-pr and Antimonopoly Committee of Ukraine Orders (2016) No. 2-pr and No. 8-pr.

[48] For example, the Cabinet of Ministers of Ukraine on Criteria for Approval of State Aid for regional development and support of SMEs No. 57 of 7 February 2018; The Cabinet of Ministers of Ukraine on Criteria for Approval of State Aid to business entities for the employment of certain categories of employees No. 33 of 31 January 2018; The Cabinet of Ministers of Ukraine on Criteria for Approval of State Aid to economic entities for research, technical development and innovation No. 118 of 7 February 2018; the Cabinet of Ministers of Ukraine on Criteria for Approval of State Aid to economic entities in coal sector No. 38 of 13 January 2021, etc. General information about the legal basis see at State aid portal http://pdd.amc.gov.ua/portal/main/content/about accessed 26 October 2022.

[49] Ukrainian Administrative Procedure, 640/65/19; Vinnytsia City Council, (2020) No. K/9901/30620/19; Kyiv City Council, 640/21523/19.

Supreme Court upheld the complainant's contention that the AMCU was wrong to use EU law sources when adopting Decision No. 652-p, since the latter contradicts the current law and the facts established by the courts. The case is significant in accepting that the EU–Ukraine AA is part of the national law of Ukraine, with its provisions imperative, and binding on the whole territory of Ukraine; it is the beginning of national courts applying the case law of the CJEU.

As far as competition law enforcement by national courts is concerned, there have been some pioneering judgements in terms of recovery of illegal state aid. Of particular note is case No. 640/65/19 based on a suit brought by the Department of Energy, Transport and Communications of Vinnytsia City Council against the AMCU regarding the rendering of illegal and quashing the decision of the AMCU of 20 November 2018 No. 652-r. The latter decision rendered state aid in the form grants to compensate for losses in providing public passenger road transport services in the amount of 407 million UAH incompatible with competition and recovery of state aid. The court of first instance ruled in favor of the AMCU, a position which was reiterated by the Supreme Court. The decision of the AMCU and the court judgments contained references to the EU–Ukraine AA, the TFEU, and EU jurisprudence (namely the *Altmark* case[50]).

Another exemplary case in enforcement of law regarding state aid is case No. 640/21523/19 involving the cassation appeal of the AMCU against the decision of the District Administrative Court of Kyiv on a suit brought by the Department of Construction and Housing of the Executive Body of Kyiv City Council. The case involved capital repairs/reconstruction/construction of educational institutions, health care facilities, residential buildings with social facilities, utilities, office buildings and sports infrastructure. The Department (as the grantor) argued that state aid rules should not be applied in this case to the provision of services of general economic interest (more specifically, with regard to the reimbursement of reasonable costs for the provision of such services). On 31 March 2021, the Supreme Court partially quashed the judgements of lower courts and refused to rule that the abovementioned support was not covered by the state aid law of Ukraine.[51] However, the Supreme Court ruled that for carrying out the functions of the ordering entity as to construction, reconstruction, major repairs of social infrastructure a tender is not required. Furthermore, the Supreme Court ruled that since the construction and reconstruction of social facilities is an investment in infrastructure, and the involvement of the contractor to perform such work is based on the results of public procurement procedures, the courts of first and appellate instance had drawn the correct conclusion that the Law of Ukraine "on State Aid to Undertakings" does not apply to the activities of municipally-owned enterprises that perform the functions of the ordering entity. This is another milestone in enforcement of law regarding state aid by the Ukrainian judiciary, as it shows the proliferation of state aid rules to yet

[50] ECJ C-280/00 *Altmark Trans GmbH and Regierungspräsidium Magdeburg v. Nahverkehrsgesellschaft Altmark GmbH, and Oberbundesanwalt beim Bundesverwaltungsgericht* (2003) EU:C:2003:415.

[51] Kyiv City Council 640/21523/19.

another industry. Moreover, the scope of this judgement covers more activities than the previous one.

From the point of view of public enforcement, the example of the Ukrainian competition authority is rather unique in terms of the sharing of "EU spirit", especially in the field of state aid.[52] National decisions on compatibility of state aid are based not only on national acts but also contain direct references to EU regulations and the practice of the CJEU.

6 Conclusion and Perspective

The pace of change in competition law reform in Ukraine has altered significantly since the country signed the EU–Ukraine Association Agreement in 2014. Recent improvements in training personnel and understanding the application of competition rules have resulted from the EU funding capacity building and loaning experienced EU personnel to work alongside national officials. The recent substantive reforms in the field of competition law have focused on merger control, vertical restraints and state aid, alongside improving the effectiveness of the competition regulator. A wide range of stakeholders have been consulted. But the reform process is piecemeal. A new form of competition law has been imposed upon the existing framework. In the future, a radical consolidation of competition law ought to take place. This would result in efficiency and clarity and enable both parties to the AA to adapt and in the future respond to new challenges, especially those involving digital markets.[53]

The implementation of the provisions of the AA in the national legislation of Ukraine and its law enforcement practice should be in compliance with EU competition law. In addition, the EU–Ukraine Association Agreement contains provisions taken from the EU's founding treaties, as well as a significant number of annexed acts of EU institutions. When applying them Ukraine must take into account the relevant practice of the EU, including that of the CJEU, in these areas. Legal positions formulated in the decisions of the CJEU, as well as on request in the preliminary rulings of the CJEU, can be an effective tool for shaping Ukrainian legislation in the context of its approximation to EU law.

Pursuant to Art. 256 AA, Ukraine is to approximate its competition legislation and application practices to the EU acquis. It is through the mechanism of implementation of this provision that not only the substantive norms of EU law practice are transposed but also enforcement of applicable law.

Therefore, given the fact that very strict and specific provisions on competition rules are contained within the EU–Ukraine AA and can also be found in Ukrainian

[52] On this aspect, see also Oles Andriychuk, 'Towards a New Digital Competition Policy of Ukraine: The EU Matrix' in this Volume.

[53] In this area, see the analysis on the current stage and perspectives of Ukrainian competition law of Anzhelika Gerasymenko and Nataliia Mazaraki, 'The "New Normal" in Competition—Filling the Gaps of Ukrainian Competition Law in the Digital Economy Age' in this Volume.

legal framework and jurisprudence, it can be assumed that the tendency of the "Europeanization" of competition law while spreading commitments on implementation of competition acquis in Ukrainian legal order has set in. Such an assumption is predicated upon the fact that the respective regulatory framework, activities of the national competition authority and other stakeholders, as well as competition rules enforcement, contain direct and indirect reference to and propagation of EU competition standards contained in primary and secondary legislation, *acquis* and case law.

References

Antimonopoly Committee of Ukraine, 'Annual Report on Providing State Aid to Undertakings in Ukraine in 2020' (Annual Report), 2020

Antimonopoly Committee of Ukraine, Guidelines on the Application of the Concept of Control, 1 November 2018 https://amcu.gov.ua/storage/app/sites/1/imported_content/5d69108d71592.pdf [Антимонопольний Комітет України, Методичні Рекомендації щодо Застосування Поняття Контролю, 1 листопад 2018]

Ondrej Blazo, 'Harmonization of Competition Law in Globalized Economy and European Law' (2010) Comenius University in Bratislava, Faculty of Law, Institute of International Relations and Comparative Law

Valerie Demedts, 'Which Future for Competition in the Global Trade System: Competition Chapters in FTAs' (2015) 49 (3) Journal of World Trade 407

Sergiy Glushcenko and Ivan Yaremchuk, 'Ukrainian Supreme Court Annulled One of the Highest Fines for Gun-jumping' *Kluwer Competition Law Blog* (19 March 2021) http://competitionlawblog.kluwercompetitionlaw.com/2021/03/19/ukranian-supreme-court-annulled-one-of-the-highest-fines-for-gun-jumping/

Cristophe Hillion, 'A New Framework for the Relation Between the Union and its East-European Neighbours' in Marise Cremona and Gabriella Meloni (eds), *The European Neighbourhood Policy: A Framework for Modernisation?—EUI Working Papers LAW 2007/21* (European University Institute Law Department 2007) 147

Jitendra Jain, *Harmonization of International Competition Laws: Pros and Cons* (Anchor Academic Publishing 2012)

Alison Jones and Christopher Townley, 'Competition Law' in Catherine Barnard and Steve Peers (eds), *European Union Law* (Oxford University Press 3rd ed. 2020) 149

Viktor Muravyov, 'Legal Approximation: Evidence from Ukraine' in Marise Cremona and Gabriella Meloni (eds), *The European Neighbourhood Policy: A Framework for Modernisation?—EUI Working Papers LAW 2007/21* (European University Institute Law Department 2007) 129

Kseniia Smyrnova and Natalia Fokina, 'The "Europeanization" of Competition Law of Ukraine' (2022) 71(1) GRUR International 1

Kseniia Smyrnova, 'Europeanization of Competition Law: Principles and Values of Fair Competition in Free Market Economy in the EU and Association Agreements with Ukraine, Moldova and Georgia' in Stefan Lorenzmeier, Roman Petrov, Christoph Vedder (eds), *EU External Relations Law* (Springer 2021)

Kseniia Smyrnova and Erika Szyszczak, 'Modern Approaches to State Aid: Ukraine' (2020) 19(1) European State Aid Law Quarterly

Kseniia Smyrnova and Iryna Berezovska, 'Association Agreements as Means of Eastern Partnership Member States' Europeization' (2018) 4(20) Social and Human Sciences, Polish-Ukrainian Scientific Journal

Kseniia Smyrnova, 'Competition Law Issues in EU–Ukraine, Moldova & Georgia Association Agreements (Comparative Aspects)' in Alexander Trunk, Susanne Rieckhof and NazarPanych (eds), *Legal Aspects of the EU Association Agreements with Georgia, Moldova and Ukraine in the Context of the EU Eastern Partnership Initiative* (Josef Eul Verlag 2017)

Kseniia Smyrnova, 'The Implementation of the Competition Provisions in the Association Agreement Between Ukraine and the European Union' (2015) 8 Law of Ukraine [Ксенія Смирнова 'Імплементація Положень про Конкуренцію в Угоді про Асоціацію між Україною та Європейським Союзом' (2015) 8 Право України]

Anastasia Usova and Denys Medvediev, 'New Merger Control Thresholds in Ukraine and Other News From the AMC' *Kluwer Competition Law Blog* (27 October 2020) http://competitionlawblog.kluwercompetitionlaw.com/2020/10/27/new-merger-control-thresholds-in-ukraine-and-other-news-from-the-amc/

Roman Petrov, Peter van Elsuwege, 'Article 8 TEU: Towards a New Generation of Agreements with the Neighbouring Countries of the European Union?' (2011) 36(5) European Law Review 688

'United Nations Conference on Trade and Development, Voluntary Peer Review of Competition Law and Policy: Ukraine Overview', UNCTAD/DITC/CLP/2013/3, 2013

Guillaume Van der Loo, *The EU–Ukraine Association Agreement and Deep and Comprehensive Free Trade Area: A New Legal Instrument for EU Integration without Membership* (Brill | Nijhof 2016)

Vertical Agreements in the Competition Law of Ukraine and the EU: A Closer Look at Resale Price Maintenance

Hanna Stakheyeva

Contents

Abstract The chapter examines resale price maintenance (RPM) in Ukraine in detail with reference to the practice of the Antimonopoly Committee of Ukraine (AMCU) and compares this with the current approach of the European Commission (EC). The comparative analysis goes beyond identifying the gaps between Ukraine and the European Union (EU) in this legal area; it provides a constructive normative analysis on means for Ukraine to advance. Following the Introduction, Sec. 2 focuses on the overview of the strict approach towards RPM in the legal framework of Ukraine. Cases of the AMCU as well as the courts are also cited here to understand the Ukrainian specifics of the subject matter. Section 3 provides highlights of RPM in the EU and its approach in this regard under the new Vertical Block Exemption Regulation, where such practices are viewed as restrictions of competition by object which may be exempted. Section 4 deals with the discussion on the weaknesses and strengths of the per se and rule of reason approaches to RPM, as well as further legislative reforms. It is suggested that when a supplier does not have significant market power, from an economic standpoint, such a small firm should be allowed to benefit from RPM. The strict approach should be relaxed at least de facto. Additionally, it is highly recommended that the AMCU improves its case search engine to allow any interested party to benefit from it.

H. Stakheyeva (✉)
Department of International Trade, Bogazici University, Istanbul, Turkey
e-mail: hanna.stakheyeva@boun.edu.tr

H. Richter (ed.), *Competition and Intellectual Property Law in Ukraine*,
MPI Studies on Intellectual Property and Competition Law 31,
https://doi.org/10.1007/978-3-662-66101-7_6

1 Introduction

RPM has been subject of competition law research and discussions for decades in various jurisdictions. Ukraine is not an exception. RPM practices are also common for the area of intellectual property (IP). Setting resale prices for licenses may be regarded as anticompetitive concerted actions under the Law of Ukraine "On Protection of Economic Competition"[1] (hereinafter "Law of Ukraine"). Recommending resale prices for licenses is not prohibited. As a general rule, there are no exemptions for IP rights; they are treated in the same way as non-IP-related conduct. Therefore, a deeper understanding of RMP practices in the EU and Ukraine may help to picture the main competition law concerns associated with RPM in the area of IP. The chosen topic is also of importance considering that there has been no deep review and analysis of RPM in Ukraine yet, despite the fact that Ukraine is committed under the EU–Ukraine Association Agreement to follow the EU approach and practice and align its legislation with the EU rules.

The term "RPM" refers to a particular type of vertical agreement in which an upstream firm controls or restricts the price (or sometimes the terms and conditions) at which a downstream firm can on-sell its product or service, usually to final consumers.[2] In other words, RPM arises when the manufacturer/producer limits the ability of a distributor/retailer to set the prices at which it may sell the products of the upstream company. Maximum (setting an upper limit on the price) and minimum (setting a minimum limit on the price) RPM may be distinguished. Some countries treat both forms of RPM in the same way under their competition law, but in the majority of jurisdictions maximum RPM does not pose competition concerns, as opposed to minimum RPM. Minimum RPM constitutes a violation of competition law, particularly when it involves monitoring and penalties for deviations from the prescribed prices, i.e. cutting off supplies, etc. The manufacturer may always recommend price levels to its retailers, but they must be pure recommendations without any threat and/or sanction involved.

According to the findings under the OECD Report,

> Resale Price Maintenance remains one of the most controversial areas of competition law and policy. Despite arguments from economists and complaints from the business community, most countries' competition laws have historically taken a hostile approach to RPM.[3]

As mentioned, how competition policy approaches RPM varies. The business community has been trying to oppose a strict approach to RPM. This opinion is supported by economists who argue that (despite a risk of facilitating collusion) RPM may often be procompetitive and help both firms and consumers[4] (e.g. improving

---

[1] The English version of the Law of Ukraine on Protection of Economic Competition 2001 is available at https://www.oecd.org/countries/ukraine/2381565.pdf accessed 27 October 2022.

[2] OECD, 'Directorate for Financial and Enterprise Affairs Competition Committee: State-owned Enterprises and the Principle of Competitive Neutrality' DAF/COMP(2008)37, 2009, 9.

[3] OECD, 'Directorate for Financial and Enterprise Affairs Competition Committee: Roundtable on Resale Price Maintenance', DAF/COMP(2008)37, 9.

[4] Dennis W Carlton and Jeffrey M Perloff, Modern Industrial Organization (Pearson 2005) 426.

interbrand competition by enhancing distribution efficiency, providing more of the pre-sale services, discouraging free-riding, protecting brand image)[5], hence it should not be per se illegal, but rather analysed on a case-by-case basis taking into account any potential efficiencies.[6] Moreover, very often RPM is carried out by small firms with little market power, and hence the effect on competition would be negligible.[7]

In the EU, RPM practices are still viewed as hardcore restrictions. At the same time this approach may slowly evolve (at least de facto) towards the rule of reason.[8] Although the new Vertical Block Exemption Regulation (VBER)[9] still treats RPM as a hardcore restriction, at the same time it states that the qualification of RPM as a restriction by object does not mean that RPM is illegal per se. Where it is believed that the RPM may bring about efficiencies, it may be exempted under Art. 101(3) Treaty on Functioning of the EU[10] (TFEU) in an individual case.

In Ukraine the AMCU follows a hostile approach to RPM. RPM/setting minimum resale prices (as opposed to maximum and recommended resale prices) is considered as anticompetitive concerted action and normally prohibited. According to the Standard Requirements for Vertical Agreements (hereinafter "Standard Requirements"),[11] RPM is regarded as a hardcore restriction. However, it is expected that

---

[5] This is an argument related to the manufacturer's investment in the image of the quality of the brand. RPM in this case may be justified as a means of preventing price reductions that may affect the sales volumes, OECD, DAF/COMP(2008)37 (n 3), 28.

[6] See for instance, Kenneth G Elzinga and David E Mills, 'Leegin and Procompetitive Resale Price Maintenance,' (2015) The Antitrust Bulletin. Also Roger D. Blair et al., 'Resale Price Maintenance and the Private Antitrust Plaintiff' (2005) 83(3) Washington University Law 657(659).

[7] Paul W Dobson and Michael Waterson, 'The Competition Effects of Industry-wide Vertical Price Fixing in Bilateral Oligopoly' (2007) 25(5) International Journal of Industrial Organization 935 (935–962).

[8] We see similarities here with the US regime, where RPM was viewed as illegal per se, but the Supreme Court ruled in 2007 that the efficiencies of RPM must be taken into account in the analysis of RPM on a case-by-case basis (see US Supreme Court *Leegin Creative Leather Products, Inc. v. PSKS, Inc* (2007) 551 U.S. 887). The EU is expected to move in this direction. In 2010 the EC started a review of the framework on vertical agreements. There has been a debate on whether it should change its strict approach towards RPM. "However, the EU policy on vertical restraints did not change substantially after the review in 2010. Despite the emphasis on economics after the modernisation process the approach taken towards RPM in the EU is still hostile.": Rebecca Johnsson, 'RPM and Object Restrictions—A Need for Change in EU Competition Policy?: A Comparative Analysis of the Different Approaches Towards RPM in EU and US Antitrust Law' (2020) Uppsala University. This is still applicable under the new VBER adopted in May 2022. According to it, the RPM is still treated as a hardcore restriction, although not illegal per se.

[9] Commission Regulation (EU) 2022/720 of 10 May 2022 on the application of Article 101(3) Treaty on the Functioning of the European Union to categories of vertical agreements and concerted practices (2022) OJ L134/4, 4–13.

[10] Treaty on European Union and the Treaty on the Functioning of the European Union, OJ C202/1 (2016).

[11] Order of the Antimonopoly Committee of Ukraine on Approval of the Standard Requirements for Vertical Concerted Actions of Business Entities and Amendments to the Standard Requirements for Concerted Actions of Business Entities for General Exemption from the Prior Authorization of the Bodies of the Antimonopoly Committee of Ukraine, No. 1364/31232.

the approach will evolve, considering that Ukraine follows the EC footprints, which in turn are very much influenced by the US approach.

The focus of this chapter is RPM under the competition policy of Ukraine. Cases of the AMCU[12] as well as the courts[13] are analysed in this chapter to bring more clarity to the Ukrainian specifics of the subject matter. Comparison with the EU approach, as well as explication of the per se rule and rule of reason rule, constitutes a vital part of the chapter, without which it is difficult to come up with practical recommendations and conclusions.

2 RPM in Ukraine

2.1 *Basic Rule*

According to Part 1 of Art. 6 Law on Protection of Economic Competition, anticompetitive concerted actions are actions that have led or may lead to the prevention, elimination or restriction of competition. Concerted actions related to the setting of prices or other conditions for the purchase or sale of goods are recognized as anticompetitive. In particular, this is the case when those actions lead to a significant restriction on competition in all or a significant part of the market, including monopolization of relevant markets and restricting access to the market of other business entities thus leading to an economically unjustified increase in prices or

[12] For instance, Decision No. 420-r dated 2 July 2020, in relation to LLC Grundfos Ukraine and 11 other companies/distributors. The supply contracts contained RPM (the minimum level of the recommended price for household goods and the minimum selling prices for household goods to third parties (resellers)). Such actions were considered as anticompetitive concerted actions relating to price setting. All 12 companies were fined a total of 5,192,736 UAH. The decision is a good source of clarification of the AMCU's approach and practical application of the Ukrainian Competition Law. For instance, see para 78 of the decision, where the AMCU emphasizes that "vertical concerted actions that contain hard-core restrictions, namely, restrictions on the ability of the buyer to determine the selling price of the contract goods, are prohibited. The hard-core restrictions contained in the supply contract concluded by ASTER-M LLC with Grundfos Ukraine LLC are prohibited, even if the supplier's shares and buyer in the market in which they, respectively, sell and buy contracts goods do not exceed 30%".

[13] For instance, Ukrainian Commercial Court of Kyiv, Decision No. 98558978 (2021) in relation to the appeal submitted by Novo Nordisk A/S (Denmark) and Novo Nordisk Health Care AG (Switzerland) against the infringement decision of the AMCU. The court ruled that AMCU's Decision No. 680-r was made with incorrect application of substantive law; there was a failure to prove the circumstances that were relevant to the case; there was incomplete clarification of the circumstances relevant to the case; the conclusions of the AMCU did not correspond to the circumstances of the case; finally, the AMCU violated procedural law, which led to an incorrect decision. Although the judgment was repealed by the Appeal Court of Kyiv later on (the text thereof is currently unavailable), it is still important to see the logic and reasoning of the Court in this case. Another case is in relation to Roche Ukraine, an indirect RPM case, i.e. in relation to the bonus mechanisms that led to allegedly (by the AMCU) unjustified overpricing of Hoffmann-La Roche Ltd medicines through public procurement procedures. For details see Sec. 2.

shortages of goods.[14] Hence, the effects of such concerted actions are important for their qualification as anti- or procompetitive.

Ukraine has implemented the EU's VBER as part of its commitments under the EU–Ukraine Association Agreement.[15] In 2017, the AMCU adopted the Standard Requirements for Vertical agreements. Paragraph 1 of Section 2 Standard Requirements deals with the vertical concerted actions that are permitted and with the situations in which the AMCU's permission is not required in accordance with Part 1 of Art. 10 Law of Ukraine. This is where the seller's share on the market in which he sells the contract goods does not exceed 30% and the share of the buyer in the market in which he buys the contract goods does not exceed 30%.

However, according to paragraph 2 of Section 2 Standard Requirements, such exemption does not apply to vertical concerted actions that contain hardcore restrictions, namely, restrictions on the ability of the buyer to determine the selling price of the contract goods.

By and large, given the lack of consistent AMCU practice on these issues, the Standard Requirements are the only source that provides at least some legal clarity. At the same time, this document contains only basic rules that are difficult to apply without taking into account the guidance of the EU on the application of the VBER. The EU had evaluated the effectiveness and relevance of EU legislation on distribution and vertical restraints for several years, and in May 2022 it adopted the new VBER and its clarifications on its application. Therefore, stakeholders in Ukraine should monitor not only the practice of the AMCU but also the status of these changes in the EU to better understand the rules set out in the Standard Requirements and their relevance.

2.2 *Grundfos* Case

In general, as seen from the review of the legislation and the AMCU's practical approach, RPM is viewed as a hardcore restriction under the VBER, but it may still be justified under Art. 10 Law of Ukraine based on efficiency claims.[16] This has also been confirmed by the AMCU in *Grundfos*.[17] Grundfos Ukraine LLC (hereinafter "Grundfos") in 2017–2018 carried out a sale of pumping equipment of the GRUNDFOS brand to its 11 retailers[18] on the basis of supply contracts, which contained the conditions of setting prices for further sales of goods, the minimum

[14] According to art 8(2) of the Law.

[15] Association Agreement between the European Union and its Member States, of the one part, and Ukraine, of the other part (2014) OJ L161/3.

[16] This is a copy-and-paste version of the EU approach to the RPM.

[17] Antimonopoly Committee of Ukraine, Grundfos, No. 143–26.13/128–18 (2020).

[18] I.e. Geiser LLC, Leon Service Plus, Vikom LLC, Romstal Ukraine, Climate Technologies, VIK XXI LLC, Unick Trading Company, Research and Production Association "Ecosoft", Aster-M LLC, LLC Propex, Snab-Reserve Group LLC.

level of the recommended price for household goods and the minimum selling prices for household goods to third parties (resellers). The main activity of Grundfos in Ukraine is wholesale of imported equipment.

According to the AMCU,[19] the analysis of supply contracts and supplementary agreements indicated that their terms contained hardcore vertical restraints that were directly related to the ability of the buyer to determine the sales price of the contract goods. These restraints functioned through the establishment of minimum sales prices of goods by one of the participants in the concerted actions and introduction of sanctions for non-compliance with the relevant minimum prices. Such actions were considered as anticompetitive concerted actions under paragraph 1 of Part 2 of Art. 6 Law of Ukraine. The companies were fined 5,192,736 UAH.

The legal assessment applied by the AMCU was based on the following grounds. According to Art. 6 Law of Ukraine, anticompetitive concerted actions are prohibited. Under Subpara. 2 of Para. 2 of Section II Standard Requirements,[20] vertical concerted actions that have as their object the establishment of minimum resale prices are recognized as containing hardcore restrictions, i.e. lead to significant restriction of competition in the market. In view of this, the AMCU qualified the actions of the undertakings regarding the conclusion of supply contracts for pumping equipment of the Grundfos brand, which contain conditions on setting prices for further sales of goods, as anticompetitive concerted actions.

It is important to emphasize that in July 2018, prior to the infringement decision, Grundfos applied to the AMCU with a request to provide preliminary conclusions on concerted actions concerning the necessity to obtain permission for concerted action through the conclusion of agreements for the supply of pumping equipment of the Grundfos brand, which contains the conditions on setting prices for further sales of goods between Grundfos and its distributors. In August 2018, the AMCU provided *preliminary conclusions*[21] to Grundfos, in which it noted the need to obtain permission for concerted actions, because it contained the RPM clause and sanctions for non-compliance with it. Thus, such concerted actions might lead to the prevention, elimination or restriction of competition.

The AMCU made an important statement in paragraph 62 of the decision that "those concerted practices may be authorized by the relevant authorities of the AMCU only if the participants of the concerted action prove the existence of conditions provided for in part one of Article 10 Law of Ukraine." Such a wording suggests

[19] Paragraph 43 of the Decision.

[20] Standard Vertical Requirements concerted actions of economic operators in relation to supply and use goods approved by the order of the Antimonopoly Committee of Ukraine from October 12, 2017 No. 20-rp, registered with the Ministry of Justice of Ukraine, 9 November 2017, No. 1364/31232.

[21] LLC No. 35-pv. In accordance with Ukrainian Law on Economic Protection Competition, Art 14 in order to prevent violations of legislation on economic protection competition, increasing the predictability of its application, the Committee may provide to the business entities on the basis of the information provided by them conclusions in the form advisory explanations on the compliance of the actions of economic entities provisions of art 6 of the Law.

that RPM is not actually a hardcore restriction since there is a chance to get approval from the AMCU if the efficiencies are proved.

Part 1 of Art. 10 Law states that:

> Concerted actions provided for in Article 6 of this Law may be authorized by the relevant bodies of the AMCU if their participants prove that these actions contribute to: improving the production, purchase or sale of goods; technical and technological, economic development; development of small or medium entrepreneurs; optimization of export or import of goods; development and application of unified technical conditions or standards for goods; and rationalization of production.

Grundfos further reported that after the receipt of the AMCU's preliminary opinions, it suspended any action aimed at application of the minimum level of recommended retail prices and/or minimum sales prices for any of their products sold to Ukrainian dealers and sent to its Ukrainian distributors messages clearly stating that the provisions on RPM would not be used in commercial relations with them. Nevertheless, the RPM was used in the commercial relations with the distributors and found to be prohibited and illegal, irrespective of the fact that the respective shares in the market did not exceed 30%.[22]

It is also interesting to see the logic and arguments of the retailers (LLC Geiser in this case) to justify the RPM clause, particularly the no intent and/or anticompetitive effect on the market, and the small and medium-sized enterprise (SME) arguments:

> The restrictions set out in the agreement were purely formal, and all issues have always been resolved through negotiations. Geiser LLC believes that such terms of the agreement took place for the purpose of keeping GRUNDFOS products in segments of high-quality products compared to cheaper ones present on the market. Also, the terms of the contract did not contain any prohibitions or recommendations regarding relationships with other pump suppliers' equipment. Thus, the actions of Grundfos were not intended to be anti-competitive in the pumping equipment market and could not lead to deficit and unjustified price increases.[23]
>
> [...]
>
> Article 7 of the Law of Ukraine states that the provisions of Article 6 shall not apply to any voluntary concerted action by small or medium-sized enterprises in relation to joint purchase of goods that does not lead to significant restrictions of competition and helps to increase the competitiveness of small and medium-sized enterprises, and Geiser LLC is a small business entity [...].[24]

The SME argument here was rejected. According to the AMCU, a small or average-sized entrepreneur is a business entity whose income (revenue) from sales products (goods, works, services) for the last financial year or the value of assets shall not exceed the amount equivalent to 500,000 EUR determined at the exchange rate of the National Bank of Ukraine, acting on the last day of the financial year, provided that on the markets in which this entrepreneur operates there are competitors with a much larger market share.

---

[22] Paragraph 79, *Grundfos* decision.

[23] Paragraph 83(b), *Grundfos* decision.

[24] Paragraph 83(d), *Grundfos* decision.

Another argument presented by one of the defendants, ASTER-M LLC, was an opinion of Mr. A.M. Isayev[25] on whether it was possible to characterize the terms of the contract for the supply of pumping equipment concluded between Grundfos and ASTER-M LLC as hardcore vertical restraints on the formation of the price of pumping equipment. According to Mr. Isayev, these could not be recognized as anticompetitive concerted actions containing strict vertical restrictions, due to the fact that ASTER-M LLC (the buyer) carried out its own activities at the level of wholesale trade, which falls under the exception provided for in paragraph 2 of Part 2 of Section II Standard Requirements, as concerted actions containing restrictions were related to only sales of goods to end consumers by a buyer operating at wholesale trade level.[26]

The AMCU rejected this conclusion as not corresponding to the actual circumstances of the case, because the strict restrictions set out in the contract concerned both the minimum level of retail prices and the minimum selling prices of goods to third parties (resellers). Furthermore, provisions for setting minimum prices were also applied to goods sold through a tender. That is why these exceptions did not apply to them.[27]

Based on the evidence gathered in the case and the responses/objections of the defendants, the AMCU concluded that the contract conditions introducing a minimum level of the recommended price for household goods and the minimum selling price for goods of household series to third parties (resellers) were regarded as concerted actions that are prohibited under Art. 6 Law of Ukraine.

The case is prominent as it sheds a light on the practical application of the legal provisions by the AMCU as well as the justificatory arguments used by the undertakings (although rejected by the AMCU). At the same time, the case can be criticized for lacking a deeper assessment of the efficiencies/effects that might result from the RPM in this case.

The effects of the concerted actions should be assessed on a case-by-case basis. This is confirmed by the Supreme Economic Court of Ukraine's statement that:

> In resolving disputes related to the evaluation of actions or inaction of business entities as concerted competitive behavior [...], commercial courts *should find out and verify the appropriate facts, appropriate means of proof related to the presence or absence of direct impact of such actions* (inaction) [...] on the conditions of production, purchase or sale of a particular product, including market parameters such as possible sales, the general level of market prices, etc.[28]

---

[25] PhD, Associate Professor of Civil Law No. 1 Yaroslav the Wise National University of Law (98), at the meeting of the Committee on 2 July 2020, the request of ASTER-M LLC was granted from 2 July 2020 No. 2/07–20 f.

[26] See para 100 of the AMCU's decision.

[27] Paragraph 101 of the AMCU decision.

[28] Item 12 of the Resolution of the plenum of the Supreme Economic Court of Ukraine of 26 December 2011 No. 15 on Some Issues of the Application Practice of Competition Law.

2.3 *Novo Nordisk*

Another informative case which provides a mix of issues, such as RPM, excessive pricing, state regulation of prices (for medicines), discounts and compensation, relates to Novo Nordisk Group and its distributors. The companies appealed the decision of the AMCU[29] in court. On 19 July 2021, the Commercial Court of Kyiv ruled[30] to invalidate the contested points of the AMCU's decision, in particular noting that competition law does not define recommended resale prices and maximum resale prices as ways to influence the distributor's price behavior, and as anticompetitive in nature. This is based on the premise that the establishment of a recommended price does not create strict obligations for the buyer and does not restrict his freedom of pricing. Also, peculiarities of procurement for budget funds prevent the occurrence of

[29] Antimonopoly Committee of Ukraine (Decision) (2020) No. 680-r.

[30] Commercial Court Kyiv, Case No. 910/508/21. The claimants were Novo Nordisk A/S (Denmark) and Novo Nordisk Health Care AG (Switzerland). In this case, Nordisk-1 and Nordisk-2 were interrelated by relations of control within the meaning of art 1 of the Law, i.e. belonged to one business entity ("Novo Nordisk Group"). During 2011–2017, Novo Nordisk Group cooperated with Medfarkom LLC, Medfarkom-Center PJSC, BaDM LLC, ZI Pharmacy LLC, Hansa PJSC, Pharmadis LLC and Medpharm LLC based on typical/standard agreements developed by Novo Nordisk Group. It was almost impossible to change any terms of cooperation under the distribution agreement (only in relation to insignificant issues). The prices for medicines remained unchanged throughout the term of the contracts. At the same time, clauses 17.1 Agreements 44–60 and clauses 16.1. Agreements 61–71 stipulated that price was subject to renegotiation and could be amended in subsequent versions of annexes to distribution agreements by mutual agreement of the parties.

The case is essentially about the discounts that the distributors received from Novo Nordisk Group in the form of credit notes and overpricing by distributors during sales in pharmacies and through public procurement. Upon receipt of a credit note containing a reference to product items, BaDM LLC reflected those discounts by reducing the price of available inventory balances or reduced the price of goods in advance by considering only the expected discount. So, in such cases, the selling price of Novo Nordisk Group drugs decreased. In some cases, credit notes were reflected in the form of reduction of total debt (additional income) of BaDM LLC, e.g. credit notes provided as compensation for exchange rate differences, in which case the received credit note did not have a direct impact on the selling price of BaDM LLC, but it did not deprive the latter of the right to reduce the selling price for its own customers based on its own decision. In this case, the company's revenue grew, but the selling price for buyers did not change, despite the possibility of BaDM LLC to reduce it.

According to the AMCU, the system of contractual relations between Novo Nordisk Group and its distributors contributed to the formation of (i) nominal pricing (on the basis of which the prices for medicines manufactured by the Novo Nordisk Group were formed on the territory of Ukraine, which is specified in the distribution agreements and serves as a basis for the calculation of customs duties, prices for end consumers), and the (ii) real pricing, which took into account the discounts introduced by the parties in the distribution agreements in force in 2011–2017, and which existed only in relations between Novo Nordisk Group and its distributors. The overpricing by distributors in pharmacies and through public procurement procedures sometimes reached 82%.

It should be noted that on 2 December 2021, the Court of Appeal recognized as legal the decision of the AMCU, which imposed a fine on the company due to non-transparent pricing of medicinal products and distortion of competition. The text of the judgment is not available. The announcement about it can be found at https://amcu.gov.ua/news/apelyacijnij-sud-viznav-zakonnim-rishennya-amku-shchodo-farmgrupi-novo-nordisk accessed 26 October 2022.

consequences in the form of price fixing.[31] According to the AMCU in this case, the discounts in the form of credit notes led to unjustified overpricing of Novo Nordisk medicines.

However, according to the analysis of the case file,[32] Novo Nordisk offered its distributors recommended maximum prices for its products in connection with tenders, which were supposed to be considered as exclusively recommended prices and not necessarily adhered to. No form of liability or incentive would be used to encourage distributors to comply with such resale prices. The recommended maximum resale prices were communicated simultaneously to all distributors involved in public procurement. Such "guiding" prices offered by Novo Nordisk via e-mail, referring to current market prices which were publicly available, did not require any discussion, negotiation, e-mail or other form of information exchange. All recommended prices aimed to ensure better competitiveness of medicines and were determined by reference to economic justification and in order to avoid excessive prices. The recommended level of maximum resale prices had to comply with the price regulations.

Such concerted actions between Novo Nordisk Group and its distributors regarding the establishment of recommended resale prices and the provision of higher discounts between May 2014 and April 2015 indicated the possibility of the impact of Novo Nordisk Group on the selling prices of its drugs, including through public procurement procedures, and the impact on pricing in supply chains. It allowed its distributors to have greater advantages over other participants in public procurement that did not have direct contracts with Nordisk. Such concerted actions strengthened the market power of their participants and restricted competition, in the AMCU's opinion.

In the Court's view, recommended maximum prices apply only to first-tier distributors, and even for them are only recommended. The AMCU did not prove the existence of any conditions, obligations, etc. that would allow the claimants to influence the price behavior of economic entities in the following links of the supply chain. The superficial nature of the AMCU's market analysis and erroneous market definition led to the AMCU's error in assessing the claimants' market power and their (even theoretical) ability to set inflated or unreasonable prices. As a result, the court concluded that the AMCU took its decision on the basis of an incorrect application of substantive law. The AMCU failed to prove the circumstances that are relevant to the case; hence, the conclusions of the AMCU in its decision did not correspond to the circumstances of the case. The AMCU violated procedural law, which led to an incorrect decision. Interestingly, the Court of Appeal upheld the AMCU's decision in December 2021.

[31] This is due to the fact that the subject of procurement (lot) consists of a large number (range) of different drugs from different manufacturers, and the choice of the winner is based on the total cost of the lot. In such conditions, fixing the price for one lot position does not fix the price of the entire lot.

[32] See Decision of the AMCU no 680-r, 106 onwards.

In our opinion, the most important takeaway of this case is that to prove the existence of the concerted actions, it is not sufficient to rely on the signs of similarities in actions (inactions) among the undertakings.[33] Anticompetitive concerted conduct shall be established and proven with the indication of relevant evidence in the decision of the AMCU. Thus, similarity should be a result of coherence with the competitive behavior rather than a simple coincidence of actions of the undertakings caused by the specificity of the relevant market. The AMCU's conclusions on the lack of objective reasons for the entity to commit similar acts (inactions) should be based on the results of a study of the whole set of factors that objectively (regardless of the entity) affect its behavior in the disputed relationships, as opposed to being the result of a limited range of factors (e.g. only the purchase price of goods). The Court also emphasized that the burden of proof in such cases lies on the AMCU.

It may be concluded, also in relation to the RPM, that to be able to qualify actions as anticompetitive concerted actions, it is obligatory to find out their consequences in the form of prevention, elimination or restriction of competition, infringement of the interests of other business entities (competitors, buyers) or consumers, in particular by causing them harm (loss) or other real violation of their rights or interests, or the occurrence of other relevant consequences.[34] Commercial courts need to clarify and reflect in court decisions what exactly are the relevant consequences that could result from the actions of economic entities that show signs of anticompetitive concerted actions.

In this case, the AMCU defined the actions of the Novo Nordisk Group with distributors as anticompetitive concerted actions under Art. 6 of the Law since they led to unjustified overpricing of the drugs. Provisions of Art. 6 of the Law concern the joint setting of prices by the undertaking concerned, while such participants should set their prices independently and individually in accordance with their own competitive strategy. The individual competitive behavior of market participants (which is a key condition of competition) was replaced by their joint (coordinated) competitive behavior towards other market participants, which limits the possibility of competitive choice for their customers. Such actions were anticompetitive in nature. The AMCU clearly stated that the conduct of the parties concerned was by nature a vertical agreement; such conduct implied the vertical restrictions; these restrictions were anticompetitive because they did not meet the conditions set out in the Law of Ukraine under Art. 8. Part 1 of Art. 8 of the Law exempts certain vertical concerted actions from the prohibition provided for in Art. 6 of the Law, namely vertical agreements, when a party to concerted actions imposes restrictions on the other party concerning: use of goods or goods of other suppliers; purchase from other business entities or sale to other business entities or consumers of other goods; purchase of goods which by their nature or in accordance with trade and other fair practices in business activities do not belong to the subject of the agreement; formation of prices

[33] Resolution of the Plenum of the Supreme Economic Court of Ukraine of No. 15 (2011) on Some Issues of Practice of Competition Law, clause 8(3).

[34] Resolution of the Plenum of the Supreme Economic Court of Ukraine No. 15 (2011) on Some Issues of Competition Law Practice, para 14.

or other conditions of the contract on sale of the delivered goods to other business entities or consumers.

Nordisk did not impose any of these restrictions on distributors, and therefore the prohibition provided for in Part 2 of Art. 8 of the Law is completely irrelevant. The only potentially (remote) relevant restriction that existed between Nordisk and their distributors is the recommended maximum price. However, this recommended maximum price is directly excluded from its assessment as anticompetitive in subject matter in accordance with Subpara. 2 of Para. 2 Standard Requirements, has a clearly procompetitive purpose (lower price), benefits end users and is essentially self-sufficient. According to the AMCU, the claimants had to limit the resale prices of distributors to ensure a fair share of discounts for end users.

One of the consequences of such a significant restriction of competition is an economically unjustified increase in prices. For example, the use of an exclusive distribution system (prohibition of active sales by distributors in the territory of other distributors) in combination with the establishment of recommended resale prices, in certain market circumstances, can significantly reduce competition in the market and thus increase prices above the level which would exist in the absence of such a restriction of competition. The AMCU's approach of proving the economic unreasonableness of the price was not based on the provisions of Part 2 of Art. 8 Law of Ukraine and in general did not meet the objectives of the legal regulation of the law.[35] Both the plaintiffs and distributors strictly adhered to the requirements for regulated prices. The AMCU did not take into account the data of the economic study of the state enterprise "Ukrpromzovnishekspertiza" of the Ukrainian insulin market, which shows the compliance of Novo Nordisk Group insulin prices with equilibrium market prices and high dependence of Novo Nordisk prices on insulin prices. This level of dependence on market prices for insulin indicates that the pricing of Novo Nordisk products was under the influence of objective economic factors and was not artificial. In addition, given this level of dependence, any "economically unreasonable overpricing" by plaintiffs or distributors would only put the plaintiffs' products at a competitive disadvantage over those of other pharmaceutical companies, which means that alleged anticompetitive concerted actions to increase prices would only be contrary to the interests of the plaintiffs.

[35] Ukraine has been regulating drug prices since the 1990s. In 2008, the government of Ukraine introduced centralized price regulation, which provided for national restrictions on wholesale and retail prices for a wide range of medicines. At the time, it was explicitly provided that the maximum mark-up should be calculated on the basis of discounted prices, i.e. discounts were allowed, but they reduced the basis for calculating the maximum mark-up and the possible maximum allowable selling price of regulated medicines. However, already in 2009 the pricing rules in Ukraine were significantly revised. The government changed the levels of mark-up restrictions and the volume of regulated products while removing any references to discounts. Therefore, according to the legislation in force since 2009, including in 2011–2017, the maximum allowance had to be calculated based on the stated price. The AMCU did not take proper note of this change in the provisions and did not consider the legislation in force during the period of the alleged offense.

In support of its position, the AMCU referred to the high level of profitability of distributors but did not investigate what level of profitability was generally characteristic of a wide range of large wholesale distributors.[36] In its decision, the AMCU had no proper grounds (including a starting point for comparison) to assess the profitability of distributors and conclude that it was inflated. It should be noted that the evidence in the AMCU case file also confirms that it is common practice in the market of large-scale wholesale distribution to provide discounts of more than 10%—in fact, they can reach and even exceed 30%—a fact which is also seen in agreements between distributors and other drug manufacturers, including Ukrainian local manufacturers. The AMCU also did not take into account the circumstances of the discount and the level of profitability as an objective result of the formation of equilibrium conditions of trade at the appropriate level of trade, to which the plaintiffs drew objections from the AMCU as well as additional explanations.

We agree with the logic and reasoning of the Commercial Court in this case. Although the judgment was repealed by the Appeal Court of Kyiv later on (the text thereof is currently unavailable), the stakeholders may still rely on the main provisions of the judgment in understanding the provision of the Law of Ukraine and in the process of self-assessing their respective actions.

2.4 *Indirect RPM*

Speaking about discounts/bonuses in the distribution contracts that are very often related to indirect RPM,[37] the AMCU issued another "pharmaceutical" decision on so-called pharmaceutical cases. It imposed fines on Roche Ukraine LLC (9,115,817 UAH) and distributors of BaDM LLC (5,407,948 UAH), Business Center Pharmacy LLC (3,207,361 UAH) and Alba Ukraine PJSC (339,999 UAH). According to the AMCU, these entities were involved in anticompetitive concerted actions regarding the setting of prices for medicines manufactured by the company F. Hoffmann-La Roche Co. Ltd., implemented through public procurement procedures. Such concerted action was taken through contracts that introduced non-transparent bonus mechanisms that led to unjustified overpricing of Hoffmann-La Roche Ltd. medicines through public procurement procedures.

In the opinion of the AMCU, the payment of bonuses to distributors which does not lead to a reduction in the cost of relevant goods but only to additional income for distributors indicates the anticompetitive nature of the concerted actions in the form of the inflated prices. It should be noted that, in general, this is a rather contradictory conclusion, as its transformation will usually lead to the loss of the incentive

[36] First-tier distributors as defined in paras 188 and 25 of the Decision.

[37] In situations where the contract between the supplier and the distributor provides for the provision of bonuses, as well as the obligation to take them into account in full resale, if the distributor adheres to its usual pricing algorithms, such as the size of the mark-up, the resale price may be predicted for the supplier. In this way, the supplier will be able to manipulate the resale price of the distributor, for example, to create barriers to entry for other suppliers.

effect of bonuses (or discounts), making them completely useless, and to possible anticompetitive effects, including the ability of the supplier to establish control over the prices of distributors. The AMCU concluded that such a bonus mechanism was not aimed at reducing the costs of medicines according to which the resale price would be calculated, but that it led to an unjustified increase in the nominal prices, i.e. prices that were ultimately paid by the consumers or the state, especially in the context of state price regulation through the application of marginal levels of trade margins.

The AMCU's decision in the case of Roche Ukraine LLC was appealed to the court.[38] The claimants here argued that contractual relations under purchase and sale agreements regarding the possibility of receiving a bonus in the form of non-refundable financial assistance from BaDM LLC and Business Center Pharmacy LLC could not be considered as anticompetitive by object (strict restrictions), as: vertical parties were not competitors; such relations did not provide for a joint definition of competitive behavior in the resale by the buyer of the goods of the supplier and the possibility of influence of the supplier on the independent decisions of the undertakings.[39]

The Court agreed with the AMCU's conclusions that Roche Ukraine LLC had an impact on the further sale of the company's medicines in bulk, especially in terms of setting prices for medicines sold to healthcare facilities fully or partially funded from state and local budgets (through state or public procurement procedures). Eventually, the claims were rejected by the Commercial Court of Kyiv as unproven, unfounded, inconsistent with the facts of the case and refuted properly and in the manner prescribed by law by the defendant, and therefore not subject to satisfaction.[40]

3 EU Approach to RPM

Shall we consider the RPM as a restriction of competition by object which may be exempted at the EU level? Yes. The new VBER[41] and the Guidelines on Vertical

[38] Decision No. 80631683 (2019), Commercial Court of Kyiv City, Case No. 910/13306/18.

[39] According to the AMCU, an important feature of the conditions of circulation of medicines manufactured by the company is that they are included in the range of medicines that are subject to state regulation in Ukraine. Almost all the company's medicines were included in the list of domestic and foreign medicines that can be purchased by health care facilities that are fully or partially financed from state and local budgets and are subject to state regulation of trade margins. Such regulation of prices for medicines in Ukraine in 2012–2016 was carried out by setting maximum levels of supply and marketing surcharges and marginal trade (retail) surcharges on registered/declared wholesale sales, depending on whether the drugs were included in the relevant state list.

[40] Commercial Court of Kyiv, Decision No. 80631683 (2019).

[41] Commission Regulation (EU) 2022/720 of 10 May 2022 on the application of Article 101(3) of the Treaty on the Functioning of the European Union to categories of vertical agreements and concerted practices (VBER). The VBER and the Guidelines provide up-to-date guidance on vertical restrictions, including RPM and online restrictions, and ensure a harmonized approach to such restrictions across the EU. The documents also incorporate the guiding principles for the assessment

Restraints[42] (hereinafter "Guidelines") explicitly state that. Vertical agreements that do not benefit from the VBER because the parties' market shares are too high, or because they contain hardcore restrictions, can, in theory, still be exempted individually under Art. 101(3) TFEU.[43]

As seen from the text of the VBER, RPM is treated as a hardcore restriction, "that is, agreements which, directly or indirectly, have the object of restricting the buyer's ability to determine its sale price, including those which establish a fixed or minimum sale price to be observed by the buyer".[44]

At the same time, as emphasized in the Guidelines, the qualification of a restriction as a hardcore restriction or as a by object restriction does not mean that it is a per se infringement of Art. 101 of the Treaty. Where undertakings consider RPM to be efficiency-enhancing in an individual case, they may rely on efficiency justifications under Art. 101(3) of the Treaty.[45]

The same is confirmed in a note of the European Commission[46] that the hardcore nature of RPM and its exclusion from the VBER "[...] does not mean that there is a "per se" prohibition of RPM. Article 81(3) EC [101 TFEU] can in principle apply to an agreement containing RPM."[47] This means that it is always possible for the firm in question to come forward with substantiated claims that the RPM will bring about efficiencies. The moment that the firm brings forward convincing evidence of efficiencies, the EC, in order to apply the hardcore rule, will be forced not only to investigate the claimed efficiencies but also to show the likely or actual negative effects. If the efficiencies outweigh the negative effects and the other conditions of Art. 101(3) TFEU, such as the indispensability test, are also fulfilled, the agreement is not prohibited.

As also emphasized by Andrés Font-Galarza, Frank P. Maier-Rigaud and Pablo Figueroa,[48] "although RPM remains a hard-core restraint, i.e., a restriction of competition by object, the Commission's Guidelines on Vertical Restraints make it clear that "undertakings have the possibility to plead an efficiency defence" under Art. 101(3) in an individual case".[49]

---

of such restrictions drawn from the case law of the Court of Justice of the EU, e.g. *Pierre Fabre* and *Coty* (in relation to online sale restrictions in distribution systems).

[42] Communication from the Commission, Guidelines on vertical restrains (2022) 2022/C 248/01.

[43] Anne C Witt, 'EJTN Training on EU Competition Law: Vertical Block Exemption Regulation' EJTN Refi (15–16 November 2021), slide 27 https://www.ejtn.eu/PageFiles/19801/5.%20Vertical%20BER%20(Witt)%20final.pdf accessed 15 May 2022.

[44] Guidelines, art 4(a) of Regulation (EU) 2022/720, para 185.

[45] Guidelines on Vertical Restraints, para 195.

[46] OECD, 'Directorate for Financial and Enterprise Affairs Competition Committee: Monopsony and Buyer Power' DAF/COMP/WD(2008)64.

[47] See the Communication from the Commission Notice—Guidelines on the Application of Article 81(3) of the Treaty (2004) OJ C101/97, 97–118, points 17–27 and 40–47.

[48] Andrés Font-Galarza et al., 'RPM Under EU Competition Law: Some Considerations From a Business and Economic Perspective' (2013) CPI Antitrust Chronicle.

[49] See Guidelines on Vertical Restraints, sec 223. See further, in the context of vertical restraints, *Pierre Fabre Dermo-Cosmétique SAS*, (Judgment) Case C-439/09 (2011), sec 47.

> [...] RPM may also lead to efficiencies, in particular where it is supplier driven. Where undertakings rely on an efficiency defence for RPM, they must be able to substantiate this with concrete evidence and show that all the conditions of Article 101(3) are fulfilled in the individual case [...].[50]

Consequently, RPM agreements can, in principle, be exempted under Art. 101(3) TFEU where four cumulative conditions are met, i.e. the agreement must: 1. contribute to improving the production or distribution of goods or to promoting technical or economic progress; 2. while allowing consumers a fair share of the resulting benefit; 3. without imposing on the undertakings concerned restrictions which are not indispensable to the attainment of those objectives; and 4. without affording such undertakings the possibility of eliminating competition in respect of a substantial part of the products in question.

The Guidelines provide some possible examples of the efficiencies that RPM may bring about. For instance, imposition of minimum release prices may be considered as procompetitive in the (distribution/franchise) systems with the uniform format if it is necessary to organize a coordinated short-term low-price campaign (up to 6 weeks), to facilitate the introduction of the new product, to prevent a distributor from using the product of a manufacturer as a loss leader or to protect the brand image of the product. This is all possible on condition that there are no less restrictive alternative means of encouraging the distributors to promote the product.

It should be mentioned that recommending a resale price or requiring a retailer to respect a maximum resale price is exempted by the VBER provided that the market share thresholds set out in the VBER are not exceeded and that the recommendation "does not amount to a minimum or fixed resale price as a result of threats, pressure or incentives. Price recommendations are considered important to communicate quality and brand position."[51]

The EU has decided to retain RPM as a hardcore restriction, irrespective of the numerous arguments made during the evaluation to take a more lenient approach. It may be viewed as a sign that RPM will continue to be the target of the scrutiny of the EC and national competition authorities.[52] For a better understanding of the EC's practical perspective on RPM we analyse here such cases as *Guess*, *Pioneer*, *Asus*, etc.

---

[50] Paragraph 197 of the Guidelines.

[51] Paragraph 32, OECD, 'Directorate for Financial and Enterprise Affairs Competition Committee: Implications of E-Commerce for Competition Policy—Note by the European Union' DAF/COMP/WD(2018)61, para 32.

[52] Marc Israel et al., 'New EU Competition Rules for Distribution Agreements', White&Case (14 July 2021) https://www.whitecase.com/publications/alert/new-eu-competition-rules-distribution-agreements accessed 29 July 2022.

The EC fined a fashion manufacturer named Guess[53] 40 million EUR in December 2018 for various anticompetitive practices, including RPM[54]:

> Guess Europe monitored pricing of third-party retailers and tried to influence them to correct resale prices "misaligned" with Guess Europe's "recommended" resale prices. E-mail exchanges show instances when one of the Guess subsidiaries signals that a distributor is deviating from the resale prices provided and requests Guess Europe to take action to "solve the problem".[55]

The EC in its analysis refers to rather old CJEU rulings[56] to eventually conclude that the RPM in this case restricted the ability of Guess's retailers to determine their resale prices, thereby restricting competition by object within the meaning of Art. 101(1) TFEU. The decision may be criticized for the lack of any assessment of the effects of the RPM on the competition on the market. It only states that the resale price maintenance by Guess could not be exempted under the VBER, because it had "as its object to restrict the ability of retailers to independently determine their sale price".[57] Additionally, Guess's conduct did not meet the conditions for an exemption under Art. 101(3) TFEU either[58] since there were

> [...] no indications that the conduct contributed to improving the production or distribution of Guess' products, or to promoting technical or economic progress, while allowing consumers a fair share of the potential benefits resulting from Guess' restrictive practices. In addition, there are no indications either that the conduct was indispensable, for example to address free-riding, or to protect Guess' brand image.[59]

The EC treated the RPM in this case as automatically anticompetitive; no proper effects analysis was conducted to establish the infringement. In our opinion, and as discussed above, while the RPM practices may be presumed to restrict competition, it should not be a per se infringement that would relieve the competition authority of its obligation to conduct an effects analysis (and especially in the situations where the undertaking concerned challenges such presumption).

We would like to draw parallels here with the conclusions of the General Court in the *Intel*[60] case. Although this is an abuse of dominance case, still it concerns in some respects the infringement that was considered to be a per se violation by the

---

[53] Commission Decision of 17 December 2018 relating to proceedings under Article 101 of the Treaty on the Functioning of the European Union and Article 53 of the Agreement on the European Economic Area—Case AT.40428 Guess (2018) C(2018) 8455 final (Case AT.40428 Guess).

[54] Vojtech Chloupek, 'Retail Price Maintenance in the EU' Bird&Bird (12 October 2020) https://www.twobirds.com/en/news/articles/2020/global/retail-price-maintenance-in-the-eu accessed 29 July 2022.

[55] Case AT.40428 Guess (n 53).

[56] *Guess* decision, para 136: "[...] agreements that impose upon retailers' minimum or fixed retail prices, thereby restricting the ability of those retailers to determine their resale prices independently, restrict competition by object within the meaning of Art. 101(1) of the Treaty".

[57] *Guess* decision, para 161.

[58] *Guess* decision, para 163.

[59] *Guess* decision, para 164.

[60] Case T-286/09 (Judgment), *RENV Intel Corporation v. Commission* (2022).

EC. The Court found this position of the EC to be incorrect and emphasized the EC's obligation to take the analysis of the effects into account while concluding that the conduct was abusive. The judgment may be considered as "a triumph of effects over form under Article 102 TFEU".[61] Such triumph may be relevant also to other pillars of competition law, i.e. the effects-based approach to Art. 101 TFEU.

In July 2018, the EC fined four consumer electronics companies, Asus, Denon & Marantz, Philips and Pioneer,[62] 111 Million EUR. The companies had restricted online retailers from deciding on the price of their products by using pricing algorithms. The manufacturers intervened with the pricing policies of the online retailers who were selling at lower prices by threatening to apply or applying sanctions. Such practices affected overall online prices for the consumers of electronics.

The EC in its analysis of the RPM stated that "certain collusive behaviour, such as resale price maintenance, may be considered so likely to have negative effects, in particular on the price, choice, quantity or quality of the goods and services, that it may be considered redundant, for the purposes of applying Art. 101(1) of the Treaty, to prove that it has actual effects on the market".[63] The conduct of Asus restricted competition "by its very nature".[64] The EC concluded that the conduct was neither exempted under the VBER nor met the conditions for exemption provided for in Art. 101(3) TFEU. Again, the decision may be criticized for the lack of a proper assessment of efficiencies, represented by a mere statement that there were "no indications that it was indispensable to induce retailer investment in certain promotional measures or pre-sale services or to alleviate the repercussions of freeriding between online and offline sales channels".[65]

Despite such shortcomings, the cases serve as good examples of RPM in e-commerce and the increased interest of the EC therein. The EC conducted an in-depth inquiry into vertical restraints in e-commerce in the EU market and concluded that RPMs are by far the most widespread restrictions of competition in e-commerce markets, which makes effective competition enforcement in this area important.[66] Additionally, both manufacturers and retailers frequently monitor online retail prices, often by means of pricing software.[67] Hence, it is easier in e-commerce markets to

---

[61] Tim Blanchard et al., 'The Intel Effect: The General Court Judgment in Case T-286/09 RENV Intel Corporation v Commission' Slaughter and May (14 February 2022) https://my.slaughterandmay.com/insights/briefings/the-intel-effect-the-general-court-judgement accessed 29 July 2022.

[62] Cases AT. 40,465 (Asus), AT. 40,469 (Denon & Marantz), AT. 40,181 (Philips), AT. 40,182 (Pioneer).

[63] *Asus* decision, para 101; see also Judgment of 11 September 2014, *CB v Commission*, C-67/13 P, EU:C:2014:2204, para 51; Judgment of 19 March 2015, *Dole Food and Dole Fresh Fruit Europe v Commission*, C-286/13 P, EU:C:2015:184, para 115.

[64] *Asus* decision, para 109.

[65] *Asus* decision, para 117.

[66] Marc Israel and Jacquelyn MacLennan, 'RPM comes Back from the Dead – EU Commission Tackles Pricing in E-commerce,' *Bird&Bird* (1August 2018) https://www.jdsupra.com/legalnews/rpm-comes-back-from-the-dead-eu-38794 accessed 29 July 2022.

[67] European Commission, 'Final Report on the E-commerce Sector Inquiry', (Report) COM(2017) 229 final.

detect deviations from manufacturers' RPM and retaliate against the ones that deviate from the "recommendations". This sector inquiry later prompted many jurisdictions to pursue such price restrictions more actively.[68]

The practice of the AMCU in e-commerce and distribution is difficult to compare with the one in the EU. RPM practices are very common in e-commerce nowadays, and Ukraine is not an exception. The only difference is that such practices have not yet been often on the radar of the AMCU. The only decision of the AMCU in this direction is the concentration permit granted at the end of 2018 to Rozetka for the acquisition of Prom.ua, Bigl.ua and other marketplaces.[69] This decision is quite interesting for the general understanding of the e-commerce market of Ukraine, but it remains uninformative in the context of the AMCU's approaches to so-called vertical concerted actions—agreements between entities operating at different levels of production or supply chains on supply, sale and resale.

In its decision to grant permission, the AMCU analyses the prospects of anti-competitive effects of concentration and concludes that they are unlikely, because, among other things, the marketplace is open to the entry and exit of new entrants, as there is significant competition with foreign players and growing sales, which are both imported into Ukraine and exported from it. At the same time, the AMCU does not pay much attention to relevant issues for e-commerce, such as selective or exclusive supply, non-compete obligations, active and passive sales, recommended prices, etc. This can be explained primarily by the horizontal (not vertical) nature of this concentration.

Given the growing volume of online sales in Ukraine and the revival of interest among antitrust authorities towards vertical restraints in other countries, it is likely

---

[68] In 2019, the German Bundeskartellamt fined bicycle wholesaler ZEG about 13.4 million EUR for imposing minimum resale prices on its 47 retailers. *The retailers were asked not to undercut the minimum sales prices set by ZEG for different bicycle models.* ZEG's representatives also checked adherence to the resale prices. They received complaints from retailers about other retailers undercutting the prices and conducted their own price research or had this carried out by others. Retailers which had undercut a certain low price were asked to strictly observe the set price. Available at https://www.bundeskartellamt.de/SharedDocs/Meldung/EN/Pressemitteilungen/2019/29_01_2019_Fahrrad.html accessed 26 October 2022.

Subsequently, in March 2020, upon the complaint of eBizcuss, Apple's largest premium reseller in France, the French Competition Authority fined Apple 1.1 billion EUR for various vertical restraints, including RPM. Apple's website displayed the prices offered in Apple stores as "suggested prices"; several clauses relating to the use of the Apple trademark for marketing and communication purposes strictly regulated promotions; and Apple monitored prices and sanctioned resellers which offered unauthorized promotions by withholding deliveries of Apple products. See F Vanherck, 'The French Competition Authority Fines Apple an Unprecedented 1.1 billion EUR for Resale Price Maintenance, Abuse of Economic Dependency, and Product and Customer Allocation', *Alert 2020.* https://www.wsgr.com/en/insights/the-french-competition-authority-fines-apple-an-unprecedented-eur-11-billion-for-resale-price-maintenance-abuse-of-economic-dependency-and-product-and-customer-allocation.html accessed 26 October 2022.

[69] Serhii Gluschenko and Olga Bobrovska, 'Distribution and E-commerce: AMCU's Practice' 2(732), *Yuridychna Gazeta.* https://yur-gazeta.com/publications/practice/antimonopolne-konkurentne-pravo/distribuciya-ta-ecommerce-praktika-amku.html accessed 26 October 2022.

that the AMCU will also change its priorities and pay more attention to distribution issues, including identifying and prosecuting such RPM in e-commerce.

4 Per Se Rule Versus Rule of Reason: Further Discussion

As seen from the previous sections, both the AMCU and the EC treat RPM as a per se violation, i.e. competition law infringement that is presumed without any proof of anticompetitive effect. There is a possibility to prove that the RPM is procompetitive, but as a starting point it is considered a violation. Businesses have been voicing their discontent and claiming that this should be changed, as RPMs are among the vital tools of doing business and as they may be procompetitive. Per se prohibition "cannot optimize the market results from an economic point of view because it means that all positive effects which are achievable through the application of price maintenance would be prohibited or only realizable in another way at greater cost".[70] Hence, RPM should not be viewed as a per se violation, or at least the current per se ban on RPM should be relaxed, since RPM may have procompetitive as well as anticompetitive effects.[71]

The per se approach offers "clarity, speed and savings in decision-making costs".[72] There is no doubt when something is permitter or not, in other words "black or white" under the per se approach. There are also less resources involved for an authority or the court deciding on it in terms of evidence collection. As correctly spotted by the OECD, "the per se approach is much like a sledgehammer: it has quick results, is relatively inexpensive and predictable, but it is not very careful. The per se rule will condemn some conduct that is actually pro-competitive."[73]

Under the rule of reason approach, competition authorities and courts are to analyse RPM on a case-by-case basis and to determine whether it is likely to cause consumer welfare harm; merely showing that RPM exists will not be enough to prove that there is a competition law infringement. Rather, all the circumstances of the case, as well as the positive effects on consumer welfare, must be carefully considered and weighed. A great deal of information is required under the rule of reason approach. And, of course, it may be very time consuming and costly to perform such analysis. This is one of the main weaknesses of the rule of reason approach. The results may be unpredictable and not always accurate.

---

[70] Rainer Olbrich and Carl-Christian Buhr, 'Who Benefits from the Prohibition of Resale Price Maintenance in European Competition Law?—The Case of Food Retailing' (2005) 26 European Competition Law Review 705 (712).

[71] Mart Kneepkens, 'Resale Price Maintenance: Economics Call for a More Balanced Approach,' (2007) 28 European Competition Law Review 656 (658).

[72] OECD, DAF/COMP(2008)37 (n 3), 36.

[73] OECD, DAF/COMP(2009)36 (n 2).

Which approach is best for RPM? The answer depends on which side of the barricade you are on—business or the regulator (as explained above). A one-size-fits-all approach to RPM is not sustainable and may entail inefficiencies and negative welfare effects.[74] I am personally in favor of the approach which was adopted by the US Supreme Court. It presumes that the rule of reason will apply unless experience shows that the practice is always or almost always anticompetitive, in which case the practice will be deemed illegal per se.[75] The US Supreme Court has held that "[t]here is a presumption in favour of a rule-of-reason standard; that departure from that standard must be justified by demonstrable economic effect, such as facilitation of cartelizing, rather than formalistic distinctions; [and] that interbrand competition is the primary concern of the antitrust laws". Per se treatment is appropriate only for conduct that almost always tends to restrict competition and reduce output or is, in other words, manifestly anticompetitive.[76] All of those factors point in favor of a rule of reason approach toward both maximum and minimum RPM.

5 Concluding Remarks

Based on the above, in our view, the current per se approach on RPM in Ukraine and in the EU should be revised and relaxed. More emphasis should be placed on the procompetitive assessment of the restrictions rather that a blunt prohibition. In any case, "the basic features of a desirable approach to RPM are no different from the basic features of a desirable approach to the abuse of a dominant position".[77] It should be relatively easy to apply, should lead to predictable results, should be understandable, should be based on widely accepted economic principles and cause minimal costs from false positives and false negatives. One of the ways to further improve the RPM assessment is to allow suppliers that do not have significant market power, from an economic standpoint, to benefit from RPM. More initiative is required from the business parties to mount a successful defense of RPM under the efficiency claims of the Ukrainian and European regimes. Irrespective of the per se approach taken by both jurisdictions, there seems to be a tendency towards a more serious economic analysis of the (procompetitive) effects of RPM. This implies that although *de jure* recognized as per se anticompetitive, RPM is de facto subject to a rule of reason assessment.

For Ukraine this means that given the lack of consistent AMCU practice on these issues, the Standard Requirements are the only source that provides at least some legal clarity. At the same time, this document contains only basic rules that are difficult to

---

[74] Andrés Font-Galarza et al., 'RPM Under EU Competition Law: Some Considerations From a Business and Economic Perspective' (2013) CPI Antitrust Chronicle.

[75] DAF/COMP(2008)37 (n 2), 37.

[76] *Continental T.V., Inc. v. GTE Sylvania, Inc.*, 433 U.S. 36, 49–50 (1977).

[77] OECD, 'Directorate for Financial and Enterprise Affairs Competition Committee: Competition on the Merits' (2006) DAF/COMP(2005)27, 23.

apply without taking into account the guidance of the EU on the application of the new VBER. Therefore, stakeholders in Ukraine should monitor not only the practice of the AMCU but also the status of these changes in the EU to better understand the rules set out in the Standard Requirements and their relevance. Additionally, the Standard Requirements may be amended with some real-life examples of possible efficiencies that the RPM may bring about (similarly to the EC Guidelines).

On the one hand, the new VBER in the EU has not changed the strict approach towards RPM, which is still being treated as a restriction by object; no legislative change is expected to happen in Ukraine due to the new VBER in relation to RPM and in light of its obligations to harmonize its laws with the EU ones. On the other hand, considering the *Intel* judgment and its endorsement of the effect-based assessments under Art. 102 TFEU, it may also be having an impact on the assessment obligations of the competition authorities under Art. 101 TFEU. The US impact on the EU law may also be observed here.

It is highly recommended that the AMCU reconcile and implement the best of the two regimes, and eventually relax its approach towards RPM, which we believe will eventually be present in the EU, at least de facto.

Finally (and not limited to the issue of RPM, but rather as a general comment), it is extremely important that the AMCU updates its website and makes the search tool operational. In its current form, it is almost impossible to find any decisions of the AMCU unless you know the precise number of the case. It would be great if each case in addition to having its number would also include the names of the undertaking(s) concerned in its title, so that it would eventually be possible to search the cases by company name. Only then may the search option of the AMCU benefit all the interested stakeholders and contribute to the improvement of the competition policy and its enforcement.

References

Roger D Blair, Jill Boylston Herndon and John E Lopatka, 'Resale Price Maintenance and the Private Antitrust Plaintiff' (2005) 83(3) Washington University Law 657(659)

Dennis W Carlton and Jeffrey M Perloff, *Modern Industrial Organization* (Pearson 2005) 426

Vojtech Chloupek, 'Retail Price Maintenance in the EU' *Bird&Bird* (12 October 2020) https://www.twobirds.com/en/news/articles/2020/global/retail-price-maintenance-in-the-eu

Paul W Dobson and Michael Waterson, 'The Competition Effects of Industry-wide Vertical Price Fixing in Bilateral Oligopoly' (2007) 25(5) International Journal of Industrial Organization 935

European Commission, 'Final Report on the E-commerce Sector Inquiry', (Report) COM(2017) 229 final Price Fixing in Bilateral Oligopoly' (2007) 25(5) International Journal of Industrial Organization 935

Kenneth G Elzinga, David E Mills, 'Leegin and Procompetitive Resale Price Maintenance', (2015) The Antitrust Bulletin

Andrés Font-Galarza, Frank P Maier Rigaud and Pablo Figueroa, 'RPM Under EU Competition Law: Some Considerations From a Business and Economic Perspective' (2013) CPI Antitrust Chronicle

Serhii Gluschenko and Olga Bobrovska, 'Distribution and E-commerce: AMCU's Practice' 2(732) *Yuridychna Gazeta* (2021) https://yur-gazeta.com/publications/practice/antimonopolne-konkurentne-pravo/distribuciya-ta-ecommerce-praktika-amku.html[Сергій Глушенко та Ольга Бобровська 'Дистрибуція та e-commerce: практика АМКУ', 2(732) *Юридична Газета* (2021)]

Marc Israel, Tilman Kuhn, Mark Powell, Yann Utzschneider, Mathis Rust and Peter Citron, 'New EU Competition Rules for Distribution Agreements', *White&Case* (14 July 2021) https://www.whitecase.com/publications/alert/new-eu-competition-rules-distribution-agreements

Marc Israel and Jacquelyn MacLennan, 'RPM comes Back from the Dead – EU Commission Tackles Pricing in E-commerce,' *Bird&Bird* (1August 2018) https://www.jdsupra.com/legalnews/rpm-comes-back-from-the-dead-eu-38794/

Rebecca Johnsson, 'RPM and Object Restrictions – A Need for Change in EU Competition Policy?: A Comparative Analysis of the Different Approaches Towards RPM in EU and US Antitrust Law' (2020) Uppsala University

Mart Kneepkens, 'Resale Price Maintenance: Economics Call for a More Balanced Approach,' (2007) 28 European Competition Law Review 656

Rainer Olbrich and Carl-Christian Buhr, 'Who Benefits from the Prohibition of Resale Price Maintenance in European Competition Law? – The Case of Food Retailing' (2005) 26 European Competition Law Review 705

Organization for Economic Co-operation and Development, 'Directorate for Financial and Enterprise Affairs Competition Committee: Implications of E-Commerce for Competition Policy – Note by the European Union' DAF/COMP/WD(2018)61

Organization for Economic Co-operation and Development, 'Directorate for Financial and Enterprise Affairs Competition Committee: Monopsony and Buyer Power' DAF/COMP/WD(2008)64

Organization for Economic Co-operation and Development, 'Directorate for Financial and Enterprise Affairs Competition Committee: State-owned Enterprises and the Principle of Competitive Neutrality' DAF/COMP(2008)37, 2009

Organization for Economic Co-operation and Development, 'Directorate for Financial and Enterprise Affairs Competition Committee: Roundtable on Resale Price Maintenance, DAF/COMP(2008)37

Organization for Economic Co-operation and Development, 'Directorate for Financial and Enterprise Affairs Competition Committee: Competition on the Merits' (2006) DAF/COMP(2005)27, 23.

Francois Vanherck, 'The French Competition Authority Fines Apple an Unprecedented EUR 1.1 Billion for Resale Price Maintenance, Abuse of Economic Dependency, and Product and Customer Allocation,' *Wilson Sonsini* (21 April 2020) https://www.wsgr.com/en/insights/the-french-competition-authority-fines-apple-an-unprecedented-eur-11-billion-for-resale-price-maintenance-abuse-of-economic-dependency-and-product-and-customer-allocation.html

Anne C Witt, 'EJTN Training on EU Competition Law: Vertical Block Exemption Regulation' EJTN Refi (15–16 November 2021) https://www.ejtn.eu/PageFiles/19801/5.%20Vertical%20BER%20(Witt)%20final.pdf

The "New Normal" in Competition—Filling the Gaps of Ukrainian Competition Law in the Digital Economy Age

Anzhelika Gerasymenko and Nataliia Mazaraki

Contents

Abstract This chapter analyses the current state of and perspectives on Ukrainian competition law and policy development to help meet the challenges arising from the evolution of the modern digital economy. It provides the technological and social framework of competition in the twenty-first century, which is substantially determined by the strategic behavior of e-platforms, a fact that holds true for economies

A. Gerasymenko
Economic Theory and Competition Policy Department, State University of Trade and Economics, Kyiv, Ukraine
e-mail: a.gerasymenko@knute.edu.ua

N. Mazaraki (✉)
International, Civil and Commercial Law Department, State University of Trade and Economics, Kyiv, Ukraine
e-mail: n.mazaraki@knute.edu.ua

H. Richter (ed.), *Competition and Intellectual Property Law in Ukraine*,
MPI Studies on Intellectual Property and Competition Law 31,
https://doi.org/10.1007/978-3-662-66101-7_7

worldwide, including Ukraine. This chapter provides a review of some Ukrainian markets marked by the presence of e-platforms. Such a framework provides the range of competition-related challenges, including those to vertical competition, market definition and procompetitive data management. Some of these challenges can be met partially with the current Ukrainian competition law, while others need the latter to be further developed. The authors suggest the introduction of the concept of vertical competition into the legislation; the development and adoption of a new methodology of market definition that accounts for the challenges of multisided contracting, zero-pricing and network effects, etc.; the management of killer-acquisitions through keeping the pre-reform merger control thresholds in the digital sphere; the cooperation of the Antimonopoly Committee of Ukraine and the National Commission for the State Regulation of Electronic Communications, Radiofrequency Spectrum and the Provision of Postal Services (NCEC) in granting gatekeeper status to e-platforms and regulating their impact on competition. This kind of regulatory cooperation does not replace the need for the soft regulation of data management, multihoming and self-preferencing, but enlarges it.

1 Introduction

The establishment of the digital economy at the turn of the twenty-first century was marked by the expansion of network goods and sharing platforms. The latter eroded the market power of conventional monopolies and set the stage for the establishment of new monopolies, mostly through the bottlenecking of modern value chains. Often such monopolies are not obvious for competition agencies because they block just one of several known value chains within a conventional market. The problem is that due to an imbalance of transaction costs in the digital economy this value chain may provide for a distinct relevant market. Hence, there is a risk of market monopolization where the conventional regulator does not even see a market. The second section of the chapter provides an economic analysis of the background of such a risk.

The major modern challenges to competition originating from that are presented in the third section, while the fourth section researches the current state of Ukrainian competition law and its capacity/incapacity to meet these challenges. The fifth section develops approaches to meet these challenges, suggesting that the Antimonopoly Committee of Ukraine (AMCU) and the National Commission for the State Regulation of Electronic Communications, Radiofrequency Spectrum and the Provision of Postal Services (NCEC) should cooperate to define the status of gatekeepers and the antimonopoly regulation of their behavior as well as to provide soft regulation of other actors of the digital economy. The last section concludes.

2 Technological and Social Framework of Competition in the 21st Century

Different economic resources have dominated different stages of the technological and economic development of society: labor (in the primitive economy), land (in the feudal economy), capital (in the industrial economy), information (in the post-industrial economy). Control over the dominant economic resource is a precondition for market power and a factor in the distortion of workable competition.

Usually, obtaining control over the key input is done gradually—it is absent or at least rather low in the infancy of an economy but high at the stage of maturity: initially, planting became popular and landowning became profitable, which stimulated the development of the agricultural economy, and eventually landowners started to concentrate land and exploit the relevant market power[1]; initially, the industrial revolution granted a competitive advantage to capital, and then the concentration of industrial capital led to the monopolization of the industrial economy.[2] The same is true for the post-industrial economy at the turn of the 21th century, with information as the key input.[3]

We first heard of the information explosion (the rapid increase in the amount and speed of information creation and publication) at the end of the twentieth century. In the early 2000s the world emitted about 20 exabytes of information per year,[4] while in 2020, each person generated 1.7 megabytes per second.[5] That means that an economic actor can go astray within a big amount of information, which makes searching and processing a source of rapidly increasing transaction costs in the information economy.[6]

Hence, there is a demand for a new kind of economic activity—the processing of big data and information personalization according to the needs and requests of consumers. It is met by information intermediaries—and often e-platforms in

---

[1] See John E Martin, *Feudalism to Capitalism: Peasant and Landlord in English Agrarian Development* (Palgrave Macmillan 1986) 3–79; Amiya K Bagchi, 'Local and Global Monopolies and the Prospects of Global Democracy' in Deepak Nayyar (ed), *Economics as Ideology and Experience: Essays in Honour of Ashok Mitra* (Frank Cass Publisher 1998) 96–98.

[2] See among others, Karl Marx, *Capital: A Critique of Political Economy, Volume 1* (Pacific Publishing Studio 2010); Paul A Baran and Paul Sweezy, *Monopoly Capital: An Essay on the American Economic and Social Order* (Monthly Review Press 1966).

[3] See among others, Alvin Toffler, *Powershift: Knowledge, Wealth and Violence at the Edge of the 21st Century* (Bantam Books 1990); Tim Wu, *The Master Switch: The Rise and Fall of Information Empires* (Vintage 2011).

[4] Peter Lyman and Hal R Varian, 'How Much Information, 2003' (2003) Technical Report, UC Berkeley.

[5] Christo Petrov, '25+ Impressive Big Data Statistics for 2021' *Techjury* (9 July 2021) https://techjury.net/blog/big-data-statistics/#gref accessed 29 July 2021.

[6] Cf Jean Tirole, *Economics for the Common Good* (Princeton University Press 2017) 381: "The most significant transactions costs are no longer transportation costs, but rather assessing what is on offer and choosing who to do business with, along with the signalling costs (seeking to convince potential trading partners of one's reliability)".

particular, such as online search engines, social media (which effectively mediate the interaction of advertisers and ads consumers), media-streaming services (which mediate the interaction of producers and consumers of media content), sharing platforms (which mediate the interaction of owners and users of assets), e-marketplaces and price comparison services (which mediate the interaction of sellers and buyers). A C Hoyng and R Mastrigt describe that "(w)hile the digital revolution has created a maze built upon a wealth of information, online platforms have provided a guiding light that helps consumers find their way".[7]

In the early 2000s such platforms were just an alternative kind of commodity flow that activated competition in the conventional markets. Some of them (crowdsourcing, sharing platforms, price-comparison services, etc.) are still in this stage of evolution, while others have changed their competitive status due to the introduction of strong network effects.

Network effect describes the distinct correspondence between the utility of the good for a person and the consumer choice of others.[8] For instance, users join a social network not just because they like it, but because others use it and such a choice facilitates their communication. The applications are developed first for one operational system and not others because the first operational system is used by a bigger number of users, which generates better sales of the developed application in return. One marketplace attracts more sellers because it is more popular among the buyers (and vice versa), which leads to larger turnover and lower transaction costs for sellers and provides a greater variety of goods and lower search costs for buyers. In the long run the scope of such individual rational decisions of different economic actors leads to so-called lock-in effect, according to which most users prefer the same information intermediary.[9] Hence, the bottleneck lies within a value chain and provides a breeding ground for monopolization and abuse of dominance.

Such expectations are confirmed by the examples of anticompetitive behavior of Amazon.com Inc., Alphabet Inc. and Facebook Inc., which are regarded as gatekeepers of the relevant bottlenecks.[10] Alphabet and Facebook control over 53% of the world's digital advertising market.[11] Moreover, dividing such a market into two complementary ones—search and display advertising markets—shows that the

---

[7] Anne C Hoyng and Robert van Mastrigt, 'Is the Current Debate About Changing the Competition Law Toolbox Warranted? A Perspective from a Digital Platform' (2020) 41(7) European Competition Law Review 327 (329).

[8] Cf Michael L Katz and Carl Shapiro, 'Systems Competition and Network Effects' (1994) 8(2) Journal of Economic Perspective 93 (95–100).

[9] Cf Carl Shapiro and Hal R Varian, *Information Rules: A Strategic Guide to the Network Economy* (Harvard Business School Press 1998) 11–13 and 103–134.

[10] House Committee on the Judiciary, 'Online Platforms and Market Power: Examining the Dominance of Amazon, Apple, Facebook, and Google' *YouTube* (29 July 2020) https://www.youtube.com/watch?v=WBFDQvIrWYM&ab_channel=HouseCommitteeontheJudiciary accessed 29 July 2021.

[11] Megan Graham and Jennifer Elias, 'How Google's $150 Billion Advertising Business Works' *CNBC* (18 May 2021) https://www.cnbc.com/2021/05/18/how-does-google-make-money-advertising-business-breakdown-.html accessed 29 July 2021.

market shares of these gatekeepers are even bigger. For instance, "Google has more than a 90% share of the 7.3 billion GBP search advertising market in the UK and Facebook has over 50% of the 5.5 billion GBP display advertising market".[12] The situation is similar in Ukraine. In 2020, the share of search advertising within the digital advertising was 51%,[13] while Google search took 85%.[14] The share of advertising costs allocated on social media and messengers was 46.2%, while 53% of Ukrainian internet users used Facebook.[15]

Digital advertising markets that are marked by anticompetitive practices are the best known but not the only examples for e-platforms. Other information intermediaries also dominate bottlenecks and restrict competition. One of the first of such antitrust cases was *US Department of Justice v. Microsoft Corporation* on the anticompetitive tying of its dominant operating system (more than 90% of the market) with its internet browser (Internet Explorer) in the mid-1990s.[16] Such a practice not only pushed the competing good (Netscape Navigator) out of the market but also maintained the dominance of the Windows operating system. Netscape Navigator used a programming language which allowed applications to run on multiple operating systems.[17] Later on, the European Commission put the identical claim to Microsoft Corporation on tying the Windows operating system to the Windows Media Player.[18]

Another example of restricting competition by gatekeepers is the behavior of the dominant actor "Cegedim SA" in the French market for medical information databases. Cegedim SA provided both the databases "OneKey" and its own customer relation management software (CRM); it refused to license its database to any laboratories using a specific competing CRM called NetReps (produced by Euris) while licensing it to laboratories using other competing CRM software.[19]

In Ukraine, the market positions of international e-platforms (Google, Facebook, Uber, Olx, AliExpress, etc.) are rather strong. Some of them dominate bottlenecks. Others meet with competition from alternative e-platforms, including from Ukraine. For instance, Uber dominates the Ukrainian taxi market with a market share of 51%,

---

[12] Stephen Smith and Elisa Lindemann, 'Spotlight on Online Platforms and Digital Advertising as CMA Calls for a New Pro-competition Regulation Regime' (2020) 31(8) Entertainment Law Review 279 (280).

[13] Liubomyr Shkil, 'Digital Advertising Market in Ukraine Have Risen Up to 13.5 billion UAH: The Top of UIA Research' *ADSIDER* (18 March 2021) https://adsider.com/ua/rynok-internet-reklamy-v-ukraini-vyris-do-13-5-mlrd-hrn-nayholovnishe-z-doslidzhennia-inau/ accessed 29 July 2021.

[14] Ivan Dubinskiy, 'Research of Number of Internet Users' *Ukrainian Internet Association* (20 January 2020). https://inau.ua/proekty/doslidzhennya-internet-audytoriyi accessed 29 July 2021.

[15] Ibid.

[16] US District Court for the District of Columbia *United States of America v. Microsoft Corporation* (1998) 98–1232.

[17] Ibid paras 66–68.

[18] Commission Decision of 24 May 2004 relating to a proceeding under art 82 EC Treaty and art 54 against Microsoft Corporation (2004) OJ L32/23 (Commission Decision against Microsoft).

[19] L'Autorité de la Concurrence 14-D-06 *relative à des pratiques mises en œuvre par la société Cegedim dans lesecteur des bases de données d'informations médicales* (2014).

but its ability to abuse a dominant position is restricted by competitors, in particular the Ukrainian e-platform Uklon (whose market share is 25%) and Estonian Bolt (whose market share is almost 13%).[20] Gig-platforms in Ukraine operate under fierce competition. None of these platforms gets more than 10% of internet users. Assumed leaders are the Ukrainian e-platforms work.ua and rabota.ua (10 and 8% of internet users respectively), American jooble.org (5% of users), Russian HeadHunter (2% of users) and trud.com (1% of users).[21] Obviously, the shares are much bigger in the upstream B2B segment, but the close run between gig-platforms in the B2C area provides sufficient evidence of their fierce competition.

The situation is different for e-marketplaces. The e-commerce market is one of the most dynamic in Ukraine—its volume grew by 41% in 2020 and reached 4 billion USD, which equals 8.8% of total retail trade; it has nearly tripled in the last five years and is expected to double in the next five years.[22] Only 22% of Ukrainian internet users deal with AliExpress, while the same indicator for Rozetka, the Ukrainian leader of e-commerce, is 40%; furthermore, 37% of users regularly deal with e-platform Prom.ua, owned by Rozetka.[23] The dominance of Rozetka and its affiliates can only be disturbed by OLX (40% of internet users deal with the platform).[24] However, it should be pointed out that in Ukraine OLX operates mostly as a C2C platform for trading second-hand goods, while Rozetka provides a B2C marketplace for new goods. That means that competition between OLX and Rozetka is not so fierce and the dominance of both e-platforms still can exist in different markets: e-markets of new and second-hand goods. Rozetka provides an online marketplace service for third-party sellers to sell their products. The monetization model is that sales commissions are paid as royalties for Rozetka trademark usage, calculated depending on the commodity type.[25] At the same time, Rozetka also sells household appliances under its own brand RZTK. Recently, Rozetka has entered an adjacent market—offline trade—creating a network of offline stores operating under franchise schemes. Rozetka is on its way to creating its own ecosystem with the launch of the Rozetka Premium subscription plan, which provides free delivery and discounts.

Another kind of e-platform is associated with state functioning at the national or municipal level. Among such e-platforms are:

(1) state-run e-platforms which provide public services by state agencies. Ukraine operates the platform Diia, which is under development now;

[20] 'Bolt Company has Assessed the Volume of the Shadow Taxi Market in Ukraine' *Economichna Pravda* (9 July 2019) https://www.epravda.com.ua/news/2019/07/9/649486/ accessed 29 July 2021.

[21] Dubinskiy, *Ukrainian Internet Association* (n 14) accessed 29 July 2021.

[22] 'The E-commerce Market in Ukraine has Reached $4 Billion' *Soul Partners* https://soulpartners.com.ua/en/news/tpost/casugamy91-the-e-commerce-market-in-ukraine-has-rea accessed 29 July 2021.

[23] Dubinskiy, *Ukrainian Internet Association* (n 14) accessed 29 July 2021.

[24] Ibid.

[25] The information on the Rozetka monetization model has been derived by the authors from agreement templates offered by Rozetka LLC to third-party sellers. No public information on the monetization model has been published officially.

(2) municipal e-platforms (smart-city services) that meanwhile operate only in the big Ukrainian cities, mainly dealing with municipally owned companies and rather few private ones;
(3) regulated e-platforms that mediate state-regulated transactions between different kinds of economic actors in certain fields of the economy. Among such platforms in Ukraine are the e-platform Prozorro, which is the obligatory intermediary for public procurement to guarantee the transparency of the procurement, and the e-platform of day-ahead and intraday electricity markets, which serves as an intermediary in competitive tendering for electricity in the relevant segments of the Ukrainian power market.

The main difference between these e-platforms and the private ones is their 100% control over a bottleneck and the institutional nature of such a monopoly.[26] The the institutional nature of such a monopoly does not prevent the abuse of dominance by such platforms. The Statistics of Antimonopoly Committee of Ukraine (hereinafter—AMCU) shows that 10–34% of competitive infringements are aligned with institutional monopolies.[27]

Summarizing the effects of the information revolution on competition, we can affirm the widespread practice of enlarging value chains by adding the link of information intermediation. Such intermediaries' activities are substantively affected by network effects that provide the breeding ground for structural dominance within a certain value chain link, while waiving such intermediation is too expensive due to the high level of transaction costs. This description of the changes is unbiased and can be affirmed by market statistics of e-platforms' activities across the world. The existence and scope of positive externalities of e-platforms due to network effects make such monopolies worthwhile and move them close to the phenomenon of natural monopolies. Nevertheless, each monopoly has a propensity for abuse sufficient for offsetting of the positive externalities.

3 Modern Challenges to Competition

The above-mentioned changes led to a range of extremely new challenges to competition and competition policies in Ukraine and all over the world. For the purposes of research, we classify the challenges into the following groups: challenges to vertical competition (Sec. 3.1); challenges to market definition (Sec. 3.2); challenges to procompetitive data management (Sec. 3.3); and other challenges (Sec. 3.4).

[26] An institutional monopoly is a monopoly provided by the institutional actor, mostly the state, through granting beneficial terms to one economic actor (a monopolist) and not to others. See Aleksey Kostusev, *Competition Policy in Ukraine* (Kyiv National Economic University Publishing House 2004) 21.

[27] Ukrainian Law on Protection of Economic Competition 2001, 2210-III, prohibit any activities of state authorities that distort competition, arts 15–17.

3.1 Challenges to Vertical Competition

Modern competition law and economics mostly focus on the defense of so-called horizontal competition that exists within a value chain link where sellers of similar goods (substitutes) compete for a consumer. In contrast, vertical competition takes place between firms from different (mostly adjacent) links of a value chain, and not for a consumer but for better sales/purchase terms and therefore for a bigger part of the profit that is generated within a value chain.

Vertical competition is not a new issue for competition law and economics. In the 1950s, John K Galbraith broached this issue while developing his theory of countervailing power.[28] The issue was also studied by Alvin Toffler, who paid attention to the change in the competition balance between producers and retailers after the introduction of the bar coding of goods, which let retailers accumulate sensitive market information and use it as a competitive advantage.[29] The introduction of so-called rules of economic dependency (*abus de dependence economique*) in France in 1986 was a response to the change in the competition balance within the trade sector. It provided some kind of prelude for vertical competition regulation.[30] Some vertical competition cases were addressed under the concept of market power leverage by natural monopolies.[31] However, these examples of addressing vertical competition are rather the exception than the rule in the theory and practice of competition policy. There is not even an established definition of vertical competition in Ukrainian competition practice.

The information revolution and the start of the era of information intermediaries' dominance discussed in the previous section have brought the research on the vertical competition phenomenon,[32] as well as its legal determination, up to date. The ad hoc application of the rules on the abuse of dominance to cases of restricting vertical competition has not proven to be sufficiently effective. While these rules can work in cases of direct infringement (like overcharging for access to e-platform essential facilities), applying the rules on the abuse of dominance are not effective enough in cases of market power leverage and self-preferencing, which are rather common practices between e-platforms and their users. Among such cases is the Google

---

[28] John K Galbraith, *American Capitalism: The Concept of Countervailing Power* (Houghton Miffin 1952).

[29] Alvin Toffler, *Powershift: Knowledge, Wealth and Violence at the Edge of the 21st Century* (Bantam Books 1990).

[30] See Frederic Marty and Patrice Reis, 'Abus de Dépendance Économique', *Dictionnaire de Droit de la Concurrence, Concurrences* art 85864 https://www.concurrences.com/fr/dictionnaire/abus-de-dependance-economique accessed 29 July 2021.

[31] See Patrick Rey and Jean Tirole, 'A Primer on Foreclosure' in Mark Armstrong and Robert H Porter (eds) *Handbook of Industrial Organization III* (North Holland 2007) 2147; Michael D Whinston, 'Tying, Foreclosure, and Exclusion' (1990) 80(4) American Economic Review 837.

[32] See among others, Robert L Steiner, 'Vertical Competition, Horizontal Competition, and Market Power' (2008) 53(2) Antitrust Bulletin 251; Global Antitrust Institute, 'Report on the Digital Economy' (Report), 2020, 263–328; Germain Gaudin, 'Vertical Bargaining and Retail Competition: What Drives Countervailing Power?' (2018) 128 (614) The Economic Journal 2380.

Shopping case, in which the European Commission considered Google's practice of favoring its own vertical comparison shopping service in Google search results a competition law infringement, while the Federal Trade Commission (USA) and the Turkish Competition Authority have failed to do so.[33]

The issues of market power leverage with respect to adjacent markets, foreclosure and self-preferencing are well worked out in the theory and practice of regulating natural monopolies.[34] The unbundling of natural monopolistic and potentially competitive segments, which was established for such cases, nipped self-preferencing in the bud. Unfortunately, there is no chance to apply this solution to modern e-platforms, even those that dominate within their bottlenecks under current Ukrainian legislation. This problem is still being approached in an ad hoc manner—a function of the AMCU's creativity in the context of applying the tools of conventional competition law to the new competition reality.

Lack of understanding of the fundamentals of vertical competition by Ukrainian regulators prevents them from applying the mechanism of market power countervailing within a value chain in cases where strong network effects keep out horizontal competition, as well as from realizing the system of vertical relations within the digital ecosystem.

3.2 Challenges to Market Definition

Another problem of competition regulation on the markets of intermediary informational services is the correct definition of their boundaries. Competition policy reasonably based on the Structure–Conduct–Performance Paradigm (hereinafter "SCP paradigm") requires one to first define the market boundaries to establish the fact of market dominance and its probable abuse. As for e-platforms, this task is complicated by a range of factors, *inter alia*, multisided contracting of an e-platform and interdependency of vertically complementary markets, zero-pricing, and the lack of focus on transaction costs and search costs while assessing substitutability.

[33] European Union, Decision C (2017) 4444 final *relating to proceedings under Art. 102 of the Treaty on the Functioning of the European Union and Art. 54 of the Agreement on the European Economic Area* (2017) Case AT.39740—Google Search (Shopping) 76–179; Federal Trade Commission 'Google Agrees to Change Its Business Practices to Resolve FTC Competition Concerns In the Markets for Devices Like Smart Phones, Games and Tablets, and in Online Search' (Official Press Release) Federal Trade Commission (3 January 2013) https://www.ftc.gov/news-events/press-releases/2013/01/google-agrees-change-its-business-practices-resolve-ftc accessed 29 July 2021; OECD, 'Abuse of Dominance in Digital Markets', 2020, 42.

[34] See among others, Michael D Whinston, 'Tying, Foreclosure, and Exclusion' (1990) 80(4) American Economic Review 837; Patrick Rey and Jean Tirole, 'A Primer on Foreclosure' in Mark Armstrong and Robert H Porter (eds), *Handbook of Industrial Organization III* (North Holland 2007) 2147; Jennifer M Clarke Smith, 'The Development of the Monopolistic Leveraging Theory and Its Appropriate Role in Antitrust Law' (2002) 52(1) Catholic University Law Review 179; Alexandre de Cornière and Greg Taylor, 'Upstream Bundling and Leverage of Market Power' (2021) 131(640) The Economic Journal 3122.

In recent times, some antitrust scholars have claimed "to put less emphasis on analysis of market definition, and more emphasis on theories of harm and identification of anti-competitive strategies".[35] However, we consider that an attempt to escape from the problem rather than a way of solving it. The same kind of activity may be pro- or anticompetitive, depending on market disposition (e.g. market dominance) and the level of the actor's market power. Not the absolute number of e-platform users or its turnover,[36] but rather the relative need of the majority of consumers for a platform's intermediary services measures its market power. To identify market power, we first need to define the boundaries and the size of a market.

Conventional tools of defining the relevant market like the SSNIP test are ineffective for e-platforms. Indirect network effects, which determine the degree of dependency of one side of a multisided market from another, may distort the results of the SSNIP test: "[I]n a two-sided market, for example, a price increase for one customer group (side A) leads to changes in demand not only on this side, A, but also on the other side, B".[37] Besides that, there is no chance to apply this price test to zero-pricing markets. Other quantitative methods—such as the estimation of demand functions, elasticities or diversion ratios—may involve similar issues. When explaining changes in demand triggered by variations in price or other strategic variables, indirect network effects should be accounted for, though it appears difficult to quantify the strength as well as the shape of network effects.[38]

Stepping away from the SSNIP test and other quantitative methods of defining the relevant market allows us to come back to factor analysis. Such an approach is rather popular in Ukraine due to the current methodology applied to determine monopoly (dominant) market position of economic entities.[39] Here we need to keep in mind the risk of an insufficient focus on transaction costs. Omitting transaction costs generates false conclusions on the substitutability of direct channels of distributing goods with those, which are intermediated by e-platforms. Digital advertising via directly contacting a certain publisher is not an adequate substitute to advertising via Google or Facebook, which widely use algorithms of personalization, because direct contracting demands much higher transaction costs for searching and checking contractors, negotiating and performing contracts, etc. and provides a lower return due to the much lower rate of advertising exposure and lack of personalization. The same is true for the substitution of supply/booking hotel rooms via booking.com, tripadvisor, etc. with supply/booking hotel rooms via individual hotels' websites, and so on. These alternatives shape different relevant markets, notwithstanding the fact

---

[35] European Commission, 'Competition Policy for the Digital Era' (Final Report), 2019.

[36] These descriptors are established by Digital Markets Act; see European Commission, 'Regulation of the European Parliament and of the Council on Contestable and Fair Markets in the Digital Sector' (Digital Markets Act 2020) (Proposal) COM(2020) 842 final 2020/0374(COD) DMA, art 3.

[37] OECD, 'Market Definition in Multi-Sided Markets—Note by Sebastian Wismer & Arno Rasek' DAF/COMP/WD(2017)33/FINAL, 2017, 12.

[38] Ibid 12–13.

[39] Antimonopoly Committee of Ukraine, Order 49-p of 5 March 2002 on Approval Methodology Applied to Determine Monopoly (Dominant) Market Position of Economic Entities 2002.

that the distinction between them is not obvious under the conventional methodology of defining market boundaries.

Another urgent and highly discussed question right now is whether different sides of multisided markets are different relevant markets or just different elements of the same market. There are arguments for each alternative in the economic literature.[40] In the example of digital advertising via an e-platform, the good is information content on the one side of the multisided market and an advertising product on the other side. The scope of contractors/consumers is different on different sides. Sales terms are also different: free and paid. Therefore, it appears that different relevant markets exist on different sides of a multisided market. By contrast, a strong indirect network effect brings different sides of the market together. Demand on ad placement via an e-platform exists because the platform has already accumulated a sufficient number of users on the other side of the platform. Free access of end users to information content is paid by advertisers. Hence, we have arguments for the existence of a single relevant market within an entire digital ecosystem. There is still no consistent practice of defining the boundaries of multisided markets. Some researches and practitioners suggest using different approaches according to the kind of e-platform (transaction/non-transaction, matching/audience providing, etc.),[41] but most experts concur on the benefits of defining such markets ad hoc and the inefficiency of universal recipes,[42] at least at the current stage of development of markets of intermediary informational services.

3.3 *Challenges to Procompetitive Data Management*

Adam Smith, David Ricardo and John Stuart Mill laid the foundation and Paul Samuelson much later specified three main questions of economics: What to produce?

[40] Cf among others, National Bureau of Economic Research, 'The Antitrust Analysis of Multi-Sided Platform Businesses' Working Papers 18783, 2013, 21–23; Lapo Filistrucchi et al., 'Market Definition in Two-Sided Markets: Theory and Practice' (2014) 10(2) Journal of Competition Law & Economics 293; OECD, 'Market Definition in Multi-Sided Markets—Note by Sebastian Wismer & Arno Rasek' DAF/COMP/WD(2017)33/FINAL, 2017, 12; Mihai M Stahie, 'Market Definition in Two-Sided Markets: An Empirical Analysis' (2017) 1 Romanian Competition Journal 80 (87–88); OECD, 'Rethinking Antitrust Tools for Multi-Sided Platforms' (Report), 2018, 41–45.

[41] Cf OECD, 'Rethinking Antitrust Tools for Multi-Sided Platforms' (Report), 2018, 41–43; OECD, 'Market Definition in Multi-Sided Markets—Note by Sebastian Wismer and Arno Rasek' DAF/COMP/WD(2017)33/FINAL, 2017, 5–7; Filistrucchi et al., 'Market Definition in Two-Sided Markets: Theory and Practice' (n 40) 293.

[42] Cf National Bureau of Economic Research, 'The Antitrust Analysis of Multi-Sided Platform Businesses' Working Paper 18783, 2013, 21–23; Jean Charles Rochet and Jean Tirole, 'Platform Competition in Two-Sided Markets' (2003) 1(4) Journal of the European Economic Association, 990; Eric Emch and T Scott Thomson, 'Market Definition and Market Power in Payment Card Networks' (2006) 5(1) The Review of Network Economics 45; OECD, 'Rethinking the Use of Traditional Antitrust Enforcement Tools in Multi-sided Markets' (2017) DAF/COMP/WD 55, 2017, 5–7.

How to produce? Whom to produce for?[43] Answering the first and the third question has been rather simplified by the evolvement of e-platforms due to large-scale collection, analysis and aggregation of consumer data. In addition, the information dominance in the resource bundle of a modern firm makes obvious that detailed and personalized information awareness is the key competitive advantage of e-platforms compared to other economic actors.

Parker and others provide the curve of value creation when data is used for a specific purpose, which demonstrates the advantage of big data over small data and explains not only the sources of e-platforms' competitive advantages but also the nature of e-platforms' market dominance, which originated in an efficiency background. "Big platforms with large amounts of data generate high value and efficient services",[44] while efficient services attract a bigger amount of consumers, which gets the ball rolling in terms of the network effect and leads to lock-in.

Different ways of coping with such a barrier to competition that are discussed in the antitrust community are e-platform break-up, unbundling, data sharing, etc., but none of them is sufficient in terms of both competition and efficiency.

Besides erecting barriers, big data concentration provides the background for two other infringements of competition law: price discrimination (*inter alia* perfect price discrimination) and collusion. Digital algorithms, based on cookies, are efficient in identifying a consumer and collecting information on his or her preferences and purchasing power, but these data can be effectively used by e-platforms and its affiliates for abuse. Among the examples is the case of Amazon.com, where removing cookies led to a price decrease on DVDs.[45] Another example is the case of Orbitz Worldwide, which suggested more expensive hotels to the consumers who used Mac OS as compared to Windows.[46] Benjamin Edelman, Michael Luca and Dan Svirsky in their experiment on Airbnb and Latanya Sweeney in her research on race discrimination while advertising via Google have proved that consumer discrimination (*inter alia* price discrimination) just becomes stronger with pricing automatization.[47]

Also, the risk of collusion becomes much higher due to the collection and exchange of information. As Libowsky writes, "technology had made a price-fixing conspiracy plausible, even among thousands of conspirators."[48] For instance, in March and April 2020 and in April 2021 when the public transport in Kyiv stopped or was substantively

[43] Paul A Samuelson, *Economics: An Introductory Analysis* (McGraw-Hill Book Company 1948).

[44] Geoffrey Parker et al., 'Digital Platforms and Antitrust' (2020) 6 Bruegel Working Paper 2 (24).

[45] OECD, 'The Regulation of Personalised Pricing in the Digital Era' DAF/COMP/WD (2018)150, 2018, 3.

[46] Dana Mattioli, 'On Orbitz, Mac Users Steered to Pricier Hotels' *The Wall Street Journal* (23 August 2012). https://www.wsj.com/articles/SB10001424052702304458604577488822667325882 accessed 29 July 2021.

[47] Ray Fisman and Michael Luca, 'Fixing Discrimination in Online Marketplaces' *Harvard Business Review* (December 2016) https://hbr.org/2016/12/fixing-discrimination-in-online-marketplaces accessed 29 July 2021.

[48] Stephen Libowsky, 'Antitrust Issues with Big Data: A United States Introduction' *Dentons* (15 January 2018) https://www.dentons.com/en/pdf-pages/www.dentons.com/-/media/208fd3e1727b492da21e58a6b81a4a38.ashx accessed 29 July 2021.

restrained due to quarantine restrictions, taxi prices coincidently rose almost threefold on each of the three dominant e-platforms (Uber, Uklon and Bolt) just by applying electronic pricing algorithms based on the big data. It would be almost impossible to reach the same collusive effect in terms of simultaneity and price identity without e-platforms, because the time expenditures and transaction costs for adjusting would be too great.

Another collusive effect of e-platforms derives from their impact on market transparency. Price comparison services increase the coordination ability of a market, as they facilitate each of the following three criteria: (a) the ability to reach the mutual equilibrium; (b) the ability to expose deviation from the mutual equilibrium; (c) the ability to punish the deviator. In the pre-digital world the hub-and-spoke model of information circulation, for example in Ukrainian retail,[49] was considered to be the basic element of collusion. Today such information exchange is not restrained by the scope of direct contractors of the info hub. It is open to the public and done in real time, just increasing the risk of collusion and complicating the substantiation of it, which previously was mostly done by confirmation of information exchange.

The above-mentioned negative effects of big data concentration by the dominant e-platform need to be balanced with positive ones and should at least be partially blocked by effective remedies to optimize competition between e-platforms.

3.4 Other Challenges

There are other challenges posed to competition among e-platforms; three should be pointed out in particular: the institutionalizing potential of gatekeepers, so-called "killer-acquisitions", and the tension between regulation and competition.

The first (the institutionalizing potential of gatekeepers) is rather strong. A dominant e-platform is disposed not only to abuse in the short run, but also to maintenance of its dominance in the long run through through enforcing special rules of access to core platform service. Often such rules are unfavorable for the users of an e-platform and for potential competitors, but because they are introduced in the early days of the market, they are likened to the nature of the market, take root and are taken for granted by market participants. As an example of such rules, let us point to exclusive dealing and the ban of multihoming. The reason why we do not dedicate a separate subsection to this challenge lies in the ability of the current *ex post* competition policy and legislation to master this challenge partially in the case of correct market definition and dominance ascertainment (see Sec. 3.2). However, what we can see from the cases in Ukrainian retail is that there is a need for additional remedies to restrict the anticompetitive potential of gatekeepers to institutionalize new markets, especially in cases of their latent dominance.

---

[49] AMCU, Decision 182-p *AMCU v. Fozzie Food, Fora, Furshet, Auchan Ukraine, ATB-Market, ECO, Adventis, Billa Ukraine, Kraj-2, Novus Ukraine, X5 Retail Group Ukraine, Spar-Centre, Bemarket, METRO Cash&Carry Ukraine, AC Nielsen Ukraine* (2015) 31–48.

In killer-acquisitions a dominant market player acquires a promising start-up to prevent potential competition. Such acquisitions already existed in the pre-digital world (in pharmacy and some other innovation-driven industries), but they were sporadic and did not provide substantial economy-wide risks.[50] They did not require the special focus of competition agencies or necessitate reforming the system of *ex ante* merger control. Today, information and innovations have become central factors of rivalry, and the speed of change of the competitive environment has increased, especially on the markets of intermediary informational services. Therefore, such acquisitions take place more often, while current turnover thresholds for their notification fail to detect the risks of potential competition removal. There is no pat answer to the question of how to facilitate such risks' detection without overburdening the merger control system.

The tension between regulation and competition is rather urgent for regulated e-platforms. Even if developing competition is an objective of regulating the introduction and functioning of e-platforms, the methods of regulation may be too imperfect to achieve the goal, restricting competition. An example is the e-platform of the day-ahead electricity market, after electricity providers lost their status as natural monopolies. The e-platform is designed to provide the competitive interaction of sellers and buyers of electricity on the relevant market. However, the establishment of the platform, whose intermediation is mandatory for every buyer and seller of electricity, has diminished the vertical competition within the industry and has blocked the value chain. It may not be a problem in the case of perfect regulation. In fact, the regulation is far from perfect. The actual access policy and price caps as well as the underlying algorithm of this platform (primarily the way bids are adjusted) that Ukrainian legislation and regulations mandate, ultimately restrict competition on the platform in practice and result in distorted prices. If the traders operated under real competition, the prices would be set at the competitive level.

Summarizing these challenges to competition, which are the manifestations of the new normal in the digital post-industrial economy, it becomes obvious that adequate answers to them are needed within both conventional competition policy and through the introduction of entirely new remedies.

[50] Cf Mark D Whitener, 'Competition and Antitrust Enforcement in the Changing Pharmaceutical Marketplace' (1995) 50(2) Food and Drug Law Journal 301 (305–307); Ove Granstrand and Sören Sjölander, 'The Acquisition of Technology and Small Firms by Large Firms' (1990) 13(3) Journal of Economic Behaviour and Organization 367.

4 Ukrainian Competition Law's (In)capacity to Meet the Challenges

The Antimonopoly Committee of Ukraine (AMCU) is the primary authority responsible for the protection of economic competition, and its competence and functions are governed by the corresponding law.[51]

The Law of Ukraine "On Protection of Economic Competition" (adopted in 2001, and amended dozens of times, the latest in June 2021) embodies the general framework for concerted practices, merger control, market dominance and its abuse, as well as investigations of competition law infringements and applicable sanctions. Despite being amended routinely, the law has neither specific concepts nor enforcement tools directly addressing the peculiarities of the business models of digital platforms, nor are there any relevant draft laws being discussed and submitted to the Parliament as of December 2021.

The AMCU also remains silent on new regulations or guidelines for digital platforms. That provides the authors an empty playground to identify gaps and formulate recommendations for how to address the competitive concerns posed by digital platforms.

4.1 AMCU Experience in Digital Markets

As of December 2021, the AMCU intervened only once in digital markets, when it approved the merger of Rozetka group and EVO group in 2018.[52] As the result of concentration, a number of Ukrainian marketplaces came under one umbrella: Prom.ua, Bigl.ua (online platforms for retail trade in consumer goods), Kabanchik.ua (an online service for finding contractors for ordering household chores and services as well as small commercial tasks), Crafta.ua (an online platform for the sale of handmade products as well as collectible and rare products), Shafa.ua (an online platform for the sale of women's and children's goods, which are usually second-hand), Zakupki.prom.ua (an online platform for participation in public procurement, a participant in the public e-procurement system Prozorro.sales and the open system of commercial procurement RIALTO) and On time (an online service for exchanging, signing and storing any documents).

The AMCU decision defined the relevant market as "the national market for the provision of services for the promotion of goods (works, services) on the Internet through online platforms (Internet platforms)".[53] The AMCU decision pointed out that:

[51] Ukrainian Law on the Antimonopoly Committee of Ukraine 1992, 3659-XII.

[52] AMCU, Decision 446-p (2018).

[53] Ibid part 67.

> This market is open to entry/exit of new entrants and there are no significant regulatory barriers to entry, in particular the ability to enter the market of new competitors depends mainly on their financial capabilities and the success of marketing strategy. Competitors do not have exclusive rights to innovation, intellectual property, logistical support, etc. In addition, there are no regulatory barriers to market entry, for example, new market participants do not need to obtain licenses, permits, etc.[54]

International online giants (Facebook, booking.com, Google, etc.) and their practices have escaped the AMCU's attention so far, and no future investigation of digital markets has yet been announced.

4.2 *Major Challenges for the National Legal Framework*

4.2.1 Legal Status of Digital Platforms

The Ukrainian competition law framework handles the term "undertaking" for all market participants—it embraces legal entities and natural persons, as well as state bodies that are engaged in economic activities. Thus, digital platforms have no specific criteria, rights and obligations with regard to economic competition, and their activities should be evaluated from a "classical" point of view, posing numerous challenges for effective legal enforcement.

Legislative changes and proposals in foreign jurisdictions predominantly apply an asymmetric approach for defining rights and obligations of market players, pressuring digital platforms recognized as "gatekeepers" to meet higher standards of competition conduct.[55] The authors believe the introduction of "gatekeeper" status into the national legal framework may be effective, but only after amendments are made to the market definition methodology, alongside a formulation of soft-law and an encouragement of extensive dialogue with digital markets participants. The approach of attaining a gatekeeper status remains another point for discussion.

4.2.2 Determining the Dominant Position of the Digital Platform

The Law of Ukraine "On Protection of Economic Competition" imposes standard economic analysis mechanisms to determine the dominant position of an undertaking:

---

[54] Antimonopoly Committee of Ukraine, 'Annual Report' 2018.

[55] Section 19a was recently added to Germany's Act against Restraints of Competition, stating that an undertaking, which is active to a significant extent on multi-sided markets and networks, is of paramount significance for competition across markets. Such undertakings would be subject to special intervention powers by German competition authorities. In the UK the statutory Digital Markets Unit will be responsible for designating firms with strategic market status, overseeing a mandatory code of conduct for those firms and implementing procompetitive interventions. The EU's Digital Market Act establishes criteria for qualifying a large online platform as a "gatekeeper".

the market share threshold of 35% is established as well as the criterion of absence of significant competition on the relevant market.

The law defines this criterion as: "does not experience significant competition due to limited access of other entities to purchase raw materials, commodities and sales of goods, the presence of *barriers to market access* for other entities, the availability of benefits or other circumstances"[56] (emphasis added). This criterion may be customized for digital platforms on the condition of defining a relevant market. Defining barriers to market access needs a thorough analysis by the competition authority based on the relevant methodology. The spectrum of potential barriers is rather diverse and includes technological and financial barriers, network effects and access to data, which poses a need for new approaches and competition authority experts with digital expertise.

4.2.3 Defining a Market

Criteria for finding dominance are detailed in the Methodology on definition of monopoly (dominant) position of undertakings on the market[57] (the Dominance Methodology), approved by the Order of the AMC dated 5 March 2002 No. 49-p. The document has not been changed since its approval, though in 2017 a draft methodology on market definition was announced that has not yet been approved.[58] The draft methodology suggests *inter alia* an analysis of the substitutability of goods, application of the SSNIP test and the method of indicators of price elasticity of demand. However, it lacks terminological consistency beyond its methodological deficiencies. Moreover, the above-mentioned quantitative methods' inefficiencies were already stressed in the previous section.

Mandrescu argues that the challenges posed by online platforms primarily concern changes to the practical application that do not exceed the boundaries of current practice.[59] Nevertheless, the authors believe that neither the old and nor the new methodology accounts for the current market tendencies; for example, the accent remains on products, not services, and on the price dimensions of competition. The legal definition of "commodity" entails any object of economic turnover, including products, works, services, documents supporting obligations and rights (including securities).

[56] Ukrainian Law on Protection of Economic Competition (PEC) 2001, 2210-III, art 12.

[57] Antimonopoly Committee of Ukraine, Order 49-p of 5 March 2002 on Approval Methodology Applied to Determine Monopoly (Dominant) Market Position of Economic Entities 2002.

[58] AMCU Draft Acy on Methodology on Market Definition 2017.

[59] See Daniel Mandrescu, 'Applying (EU) Competition Law to Online Platforms: Reflections on the Definition of the Relevant Market(s)' (2018) 41f(3) World Competition: Law and Economics Review.

In fact, AMCU practice shows that instead of studying the commodity/product substitutability of services (in fuel, pharmacy retail) of intermediaries, the substitutability of commodities (gasoline and medicines respectively) has been examined.[60]

Another example of the need to switch the focus is the substitutability criterion: the current methodology provides for the "substitutability of goods (product group) in terms of their production, i.e. the ability of manufacturers to offer new products to replace existing ones".[61] It should be stressed that it is not only about the absolute ability to offer an identical product (in case of digital markets: a service), but also about taking into account the opportunity cost of such supply. The assessment of such cost should consider not only production but also transaction costs. Also, neither methodology has embraced limitations to substitution due to switching costs, though they are vital for competition enforcement in digital markets.

4.2.4 Abuse of Dominance

For determining the abuse of dominance, Ukrainian competition law takes both a formalistic approach (e.g. "setting prices or other conditions for the purchase or sale of goods that could not be set in the face of significant competition in the market", "creating barriers to market access (exit from the market) or elimination of sellers, buyers and other business entities from the market") and an effects-based approach (e.g. "restrictions on production, markets or technical development that have caused or may cause damage to other entities, buyers, sellers").[62]

Based on foreign competition authorities' cases and academic research, the authors believe an effects-based approach should be a determinant in handling anti-competitive behavior in the digital economy.[63]

However, practices constituting an abuse of dominance that are listed in Art. 13 Law of Ukraine "On Protection of Economic Competition" may be well suited to online platforms, for example:

- "setting prices or other conditions for the purchase or sale of goods that could not be set in the face of significant competition in the market"—for self-preferencing of platform's products and services, imposing retail most-favored-nation clauses (dictating that the seller may not offer better terms and conditions on its own website or other platforms);

---

[60] AMCU, Decision 680-p *AMCU v. Novo Nordisk A/C, Novo Nordisk Health Care AG, BaDM, BaDM-B, Apteka ZI, Ganza, Farmadix, Medfarm* (2020) 33–49; AMCU, Decision 329-p *AMCU v. WOG, OKKO-Retail, Socar Petroleum* (2019), 6–11.

[61] Antimonopoly Committee of Ukraine, Order 49-p of 5 March 2002 on Approval Methodology Applied to Determine Monopoly (Dominant) Market Position of Economic Entities 2002.

[62] PEC, art 2.

[63] European Commission, 'DG Competition Discussion Paper on the Application of art 82 of the Treaty to Exclusionary Abuses' 2005; OECD, 'Abuse of Dominance in Digital Markets', 2020, 42; Payal Malik et al., 'Legal Treatment of Abuse of Dominance in Indian Competition Law: Adopting an Effects-Based Approach' (2019) 54(2) Review of Industrial Organization.

- "creating barriers to market access (exit from the market) or elimination of sellers, buyers and other business entities from the market"—for creating obstacles to users' multihoming. Yet the cornerstone of adapting current legislation remains the same—market definition methodology.

4.2.5 Merger Control

Current law[64] provides that a transaction qualifying as a concentration requires merger clearance by the AMC if it satisfies the following criteria:

- the combined worldwide value of assets or turnover of the parties to the concentration exceeds 30 million EUR and the value of Ukrainian assets or turnover of each of at least two parties exceeds 4 million EUR; or
- Ukrainian value of assets or turnover in Ukraine of the target or of at least one of the founders of a new entity exceeds 8 million EUR and worldwide turnover of at least one other party exceeds 150 million EUR.

All figures shall be taken for the last financial year immediately preceding the year of the concentration.

A current draft law[65] aims to amend the calculation of the thresholds of the parties to the concentration. Only the object of acquisition is considered since in the Ukrainian markets the indicators of the part of the seller's group with which the relationship is terminated do not affect competition. In order to prevent the acquisition of parts, a fuse is introduced—transactions between the same entities for two years are considered as one concentration. In order to minimize the regulatory burden and regulatory costs given that the seller's group is not taken into account when calculating the thresholds, the value in Ukraine of the entity which is controlled or partly controlled is reduced from 4 million EUR to 2 million EUR. This amendment fails to meet the "killer-acquisition" challenge, which would require keeping the pre-reform merger control thresholds or introducing other remedies. For instance, Art. 12 DMA obligates gatekeepers to notify authorities of all their M&A activity (essentially bringing the notification threshold to zero for gatekeepers), and such an approach seems to be well-suited to digital markets and constitutes an integral part of the legal framework of online platforms.

4.2.6 Vertical Competition Regulation

Current Ukrainian competition law does not include the term "vertical competition" at all. The definition of economic competition, presented in the Law of Ukraine "On Protection of Economic Competition" states:

---

[64] PEC, art 24.

[65] Ukrainian Draft Law on Amendments to Certain Legislative Acts of Ukraine on Improving the Activities of the Antimonopoly Committee of Ukraine 2021, 5431, 10.

> [D]enoting such a contest among economic entities with a view to gaining advantages over other economic entities thanks to their own achievements, which results in the situation where consumers and economic entities have an opportunity to choose from among several sellers, buyers, whereas an individual economic entity is not able to set conditions for the turnover of products on the market.[66]

It reveals that the law mostly deals with the concept of horizontal competition, notwithstanding the fact that the range of the biggest antitrust cases of the AMCU in recent years included vertical competition issues. The previous section has pointed out that this is also true for the digital sector.

5 Alternative Approaches to Meet the Challenges: Which Way Is Better for Ukraine?

To meet the challenges, Ukrainian competition law needs to be amended. Among other things, it should cover the legal introduction of the concept of vertical competition and development of the scope of regulation of the latter; development of and adoption of a new methodology of market definition which is open to the challenges of multisided contracting, zero-pricing and network effects, etc.; killer-acquisition management through keeping the pre-reform merger control thresholds in the digital sphere.

As a number of challenges for competition cannot be solely met by *ex post* competition policy measures (even in the case of competition policy modification in the above-mentioned way), the authors would recommend supplementing *ex post* competition measures with specific elements of *ex ante* ones, which should be applied only to those e-platforms which are recognized as dominant players in the market of information and intermediary services (a certain analogy with the UK model of the strategic status market test). In this case, the procedure for assigning such a status should be different from that proposed by the DMA and is more a procedure for notifying powerful operators of the digital economy than establishing the prerequisites and practices of real dominance of e-platforms.

No matter how difficult the task of correctly defining the boundaries of the markets of information and intermediary services and establishing the fact of dominance of e-platforms on these markets would be, we believe that this is the cornerstone of attaining a gatekeeper status and introducing additional regulation.

The AMCU pursues a well-established practice of selecting priority markets to study the boundaries and state of competition on an annual basis. Hence, the authors deem it appropriate for the AMCU to conduct a study of digital markets in order to set the boundaries of the relevant market(s) for online platforms and determine the presence/absence of the fact of their dominance. If the fact of dominance is confirmed, the relevant market and its dominant operator should be included in the

[66] PEC, art 1.

newly created list of dominant platforms in the field of information intermediation, which would be subject to *ex ante* regulation.

The authors strongly believe that the NCEC should be in charge of monitoring the competition in the markets of information and intermediary services where dominance has been established. The NCSRC tasks in these spheres may be divided into two groups:

(1) constant monitoring of the existence of dominance on given markets. Markets of information and intermediary services, in contrast to the markets of natural monopoly, are very dynamic. Their boundaries and their structural and behavioral preconditions of dominance can change quickly enough to create or eliminate grounds for additional regulation. For these reasons, the NCEC should introduce constant monitoring of relevant markets according to the criteria established by the AMCU. If the results of such monitoring indicate the presence of significant deviations from the established AMCU indicators of stability of market boundaries and structure, the NCEC should send a request to the AMCU to conduct a special study of the market and confirm or deny the dominance of the e-platform as a prerequisite for its preservation in or exclusion from the list of dominance in the field of information intermediation;
(2) introduction of *ex ante* measures to stimulate the development of competition in the markets of information and intermediary services with signs of dominance. Their range can be quite wide. We now see the feasibility of at least two remedies that have proven themselves in natural monopolies, avoiding excessive substitution of the "first best" mechanism for regulating the "second best": unbundling and access regulation.

In this regard it appears informative to characterize the peculiarities of the application of unbundling and access regulation in the markets of information and intermediary services. Unbundling is the practice of vertically separating naturally monopolistic activities from potentially competitive ones. It aims to minimize the scope of direct government regulation and stimulate competition in markets not burdened with natural monopoly status, which blocks market power leverage from natural monopolistic to adjacent markets and self-preferencing. As the latter are widespread ways of spreading and exploiting market power by dominant e-platforms in the world and Ukraine (see Microsoft tying its operating system with Internet Explorer and Windows Media Player, Google Shopping, RZTK Private brand, etc.), it would be advisable to take advantage of this remedy in cases of confirmed dominance of e-platforms. At the same time, realizing the above-mentioned dynamism of the markets of information and intermediary services in comparison with the natural monopolies, it would be helpful to provide not a full ownership unbundling, but a partial one and to supplement the latter with compliance measures in the first stages of the introduction of appropriate regulation.

If full ownership unbundling prohibits the operator of an essential facility (e.g. search engine, operating system, e-marketplace, etc.) not only from independently carrying out any activity in related markets, but also from being connected by control relations with entities in such markets, partial unbundling allows related parties to operate in related markets. However, it would require the legal, managerial and operational separation of the essential facility operator's functions from other activities in the relevant value chain. In this e-marketplace model, Rozetka would still have the right to sell its own products on its marketplace, but the production and sale of such products would have to be carried out by a separate legal entity, which would have to keep separate management and accounting records and be managed without direct subordination to the management of the e-marketplace, and subordination to the owners would be limited to financial control. The management of the e-marketplace and the owners of the group as a whole would not be entitled to interfere in the operational activities of manufacturers of goods under the RZTK brand. Continuous monitoring of compliance with the relevant rules would be carried out by a special compliance officer and would be subject to control by the NCEC. The option of introducing full ownership unbundling in a certain market of information and intermediary services can be considered separately if such a market retains signs of dominance for at least five years.

With regard to regulation of access to core platform services, a simple commitment by the dominant e-platform to ensure freedom of such access is, in our view, insufficient, although it is clear that this is what should underlie the access regulation. Regulation of access from the NCEC should include:

- defining the core platform services and the operator of such services;
- fixing the range of related services (i.e. related to the provision of core platform services), ensuring their proper quality;
- determining the capacity of the e-platform (the maximum number of users who can simultaneously use the platform without compromising the quality of services provided, such as the speed of information exchange) and the order of access to it in case of exhaustion of such capacity;
- approaches and methods of setting tariffs for access to the core platform service to avoid their discrimination and direct abuse. At the same time, in order to avoid negative externalities of state regulation such as those mentioned above in the context of the e-platform of the day-ahead electricity market, we do not consider it appropriate to introduce direct state regulation of the level of access prices. Pricing should remain market-based, and in case of detection of price abuses by the dominant e-platform, Arts. 13, 50 and 52 Law of Ukraine "On Protection of Economic Competition" should be applied to it.

This is a rather rough outline of our vision of the competition system in the markets of information and intermediary services in Ukraine, whose role is growing in the digital economy of the twenty-first century, but it gives a general idea of the appropriate vectors of competition policy in Ukraine in the context of challenges.

6 Conclusion

To meet the "new normal" of competition in the current digital world, Ukrainian competition law and policy require huge modification in three vectors: the first is the reform of the *ex post* mechanism of economic competition protection through the introduction of a range of slight changes to the Law of Ukraine "On Protection of Economic Competition" to widen the sphere of the state control of competition. The second is to develop a new methodology of market definition open to the challenges of multisided contracting, zero-pricing and network effects, as well as to other complications driven by the economy's digitalization. The third is for the AMCU and NCEC to cooperate in order to constantly monitor and regulate digital markets marked by the dominance of an e-platform. This three-vector reform would enable Ukrainian competition law and policy to cope with the digital competition challenges and provide an effective regulatory framework not only for e-platforms but also for their small contractors and society at large.

References

Antimonopoly Committee of Ukraine, 'Annual Report' 2018 [Антимонопольний комітет України, 'Річний звіт' 2018]

Amiya K Bagchi, 'Local and Global Monopolies and the Prospects of Global Democracy' in Deepak Nayyar (ed), *Economics as Ideology and Experience: Essays in Honour of Ashok Mitra* (Frank Cass Publisher 1998)

Paul A Baran and Paul M Sweezy, *Monopoly Capital: An Essay on the American Economic and Social Order* (Monthly Review Press 1966)

Jennifer M Clarke Smith, 'The Development of the Monopolistic Leveraging Theory and Its Appropriate Role in Antitrust Law' (2002) 52(1) Catholic University Law Review 179

'Bolt Company has Assessed the Volume of the Shadow Taxi Market in Ukraine' *Economichna Pravda* (9 July 2019) https://www.epravda.com.ua/news/2019/07/9/649486/ ['У Компанії Bolt Оцінили Розмір Тіньового Ринку Таксі в Україні' *Економічна Правда* (9 липня 2019]

Alexandre de Cornière and Greg Taylor, 'Upstream Bundling and Leverage of Market Power' (2021) 131(640) The Economic Journal 3122

Ivan Dubinskiy, 'Research of Number of Internet Users' *Ukrainian Internet Association* (20 January 2020) https://inau.ua/proekty/doslidzhennya-internet-audytoriyi [Іван Дубінський 'Дослідження Інтернет-Аудиторії' *Інтернет Асоціація України* (20 січня 2020)]

Eric Emch and T Scott Thomson, 'Market Definition and Market Power in Payment Card Networks' (2006) 5(1) The Review of Network Economics 45

European Commission, 'Competition Policy for the Digital Era' (Final Report), 2019

Lapo Filistrucchi, Damien Geradin, Eric van Damme and Pauline Affeldt, 'Market Definition in Two-Sided Markets: Theory and Practice' (2014) 10(2) Journal of Competition Law and Economics 293

Ray Fisman and Michael Luca, 'Fixing Discrimination in Online Marketplaces' *Harvard Business Review* (December 2016) https://hbr.org/2016/12/fixing-discrimination-in-online-marketplaces

John K Galbraith, *American Capitalism: The Concept of Countervailing Power* (Houghton Miffin 1952)

Germain Gaudin, 'Vertical Bargaining and Retail Competition: What Drives Countervailing Power?' (2018) 128 (614) The Economic Journal 2380

Global Antitrust Institute, 'Report on the Digital Economy' (Report) 2020, 263

Megan Graham and Jennifer Elias, 'How Google's $150 Billion Advertising Business Works' *CNBC* (18 May 2021) https://www.cnbc.com/2021/05/18/how-does-google-make-money-advertising-business-breakdown-.html

Ove Granstrand and Sören Sjölander, 'The Acquisition of Technology and Small Firms by Large Firms' (1990) 13(3) Journal of Economic Behaviour and Organization 367

House Committee on the Judiciary, 'Online Platforms and Market Power: Examining the Dominance of Amazon, Apple, Facebook, and Google' *YouTube* (29 July 2020) https://www.youtube.com/watch?v=WBFDQvIrWYM&ab_channel=HouseCommitteeontheJudiciary

Anne C Hoyng and Robert van Mastrigt, 'Is the Current Debate About Changing the Competition Law Toolbox Warranted? A Perspective From a Digital Platform' (2020) 41(7) European Competition Law Review 327

Michael L Katz and Carl Shapiro, 'Systems Competition and Network Effects' (1994) 8(2) Journal of Economic Perspective 93

Aleksey Kostusev, *Competition Policy in Ukraine* (Kyiv National Economic University Publishing House 2004) [Алексей Костусев, *Конкурентная Политика в Украине* (Издательство Киевского Национального Экономического Университета 2004)]

Stephen Libowsky, 'Antitrust Issues with Big Data: A United States Introduction' *Detons* (15 January 2018) https://www.dentons.com/en/pdf-pages/www.dentons.com/-/media/208fd3e1727b492da21e58a6b81a4a38.ashx

Peter Lyman and Hal R Varian, 'How Much Information, 2003' (2003) Technical Report, UC Berkley

Payal Malik, Neha Malhotra, Ramji Tamarappoo and Nisha Kaur Uberoi, 'Legal Treatment of Abuse of Dominance in Indian Competition Law: Adopting an Effects-Based Approa*ch'* (2019) 54(2) Review of Industrial Organization

Daniel Mandrescu, 'Applying (EU) Competition Law to Online Platforms: Reflections on the Definition of the Relevant Market(s)' (2018) 41 (3) World Competition: Law and Economics Review

John E Martin, *Feudalism to Capitalism: Peasant and Landlord in English Agrarian Development* (Palgrave Macmillan 1986)

Karl Marx, *Capital: A Critique of Political Economy, Vol. 1* (Pacific Publishing Studio 2010)

Dana Mattioli, 'On Orbitz, Mac Users Steered to Pricier Hotels' *The Wall Street Journal* (23 August 2012) https://www.wsj.com/articles/SB10001424052702304458604577488822667325882

National Bureau of Economic Research, 'The Antitrust Analysis of Multi-Sided Platform Businesses' Working Paper 18783, 2013

Organization for Economic Co-operation and Development, 'Abuse of Dominance in Digital Markets', 2020, 42

Organization for Economic Co-operation and Development, 'Rethinking Antitrust Tools for Multi-Sided Platforms' (Report), 2018

Organization for Economic Co-operation and Development, 'The Regulation of Personalised Pricing in the Digital Era' DAF/COMP/WD (2018)150, 2018

Organization for Economic Co-operation and Development, 'Market Definition in Multi-Sided Markets—Note by Sebastian Wismer & Arno Rasek' DAF/COMP/WD(2017)33/FINAL, 2017

Organization for Economic Co-operation and Development, 'Rethinking the Use of Traditional Antitrust Enforcement Tools in Multi-sided Markets' DAF/COMP/WD (2017)55, 2017

Geoffrey Parker, Georgios Petropoulos and Marshall van Alstyne, 'Digital Platforms and Antitrust' (2020) 6 Bruegel Working Paper 2

Christo Petrov, '25+ Impressive Big Data Statistics for 2021' *Techjury* (9 July 2021) https://techjury.net/blog/big-data-statistics/#gref

Patrick Rey and Jean Tirole, 'A Primer on Foreclosure' in Mark Armstrong and Robert H Porter (eds), *Handbook of Industrial Organization III* (North Holland 2007)

Jean-Charles Rochet and Jean Tirole, 'Platform Competition in Two-Sided Markets' (2003) 1(4) Journal of the European Economic Association 990

Paul A Samuelson, *Economics: An Introductory Analysis* (McGraw-Hill Book Company 1948)
Carl Shapiro and Hal R Varian, *Information Rules: A Strategic Guide to the Network Economy* (Harvard Business School Press 1998)
Liubomyr Shkil, 'Digital Advertising Market in Ukraine have Risen up to 13.5 billion UAH: The Top of UIA Research' *ADSIDER* (18 March 2021) https://adsider.com/ua/rynok-internet-reklamy-v-ukraini-vyris-do-13-5-mlrd-hrn-nayholovnishe-z-doslidzhennia-inau/ [Любомир Шкіль, 'Ринок Інтернет-Реклами в Україні Виріс до 13,5 млрд грн. Найголовніше з Дослідження ІнАУ' *ADSIDER* (18 березня 2021)]
Stephen Smith and Elisa Lindemann, 'Spotlight on Online Platforms and Digital Advertising as CMA Calls for a New Pro-competition Regulation Regime' (2020) 31(8) Entertainment Law Review 279
Mihai M Stahie, 'Market Definition in Two-Sided Markets: An Empirical Analysis' (2017) 1 Romanian Competition Journal 80
Robert L Steiner, 'Vertical Competition, Horizontal Competition, and Market Power' (2008) 53(2) Antitrust Bulletin 251
Jean Tirole, *Economics for the Common Good* (Princeton University Press 2017)
'The E-commerce Market in Ukraine has Reached $4 Billion' *Soul Partners* (22 June 2021) https://soulpartners.com.ua/en/news/tpost/casugamy91-the-e-commerce-market-in-ukraine-has-rea
Alvin Toffler, *Powershift: Knowledge, Wealth and Violence at the Edge of the 21st Century* (Bantam Books 1990)
Michael D Whinston, 'Tying, Foreclosure, and Exclusion" (1990) 80(4) American Economic Review 837
Mark D Whitener, 'Competition and Antitrust Enforcement in the Changing Pharmaceutical Marketplace' (1995) 50(2) Food and Drug Law Journal 301
Tim Wu, *The Master Switch: The Rise and Fall of Information Empires* (Vintage 2011)

Towards a New Digital Competition Policy of Ukraine: The EU Matrix

Oles Andriychuk

Contents

Abstract The leading antitrust jurisdictions are introducing a paradigmatic reform of the rules regulating competition in digital markets. Not only do they revolutionize the enforcement mechanism, they are equally innovative in terms of the constitutional and ideological questions concerning the very role of economic competition in the broader constellation of societal values. Against this background, the system of competition law of Ukraine is following a different path. The chronologic gap keeps it somewhere in the 1990s with the dominance of the reductionist beliefs in the omnipotent power of neoclassical economics to solve axiomatically all antitrust conundrums. The Ukrainian competition policy is currently being shaped by the normative imperative of non-intervention, invoked in opposition to the previous central planning system inherited from the Soviet past. This situation is counterintuitive because the main influencer behind this paradigm—the European Union—itself is undergoing a U-turn in many questions of its own competition policy. Now, when the approach is being so fundamentally revised, it would be a dead-end street for Ukraine to continue pursuing it without a systemic readjustment. The new philosophy of "smart regulation" should be transposed. After the illegal war against Ukraine was brutally initiated by Russia, it became clear that Ukraine will be ultimately offered a meaningful perspective of joining the EU. This requires a fundamental revision of the current conception of Ukraine's digital competition policy. This chapter aims to articulate the key elements of the emerging EU digital competition law, indicating the areas requiring transposition to competition policy of Ukraine.

O. Andriychuk (✉)
Newcastle University, Law School, Newcastle, UK
e-mail: oles.andriychuk@newcastle.ac.uk

H. Richter (ed.), *Competition and Intellectual Property Law in Ukraine*,
MPI Studies on Intellectual Property and Competition Law 31,
https://doi.org/10.1007/978-3-662-66101-7_8

1 Introduction

One of the most vibrant, dynamic and rapidly developing areas of competition policy concerns the digital economy. All mature jurisdictions are currently revising their attitude to the digital markets.[1] There is a clearly observable transition from the phase of Internet-optimism characterised by a laissez-faire approach to the digital gatekeepers towards a new phase of Internet-pragmatism, with much more proactive (and often targeted) regulatory, enforcement and judiciary options being considered.

If the period from 2018 to 2020 was the period of reports,[2] the period from 2020 to 2022 is clearly a period of action: Important investigations have been launched, landmark cases adjudicated,[3] and vital pieces of legislation introduced in various jurisdictions across the globe. The situation in the digital markets is changing with unprecedented dynamics, and the regulatory responses follow suit. One of the most ambitious systemic legislative initiatives in this field is the introduction of the proposal for an EU Digital Markets Act (DMA).[4]

The purpose of this chapter is to summarise the central features of the emerging digital competition law, as envisaged mainly by the DMA, to explore how the reform changes our understanding of the role and function of economic competition in the digital society, and to extrapolate this new modality from the EU to the Ukrainian context.

Section 2 of this chapter explores the emergence of EU digital competition law, focusing mainly on the question of goals. It explains why the question of goals has been reopened in the context of EU competition rules, and why this discussion should be equally relevant to the legal and economic analysis of the emerging competition

---

[1] H.R.3825 – Ending Platform Monopolies Act, Bill referred to the House Committee on the Judiciary, 11 June 2021; H.R.3816 – American Choice and Innovation Online Act, Bill referred to the House Committee on the Judiciary, 11 June 2021; H.R.3826 – Platform Competition and Opportunity Act of 2021, Bill referred to the House Committee on the Judiciary, 11 June 2021; President of the US Executive Order 14036, 'Promoting Competition in the American Economy', 9 July 2021; German Act to amend the Act against Restraints of Competition for a focused, proactive and digital Competition Law 4.0 and other competition law provisions 18 January 2021; UK Department for Digital, Culture, Media & Sport and Department for Business, Energy & Industrial Strategy, 'A New Pro-Competition Regime for Digital Markets', Open Consultation, 20 July 2021; The Parliament of the Commonwealth of Australia, House of Representatives, 'News Media and Digital Platforms Mandatory Bargaining Code Act', Act No. 21, 2 March 2021.

[2] European Commission, 'Competition Policy for the Digital Era' (Report) 2019. See also Digital Competition Expert Panel, 'Unlocking Digital Competition: Report of the Digital Competition Expert Panel' (Report) (2019); Open Forum Academy, 'Interoperability as a Tool for Competition Regulation' (Report) (2020); European Commission, Uncovering Blindspots in the Policy Debate on Platform Power: Final Report' (Report) (2021).

[3] ECJ C-612/17 *Google and Alphabet v Commission* (2021) ECLI:EU:T:2021:763; 'Notice of Intention to Accept Commitments Offered by Google in Relation to its Privacy Sandbox Proposals-Case number 50972' (2021) *Competition and Markets Authority*; Bundeskartellamt, 6th Decision Division B6-22/16 (2019); *Facebook v Apple* discussions on the new iOS 14.5 feature requiring the user's explicit consent to be tracked.

[4] European Commission, 'Regulation of the European Parliament and of the Council On Contestable and Fair Markets in the Digital Sector (Digital Markets Act)' (Proposal) COM(2020) 842 final, 2020.

rules of Ukraine. It identifies an important shift in the understanding of the goals of competition law. While in the previous modality the focus was placed almost consensually on consumer welfare and economic efficiency, the emerging trend on the one hand focuses more on the phenomenon of economic competition as such (contestability, rivalry), and on the other it is characterised by the greater openness of competition to other important economic and non-economic societal goals (fairness, sustainability, trade). Furthermore, the shift is present not only on a normative level. It is equally visible at (and directly connected to) the methodological level. While the former period was the period of a holistic, "scientific" approach of law and economics, which by definition treated the phenomenon of economic competition as an object of natural science (discoverable, provable, measurable), the current trend is characterised by the co-existence of several conflicting methodological approaches with none being capable of becoming a new absolute.[5]

For Ukraine such a revolution in the very conceptual toolkit of competition law, economics and policy requires a relevant conceptualisation. The normative transition from mono—to polycentricity as well as the methodological transition from the singularity of law and economics to a more pluralistic modality has to be adequately captured and internalised. Focussing on implementing the old paradigm is economically inefficient and conceptually wrong.

Section 3 summarises and analyses the main provisions of the DMA as proposed by the European Commission to the European Parliament in December 2020. It demonstrates how and why the evolution of the digital economy is leading to the re-interpretation of the established objectives of competition law and the recalibration of the available instruments of competition enforcement, thereby modifying the very nature of competition law, economics and policy. Our understanding of the phenomenon of economic competition (and its regulation) is becoming much less axiomatic and much more contextual, communicative, participatory, interpretative and flexible. The proposed rules reflect this newly emerging modus vivendi.

Section 4 projects the DMA discussions from the EU to Ukraine, asking if the rules that fundamentally recalibrate not only the methodology of pursuing competition policy in the digital economy, but also many normative postulates of competition law, economics and policy, should be transposed from one jurisdiction to the other. It would appear very impractical and simply logically absurd to steer and direct Ukraine towards reforming (or rather developing properly) its still emerging competition philosophy according to the rationale of the "old" paradigm while simultaneously fundamentally reforming the EU approach to the matter. Clearly, from the perspective of its potential membership in the EU, Ukraine should begin approximating its rules on regulating—as well as the proper understanding of—the competitive process in the digital economy as early as realistically possible. There could be of course "second-mover" advantages, where the rules are adopted into the Ukrainian matrix once they have been tested and refined in the EU. This, however, would imply at least some legal or political document manifesting the need for such approximation

---

[5] Oles Andriychuk, 'Between Microeconomics and Geopolitics: On the Reasonable Application of Competition Law' (2022) 85 Modern Law Review.

in the (nearest) future as well as a roadmap of its implementation. Such a trajectory should be explicitly and officially articulated.

In any case, Ukraine should not be encouraged to adopt (and should be discouraged from adopting) the rules, principles and vision that characterise the previous paradigm, in particular those that are in direct contradiction with the emerging paradigm (for example, increasing jurisdictional thresholds for merger evaluation (to promote innovation and encourage investment) at the time when the EU[6] and its Member States[7] are so enthusiastically seeking to improve merger control[8] with the aim of examining more—not fewer—mergers).

If the issue of EU membership remains open and hypothetical, this still does not make the need for Ukraine to adopt the EU-style *ex-ante* rules on digital markets less relevant. The challenges that the DMA, Digital Service Act (DSA), Digital Governance Act (DGA) and other EU legislative proposals aim to address are not specific to the EU, and they are as—if not more—relevant to the Ukrainian digital markets. The main conclusion in this respect is that the Ukraine's approximation to the rules regulating economic competition in digital markets should be pursued taking into account of, and in some conceptual conformity with, the EU reforms in general, and the DMA as the main embodiment of these reforms in the domain of digital competition in particular. An important systemic obstacle emerging in the context of implementing this normative goal concerns the way the DMA vision is integrated into the digital competition policy discourse of Ukraine. Evidently, the more proactive modality of a regulatory approach to digital markets envisages a deeper understanding of the broader macroeconomic policy by the competition agency. The Ukrainian national competition authority would have to be more involved in the governmental agenda.[9] This requires establishing stronger communicative channels between the Government and the Antimonopoly Committee of Ukraine (AMCU). Another aspect of this challenge concerns staffing the AMCU with technical experts in data science and digital markets. The authority would be expected to demonstrate its specific expertise in investigating concrete cases, but also its embeddedness in the long-term strategic approach to shaping the digital markets of Ukraine. The relevant part of this paper will address specific aspects of the evolution of competition policy in Ukraine from the normative and strategic perspectives articulated in the introduction.

---

[6] Commission Guidance on the application of the referral mechanism set out in art 22 of the Merger Regulation to certain categories of cases, 26 March 2021.

[7] German Federal Ministry for Economic Affairs and Energy, 'Article 114 TFEU as a Legal Basis for Strenghtened Control of Acquisitions by Digital Gatekeepers' (Legal Opinion) (2021).

[8] Council of the European Union, 'Council Regulation (EC) No 139/2004 of 20 January 2004 on the control of concentrations between undertakings (the EC Merger Regulation)' (2004) (024) Official Journal (1–22).

[9] This is a trend that is being discussed in the pioneering antitrust jurisdictions. See e.g., UK House of Lords Communications and Digital Committee Inquiry into Digital Regulation, 'An Inquiry into the Work of Digital Regulators' (2021) https://committees.parliament.uk/writtenevidence/40230/pdf/ accessed 2 December 2021.

The current situation with the illegal and inhumane Russian war in Ukraine has triggered the longstanding question about the geopolitical future of Ukraine in general and the format of its co-existence with the EU specifically. Before the war, there were three possible societal vectors of Ukraine's relationship with the EU development: (1) the gradual absorption into Russia's economic sphere of influence; (2) Ukraine as a buffer zone between the EU and Russia; or (3) Ukraine as a prospective EU Member. Before the war, the critical mass of European establishment was tacitly in support of the second option, positioning Ukraine somewhere in between the EU and the Eurasian Economic Community with only a hypothetical possibility of joining the EU at some indeterminate point in the future. This buffer-zone condition was marked with catchy labels EU–Ukraine neighbourhood, friendship, partnership or association. All these formats ultimately envisage some selective approximation of legal and economic systems, however, without any meaningful and realistic perspectives of joining the EU. The possibility of EU integration was illusionary and hypothetical. The fundamental rationale of the relationship between the EU and Ukraine was shaped in the format of a mutually beneficial, pragmatic cooperation of two independent entities. After the war started, the atmosphere began to change rapidly. After a delicate, very contestable (and long awaited) issue of awarding Ukraine with the formal status of an EU Candidate State has been finally sorted, there is an increasing understanding that the road to full membership should be realistic. Afterall, the choice about Ukraine's future becomes binary. The early preferred buffer-zone option is disappearing from the geopolitical constellation. Not accepting Ukraine in the EU would ultimately mean its coercive incorporation into the *Russian World*. This is an existential moment not only for Ukraine, but also for the EU.

The possibility of the eventual accession raises a number of foundational challenges about the adaptation of Ukraine's political, economic, social and legal systems into the existing mechanisms and institutions of the EU. This would also require a paradigmatic recalibration of the current formats of cooperation between the EU and Ukraine. Many of the mechanisms of EU accession would require time and strategic planning. The reform of Ukraine's competition law, economy and policy are among those areas. It is therefore absolutely crucial to begin the process of the continuous systemic redesigning of the optics through which EU competition law is perceived by the Ukrainian antitrust stakeholders (enforcers, judges, practicing lawyers and academics) as soon as possible. Even under the most optimistic scenario, the issue of a gradual conversion of the Ukrainian competition system into the EU would require thorough systemic work in different sectors and would require the comprehensive knowledge and understanding of the mechanisms and legal matrix of the EU.

The main thesis of this contribution is twofold: Normative and substantive. The normative thesis is that Ukraine should be perceived and treated as a future EU Member State, implying thereby that all the complexity of the intellectual regulatory conundrums related the future of digital markets should be transposed to Ukraine as a future EU Member State. Ukraine is not a neighbour; it is a Member. The substantive thesis outlines the contours of the regulatory reform of digital markets.

2 The Re-Emerging Discussions on the Goal(s) of Competition Policy

Competition law in the digital economy can be drafted and applied in a way that promotes different objectives. It can be interpreted narrowly, axiomatically and commensurably as having a consumer welfare or utility function, as envisaged by neoclassical price theory economics.[10] It can also be interpreted broadly, deontologically and incommensurably as fairness or freedom, as reflected in various constitutional theories of economic competition,[11] also with various approaches in-between. Such a co-existence of different legitimate visions about competition law, many of which are either in direct opposition to or in categorical ignorance of one another, leads to an epistemic conflict. It could be solved in two ways: Monistically or pluralistically.

The monistic perception of the relationship between the disciplinary goals ("our approach is correct, all the others are not") implies a clash between the approaches. In contrast, a more pluralistic perception implies a coexistence between the goals and methods of competition policy ("our approach is correct, all/some of the others may be correct too").[12] The law and economics consensus, which dominated the discipline until recently, may be seen as an example of the monistic approach. Its "universalistic", "science-led", "axiomatic" apparatus converts into the price theory all the relevant facts, values and interests.[13] Such an inward-looking period of competition law, underpinned and exhausted by narrow technical expertise, is losing its momentum. The views arguing that the competition policy apparatus may embrace more than what is implied by neoclassical economics are re-emerging rapidly. The discipline is in an epistemic transition from mono- to polycentricity,[14] becoming more open to unorthodox, future-proof approaches with an increasing role played by political or non-axiomatic choices. The DMA epitomises this trend.[15]

With a degree of stylisation, one can identify the following eight legitimate societal values that are often associated with the goals of EU digital competition law:

---

[10] Richard Posner, 'The Decline of Law as an Autonomous Discipline: 1962–1987' (1987) 100(4) Harvard Law Review 761.

[11] Ariel Ezrachi, 'Sponge' (2016) 5(1) Journal of Antitrust Enforcement 49.

[12] Stavros Makris, 'Openness and Integrity in Antitrust' (2021) 17(1) Journal of Competition Law & Economics 1 (3–4).

[13] Andriychuk, 'Between Microeconomics and Geopolitics: On the Reasonable Application of Competition Law' (n 5).

[14] Ioannis Lianos, 'Polycentric Competition Law' (2018) 71(1) Current Legal Problems, 1 (6): "The mainstream model of competition law disregards questions that the current methods and tools of economics, and in particular Neoclassical Price Theory (NPT), have difficulty integrating and processing analytically. Issues, such as fairness, are considered controversial from the point of view of economics and are deemed to belong to the separate realm of politics. A similar intellectual scheme distinguishes the domain of competition law, which is considered as a field of applied economics, and thus intrinsically allergic to any form of political content".

[15] Oles Andriychuk, 'Shaping the New Modality of the Digital Markets: The Impact of the DSA/DMA Proposals on Inter-Platform Competition' (2021) 44(3) World Competition 261(266).

(i) protection of overall welfare; (ii) protection of consumer welfare; (iii) protection of end-user interests; (iv) protection of business user interests; (v) protection of innovation; (vi) protection of economic growth; (vii) protection of rivalry; (viii) protection of the internal market. These eight societal values—and various combinations thereof—constitute the main parameters of the discussions on the goals of EU digital competition law. They all also have their strong established intellectual pedigree in traditional *ex-post* competition law. A more creative interpretation and application of the current and the proposed competition rules allow the modality of "protection" to be complemented with the modality of "promotion" for all eight, thereby enabling a more proactive role of the enforcers and a wider application of the instruments of legal interpretation. The macroeconomic processes in the area of the digital economy are among the main driving forces, necessitating the revision of the traditional function of competition law and complementing its "protective" modality with the "promoting" one.

The complexity of the normative values which are commonly seen as goals of competition law is further expanded by the different methodologies underpinning different approaches to competition. Clearly, the same normative values could be promoted by different means and measured by different parameters, which allows for a meaningful disagreement even between those who agree on the normative aspects. Last but not least, there is a myriad of societally legitimate interests that in one way or another influence competition analysis. Those interests may be seen as external by the proponents of a narrower perception of competition theory, or as internal by the supporter of more inclusive conceptions.

The routine functioning of competition law allows for a mutual support and simultaneous enhancement of these different goals and methodologies. Conventionally, the technical differences between various approaches are either shifted to the layer of purely academic discussion or referred to by skilful legal and economic teams in atypical, difficult cases as an *ultima ratio*. The situation becomes very different at times of paradigmatic change, like the one we are experiencing at present in the area of the digital economy. The revival of the broader societal discussions on the goals of competition law, the methods of competition economics and the very mission of competition policy necessitates a critical reassessment of each of these approaches, as well as a proper analysis of the relationships between them.

As most of these goals and the theories underpinning them are not in an antithetical relationship to each other, the professional discussions take place not about the legitimacy of each of the goals of competition policy or their hierarchical taxonomy, but rather about the advantages and disadvantages of each: The discussions are less about the categorical primacy of one over the other but rather about their relative priority case by case. Such discussions are more productive and inclusive than the more rivalrous juxtapositions of one approach to the other(s). The central role in such discussions is assigned to the focus, the prism, the perspective, the narrative.

3 The DMA as a New Paradigm for Shaping Competition in Digital Markets

Given the potentially far-reaching implications of the Act on the very architecture of the digital economy and digital communications more broadly, the DMA proposal has been discussed intensively by various stakeholders and from different perspectives. The Commission has helpfully summarised most of the developed narratives and ideas in a condensed 20-page text of the Preamble of the DMA. It begins with explaining the obvious advantages of the digital markets and their key potential shortcomings predetermined by the objective characteristics of tipping, zero-price, the power of default settings, low marginal costs, lack of multihoming, lock-in and other network effects, multi-sidedness, the ability to eliminate competition and steer innovation, manipulating algorithmically the rankings and giving priority to one's own products and services or those of the commercial partners by inter alia tying, leveraging or margin squeezing, vertical integration and the tendency of the most successful players to expand and transform into closed, self-sufficient digital ecosystems offering the end-users most if not all services on the one-stop-shop basis—the features enabling quick (if not unlimited) scaling up.

These objective factors are underpinned and intensified by two external conditions making competition for (rather than on) the digital markets particularly fierce if not antagonistic. Those two external conditions are (i) nearly exponential growth of the digital element in the global economy, explaining high profits and rapid growth of the main market players and (ii) the future prospects of a further percentual increase of the digital components in all goods and services, making the role of the biggest platforms decisive in shaping the global economy, culture and society more generally. There is already a rich literature developing the 4th industrial revolution narrative,[16] the central proposition of which is the attribution and analysis of the quintessential role of the digital gatekeepers in designing the conditions, rules and parameters of

---

[16] UK Department for Business, Energy and Industrial Strategy, 'Regulation for the Fourth Industrial Revolution' (2019) Policy Paper, 5: "The Fourth Industrial Revolution presents challenges for regulatory systems across the globe, as they struggle to keep pace with rapid, complex technological innovation. [...] We need to act now to maintain our world-beating regulatory system in this period of transformational change"; Klaus Schwab, 'The Fourth Industrial Revolution: What it Means and How to Respond' Foreign Affairs (12 December 2015) https://www.foreignaffairs.com/articles/2015-12-12/fourth-industrial-revolution accessed 2 December 2021; John Gibson, 'Tools for Fourth Industrial Revolution' *C&M Litigation Forecast* (9 January 2019) https://www.crowell.com/files/Litigation-Forecast-2019-Antitrust-Crowell-Moring.pdf accessed 2 December 2021; Matthias Schäfer, 'The Fourth Industrial Revolution: How the EU Can Lead It' (2018) 17(1) European View 5; Katherine Woodhouse, 'South Africa: Competition Regulation and the 4th Industrial Revolution – Finding Some Middle Ground' *Mondaq* (21 August 2019) https://www.mondaq.com/southafrica/antitrust-eu-competition-/838520/competition-regulation-and-the-4th-industrial-revolution-finding-some-middle-ground accessed 2 December 2021; BRICS Competition Law and Policy Centre, 'Digital Era Competition: BRICS View' (Academic Report) (2019), 1295; Alexandre de Streel, 'Should Digital Antitrust Be Ordo-Liberal?' (2020) 18(1) Concurrences: Competition Law Review 2: "History [...] tells us that at the beginning of each industrial revolution, economic power tends to concentrate among the first few firms that master the new technologies. Indeed today, at the dawn of the fourth Industrial Revolution, few big digital

the future economy. The role of the big digital players is compared to the transport infrastructure, and the role of big data is comparable to natural resources in the previous phases of industrial development. This explains the strategic importance of the sector, and the growing engagement in the prima facie purely economic discussions of the geopolitical zero-sum interests and discourses as well as the emergence of the concept of digital sovereignty.[17] The new emphasis of the contestability of the markets as their ability to enable easy entry and exit has been given priority over the conventional vocabulary of competition on the merits as the yardstick for distinguishing good and bad instances of competition.

The DMA is being introduced under Art 114 TFEU, which implies a focus on harmonisation and anti-fragmentation objectives.[18] This also implies that the DMA should not be seen as an explicit extension of the apparatus of *ex-post* competition law, but rather as an instrument of the pursuit of a broader set of EU policies, with competition seen as an indispensable element of the Internal Market, the meaning of which is not exhausted by the provisions of Title VII Chap. 1 TFEU.

Following extensive discussions, the final draft of the Commission's proposal abandoned the original legislative terminology of the "New Competition Tool" (only summarising the outcomes of the public consultation in Part 3 of the Explanatory Memorandum to the DMA).[19] However, even without the name being mentioned explicitly, the DMA is indeed a new competition tool,[20] which aims to bring significant regulatory synergies by introducing new enforcement standards of the targeted, individualised *ex-ante* competition rules, based on, elaborating on and going beyond the fruitful intellectual soil of the traditional *ex-post* competition law.

The vocabulary of "digital markets", preferred over the "new competition tool", may have several advantages and explanations:

(i) as the Act goes further than the rationale of the traditional established *ex-post* competition rules, focusing on a broader set of issues in the digital markets design rather than exclusively on protecting competition in those markets, such terminology is semantically more accurate.

---

conglomerates have accumulated not just important economic but also informational and quasi-regulatory powers. Europe should be particularly worried because most of those conglomerates are based in the US or in China".

[17] Anupam Chander and Haochen Sun, 'Sovereignty 2.0' (2020) 041 University of Hong Kong Faculty of Law Research Paper 3 (7): "[O]bservers generally welcome digital sovereignty efforts by governments in the Global North, but deplore such efforts by governments in the Global South. [...] In the former case, digital sovereignty is recognized as the government protecting citizens—either from foreign governments or corporations. In the latter case, digital sovereignty is seen as the government hijacking the internet to protect itself".

[18] The very functionality of the EU with such a pervasive use of the unanimity rule and proposals for abandoning it is being discussed by EU constitutional law scholars: Bruno De Witte, 'Overcoming the Single Country Veto in EU Reform?' (2020) 5(2) European Papers 983.

[19] COM(2020) 842 final (n 4), 7.

[20] As noted by EVP Vestager in the joint press conference with Commissioner Breton on 15 December 2020, the idea of the NCT has been implemented in the DMA. Indeed, some discrepancies between the leaked version of the NCT early draft and the final DMA proposal—towards the eventual softening of the latter—do not make the very idea of the NCT less important or central.

(ii) this change responds to criticism of the interventionist nature of the proposal and the claims that it goes against the rationale of traditional *ex-ante* competition law. The proposal essentially accepts this rather rhetorical claim of the proponents of the purity of competition law that such targeted proactive interventions are not competition law sensu stricto.[21] Indeed, these interventions are formally justified by the reasons that go beyond the apparatus of competition law. This tactical move mitigates the formal categorical nature of the proposal without compromising on its effectiveness.

(iii) while the addressees of the Act are only gatekeepers—which creates obvious parallels with undertakings with a dominant position—the subject matter of the Act does indeed cover a much broader spectrum of issues. Essentially, the proposal elaborates a long list of areas, the identifying gatekeeping of which would allow the Commission to take a much more proactive role in steering, shaping, designing and policing the evolution of the digital markets. This Act manifests (or at least explicitly allows for) a paradigmatic shift towards a more proactive, more engaged and interventionist enforcement. This is an ideological and strategic, not a merely methodological and tactical choice.

The objective of the DMA is to equip the Commission with more effective tools to deal with the growing socio-economic power of the biggest online players. These stronger, faster and better-calibrated powers of monitoring, controlling and remedying the competition-related side of the problems of unprecedented growth and concentration of the data-driven economy is expected to enable the Commission to play a more proactive role in protecting and promoting EU public interests in the field.

In the spirit of the *ex-post* competition law regulating unilateral conduct, out of thousands of online market players the DMA focuses on a small number of the biggest and most significant for the architecture of the data-driven economy, imposing on them significantly stricter regulatory requirements than on all others. Similarly, in the logic of Art. 102 Treaty on the Functioning of the European Union (TFEU), the DMA acknowledges that the gatekeeping status in itself is neither prohibited nor penalised.[22] The eventual liability of the gatekeepers could be introduced only at the moment of non-compliance with the stricter requirements, not at the moment of their being qualified as gatekeepers. The proposal envisages pecuniary (for first offenders) and structural (for repeated non-compliance) remedies and allows the possibility of a closer look at the eventual acquisitions by the gatekeepers of the undertakings,

[21] The very provision of DMA, art 1(6) makes it clear that "[t]his Regulation is without prejudice to the application of Articles 101 and 102 TFEU".

[22] COM(2020) 842 final (n 4), preamble recital 15: "The fact that a digital service qualifies as a core platform service in light of its widespread and common use and its importance for connecting business users and end users does not as such give rise to sufficiently serious concerns of contestability and unfair practices. It is only when a core platform service constitutes an important gateway and is operated by a provider with a significant impact in the internal market and an entrenched and durable position, or by a provider that will foreseeably have such a position in the near future, that such concerns arise".

the investigation of which would not be initiated under current merger rules as not meeting the necessary thresholds.

The emerging *sui generis* digital competition rules are unique. Comparing them with the liberalisation policy of the early 2000s is only partially correct. The specificity of the liberalisation policy was that the rules were restrictive for the incumbents only with regard to the requirements of providing access to their infrastructure to newcomers; on the other hand, most of the newcomers were the incumbents from other EU jurisdictions themselves, thus achieving the Solomonic solution: Competition was triggered but those who abandoned their monopolistic status were its main beneficiaries on other EU markets. The current wave of regulatory initiatives does not appear to be drafted in the win–win format, targeting the undertakings with gatekeeping status without aiming to offer them any regulatory compensation. Furthermore, the landmark legislative proposal, which constitutes the core of the analysis of this chapter, is characterised by a very nuanced approach, aiming not only to achieve the intended objectives but also to minimise the scope for circumventing the rules.[23] The field is evolving in the broader context of digital constitutionalism[24] as well as digital sovereignty.[25]

[23] Regulating the digital society is a particularly problematic task *inter alia* due to the dynamism of its evolution as well as the unique position of the digital gatekeepers that allows them to interpret most of the legislative initiatives in an opportunistic (though formally legal) way, justifying their actions against competitors. The most remarkable recent example is discussed in e.g. Damien Geradin et al., 'GDPR Myopia: How A Well-Intended Regulation Ended Up Favouring Large Online Platforms – The Case of Ad Tech' (2020) 16(2) European Competition Journal 1: "In an ideal world, the regulatory requirements contained in the GDPR, [...] should deliver the best outcome for society in terms of enhancing the privacy of individuals without undermining other components of social welfare, such as competition, investment and innovation. However, [...] while the GDPR has delivered positive outcomes by enhancing the protection afforded to users of digital services and strengthening the rights of data subjects, it has also had adverse effects on competition by strengthening the position of large online platforms on digital markets [...] This is what we understand by 'GDPR Myopia': in its effort to improve the protection of data subjects, the GDPR worsened one of the main problems experienced in digital markets today, which is increased market concentration and reduced contestability. In addition, the GDPR seems to have given large platforms a tool to harm rivals by reducing access to the data they need to run their business".

[24] Giovanni De Gregorio, 'The Rise of Digital Constitutionalism in the European Union' (2021) 19(1) International Journal of Constitutional Law 41: "In the last twenty years, the policy of the European Union in the field of digital technologies has shifted from a liberal economic perspective to a constitution-oriented approach. This change of heart has resulted primarily from the rise of the information society which has created not only new opportunities but also challenges to fundamental rights and democratic values. Even more importantly, this technological framework driven by liberal ideas has empowered transnational corporations operating in the digital environment to perform quasi-public functions on a global scale".

[25] Chander and Sun, 'Sovereignty 2.0' (n 17) 8: "When Thomas Hobbes imagined an "Artificial Man" in the form of a state, [...] he was not picturing Facebook. But the reality is that modern leviathans like Facebook and Google, and even Reddit and Twitter, exercise enormous power over our lives. Increasingly, governments across the world have sought to bring these companies under their control. While China pioneered data sovereignty, it is now the demand of governments from Australia to Zimbabwe. The era of countries unsure whether they had the power to regulate the internet is over".

4 Ukraine's Adaptation to the New Reality

While there was never a genuine international consensus on the role and function of competition policy, there was definitely an illusion of such a consensus. The universal glue keeping all antitrust paradoxes together was neoclassical microeconomics. The omnipotent and omnipresent price theory in tandem with the omnipotent and omnipresent sophisticated mathematics was able to reduce the whole spectrum of economic life to the simple calculable common denominator of the rational choice, underpinned by robust, technical econometric modelling: A perfect harmony of simplicity and technicality, the harmony creating an illusion of scientific truth—reassuring, universal, stable, reliable, but also illusionary, reductionist and confusing.[26] For decades opposition to this regulatory idyll was raised either by heterodox economics or the conservative side of the legal profession. The former was successfully marginalised; the latter colonised and modified into an interdisciplinary hybrid of law and economics. The discussion about the policy as well as the policy itself became autonomous, self-sufficient, self-centred and self-referential. Any external interference in competition discussions was seen as obscuring the clarity of the metrics and spoiling the purity of the analysis. The small communicative channels for non-competition interests and non-competition metrics remain shallow and excessively complex for navigation. Competition evangelism reporting success after success with over a hundred new jurisdictions adopting competition laws became the reassuring indicator of the globalised, end-of-history scientific competition movement; the independence of the national competition authorities from government interference (and discussion) became the undisputable benchmark of the successful implementation of the objective, neutral, evidence-based policy.

Competition law was diagnosed as suffering from an excessive vagueness. The authoritative remedy prescribed by the leading minds in the field was a broader and a more systematic use of microeconomic price-oriented theories. Law and economics is an apotheosis of such a theory. It is a universalist toolkit, capable of calculating any societal phenomenon: From love to astrophysics. Calculability implies clarity and scientific unambiguity, needed so much in a field characterised by its excessive vagueness. Relative vagueness is a part of the interpretative and relatively indeterminate nature of law. The very phenomenon of economic competition is equally interpretative and indeterminate in its very nature. Under the currently dominant approach to competition law, these two ontological features of the discipline are perceived as being its two fundamental shortcomings. In reality, however, these are the main advantages of the emerging digital competition law.[27]

---

[26] Oles Andriychuk, 'Between Microeconomics and Geopolitics: On the Reasonable Application of Competition Law' (2021) 84 Modern Law Review 1.

[27] Oles Andriychuk, 'Will the DMA deliver? On Carrots and Sticks (and Some Magic Tricks)' *Chillin'Competition* (20 October 2021) https://chillingcompetition.com/2021/10/26/chillincompetition-dma-symposium-will-the-dma-deliver-on-carrots-and-sticks-and-some-magic-tricks-by-oles-andriychuk/ accessed 2 December 2021.

The digital society can be characterised by a number of systemic features, changing which may be possible either with radical interventionism or by the evolutionary emergence and maturing of the new trends. None of these options is within the mandate and scope of competition law. Even its proactive regulatory shift (at least in democratic societies) would go beyond shaping the format of the markets and should never be used for promoting its specific participants. Equally unrealistic and futile may sound the enthusiasm of those who believe that the regulatory rules are capable of reconfiguring the systemic features of the digital economy.[28] Gatekeepers possess incomparably greater knowledge and expertise than those who aim to re-channel their most successful business practices. The changes are likely to be only temporary, tactical and marginal; not permanent, strategic and systemic.

The proactive mode implies not merely the protection of competition from the established infringements, but also the greater engagement of public authorities in designing the specific features of the markets. The traces of the trend can be seen in the mechanism of commitments introduced during the modernisation reform in 2003.[29] Following the preliminary assessment of the Commission, the potential infringer may offer specific remedies that would meet the concerns expressed by the Commission. The main function of this mechanism, however, is related to restoring the problem, and the Commission is not in the position to negotiate the specificities of the commitments: It either accepts them or not. The situation is fundamentally advanced by the DMA proposal. The catalogue of the obligations envisaged by Art. 6 DMA is very broad, and the addressees of the rules—the gatekeepers—may enter into a regulatory dialogue with the Commission, discussing their calibration for each specific gatekeeper. Such a modality shift allows for a significantly more proactive role of the enforcer.

In the light of the paradigmatic transformation of EU competition rules, it is important for Ukraine to capture the spirit of the current reforms. It should also start exploring the avenues for introducing comparable legislation. Even more so, the trend is not limited to the EU. Equally proactive robust initiatives are being

---

[28] Pablo Ibáñez Colomo, 'Will the DMA deliver on its Promises? Part I: substantive aspects (or markets do not become contestable by decree)' *Chillin'Competition* (20 October 2021) https://chillingcompetition.com/2021/10/20/will-the-dma-deliver-on-its-promises-part-i-substantive-aspects-or-markets-do-not-become-contestable-by-decree/ accessed 2 December 2021.

[29] Council of the European Union, 'Council Regulation (EC) No 1/2003 of 16 December 2002 on the implementation of the rules on competition laid down in Articles 81 and 82 of the Treaty' (2002) Official Journal of the European Communities L 1/9, art 9.

discussed in many other jurisdictions.[30] In Germany, they are being implemented.[31] The reforms have been conceptualised theoretically[32] and practically.[33] The new rules are being proposed in the UK,[34] the EU[35] and the US.[36] This is an objective shift of paradigmatic importance, which is still neither reflected upon nor even taken into consideration in the Ukrainian context.

Against the background of a significant underperformance in terms of developing its competition regime in line with the current development, Ukraine is simultaneously focused on mastering policies which are directly relevant neither to the conceptual foundations of economic competition in general nor to the situation of competition law in particular.

Digital competition is an emerging area which raises myriad of challenges and offers numerous opportunities not only to undertakings and end users but also to polities. Each country develops a unique approach to addressing this issue. Such an

---

[30] Australian Competition and Consumer Commission 'Digital Advertising Services Inquiry' (Final Report) (2021); UK Competition and Market Authority, 'Online Platforms and Digital Advertising Market Study' (Final Report) (2020); European Parliament, 'Online advertising: the impact of targeted advertising on advertisers, market access and consumer choice' (Commissioned Report) (2021); French Competition Authority, Decision 21-D-11 (2021); The Parliament of the Commonwealth of Australia, House of Representatives, 'News Media and Digital Platforms Mandatory Bargaining Code Act', Act No. 21, 2 March 2021; See above BRICS Competition Law and Policy Centre, 'Digital Era Competition: BRICS View' (Academic Report) (2019), 1295 (n 16).

[31] German Act to amend the Act against Restraints of Competition for a Focused, Proactive and Digital Competition Law 4.0 and Other Competition Law Provisions, 18 January 2021.

[32] Pablo Ibáñez Colomo, 'The Draft Digital Markets Act: A Legal and Institutional Analysis' (2021) 12(7) Journal of European Competition Law & Practice 576; Niamh Dunne, 'The Role of Regulation in EU Competition Law Assessment'(2021) 44(3) World Competition 287; Martin Eifert et al., 'Taming the Giants: The DMA/DSA Package' (2021) 58(4) Common Markets Law Review 987; Philipp Bongartz et al., 'The Digital Markets Act: Moving from Competition Law to Regulation for Large Gatekeepers' (2021) 10(2) Journal of European Consumer and Market Law 60; Pierre Larouche and Alexandre de Streel, 'The European Digital Markets Act: A Revolution Grounded on Traditions'(2021) 12(7) Journal of European Competition Law & Practice 542; Nicolas Petit, 'The Proposed Digital Markets Act (DMA): A Legal and Policy Review' (2021) 12(7) Journal of European Competition Law & Practice 529; Assimakis Komninos, 'The Digital Markets Act and Private Enforcement: Proposals for an Optimal System of Enforcement', Concurrences, 2022, Forthcoming; Giorgio Monti, 'The Digital Markets Act – Institutional Design and Suggestions for Improvement' (2021) (2021–04) TILEC Discussion Paper 1; Peter Georg Picht and Heiko Richter, 'The Proposed EU Digital Services Regulation 2020: Data Desiderata' (2021) 21 Max Planck Institute for Innovation & Competition Research.

[33] For a full catalogue of the reports analysing the situation on digital markets and the ways of reforming competition rules, see the University of Chicago Stigler Centre database: https://www.chicagobooth.edu/research/stigler/events/antitrust-competition-conference/world-reports-on-digital-markets accessed 2 December 2021.

[34] UK Department for Digital, Culture, Media & Sport and Department for Business, Energy & Industrial Strategy, 'A New Pro–Competition Regime for Digital Markets' (Report) (2021).

[35] COM(2020) 842 final (n 4).

[36] H.R.3816 – American Choice and Innovation Online Act, Bill referred to the House Committee on the Judiciary, 11 June 2021; H.R.3825 – Ending Platform Monopolies Act, Bill referred to the House Committee on the Judiciary, 11 June 2021; H.R.3826 – Platform Competition and Opportunity Act of 2021, Bill referred to the House Committee on the Judiciary, 11 June 2021.

approach takes into account the macroeconomic interests of this country, the role of its undertakings and industries in the global digital supply chain, mechanisms and processes that could be triggered or limited by competition law.[37]

Another example of a policy requiring reconceptualisation is Ukraine's current approach and its obligations vis-à-vis the mechanism of state aid.[38]

While the wordings of Arts. 101 and 107 TFEU both refer to actions restricting competition and declare these actions to be incompatible with the internal market, the ontology of the mechanism of state aid—unlike the ontology of the mechanism of the prohibition of anticompetitive agreements—concerns competition only peripherally. The main ontology, the main essence and the main logic of state aid control is the protection and promotion of the Internal Market, making it more homogeneous and centralised. The interest of protecting competition is used mainly as a concurrent proxy.

The argument underpinning the proposition that the economic phenomenon of state aid is inseparably linked to the idea of market integration, not economic competition, is threefold:

First, no other jurisdiction—however diverse, autonomous and heterogeneous its different regions may be—operates an established and robust mechanism of protecting its undertakings from anticompetitive regional aid. Arguably such regional aid may be as harmful for competition as the aid granted by the EU Member States to domestic undertakings. Evidently, it is never anticompetitive enough to trigger the adoption of federal state aid rules. The situation in the EU (qua primarily economic polity) is fundamentally different, as the main objective of the mechanism of state aid control is the protection and cementing of the Internal Market (with protection of competition as a positive but adjacent effect). In other words, it is fundamentally different because of the overarching objective of market integration, and not because European undertakings benefit and suffer from state aid more than undertakings in other jurisdictions.

The second aspect of the argument is apagogical: If the overarching rationale of state aid were indeed the protection of competition, the values and interests of such EU initiatives as—for example—the European Green Deal would harm competition, as they would provide a disproportionate advantage to sectors, countries and regions with higher green awareness and pedigree, thereby increasing the technological gap between the greener and the redder territories. If the main rationale of state aid is market integration rather than competition, it is logically acceptable to shift the priority from the objective of homogeneity (market integration) to the qualitative features of the Internal Market (market greening). This trade-off would be much

[37] Harry First, 'Digital Platforms and Competition Policy in Developing Countries' (2021) 19(2) Concurrences: Competition Law Review 3: "The power of platforms is not just a first world problem, however, but is also an issue of importance for competition policy in developing countries. These platforms present different costs and benefits for developing countries than for developed countries; in particular, the major big tech platforms have become important tools for further digital platform innovation in developing economies".

[38] See Ksenia Smyrnova, 'The "Europeanization" of Competition Law in Ukraine' in this Volume.

more difficult to explain and justify should the overarching objective of state aid control be in fact protection of competition rather than market integration.

Third, even if the above two propositions are not sufficiently convincing, state aid is neither a central nor an essential mechanism of Ukraine competition policy. The focus should be placed on shaping markets in general, and digital/energy markets in particular, in the light of the broader societal context. This context has hitherto been acknowledged as far as the ethos of the privatisation of economic life of Ukraine was concerned. Such an approach is important indeed, given Ukraine's tragic legacy of the USSR with its radical distortion of the mechanisms and principles of the market economy. In the bipolar world, such a revision implied a categorical counter-narrative: The role of state intervention is characterised as harmful by default.[39] Implementing this categorical counter-narrative into Ukraine competition policy implies that pretty much any instance of state aid is considered to be against the principles of the market economy. In times of polycentricity and the convergence of ideological polarities, discussions on the role of national champions and the global digital race, Ukraine has to reconsider its approach to the prohibition of state aid, making it more nuanced and context-dependent.[40]

Two avenues require articulation in this respect: (i) a decision must be made whether Ukraine has realistic chances to join the EU in the short-or medium-term perspective. If the answer is positive, then the mechanism of state aid has to continue to be developed in unison with EU development—as a matter of the approximation of laws. Otherwise, the Ukraine competition regime should give priorities to the much more urgent and central areas of competition law than protecting (usually) big (usually) foreign (usually) corporations from any state interventions, and aim to shape some of its industrial policies—a legitimate and indispensable function of every government in every country; (ii) the rationale of state aid should be removed from competition policy and allocated to international trade policy—in line with Ukraine's commitments within the World Trade Organisation and trade agreements with individual jurisdictions. Co-opting state aid into the area of competition makes little sense in a context other than the EU (or economic unions of a similar level of integration). What is currently considered to be a state aid mechanism should be treated within the antidumping, subsidies and foreign direct investment matrix.[41]

This delusional approach of incorporating the worst elements of both orthodoxies (the legacy of the USSR-style planned economy and the remedy of reductionist non-interventionism of the Chicago School) goes far beyond the mechanism of state aid (and the scope of this contribution). The most important of these appears to be a reconceptualisation of the relationship between competition law, IP and innovation.

---

[39] See Oleg Podtserkovnyi 'Legal Support of State Economic Policies of Ukraine in the Context of Investment Development and Protection of Competition' in this Volume.

[40] Kseniia Smyrnova and Erika Szyszczak, 'Modern Approaches to State Aid: Ukraine' (2020) 8(1) European State Aid Law Quarterly 8.

[41] See Zvenyslava Opeida, 'Competition and International Trade: Complementing Trade Defense Policy with Effective Competition Policy in Ukraine' in this Volume.

Many universally acknowledged shortcomings of the digital society are underpinned by robust innovation.[42]

5 Outlook: Towards a Genetically Modified Competition Policy

The fundamental question for Ukraine is how much of the logic and the mechanism of the new digital competition rules it is capable of implementing. The implementation should not be done mechanistically. It is not a box-ticking activity. The new rules imply a much more proactive approach to the digital markets. The new rules also imply a paradigmatic recalibration of the very understanding of the role and function of the enforcer in the digital economy.

Ukraine is also in need of a revision and update of its regulatory philosophy concerning the digital markets. It must be synchronised with the current processes taking place in the EU. This paper aims to articulate the key features of the reform of digital competition policy currently taking place in the EU. This has been done by summarising the key novelties of the DMA proposal and explaining the macroeconomic preconditions necessitating the reform and the implications for the future functioning of digital services in the digital markets.

References

Oles Andriychuk, 'A New Pro-Competition Regime for Digital Markets: Individual Response to Public Consultation by Oles Andriychuk' (2021) Centre for Internet Law and Policy University of Strathclyde

Oles Andriychuk, 'Between Microeconomics and Geopolitics: On the Reasonable Application of Competition Law' (2021) 84 Modern Law Review

Oles Andriychuk, 'Will the DMA deliver? On Carrots and Sticks (and some magic tricks)' Chillin' Competition (20 October 2021) https://chillingcompetition.com/2021/10/26/chillincompetition-dma-symposium-will-the-dma-deliver-on-carrots-and-sticks-and-some-magic-tricks-by-oles-andriychuk/

Oles Andriychuk, 'Shaping the New Modality of the Digital Markets: The Impact of the DSA/DMA Proposals on InterPlatform Competition' (2021) 44(3) World Competition

[42] Oles Andriychuk, 'A New Pro-Competition Regime for Digital Markets: Individual Response to Public Consultation by Oles Andriychuk' (2021) Centre for Internet Law and Policy University of Strathclyde, 4: "Innovation is a term having various overlapping meanings and dimensions. There is no single objective metric for measuring innovation. The key question is who benefits from the innovation? Is innovation evolving in the direction expected by the enforcer? What type of innovation should [… we] accept? Is it the innovation in delivering a greater online experience for end users? Their greater experience from engaging more comprehensively in filter-bubbles and echo-chambers? Is it the innovation in developing more advanced and robust tailoring and matching expertise? Is it the innovation in improving surveillance techniques of the Digital Panopticon?".

Philipp Bongartz, Rupprecht Podszun and Sarah Langenstein, 'The Digital Markets Act: Moving from Competition Law to Regulation for Large Gatekeepers' (2021) (1082) Journal of European Consumer and Market Law

Anupam Chander and Haochen Sun, 'Sovereignty 2.0' (2021) (041) University of Hong Kong Faculty of Law Research Paper

Niamh Dunne, 'The Role of Regulation in EU Competition Law Assessment' (2021) 44(3) World Competition

Martin Eifert, Axel Metzger, Heike Schweitzer and Gerhard Wagner, 'Taming the Giants: The DMA/DSA Package' (2021) 58(4) Common Markets Law Review

Ariel Ezrachi, 'Sponge' (2016) 5(1) Journal of Antitrust Enforcement

Harry First, 'Digital Platforms and Competition Policy in Developing Countries' (2021) 19(2) Concurrences: Competition Law Review

Damien Geradin, Theano Karanikioti and Dimitrios Katsifis, 'GDPR Myopia: How A Well-Intended Regulation Ended Up Favouring Large Online Platforms—The Case of Ad Tech' (2020) 16(2–3) European Competition Journal

John Gibson, 'Tools for Fourth Industrial Revolution' *C&M Litigation Forecast* (9 January 2019) https://www.crowell.com/files/Litigation-Forecast-2019-Antitrust-Crowell-Moring.pdf2021

Giovanni de Gregorio, 'The Rise of Digital Constitutionalism in the European Union' (2021)19(1) International Journal of Constitutional Law

Pablo Ibáñez Colomo, 'Will the DMA deliver on its Promises? Part I: substantive aspects (or markets do not become contestable by decree)' Chillin'Competition (20 October 2021) https://chillingcompetition.com/2021/10/20/will-the-dma-deliver-on-its-promises-part-i-substantive-aspects-or-markets-do-not-become-contestable-by-decree/

Pablo Ibáñez Colomo, 'The Draft Digital Markets Act: A Legal and Institutional Analysis'(2021) 12(7) Journal of European Competition Law & Practice

Alexey Ivanov, 'Digital Era Competition: A BRICS View' in Ioannis Lianos (ed), *Competition Law for the Digital Era: A Complex Systems' Perspective* (BRICS Competition Law and Policy Centre 2019)

Assimakis Komninos, 'The Digital Markets Act and Private Enforcement: Proposals for an Optimal System of Enforcement', in Eleanor M. Fox Liber Amicorum, Antitrust Ambassador to the World (Concurrences, 2021) https://ssrn.com/abstract=3914932

Pierre Larouche and Alexandre de Streel, 'The European Digital Markets Act: A Revolution Grounded on Traditions' (2021) 12(7) Journal of European Competition Law & Practice

Ioannis Lianos, 'Polycentric Competition Law' (2018) 71(1) Current Legal Problems

Stavros Makris, 'Openness and Integrity in Antitrust' (2021) 17(1) Journal of Competition Law & Economics

Giorgio Monti, 'The Digital Markets Act—Institutional Design and Suggestions for Improvement' (2021) (2021–04) TILEC Discussion Paper

Open Forum Academy, 'Interoperability as a Tool for Competition Regulation' (Report) 2020

Peter G Picht and Heiko Richter, 'The Proposed EU Digital Services Regulation 2020: Data Desiderata' (2021) 21–21 Max Planck Institute for Innovation & Competition Research Paper

Nicolas Petit, 'The Proposed Digital Markets Act (DMA): A Legal and Policy Review' (2021) 12(7) European Competition Law & Practice

Richard Posner, 'The Decline of Law as an Autonomous Discipline: 1962–1987' (1987) 100(4) Harvard Law Review

Matthias Schäfer, 'The Fourth Industrial Revolution: How the EU Can Lead It' (2018) 18(1) European View

Klaus Schwab, 'The Fourth Industrial Revolution: What It Means and How to Respond' *World Economic Forum* (14 January 2016) https://www.weforum.org/agenda/2016/01/the-fourth-industrial-revolution-what-it-means-and-how-to-respond/

Kseniia Smyrnova and Erika Szyszczak, 'Modern Approaches to State Aid: Ukraine' (2020) 8(1)

Alexandre de Streel, 'Should Digital Antitrust Be Ordo-Liberal?' (2020) 18(1) Concurrences: Competition Law Review

Bruno de Witte, 'Overcoming the Single Country Veto in EU Reform?' (2020) 5(2) European Papers
Katherine Woodhouse, 'South Africa: Competition Regulation and the 4th Industrial Revolution – Finding Some Middle Ground' *Mondaq* (21 August 2019) https://www.mondaq.com/southafrica/antitrust-eu-competition-/838520/competition-regulation-and-the-4th-industrial-revolution-finding-some-middle-ground

The Intersection Between Intellectual Property and Competition Laws in the Pharmaceutical Sector: A Ukrainian Perspective

Olga Gurgula

Contents

Abstract Robust protection of competition is particularly important in the field of pharmaceuticals as this may help to improve access to affordable medicines and foster medical innovation. While the Antimonopoly Committee of Ukraine (AMCU) has undertaken certain activities in the pharmaceutical sector aimed at combating price increases, these activities do not cover practices that rely on intellectual property (IP) rights that may have a negative effect on the pharmaceutical market. The aim of this chapter is to explore the current competition law approach to IP-related practices in Ukraine. It will discuss certain exemptions related to IP agreements and will suggest that the current competition law rules may require clarification. Specifically, to ensure that only genuinely procompetitive IP agreements are allowed, it will

---

O. Gurgula (✉)
Brunel Law School, Brunel University London, Uxbridge, UK
e-mail: Olga.Gurgula@brunel.ac.uk

H. Richter (ed.), *Competition and Intellectual Property Law in Ukraine*,
MPI Studies on Intellectual Property and Competition Law 31,
https://doi.org/10.1007/978-3-662-66101-7_9

be suggested that it may be necessary to develop specific guidance on the correct interpretation of the law and its application to IP-related agreements. By way of example, the chapter will discuss anticompetitive IP-related agreements that are unique to the pharmaceutical industry, i.e. “pay-for-delay” agreements. While such agreements have not been the subject of investigation by the AMCU, they have attracted particular attention in the European Union (EU) and the US. The chapter will discuss the approaches for assessing such agreements developed in the EU and the US, and will provide some recommendations that, it is believed, will help to create more effective competition law enforcement in the field of pharmaceuticals for the benefit of Ukrainian patients. The discussion in this Chapter, while focusing on Ukraine, may also be useful to other jurisdictions that seek to improve their competition law enforcement in the field of IP to facilitate access to medicines.

1 Intersection Between IP Law and Competition Policy in the Pharmaceutical Industry

1.1 The Role of IP Law and Competition Policy in Incentivising Innovation

Intellectual property (IP) law is closely intertwined with competition law. The essential features of IP rights are that they confer upon their owners certain exclusivities that enable them to behave in a particular way. Taking patents as an example, patents provide exclusive rights to their holders, allowing them to prevent others from exploiting patented inventions without their consent. In other words, patent holders are able to prevent their competitors from marketing a product protected by the patent.[1] This, in turn, allows them to charge supra-competitive prices for a limited period.[2] In the past, due to these characteristics IP rights were considered to be in conflict with competition law.[3] This is because, while IP rights create monopoly, which was seen to be contrary to competition, competition law favours free entry and asset mobility, which IP rights limit in order to create incentives.[4] However, more recently this view has been revised and these two bodies of laws are now seen as complimentary: both IP and competition laws aim at incentivising innovation, although they achieve this aim through different means. From the IP law perspective, a temporary monopoly is justified by the need to reward inventors for their innovative efforts, allowing them to recoup investments and gain profit, as well as

[1] See e.g. EGC, Case T-321/05 *AstraZeneca AB v. European Commission* (2010) EU:T:2010:266, para 362 (the possession of an exclusive right “normally results in keeping competitors away, since public regulations require them to respect that exclusive right”).

[2] OECD, ‘Licensing of IP Rights and Competition Law’ DAF/COMP (2019) 3, 8.

[3] Herbert J Hovenkamp, ‘Intellectual Property and Competition’ (2019) Faculty Scholarship at Penn Law 1807, 1.

[4] Ibid.

providing further incentives to innovate. From the competition law perspective, while it generally condemns practices of monopolists that restrain competition, the grant of this exclusivity is seen as a just balance between competing interests of patent and competition laws. On the one hand, the exclusive right granted by the patent system allows the rightholder to prevent the invention from being copied and thus blocks competition by imitation (price competition); this, in turn, facilitates innovation in the form of developing alternative products and thus generates competition by substitution (dynamic competition).[5]

While preventing competitors from using the IP-protected technologies and thus gaining a competitive advantage is typically considered to be a lawful exercise of the IP rights, some IP-related practices may be considered anticompetitive as they significantly impede competition and harm consumer welfare. This raises the question of when competition law should cease to "tolerate" the exercise of the exclusive IP rights. As could be seen from the activities of the competition authorities in the EU and the US, practices in which IP rights are used as an "instrument of abuse" or as a tool for restricting competition[6] may raise competition law concerns and, thus, need intervening. It is this type of practice by pharmaceutical companies that will be analysed in this Chapter.

1.2 Competition Law as a Tool for Improving Access to Medicines

Robust protection of competition is especially important in the field of pharmaceuticals. Active competition law enforcement in this sector may help, under certain conditions, to foster innovation in the pharmaceutical sector, as well as facilitate better access to affordable medicines. It is also widely acknowledged that competition law can supplement other tools that are aimed at promoting innovation and

[5] Andreas Heinemann 'Abusive Filing of IP Rights' in Duncan Matthews and Herbert Zech (eds), *Research Handbook on Intellectual Property and the Life Sciences* (Edward Elgar Publishing Ltd 2017) 479; See also Max Planck Institute for Intellectual Property and Competition Law, 'Copyright, Competition and Development' (Report), 2013, 5: "both IP law and competition law are designed to promote a system that creates incentives for dynamic competition [...] by excluding competition by imitation and enhancing competition by substitution".

[6] Steven D Anderman and Hedvig Schmidt, *EU Competition Law and Intellectual Property Rights: The Regulation of Innovation* (Oxford University Press 2011) 6 (referring to ECJ C-85/76 *Hoffman-La Roche v. Commission* (1979) ECLI:EU:C:1979:36, para 51, and ECJ C-262/81 *Coditel SA v. Cine-Vog Films SA and others (Coditel II)* (1982) ECLI:EU:C:1982:334, para 14.

improving access.[7] The UN High Level Panel on Access to Medicines has emphasised the importance of using competition law.[8] It finds that "competition policies are important levers that governments can employ to ensure that health technologies markets operate competently and that the public benefits from low prices and innovation."[9] The need for greater use of competition law to facilitate access to medicines has also been highlighted by the Global Commission on HIV and the Law, stating that "countries must proactively use other areas of law and policy, such as competition law, price control policy and procurement law which can help increase access to pharmaceutical products."[10] More recently, South Africa and China have initiated a discussion on "Intellectual Property and the Public Interest: Promoting Public Health Through Competition Law and Policy" at the World Trade Organization (WTO) Council for TRIPS.[11] They urged Members "to share their national experiences and examples of how competition law is used to achieve public health and related national objectives."[12]

While robust competition may facilitate pharmaceutical innovation and access to medicines, restrictions of competition may have the opposite effect. In particular, certain IP-related practices by originators[13] aiming to prolong the commercial life of their existing successful products have attracted the attention of competition authorities in different jurisdictions. For example, in 2008 the European Commission undertook a major investigation into the pharmaceutical sector with a specific focus on patent strategies.[14] It identified a number of such strategies it described as aiming "to extend the breadth and duration of [originators'] patent protection"[15] and "to delay or block the market entry of generic medicine."[16] These include, *inter*

---

[7] UNDP, 'Using Competition Law to Promote Access to Medicines and Related Health Technologies in Low- and Middle-Income Countries' *UNDP* (7 December 2017) https://www.undp.org/publications/using-competition-law-promote-access-medicines-and-related-health-technologies-low-and accessed 27 December 2021.

[8] United Nations Secretary-General's High-Level Panel on Access to Medicine, 'Promoting Innovation and Access to Health Technologies' (Report), 2016.

[9] Ibid 24.

[10] UNDP, 'Global Commission on HIV and the Law: Risk, Rights and Health' (Report) 87, 2012.

[11] World Trade Organization, 'Intellectual Property and the Public Interest: Promoting Public Health Through Competition Law and Policy: Communication from China and South Africa' (Communication) IP/C/W/643, 2018.

[12] Ibid para 9.

[13] European Commission, 'Pharmaceutical Sector Inquiry' (Final Report), 2009, 9 ('"Originator company" is defined as a company that sells originators', while '"Originator" is defined as a novel drug that was under patent protection when launched onto the market').

[14] Ibid.

[15] European Commission, 'Executive Summary of the Pharmaceutical Sector Inquiry Report' (Communication) COM(2007)165, 2009, 10.

[16] European Commission, 'Pharmaceutical Sector Inquiry' (Final Report) 2009 (n 13) 7–8 ('"Generic company" is defined as a company that sells generics', while '"Generic" is defined as a medicinal product which has the same qualitative and quantitative composition in active substances and the same pharmaceutical form as a reference (originator) medicinal product and whose bioequivalence with the reference medicinal product has been demonstrated').

alia, such practices as "pay-for-delay" agreements, life-cycle management strategies, sham litigation, divisional patent applications and strategic patenting.[17] These practices have the capacity not only to increase drug prices, making them unaffordable for patients, but also may affect dynamic competition by stifling innovation of both originators and generic companies.[18]

1.3 Access to Medicines in Ukraine and the Importance of Robust Competition Law Enforcement

A 2018 World Health Organisation (WHO) study revealed that public spending on health as a share of GDP had been consistently low in Ukraine, i.e. in 2014 it fell from a peak of 3.8–2.9% and remained at this level in 2015.[19] Until very recently, there was no system for public reimbursement of prescription medicines in the outpatient sector in Ukraine and, thus, patients provided with prescriptions had to buy medicines in pharmacies and pay their full cost out of pocket.[20] As a result, spending on medicines has been the main driver of financial hardship for Ukrainian citizens, representing 46% of out-of-pocket payments among all households, and accounting for 69% of household spending for the poorest.[21] A similar situation exists in relation to inpatient treatment.[22] While the regional budgets cover the procurement and provision of certain inpatient medicines, constant underfunding and inefficiencies result in only a small share of the inpatient budget being spent on medicines.[23] This means that patients have to buy their medicines and other supplies in hospitals.[24]

The first pilot scheme that introduced the public reimbursement for prescription drugs to patients in the outpatient setting, which covered only antihypertensive medicines, was launched by the Ministry of Health only in 2012–2013.[25] This project was carried on until the allocated funds were exhausted.[26] More recently, in 2017,

---

[17] Olga Gurgula, 'Strategic Patenting by Pharmaceutical Companies—Should Competition Law Intervene?' (2020) 51 International Review of Intellectual Property and Competition Law 1062.

[18] Ibid 1071.

[19] World Health Organisation, 'Can People Afford to Pay for Health Care? Ukraine' (Review), World Health Organisation 2018 (this is considerably below the average for countries in the WHO European Region (5%) and the European Union (6%)).

[20] Ibid 9 (in 2017, 96% of people who were prescribed outpatient medicines paid for them out of pocket). See also Tetiana Stepurko et al., 'Informal Payments for Health Care Services: The Case of Lithuania, Poland and Ukraine' (2015) 6(1) Journal of Eurasian Studies 46–58.

[21] World Health Organisation 'Evaluation of The Affordable Medicines Programme in Ukraine' (Report) WHO 2019, 3.

[22] WHO 2018 (n19) 9.

[23] Ibid.

[24] Ibid. See also Oksana Kashyntseva, 'Patent Law and Access to Medicines in Ukraine' in this Volume.

[25] WHO 2019 (n 21) 2.

[26] Ibid.

Ukraine launched the Affordable Medicines Programme (AMP), which is considered to be one of the key components of the healthcare system reform.[27] The AMP introduced public coverage for some outpatient medicines, in particular, for patients diagnosed with cardiovascular diseases, type 2 diabetes and bronchial asthma (it initially covered 23 international non-proprietary names). In 2021, the programme was broadened to include a number of treatments for several additional chronic diseases, and it currently covers cardiovascular diseases, several types of diabetes, prevention of strokes and heart attacks, bronchial asthma, mental and behavioral disorders and epilepsy.[28] The treatment for all other diseases continues to be covered by patients out-of-pocket.

In the light of the insufficient state support of patients in providing access to medicines, controlling business strategies that affect drug prices is of paramount importance in Ukraine. In this regard, as was mentioned, competition law can play a key role in facilitating access to medicines, as well as incentivising pharmaceutical innovation. However, while some countries have successfully used competition law, it is an underutilised tool in the field of healthcare in many jurisdictions, including in Ukraine.[29] The Ukrainian competition authority, the Antimonopoly Committee of Ukraine (AMCU), has been relatively active in the pharmaceutical sector, but its investigations have been focused on a small number of abusive practices by stakeholders, and it has not yet dealt with any IP-related practices by pharmaceutical companies that may have a negative effect on the market and consumers. This may be because the AMCU, due to the limited resources it possesses, has been prioritising those cases it considers the most significant. However, it may also be due to an insufficient understanding of the role that the IP plays in this field. Therefore, guidance on specific IP-related anticompetitive practices in this sector, as well as studying the approaches to the assessment of such practices in mature competition law jurisdictions, including the EU and the US, may be required. This will, on the one hand, draw the attention of the AMCU to such practices, while on the other hand assisting in their appropriate analysis.

This chapter, therefore, will first discuss the anticompetitive practices that have been the main focus of the AMCU's investigative activities in the pharmaceutical sector to date. It will then explain the Ukrainian competition law rules, focusing on anticompetitive agreements and specific exemptions concerning IP-related agreements, as well as a new technology transfer block exemption regulation adopted in 2018. It will be suggested that the application of these provisions with respect to IP-related agreements may need to be clarified and may require the development of specific guidance by the AMCU on their correct interpretation. Such guidance will ensure that only genuinely procompetitive IP agreements are allowed, while also

---

[27] Ibid 4.

[28] Ministry of Health Decree No. 2077 on the Approval of the Register of Medicines which are Subject to Reimbursement under the Programme of State Guarantee of Provision of Medical Services for the Population, as of 1 October 2021, 27 September 2021.

[29] Duncan Matthews and Olga Gurgula, 'Patent Strategies and Competition Law in the Pharmaceutical Sector: Implications for Access to Medicines' (2016) 38(11) European Intellectual Property Review 661.

preventing pharmaceutical companies from relying on the exemptions provided by the law to immunise anticompetitive agreements that stifle competition and harm consumer welfare. The chapter will discuss a specific example of anticompetitive IP-related agreements that is unique to the pharmaceutical sector, namely "pay-for-delay" agreements, and the approaches to the competition law assessment of such agreements taken by the competition authorities in the EU and the US. Finally, it will provide some recommendations to the AMCU, which, it is believed, will help to create a more effective competition law enforcement in the field of pharmaceuticals for the benefit of Ukrainian patients.

2 The Pharmaceutical Market in Ukraine and Recent Activities of the AMCU in This Field

2.1 The Structure of the Pharmaceutical (Supply) Market in Ukraine

As of the end of 2020, the total volume of the pharmaceutical market amounted to 2.2 billion USD.[30] The Ukrainian pharmaceutical sector is characterised by a fair share of domestic production[31] and is dominated (in both volume and value) by generic medicines.[32] At the same time, according to the 2020 AMCU analysis, 70% of medicines in circulation in Ukraine are imported, and domestic medicines are mostly made from raw materials imported to Ukraine.[33] This makes the market dependent on the import, and the price of both imported and domestic drugs dependent on fluctuations in the exchange rate of the Ukrainian hryvnia to foreign currency.[34]

According to the type of activities at different levels of the system that supplies medicines ready for use by Ukrainians, the AMCU identifies several groups, which include local producers of medical products, representatives of foreign producers, importers (distributors), wholesalers and retail.[35] The participants in the medicine supply chain act on different product markets.[36] At the level of production/import of

---

[30] 'The Ukrainian Pharmaceutical Market in 2020 Grew by 13%'—Experts' *Interfax* (31 March 2021) https://ua.interfax.com.ua/news/press-conference/734294.html accessed 27 December 2021.

[31] WHO 2019, (n 21) 2.

[32] Ibid.

[33] AMCU, 'Recommendations on Implementing Actions Directed for Preventing Violations of the Law on the Protection of Economic Competition' 2020, No. 14-рк, para 3.16.

[34] Ibid para 3.16 (This means that changes in exchange rates and the devaluation of the hryvnia lead to the increase in drug prices at all levels of supply, which, however, affects the expenditure of only the final consumer. At the same time, the consumer has a fixed wage, pension and other social benefits in national currency, and this income does not change along with the changes in the exchange rate of the Ukrainian hryvnia to foreign currency); Ibid para 4.28.

[35] Ibid para 2.4.

[36] Ibid para 2.5.

medicines, the main participants in the markets of relevant medicines are domestic manufacturers of medicines, representative offices of foreign manufacturers and importers.[37] The AMCU found that at this level concentration can be high if a medical product is patent-protected (i.e. generics are not available) or the number of brand name products with the same active ingredient is limited.[38] During the past several years at the distribution/wholesale level there have been three large local distributors that have significant market power in the supply of wholesale batches of a wide range of medicines and that have not experienced significant competition due to the relatively small shares owned by competitors.[39] Finally, retail markets for medicines are regional and are mostly competitive.[40] However, within certain territorial boundaries, such markets may have structural features of a monopoly position/collective monopoly.[41]

According to the AMCU the main competitive concerns with the pharmaceutical market in Ukraine include the establishment of administrative barriers to entry into markets by the regulators; the ability of the regulator to omit or exercise power to give preference to individual market participants; market consolidation processes; creation of economic barriers to entry by monopolists; the possibility of transferring financial risks to the patient at each stage of the medicinal product turnover; and rising prices for medicines.[42]

2.2 *Recent Activities of the AMCU: Distribution Agreements in the Ukrainian Pharmaceutical Sector*

In recent years, the AMCU has increased its activities in the field of pharmaceuticals, conducting market analysis[43] and issuing guidelines[44] and recommendations to relevant stakeholders,[45] including recommendations to market participants to restrain from raising the prices on pharmaceutical products during the COVID-19

[37] Ibid para 2.7.

[38] Ibid para 2.8.

[39] Ibid para 2.10.

[40] Ibid para 2.12.

[41] Ibid.

[42] OECD, 'Excessive Pricing in Pharmaceutical Markets—Note by Ukraine' DAF/COMP/WD(2018)119, 2018, para 60.

[43] AMCU 'Report on the Results of the Analysis of the Pharmaceutical Markets (For the Period of 2014—the First Half of 2016)' (Report) (2016).

[44] AMCU, 'Recommendations on the Application of Legislation on the Protection of Economic Competition by the Participants of the Medicinal Products Markets in Vertical Relationships of Supply and Promotion of Medicines' (2019), No. 5-pp.

[45] AMCU, 'Recommendations on Implementing Actions Directed for Preventing Violations of the Law on the Protection of Economic Competition' (n 33).

pandemic.[46] In addition, the AMCU has been actively investigating specific anticompetitive practices in this sector.[47] One type of such cases relates to pricing practices by pharmacies.[48] For example, during its 2016 market analysis, the AMCU found that there had been a number of violations of state price regulations by local pharmacies.[49]

However, perhaps the most important investigations to date concern vertical agreements between pharmaceutical market participants, which the AMCU suspects represent anticompetitive concerted practices. In this respect, the AMCU has devoted particular attention to distribution agreements between foreign pharmaceutical companies (or their subsidiaries) and large domestic wholesale distributors.[50] The investigations of the AMCU revealed that some of these agreements related to medicines for which the price is specifically regulated.[51] Importantly, the agreements included, among other things, a non-transparent system of discounts provided by a foreign pharmaceutical company for the benefit of its distributors.[52] The AMCU concluded that such agreements may lead to negative consequences in the form of restriction of competition in the pharmaceutical market by distorting the price regulation resulting in the increase of drug prices that are sold through public procurement procedures.[53]

One recent AMCU decision,[54] which was confirmed by the first instance[55] and appellate[56] courts, concerned the distribution agreements that were concluded between GlaxoSmithKline LLC (GSK), which was a part of the GlaxoSmithKline

[46] AMCU, 'Report on the Detection and Termination of Anti-Competitive Practices During the Quarantine Measures Implemented Due to Covid-19. The Implementation of Compliance Control Legislation on Economic Protection of Competition by Participants of Pharmaceutical Markets During the Increase of Covid-19 Infections in Ukraine' (Report), 2020.

[47] See e.g. Annual Reports of the AMCU from 2020, 2019, 2018 and 2017 https://amcu.gov.ua/pro-nas/zvitnist/richni-zviti accessed 27 December 2021.

[48] AMCU 'Report on the Results of the Analysis of the Pharmaceutical Markets (For the Period of 2014—the First Half of 2016)' (n 43).

[49] Ibid 5.3.3, para 28.

[50] Decision of the AMCU No. 628-p of 14 November 2017 (in which it fined Sanofi-Aventis Ukraine in the amount of 69,547,184 UAH and its two wholesale distributors in the amount of approx. 800,000 UAH each); Decision of the AMCU No. 377-p of 2 August 2018 (in which it fined Roche Ukraine in the amount of 9,115,817 UAH and its distributors BaDM—5,407,948 UAH, Business Centre 'Farmacia'—3,207,361 UAH and Alba Ukraine 339,999 UAH); Decision of the AMCU No. 680-p of 30 November 2020 (in which it fined Novo Nordisk A/C and its several distributors in the total amount of 188,130,255 UAH).

[51] AMCU 'Report on the Results of the Analysis of the Pharmaceutical Markets (for the Period of 2014—the First Half of 2016)' (n 43) 5.1, para 9.

[52] Ibid 5.1, para 11 (other terms of these agreements included export ban of medicines outside Ukraine; The obligation to prevent third parties from exporting goods outside Ukraine; The obligation to provide reports and the introduction of payment terms that ensure the control of the pharmaceutical company over the flow of goods in the medicinal markets of Ukraine).

[53] Ibid 5.1, para 12.

[54] Decision of the Antimonopoly Committee of Ukraine (2019) No. 830-p regarding a competition law violation and imposition of a fine.

[55] Commercial Court of Kyiv, Decision (2020) 910/4801/20.

[56] Northern Appellate Commercial Court, Decision (2021) 910/4801/20.

group companies and the sole importer of the GSK medicines in Ukraine, and several large wholesale distributors in Ukraine. In this case the AMCU investigated the setting of prices for GSK drugs when imported to Ukraine and the subsequent resale by distributors of such medicines through public procurement procedures. Specifically, drug prices are subject to state regulation in Ukraine. During the period under investigation (2011–2016), this was done by setting a maximum level of wholesale and retail margins. In particular, the maximum price margins of drugs purchased through public procurement procedures could not exceed 10% of their wholesale price.[57]

The key problematic issue in these distribution agreements, according to the AMCU analysis, were discounts. These discounts were set at two different levels. Specifically, GSK's activity with respect to import and distribution of medicines was carried out on the basis of foreign economic agreements with its foreign suppliers. The AMCU found that the discounts received by GSK from the suppliers (that were also part of the GSK group) reduced the total amount of the cost of imported drugs and the GSK's debt before these suppliers. Thus, already at the stage of importing the GSK medicines, the price setting with respect to all GSK medicines imported to Ukraine envisaged the difference between the purchase price established in the contracts between GSK and its foreign suppliers and the real price paid for these medicines due to the existent discount system.

In turn, GSK was selling its products in Ukraine through local distributors, five of which were buying the majority of the supply. The distribution agreements included a system of incentives, including discounts, which were not reflected in the pricing.[58] The size of the discount for achieving the quarterly goal directly depended on the volume of actual purchases of the distributor and its share in the total sales of GSK: the larger the share—the greater the amount of the discount for the distributor.[59] There were a variety of discounts, which were provided by signing of debt reconciliation acts and were subject to fulfilling the terms of the corresponding agreement. By signing these acts, the distributor could reduce its debt to GSK by the amount of this discount. This essentially meant that such discounts did not reduce the price of medicines, including the medicines that were sold by distributors through state procurement procedures, but rather were an additional income of the distributors. In other words, this system of granting discounts between GSK and its distributors created conditions for further sale of medicines by distributors under which discounts received from GSK were not taken into account when forming the price of medicines during their sale through public procurement procedures. Namely, during such a sale, the distributors were able to set the maximum possible margins within the state regulation based on the purchase price of drugs from GSK, i.e. the nominal price. At the same time, the distributors were able to offset part of their costs incurred during the purchase of the medicines by later receiving the discounts when signing acts of

[57] Decision of the Antimonopoly Committee of Ukraine No. 830-p (n 54), paras 103–109.

[58] Other conditions included restrictions on export by the distributors of GSK medicines and a control system of distributors' compliance with the relevant terms of contracts.

[59] Commercial Court of Kyiv, Decision (2020) (n 55).

debt reconciliation. This, while increasing their income, did not reduce the price for the final consumer, i.e. the state.

Therefore, the AMCU found that the system of contractual relationships between the GSK group companies and GSK on the one hand, and between GSK and its local distributors on the other hand, created conditions for establishing nominal and real prices for the purchase of medicines on the territory of Ukraine at two levels: first, at the stage of importing medicines into the territory of Ukraine and, second, at the stage of the sale of medicines on the wholesale market in Ukraine. The differences between the nominal and actual prices led to an unjustifiable increase in sales prices of GSK drugs, as sales prices for medicines through public procurement procedures were set taking into account the registered wholesale prices, i.e. the nominal price, and not the actual price. For example, the margins set by one of the distributors for Ventolin Nebula based on the nominal price, which it sold through public procurement procedures, was close to 10% (the maximum allowed margin under the law); however, considering the actual purchase price of this drug the margin exceeded 29%.

The AMCU concluded that the parties to these distribution agreements deliberately introduced a mechanism to circumvent the rules of price regulation and inflated prices during the sale of GSK drugs through public procurement procedures. In view of the above, the AMCU found that these distribution agreements between GSK and its several distributors, which introduced a non-transparent mechanism of discounts, led to unjustified overpricing of GSK drugs sold through public procurement procedures and, thus, violated Art. 6(1) Law on the Protection of Economic Competition, which prohibits anticompetitive concerted actions.[60]

To provide some guidance on the assessment of vertical agreements, the AMCU issued the 2019 Recommendations "On the application of legislation on the protection of economic competition by the participants of the medicinal product markets in a vertical relationship of supply and promotion of medicines."[61] In these Recommendations, while the AMCU acknowledges that the use of discounts is a common commercial practice and can have many procompetitive effects, it notes that discounts can also have anticompetitive effects.[62] In particular, the AMCU noted the following anticompetitive effects[63]:

- discounts as an element of a mechanism to exclude competitors from the market by setting prices below production costs and the sale of goods;
- discounts as a tool to circumvent price regulation thereby overpricing bids in public procurement;
- discounts as a dealership tool (restriction of access to customers) and as a tool to increase the costs of competitors;

[60] This provision will be discussed in more detail in the following section.

[61] AMCU, 'Recommendations on the Application of Legislation on the Protection of Economic Competition by the Participants of the Medicinal Products Markets in Vertical Relationships of Supply and Promotion of Medicines' (n 44).

[62] Ibid para 28.

[63] Ibid para 30.

- discounts as a means of restricting access to key resources, which can be raw materials or access to the main supply links, in particular, access to powerful distributors;
- discounts on bulk goods may have the effect of strengthening the market power of the supplier in competitive markets, by including in one list that is subject to discounts both unique drugs and drugs that have many substitutes. The use of such discount lists along with the conditions for achieving certain levels of sales has an additional exclusivity effect;
- discounts on lists of goods can have the effect of imposing a wider range of goods compared to the situation when the discount is set for each drug separately.

The Recommendations further explain that agreements between manufacturers/suppliers (importers) and distributors may qualify as anti-competitive concerted actions if they contain provisions on: providing benefits to individual distributors (unless such conditions are expressly permitted under the Standard requirements [in accordance with the law][64]); introduction of non-transparent pricing mechanisms (discounts, bonuses, credit notes), the purpose or consequence of which is: restriction, elimination, prevention of competition from generics; market sharing (except where allowed according to the Standard requirements); fixing a certain inflated level of market prices; and overpricing of drugs sold through public procurement procedures.[65]

It is outside of the scope of this chapter to analyse the correctness of the approach taken by the AMCU in relation to this type of agreement by pharmaceutical companies. However, it is clear that in pursuing them the AMCU seems to focus on practices that affect the trade of drugs in terms of their pricing and availability in Ukraine. The ultimate goal is, thus, to improve access to medicines in Ukraine, which, of course, in the light of the current critical level of access, is crucial. It remains to be seen how the practice in this area will develop in the future. At the time of writing the AMCU decision in this case is under appeal at the Supreme Court and GSK has also initiated an investment litigation against Ukraine to protect its interests as a result of this decision.[66]

3 IP-Related Anticompetitive Agreements

While the AMCU has been actively investigating certain anticompetitive practices in the pharmaceutical sector, it has considered no IP-related practices in this field

[64] Ukrainian Law on the Protection of Economic Competition 2001, art 11.

[65] AMCU, 'Recommendations on the Application of Legislation on the Protection of Economic Competition by the Participants of the Medicinal Products Markets in Vertical Relationships of Supply and Promotion of Medicines' (n 44), para 31.

[66] Roman Bryl 'Pharmaceutical Giant GSK has Filed an Investment Lawsuit Against Ukraine' *Liga Business* (17 December 2021) https://biz.liga.net/ua/ekonomika/all/novosti/farmatsevticheskiy-gigant-gsk-podal-investitsionnyy-isk-protiv-ukrainy accessed 27 December 2021.

to date. The following sections, therefore, will discuss the competition law rules in Ukraine with the focus on anticompetitive agreements. While analysing these provisions, guidance on their application with reference to case law in the EU and the US will be provided.

3.1 Regulation of Anticompetitive Agreements in Ukraine

3.1.1 The Prohibition of Anticompetitive Concerted Actions and Specific Exceptions

The main law that regulates anticompetitive practices in Ukraine is the Law "On the Protection of Economic Competition"[67] (LPEC), which was adopted in January 2001 and largely follows the model of EU competition rules, aligning Ukrainian law more closely with international standards.[68] It applies to practices that influence or may influence economic competition in the territory of Ukraine.[69] Article 6 LPEC contains a prohibition of anticompetitive concerted actions that "have led or may lead to the prevention, elimination or restriction of competition".[70] The rules set in Art. 6 LPEC follow the same approach as Art. 101 Treaty on the Functioning of the European Union (TFEU) and Section 1 Sherman Act as they do not distinguish between horizontal and vertical restraints, prohibiting both of them.[71] Article 10 LPEC contains an exception to the prohibition of Art. 6 LPEC. This is subject to obtaining an individual authorisation from the AMCU or the Cabinet of Ministers of Ukraine with respect to concerted actions if the parties can prove that such actions facilitate: the improvement of production, purchase or sale of goods; technical, technological or economic development; development of SMEs; optimisation of export or import of goods; development and application of unified technical conditions or

[67] Ukrainian Law on the Protection of Economic Competition 2001 (LPEC), 2210-III.

[68] Michael Emerson and Veronika Movchan, '*Deepening EU–Ukrainian Relations. What, Why, How?*' (Centre for European Policy Studies, 2018); Malgorzata Jakubiak, 'Analysis of Factors Contributing to the Adoption of Competition Law in Ukraine: Implications for Other Developing Countries' (2005) CASE Doradcy.

[69] LPEC, art 2(2).

[70] OECD, 'OECD Reviews of Legislation and Policy in the Field of Competition: Ukraine' (Report), 2016, 36 ('"Article 6 makes no distinction between horizontal and vertical concerted actions, but does include a non-exclusive list of anticompetitive practices that constitute potential violations. The list covers price-fixing, market division, restriction of outputs or inputs, discrimination between similarly situated parties and tying, and adds bid-rigging, boycotts and other conduct restraining market entry or exit, and actions designed to impede the competitive ability of other companies 'without an objective basis'").

[71] UNCTAD, 'Voluntary Peer Review of Competition Law and Policy: Ukraine' (Report) UNCTAD/DITC/CLP/2013/3, 2013, 18.

standards for goods; or rationalisation of production, if such concerted actions do not lead to a substantial lessening of competition in the entire market or a part thereof.[72]

At the same time, the LPEC contains certain specific exemptions to the Art. 6 prohibition in Arts. 7–9. These exemptions reflect similar provisions contained in the German Act against Restraints of Competition at a time when a draft Ukrainian law was being prepared (which were later removed from German law).[73] In particular, the exemptions include:

(a) Concerted actions of SMEs relating to joint purchase of goods that do not lead to substantial restriction of competition and facilitate increased competitiveness of SMEs (Art. 7);
(b) Concerted actions relating to the supply and use of goods if such concerted actions do not lead to substantial restriction of competition on the whole market or a part thereof, do not restrict access of other economic entities to the market, and do not lead to an economically unjustified price increase or a shortage of goods (Art. 8);
(c) Concerted actions relating to intellectual property rights (Art. 9);
(d) Other concerted actions meeting the standard requirements established by the AMCU under Art. 11.

As these types of potentially anticompetitive actions are exempted from the general prohibition set in Art. 6, their performance is not considered illegal.[74] However, the exemptions in Arts. 7 and 8 would only be applicable if the concerted actions do not present a substantial threat to competition on the market while having a concrete positive effect on the economic development of Ukraine.

At the same time, Art. 9 LPEC limits the exemption with respect to concerted practices related to the transfer and use of IP rights less strictly than the other two specific exemptions in Arts. 7 and 8. It allows any restrictions imposed on the party to which the IP right is transferred if they do not go beyond legal rights of the

---

[72] This is similar to the approach taken by European Union law, i.e. in art 101 TFEU. In particular, under art 101 TFEU, an agreement that falls within art 101(1) TFEU is not necessarily unlawful, because art 101(3) provides for an exception to the general prohibition of art 101(1) by stating that this provision may not apply to agreements that satisfy four conditions. Specifically, the provisions of art 101(1) may be "declared inapplicable in the case of [an agreement] which contributes to improving the production or distribution of goods or to promoting technical or economic progress, while allowing consumers a fair share of the resulting benefit, and which does not: (a) impose on the undertakings concerned restrictions which are not indispensable to the attainment of these objectives; (b) afford such undertakings the possibility of eliminating competition in respect of a substantial part of the products in question." However, currently undertakings are not required to notify the European Commission and obtain an exception. Such a system of "individual exemptions" under art 101(3) TFEU was abolished by Council Regulation 1/2003 of 16 December 2002 on the implementation of the rules on competition laid down in arts 81 and 82 Treaty (2002) OJ L1/1, which established the principle that undertakings must self-assess whether their agreements comply with art 101 TFEU.

[73] OECD, 'Competition Law and Policy in Ukraine: An OECD Peer Review' (Report) 2008, 109.

[74] UNCTAD/DITC/CLP/2013/3, (n 71) 19.

rightholder.[75] The restrictions not considered to go beyond such rights are those concerning the scope of rights, the term and territory of the licence, the type of activity, the field of use and the minimum volume of production.[76] Importantly, as will be explained below, there are no specific thresholds for applying this provision.

The rationale of Art. 9 essentially reflects the so-called "scope of the patent" concept, under which restrictions in patent licensing agreements are allowed provided that they do not go beyond the scope of the patent rights of the licensor.[77] In the US, this concept takes its roots from the patent misuse doctrine that had evolved from patent law and was later adopted by antitrust law to condemn clauses that extend the scope of the exclusivity granted by the patent and considered these to be a patent abuse.[78] Similarly, in the past, the German Act against Restraints of Competition, which, as mentioned, inspired the drafters of Art. 9, contained a provision that forbade practices which extended exclusivity beyond the rights granted by the patent.[79] Such practices were considered illegal per se, and included, for example, tie-ins of non-patented products with patented products and post-expiration royalties.[80]

3.1.2 New Block Exemptions on Technology Transfers in Ukraine and Art. 9 LPEC

As part of its obligations under the Association Agreement with the European Union,[81] which was signed in 2014, Ukraine undertook an obligation to fill certain gaps in Ukrainian legislation with respect to the lack of a block exemption system,

---

[75] LPEC, art 9(1): "The provisions of Art. 6 of this Law shall not apply to agreements on the transfer of intellectual property rights or on the use of the object of intellectual property insofar as they restrict the party to the agreement to which the right is transferred, if these restrictions do not exceed limits of legal rights of the [holder] of intellectual property rights".

[76] LPEC, art 9(2): "It is considered that restrictions on the scope of rights transferred, the term and territory of the permit for use of the object of intellectual property rights, as well as the type of activity, field of use, minimum amount of production do not go beyond the rights specified in part one of this article".

[77] Anderman and Schmidt (n 6) 235.

[78] See e.g. US Supreme Court *Mercoid Corp v. Mid Continent Investment Co.* (1943) 320 U.S. 661.

[79] Anderman and Schmidt (n 6) 235; Section 20(1) of the German Act against Restraints of Competition 1957 provides that patent licensing agreements are void to the extent that they impose restraints on the licensee which exceed the scope of the patent grant. Certain restrictions are deemed not to exceed the patent right).

[80] See e.g. EC, Judgement C-193/83 *Windsurfing International v. Commission of the European Communities* (1986) ECR 61, that concerned restrictions in a patent licence which went beyond the specific subject matter of a patent by tying a patented product with a non-patented product. This case law still remains good law and was referred to by the Commission in its most recent decisions in case AT.39226 *Lundbeck.*

[81] Association Agreement between the European Union and its Member States, of the one part, and Ukraine, of the other part 2014, OJ L161/3 (EU–Ukraine Association Agreement).

in particular, for agreements on technology transfer.[82] In the EU, these were to be found in EU Regulation 772/2004[83] and after its expiry such technology transfer agreements have been governed by Commission Regulation (EU) No. 316/2014 of 21 March 2014 on the application of Art. 101(3) TFEU to categories of technology transfer agreements. This technology transfer block exemption regulation (TTBER 316/2014) provides a "safe harbour" type of exemption for licensing agreements, while the Commission's Guidelines on the application of Art. 101 TFEU to technology transfer agreements (TTA Guidelines)[84] explain how to apply the TTBER 316/2014.[85] Importantly, the TTA Guidelines also provide guidance on the application of Art. 101(3) TFEU[86] to licensing agreements that fall outside the scope of TTBER 316/2014.[87] Following the signing of the Association Agreement with the European Union, the AMCU, responsible for implementing Chapter 10 "Competition Law" provisions, undertook steps to harmonise Ukrainian competition law with the EU standards by drafting block exemptions on technology transfers.[88] In 2018, Ukraine adopted, among other things, the AMCU Resolution on the Standard Requirements of Concerted Practices of Undertakings concerning Technology Transfer Agreements.[89]

According to this Resolution, a technology transfer agreement is exempted if either: (a) it is concluded between competitors and their combined market share does not exceed 20% of the relevant market(s), or (b) it is concluded between non-competitors and the market share of each of the parties does not exceed 30% of the relevant market(s). The Resolution also states that a technology transfer agreement, as a whole, will not benefit from the exemption if it contains hardcore restrictions (subject to certain exceptions), specifically: (a) in agreements between competitors, restrictions on resale prices, limitation of output, allocation of markets or customers, restriction of the licensee's ability to exploit its own technology rights or the restriction of the ability of any of the parties to carry out research and development; and (b) in agreements between non-competitors, restrictions on resale prices, restrictions of passive sales or restriction of active or passive sales to end-users by a licensee

---

[82] Kseniya Smyrnova, 'Enforcement of Competition Rules in the Association Agreement between the EU & Ukraine' (2014) 7(10) Yearbook of Antitrust and Regulatory Studies; See also Kseniia Smyrnova, 'The "Europeanisation" of Competition Law in Ukraine' in this Volume.

[83] Commission Regulation 772/2004 of 27 April 2004 on the application of art 81(3) of the Treaty to categories of Technology Transfer Agreements (2004) OJ L123/11.

[84] Communication from the Commission—Guidelines on the application of art 101 of the Treaty on the Functioning of the European Union to Technology Transfer Agreements (2014) OJ C89/03 (TTA Guidelines).

[85] Anderman and Schmidt (n 6) 255.

[86] If an agreement is caught by art 101(1) prohibition, it can nevertheless be saved from non-enforceability by being exempted under art 101(3) if it meets its conditions.

[87] Anderman and Schmidt (n 6) 255.

[88] OECD, 'OECD Reviews of Legislation and Policy in the Field of Competition: Ukraine' (n 70) 70.

[89] OECD, 'Competition Provisions in Trade Agreements—Contribution from Ukraine' DAF/COMP/GF/WD (2019).

which is a member of a selective distribution system and which operates at the retail level.[90]

It should be noted that this Resolution on technology transfer does not cover the transfer and use of such IP rights as trade marks and copyright (except for software copyright).[91] The rationale for this seems to be that the licensing of such IP rights would not typically entail the transfer of technology.[92] Therefore, Art. 9 is broader in this respect, as it covers the transfer and use of all IP rights. Moreover, considering the content of the new Resolution and Art. 9, their mutual operation may need to be clarified. While Art. 9 establishes general exemption from Art. 6 prohibition for agreements on the transfer or use of IP rights, if they impose restrictions that do not go beyond the scope of legitimate rights of the rightholder, the Resolution has a different approach. The latter (mirroring the TTBER 316/2014), as was discussed above, establishes certain thresholds with respect to market shares of the parties to the agreement, along with the prohibition of certain hardcore restrictions. As per the rationale of the TTBER 316/2014, if an agreement meets these requirements there is a presumption that it generally leads to an improvement in production or distribution and allows consumers a fair share of the resulting benefits.[93] Therefore, in contrast with the provisions of Art. 9 LPEC, exemptions under the Resolution from the prohibition on restrictions with respect to the territory of the licence for the use of IP rights, the scope of their use or the volume of production apply subject to certain conditions.[94] This may lead to a situation in which some restrictions set out in technology transfer agreements may be exempted from the prohibition by Art. 9 LPEC, while they are not permitted under the Resolution.[95] The provisions of Art. 9 and the Resolution, however, have not been applied in practice and there is no guidance on their application available from the AMCU or the courts.

[90] Section 4 of the Resolution; See also Igor Svechkar et al., 'Restraints of Trade and Dominance in Ukraine: Overview' *Thomson Reuters Practical Law* (1 February 2021) https://ca.practicallaw.thomsonreuters.com/7-569-9990?transitionType=Default&contextData=%28sc.Default%29 accessed 27 December 2022.

[91] See recital 2 of the Resolution.

[92] See, however, para 47 of the TTA Guidelines, which states that "[p]rovisions in technology transfer agreements relating to the licensing of other types of intellectual property such as trademarks and copyright, other than software copyright [...], are only covered by the TTBER if, and to the extent that, they are directly related to the production or sale of the contract products [...] For instance, where a licensor authorises a licensee to use its trademark on the products incorporating the licensed technology, this trademark licence may allow the licensee to better exploit the licensed technology by allowing consumers to make an immediate link between the product and the characteristics imputed to it by the licensed technology rights".

[93] See recitals 10 and 11 TTBER No. 316/2014.

[94] See e.g. Explanatory Note on Ukrainian Draft Law on the Amendments to Certain Laws of Ukraine on the Protection of Economic Competition 2017, No. 6723.

[95] Ibid.

3.1.3 Guidance Regarding the Application of Article 9 LPEC is Needed

To improve the operation of legal provisions relating to the transfer and use of IP rights it may be necessary to clarify their application. One option would be to remove Art. 9 and follow the EU approach to the assessment of this type of agreement. In the EU the law, first, provides exemptions for a technology transfer agreement under the TTBER 316/2014 that meets certain market thresholds and does not contain hardcore restrictions. Second, if such an agreement falls outside the scope of the safe harbour provided by the TTBER 316/2014, it may nevertheless be exempted under Art. 101(3) TFEU.[96] In Ukraine, the latter could be done under Art. 10 LPEC by seeking authorisation from the AMCU if the parties are able to meet the requirements of this provision. To assist the AMCU in deciding on an exception with respect to a particular IP agreement under Art. 10 LPEC guidance similar to that discussed below may need to be developed. Another option is to provide guidance on the appropriate interpretation of Art. 9 to avoid granting exemptions to IP agreements that may in fact be anticompetitive. As the TTA Guidelines explain:

> The fact that intellectual property laws grant exclusive rights of exploitation does not imply that intellectual property rights are immune from competition law intervention. Article 101 of the Treaty is in particular applicable to agreements whereby the holder licenses another undertaking to exploit its intellectual property rights.[97]

While competition law acknowledges that the process of technology transfer in the form of IP licensing is in principle procompetitive as it "helps to increase the reward for innovative effort and the incentives for others to invest in R&D",[98] some restrains in an IP licensing agreement may be used as a tool to create restrictions of competition. In particular, "some IP licensing agreements have the potential to create conditions of dominant market power or collusion in the licensed market which foreclose competitors from entering that market" and, thus, can be used to exclude competitors from markets and may harm consumers.[99] Therefore, it is paramount to develop guidelines that would assist the AMCU and the courts in interpreting the boundaries of Art. 9 application. In particular, such guidance would need to define what is actually meant by licensing and what will fall outside of the scope of this term. In addition, certain factors that would help to make the scope of licensing clear, such as market definition, would need to be explained. The latter, for example, is important when assessing whether the cross-licensing of competing technologies may in fact be entered into for the purpose of market allocation to avoid the scrutiny of competition law. The explanations would need to elaborate on what should be taken into account when assessing whether the licence itself does not serve a specific purpose for the

---

[96] See e.g. Commission Regulation 330/2010 of 20 April 2010 on the application of art 101(3) of the Treaty on the Functioning of the European Union to Categories of Vertical Agreements and Concerted Practices (2010) OJ L102/1, 1–7, and Commission Notice on Guidance on Vertical Restraints (2010) OJ C130/1, 1; Anderman and Schmidt (n 6) 204.

[97] TTA Guidelines (n 84), para 7.

[98] Anderman and Schmidt (n 6) 202.

[99] Ibid 203.

parties to escape the prohibition of competition law (such as licensing in the context of pay-for-delay agreements, which will be discussed below). It needs to convey to the AMCU and the courts that IP licensing that falls under the Art. 9 exemption should be genuine in the sense that it serves a clear economic and existing purpose for both the licensee and the licensor. A clear application of this provision within the context of technology transfer will give investors, including foreign companies, confidence to license their technologies to Ukrainian business.

As was mentioned, Art. 9 is broader than the Resolution as it also covers IP rights that do not entail the transfer of technology, such as trade marks and copyright (except for software copyright). Therefore, it may be necessary to develop guidance on the application of Art. 9 to these types of IP rights as well. Typically, agreements concerning trade marks relate to distribution and resale of goods and services, which may include such restrictions as resale prices and territorial restrictions. The former would likely be outside of the scope of Art. 9, because the trade mark holders cannot impose prices on a licensee as this would go beyond the scope of their legitimate rights. This would also restrain the economic freedom of the licensee, which would be against the fundamental principle of competition law. With respect to the territorial restrictions, it may be permitted to put restrictions on active sales outside the territory, but it is unlikely that Art. 9 can restrict passive sales. This is because passive sales by definition are unsolicited sales. Therefore, to create a harmony between Art. 6 and Art. 9 it is advisable that the AMCU exclude passive sales from the exception of Art. 9 because they restrict the actions of third parties and are essentially restrictions on consumers. The analysis in relation to copyright agreements would follow in general the same logic as the assessment of patent-related agreements, but the particularities of this right would need to be taken into account (including the difference between performing and non-performing rights).[100]

4 The EU and US Approaches to the Assessment of Pay-for-Delay Agreements

Despite the recent legislative and investigative activities of the AMCU in the pharmaceutical sector, there have been no cases with respect to IP-related practices by pharmaceutical companies. Therefore, considering the limited experience of the AMCU in investigating IP-related practices and virtually non-existent practice in this regard in the field of pharmaceuticals some possible guidance on the application of competition law rules to certain types of IP-related agreements in the pharmaceutical sector will be considered in this section. In particular, this section will focus on pay-for-delay agreements.

[100] Richard Whish and David Bailey, *Competition Law* (Oxford, 8th ed. 2015) 819; Anderman and Schmidt (n 6) 244.

4.1 The Assessment of Pay-for-Delay Agreements in the EU and the US

While many IP-related agreements are usually procompetitive and lawful, certain agreements that involve IP rights may be considered anticompetitive. One type of problematic agreement in the pharmaceutical field is the so-called "pay-for-delay" or "reverse payment" agreement.[101] This type of agreement has attracted the attention of competition authorities in a number of jurisdictions, including in the US and the EU. These agreements are typically entered into to settle patent litigation between the originator company (the patent holder who alleges patent infringement) and the generic company (the potential competitor who asserts that the patent is invalid or not infringed). A salient element of these agreements is that they involve some kind of consideration flowing from the originator to the generic company[102] in exchange for the promise by the latter to refrain from entering the market. The competition law concern is that the originator uses its patent in an anticompetitive way in order to extend its monopoly by paying a generic company for staying out of the market, and thus eliminating its direct competitor. This, therefore, stifles competition and harms consumers, who are deprived of access to a cheaper generic version of the drug, which could have entered the market in the absence of such an agreement.[103]

In the US, pay-for-delay agreements have been one of the top priorities for the Federal Trade Commission (FTC).[104] In the last several decades, the courts have applied various tests to assess these agreements,[105] the most commonly applied of which, up until recently, was the "scope of the patent" test. This, however, changed when the US Supreme Court delivered its decision in *FTC v Actavis*.[106] This case concerned a pay-for-delay agreement between an originator company Solvay and a generic company Actavis, under which the latter agreed not to bring its generic to the market for nine years (but 65 months before Solvay's patent expires) and promised

---

[101] Matthews and Gurgula (n 29); Josef Drexl, '"Pay-for-Delay" and Blocking Patents—Targeting Pharmaceutical Companies Under European Competition Law' (2009) 40 International Review of Intellectual Property and Competition 751; Joseph Straus, '"Pay for Delay"—A Subtly Hidden, Overlooked or Ignored Transatlantic Divide: Exemplified on the *Actavis* Decision of the US Supreme Court and the *Servier* Decision of the EU Commission' (2016) 76 Zbornik Znanstvenih Razprav 197; Michael A Carrier, 'Drug Patent Settlements Around the World' (2017) 62(4) The Antitrust Bulletin 770.

[102] Hence the "reverse payment", as normally it is the alleged infringer who pays the patent holder.

[103] Matthews and Gurgula (n 29).

[104] Federal Trade Commission, 'Pay-For-Delay: When Drug Companies Agree Not to Compete' *Federal Trade Commission*https://www.ftc.gov/news-events/media-resources/mergers-competition/pay-delay accessed 27 December 2021.

[105] Olga Gurgula, 'US Supreme Court Decision on Reverse Payment Agreements: New Era in Patent Litigation Settlements—*FTC v. Actavis, Inc.*, 570 US' (2013) 3(4) Queen Mary Journal of Intellectual Property 325; Olga Gurgula, 'Restrictive Practices in the Pharmaceutical Industry: Reverse Payment Agreements Seeking for a Balance between Intellectual Property and Competition Law' (2012) 5 Global Antitrust Review.

[106] US Supreme Court, *Federal Trade Commission v. Actavis, Inc.*, (2013) 570 U.S. 136.

to promote Solvay's patented drug AndroGel to doctors in exchange for millions of dollars.[107] The FTC challenged this agreement, but its complaint was dismissed by the district court.[108] On appeal, confirming the dismissal, the Eleventh Circuit concluded that "as long as the anticompetitive effects of a settlement fall within the scope of the patent's exclusionary potential, the settlement is immune from antitrust attack."[109] The Appellate Court explained that patent holders have a "lawful right to exclude others from the market,"[110] and, therefore, a patent "conveys the right to cripple competition."[111] Such an approach, which was largely followed by other courts, essentially gave an almost automatic immunity to this type of agreement.[112] However, the Supreme Court disagreed with the lower courts. It explained that the payment allowed the originator to eliminate the "risk of competition" and "induce[d] the generic challenger to abandon" its patent challenge in return for "a share of [the originator's] monopoly profits that would otherwise be lost in the competitive market."[113] The Court noted that lawfulness of these agreements depends on whether the payment can be justified by "traditional settlement considerations, such as avoided litigation costs or fair value for services" that the generic has agreed to perform.[114] The Court also indicated that patent and antitrust policies are both relevant to determining the scope of the patent monopoly. It stated that:

> Although the anticompetitive effects of the reverse settlement agreement might fall within the scope of the exclusionary potential of Solvay's patent, this does not immunize the agreement from antitrust attack. For one thing, to refer simply to what the holder of a valid patent could do does not by itself answer the antitrust question…It would be incongruous to determine antitrust legality by measuring the settlement's anticompetitive effects solely against patent law policy, and not against procompetitive antitrust policies as well.

It therefore concluded that these agreements must be analysed, along with other antitrust cases, under the antitrust "rule-of-reason" test.

Similarly, in the EU, in the aftermath of its 2008 pharmaceutical sector inquiry, the European Commission launched several investigations against originators and generic companies for entering into pay-for-delay agreements, alleging violations of Arts. 101 and 102 TFEU.[115] The Commission concluded that these agreements

---

[107] Ibid 5.

[108] US District Court for Northern District of Georgia, Atlanta Division *In re AndroGel Antitrust Litigation (No. II)* (2010) 687 F. Supp. 2d 1371, 1379.

[109] US Court of Appeals for the Eleventh Circuit *Federal Trade Commission* v. *Watson Pharmaceuticals, Inc.*, (2012) 677 F.3d 1298, 1312.

[110] Ibid.

[111] Ibid 1310.

[112] US Supreme Court, *Federal Trade Commission v. Actavis, Inc.*, (2013) 570 U.S. 136, 158.

[113] US Supreme Court, *Federal Trade Commission v. Actavis, Inc.*, (2013) 570 U.S. 136, 154, 157.

[114] Ibid 156; see e.g. US Court of Appeals for the Fifth Circuit, *Impax Laboratories, Inc. v. Federal Trade Commission* (2019) 19-60394.

[115] For example, in 2014, the European Commission fined Servier 330 million EUR and several producers of generic medicines 97 million EUR for delaying the market entry of generic perindopril, a medicine used to treat high blood pressure. In 2013, it fined Johnson & Johnson and Novartis 16 million EUR for delaying the market entry of generic pain-killer fentanyl.

caused consumer harm by delaying generic entry and maintaining unjustifiably high prices. The current approach to the assessment of this type of agreement in the EU is reflected in the *Lundbeck* case, which, at the time of writing, is the latest agreement reviewed by the Court of Justice of the European Union (CJEU). On 25 March 2021, the CJEU dismissed the appeals against the Commission's decision to fine Lundbeck and several other companies for entering into anticompetitive pay-for-delay agreements.[116] The case concerned the blockbuster antidepressant containing the active pharmaceutical ingredient (API) citalopram. Lundbeck obtained patent protection for the API and two processes for its manufacture in several European countries. While its compound patent expired in January 2002, Lundbeck still had a number of process patents that covered certain ways to produce citalopram. Four generic companies had been planning to enter the market with their generic versions of citalopram after the expiration of the compound patent. However, Lundbeck initiated or threatened to initiate patent infringement proceedings against them, and generics, in turn, raised arguments of non-infringement or invalidity of the patents. Eventually, Lundbeck entered into an agreement with each generic company (Merck, Alpharma, Arrow, and Ranbaxy), according to which it transferred to them a significant consideration in exchange for a promise not to enter the citalopram market for a certain period of time.

The Commission found that Lundbeck and the generic companies were at least potential competitors, and that the agreements restricted competition "by object" since the amounts that Lundbeck paid to the generic companies roughly corresponded to the profits that the generic companies anticipated making had they entered the market. It fined Lundbeck 93.7 million EUR and the generic companies 52.2 million EUR for delaying market entry of the generic antidepressant citalopram. In September 2016, the General Court upheld the Commission's decision, which was appealed by Lundbeck to the CJEU. The CJEU agreed with the General Court that the agreements were characterised as restriction by object, since it was the payments by Lundbeck, rather than its patents, that induced the generic companies to delay their market entry. The CJEU rejected Lundbeck arguments that the settlement agreements were limited to the scope of Lundbeck's new process patents, stating, with reference to the GC's judgment, that patent rights do not include "the right to conclude agreements by which actual or potential competitors were paid not to enter the market."[117]

---

[116] Judgment in Cases ECJ C-586/16p *Sun Pharmaceutical Industries and Ranbaxy (UK) v. Commission* (2021) ECLI:EU:C:2021:24; ECJ C-588/16p *Generics (UK) v. Commission* (2021) ECLI:EU:C:2021:242; ECJ C-591/16p *Lundbeck v. Commission* (2021) ECLI:EU:C:2021:243; ECJ C-601/16p *Arrow Group and Arrow Generics v. Commission* (2021) ECLI:EU:C:2021:244; C-611/16p *Xellia Pharmaceuticals and Alpharma v. Commission* (2021) ECLI:EU:C:2021:245; and C-614/16p *Merck v. Commission* (2021) ECLI:EU:C:2021:246.

[117] Ibid para 122.

4.2 *Specific Considerations When Applying Art. 9 to Pay-for-Delay Agreements*

Considering the practice of assessing pay-for-delay agreements in the EU and the US, it seems that while the patent may allow its holder to prevent competitors from using its patented product, it does not allow it to collude with competitors by paying them off for not entering the market. It is important to note that some pay-for-delay agreements may include not only a value transfer in the form of a monetary payment, but also a licence to use a patent held by the originator. The provisions of such an agreement may include certain limitations on the generic's ability to sell its generic version of the drug. Viewing such an agreement separately, it may potentially fall within the exemption provided by Art. 9 LPEC, which allows the licensing of IP if it falls within the scope of the IP rightholder. However, such an agreement must be analysed as part of the overall anticompetitive strategy by the originator to delay or eliminate generic competition. As the European Commission explains in its TTA Guidelines:

> 'pay-for-delay' type settlement agreements often do not involve the transfer of technology rights, but are based on a value transfer from one party in return for a limitation on the entry and/or expansion on the market of the other party and may be caught by Article 101(1). If, however, such a settlement agreement also includes a licensing of the technology rights concerned by the underlying dispute, and that agreement leads to a delayed or otherwise limited ability for the licensee to launch the product on any of the markets concerned, the agreement may be caught by Article 101(1) and would then need to be assessed in particular in the light of Articles 4(1)(c)[118] and 4(1)(d)[119] of the TTBER [...] If the parties to such a settlement agreement are actual or potential competitors and there was a significant value transfer from the licensor to the licensee, the Commission will be particularly attentive to the risk of market allocation/market sharing.[120]

The European Commission categorises patent settlement agreements based on two main criteria: (a) whether the agreement envisages a limitation on the generic company's ability to market its own medicine, and (b) whether it provides for a value transfer from the originator to the generic company.[121] Licences may fulfil both criteria. With respect to the first criterion, the Commission noted that a licence granted by the originator company allowing the generic to be on the market counts as limiting generic entry if the generic company cannot enter the market with its own product or it cannot set the conditions for the commercialisation of its product freely.[122] Therefore, the generic company's entry is at least partly controlled by

---

[118] TTBER, art 4(1)(c) "the allocation of markets or customers".

[119] TTBER, art 4(1)(d) "the restriction of the licensee's ability to exploit its own technology rights or the restriction of the ability of any of the parties to the agreement to carry out research and development".

[120] TTA Guidelines (n 84), paras 238–239.

[121] European Commission, '8th Report on the Monitoring of Patent Settlements (Period: January–December 2016)' (Communication) (2018), para 8.

[122] Ibid para 9.

the originator company through the terms of the licence agreement.[123] With respect to the second criterion, a value transfer could be in the form of a licence to the generic company enabling it to enter the market.[124] The Commission concludes that agreements that restrict the generic company's ability to market its own product and provide for a value transfer from the originator to the generic company are likely to attract the highest degree of antitrust scrutiny.[125]

Commenting on this type of agreement Hovenkamp explains:[126]

> [O]ne thing that makes an *Actavis* style pay-for-delay settlement unusual is that it does not involve a license at all, but at most an agreement to license at some future date. That is why Justice Breyer's opinion for the Court observed that, while the Patent Act explicitly permits licensing, the agreement providing for delayed entry was not authorized by the Patent Act. Indeed, an equilibrium agreement under the scope-of-the-patent test advocated by the dissenters would *never* be a license: for the entire remaining duration of the patent the generic would not produce. Once the patent expires the generic is free to produce without a license. Until actual production under a license occurs, the settlement is nothing more than a naked market division agreement.

Therefore, based on these principles it is important to differentiate between genuine patent licences and licences that mask other agreements, such as pay-for-delay agreements. In the latter case, a licensing agreement must be analysed in the context of the overall strategy to delay generic entry. In such a scenario, Art. 9 LPEC must not apply, to avoid a plainly anticompetitive agreement being saved by this provision. Thus, the AMCU should construe this provision appropriately, i.e. in some cases even a seemingly lawful exercise of IP rights under IP laws may still be a violation of competition law, and therefore the AMCU should not be prevented from intervening. These considerations may also be useful beyond the assessment of pay-for-delay agreements and should be taken into account by the AMCU when assessing any IP-related agreement.

5 Conclusions

Competition law may be a useful tool in facilitating better access to affordable medicines and incentivising medical innovation. However, it is not sufficiently utilised in many jurisdictions, including in Ukraine. Some IP-related practices that have been condemned by competition authorities in other jurisdictions have not yet attracted the attention of the AMCU. Therefore, to ensure robust and healthy competition in the pharmaceutical market the AMCU may need to take a proactive role in promoting competition and innovation, as well as raising awareness of the right

[123] Ibid.

[124] Ibid para 12.

[125] Ibid para 17.

[126] Herbert J Hovenkamp, 'Intellectual Property and Competition' (2019) Faculty Scholarship at Penn Law 1807 (n 3)10.

holders about the limits that competition law imposes on the utilisation of their IP rights. Importantly, the AMCU must pay closer attention to the IP-related practices that may delay or block competition in the pharmaceutical market. These include such practices as pay-for-delay agreements, which have been the subject of special attention by both the European Commission and the US Federal Trade Commission. To avoid this type of anticompetitive agreement being exempted under Art. 9 LPEC it is advisable to develop guidance on its application, so that only genuinely procompetitive IP agreements that serve a clear economic purpose for both the licensee and the licensor would be allowed, while anticompetitive agreements would fall outside of this provision. It is believed that the combination of an active enforcement of the competition law rules by the AMCU in the pharmaceutical sector and the development of specific guidance on the correct application of such rules to IP-related practices, following the approaches to the assessment of these agreements in mature jurisdictions, will help to ensure the timely arrival of an affordable generic treatment for the benefit of Ukrainian patients.

Acknowledgement I am very grateful to Dr. Amir Nabil Ibrahim (the former chair of the Egyptian Competition Authorities) for his useful critique and feedback to the earlier versions of this chapter, as well as to my colleagues from Max Planck Dr. Heiko Richter and Dr. Daria Kim for their valuable comments. I would also like to thank Inesa Shumilo (Associate Professor of Private International Law and Comparative Law Department, Yaroslav Mudriy National Law University) and Taras Kyslyy (Partner, attorney-at-law at Arzinger) for their help in gathering materials for this chapter, and to Sophia Sorg for her kind assistance with the formalities when finalising this chapter.

References

Steven D Anderman and Hedvig Schmidt, *EU Competition Law and Intellectual Property Rights: The Regulation of Innovation* (Oxford University Press 2011)

Antimonopoly Committee of Ukraine, 'Recommendations on Implementing Actions Directed for Preventing Violations of the Law on the Protection of Economic Competition' (2020) [АМКУ, 'Про Здійснення Заходів, Спрямованих на Запобігання Порушенням Законодавства Про Захист Економічної Конкуренції' (2020)]

Antimonopoly Committee of Ukraine, 'Report on the Detection and Termination of Anti-Competitive Practices During the Quarantine Measures Implemented Due to Covid-19. The Implementation of Compliance Control Legislation on Economic Protection of Competition by Participants of Pharmaceutical Markets During the Increase of Covid-19 Infections in Ukraine' (Report), 2020 [АМКУ, 'Звіт Виявлення та Припинення Антиконкурентних Практик під час Карантинних Заходів, Запроваджених через Covid-19. Здійснення Контролю за Дотриманням Законодавства Про Захист Економічної Конкуренції Учасниками Фармацевтичних Ринків під Час Спалаху в Україні Коронавірусної Інфекції COVID-19' (2020)]

Antimonopoly Committee of Ukraine, 'Recommendations on the Application of Legislation on the Protection of Economic Competition by the Participants of the Medicinal Products Markets in Vertical Relationships of Supply and Promotion of Medicines' (2019) [АМКУ, 'Рекомендаційні Роз'яснення щодо Застосування Законодавства про Захист Економічної Конкуренції Учасниками Ринків Лікарських Засобів у Вертикальних Відносинах щодо Постачання та Просування Лікарських Засобів' (2019)]

Antimonopoly Committee of Ukraine, 'Report on the Results of the Analysis of the Pharmaceutical Markets —the First Half of 2016)' (Report) (2016) [АМКУ, 'Звіт за Результатами Дослідження Фармацевтичних Ринків (за Період 2014—Перше Півріччя 2016 (2016)]

Michael A Carrier, 'Drug Patent Settlements Around the World' (2017) 62(4) The Antitrust Bulletin 770

Josef Drexl, '"Pay-for-Delay" and Blocking Patents—Targeting Pharmaceutical Companies Under European Competition Law' (2009) 40 International Review of Intellectual Property and Competition 751

Michael Emerson and Veronika Movchan, '*Deepening EU–Ukrainian Relations. What, Why, How?*' (Centre for European Policy Studies 2018)

European Commission, 'Pharmaceutical Sector Inquiry' (Final Report) 2009

Explanatory Note on Ukrainian Draft Law on the Amendments to Certain Laws of Ukraine on the Protection of Economic Competition 2017 [Пояснювальна Запискадо проекту Закону України «Про внесення змін до деяких законів України про захист економічної конкуренції» (2017)]

Federal Trade Commission, 'Pay-For-Delay: When Drug Companies Agree Not to Compete' *Federal Trade Commission* https://www.ftc.gov/news-events/media-resources/mergers-competition/pay-delay

Olga Gurgula, 'Strategic Patenting by Pharmaceutical Companies—Should Competition Law Intervene?' (2020) 51 International Review of Intellectual Property and Competition Law 1062

Olga Gurgula, 'US Supreme Court Decision on Reverse Payment Agreements: New Era in Patent Litigation Settlements—*FTC v. Actavis, Inc.*, 570 US' (2013) 3(4) Queen Mary Journal of Intellectual Property 325

Olga Gurgula, 'Restrictive Practices in the Pharmaceutical Industry: Reverse Payment Agreements Seeking for a Balance between Intellectual Property and Competition Law' (2012) 5 Global Antitrust Review

Andreas Heinemann 'Abusive Filing of IP Rights' in Duncan Matthews and Herbert Zech (eds), *Research Handbook on Intellectual Property and the Life Sciences* (Edward Elgar Publishing Ltd 2017)

Herbert J Hovenkamp, 'Intellectual Property and Competition' (2019) Faculty Scholarship at Penn Law 1807

Malgorzata Jakubiak, 'Analysis of Factors Contributing to the Adoption of Competition Law in Ukraine: Implications for Other Developing Countries' (2005) CASE Doradcy

Duncan Matthews and Olga Gurgula, 'Patent Strategies and Competition Law in the Pharmaceutical Sector: Implications for Access to Medicines' (2016) 38(11) European Intellectual Property Review 661

Organisation for Economic Co-operation and Development, 'Competition Provisions in Trade Agreements – Contribution from Ukraine' DAF/COMP/GF/WD (2019)

Organisation for Economic Co-operation and Development, 'Licensing of IP Rights and Competition Law' DAF/COMP(2019)

Organisation for Economic Co-operation and Development, 'Excessive Pricing in Pharmaceutical Markets – Note by Ukraine' DAF/COMP/WD (2018)119, 2018

Organisation for Economic Co-operation and Development, 'OECD Reviews of Legislation and Policy in the Field of Competition: Ukraine' (Report), 2016

Organisation for Economic Co-operation and Development, 'Competition Law and Policy in Ukraine: An OECD Peer Review' (Report) 2008

Kseniya Smyrnova, 'Enforcement of Competition Rules in the Association Agreement between the EU & Ukraine' (2014) 7(10) Yearbook of Antitrust and Regulatory Studies

Joseph Straus, '"Pay for Delay"—A Subtly Hidden, Overlooked or Ignored Transatlantic Divide: Exemplified on the *Actavis* Decision of the US Supreme Court and the *Servier* Decision of the EU Commission' (2016) 76 Zbornik Znanstvenih Razprav

Tetiana Stepurko, Milena Pavlova, Irena Gryga, Liubove Murauskiene, Wim Groot, 'Informal Payments for Health Care Services: The Case of Lithuania, Poland and Ukraine' (2015) 6(1) Journal of Eurasian Studies

Igor Svechkar, Oleksandr Voznyuk, Alexey Pustovit and Tetiana Vovk, 'Restraints of Trade and Dominance in Ukraine: Overview' *Thomson Reuters Practical Law* (1 February 2021) https://ca.practicallaw.thomsonreuters.com/7-569-9990?transitionType=Default&contextData=%28sc.Default%29

United Nations Development Programme, 'Using Competition Law to Promote Access to Medicines and Related Health Technologies in Low- and Middle-Income Countries' *UNDP* (7 December 2017) https://www.undp.org/publications/using-competition-law-promote-access-medicines-and-related-health-technologies-low-and

United Nations Development Programme, 'Using Competition Law to Promote Access to Health Technologies: A Guidebook for Low-and Middle-Income Countries' (Guidebook) 2014

United Nations Conference on Trade and Development, 'Voluntary Peer Review of Competition Law and Policy: Ukraine' (2013) (Report) UNCTAD/DITC/CLP/2013/3, 2013

United Nations Development Programme, 'Global Commission on HIV and the Law: Risk, Rights and Health' (Report) 87, 2012

United Nations Secretary-General's High-Level Panel on Access to Medicine, 'Promoting Innovation and Access to Health Technologies' (Report) 2016

Richard Whish and David Bailey, *Competition Law* (Oxford 8th ed. 2015)

World Health Organization 'Evaluation of The Affordable Medicines Programme in Ukraine' (Report) WHO 2019

World Health Organization, 'Can People Afford to Pay for Health Care? Ukraine' (Review) WHO 2018

World Trade Organization, 'Intellectual Property and the Public Interest: Promoting Public Health Through Competition Law and Policy: Communication from China and South Africa' (Communication) IP/C/W/643, 2018

Legal Mechanisms of Protection Against Unfair Competition in Ukraine—Prerequisites, Problems and Trends

Olga Bakalinska

Contents

Abstract Fair competition embodies certain moral-ethical and socio-historical ideas about good and evil in business activity, determining the limits of permitted behaviour, especially in competition. Studying the issues of economic competition legislation, we found that researchers have not tried to define the concept and content of fair competition in their research, although each of them pointed to the need to

O. Bakalinska (✉)
The Academician F. H. Burchak Scientific-Research Institute of Private Law and Entrepreneurship of the National Academy of Legal Sciences of Ukraine, Kyiv, Ukraine
e-mail: bakalinskaya@ukr.net

H. Richter (ed.), *Competition and Intellectual Property Law in Ukraine*,
MPI Studies on Intellectual Property and Competition Law 31,
https://doi.org/10.1007/978-3-662-66101-7_10

provide conditions for its development and protection. Thus, fair competition serves as a certain ideal or goal of legal regulation for most researchers, but there is no specific objective form of its implementation. The judicial and administrative practices of terminating unfair competition in business activity are based on a similar position, although the decisions of the Antimonopoly Committee of Ukraine and the courts sometimes differ. For 20 years, the Antimonopoly Committee of Ukraine has been the leader of legal protection against unfair competition, having promoted the ideas of pro-competitive awareness through competition advocacy mechanisms. In the last few years, the leading role in ensuring an effective mechanism for protection against unfair competition has lain with the courts, in particular the Commercial Division of the Supreme Court of Ukraine. That is why we have been observing changes in approaches to the definition of unfair competition and the combination of a general prohibition of unfair competition with related categories of the abuse of rights and the protection of intellectual property rights over the last three to five years.

1 Introduction

The development of competition legislation and law in Ukraine are inextricably linked with the independence of our state, the implementation of economic and political transformations and our country's decision to integrate with Europe.

What is to be considered as the starting point in the development of competition law in Ukraine is solved differently by different researchers. Some believe that the history of competition law begins with the first acts aimed at creating conditions for competitive competition and demonopolization in the 1990s, while others believe that the origins of the formation of competition law should be sought earlier—in the 19th, the 17th and even the tenth century. Indeed, attempts to regulate competition relations are found in the earliest sources of law, although modern competition law has been formed in our time. Moreover, competition law is one of the few complex subsystems of legal regulation in the sphere of the economy that was fully formed at the end of the twentieth century without absorbing the legal material that existed before. Nevertheless, the academic basis of competition law was laid at the end of the nineteenth century by French, German, American and Russian researchers (B. Zeller, E. Ehrlich, E. Puglier, O. Venediktov, V. Synaisky, O. Kaminka, G. Shershenevych, V. Schreter).

The rejection of competition in the Soviet Union and the construction of a state monopoly system did not stop the development of competition law theory, and in particular academic research on the legal nature and features of the development of competition in bourgeois economies were the subject of study by many researchers (V. Eremenko, V. Mozolina, O. Zhidkova, M. Kulagina, O. Zimenkova, Yu. Svyadosets). In addition, certain obligations to ensure fair competition, although formal, extended to the USSR, since the state was a member of the Paris Convention for the protection of industrial property and other international conventions. It is worth noting that the research of European and Soviet academics became the basis for the formation of the theoretical foundations for the development of competition legislation and law after Ukraine gained independence.

Ukraine's international obligations both within the World Trade Organisation (WTO) and the association agreement between Ukraine and the European communities have a significant impact on modern competition legislation and the development of the law. They determine the vector of the development of Ukraine competition legislation, allow the improvement of processes and procedures in the activities of the Antimonopoly Committee of Ukraine (AMCU) and other state authorities in the field of competition, ensure proper protection of the interests of business entities, consumers and the state in competitive legal relations and establish a dialogue between the state and business on a civilized basis, in particular through the advocacy of competition, compliance with competition law, etc.

An important factor in ensuring the development of competitive competition is the presence of certain ideas about good and evil in competition, about integrity and bad faith in competitive behaviour. Honest, good customs, business practices, rules of corporate and entrepreneurial ethics that take into account the historical, social and mental features of how the representatives of the Ukrainian nation perceive and assess phenomena of objective reality, have a significant impact on the formation of a competition culture in economic activity.

Modern competition legislation is the result of the long-term multifaceted work of adapting competition legislation formed according to best international practices to constantly changing economic, political and social conditions. Since its inception, competition law has undergone significant changes. These began with the change in the model of legal regulation as adopted from the USA in the law of Ukraine on limiting monopolism and preventing unfair competition in business activities to the European influence on the law of Ukraine "On the Protection of Economic Competition", followed by changes in the organizational mode of economic competition support and protection, changes in the terminological basis and principles of state policy in this field, and ending with the content revision of the individual competition laws and institutional norms in order to expand the scope of legal regulation through the formation of new competition legislation institutions, such as state assistance to business entities and public procurement.

Over the past few years, Ukrainian academics have presented thorough scientific research on the problems of developing competition legislation and law. Thanks to the scientific research of A. Bezukh, S. Valitov, N. Korchak, V. Polyukhovich, O. Podtserkovny, K. Smirnova, T. Shvydkaya, S. Shklyar and others, it has been possible to determine the features of competition law doctrine content and structure, trends in the development of its institutions, and ways to improve law-making and law enforcement practice.

Today, we are on the threshold of fundamental changes in competition legislation and law, which are related to the need to take account of changes in the economy and law enforcement, as well as the need to respond to the consequences of global economic and social crises, especially in the context of modern globalization and regionalization processes.

2 General Approaches to the Definition of "Unfair Competition" in Ukrainian Legislation

The awareness of the dangers of violations of the principles of good faith in competition determined the need for international legal protection of business entities and consumer rights from the effects of unfair competition back in the late nineteenth century. In particular, at the Brussels Diplomatic Conference of 1900 on the revision of the 1883 Paris Convention on the Protection of Industrial Property, it was agreed that any act of competition in conflict with fair practices in industrial and commercial matters was considered to be an act of unfair competition under Art. 10bis (unfair competition) of the Convention. The article also contains a list of actions that should be prohibited as unfair competition, namely:

- all acts of such a nature as to create confusion by any means whatever with the establishment, the goods, or the industrial or commercial activities, of a competitor;
- false allegations in the course of trade of such a nature as to discredit the establishment, the goods, or the industrial or commercial activities, of a competitor;
- indications or allegations the use of which in the course of trade is liable to mislead the public as to the nature, the manufacturing process, the characteristics, the suitability for their purpose, or the quantity, of the goods.

It should be noted that in accordance with Art. 10ter of the Paris Convention, the governments of all states that have signed the Convention are obliged to provide administrative and judicial protection of the rights of business entities and citizens against acts of unfair competition. So, if an entrepreneur cannot receive adequate protection within the national system of protection against unfair competition, they have the right to apply for protection of their rights to international legal institutions both with a claim for recognition of the fact of the offence and with a claim against state bodies that did not provide effective protection of their rights.

Therefore, the acknowledgement of unfair competition as an offence, in fact, gives grounds for regarding fair competition as a universally recognized good requiring proper and effective protection. According to N. Korchak, the right to participate in fair competition is derived from the right to entrepreneurial activity as a subjective right. So, the right to participate in fair competition is a natural and inalienable human right. In addition, since the state is accountable to the individual for its activities, the content of its obligation to be a guarantor of fair competition is the implementation of a system of organizational and legal measures to counteract, restrict or eliminate the negative economic consequences that may arise in the absence of competition.[1] The first legal definition of unfair competition appeared in Art. 1 Law of Ukraine "On Protection against Unfair Competition" (Unfair Competition Law) of 7 June 1996. In accordance with this Law, any actions in competition contrary to the rules, trade and other fair practices in business activity are deemed to be unfair competition. A. Deringer stated in a commentary to the Unfair Competition Law that the Law is

[1] Natalia Korchak, 'General Provisions of State Protection of Competition in Business' (2001) 2 Entrepreneurship, Economy and Law 7(8).

intended to regulate relations in business, and must therefore be applied provided that the actions taken meet two criteria:

(1) they must take place in business activity, that is under the conditions of economic turnover;
(2) they must be committed with a competitive intention, namely with the intention to improve the competitive situation of the offending party or a third party in relation to their competitors.

For the provisions of the Unfair Competition Law to apply, it must first be determined whether there is a competitive relationship between the offender and the person whose rights have been violated.

Whether a competitive act is unfair is determined according to fair practices in the relevant field. This wording also complies with the principle of faith and trust, well-known in almost all civil law, according to which, in the absence of legal or contractual provisions, obligations must be fulfilled in accordance with the traditional rules for this type of relationship. However, A. Deringer notes that the term "rules" in Art. 1 does not mean legislative rules, but rules or customs that have been developed in the economy. Nevertheless, the existence of such rules in the trade is not yet absolute proof that the actions they regulate are fair competition, as there may be cases of abuse in the trade which, in the interests of other market participants or the public, cannot be considered fair.[2]

The uncertainty and vagueness of the legislative definition of unfair competition has given rise to the academic understanding of this concept as well as the search for clear criteria for assessing the good faith or bad faith of a particular business practice.

For instance, it was held in the judgment of the High Commercial Court of Ukraine on 2 March 2010 in case No. 38/108[4] that the Unfair Competition Law does not contain an exhaustive list of actions that fall under the definition of unfair competition, and therefore its scope is not limited exclusively by the actions specified in Chapters 2–4 of the Law. At the same time, the Law directly refers to the relevant fair practices in business (economic) activities (in particular, regarding the illegality of the use of another's business reputation [Chapter 2], regarding the creation of obstacles to business entities in the process of competition and the achievement of undue competitive advantages [Chapter 3], illegal acquisition, disclosure and use of commercial secrets [Chapter 4], etc.). Unfair competition is a form of illegal action by business entities in the competition process which violates the rights of individual business entities, as well as rules, trade and fair practices in business activity. As P. Kharchenko rightly points out, the objective criterion for establishing bad faith in the actions of the offender is the hypothetical sense of the "honesty" of a certain "respectable and honest entrepreneur". The main criterion for determining "bad faith" in the market is in the purpose of the rules of law relating to unfair competition. In theory, the free action of competition mechanisms can regulate the behaviour of a

[2] On the Unfair Competition Law see Arved Deringer, 'Commentary to the Law of Ukraine "On Protection against Unfair Competition"' in Gennady Androschuk and Sergiy Shklyar (eds), *Competition Law: Protection Against Unfair Competition—Scientific and Practical Publication* (Justinian 2012) 285.

dishonest entrepreneur because the consumer, acting in this competition as an arbitrator, can make a choice in favour of goods, works or services of honest competitors. However, with the increasing complication of the economic situation, such a role of the consumer is becoming less significant, because consumers they can often not only respond but inadequately to dishonest behaviour by the entrepreneur, but are also unable to recognize such behaviour. At the same time, both the entrepreneur-competitor and the consumer need protection from unfair competition, and in this connection, public interests, the protection of which is one of the main functions of the state, become a priority in the prevention and termination of unfair competition by the bodies of the AMCU.[3] It should be noted that the analysis of the application practice of Ukrainian competition law allows the conclusion that during almost twenty-five years of its existence, it was the provision of Art. 1 Unfair Competition Law that was applied the most frequently. Even in cases when qualifying certain offences gave the opportunity to justify and properly confirm the dishonest behaviour of an individual business entity, both the AMCU and representatives of the parties have used references to the general prohibition of unfair competition in Art. 1 Unfair Competition Law and in Art. 10bis Paris Convention for the Protection of Industrial Property to prove and justify their position. However, the uncertainty and vagueness of the concept of unfair competition contained in Art. 1 of the Law has often led to the non-recognition of and appeals against decisions of the antimonopoly authorities by both entrepreneurs and the courts. In some cases, this uncertainty is still a reason for the abuse of rights by some lawyers and judges in appealing the decisions of the AMCU and its bodies and the decision of the courts on specific cases. According to the Unfair Competition Law as amended on 18 December 2008, any actions in competition in conflict with trade and other fair customs in economic activity are recognized as unfair competition.

The clarification of the legal definition of "unfair competition" in the Unfair Competition Law as of 18 December 2008 is associated primarily with the fact that the uncertainty of the term "rules" in the current competition law and its ambiguity in lexicographic sources (dictionaries) led to a significant complication in qualifying violations, especially in the case of certain actions being qualified solely on the basis of Art. 1 of the Law. In addition, because of these changes, the concept of unfair competition contained in Art. 1 Unfair Competition Law was brought into line with the definition of "act of unfair competition" contained in Art. 10bis Paris Convention for the Protection of Industrial Property of 20 March 1883, an international legal standard for protection against unfair competition. In view of this, the provisions of Art. 10bis Paris Convention should be considered as rules of direct action that can be applied directly by the courts of Ukraine and the bodies of the AMCU. Where certain actions in competition are to be qualified as unfair competition based on Art.

[3] Petro Kharchenko, *Administrative and Legal Measures to Ensure Protection Against Unfair Competition in the Activities of the Antimonopoly Committee of Ukraine* (Institute of Legislation of the Verkhovna Rada of Ukraine 2005) 30.

10bis(3)(1), (2), (3) Paris Convention, reference should be also made to the provisions of Art. 1(1) Unfair Competition Law.[4]

Thus, the concept of unfair competition enshrined in Art. 1 Unfair Competition Law has finally acquired the characteristics of a general prohibition (general offence), regardless of whether a particular business practice complies with the applicable law or merely violates moral and ethical norms and requirements of economic activity. At the same time, the establishment of a general prohibition of unfair competition covers all actions that go beyond trade and other fair practices in economic activity.

The concept of unfair competition comprises the following features:

- the presence of business entities' actions;
- the performance of business entities' actions takes place in economic activity;
- the focus of action is to gain an advantage in competition;
- the existence of a conflict between the actions committed by the offender and trade and other fair practices in economic activity.

Thus, to qualify certain behaviour as unfair competition, it is necessary to prove that the relevant business entity or group of entities is active in the market. Thus the definition of unfair competition in Ukrainian law does not cover inactivity by business entities. At the same time, the scope of implementation of a business entity's active behaviour can be diverse: the production and sale of goods, the provision of services or the performance of works. In terms of the differences in the legal content of the regulation, the concept of "priority", is used in the Unfair Competition Law in the sense of the priority right to use the results of lawful, fair and honest business activity, and is not identical to the concept of "priority" according to the Laws of Ukraine "On Protection of Rights to Industrial Designs", "On Protection of Rights to Inventions and Utility Models" and "On Protection of Rights to Marks for Goods and Services", which defines priority as the priority of the application for registration of relevant rights. When resolving a dispute over the priority of intellectual property rights (trademarks, industrial designs, etc.), the court must proceed not only from the owner's exclusive rights to the use of the registered trademark, but also from a person's general rights to use the results of their own activities (if not stipulated otherwise by law), and the exclusive competence of the Antimonopoly Committee of Ukraine in the field of protection against unfair competition. One example was the consideration of the actual circumstances of the use of two labels for one product by two manufacturers in the same market, where the external design of the labels (overall composition, colour, placement of basic elements and inscriptions, as well as individual elements, product names, technical inscriptions and fonts) is similar to the degree of confusion and may lead to confusion of the business entities' activities.[5]

The current legislation does not link the possibility of protection against unfair competition only to the existence of the injured party's right to the relevant intellectual

[4] Olga Bakalinska, 'Improving Legislative Protection Against Unfair Competition: A New Step Towards the European Economic Space' (2009) 2 Competition Bulletin of the AMC of Ukraine 29.

[5] Resolution of the Supreme Economic Court of Ukraine on Some Issues of Dispute Resolution Practice Related to the Protection of Intellectual Property Rights, 2012, No. 12, v0012600-12.

property. At the same time, to prove that certain competitive actions are in conflict with trade and other fair customs in economic activity, and that therefore such actions are unfair competition under Art. 1(1) Unfair Competition Law, it is necessary to determine which rule of behaviour or custom is violated by the business entity, and to establish the content of this rule, as well as to refer to the evidence used to establish its content.[6]

A prerequisite for recognizing certain actions of business entities as unfair competition is the performance of these actions "in competition". Given that economic competition is competition between participants in competitive economic relations, unfair competition as a form of abuse of the right to fair competition is displayed in these relations between business entities competing for the market, product or consumer. Thus, to recognize a certain business practice as unfair competition, it is necessary to prove that business entities are rivals in a specific field of economic activity, have a common or similar circle of consumers, offer identical or similar (interchangeable) goods and gain an advantage in competition due to their own achievements.[7] For instance, in the judgment of the High Commercial Court of Ukraine as of 9 July 2013 in case No. 913/417/13-г[8] the Court held that the use of a designation is unfair competition only where it is used unfairly and leads to an advantage over competitors and/or it misleads consumers. The same approach is seen in the decision of the High Commercial Court of Ukraine as of 25 January 2011 in case No. 14/460[9] where the Court upheld the decision of the AMCU on the sale of medicines and medical devices using designations on the package similar to the designations of another business entity, which it held to be a violation in the form of an improper use of designations.[10] At the same time, the fact that a business entity uses designations that are already used by another business entity may not be considered unfair competition if it does not lead to confusion with the activities of the other business entity, in particular if the designations are significantly different and the business entities are separated geographically (carry out their activities in different cities), and therefore there is no fact of competition between them (including unfair).[11] On the other hand, in it is necessary to assess the compliance of a specific business entity in a contractual relationship with the requirements of good faith or

[6] Overview of case law of the Supreme Economic Court of Ukraine and the Supreme Court of Ukraine on the Application of Legislation into Protection of Economic Competition as of 31 December 2017, 79–90 https://amcu.gov.ua/npas/oglyad-sudovoyi-praktiki-vishchogo-gospodarskogo-sudu-ukrayini-ta-verhovnogo-sudu-ukrayini-z-pitan-zastosuvannya-zakonodavstva-pro-zahist-ekonomichnoyi-konkurciyi accessed 11 June 2022.

[7] Olga Bakalinska, *Protection of Economic Competition: Organizational and Legal Principles of Public Administration* (VM Koretsky Institute of State and Law 2003) 68.

[8] High Commercial Court of Ukraine 01-24/152 (2013) 913/417/13-г; Review Letter of the High Commercial Court of Ukraine, 24 December 2014, 01-06/2304/14, 3.

[9] AMCU (Decision) 16 July 2009 256-p.

[10] High Commercial Court of Ukraine (2013) 5015/6832/11.

[11] High Commercial Court of Ukraine (2011) 5002-29/5051.1-2010 https://zakononline.com.ua/court-decisions/show/30380450 accessed 11 June 2022.

bad faith, in combination with the criteria of good faith actions on the part of competitors, it is appropriate to apply general criteria of good faith, such as the actions of business entities and their caution with respect to the rights and interests of the other party, and it may be reasonable to anticipate harm to these rights and interests and to prevent a violation of the fair balance of rights and interests of the parties to the contractual obligation.[12] At the same time, it is necessary to check the compliance of the content of the agreement or actions of the participants in competition and their consequences with the requirements of competition legislation.

The Resolution of the Plenum of the High Commercial Court of Ukraine "On Some Issues of Dispute Resolution Practice Related to the Protection of Intellectual Property Rights" states that the AMCU must determine in its decisions which rule of behaviour or custom has been violated by the business entity, the content of this rule, and refer to the evidence on the basis of which this content is determined to establish that the business entity's actions contradict these rules of behaviour or other fair practices in industrial and commercial cases (Art. 1(1) Unfair Competition Law). The duty of proving the relevant circumstances in court rests with the Committee. The court, for its part, must assess the related evidence in accordance with the requirements of Chapter 5 of the Commercial Procedural Code of Ukraine. It should be pointed out that the rules of behaviour, regulated by the Civil Code of Ukraine and other legislative acts governing the protection of intellectual property rights, including those that define fairness, good faith and reasonableness as general principles of civil law, do not fall under the term of "fair customs" in business activity.[13]

It should be noted that in the process of developing the practice of applying competition law, the attitude to the assessment and definition of this criterion in the classification of actions as unfair competition has changed. However, it is not necessary for a business entity to be a competitor of an honest party to act in bad faith. A classic example was given by A. Kur, in which the German competition court recognized the existence of a competitive relationship between a business entity whose business was roasting coffee beans and one whose business was trading in flowers. In making its decision, the court proceeded from the fact that the entrepreneur who used the phrase "Coffee instead of flowers" for advertising established a competitive relationship.[14] Unfair methods of competition are increasingly being used by business entities that act for the benefit of other market participants. In many cases, the lack of a competitive relationship between the offender and the person whose rights have been violated by unfair acts allows the offender to avoid liability. Such actions are quite often the result of marketing strategies by the business entity to promote the product on the market, such as product placement and ambush marketing. The use of such marketing strategies is usually associated with the ever-increasing influence

[12] Yuriy Tobota, *The Principle of Justice, Good Faith and Reasonableness in Civil Law* (Law Academy of Ukraine named after Yaroslav the Wise 2011) 175.

[13] Resolution of the Supreme Economic Court of Ukraine on Some Issues of Dispute Resolution Practice Related to the Protection of Intellectual Property Rights, 2012, No. 12, v0012600-12.

[14] Speech by Annette Kur at the International Conference in Kyiv (1995) on the topic "Principles of Law on Unfair Competition, with a Focus on German Law".

of PR technologies on the development of commercial relations and trade and thus provides the opportunity to obtain maximum commercial results with minimal use of their own intellectual, financial and production resources.

For example, actions that lead to an unauthorized or deceptive association (commercial or non-commercial) with the Olympic Games, and thus violate the legal rights arising from the relevant agreement with the official marketing partners of the Olympic Games, are considered as an act of unfair competition. Such a strict attitude does not prevent such brands as Nike, Adidas and Reebok acting as sponsors, ambushers of the Olympic Games and other events in the sports world from time to time. In view of this, in qualifying certain actions of business entities as unfair competition, it is necessary, in our opinion, to prove not only the presence of a competitive situation or a special competitive relationship that arises in the course of competition, but also the intention of the business entity to obtain or maintain a competitive advantage in economic activity through the use of unfair means of competition.

When a certain action is to be qualified as an act of unfair competition, the business entity's behaviour is assessed in accordance with the requirements of good faith. The good faith of a business entity's behaviour in a competitive relationship should be assessed on the basis of an analysis of the entity's behaviour towards competitors, consumers and the state. The criterion of good faith is the standard of the conscious and responsible behaviour of a business entity which in the process of competition uses its own achievements to win over competitors, shows the necessary care and concern to balance its rights and interests with the interests of its competitors, the state and society as a whole, does not intend to harm competitors or consumers by its actions, and whose conduct corresponds to the rules and customs of economic turnover as well as the moral principles of society.

The general prohibition of unfair competition contained in the current legislation of Ukraine is supplemented by a number of private prohibitions on the most common and dangerous acts of unfair competition. In accordance with Art. 1(1) Unfair Competition Law an act of unfair competition is an action in competition as defined in Chapters 2–4 of this Law; thus, in determining certain unfair competitive actions, the legislator has also classified them, in particular:

(1) illegal use of a business entity's business reputation (Chapter 2 of the Law);
(2) creation of obstacles for business entities in the process of competition and achieving illegal advantages in competition (Chapter 3 of the Law);
(3) illegal acquisition, disclosure and use of commercial secrets (Chapter 4 of the Law).

The following sections will discuss the peculiarities of these specific acts of unfair competition in the practice of the law enforcement agencies.

3 Illegal Use of the Business Reputation of a Business Entity

3.1 Overview

The practice of the application of the legislation on protection against unfair competition shows that the most common violations of the current legislation in this area vary in the nature and the legal consequences of the encroachment on the business entity's reputation. In the law enforcement practice of the Romano-Germanic legal system, these types of violations are the most common. The names used vary: "the illegal use of another's reputation" under French law; "the illegal use of another's reputation and the results of another's work" under German law; "actions leading to confusion between the goods and enterprises of competitors" in Italy. A common feature of all these actions is their focus on obtaining an economic effect (attracting consumers) using a competitor's business reputation, leading to confusion between the competitor's goods and enterprise in the minds of consumers.[15] In the UK and Canada, these actions are called "doing business under another's name".[16]

In terms of the characterization of this type of violation, it should be noted that, as a rule, the business reputation is not the direct object of encroachment in the commission of unfair acts. The illegal use of a business reputation is carried out by encroachments by a competitor on its material media: products, brand names, marks for goods and services or other designations. These media should be well known in the relevant market and associated with certain, usually high, quality characteristics of the product by consumers. Under such conditions, the offender who illegally uses these objects is able to use the achievements of a law-abiding competitor, namely, their owner.

The business entity's reputation is considered to be the result of others' perception of its owner's activity. For legal entities, the object of assessment are the goods, works or services produced by the business entity. In the process of carrying out their activities, business entities enter various relations, the result of which has a direct impact on the formation of the business reputation and its assessment. For instance, I. Koval distinguishes three groups of such relations: relations with consumers (buyers) of goods and services, relations with business partners, contractors and competitors, and relations between the business entity and public authorities, controlling bodies and the mass media.[17] Hence, the business reputation must be assessed in the light of these parameters.

Such a use of a business entity's reputation is considered illegal if it in whole or in part encroaches on a specific object of the intellectual property or tangible property of the business entity that embodies a specific element of the business

---

[15] Vladimir Eremenko, *Legislation on the Suppression of Unfair Competition of Capitalist Countries* (Moskva VNIIPI 1991) 9–11.

[16] Sergey Paraschuk, *Unfair Competition: Content and Legal Means of its Suppression* (Lomonosov Moscow State University 1995) 150.

[17] Irina Koval, *Illegal Use of Business Reputation of the Business Entity as a Form of Unfair Competition* (2002) 10 Entrepreneurship, Economy and Law 23 (25).

entity's reputation or affects the assessment of this reputation. It should be noted that the object of encroachment can be both an object, such as the brand name, and the set of objects in which it is embodied.

Proving the "bad faith" of the use of a business reputation is always associated with the establishment of the fact of an unauthorized use of a particular object that is part of the business reputation of a particular business entity. Unauthorized is the use of objects without permission from their owners or from persons who have a priority over the use of certain assets (authorized by the state through registration) or who are the first to put the object into circulation (priority of use). For certain actions to be qualified as the illegal use of a business entity's reputation, a necessary condition is that these objects are directly put into circulation. Putting into circulation is to be understood as the sale, import, offer for sale, in particular through the internet, storage for the purposes of further resale, etc.[18]

At the same time, it is not necessary to prove the existence of damage to the owner, but the fact that the offender makes a profit is only an additional condition of the offence, because the very fact of misuse is the basis for liability. Common to all types of violations identified in Chapter 2 Unfair Competition Law is that they are all aimed at gaining an advantage in competition using a competitor's business reputation, which in turn leads or may lead to confusion with the competitor's goods, works or services. In this case, the competitor as a rule loses consumers and contractors and does not make a profit. At the same time, contractors and consumers lose the right to freely choose the relevant product due to the confusion, and the distinctive properties of the fair competitor's designations, its products and packaging are blurred or totally lost.

The most common type of confusion is when the designation is so similar to the protected designation that consumers cannot identify which is authentic. When establishing the fact of confusion, the following factors relating to the degree of distinctiveness of the protected designation should be taken into account: volume of activity; owner's business reputation; the level of consumer awareness; and the similarity of the designations.

Types of misuse of the business entity reputation are laid down in Chapter 2 Unfair Competition Law. They are classified according to the objects of encroachment and are grouped into four types of violations: misuse of another's designations (Sec. 3.2); misuse of goods from another manufacturer (Sec. 3.3); copying the look of the product (Sec. 3.4); comparative advertising (Sec. 3.5).

[18] Gennady Androschuk et al., *Scientific and Practical Commentary to the Law of Ukraine on Protection against Unfair Competition—Scientific and Practical Edition* (Ûridična Gazeta 2013) 40.

3.2 Improper Use of Designations

In accordance with Art. 4 Unfair Competition Law, it is considered illegal to use the name, commercial (brand) name, trademark (mark for goods and services), advertising materials, packaging of goods and periodicals, and other designations without the permission (consent) of a business entity that has previously begun to use them or similar designations in economic activity, which has led or may lead to confusion with the activities of this business entity. For this violation, proof is required that:

- the designations are used without the owner's permission, i.e. illegally;
- there is a use of designations registered as objects of intellectual property or that have priority protection due to long-term use in economic turnover;
- the relevant designations are associated by business entities and consumers with the goods, works or services of a particular business entity with a good reputation (high quality);
- such activity leads to the confusion of the goods, works and services of the offender with the corresponding goods (works, services) of the honest business entity;
- by committing such an unfair act, the offender gains an advantage in competition without making any intellectual or financial effort.

The provisions of Art. 4 Unfair Competition Law provide protection against unfair competition in the form of the misuse of business reputation that is based not on a protection document, such as a patent for an industrial design or a certificate for a mark for goods and services, but on the priority of any designation or set of designations that distinguishes the activity of the corresponding business entity from others. It should be noted that this approach has become common in judicial practice.

For example, the private enterprise Dyvotsvit in its business activity has been using the design of packaging adhesives "MetaFix Flizelin Premium", "MetaFix Vinyl Indicator" and "MetaFix Universal Special", which are similar to the design of adhesive packaging like "Metylan Flizelin" and "Metylan Vinyl Premium" manufactured by the limited liability company with foreign investment HENKEL BAUTEHNIK (UKRAINE). HENKEL BAUTECHNIK (UKRAINE) II Ltd. did not grant permission to either use a similar design or sell on the same commodity market. The violation was not recognized and not stopped. A fine of 1.6 million UAH was imposed, because this similarity could lead to confusion with the business activity of HENKEL BAUTECHNIK (UKRAINE) II Ltd. The Committee recognized the usage of MetaFix Flizelin Premium, MetaFix Vinyl Indicator and MetaFix Universal Special by Dyvotsvit as a violation of Art. 4 Unfair Competition Law. Dyvotsvit was fined and obliged to cease the violation within two months.[19]

Based on the results of this case in 2020, the AMCU issued a decision, by which the actions of the Pharmaceutical Company Zdorovya were recognized as a violation. That was provided under Art. 4 Unfair Competition Law as in the form of "usage without permission". The design of the "Citramon-Health" medicine packaging was

---

[19] AMCU Ukraine (Decision) 23 December 2021, No. 716-p https://amcu.gov.ua/storage/app/uploads/public/627/ccb/c10/627ccbc10ef3d640199715.pdf accessed 11 June 2022.

similar to the design of the medicine "CitramonDarnitsa" from PJSC Pharmaceutical Company Darnytsia, which it had started to use earlier than Pharmaceutical Company Zdorovya Ltd. in its business activities, which could lead to confusion with the PJSC Pharmaceutical Company Darnytsia.[20]

An example of a violation of the law on protection against unfair competition is the case of "Strongdrink" LLC regarding the use without permission (consent) of the international corporation "Jack Daniel's Properties, Inc." (California, USA) of labels for Black Jack and Black Jack Silver strong malt ("Solodovyi") alcoholic beverages that were similar to the label design of Jack Daniel's alcoholic products, previously used by the international corporation "Jack Daniel's Properties, Inc.", which could lead to confusion with the activities of the latter corporation. In its decision of 1 October 2020 in case No. 910/16373/18, the Supreme Court dismissed the appeal on the law of "Strongdrink" LLC against the decision of the lower courts in the dispute, with the AMCU appealing the finding of a violation of the law on protection against unfair competition.[21]

Commercial Courts should take into account in their proceedings, that Art. 5 Law of Ukraine "On Protection of Trademarks for Goods and Services" and Art. 4 Unfair Competition Law, differently determine the date from which the right to protection against illegal use is granted to the owner of the mark for goods and services. According to the first law, it is the date of submission of the application; according to the second, it is the date of the beginning of a trademark usage in business activity.[22]

In general, the provisions of Art. 4 Unfair Competition Law provide protection against such competition in the form of usage of designations not on the basis of a security document, but on the grounds of the priority in using designations or a set of designations, providing individualization of the indicated business entity.

The precondition for the application of the Unfair Competition Law to the disputed legal relations is the existence of competition relations between entities to which the violation relates. If the infringement of intellectual property rights occurs outside the sphere of competition, then it is exclusively the Central Committee of Ukraine, the Civil Code of Ukraine and other legislative acts governing the protection of intellectual property rights and relevant procedural law, that ensure the protection of such rights.

---

[20] AMCU (Decision) 17 December 2020, No. 793-r https://amcu.gov.ua/storage/app/uploads/public/605/4a0/e26/6054a0e268fc0702551413.pdf accessed 11 June 2022.

[21] The Supreme Court of Ukraine composed of a panel of judges of the Commercial Court of Cassation (2020) 910/16373/18.

[22] Resolution of the Supreme Economic Court of Ukraine on Some Issues of Dispute Resolution Practice Related to the Protection of Intellectual Property Rights, 2012, No. 12, v0012600-12, paras 91–94.

3.3 Illegal Use of the Goods of Another Manufacturer

The illegal use of the goods of another manufacturer is the putting into circulation of the goods of another manufacturer under a wrong designation by changing or removing the designations of the manufacturer without the permission of the authorized person.

In this way, an unfair competitor tries to gain a certain image in the market and "promote" their brand at the expense of an honest business entity that duly monitors the quality and range of products while investing a large amount of money. Such dishonest behaviour may result in significant harm to the honest business entity.

For a finding of a violation under Art. 5 Unfair Competition Law, in the form of misuse of goods from another manufacturer the following conditions must be satisfied:

- the goods put into circulation are the goods of another manufacturer;
- the corresponding product is in demand and is characterized by a fairly high quality;
- the use of the goods is illegal, i.e. the goods are put into circulation without the permission of the rightful owner;
- the competitor deliberately removes the designations of the rightful owner and aims to use the competitor's achievements for its own purposes;
- the putting of such goods with the offender's own designations into circulation will contribute to the formation of a positive reputation of the offender;
- the putting of such goods into circulation will contribute to the partial outflow of consumers from a fair competitor;
- such behaviour may cause damage to a competitor.

This offence can be committed by substituting a less-known product for a better-known product or a product of inferior quality for a better-quality product. Such an offence not only misleads the consumer but also damages the good name of the product and the business reputation of the manufacturer or supplier of the product. Such "substitution" of goods is unfair competition, even if no other trademark or brand name is used.

3.4 Copying Product Appearance

Copying product appearance is the reproduction of the product look of another business entity (entrepreneur) and putting it into circulation without an unambiguous indication of the manufacturer of the copy, which may lead to confusion with the activities of another business entity (entrepreneur).

The entrepreneur uses the appearance of a product to distinguish it from the total mass of similar products. This is done by giving the product a new and original shape, pattern, colour scheme, etc.[23] The product appearance is quite often the result of creative activity on the part of the business entity. To give a product uniqueness and individuality, an honest competitor expends significant mental and material resources. The product appearance is thus a business card of the business entity or an extra feature individualizing its activities. That is why any improper use of the product appearance can cause damage to a fair competitor.

A finding of a violation in the form of copying the product appearance requires the establishment and proof of the following:

- the appearance of the copied product is original and distinguishes that particular product from other similar ones;
- the product whose appearance is copied, is in demand;
- consumers associate the appropriate appearance of a product with high quality goods;
- putting the goods that look similar to the known product into circulation will lead to confusion with the activities of a competitor with a good reputation;
- giving a certain appearance to a product will help expand the circle of consumers and create an opportunity to earn extra income.

It should be noted that the current legislation allows the product appearance to be copied if such copying is functionally necessary. The peculiarity of the qualification of this violation is that the provisions of Art. 6 do not cover cases where the objects of the unfair action are products protected as objects of intellectual property rights.

3.5 Comparative Advertising

Advertising that contains a comparison with the goods, works, services or activities of another business entity is considered comparative. According to Art. 1 Law of Ukraine "On Advertising", advertising is information about a person or product, disseminated in any form and in any way and intended to form or maintain consumer awareness of the advertising and an interest in such persons or goods. At the same time, consumers of advertising are recognized as an indefinite number of people to whom advertising is addressed.

On 11 December 2019, the Law of Ukraine "On Amendments to Certain Legislative Acts of Ukraine" (on Harmonization of Legislation in the Field of Comparative Advertising with European Union Law) No. 0953 of 29 August 2019 (Law on Amendments) entered into force according to the conditions of using comparative advertisement in Ukraine.

The Law unifies the definition of comparative advertisement in various legislative acts. As of now, the comparative advertisement should be understood as advertising that contains comparisons with other persons, goods (activities) of another person,

[23] T Udalov, *Competition Law* (Shkola 2004) 200–202.

directly or indirectly identifying the competitor or goods and services offered by the competitor.

Also, in accordance with the Law on Amendments, Ukraine has lifted the ban on comparative advertisement in order to enhance the advertising effect with respect to medicines, medical devices, treatment methods, etc. We may find ourselves in a situation where, under conditions of fierce competition within the pharmaceutical market, we see a large amount of comparative advertising, which will compare some of the more beneficial aspects and will not take into account other significant ones. For example, comparing the prices on medicines, without taking into account the innovative level of such medicines, may influence the choices of consumers, who usually do not have specialist knowledge in the field of pharmaceuticals.

From now on, it will not be possible to prevent the use of a trademark or trade name when used for comparative advertisement of competing products. The use of a trademark in comparative advertisement is now a legitimate case of free use of a trademark without the consent of the copyright holder, if the comparative advertisement does not show indications of unfair business practices.

It should be borne in mind that the current legislation contains provisions that allow the use of comparative advertisement in the following cases:

- if the advertisement does not contain indications of unfair business practice specified by the legislation on consumer protection;
- if the advertisement compares homogeneous (similar) products that meet the same needs or have the same purpose, or compares the activities covered by one area or one activity;
- if the advertisement objectively compares one or more essential, comparable and representative characteristics of a homogeneous (similar) product, activity (in particular, price), information about which may influence the consumer's decision when making a choice;
- if the competitor's product, protected by trademark or trade name, is not depicted by the way of imitation. The Law of Ukraine "On Advertisement" determines the legality of comparisons in advertising and the responsibility for non-compliance with the requirements established by the Law for the content of comparative advertisement. When launching a comparative advertisement campaign, any business entity should comprehend that comparative advertisement must be based on an in-depth analysis of all components for such type of advertising, i.e. the idea, advertising text, design, text font, etc. It must meet clear requirements of the Law of Ukraine "On Advertisement on Comparative Advertising", as well as the Unfair Competition Law.

Examples of comparative advertisement on the verge of running afoul with the law can be found in Ukraine. The goals of the "competition of *trolls* from marketing" has unfolded before the eyes of Kyiv residents. The company Autobereg, a dealer of Hyundai, organized a campaign with the #liviyberegkrutishiy hashtag, whose slogan was: "There is no Maidan, but Boryspil is closer". Their competitors, AutoAlliance, a dealer of Nissan gave an answer in the best traditions of the genre: "Dynamo plays on the right", #the right embankment is steeper (that is tougher, awesome). Moreover, the third participant, Bogdan Corporation, which promotes Subaru cars on the Ukrainian market, put the full stop to this discussion: "It doesn't matter what the shore is, if you're in a Subaru car", backing up the board with the #girlsdon'tquarrel.[24]

A striking example of illegal comparative advertisement is the case of "Farby Kolorit" ("Paints Color") Ltd., which distributed leaflets in eight "Epicenter" hypermarkets, containing comparative advertisements of anti-corrosion coatings of its own manufacture with the products of some five other businesses. These leaflets contain links to the results of tests published in the magazine "Private House" of June 2015, however, as established by the Department, do not correspond to the original of this article and encourage customers to purchase products "Farby Kolorit". Moreover, the conclusions in the leaflets, which are allocated in a separate block, speak of its advantages over others. At the same time, during the investigation in the case it was established that said article in the magazine "Private House" of June 2015 was designed and issued by the Farby Kolorit Ltd. Order. In addition, the leaflets were not attached with the label "On the rights of advertising". That contributes to the consumers' imagination of misconception that they were offered not just an advertisement, but informational material, and therefore they perceived it with more confidence, which could affect their choice, because information for this segment of products was distributed directly at the place of sales and purchase.[25]

The distribution of advertising that compares the prices of goods sold by a competitor, not with the price of a specific product sold by the advertising entity but with the price of certain abstract products that are not objective and useful for informing customers, is a violation of the legislation on the protection of economic competition, provided by Art. 7 Unfair Competition Law in the form of comparative advertising.[26]

Dissemination of information by the business entity alleging an insufficient capacity of other business entities such that it is unable to provide the required number of relevant services, without reference to its own capacity, as a result of which the consumer may conclude that the advertising entity is able to meet all consumer demand for these services, is a violation of Art. 7 Unfair Competition Law in the form of comparative advertising.

Comparisons in advertising are not considered illegal if the information about goods, works or services, as confirmed by actual data, is reliable, objective and useful for informing consumers. That is, the qualification of certain information as

---

[24] Oleksandr Rozdorozhny, 'Comparative Advertisement and Advertising Trolling: On the Verge of what is Allowed' *Juridiczna Gazeta Online* (2 April 2018) https://yur-gazeta.com/publications/practice/inshe/porivnyalna-reklama-ta-reklamniy-troling-na-mezhi-dozvolenogo.html/ accessed 11 June 2022.

[25] "Paints Color" Ltd. was fined for using illegal comparative advertising, Kyiv Regional Territorial Branch of the Antimonopoly Committee of Ukraine.

[26] Overview of case law of the Supreme Economic Court of Ukraine and the Supreme Court of Ukraine on the Application of Legislation into Protection of Economic Competition as of 31 December 2017, 79–90 https://amcu.gov.ua/npas/oglyad-sudovoyi-praktiki-vishchogo-gospodarskogo-sudu-ukrayini-ta-verhovnogo-sudu-ukrayini-z-pitan-zastosuvannya-zakonodavstva-pro-zahist-ekonomichnoyi-konkurciyi accessed 11 June 2022.

comparative advertising requires proof that such information is not confirmed by actual data. We agree with studies that argue that such a definition of "comparative advertising" is not complete and sufficient for a clear regulation of the legal relations arising in connection with its application in practice.[27]

The qualification of specific advertising information as comparative requires proof of the following:

- the information provided is advertising information;
- the advertising information contains comparisons with the goods, works or services of a particular business entity;
- the customer of advertising (the person who disseminates information) is a competitor of the business entity whose goods, works or services are the subject of the comparison;
- the information contained in the advertising is not confirmed by actual data;
- by using comparisons in advertising information, the business entity will expand or be able to expand the range of contracting partners (consumers and suppliers);
- dissemination of such information may adversely affect the competitor's business activity.

4 Creation of Obstacles for Business Entities in the Process of Competition and Achieving Illegal Advantages in Competition

4.1 Overview

The second group of unfair competitive activities defined by Chapter III Unfair Competition Law includes various unfair activities of business entities in terms of their legal nature and content aimed at creating obstacles to business entities in competition and consequently gaining illegal advantages in competition. Obstacles to competition may be administrative or market-related in nature. In any case, barriers to competition are associated with restrictions on doing business, which complicate the business process making it, in some cases, impossible or ineffective. The main peculiarity of these actions is that they are usually carried out not in the field of information or intellectual property, but mainly in the field of trade circulation. The main feature of this group of unfair activities is that the subjects of these violations are both business entities and the individuals (employees or managers of business entities) who intentionally or negligently act in the interests of competitors of a fair business entity acting conscientiously and in good faith in the market. Important differences in some unfair activities, combined in Chapter III Unfair Competition Law significantly complicate the process of classification of violations on the one hand, and the qualification of violations on the other hand. We will consider the most

[27] Tkachenko, 'Comparative Advertising—No Rules of the Game?' (2003) 1 Ûridičnij žurnal 39.

common in the light of the practice of the application of the legislation on protection against unfair competition.

4.2 Discrediting a Business Entity

Discrediting is dissemination of false, inaccurate or incomplete information in any form relating to the person or activity of a business entity, including its goods, that causes damage or may cause damage to the business entity's reputation.

A characteristic feature of this wrongful act is that the person committing the act of discrediting does not necessarily receive specific advantages or benefits. In addition, when qualifying a certain action as discrediting the entrepreneur, it is not necessary to prove the existence of damage, the possibility of causing the damage is sufficient. For instance, in the decision of the High Commercial Court of Ukraine of 17 May 2011 in case No. 15/910-10 the Court determined that a business entity that sends false information about the bankruptcy of a direct competitor to one of its potential customers is guilty of unfair competition in the form of discrediting the business entity.

It is worth noting the position of the High Commercial Court on the assessment of compliance with the requirements of good faith and the dissemination by a business entity to an indefinite circle of customers of false information about the lack of intention of another entity that is its competitor in the market to carry out certain activities, information that could damage the latter's business reputation (refusal to cooperate with consumers and reorientation to another partner), which was recognized as a violation under Art. 8 Unfair Competition Law.[28]

The actus reus of discrediting comprises the following:

- there is dissemination of data (information);
- the data disseminated are inaccurate, incomplete or unreliable;
- the data are disseminated by a competitor or in the interests of a competitor by another person, provided that this connection can be established;
- the dissemination of such data caused or may cause damage to an honest competitor.

For example, on 2 December 2021, by the AMCU Resolution No. 649-p,[29] it has been ruled to discredit (Art. 8 Unfair Competition Law) the distribution of information on the "Prozorro" system. That involves the fact that a competitor "offers substandard or dubious products, or the questionable origin of materials". The qualification of employees working on the imported equipment is also questionable, or

[28] Overview of case law of the Supreme Economic Court of Ukraine and the Supreme Court of Ukraine on the Application of Legislation into Protection of Economic Competition as of 31 December 2017, 79–90 https://amcu.gov.ua/npas/oglyad-sudovoyi-praktiki-vishchogo-gospodarskogo-sudu-ukrayini-ta-verhovnogo-sudu-ukrayini-z-pitan-zastosuvannya-zakonodavstva-pro-zahist-ekonomichnoyi-konkurciyi accessed 11 June 2022.

[29] AMCU (Decision) 2 December 2021, No. 649-r.

wages do not comply with the Ukrainian legislation requirements. Thus, the infringer made such conclusions on the basis of his own analysis as for the price offers from competitors.

Dissemination of information should be understood as: its publication in the mass media, broadcast on radio, television or using other media; dissemination on the Internet or using other means of telecommunications; narrations, descriptions, statements, letters addressed to other persons; messages in public speeches, in electronic networks, or in any other form to at least one person. Dissemination of information is also the display (demonstration) of posters, slogans or other works in public places as well as the distribution of leaflets whose content or form discredits the dignity or honour of the individual or the business reputation of individuals and legal entities. The Constitution of Ukraine guarantees everyone the right to freedom of thought and speech, to free expression of their views and beliefs (Art. 34). However, according to Art. 68 Constitution, everyone is obliged to strictly refrain from encroaching on the rights and freedoms, honour and dignity of others as granted by the Constitution and laws of Ukraine. The right to freedom of thought and speech, to the free expression of one's views and beliefs corresponds to the obligation not to disseminate inaccurate information about a person to discredit their dignity, honour or business reputation.

For a finding of discrediting, the data disseminated must be untrue, inaccurate or incomplete, hence does not comply with reality (false in nature), or must be stated in an untrue, inaccurate or incomplete way. When holding disseminated information to be unreliable, the courts should determine the nature of such information and determine whether it is a factual statement or an evaluative judgment, since evaluative judgments, opinions, beliefs and critical assessments of facts and shortcomings, as an expression of the subjective opinion and views of a competitor, in accordance with Art. 30 Law of Ukraine "On Information", cannot be checked for validity (as opposed to verifying the truth of facts) and refuted, which is in line with the case law of the European Court of Human Rights in interpreting the provisions of Art. 10 Convention for the Protection of Human Rights and Fundamental Freedoms.

4.3 Achievement of Illegal Advantages in Competition

The achievement of illegal advantages in competition is the receipt of such advantages over another business entity by violating current legislation as confirmed by a decision of the state body endowed with the relevant competence. For a finding of this type of unfair activity, the following should be established:

- there is a violation of current legislation;
- the fact of the offence is established and there is a relevant decision of the competent state body, which confirms and terminates it;
- the decision has entered into force;
- as a result of the violation, the competitor has gained an advantage in competition over other market participants;

- the use of these competitive advantages puts a business entity in a privileged position and is contrary to commercial and other fair practices, the requirements of good faith, reasonableness and fairness.

It should be noted that this type of unfair action is one of the most controversial. In a comment on the Unfair Competition Law, A. Deringer noted that the provisions of Art. 15 of the Law are applied to actions that are a violation of another law. As such, they are not unfair competition. But if they were committed to gain an advantage in competition over a law-abiding competitor, then they are considered to be unfair competition.[30]

Advantages which a business entity gains in competition by restricting or infringing the rights of competitors, or those obtained without sufficient grounds, may be considered illegal. In such cases, special agencies establish the fact of violation, order its cessation, and may apply penalties, and in some cases may even revoke the license to carry out further activities. However, this will not help a law-abiding competitor, because the violation sometimes lasts a long time, and only a decision by a special agency can stop the relevant actions.[31]

According to the current legislation, the relevant state bodies are ordinary courts, commercial courts, executive bodies, local government bodies, administrative and economic management and control bodies responsible for monitoring compliance with legislation in a particular area and adopting decisions establishing the fact of a violation. O. Dzhurynskyi is to be agreed with in his argument that if the fact of a violation of current legislation has been established in court or by a competent body of the state power, or local government bodies,—this means that the person was made responsible and received the relevant punishment.[32] Therefore, the recognition of specific unfair actions as obtaining illegal advantages in competition as an independent component of the offence in the field of unfair competition raises the question of the extent to which consideration is to be given to Art. 61 Constitution of Ukraine, which lays down that no one can be brought to justice of the same kind twice for the same offence.

4.4 Dissemination of Misleading Information

Dissemination of misleading information is the communication by a business entity, directly or through another person, to one, several or an indefinite number of persons, including through advertising, of incomplete, inaccurate or false information, in particular by virtue of the chosen method of presentation, the omission of certain facts or vagueness of wording, that has influenced or may influence the intentions of

---

[30] Arved Deringer, 'Commentary to the Law of Ukraine "On Protection Against Unfair Competition"' in Androschuk and Shklyar (n 2) 308.

[31] Ibid 309.

[32] Oleg Dzhurynsky, *Protection Against Unfair Competition (Civil Law Aspect)* (Kyiv Taras Shevchenko University 2010) 114.

these people to purchase (order) or distribute (sell, supply, perform, provide) goods, works or services of the business entity mentioned.

In particular, misleading information is information that:

- contains incomplete, inaccurate or false data about the origin of goods, manufacturer, seller, method of manufacture, sources and method of purchase, sale, quantity, consumer properties, quality, completeness, suitability for use, standards, characteristics, features of the sale of goods, works or services, prices and discounts on them, as well as the essential terms of the contract;
- contains incomplete, inaccurate or false data about the financial condition or economic activity of the business entity;
- attributes powers and rights to the entity that it does not have, or relationships which it is not in;
- contains references to the output, purchase, sale or delivery of goods, performance of works or provision of services that in fact did not exist on the day of the dissemination of the information.

Information is considered to be misleading if it is aimed at creating a false impression of a competitor's products or services. Considering that the credibility and the availability of information are amongst the basic principles of fair competition practice, there is a general rule enshrined in Art. 10bis(3) Paris Convention according to which the dissemination of any misleading information is incompatible with good competition practices. For this reason, the legislations of most countries of the Paris Union prohibit practices that may be misleading. According to the practice of EU countries, this is the most common and a very dangerous form of unfair competition. Misleading information can have very serious consequences, both for the producer and for the consumer.[33] Losses due to misleading information are inflicted not only on competitors who honestly disseminate information about their products, but also on consumers who rely on this information.

In the light of the fact that the main area of misleading information is trade, and that the information disseminated in this area is often advertising, most countries have developed their own system to prevent "misleading" information based on provisions on the prevention of misleading advertising.[34] In particular, Art. 2b EU Directive concerning misleading and comparative advertising (2006/114/EC), which is now the standard for EU countries, defines misleading advertising as any advertising which in any way, including its presentation, deceives or is likely to deceive the persons to whom it is addressed or whom it reaches and which, by reason of its deceptive nature, is likely to affect their economic behaviour or which, for those reasons, injures or is likely to injure a competitor.[35]

In recent years, unfair competition in the form of dissemination of misleading information has accounted for the lion's share of unfair competition phenomena

---

[33] WIPO, 'Protection Against Unfair Competition', WIPO 725(E) 1994–2004, 114.

[34] WIPO, 'Introduction to Intellectual Property', (WIPO 1999) 128.

[35] Parliament and Council Directive 2006/114/EC of 12 December 2006 concerning misleading and comparative advertising (2006) OJ L376/21.

detected and terminated by the AMCU and the subject of appeal in the courts of Ukraine. In view of this, it is necessary to examine administrative and judicial practice to understand the content and role of these violations and their impact on the development of ideas of good faith in competition legislation and law.

Let us consider several cases in which the actions of business entities were classified as unfair competition in the form of dissemination of misleading information, i.e. under Art. 15-1 Unfair Competition Law. For example, Volyngas Zbut Ltd. reported to an indefinite number of people in informational messages containing false information about its own conditions for the sale of natural gas as a fuel through local pipelines in the Volyn region. This concerns the statement that Volyngas Zbut Ltd. has always indicated the real price of gas and that there are no cases (practice) where this business entity, when after concluding a contract with it has offered additional agreements for gas supply at higher prices than that offered in the proposals. This means that in order to win the tenders, the offered price (unlike other market participants) is not deliberately underestimated. Furthermore, the information provided on the percentage of purchases in which Volyngas Zbut Ltd. is recognized as the winner (97 and 93% and/or more than 90%) includes the beginning of the 2018 to September 26. The chosen method of presenting information may affect the intentions of individuals to purchase goods from this entity and can lead to illegal advantages in competition. This is recognized as a violation of Art. 15-1 Unfair Competition Law in the form of dissemination of misleading information.[36]

According to the results of consideration of the case, the AMCU issued a decision where the actions of NVK Ecopharm Ltd. were recognized as a violation. This resolution was made under Art. 15-1 Unfair Competition Law. The violation was committed in the form of reporting false information to websites on the internet at https://ecopharm.ua/ and https://proteflazid.com.ua/ concerning the drug "Proteflazid". The table of contents concerned treatment and/or prevention of the acute respiratory disease COVID-19 caused by SARS-CoV-2 coronavirus, without proper justification in accordance with applicable law, in particular without official recommendations of the Ministry of Health of Ukraine on its use while cure and/or prevention of acute respiratory disease COVID-19.[37]

A new approach of the AMCU in the application of Art. 15-1, which deserves attention, is the simultaneous application of two articles of the Unfair Competition Law to the same actions of a business entity. Namely, according to the AMCU, a company's use of a disputed designation on product labels may lead to confusion with the activities of the applicant, who previously began to use such designation in their business, which contains signs of violation of Art. 4. At the same time, such actions contain indications of a violation of Art. 15-1 of the Law, as they may create a misleading impression on the part of consumers regarding the company's products, and influence their intentions to purchase products. It should be noted that such a

[36] AMCU (Decision) 13 October 2020, No. 31-p https://amcu.gov.ua/storage/app/uploads/public/605/4a0/e26/6054a0e268fc0702551413.pdf accessed 11 June 2022.

[37] AMCU (Decision) 10 July 2020, No. 430-p https://amcu.gov.ua/storage/app/uploads/public/605/4a0/e26/6054a0e268fc0702551413.pdf accessed 11 June 2022.

double "qualification" of some actions is atypical of the previous practice of the regulator. Influence on the intentions of consumers to purchase products that carry a qualifying characteristic feature of the violation under Art. 15-1 of the Law, may be stipulated by its confusion in relation to the person who produces such products, which is a qualifying feature of the violation under Art. 4 of the Law.

The similarity of the qualification of violations in practice can also be seen in previous decisions of the AMCU, for example, regarding the case of unfair competition of the AMCU against the Limited Liability Company Simferopol Wine and Cognac Factory (Company). The reason for initiating proceedings in the actions of the Company during manufacture process and then sale of alcoholic beverages such as the rum/alcoholic beverage "Cane" and "Captain Jack" in Ukraine was a statement of the international corporation Diageo Scotland Limited (Corporation, the applicant).[38] The Corporation's products are represented on national and international markets for alcoholic beverages by a number of well-known brands, one of which is the "Captain Morgan" brand—a brand also recognized in Ukraine. The Company's alcoholic beverages were introduced to the Ukrainian market under the name "Captain Jack". As a result of consideration of the case, the AMCU determined that rum and the strong alcoholic beverage "Cane" are different products that are distinguished from each other in their consumer properties, and therefore the spreading of false information about the type of product when labeling drinks is qualified under Art. 15-1 of the Law.[39]

At the same time, the decision in the case contains a detailed description of the applicant's and the Company's activities. The Corporation's acquisition of business reputation under the "Captain Morgan" trademark, the date of commencement of the applicant's products under that trademark in Ukraine and business reputation, including priority in the use of symbols is fulfilled in accordance with Art. 4 of the Law. The decision also mentions a lawsuit No. 911/4825/14 on the Corporation's claim against the Company for termination of intellectual property rights violations of the well-known trademark "Captain Morgan". The decision of the Regional Commercial Court of Kyiv from 24 February 2015 in this case left unchanged by the decision of the Kyiv Commercial Court of Appeal from 2 June 2016, and the claim of the Corporation was satisfied. The Courts, in particular, found that the Corporation's intellectual property rights were infringed by the production and sale of alcoholic cane (rum) under controversial terms that are similar to the well-known Ukrainian brand "Captain Morgan" in such a way that they can be confused.[40] However, the conclusions of the AMCU in the decision relate exclusively to the spread of misleading information about the type of product—rum by the Company. The AMCU did not provide an assessment as to the possibility of consumer confusion due to the Company's use

[38] AMCU (Decision) 20 December 2016, No. 554-r https://amcu.gov.ua/storage/app/sites/1/imported_content/5d690c3c87379.pdf accessed 11 June 2022.

[39] AMCU https://amcu.gov.ua/news/do-uvagi-tov-simferopolskij-vino-konyachnij-zavod-kod-yedrpou-35112619 accessed 11 June 2022.

[40] Commercial Appelate Court of Kyiv, 911/4825/14 (2015).

of controversial designations, which had been established previously by the Courts as illegal use of designs in accordance with Art. 4 of the Law.

5 The Illegal Acquisition, Disclosure and Use of Commercial Secrets

5.1 Scope and Legal Basis

The third group of unfair activities that can be qualified as unfair competition are the activities of business entities aimed at the illegal acquisition, disclosure and use of commercial secrets. According to G. Slyadneva, the strengthening of economic competition in the development of market relations in Ukraine has meant that greater importance is being attached to the commercial secrets of business entities and their protection. The development of economic competition as well as the need to achieve market advantage have created a need for commercial secrets of business entities to be protected by means of the law.[41]

Commercial secrets can include: production technology; technological methods and equipment; the modification of previously known technologies and processes; research results and programmes; promising management methods; pricing and sales policy; comparative characteristics of the entity's own product range and that of competitors in terms of quality, look, packaging, etc.; production, commercial, financial and credit relations with partners; enterprise plans to expand (reduce) production; facts relating to sales and purchase negotiations; data that can be used to damage the reputation of the enterprise; information about the company's staff; availability of the means and conditions for the protection of commercial secrets. Of the information that needs to be protected under market conditions, foreign firms consider the following as industrial property: inventions, data on equipment and tools developed or purchased by the entity and not available for general use.

Adequate measures to protect commercial secrets are the adoption of in-company provisions—orders and instructions on the approval and implementation of the regulations on commercial secrets. These provisions should contain a list of the data that constitutes a particular enterprise's commercial secrets, as well as a list of the consequences and the types of legal liability for loss of information that is the intellectual property of the enterprise. To ensure the conditions for the preservation of commercial secrets it is important to approve the form of the obligation (agreement) about non-disclosure of the information that constitutes a commercial secret. Employees who have access to confidential information should be familiar with the object of legal protection and their liability for any violation of the rules concerning its use, and should sign an agreement on the non-disclosure of information that constitutes

---

[41] Ganna Slyadneva, *The Right of a Business Entity to Trade Secret and its Protection* (Institut Ekonomìko-Pravovih Doslìdžen′ NAN Ukraïni 2004) 26.

a commercial secret. If the list of information that constitutes a commercial secret of the enterprise is significant in volume, it is advisable to hand out the list to the employees so that they could recall it if necessary.

The obligation not to disclose a commercial secret may also include clauses on the non-disclosure of commercial information not only during the period of the employee's employment at a particular company, but also for a certain period after they have left the company. This obligation must be kept in the employee's personal file. However, the obligation not to disclose information that constitutes a commercial secret of the enterprise may include only those provisions that do not contradict the Constitution of Ukraine and current legislation. It should be noted that the composition and amount of information that constitutes a commercial secret and the methods of their protection are determined by the business entity independently, taking into account the provisions of the Resolution of the Cabinet of Ministers of Ukraine No. 611, as well as the requirements of applicable law.

In accordance with the Unfair Competition Law and Art. 36 Economic Code of Ukraine, the offence is the illegal acquisition, disclosure and use of commercial secrets. In particular, these are as follows: (1) illegal acquisition of commercial secrets; (2) disclosure of commercial secrets; (3) incitement to disclose commercial secrets; (4) illegal use of commercial secrets.

5.2 Illegal Acquisition of Commercial Secrets

The illegal acquisition of commercial secrets in accordance with Art. 16 Unfair Competition Law is the illegal extraction of information that, in accordance with the legislation of Ukraine, constitutes a commercial secret, if such has caused or could cause damage to a business entity (entrepreneur).

For a finding that an activity constitutes the illegal acquisition of a commercial secret, it must be established whether:

- the information is a commercial secret;
- the information was obtained in an illegal manner;
- as a result of such actions, damage has been caused or may be caused to a fair competitor.

An illegal method of obtaining information that constitutes a commercial secret means extraction regardless of the access regime established by the owner of the commercial secret. It is considered illegal to acquire a commercial secret, regardless of the manner in which the illegal actions were carried out: theft of documents, eavesdropping on conversations, obtaining such information from persons possessing it, for a fee, etc. According to German law, as A. Deringer notes, the acquisition of information is illegal only if it is carried out without obtaining authority "with the use of technical means" (copying equipment, cameras, television cameras, listening devices, etc.), "through the making of an accurate display of the secret" (copies, drawings, reprints, recording on magnetic tape) or "by removing the object in which the secret is embodied". Thus, illegal acquisition covers two processes: first, the method, valid only with the consent of the authorized person, and secondly, the fact of using this method without obtaining authorization or consent.[42]

Every owner of a commercial secret establishes the regime and method of protection of this information independently, and therefore determines to whom and in what cases it may or may not be disclosed. Any actions contradicting the established protection regime (except those specified by law) are illegal. The actions specified by law include access to commercial secrets of persons legally entitled to such access. These persons include in particular employees of state executive bodies, law enforcement agencies and banking institutions which in accordance with the law have the right to access confidential information by the nature of their professional or official functions. They enjoy, in particular, the right to familiarize themselves with information that constitutes a commercial secret, and at the same time are subject to the obligation to comply with the regime concerning this secret, that is not to disclose it to third parties. It should also be noted that the illegal acquisition of commercial secrets can only be actions that cause or could cause damage to the business entity. In this case, the amount of the damage or the hypothetical damage is irrelevant for the grant of appropriate protection. Therefore, if such actions cannot cause damage, they will not be recognized as an offence even in the presence of other components of an unfair action. A peculiarity of the qualification of actions as the illegal acquisition of commercial secrets may be the inability to prove the existence of property damage. However, there is almost always non-pecuniary (moral) damage, although it is very difficult to prove.

According to para 5.12 of the information letter of the AMCU on peculiarities of the application of legal provisions on the protection against unfair competition in connection with the entry into force of the Law of Ukraine "On the Modification of the Law of Ukraine on Protection Against Unfair Competition" as of 18 December 2008 No. 689-VI "when applying Arts. 16–19 of the Law of Ukraine on protection against Unfair Competition it should be borne in mind that according to Art. 508 Civil Code of Ukraine the term of legal protection of commercial secrets is limited to the existence of all its features, in particular, inaccessibility of the relevant information to third parties".

5.3 *Disclosure of Commercial Secrets*

Disclosure of commercial secrets is the familiarization of another person with information that in accordance with current legislation of Ukraine constitutes a commercial secret, without the consent of a person authorized to do so, by a person to whom this information was entrusted in the prescribed manner or to whom it became known

[42] Arved Deringer, 'Commentary to the Law of Ukraine "On Protection Against Unfair Competition"' in Androschuk and Shklyar (n 2).

in connection with the relevant obligations, if it causes or could cause damage to the business entity.

For actions to be qualified as the illegal disclosure of commercial secrets, proof must be provided that:

- the information that a person familiarized another with is a commercial secret;
- the information is disseminated without the permission of the owner or the person who legally controls it;
- the information has been communicated to a person to whom this information has become known in the prescribed manner or in connection with the performance of relevant duties (for example, the person is aware that this information is confidential and properly protected);
- the dissemination of the information causes or may cause damage.

Disclosure should be understood as the illegal familiarization of other persons with information that is a commercial secret, as well as the creation by a person who has become aware of the information (in connection with their professional or official activities, and who must keep it secret) of conditions favourable for access to the information by third parties. Such persons include law enforcement officials, banking institutions, tax authorities, public authorities and management, as well as other persons who, in accordance with the law, have the right to access information that is a commercial secret, or have access to such information by nature of the professional or official responsibilities that they perform.

The manner of disclosure of a commercial secret (notification to others, in the media or otherwise) is irrelevant. Disclosure of information that is a commercial secret necessarily implies damage or the possibility of damage. Although it may be difficult or impossible to prove and substantiate the material damage under certain conditions, the economic entity whose rights have been violated has the right to claim compensation for non-pecuniary damage in accordance with Art. 23 Civil Code of Ukraine, taking into account the provisions of para 3 of the Resolution of the Plenum of the Supreme Court of Ukraine on judicial practice in cases of compensation for moral (non-pecuniary) damage, according to which non-pecuniary damage caused to a legal entity should be understood as losses of a non-pecuniary nature arising in connection with the denigration of its business reputation, encroachment on its brand name, trademark or industrial mark, the disclosure of commercial secrets, as well as actions aimed at lowering the prestige of or undermining confidence in its activities.

5.4 *Incitement to Disclose Commercial Secrets*

Incitement to disclose commercial secrets is the inducement of a person to disclose information to whom information that is a commercial secret under the legislation of Ukraine has been entrusted in the prescribed manner or has become known in connection with the performance of relevant duties, if this has caused or could cause damage to the economic entity.

To qualify an action as incitement to disclose a commercial secret, it should be determined that:

- the information is a commercial secret;
- the person who encourages the disclosure of a commercial secret is a competitor of the owner of the information;
- the person who is encouraged to disclose understands that the relevant information is a commercial secret and they received it with the permission of the owner in a lawful manner;
- disclosure will or may cause damage to a fair business entity.

The legislator does not specify what exactly can be recognized as incitement, hence it can be assumed that it covers any intentional acts that are aimed at ensuring disclosure by the person to whom the commercial secret was entrusted in the prescribed manner or became known in connection with the relevant obligations. Persons who legally possess a commercial secret may be persons who have become aware of the relevant information as a result of performing not only official but also other, in particular, contractual duties (for example, auditors, employees of law firms or consulting firms).

5.5 Illegal Use of a Commercial Secret

Illegal use of a commercial secret is the introduction into production of illegally obtained information that constitutes a commercial secret under Ukrainian legislation or taking it into account during the planning or implementation of economic activity without the permission of the authorized person.

To qualify actions as the illegal use of commercial secrets, it must be proven that:

- when planning and implementing innovations in the production process, information is used that is a commercial secret of another business entity, and that the person who encourages the disclosure of commercial secrets is a competitor of the information owner;
- a commercial secret has been obtained as a result of illegal actions, i.e. without the permission of the owner;
- the use of relevant information eliminates or significantly reduces the business entity's costs for innovation and the improvement of production;
- the use of a competitor's commercial secret enables the economic entity to achieve an advantage in competition or improve its position.

The peculiarity of these unfair actions is that the information that constitutes the commercial secret of a fair competitor is used by another business entity in its business activities. At the same time, current legislation does not require that the dishonest business entity has acquired or disclosed a commercial secret, or has funded the process sufficiently, has used that information in a production or management process and understands that the relevant information is a competitor's commercial secret and that its use will enable the business entity to gain an advantage in competition or to win the competition by controlling and using the information. We agree with V. Eremenko that the nature of a commercial secret itself, which implies its secret nature for as long as possible, excludes its publication and subsequent transfer to the public domain after a certain period of time.[43]

5.6 Discussion

Legal protection against unfair competition in the field of commercial secrets (know-how) is known to the laws and law enforcement practices of many foreign countries. Of particular interest are the provisions of EU law on liability for the disclosure of commercial secrets by former employees who, shortly after leaving the company, pass on commercial secrets to competitors or use them themselves by opening a competing business entity. In principle, the former employee is free to use secret information and knowledge gained by them while working at the former enterprise. In this regard, A. Kaminka noted: "[...] it is unfair if the owner, inviting the employee, deprives them at the same time of the right to use the personal experience, knowledge and the means that they acquired during a long, difficult and conscientious service to change from being an employee to an entrepreneur. On the other hand, it may sometimes seem unfair if the employee is entitled to immediately compete with the employer after leaving the latter's employment, and if the employee could compete with the employer using the special knowledge about the latter's state of affairs that he has acquired from the employer during the service".[44] It is only if there are special circumstances that these actions are unfair. Unfortunately, the current legislation of Ukraine does not provide for liability for such unfair actions of competitors as enticing employees. Manifestations of unfair advertising, abuse of the trust and social responsibility of competitors and consumers, as well as unregulated conditions of sales, lotteries and other forms of incentives to purchase and sell goods, works and services remain unregulated. The Unfair Competition Law contains only a limited list of the most common and dangerous unfair acts that under certain conditions can be defined as unfair competition. It should be noted that in the legislation and law enforcement practice of most foreign countries there are between twenty and five hundred forms of unfair competition. The specifics of competition and the need to ensure the dominance of good and fair practices in competition causes the emergence of new forms of unfair competition.

---

[43] Vladimir Eremenko, *Legal Regulation of Competitive Relations in Russia and Abroad* (Lomonosov Moscow State University 2001) 259.

[44] Avgust Kaminka, *Essays on Commercial Law Vol. 1* (Ûridičeskij Knižnыj Sklad "Pravo" 1912) 206–207.

6 Conclusion

Protection against unfair competition in Ukraine is not limited to the provisions of the Unfair Competition Law. Relevant legal norms are also contained in the laws of Ukraine on advertising, on foreign economic activity and on consumer protection. At the same time, the provisions of the Unfair Competition Law, together with the relevant provisions of the Commercial Code and the Civil Code of Ukraine create the necessary general “background” for the development of fair competition and provide necessary legal guarantees not only because the effectiveness of any right must be ensured by an appropriate mechanism for its protection. Thus, protection against unfair competition is a necessary and an appropriate guarantee for the development of fair competition in Ukraine.

Studies of the problems of the legal regulation of fair competition suggest that in Ukraine the repeated efforts of legislators and representatives of the AMCU to form more or less defined rules of fair competition have not been successful. The rules of professional ethics developed by entrepreneurs in cooperation with chambers of commerce and industry and agreed with the AMCU, recommendations of advisory bodies and international non-governmental organizations and unions, and decisions of the European Court of Human Rights remain an effective mechanism for implementing the principles of good faith.

To ensure the normal and effective development of the socio-economic system of our state, it is necessary to have honest and civilized relations between competing businesses, and compliance with certain rules of conduct in the market. For freedom of competition not to turn into anarchy, certain guarantees and mechanisms are required to maintain fair and equal conditions of entrepreneurship and competition for all market participants. The state plays a special role in this process, establishing the principles of fair and lawful competitive behaviour through the norms of competition law. However, it should be noted that the formation of effective competitive relations largely depends on the characteristics of the interaction of individual businesses in the market, corporate culture, rules of professional ethics and business practices, the formation of which is influenced by entrepreneurs themselves.

Thus, fair competition can be defined as a system of ideas that is well-established in society, recognized by law, custom and judicial and administrative practice, about the proper behaviour of business entities in the market in competition, allowing the business entity to compete freely and to prevail in competition without violating the rights of third parties.

Fair competition is a means of balancing the private and public interests of economic entities, consumers and the state in competitive relations, and at the same time is a universally recognized interest that is acknowledged by all participants in economic turnover and protected by the state. The development of fair competition in the market is impossible without the formation of a system of self-regulation based on the interaction of entrepreneurs. The basis of such self-regulation can be the rules and principles of professional ethics in various areas of the economy; the proposals, decisions and conclusions of associations and other non-governmental organizations aimed at the formation of general approaches to counteracting unfair competition and the development of fair competition in the market, the promulgation of leading decisions of international judicial bodies in cases of protection against unfair competition, and the expansion of the scope of arbitration in the field of protection against unfair competition.

References

Gennady Androschuk, *Scientific and Practical Commentary to the Unfair Competition Law– Scientific and Practical Edition* (Ûridična gazeta 2013) [Геннадій Андрощук та інші, *Науково-практичний Коментар до Закону України "Про захист від Недобросовісної Конкуренції"* (Юридична газета 2013)]

Olga Bakalinska, 'Improving Legislative Protection Against Unfair Competition: a New Step Towards the European Economic Space' (2009) 2 Competition Bulletin of the AMC of Ukraine 29 [Ольга Бакалінська, 'Удосконалення Законодавчого Захисту від Конкуренції: Новий Крок до Європейського Економічного Простору' (2009) 2 Вісник Антимонопольного Комітету України 29]

Olga Bakalinska, *Protection of Economic Competition: Organizational and Legal Principles of Public Administration* (V. M. Koretsky Institute of State and Law 2003) [Ольга Бакалінська, *Захист Економічної Конкуренції: Організаційно-Правові Засади Державного Управління* (Інститут держави і права ім. В. М. Корецького 2003)]

Arved Deringer, 'Commentary to the Law of Ukraine "On Protection Against Unfair Competition"' in Gennady Androschuk and Sergiy Shklyar (eds), *Competition law: protection against unfair competition. Scientific and practical publication* (Justinian 2012) [Арвед Дерингер, 'Коментар до Закону України "Про Захист від Недобросовісної Конкуренції"' у Геннадій Андрощук та Сергій Шкляр (ред), *Конкурентне Право: Захист від Недобросовісної Конкуренції* (Юстініан 2012)]

Oleg Dzhurynsky, *Protection Against Unfair Competition (Civil Law Aspect)* (Kyiv Taras Shevchenko University 2010) [Олег Джуринський, *Захист від Недобросовісної Конкуренції (Цивільно-Правовий Аспект)* (Київський Національний Університет імені Тараса Шевченка 2010)]

Vladimir Eremenko, *Legal Regulation of Competitive Relations in Russia and Abroad* (Lomonosov Moscow State University 2001) [Владимир Еременко, *Правовое Регулирование Конкурентных Отношений в России и за Рубежом* (Московский Государственный Университет имени М. В. Ломоносова 2001)]

Vladimir Eremenko, *Legislation on the Suppression of Unfair Competition of Capitalist Countries* (Moskva VNIIPI 1991) [Владимир Еременко, *Законодательство о Пресечении Недобросовестной Конкуренции Капиталистических Стран* (Москва ВНИИПИ 1991)]

Avgust Kaminka, *Essays on Commercial Даw. Vol. 1* (Ûridičeskij knižnыj sklad "Pravo" 1912) [Август Каминка, *Очерки Торгового Права. Выпуск 1*-й (Юридический книжный склад "Право" 1912)]

Petro Kharchenko, *Administrative and Legal Measures to Ensure Protection Against Unfair Competition in the Activities of the Antimonopoly Committee of Ukraine* (Institute of Legislation of the Verkhovna Rada of Ukraine 2005) [Петро Харченко, *Адміністративно-правові Заходи Забезпечення Захисту від Недобросовісної Конкуренції в Діяльності Органів Антимонопольного Комітету України* (Інститут Законодавства Верховної Ради України 2005)]

Natalia Korchak, 'General Provisions of State Protection of Competition in Business' (2001) 2 Entrepreneurship, Economy and Law 7 [Наталія Корчак, 'Загальні Положення Державного

Захисту Конкуренції у Підприємницькій Діяльності' (2001) 2 Підприємництво, Господарство і Право 7]

Irina Koval, 'Illegal Use of Business Reputation of the Business Entity as a Form of Unfair Competition' (2002) 10 Entrepreneurship, Economy and Law 23 [Ирина Коваль, 'Неправомерное Использование Деловой Репутации Субъекта Хозяйствования как Форма Недобросовестной Конкуренции' (2002) Підприємництво, Господарство і Право 23]

Sergey Paraschuk, *Unfair Competition: Content and Legal Means of its Suppression* (Lomonosov Moscow State University 1995) [Сергей Паращук, *Недобросовестная Конкуренция: Содержание и Правовые Средства ее Пресечения* (Московский Государственный Университет имени М. В. Ломоносова 1995)]

Oleksandr Rozdorozhny, 'Comparative advertisement and advertising trolling: on the verge of what is allowed' *Juridiczna Gazeta Online* (2 April 2018) https://yur-gazeta.com/publications/practice/inshe/porivnyalna-reklama-ta-reklamniy-troling-na-mezhi-dozvolenogo.html/ [Олександр Роздорожний, 'Порівняльна Реклама та Рекламний Тролінг: на Межі Дозволеного' *Юридична Газета Online* (2 квітня 2018)]

Ganna Slyadneva, *The Right of a Business Entity to Trade Decret and its Protection* (Institut ekonomìko-pravovih doslìdžen′ NAN Ukraïni 2004) [Ганна Сляднєва, *Право Суб'єкта Господарювання на Комерційну Таємницю та його Захист* (Інститут економіко-правових досліджень НАН України 2005)]

S Tkachenko, 'Comparative Advertising. No Rules of the Game?' (2003) 1 Ûridičnij žurnal 39 [С. Ткаченко, 'Порівняльна Реклама. Правила Гри Відсутні? (2003) 1 Юридичний журнал 39]

Yuriy Tobota, The Principle of Justice, Good Faith and Reasonableness in Civil Law (Law Academy of Ukraine named after Yaroslav the Wise 2011) [Юрій Тобота, Принцип Справедливості, Добросовісності і Розумності у Цивільному Праві (Юридична Академія України ім. Ярослава Мудрого 2011)]

T Udalov, *Competition Law* (Shkola 2004) [Т. Удалов, Конкурентне Право (Школа 2004)]

Protecting Intellectual Property Rights from Unfair Competition in Ukraine

Olha Kronda

Contents

Abstract This chapter examines the protection of intellectual property from unfair competition in Ukraine. Infringements in this area have now become widespread. The objects of intellectual property rights (such as trademarks, trade names, trade secrets, geographical indications) are a means by which some business entities can obtain illegal benefits by exploiting the reputation of other business entities. In order to maintain or restore their reputation on the market and ensure their competitiveness,

O. Kronda (✉)
Intellectual Property and Information Law Department of the Educational and Scientific Institute of Law, Taras Shevchenko National University of Kyiv, Kyiv, Ukraine
e-mail: OlgaKronda@knu.ua

H. Richter (ed.), *Competition and Intellectual Property Law in Ukraine*,
MPI Studies on Intellectual Property and Competition Law 31,
https://doi.org/10.1007/978-3-662-66101-7_11

business entities pay great attention to monitoring and preventing possible infringements of their intellectual property rights on the market. This, in turn, requires the use of effective remedies. This chapter discusses the general concepts of and the charged relationship between unfair competition and intellectual property, and specific forms of unfair competition with regards to intellectual property rights (i.e. the illegal use of designations, the illegal use of comparative advertising, the dissemination of misleading information, and violations of trade secrets). Since Ukraine became independent, it has become the practice to consider such cases, and this chapter will analyse key cases in detail. Finally, this chapter will discuss the role of and the protection procedure applied by the Antimonopoly Committee of Ukraine in courts. In the future, all disputes concerning infringements in the field of unfair competition and intellectual property rights will be considered by the High Court on Intellectual Property.

1 Introduction

This section addresses general features of unfair competition in intellectual property, as well as the main features and types of such unfair competition. It sets out a list of intellectual property rights used in unfair competition and analyzes the relevant offenses. It also presents the practice of the Antimonopoly Committee of Ukraine (AMCU) in this field.

Competition has always been one of the key elements of business activities. Overall, competition has a positive effect on the economy and businesses themselves. Competition ensures that the quality of goods and services improves, encourages goods that use new technologies, etc. However, it is sometimes more beneficial for businesses to capitalize on a competitor's business reputation by imitating a well-known trademark than for them to develop their own. Such offenses are classified as unfair competition, and also damage the national economy. Businesses need clear guarantees and mechanisms for the creation of a level playing field to maintain fair business and competitive positions for all market players. It is either for the government to adopt relevant regulations, or for businesses themselves to develop relevant good business practices through specific conduct.

In Ukraine, more and more intellectual property infringements take place each year under the heading of unfair competition. These cases are heard by both the AMCU and the courts at various levels. Ukraine has developed a practice of hearing cases on the protection of intellectual property rights in the field of unfair competition. Each year, intellectual property becomes an increasingly valuable asset for businesses around the world, and hence reliable protection of intellectual property against unfair competitive activities is a key to business success and security. Moreover, intellectual property is a driving force that ensures the beneficial development not only of each enterprise but also of the state as a whole.

According to its 2016 annual report, the AMCU terminated 276 violations of the Ukrainian Law on Protection Against Unfair Competition[1] (hereinafter the Unfair Competition Law). Orders were issued imposing penalties for infringements in 75 cases, and 201 practices involving elements of the offense were terminated by notifying the businesses appropriately.[2] In total, the penalties imposed amounted to approx. 5 million UAH. The number of violations was approximately the same in 2017, while the penalties imposed amounted to approx. 50 million UAH.[3] According to the 2018, 2019 and 2020 annual reports, the penalties imposed amounted in total to 0.024 million UAH,[4] 9.3 million UAH,[5] and 218.8 million UAH[6] respectively. Even though the amount varies significantly from year to year, a tendency towards businesses committing more serious offenses can be observed throughout Ukraine.

According to the AMCU's 2020 annual report, the most common violations are in the field of unfair competition within the meaning of Art. 15(1) Unfair Competition Law, namely in the form of the dissemination of misleading information (85% of all violations).[7] The next in terms of numbers is the illegal use of marks and indications (as provided for in Art. 4 Unfair Competition Law), which only accounts for 9% of the total.

2 Unfair Competition in the Field of Intellectual Property and Forms Thereof

Article 1(1) Unfair Competition Law provides: "Unfair competition shall be understood as any action performed in the course of competition running counter to the trade and other fair practices in business activities".[8] Fair business practices include, as a rule, those established and widely followed within the framework of any code of conduct not laid down by the applicable legislation. Under provisions of the Ukrainian laws in force, good business practices are assumed to be related to general provisions on contracts. However, in real terms, it is difficult to argue on the basis of trade and fair customs. Such rules have as yet not been approved by any competent body, and are consequently a purely subjective interpretation. Moreover, during court proceedings, it is necessary to define clearly the custom as a rule of conduct, prove its existence and identify its substance. In this connection, reference can be made to

---

[1] Ukrainian Law on Protection Against Unfair Competition 1996.

[2] Antimonopoly Committee of Ukraine, 'Annual Report', 2016.

[3] Antimonopoly Committee of Ukraine, 'Annual Report', 2017.

[4] Antimonopoly Committee of Ukraine, 'Annual Report' 2018.

[5] Antimonopoly Committee of Ukraine, 'Annual Report' 2019.

[6] Antimonopoly Committee of Ukraine, 'Annual Report' 2020.

[7] Ibid.

[8] On the doctrine and application of the Ukrainian Law on Protection Against Unfair Competition; see also Olga Bakalinska, 'Legal Mechanisms of Protection Against Unfair Competition in Ukraine—Prerequisites, Problems and Trends' in this Volume.

litigation between E.I. Du Pont de Nemours and Company and the AMCU aimed at a finding that the latter's decision was partially invalid. The AMCU held the actions of the company to be an infringement of Art. 1 Ukrainian Law "On Protection Against Unfair Competition", in particular finding that the company's conduct conflicted with good trade practices in business. The case was heard by various courts at different levels, and the AMCU's decision was reversed on the grounds that the AMCU did not refer to specific rules, fair trade or other good business practices infringed by the plaintiff, and had failed to identify their substance and provide evidence for the existence of such rules as a custom.[9]

Article 1(2) Ukrainian Law "On Protection Against Unfair Competition" refers to other provisions of the same law in which specific elements of such offenses are defined. The list of elements is not exhaustive.

Article 10*bis*(2) Paris Convention for the Protection of Industrial Property provides that "any act of competition contrary to honest practices in industrial or commercial matters constitutes an act of unfair competition."[10] It should be noted that the two definitions are almost identical.

Not every practice as such can be considered as an act of unfair competition. Thus, for a certain action to be qualified as unfair competition, certain characteristics must be satisfied. We propose to identify these characteristics of unfair competition, including in the field of intellectual property:

- Unfair competition is characterized by active involvement.
- Unfair competition is aimed at gaining advantages in business activities.
- Unfair competitors are business entities.
- Practices in connection with unfair competition are considered to be illegal if they conflict not only with applicable laws and regulations but are also contrary to good business practices, good faith, fairness and reasonableness requirements.
- As a result of practices in connection with unfair competition, damage may be caused to competitors, or their business reputation (goodwill) may be harmed.

It should be noted that unfair competition can be carried out only by actions, there being no provision for the possibility of passive behavior (inaction).

Unfair competitors are business entities, i.e. commercial or business organizations and individuals competing with each other. However, this constellation does not include the consumer who is also affected by offenses in the field of unfair competition. The consumer is not a competitor, but he is a party to market relations, and is almost in the same position as competitors in terms of the scope of rights granted in the field of protection against unfair competition. Hence the concept of unfair competition covers not only the relationship between competitors but also unfair practices that adversely affect consumers.

Unfair competition may cause damage to competitors or their business reputation (goodwill). Apart from actual losses (if any), even the threat of such damage or loss of business reputation will be enough. It is important to note that there is no

[9] Kyiv Economic Court of Appeal, Decision 21/17-54/220 (2019).

[10] Paris Convention for the Protection of Industrial Property 1983, art 10*bis*(2).

requirement to establish the actual amount of damage or harm to business reputation, and it is sufficient for there to be a hypothetical possibility. In addition, alongside the proof of a set of elements of unfair competition, it is necessary first of all to prove that the practices have been committed by a competitor. For example, it is not unfair competition for a non-competitor to disseminate false information about a company.

Sections 4–7 will address what are in practice the most relevant types of unfair competition in the field of intellectual property: unauthorized use of designations, illegal use of comparative advertising, misleading information about intellectual property (geographical indications), misappropriation of trade secrets. But before examining these in depth, the following Sec. 3 outlines the basic characteristics of administrative and judicial enforcement in the field of unfair competition in Ukraine.

3 Administrative and Judicial Enforcement

3.1 Need for Effective Protection

Intellectual property rights that have been infringed in the field of unfair competition can be protected today both in court and through the bodies of the AMCU. The need for effective protection follows from international treaties: Article 10*bis*(1) Paris Convention for the Protection of Industrial Property, to which Ukraine has been a party as of 25 December 1991, provides that the countries of the Union are bound to assure to nationals of other countries of the Union effective protection against unfair competition.[11] Moreover, Art. 10*ter*(1) of the Convention provides that the countries of the Union undertake to assure to nationals of the other countries of the Union appropriate legal remedies effectively to repress all the acts referred to in Arts. 9 to 10*bis*.

3.2 Enforcement Through the Antimonopoly Committee of Ukraine

The AMCU is a specially qualified body that ensures the state protection of competition in business. Every year, the AMCU hears many intellectual property cases, including cases of the unauthorized use of a commercial (brand) name, trademark, illegal actions concerning trade secrets, etc.

The AMCU is the governmental authority that provides state protection to competition in business, and is a specially qualified state body by virtue of the powers and functions vested in it. Its main task in the field of intellectual property is to create and implement competition policy, i.e. by exercising state control over compliance

[11] Ibid 995 (123).

with unfair competition legislation, it puts an end to violations that constitute unfair competition. It also promotes fair competition and participates in the due elaboration and implementation of proposals on laws and other regulations governing the development of competition, competitive policy and demonopolization of the economy.

Article 28(4) Unfair Competition Law provides that persons whose rights are infringed by acts defined by this Law as unfair competition may within six months from the day when they became aware or should have become aware of the infringement of their rights, apply to the local offices of the AMCU for the protection of these rights.[12] Therefore, if a business entity becomes aware of an infringement of its rights by a competitor, it may apply to the AMCU or directly to the court. However, if an entity decides to apply to the AMCU, it must not be deprived of the right to seek legal redress, and is entitled to appeal the AMCU decision in court.

In practice, applying to the AMCU is more effective and faster than seeking legal redress. Moreover, this alternative remedy allows the right holder to put an end to the infringement of his exclusive rights to use the intellectual property not only in the shortest (fastest) possible way but also with the help of a government authority, the AMCU, which has broad opportunities and powers to collect a wide range of evidence to prove the fact of the offense.

Article 21 Unfair Competition Law provides that the AMCU may impose a fine of up to 5% of income (proceeds) gained from the sale of products (goods, works, or services) by the offender for the last reporting year that precedes the year in which the fine is imposed.

The trial practice approached by the AMCU in the examination of cases involving unfair competition in respect of intellectual property is quite broad. The AMCU also prepares annual reports on its activities, specifically highlighting the highest-profile cases. The annual report is published on the AMCU website.

An ever-increasing number of appeals from businesses to the AMCU bodies is, in turn, the result of both increased confidence in the qualifications and the improved practical experience of the AMCU staff, and the fact that these bodies have the authority to apply effective enforcement measures against offenders (in particular, the above-mentioned fines).

Mykola Pototskyi notes the advantages of filing a complaint with the ACMU: it can independently investigate the facts of an infringement, there is no need for a mandatory registration of intellectual property or legal expertise, the decision comes into effect and becomes binding immediately after it has been awarded, if the judgment is worded appropriately, and there is a possibility to impose a fine and an order for the withdrawal of the goods.[13]

---

[12] Ukrainian Law on Protection Against Unfair Competition 1996, 236/96-VR, art 28.

[13] Mukola Potockyi, 'Counterfeiting in the Field of Medicines as Unfair Competition' *DD&I IP Agency* (17 May 2019) https://uba.ua/documents/text/Potockiy_Mykola.pdf accessed 22 September 2021.

3.3 *Enforcement Through the Courts*

However, the business entity may decide not to have recourse to the AMCU, but instead to go directly to a court. A practical reason for this choice is where the interested parties fail to act within the six months laid down in Art. 28 Unfair Competition Law, or for reasons of a personal nature, as well as the possibility to claim damages. Indeed, most cases are heard by the courts after decision by the AMCU.

According to the Ruling of the Plenum of the High Commercial Court of Ukraine of 26 December 2011, No. 15 on Certain Practical Issues Related to the Application of the Competition Law, both commercial and administrative courts continue to hear cases involving the AMCU, thus leading to ambiguous judicial practice.[14] Disputes regarding protection against unfair competition in respect of intellectual property are today settled in administrative, commercial, civil and criminal (disclosure of trade secrets) litigation. Immediately after the Intellectual Property High Court of Ukraine has been established, all disputes concerning unfair competition will be heard by this court.[15] Hence, pursuant to Art. 20(6), Part 2, Commercial Procedure Code, the Intellectual Property High Court will deal with cases on intellectual property rights, in particular disputes arising from relationships related to protection against unfair competition, i.e. in respect of the unauthorized use of designations or goods of another manufacturer, copying (imitating) the appearance of the product, and the acquisition, disclosure and use of trade secrets, as well as appeals against AMCU decisions with regard to any issue specified in the Code.

Such hearings should be subject to prompt and qualified examination. The judicial statistics on the time limits for the consideration of disputes arising in the field of the protection of intellectual property rights in Ukraine show that such cases take about two years (minimum) to be heard, not including the time during which consideration is suspended for the obtaining of a legal expertise (if any). Therefore, the trial of such cases takes on average three to four years. In contrast, patent courts in European countries usually take about one and a half to two years to resolve such disputes. For example, the time for the consideration of disputes in the Swiss Federal Patent Court is limited to 12 months, and to a maximum of 18 months in the German Federal Patent Court.[16]

The idea of establishing a specialist court to settle disputes in the field of intellectual property originated in the late twentieth century. It was discussed for a long time, and after it had been gradually set up through regulations, a reform of the Ukraine judicial system in 2016 created a new legislative framework, the Ukrainian

---

[14] Issued by the Plenum of the High Commercial Court of Ukraine on 26 December 2011 on Certain Practical Issues Related to the Application of the Competition Law, 15.

[15] See Anna Shtefan and Olga Gurgula, 'The New Intellectual Property Court in Ukraine: Its Creation and Exclusive Jurisdiction' in this Volume.

[16] Iruna Bezzub, 'Specialist Court for the Settlement of Intellectual Property Disputes: Foreign Experience and Ukrainian Opportunities' *Social Communications Research Center* (11 December 2017) http://www.nbuviap.gov.ua/index.php?option=com_content&view=article&id=3181:spetsializovanij-sud-iz-rozglyadu-sprav-u-sferi-intelektualnoji-vlasnosti&catid=8&Itemid=350 accessed 22 September 2021.

Law on the Judiciary and the Status of Judges a provision of which established a specialist court for the settlement of intellectual property disputes, the Intellectual Property High Court of Ukraine. The lack of relevant judicial practice, the difficulty in resolving the question of jurisdiction for disputes and the growing number of infringements in the field of intellectual property formed the background for the creation of this judicial body.

The updated legal framework includes provisions on the organizational preconditions for the functioning of the specialist court, as well as the rules for submission to jurisdiction within the framework of the applicable code of procedure. The competition to fill vacant positions of judges of the Intellectual Property High Court of Ukraine has been suspended for now as the High Qualification Commission of Judges is not operating. Hence, although this court has been formally established, it is not yet active.

A significant difference between court proceedings and case investigation by the AMCU is that during court proceedings the parties have the opportunity to change the grounds or subject matter of the claim, seek additional demands for relief or otherwise amend the claims. In contrast, when applying to the AMCU, the business entity may face such problems as the uncertainty of the time limits for the investigation of the case, a more "closed" procedure, etc. But there are also drawbacks to litigation, including the judges' lack of experience in infringements in the field of competition, much longer time limits for trials, etc.

Despite the difficulties that a business entity may face in litigation or during the investigation of cases concerning protection against unfair competition in the field of intellectual property by the AMCU bodies, it should be noted that there is a partially implemented common practice of protecting the rights of business entities in this field. Moreover, the establishment of the Intellectual Property High Court of Ukraine will have a favorable effect on the harmonization of approaches to law enforcement, as well as encouraging investment and innovation, thus having a positive effect on the economic growth and prosperity of the state.

4 Unauthorized Use of Designations

4.1 Relevance and Legal Basis

Article 4(1) Unfair Competition Law treats the following as unauthorized uses: the use of the name, trade name, trademark (mark for goods and services), promotional materials, design of packaging of goods, titles of periodicals and other designations without the consent of an entity that previously began to use such or similar designations in its business activities, and where such use leads or may lead to confusion with the activities of such an entity. However, according to Art. 4(2), the use of an individual's own name is not considered to be illegal, if it is followed by a distinctive element that eliminates a possibility of confusion with another entity's activities.[17] In most cases, Art. 4 applies to the unauthorized use of trademarks.

In Ukraine, the courts and the AMCU are engaged in the practical application of Art. 4. The AMCU ensures the protection, which includes the restoration of an entity's infringed intellectual property rights, the termination of violations, the imposition of fines, etc. In particular, it can impose a fine on the offender and order a formal rebuttal of false, inaccurate or incomplete information. However, in such cases, no reimbursement is made for losses or indemnification for non-pecuniary damages through the recovery of the appropriate sum of money from the offender to the benefit of the injured party. Fines imposed by the AMCU are payable to the state budget.

4.2 *Packaging Design*

Several cases involve the unauthorized use of a design for the packaging of a product which has been previously registered for the corresponding trademark, thus leading to confusion. In 2019, the Antimonopoly Committee local office investigated the case relating to the use by Lesaffre Ukraine Ltd. from 24 September 2017 to 24 October 2019 without the permission of Balex Company LLC of the distiller's yeast packaging designs bearing the designation Zelenyi Zmii (in Ukrainian, Green Firedrake in English) in a design similar to that of the distiller's yeast packaging bearing the designation Mitsnyi Zmii (in Ukrainian, Strong Firedrake in English), which had previously been used by Balex for its business activities, such use thus giving rise to a risk of confusion between the activities of Lesaffre Ukraine Ltd. and those of Balex. These practices were held to be an unauthorized use of designations and hence a violation within the meaning of Art. 4 Unfair Competition Law. The claimant provided proof of the registration of its trademark, which the respondent failed to do. The offender was therefore fined 2 million UAH.[18]

Another high-profile case in 2020 was pursued by the ACMU and resulted in a decision according to which practices of the Zdoroviya Pharmaceutical Company were held to be a violation within the meaning of Art. 4 Unfair Competition Law. Zdoroviya had used without the consent of Darnitsa Pharmaceutical Company a design for the packaging of the pharmaceutical Citramon-Zdoroviya similar to that of the pharmaceutical Citramon-Darnitsa, which Darnitsa had began to use in its business activities immediately before Zdoroviya began to do so, such use by the latter thus giving rise to a risk of confusion with Darnitsa's activities. A fine of 10,191,755 UAH was imposed on the offender.[19]

[17] Ukrainian Law on Protection Against Unfair Competition 1996, 236/96-BP, art 4.

[18] Antimonopoly Committee of Ukraine, Decision (2019) 54/19-18.

[19] Antimonopoly Committee of Ukraine, Decision (2020) 793-p.

4.3 Geographical Indications

It should be noted that Art. 4 Unfair Competition Law does not directly refer to geographical indications.[20] However the wording "other designations" gives us every reason to believe that the unauthorized use is to apply to geographical indications as well. Moreover, before being amended, this article contained the phrase "names of localities of the origin of the goods", which was then replaced by indications of the origins of goods, and subsequently the legislature finally resolved to simply state "other designations" without further details.

One case involving the unauthorized use of a geographical indication, the parties to which were the Niva Research, Development and Production Company and three Italian manufacturers (AMCU Decision (2018) No. 501-p), is not without interest. Niva's practice was investigated by the AMCU and held to be a violation of Art. 4 Unfair Competition Law, namely on the grounds of the unauthorized use in its business activities of the Asti designation on a number of labels, as well as the use of a bottle similar to the Twist bottle made by Santero 2 Fratelli & C.—Industria Vinicola Agricola Santo Stefanese—s.p.a. while simultaneously using the Asti designation, which was likely to lead to a risk of confusion with the activities of the members of the Consorzio per la Tutela dell'Asti.[21]

An ambiguous situation arose with the Asti designation when the verbal element of the trademark (which is registered in Ukraine) coincided with the geographical indication (Asti which is protected in the EU geographical indication). Trademarks that included the word element Asti were registered in Ukraine by the Ukrainian manufacturer Niva as far back as 2011, i.e. before the Association Agreement became effective. However, it was found that the Asti designation was also used for marking the packaging of Italian wines.

Since the Asti geographical indication was given protection by Ukraine when the provisions of the Association Agreement became fully effective as of 1 September 2017, such a constellation is to be considered in the context of Arts. 198 and 206 Association Agreement and in accordance with the Ukrainian laws and regulations in force.

The AMCU held that in the case of well-known marks, if they coincide with a geographical indication, they continue to enjoy legal protection provided that the consumer is not misled by such marks for goods and services with respect to their nature, quality or origin. At the same time, only a court may hold the certificate invalid, as provided for by Art. 19 Ukrainian Law on Protection of Rights to Marks for Goods and Services.[22]

In this case, Niva's business activity was not held to be an unauthorized use of the Asti designation similar to that used by Italian businesses previously.

---

[20] See Anastasiia Kyrylenko, 'Why so Few Geographical Indications in Ukraine? Legal, Political and Socio-Economic Perspective' in this Volume.

[21] Antimonopoly Committee of Ukraine, Decision (2018) 501-p.

[22] Ibid.

4.4 Trade (Brand) Name

The most frequent application of Art. 4 Unfair Competition Law by the AMCU bodies involves cases of the unauthorized use of trademarks. However, in practical terms, of interest are decisions rendered by the AMCU on the unauthorized use of a trade (brand) name, which we will focus our attention on here.

One important case involving such a use involved the competing business entities LLC Ramintek LTD. and LLC Ramintek Innovation and Production Company (case No. 69/9-r-02-02-18).[23] This case was initially heard in 2018 by the AMCU local office for Kyiv Region, after which it was reviewed by courts at different levels. It was finally resolved by a review of the decision of 17 October 2018, No. 60/26-p/k awarded by the Administrative Panel of the AMCU local office for Kyiv Region in case No. 69/9-r-02-02-18.

LLC Ramintek Innovation and Production Company (LLC IVK Ramintek) asked the AMCU local office for Kyiv Region to clarify whether LLC Ramintek LTD.'s practices involved elements of a violation of the legislation on protection against unfair competition, namely an illegal use of a part of the commercial (brand) name Ramintek.

On 17 October 2018, the AMCU local office held that LLC Ramintek LTD. had committed a violation within the meaning Art. 4 Unfair Competition Law, i.e. through the unauthorized use of a part of the commercial (brand) name Ramintek in its business name, website's domain name and e-mail address without the consent of LLC IVK Ramintek, which had previously begun to use the name for its business activities, leading to confusion with the practice of the said business entity.[24]

LLC Ramintek LTD. was fined 68,000 UAH and ordered to cease the violation of the law by removing within 30 consecutive days from receipt of the order from its name, e-mail address and its website domain name, including the content of the latter, the Ramintek part of the commercial (brand) name and to refrain from using it in its business activities. Information on compliance with the order was to be communicated to the AMCU office by submitting appropriate evidence.

LLC Ramintek LTD. contested this decision. The case was heard by the Commercial Court of Kyiv, the Northern Commercial Court of Appeal and the Supreme Court of Ukraine. All three instances upheld the AMCU office decision. In particular, the Supreme Court ruling of 26 September 2019 in case No. 910/17070/18 held that the procedure for acquiring rights to a commercial (brand) name does not require compliance with formal procedures for registration and the grant of the status as an intellectual property right. For this reason, any actions that may lead to confusion concerning the company, goods, industrial or trading activities of a competitor, including actions related to the use of designations that have not been duly registered as intellectual property rights (trademarks, industrial designs, etc.) may be held to be an act of unfair competition.[25]

---

[23] Ukrainian Supreme Court, Decision 910/17070/18 (2018).

[24] Ibid.

[25] Ibid.

After the Supreme Court brought this issue to a close, the decision of the local office for Kyiv Region was reviewed by the AMCU. The decision of 17 October 2018, No. 60/26-p/k awarded by the Administrative panel of the AMCU local office for Kyiv Region in case No. 69/9-r-02-02-18 was upheld.

This case involved the unauthorized use of a part of the commercial (brand) name in a company's own name, website domain name and e-mail address.

However, there are many cases in which an appeal against the decision awarded by the AMCU bodies is not filed with the courts. For example, the AMCU local office for Sumy Region initiated proceedings at the request of Kerameya Ltd. (the claimant) concerning unfair competition by Kerameya Trading House Ltd., whose practices involved elements of a violation of the law through the unauthorized use of the commercial (brand) name TH Kerameya Ltd. that could lead to confusion between the business activities of Kerameya Ltd. and TH Kerameya Ltd.

According to the Certificate of Incorporation of 18 May 2006, the claimant was incorporated as a business entity under the registered name of Kerameya Ltd. (limited liability company). The company also held the right to the mark Kerameya for goods and services registered as of 25 December 2008. The state registration of LLC TH Kerameya took place on 22 March 2013.

During the proceedings, the AMCU local office spoke with business representatives (potential consumers, i.e. construction companies purchasing construction materials in the course of their business) within Ukraine. According to the results of the survey conducted by the AMCU local office, it was found that for some (over a quarter) of the respondents, the use of the similar name Kerameya by both business entities could lead to confusion between the activities of these entities on the market.

Accordingly, TH Kerameya Ltd.'s practices involving the use of the Kerameya brand name identical to the brand name of Kerameya Ltd. were held to be a violation within the meaning of Art. 4 Unfair Competition Law, namely the unauthorized use of the commercial (brand) name Kerameya without the consent of the business entity that had previously begun to use it in its business activities, which could lead to confusion with activities of the latter business entity.[26] The company was fined 68,000 UAH, which was paid into the state budget.

4.5 Conclusion

These cases demonstrate that a prompt and efficient hearing is possible, thus providing the objective opportunities for the rapid restoration of infringed rights. We fully support the view of Oleg Dzhurynskyi, who considers that the main way to protect the market player's rights against unfair competition is to make use of civil law remedies in litigation. The administrative procedure for hearing and settling such disputes should be an ancillary tool. As a rule, this procedure precedes the relevant

[26] Antimonopoly Committee of Ukraine, Decision 02-06/15-2016 (2017).

legal proceedings and serves as a way of responding promptly to infringements, thus creating the means to terminate illegal activities and punish the offender.[27]

After analyzing the decisions of both courts and the AMCU on the unauthorized use of designations, we should draw attention to the increase in the number of claims for the protection of infringed rights in this area, and the variety and complexity of such infringements. At the same time, the establishment of the Intellectual Property High Court of Ukraine will ensure a generalizing judicial practice,[28] working out common approaches to law enforcement along with the Antimonopoly Committee activities in this field.

5 Illegal Use of Comparative Advertising

Comparative advertising is common along with other types of advertising used in all areas of the economy. Such advertisements emphasize the advantages of the advertiser's own goods or services, by making a comparison with similar goods or services that might be better known on the market. It is a type of advertisement in which one product is directly or indirectly compared with another competing product.

At first glance, intellectual property legislation does not play a significant role in the area of comparative advertising. However, this law is crucial if a competitor's intellectual property rights are infringed by this practice. The most common intellectual property right used in comparative advertising is trademarks, which therefore has the greatest impact on the competitive aspects of comparative advertising. However, it may involve more than just trademarks.

Creating successful and legally safe comparative advertisements requires considerable investment and time. It usually involves using the reputation, well-known brands, creative potential and efforts of an innovative company. For this reason, it is essential for a business entity to understand the importance of intellectual property in the context of comparative advertising and to apply a strategy to develop and protect its advertising using the legal instruments available in the field of intellectual property.

On 12 November 2019, the Ukrainian Parliament (the Verkhovna Rada of Ukraine) adopted the Ukrainian Law "On Amending Certain Legislative Acts of Ukraine" regarding Harmonization of Legislation in the Field of Comparative Advertising with Laws of the European Union, making comparative advertising legal in Ukraine.[29] In recent years, Ukraine has been harmonizing its legislation with EU laws. To this end, a number of international cooperation agreements have been concluded, of which the most decisive has been the EU–Ukraine Association Agreement, which was

[27] Oleg Dzhurynskyi, 'Protection Against Unfair Competition' (2010) Civil Law Aspects,153.

[28] See Anna Shtefan and Olga Gurgula, 'The New Intellectual Property Court in Ukraine: Its Creation and Exclusive Jurisdiction' in this Volume.

[29] Olena Bakalinska, Bogdan Voievodin, Olena Kokhanovska, Nina Saniakhmetova and others were among those involved in research of unfair advertising and general promotion related issues.

ratified in 2014 and became effective in 2017.[30] Accordingly, to fulfill the obligations assumed under the Association Agreement, appropriate changes were required to be made in the laws concerning comparative advertising. Ultimately, the Ukrainian Law "On Amending Certain Legislative Acts of Ukraine" regarding Harmonization of[31] Legislation in the Field of Comparative Advertising with Laws of the European Union of 2019 was adopted, which allows the use of images, product references, trade and other marks to refer to the comparable product.[32]

However, although at that time Ukrainian legislation did not prohibit comparative advertising, in fact, its use in practice was virtually impossible since the use of a competitor's intellectual property (trademarks) in such advertising was not regulated. The resulting legal uncertainty disincentivized businesses from placing comparative advertising. The adopted amendments merely regulate these aspects of the use of intellectual property in comparative advertising. Before the amendment, the old version of Art. 7(1) (effective until 12 November 2019) Unfair Competition Law defined comparative advertising as advertising containing a comparison with goods, works, services or activities of another business entity. After the amendment, Art. 7(1) Unfair Competition Law provides that comparative advertising is advertising containing a comparison with the persons and goods (activities) of another person in which the competitor or goods and/or services offered by such a competitor are directly or indirectly identified.[33]

The changes adopted have thus significantly expanded the concept of comparative advertising, such that the direct or indirect identification of a competitor is considered to be a beneficial innovation.

Before the amendments, Art. 7 Unfair Competition Law laid down that comparative advertising was lawful if its claims were confirmed by facts and if such advertising was authentic, adequate and valuable (good to know) in terms of consumer information.[34] However, such categories as authenticity, adequacy and goodness are subjective concepts and would require proving in litigation (if any). Ultimately, the amendment abolished this requirement, and Art. 7 Unfair Competition Law now provides that the legality of comparisons in advertising and liability for non-compliance of the content of comparative advertising with statutory requirements

[30] On 16 September 2014 the Verkhovna Rada of Ukraine and the European Parliament simultaneously ratified the Association Agreement. The agreement became effective as of 1 September 2017; see Roman Petrov, 'The EU–Ukraine Association Agreement as a General Framework of Contemporary EU–Ukraine Relations' in this Volume.

[31] Ukrainian Law on Amending Certain Legislative Acts of Ukraine Regarding Harmonization of Legislation in the Field of Comparative Advertising with Laws of the European Union 2019, 286-IX.

[32] Parliament and Council Directive 2006/114/EC of 12 December 2006 concerning misleading and comparative advertising (2006) OJ L376/21 (Misleading and Comparative Advertising Directive); Parliament and Council Directive 2005/29/EC of 11 May 2005 concerning unfair business-to-consumer commercial practices in the internal market and amending Council Directive 84/450/EEC, Directives 97/7/EC, 98/27/EC and 2002/65/EC of the European Parliament and of the Council and Regulation (EC) No 2006/2004 of the European Parliament and of the Council (2005) OJ L149/22.

[33] Ukrainian Law on Protection Against Unfair Competition 1996, 236/96-BP, art 7.

[34] Ibid.

is determined by the Ukrainian Law "n Advertising".[35] In particular, its Art. 11 Ukrainian Law "On Advertising" allows the use of comparative advertising if the advertisement:

(1) does not contain the elements of unfair business practices as set forth by applicable consumer protection laws;
(2) compares homogeneous (similar) goods that meet the same needs or have the same purpose, or compares activity in one and the same industry or one and the same type of activity;
(3) objectively compares one or more material, comparable and representative characteristics of a homogeneous (similar) product or activity, including price, information about which may influence a consumer's decision when making a choice;
(4) does not discredit or contain false information about the quality of homogeneous (similar) goods of other manufacturers or sellers, or discredit activity or standing of other persons, or denigrate the trademarks, trade names, other identifiers of competitors or designation of origin;
(5) for a product with a designation of origin (plain or qualified), it relates to a product with the same designation;
(6) does not create confusion between the advertiser and a competitor or between the advertiser's goods, trademarks, trade name and other identifiers and those of competitors; and
(7) it does not present goods as imitations of the competitor's goods protected by a trademark or trade name.[36]

As can be seen, Art.11 Ukrainian Law "On Advertising" now defines the scope of use of comparative advertising more clearly. Comparative advertising being a powerful tool for influencing consumers, it is regulated by law in almost all countries of the world. Anyone creating comparative advertisements is required to comply with laws and regulations governing intellectual property rights, labeling and marking, and their use in advertising. Of course, such laws differ somewhat depending on peculiarities in each country and sometimes may be very different from each other. For this reason, when creating and using comparative advertisements today.

Given that these significant amendments of the Ukrainian Law "On Comparative Advertising" were only adopted recently, there is as yet no established practice of the courts and the AMCU on them. However, such a practice will surely develop over time.

In the EU, the Misleading and Comparative Advertising Directive 2006/114/EC was adopted by the European Union and allows the Member States of the EU to permit the use of comparative advertising under certain conditions, namely the comparison should concern the same goods or services, material characteristics should be compared objectively, no confusion should be caused, and competitors' trademarks,

[35] Ibid.

[36] Ukrainian Law on Advertising 1996, 270/96-BP.

etc. should be not denigrated.[37] By adopting the relevant changes concerning such advertising, Ukraine harmonized its laws in accordance with the provisions of the Association Agreement. It is for this reason that the positive changes in the existing laws in the field of intellectual property are gradually bringing Ukrainian legislation closer to that of the EU.

6 Misleading Information About Intellectual Property (Geographical Indications)

6.1 Relevance of Geographical Indications

With unfair competition practices becoming more frequent with each passing year,[38] there have also been many instances of business entities engaging in activities that can be classified as unfair competition with respect to geographical indications. Attempts are made to obtain a competitive advantage over other manufacturers by using a geographical indication.

In Ukraine, there have been cases of unfair competition involving the misleading use of geographical indications. Interest in geographical indications as an intellectual property right increased after the signing of the Association Agreement between Ukraine and the European Union, due to the fact that Ukraine has granted protection to more than 3,000 EU geographical indications, while less than ten geographical indications were filed by Ukraine for EU protection.[39] After the expiry of the transition period (years for alcoholic products and seven years for cheese), Ukrainian producers will not be able to use EU geographical indications to designate their products in Ukraine. They will therefore have to pay even greater attention to the unfair competition regulations to ensure that their business activities remain compatible with the good faith and fairness requirements. As a consequence, a number of questions arise about the possible misleading use of geographical indications as a form of unfair competition.[40]

[37] Misleading and Comparative Advertising Directive.

[38] Koznova Olexandra, 'Increased Activity of the Antimonopoly Committee of Ukraine: A New Reality? (20 January 2021) https://biz.ligazakon.net/analitycs/201058_zrostannya-aktivnost-antimonopolnogo-komtetu-ukrani-nova-realnst accessed 22 December 2021.

[39] See Anastasiia Kyrylenko, 'Why so Few Geographical Indications in Ukraine? Legal, Political and Socio-Economic Perspective' in this Volume.

[40] Prominent academics such as Hennadiy Androshchuk, Oleksandr Bezukh, Yuriy Boshytskyi, Oleg Dzhurynskyi, Yuriy Kapitsa, Anatoliy Kodynets, O. Melnychenko, Yuriy Nosik are among those who have dealt with various unfair competition issues. Academics such as M. Arkhipova, Y. Boshytskyi, Yuriy Kapitsa, Anatoliy Kodynets, Oksana Kovalchuk, Mariia Kovalchuk, Yuriy Melnychenko and others have applied themselves to the academic and theoretical problems of geographical indications.

At the same time, the signing of the Association Agreement between Ukraine and the European Union led to an increase in the number of geographical indication registrations in Ukraine. Amongst the best known are Hutsul brinsen cheese (sheep brynza), Melitopol sweet cherries, Krolevets towels and Petrykivka painting. The signing of the Association Agreement was an incentive for Ukraine to develop its geographical indications. The activities of Ukrainian producers are required to comply with the rules of fair competition, which is both the key to economic efficiency and an effective tool for the collective promotion of goods on the market.

The World Intellectual Property Organization (WIPO) reported that in 2018 there were about 65,900 protected geographical indications in the world (according to data shared by 92 national authorities). The largest number of geographical indications were registered in Germany (15,566), China (7,247), Hungary (6,683), the Czech Republic (6,285), Bulgaria (6,038), Italy (6,015) and Portugal (5,998). There are several countries that boast a middle-income economy combined with a large number of geographical indications, such as Moldova with 4,732, Bosnia and Herzegovina 4,499, and Georgia 4,426 geographical indications in 2018.[41] In contrast, India and Brazil had only 330 and 68 geographical indications respectively. There are thus many countries around the world that have long understood the value and potential of geographical indications, as well as the importance of granting them comprehensive legal protection. The countries with many geographical indications include not only the most advanced economies in the world but also many with a low-income economy. Ukraine will certainly have to follow the example of these as far as concerns the registration of its own geographical indications.

6.2 *Legal Basis*

Article 8 Ukrainian Law "On Legal Protection of Geographical Indications" provides that grounds for the denial of legal protection to a geographical indication include the use or reproduction of the name of a plant variety or animal breed which may mislead consumers regarding the actual origin of the goods, or the use of an indication that is identical or similar to and hence can be mistaken for a trademark the rights to which are acknowledged in Ukraine, if, considering the reputation, public awareness and duration of this trademark use, such legal protection may mislead consumers concerning the authenticity of the goods.[42] However, this clause does not apply unless consumers are misled.

The CIS Agreement on Measures for the Prevention and Repression of the Use of False Trademarks and Geographical Indications of 4 June 1999 is also still in

[41] World Intellectual Property Organization, *World Intellectual Property Indicators 2019* (WIPO 2019) 179.

[42] Ukrainian Law on Legal Protection of Geographical Indications 1999, 752-XIV.

force.[43] Art. 4 of this Agreement provides that concerning geographical indications, the parties shall provide legal remedies to interested parties to prohibit: (a) the use in the designation or presentation of goods of any element that identifies (or suggests an association with) a place of origin other than the true place of origin of the goods and which is liable to mislead consumers as to the geographical origin of the goods.[44] This Agreement also stipulates that the parties shall refuse or invalidate the registration of a trademark containing a geographical indication if its use misleads consumers as to the true place of origin of the goods.

Notwithstanding the absence of explicit provisions on infringements of geographical indications in the text of the Unfair Competition Law, such violations are judged under Art. 4 (unlawful use of marks and indications) and Art. 15(1) (dissemination of misleading information). This latter article provides that the dissemination by a business entity, either directly or through another person, to one, more than one or an indefinite number of persons, including in advertisements, of incomplete, inaccurate, or false information, in particular as a result of choosing the manner it is presented, the omission of facts or an ambiguity of the wording that affects or may affect the intentions of such persons to purchase (order) or commercialize (sell, deliver, perform or provide) goods, works or services of such business entity is unlawful.[45]

Oksana Kovalchuk identifies two types of misleading use of geographical indications, namely direct (when the same denominations are used to indicate the true origin of the goods) and indirect (when goods are produced without any indication of origin or when a geographical indication is erroneously applied to the goods originating from another locality, or if a geographical indication has the form of an image causing a misconception as to the origin of goods).[46]

6.3 *Judicial Practice*

The continuous increase of the number of geographical indication registrations in Ukraine has been accompanied by frequent cases of the unfair use of these indications. Most cases involve the misleading use of geographical indications concerning the origin of the goods, i.e., where consumers have a misconception about such an origin. The AMCU and the courts at different levels hear the cases on both direct and indirect misleading use of geographical indications.

[43] The agreement was signed between the CIS countries and ratified by Ukraine on 21 September 2000.

[44] Agreement on Measures for the Prevention and Repression of the Use of False Trademarks and Geographical Indications 1999, 997(225).

[45] Ukrainian Law on Protection Against Unfair Competition 1996, 236/96-BP, art 15.

[46] Oksana Kovalchuk, 'Intellectual Property Right for the Geographical Indications in Ukraine and Member States of the European Union' (2014), 200.

One case[47] heard by the AMCU related to the Aquavintex Joint Venture, which provided inaccurate information on the labels of its own Alazani Valley Shereuli wine (semi-sweet white and semi-sweet red) that was capable of indicating and being understood as information about a foreign origin of the wine. In particular, the wine labels bore the flag of Georgia and a number of inscriptions in Georgian, as well as the text "Georgian Collection", which was certainly capable of misleading the consumer as to the country of origin. Aquavintex attempted to support its position by arguing that it held a registered trademark in the Georgian language and a pictorial trademark that was similar to the Georgian flag. The "Georgian Collection" trademark had also been submitted for registration. In addition, the label contained information on the origin of the goods, namely Alazanska dolyna Shereuli (in Ukrainian) and Alazani Valley Shereuli (in English). All the products were of Ukrainian origin. From the very beginning, the AMCU ordered the elimination of these infringements, but they were not terminated in full. For this reason, on 12 November 2020, the AMCU held that Aquavintex was held liable for c a violation within the meaning of Art. 15(1) Unfair Competition Law, i.e. by providing inaccurate information on the labels of its own wines that was capable of indicating and being understood as information about the foreign origin of the wine. The company was fined 693,252 UAH.

A similar case between the AMCU and Kamyanka Global Wine LLC also involved Georgian wine and concerned the dissemination of misleading information as to the country of origin of goods. The product labels and the website http://www.kgwines.com contained trademarks such as Didi Godori, Grandpa Valiko (Dedushka Valiko in Russian), Mountain wine (Hornoye vino—in Russian), Tellavani, Jorgewine, Kakhetipremium, LAZURI (in both Ukrainian and English) and Alaverdi (in both Ukrainian and English). On 1 December 2017, the AMCU held that the indications placed by Kamyanka Global Wine LLC on packaging and labels of several of its own wines,[48] as well as on the website http://www.kgwines.com constituted the communication of false information, i.e. inscriptions in the Georgian language, the flag of Georgia, the wording 100% Georgian wine, Georgia, Georgian, Georgian traditions, Georgian wines (in the original Russian), etc. to an indefinite circle of persons and were thus misleading information. This may have had an effect on the decisions of such persons to purchase the wines made by Kamyanka Global Wine thinking them to be Georgian wines. The defendant was also found guilty of actions whose purpose was to distribute on Kamyanka Global Wine's website http://www.kgwines.com and letterhead paper misleading information, thereby communicating false information, i.e. the wording "Wines from around the world" (in the original Russian) to an indefinite circle of persons. This may have had an effect on the decisions of such persons to purchase the wines made by Kamyanka Global Wine and was held to be a violation of Art. 15(1) Ukrainian Law on Protection Against Unfair Competition.[49] The

[47] Antimonopoly Committee of Ukraine, Decision (2017) 670-p.

[48] Under Didi Godori, Grandpa Valiko (Dedushka Valiko in Russian), Mountain wine (Hornoye vino in Russian), Tellavani, Jorgewine, Kakhetipremium, LAZURI (both in Ukrainian and English) and Alaverdi (both in Ukrainian and English) trademarks.

[49] Antimonopoly Committee of Ukraine, Decision (2017) 670-p.

company was fined 7,010,000 UAH. Penalties imposed by the AMCU bodies are payable to the state budget.

Such AMCU decisions are not a rare event. There have been similar judgments regarding "Kamchatskaya zernistaya"[50] (in Russian)—salmon roe, "Grapes of Italian origin"[51] (in Ukrainian), "Made with Italian technology"[52] (in Ukrainian) and so on.

7 Misappropriation of Trade Secrets

7.1 Relevance and Legal Basis

The unauthorized acquisition, disclosure and use of trade secrets is a common form of unfair competition in the field of intellectual property. Unfortunately, there is as yet no specific law that regulates relationships in terms of providing legal protection for trade secrets.[53] Back in 2008, the Cabinet of Ministers of Ukraine adopted an ordinance on the Approval of the Concept of the Draft Ukrainian Law on Protection of Trade Secrets of 5 November 2008, No. 1404-p.[54] This law would provide that a trade secret as the totality of information of a technical, organizational, commercial, production or other nature was of significant economic interest to its owner who conducted business activities in a competitive environment. Ensuring a proper legal regulation of relationships related to the protection of trade secrets was to be an important task within the framework of the state policy implemented in the field of economic competition and the restriction of monopoly. The adoption of the new Ukrainian Law "On Protection of Trade Secrets" would ensure reasonable protection of intellectual property rights to trade secrets and create the conditions necessary to prevent unfair competition in business.[55]

In Ukraine there is no normative legal document that regulates the legal position of know-how. Nor does the Civil Code of Ukraine regard know-how as an object of intellectual property rights. By signing the Association Agreement with the EU, Ukraine did not commit itself to Directive (EU) 2016/943 of the European Parliament and of the Council of 8 June 2016 on the protection of undisclosed know-how

---

[50] 'With Thoughts About Supermarkets and New Year, Producer of Caviar Lies on the Label "Kamchatskaia Zernierstaia"—AMCU (2019)' *Our Money* (10 December 2019) https://nashigroshi.org/2019/12/10/z-dumkamy-pro-supermarkety-i-novyy-rik-vyrobnyk-ikry-breshe-na-etyketkakh-kamchatskay-ziernistay-amku/ accessed 22 December 2021.

[51] Antimonopoly Committee of Ukraine, Decision (2020) 740-p.

[52] Ibid.

[53] On the regulation of trade secrets in Ukraine, see also Olga Bakalinska, 'Legal Mechanisms of Protection Against Unfair Competition in Ukraine—Prerequisites, Problems and Trends' in this Volume.

[54] Ordinance of the Cabinet of Ministers of Ukraine on the Approval of the Concept of the Ukrainian Draft Law on Protection of Trade Secrets 2008, 1404-p.

[55] Ibid.

and business information (trade secrets) against their unlawful acquisition, use and disclosure.

Article 159(1) Association Agreement only generally indicates that the parties agree to exchange views and information on their domestic and international practices and policies affecting transfer of technology. This shall in particular include measures to facilitate information flows, business partnerships, and licensing and subcontracting deals on a voluntary basis. Particular attention shall be paid to the conditions necessary to create an adequate enabling environment for technology transfer in the host countries, including issues such as the relevant legal framework and development of human capital.[56]

An analysis of judicial practice indicates that the courts do not uphold claims for protection from unfair competition related to know-how, and do not award damages (or other claims) relating to rights to know-how, arguing that no evidence has been submitted of the circumstances invoked and that know-how is not regulated by law.[57] As of today, there are no laws and draft laws that regulate the legal status of know-how.

With regard to the unauthorized acquisition, disclosure and use of trade secrets, the Law "On Protection from Unfair Competition" stipulates that the main subtypes of this form of unfair competition include unauthorized acquisition or disclosure, or persuasion to disclose, and the illegal use of trade secrets. Hence, the unauthorized acquisition of trade secrets is to be understood as the illegal obtaining of information, which, under the Ukrainian laws in force, constitutes a trade secret if it has caused or could have caused damage to the business entity. Disclosure of a trade secret is to be understood as making a third party (or another person) aware of information which is a trade secret within the meaning of the Ukrainian laws in force without the permission of a person authorized to do so or a person to whom such information was entrusted or became known by virtue of their duties, if it has caused or could have caused damage to the business entity. A special subtype of such activities is the tendency to disclose trade secrets, which should be understood as motivating a person who has been entrusted with information in the prescribed manner, or to whom the information has become known in connection with their relevant duties, to disclose information that under Ukrainian Law constitutes a trade secret, before the disclosure of that information, if it has caused or could have caused damage to the entity.[58]

Unauthorized use of a trade secret is to be understood as the implementation in production or consideration for planning purposes or conducting business activities on the basis of information which is a trade secret within the meaning of the Ukrainian laws in force, without the consent of the authorized person.

---

[56] Association Agreement between the European Union and its Member States, of the one part, and Ukraine, of the other part (2014) OJ L161/3 (EU–Ukraine Association Agreement), 984 (11).

[57] Kharkiv Region District Court, Decision 922/356/17 (2017); Shevchenkivskiy District Court of Kyiv Decision 761/29788/14-ц (2015).

[58] Ukrainian Law on Protection Against Unfair Competition 1996, 236/96-BP.

7.2 *Judicial Practice*

A crucial decision of the AMCU concerning the unauthorized use of trade secrets is the Ergon-Electric Ltd. case.[59] This is the only case since Ukraine became independent in which the AMCU held an offender liable for the unauthorized use of trade secrets. It held that in its business activities Ergon-Electric Ltd. used information that was a trade secret of its competitor TVK Vector-VS Ltd. without the latter's consent, namely the full list of suppliers and customers together with their representatives' contact details, as well as contracts signed with them, purchase and sales volumes of electrical products (distribution, control and measuring equipment and instrumentation, busbars, etc.), purchase and sale prices for the said products (including information on the trade margins and discounts for the purchase of products).

Ergon-Electric Ltd. obtained the information that constituted a trade secret of TVK Vector-VS Ltd. through its founding shareholders, who had previously been employed by TVK Vector-VS Ltd. and therefore had access to the trade secrets. Moreover, they had signed a non-disclosure agreement in which they undertook to maintain trade secrets and in particular not to use such information for three years after leaving the company for any competitive activity that could harm TVK Vector-VS Ltd. Nevertheless, before leaving the company, they illegally copied information that constituted the company's trade secret and which was then used for the planning and conduct of the business activities of Ergon-Electric Ltd., which they had set up as a competitor to the claimant. The case concluded with Decision No. 30-p of 13 December 2018 issued by the Interim Administrative Panel of the AMCU, holding that the actions of Ergon-Electric Ltd. constituted unfair competition in the form of its unauthorized use of trade secrets of TVK Vector-VS Ltd. in violation of Art. 19 Unfair Competition Law.

It should be emphasized that it is extremely difficult to prove the fact of an unauthorized use of trade secrets. There are many cases in which it has been held that the claimant did not prove in court that the respondent had illegally used the claimant's trade secret.[60]

Thus, in its ruling of 28 February 28, 2019 in case No. 752/5775/16-c, the Supreme Court rejected the appeal on a point of law claiming the defendant's liability for misappropriation and unauthorized use for its own purposes of a legal entity's trade secret, since the claimant had failed to prove the fact of disclosure and provide evidence of the infringement of its right by the defendant. In short, the claimant failed to prove in court that the respondent was illegally using its trade secret.[61]

---

[59] Antimonopoly Committee of Ukraine, Decision 30-p/tk (2018).

[60] Ibid.

[61] Ibid.

7.3 Conclusion

The analysis of the judgments awarded by the AMCU and the courts concerning the unauthorized use of trade secrets allows us to conclude that if the actus reus of unauthorized acquisition or use of information that constitutes a trade secret is to be upheld, it is necessary to report in as much detail as possible each component of the violation and provide evidence of the damage caused as a result in order to protect the claimant's rights in litigation. An effective system for the protection of trade secrets will help improve the ability of entities to use their business and production processes for their own benefit but not for that of their competitors.

References

Antimonopoly Committee of Ukraine, 'Annual Report' 2020

Antimonopoly Committee of Ukraine, 'Annual Report' 2019

Antimonopoly Committee of Ukraine, 'Annual Report' 2018

Antimonopoly Committee of Ukraine, 'Annual Report', 2017

Antimonopoly Committee of Ukraine, 'Annual Report', 2016

Iruna Bezzub, 'Specialist Court for the Settlement of Intellectual Property Disputes: Foreign Experience and Ukrainian Opportunities' *Social Communications Research Center* (11 December 2017) http://www.nbuviap.gov.ua/index.php?option=com_content&view=article&id=3181:spetsializovanij-sud-iz-rozglyadu-sprav-u-sferi-intelektualnoji-vlasnosti&catid=8&Itemid=350 [Ирина Беззуб, 'Спеціалізований Суд із Розгляду Справ у Сфері Інтелектуальної Власності: Зарубіжний Досвід та Українські Перспективи' Центр дослідження соціальних комунікацій (11 грудня 2017)]

Oleg Dzhurynskyi, 'Protection Against Unfair Competition' (2010) Civil Law Aspects [Олег Джуринський, 'Захист від Недобросовісної Конкуренції' (2010) Цивільно-Правовий Аспект]

European Commission, 'Report on the Protection and Enforcement of Intellectual Property Rights in Third Countries' (Working Document) SWD (2021)

Oksana Kovalchuk, 'Intellectual Property Right for the Geographical Indications in Ukraine and Member States of the European Union' 2014 [Оксана Ковальчук, 'Суб'єкти Права Інтелектуальної Власності на Географічне Зазначення']

Koznova Olexandra 'Increased Activity of the Antimonopoly Committee of Ukraine: A New Reality?' (20 January 2021) https://biz.ligazakon.net/analitycs/201058_zrostannya-aktivnost-antimonopolnogo-komtetu-ukrani-nova-realnst [Match Match Match Match'Зростання Активності Антимонопольного Комітету України: Нова Реальність?' (20 січня 2021)]

Mukola Potockyi, 'Counterfeiting in the Field of Medicines as Unfair Competition' *DD&I IP Agency* (17 May 2019) https://uba.ua/documents/text/Potockiy_Mykola.pdf [Микола Потоцький, 'Контрафакція у Сфері Лікарських Засобів, як Недобросовісна Конкуренція' *DD&I IP Agency* (17 травня 2019)]

World Intellectual Property Organization, '*World Intellectual Property Indicators 2019*' (WIPO 2019)

'With Thoughts About Supermarkets and New Year, Producer of Caviar Lies on the Label "Kamchatskaia Zernierstaia" – AMCU (2019)' *Our Money* (10 December 2019) https://nashigroshi.org/2019/12/10/z-dumkamy-pro-supermarkety-i-novyy-rik-vyrobnyk-ikry-breshe-na-etyketkakh-kamchatskay-ziernistay-amku/ ['З Думками про Супермаркети і Новий Рік, Виробник Ікри Бреше на Етикетках "Камчатскай Зєрністай" – АМКУ (2019)' *Наші гроші* (10 грудня 2019)]

Policies and Law on Intellectual Property

Association Agreements and Problems Approximating Intellectual Property Legislation of Third Countries with the EU Acquis: The Case of Ukraine

Yuriy Kapitsa

Contents

Y. Kapitsa (✉)
Centre for Intellectual Property Studies and Technology Transfer of the National Academy of Sciences of Ukraine, Kyiv, Ukraine
e-mail: kapitsa@nas.gov.ua

H. Richter (ed.), *Competition and Intellectual Property Law in Ukraine*,
MPI Studies on Intellectual Property and Competition Law 31,
https://doi.org/10.1007/978-3-662-66101-7_12

Abstract Is it possible for a non-EU country to reach a level of IP legislation compatible with that of the EU and to apply it effectively? This chapter explores this issue based on the analysis of the content and the implementation practices of EU Partnership and Cooperation Agreements with Ukraine and other Newly Independent States and the Association Agreements with Ukraine, Moldova and Georgia, as well as other EU free trade agreements. It examines the problem of incompleteness of the IP provisions of these Association Agreements compared to the respective EU acts, the lack of an approximation mechanism in the Agreements and the problem of interpretation of the implemented EU provisions. The chapter considers possible measures to create a sustainable mechanism for approximating Ukrainian IP legislation to EU law and for efficiently applying the implemented provisions of the Agreement and EU acts. Furthermore, it discusses methodological issues of approximation of the IP legislation of third countries to EU law, including EU candidate countries, and illustrates the specifics of approximation of national legislation to EU law by focusing on certain IP subject matter.

1 Introduction

Efforts to unify national intellectual property (IP) legislation in different countries traditionally have been made at many levels: WIPO Agreements, Council of Europe Conventions, TRIPS Agreement, etc. Within the EU, massive initiatives between 1980 and 2000 resulted in the creation of a regionally harmonised environment for IP protection with regional protection of geographical indications (1992), trademarks (1993), plant varieties (1994), designs (2001) and unitary patents (underway), as well as harmonising and unifying national legislation by adopting more than 30 EU directives and regulations on various aspects of protection of intellectual property rights.

Concluding EU Partnership and Cooperation Agreements (PCA), Association Agreements, and other agreements with third countries, including Ukraine, as well as creating free trade areas became a common EU way of expanding the regional model of IP protection to other countries. By that means the EU introduces requirements into its international treaties to make third countries' legislation compatible with that of the Community. That was supposed to safeguard the interests of right holders and provide a uniform intellectual property environment for the economic activity of European companies in these countries and vice versa.

Such international agreements raise several questions, which this chapter will discuss, e.g.: To what extent have the EU plans in the area been realised as regards the Newly Independent States[1] (NIS) and Ukraine in particular? Have the goals of the PCA been achieved? Have the provisions of the PCA and the Association Agreements laid an efficient legal foundation for legislative approximation? Is it possible to

[1] Newly Independent States: Azerbaijan, Belarus, Armenia, Georgia, Kazakhstan, Kyrgyzstan, Moldova, Russian Federation, Tajikistan, Uzbekistan, Ukraine.

achieve a level of IP protection under the agreements with Ukraine, Georgia and Moldova similar to that provided in the EU? What problems have emerged along the way? Taking into account the decision of the European Council of 23 June 2022 to grant the status of candidate country to Ukraine and Moldova: Are the respective Association Agreements an appropriate basis for legislation approximation for EU accession or should a special mechanism be adopted?

This chapter considers these issues in the context of the practice of realising the PCA with NIS and fulfilling the Association Agreement between the EU and Ukraine and similar agreements with Georgia and Moldova. It also reveals some drawbacks in the 2014 Association Agreements that have greatly complicated the legislative approximation. Based on the legislative approximation practices in Ukraine and other countries, ways of establishing a sustainable mechanism to approximate domestic IP legislation to that of the EU are suggested for the countries that: (a) made commitments to approximate their legislation with that of the EU without seeking EU membership or broader integration; (b) concluded association agreements with the EU that involved creating a free trade area; and (c) EU candidate countries.

2 Agreements Between the EU and Ukraine and Problems of Approximating IP Legislation

2.1 Interim Agreement and Partnership and Cooperation Agreement

2.1.1 The Interim Agreement Between the EC and Ukraine of 1995

Ukraine's commitments to improve its IP legislation along European Community lines were first set forth in the Interim Agreement on trade and trade-related matters between the EC and Ukraine of 1 June 1995,[2] which was effective until 1 March 1998, when the PCA came into force. It is worth mentioning that IP protection was the only branch of law whose commitment to legislative approximation was laid down in the Interim Agreement. Its Art. 18 reads:

> Pursuant to the provisions of this Article and of Annex III, Ukraine shall continue to improve the protection of intellectual, industrial and commercial property rights in order to provide, by the end of the fifth year after the entry into force of this Agreement for a level of protection similar to that provided in the Community by Community acts, in particular those referred to in Annex III, including comparable means of enforcing such rights.

[2] Interim Agreement on trade and trade-related matters between the European Community, the European Coal and Steel Community and the European Atomic Energy Community, of the one part, and Ukraine, of the other part (1995) OJ L311/2.

Annex III includes six directives and two regulations as secondary law which had been adopted by the European Community before the Agreement was signed.[3]

2.1.2 The PCA Between the EC and Ukraine of 1998 in Context

The "Partnership and Cooperation Agreement between the European Communities and their Member States, and Ukraine" was signed on 14 June 1994 and entered into force on 1 March 1998.[4] This agreement includes Art. 51, which identifies 16 areas including IP. It states that an important condition for strengthening the economic links between Ukraine and the Community is the approximation of Ukraine's existing and future legislation to that of the Community. Ukraine shall ensure that its legislation will gradually be made compatible with that of the Community. However, unlike other law branches, IP protection is given a separate Art. 50 in the Agreement, which specifies requirements for Ukraine that were supposed to be fulfilled by 1 March 2003 (five years after the PCA entered into force). Art. 50 reads:

> (1) Pursuant to the provisions of this Article and of Annex III, Ukraine shall continue to improve the protection of intellectual, industrial and commercial property rights in order to provide, by the end of the fifth year after the entry into force of the Agreement for a level of protection similar to that existing in the Community, including effective means of enforcing such rights.
>
> (2) By the end of the fifth year after entry into force of the Agreement, Ukraine shall accede to the multilateral conventions on intellectual, industrial and commercial property rights referred to in paragraph 1 of Annex III.

These provisions are identical to those in the PCAs of the EC with other NIS as well as to the Association Agreements between the EC and Bulgaria, Czech Republic, Hungary, Poland, the Baltic states and other countries in Central and Eastern Europe. The analysis of the PCA implementation in NIS shows that their commitments to join international conventions were mostly fulfilled, while their IP laws had not been

[3] Council Directive 89/104/EEC of 21 December 1988 to Approximate the Laws of the Member States Relating to Trade Marks (1988) OJ L40/1 (Trade Mark Directive); Council Directive 87/54/EEC of 16 December 1986 on the Legal Protection of Topographies of Semiconductor Products OJ L24/36; Council Directive 91/250/EEC of 14 May 1991 on the Legal Protection of Computer Programs OJ L122/42; Council Directive 93/83/EEC of 27 September 1993 on the Coordination of Certain Rules Concerning Copyright and Rights Related to Copyright Applicable to Satellite Broadcasting and Cable Retransmission OJ L248/15 (Satellite Broadcasting and Cable Retransmission Directive); Council Directive 93/98/EEC of 29 October 1993 on Harmonizing the Term of Protection of Copyright and Certain Related Rights OJ L290/9; Council Directive 92/100/EEC of 19 November 1992 on Rental Right and Lending Right and on Certain Rights Related to Copyright in the Field of Intellectual Property OJ L346/61; Council Regulation No. 1768/92 of 18 June 1992 Concerning the Creation of a Supplementary Protection Certificate for Medicinal Products OJ L182/1; Council Regulation No. 2081/92 of 14 July 1992 on the Protection of Geographical Indications and Designations of Origin for Agricultural Products and Foodstuffs OJ L208/1.

[4] Partnership and Cooperation Agreement between the European Communities and their Member States, and Ukraine (1998) OJ L49/3 (EU–Ukraine PCA).

approximated to EU laws[5] by 2003–2004, which was the deadline for upgrading the level of protection to that provided in the EU.[6] Various reasons explain this deficit, including the significant volume of EU acts, the absence of translations and working institutional mechanisms for adapting legislation, and—most importantly—the absence of EU policy documents regarding the scope and the stages of legislative approximation.

The PCA stipulated that the EU should provide technical assistance, as appropriate, to approximate legislation. This may involve the exchange of experts, the provision of early information especially on relevant legislation, the organization of seminars, training activities, and aid for translation of Community legislation.[7] However, the so-called TACIS IP projects undertaken in Russia, Ukraine and other countries in 1995–2002 and the activities of the European Policy and Legal Advice Centres did not lead to systematically reviewing the legislation system with the preparation of new draft laws. Another shortfall was the absence of translated EU legislation following the standards and using the glossaries accepted by the EU to translate official documents into the languages of EU Member States.[8] As a result, there was a discrepancy in terminology used by different translators.[9]

In contrast, the situation was totally different for Central and Eastern European countries and the countries of the European Economic Area. In 1995, The European Commission prepared the "White Paper in Preparation of the Associated Countries of Central and Eastern Europe to Integration into the Internal Market of the Union".[10] This document was developed for the countries with which an association agreement had been concluded or was to be concluded. The paper provides recommendations for sequencing in legislative approximation, a list of EU regulatory acts which should be taken into account first of all, and it sets out conditions for harmonising the legislation. The White Paper Annex lists 899 EU directives and regulations. Each of

[5] The following data is provided for each country: date when the PCA was signed, date when the PCA came into force, date when the commitment to provide the level of IP protection similar to that existing in the EU should be fulfilled: Azerbaijan—1996, 1999, 2004; Belarus—1995, PCA was not ratified; Armenia—1996, 1999, 2004; Georgia—1996, 1999, 2004; Kazakhstan—1995, 1999, 2004; Kyrgyzstan, 1995, 1999, 2004; Moldova—1994, 1998, 2003; the Russian Federation—1994, 1997, 2002; Tajikistan—2004, 2010, 2014; Uzbekistan—1996, 1999, 2003; Ukraine—1994, 1998, 2003.

[6] Yuriy Kapitsa, 'Features of Harmonization of Legislation of the NIS Countries with the Legislation of the European Union in the Field of Intellectual Property Protection' (2011) 3 The Law of Ukraine Journal 2011 92 (93–99).

[7] See art 43 PCA with Armenia, art 43 PCA with Azerbaijan, art 50 PCA with Moldova, art 51 PCA with Ukraine.

[8] European Commission Guide for External Translators 2008.

[9] The analysis of the translation of EU acts as part of the project TACIS Intellectual Property in Ukraine (1998–2000) showed different translations of the same terms and expressions in EU directives, the lack of legal editing, and the possibility to use these translations to obtain an overview of the content of the EU acts rather than as a basis to introduce changes to the national legislation. Kapitsa, 'Features of Harmonization' (n 6).

[10] European Commission, 'Preparation of the Associated Countries of Central and Eastern Europe to Integration into the Internal Market of the Union' (White Paper) COM (95) 163 final, 1995.

the 23 sections deals with a certain branch of law, describes its legislation, identifies organizational conditions and mechanisms for enforcing respective acts, and suggests a concrete sequence in considering them. In addition to the list of EU directives and regulations, the section on IP includes the requirement that all the countries join the European Patent Convention by 1997. It emphasises the importance of administrative actions to enhance the enforcement of IP rights and to improve the performance of the judicial authorities.

High requirements to organize the approximation of legislation were established for the "second wave" of associated countries. Every month, Bulgaria and Romania had to translate 6,000 out of the total 90,000 pages of the *acquis communautaire* to comply with the EU translation standards.[11] These translations were published in the respective native languages in the Official Journal of the EU.[12] Moreover, the Bulgaria 2005 Comprehensive Monitoring Report[13] shows that the ECJ selected its key rulings that were to be translated, which totalled approximately 15,000 pages.

As the practice of applying the White Paper indicates, when considering the countries' accession applications the European Commission took into account first of all changes to the national legislation based on the White Paper.[14] The experience of Bulgaria, Poland and the Baltic states regarding an efficient enforcement of IP rights indicates that some of those countries joined the EU with a level of piracy which significantly exceeded that of the other EU countries.[15] Thus, the most important action for the associated countries was to align their legislation *formally* with the specific EU acts.

Moreover, there was a fundamental difference in the goals of legislative approximation between the associated countries and the NIS. Associated countries had to adapt their legislation to the most important EU acts in terms of the internal market. Moreover, the ECJ's judgments on the interpretation of EU acts were not taken into consideration when the first wave of countries joined the EU. It meant that when these countries joined the EU, the *acquis* would apply automatically to their domestic legal relations. Most NIS, in contrast, did not set accession to the EU as their political goal; and regarding those NIS that declared their intention to become a EU Member State in the 1990s, the EU was not ready to consider the accession of new EU Member States from Eastern Europe.

---

[11] European Commission, 'Comprehensive Monitoring Report on the State of Preparedness for EU Membership of Bulgaria and Romania' (Communication) COM (2005) 534 final.

[12] Act concerning the conditions of accession of the Republic of Bulgaria and Romania and the adjustments to the Treaties on which the European Union is founded (2005) OJ L157, art 58.

[13] European Commission, 'Bulgaria: 2005 Comprehensive Monitoring Report' (Report) COM (2005) 534 final, 30–31 and 75.

[14] See European Commission, 'Agenda 2000—Commission Opinion on Poland's Application for Membership of the European Union' (White Paper) DOC 97/18, 1997, 30–31 and 87.

[15] See Annual Reports of International Intellectual Property Alliance https://www.iipa.org/ accessed 5 July 2021.

2.1.3 The Application of PCA Provisions in NIS

In practice, and in the absence of EU recommendations, the NIS applied the PCA provisions on IP protection to the extent those countries were politically prepared to take integration actions. The EU "Euro Aid" projects, which were undertaken in Azerbaijan, Ukraine, Moldova and other countries between 2005 and 2014, usually responded to the request of the public authorities to work at legislative approximation. However, the project recommendations on the scope of approximation varied dramatically from country to country. Among all NIS, Azerbaijan, Russia, Ukraine, and Moldova gained the most extensive experience in the approximation of IP legislation in this period.

For example, under the EU project "Support to the National Coordination Unit and the Partnership and Cooperation Agreement Implementation in Azerbaijan" (2008–2010),[16] the national plan of legislative approximation was developed in cooperation with the Azerbaijani executive authorities. In the IP area, attention was focused on fulfilling the TRIPS Agreement and implementing certain provisions of the EU acts including the term of protection of design rights and plant variety rights similar to that in the EU. Due to Azerbaijani IP authorities' interest in providing a high degree of IP enforcement, this author was involved in developing a number of regulatory acts in cooperation with experts of the State Copyright Committee of the Republic of Azerbaijan, which reflected, on the one hand, the requirements of the Enforcement Directive 2004/48/EC,[17] and on the other hand, NIS experience (including that of Ukraine) in introducing holograph protection; regulating the sale of audio-visual products, phonograms and software; enhancing the coordination of IP enforcement measures at the level of central government authorities and regions; and improving the regulation of the activities of collective management organisations.

The Russian Federation took a selective approach to applying EU legislation by adopting Part 4 of the RF Civil Code in 2006, which among other things introduced database protection by *sui generis* right and increased the duration of design rights to 25 years.

In Ukraine, the 1998–2003 EU projects of technical assistance did not set an objective either to prepare draft laws in line with EU legislation or to translate the entire EU *acquis* on intellectual property. The scope and stages in legislative approximation were identified in Ukraine in 2001–2007 based on the political decisions of the Ukrainian government and the legislative approximation mechanism established at the legislative and organisational level (see Part 4).

Moldova, in contrast, employed an approach to ensure the entire harmonisation of the national acts with EU acts and adopted amended IP laws in 2007–2010 taking

---

[16] European Commission, 'International Cooperation—Calls for Proposals and Tenders: Support to the National Coordinating Unit (NCU) and to the Partnership and Cooperation Agreement (PCA) Implementation in Azerbaijan' EuropeAid/124289/C/SER/AZ, 2006.

[17] Parliament and Council Directive 2004/48/EC of 29 April 2004 on the Enforcement of Intellectual Property Rights (2004) OJ L157 (Enforcement Directive) 45.

into consideration the requirements of EU acts.[18] However, analysis of the degree of legislative approximation made by the project "Support for the Implementation of Agreements between the Republic of Moldova and the EU" (2008–2011),[19] while confirming the existence of formal legislative approximation, noted the most sustention for the point of authors lack—the necessity of more IP enforcement actions to achieve complete legislative approximation.[20] The enforcement of IP rights was also emphasised in the action plans which the EU concluded with NIS within the PCA framework.

2.1.4 Conclusion

To sum up, there has been an evident policy shift of the EU from the priority of formal legislative approximation as regards the associated countries in Central and Eastern Europe to a focus on enforcement of IP rights, rather than conformity with the EU law, in relations with the NIS.

The practice of concluding EU Association Agreements with Central and Eastern European countries as well as PCAs with NIS indicates that despite the formally similar requirements made in these agreements to ensure a level of IP protection similar to that provided in the EU (including efficient ways of ensuring the enforcement of these rights), their mechanisms and the extent of legislative approximations are different: The main requirement for the associated countries of Central and Eastern Europe was to bring their IP legislation in compliance with the regulations, directives and in some cases certain European court rulings identified by the EU. It was supposed that after the countries joined the EU, the IP protection *acquis* would automatically apply to them. In contrast, the EU has not developed an approach or recommendations on the legislative approximation mechanism for the NIS that have no intention to join the EU at all or in the near future, but instead placed an emphasis on ensuring the enforcement of intellectual property rights.

Moreover, the analysis reveals a lack of clear EU recommendations regarding NIS legislative approximation and the lack of targeted technical assistance with translating the *acquis* and drafting respective laws. Further striking features are the difference in NIS political priorities concerning EU integration, the undeveloped organisational mechanisms for legislative approximation resulting in different approaches of these countries to the timeframe, and the extent of legislative approximation. As a

[18] Moldova Law on Protection of Industrial Designs 2007, 161-XVI; Moldova Law on Protection of Inventions 2008, 50-XVI; Moldova Law on Protection of Trademarks 2008, 38-XVI; Moldova Law on Protection of Geographical Indications, Appellations of Origin and Traditional Specialities Guaranteed 2008, 66-XVI; Moldova Law on Protection of Plant Varieties 2008; Moldova Law on Copyright and Related Rights 2010, 139, etc.

[19] European Commission, 'International Cooperation—Calls for Proposals and Tenders: Rural SME Policy Support Window' EuropeAid/125947/C/SER/MD, 2017.

[20] Eugene Stuart et al., *Intellectual Property Law and Policy—Law Approximation to EU Standards in the Republic of Moldova* (Sinectica-Com 2010) 218.

result, the requirements of the Partnership and Cooperation Agreements with NIS on approximating national IP legislations with the EU law have not been fulfilled.

2.2 The EU–Ukraine Association Agreement (2014) and Intellectual Property

2.2.1 Context and Goal

The Association Agreement between Ukraine and the European Union, signed in 2014, is a dramatic turning point in the development of Ukrainian society.[21] The Agreement created conditions for gradually integrating Ukraine into the EU internal market based on a Deep and Comprehensive Free Trade Area. The Preamble of the Agreement states that the Parties want to achieve economic integration, inter alia, "through extensive regulatory approximation" and recognise that "such a Deep and Comprehensive Free Trade Area, linked to the broader process of legislative approximation, will contribute to further economic integration with the European Union Internal Market as envisaged in this Agreement". Furthermore, it contains the commitment to "gradually approximating Ukraine's legislation with that of the Union along the lines set out in this Agreement and to effectively implementing it". Among the goals of the association is "to support Ukrainian efforts to complete the transition into a functioning market economy by means of, inter alia, the progressive approximation of its legislation to that of the Union" (Art. 1(2)(d)).

2.2.2 Approximation Requirements of the Association Agreement

The Agreement includes annexes that list EU acts with which Ukraine is to approximate its legislation. The only exception is made for IP: Title IV, Chapter 9 ("Intellectual property") directly incorporates an extensive body of specific provisions of EU IP acts. This raises several issues related to Chapter 9,[22] such as whether provisions related to IP in Chapter 9 and other chapters of the Agreement cover all the provisions of the EU *acquis*; whether the Agreement contains commitments to approximate the Ukrainian legislation to both the existing EU acts and new EU acts adopted after the Agreement was signed; whether the Agreement includes new IP provisions which are absent from the EU *acquis*; whether the Agreement has a mechanism for Ukrainian courts to take into account European case law on the interpretation

---

[21] The political part of the Agreement was signed on 21 March 2014. The economic part of the Agreement was signed on 27 June 2014. For further background and analysis, see also Roman Petrov, 'The EU–Ukraine Association Agreement as a General Framework of Contemporary EU–Ukraine Relations' in this Volume.

[22] Yuriy Kapitsa, *Intellectual Property Rights of the European Union: Formation, Institutions, Directions of Development* (Academiperiodica 2017) 450.

of the EU acts when applying the implemented provisions of EU acts; and how the legislative approximation mechanism is related to the approaches taken by the EU agreements on the EEA, EFTA etc., in the context of creating a free trade area between the EU and Ukraine.

Various experts have reviewed the requirements of the Association Agreement to approximate the Ukrainian legislation with the EU legislation[23] and the issues of IP protection.[24] A key characteristic of the Association Agreement is its lack of uniform legislative approximation requirements for different areas of the Agreement. In general, Art. 474 "Gradual Approximation" applies to Titles IV, V and VI of the Agreement, stating that

> […]in line with the objectives of this Agreement as set out in Article 1, Ukraine will carry out gradual approximation of its legislation to EU law as referred to in Annexes I to XLIV to this Agreement, based on commitments identified in Titles IV, V and VI of this Agreement, and according to the provisions of those Annexes.

In particular, the Agreement contains specific legislative approximation requirements for different areas, which the following examples illustrate[25]:

The legislation of sanitary and phytosanitary measures, for instance, shall be approximated based on the EU acts and their implementation timeframe established in Annex V to the Agreement (Arts. 59, 64). Moreover, the "EU Party shall inform Ukraine well in advance of changes to the EU Party legislation to allow Ukraine to consider amending its legislation accordingly" (Art. 67).

As regards legislation on financial services, telecommunication services, postal and courier services and international maritime transport services, it is set forth that "an act corresponding to a EU Regulation or Decision shall as such be made part of the internal legal order of Ukraine"; as far as the directive is concerned, the Ukrainian authorities of Ukraine are entitled to choose the form and method of implementation (Art. 2(2), Annex XVII). In order to guarantee legal certainty, the EU Party "will inform Ukraine and the Trade Committee regularly in writing on all new or amended

---

[23] Viktor Muraviov, 'Legal Mechanism of Implementation of the Association Agreement between Ukraine and the European Union' (2015) 8 Journal Viche 7; Guillaume Van der Loo, *The EU–Ukraine Association Agreement and Deep and Comprehensive Free Trade Area* (Brill–Nijhoff 2016); Roman Petrov, 'EU–Ukraine Association Agreement's Effective Implementation Into the Legal Order of Ukraine: Challenges and Successes' in Ondrej Hamulák and Naděžda Sisková (eds) *European Studies The Review of European Law, Economics and Politics* (Wolters Kluwer 2019) 155 (155–174).

[24] E.g. Gennadiy Androschuk, Mykhailo Mykiyevych, Elena Kadetova, Andriy Olefir and others.

[25] In particular, sanitary and phytosanitary measures (arts 59, 64), customs legislation (art 84), financial, electronic communications, postal and courier, international maritime transport services (arts 114, 124, 133, 138), public procurement (arts 152, 153), competition (art 256)—see Kseniia Smyrnova, '"Europeanization" of Competition Law in Ukraine' in this Volume.

sector-specific EU legislation" (Art. 3(2)).[26] In this respect, the provisions of Art. 6 "Interpretation" of Annex XVII are of importance:

> Insofar as the provisions of this Annex and the applicable provisions specified in the Appendices are identical in substance to corresponding rules of the Treaty on the Functioning of the European Union and to acts adopted pursuant thereto, those provisions shall, in their implementation and application, be interpreted in conformity with the relevant rulings of the Court of Justice of the European Union.

The amendments to the Annex list respective directives and regulations and the timelines for their implementation.

As far as the public procurement legislation is concerned, Art. 153 sets out that during the legislative approximation "due account shall be taken of the corresponding case law of the European Court of Justice and the implementing measures adopted by the European Commission as well as, if this should become necessary, of any modifications of the EU *acquis* occurring in the meantime".

However, Chapter 9 of Title IV, "Intellectual property", lacks such annexes[27] to the Agreement that would specify EU acts to be integrated into the Ukrainian legislation. Rather, the IP Chapter only incorporates certain provisions of the EU intellectual property acts, which were selected by the developers of the Agreement together with mutual commitments of the Parties to complying with them. Also, Chapter 9 does not stipulate any legislative approximation timelines, as are provided in the other chapters. Furthermore, the chapter lacks commitments to approximate the Ukrainian legislation with the existing and new EU IP acts,[28] nor does it contain any commitments for the EU to inform Ukraine about newly adopted EU acts. Finally, there are no guidelines on the mechanism for adapting the provisions of Chapter 9 to the Ukrainian legislation in terms of different requirements which are related to the implementation of EU directives and regulations.

In sum, the analysis of the provisions in the Agreement and the respective provisions in the EU acts reveals that the reflection of EU IP acts in Chapter 9 is selective and incomplete. In some cases, the wording of the provisions is even different from that in EU acts. If the European Commission had selected certain provisions from the copyright and related right directives, as the Association Agreement does, and then suggested that its Member States harmonise their national legislations along only those lines without considering the EU court rulings, these states would have encountered significant problems.

---

[26] According to Annex XVII, the Trade Committee shall add within three months any new or amended EU legislative act to the Appendices. Once a new or amended EU legislative act has been added to the relevant Appendix, Ukraine shall transpose the legislation into its domestic legal system in accordance with art 2(2) (art 3(2)). The Trade Committee shall also decide on an indicative period for the transposition of the act (art 3(3)).

[27] Except for Annexes XXII-A–XXII-D concerning geographical indications.

[28] As envisaged in certain other areas in the Agreement.

2.2.3 Conformity of the Association Agreement's IP Provisions with EU Acts?

The conformity of certain provisions of the Agreement to EU acts is discussed in the following.[29] Several divergences become evident and are worth a critical review:

Copyright and related rights. As regards the InfoSoc Directive 2001/29/EC,[30] Arts. 171, 173–177 of the Agreement include some of its provisions. However, out of a significant number of exceptions and limitations, only one exception, that related to temporary acts of reproduction, is provided.[31] The lack of exceptions from Art. 5 InfoSoc Directive in the Agreement, which are meant specifically for the information society and could be used in Ukraine, is detrimental to the Agreement, which does not promote the development of the knowledge economy and modern information relations in Ukraine in a way similar to that in the EU. Furthermore, the Agreement is missing a provision similar to Art. 3(3) of the Directive regarding the non-exhaustion of rights by any act of communication to the public or making available to the public.[32] In addition, Art. 6(4) of the Directive "Obligations as to technological measures" is missing as well, although it contains an important provision on abuse prevention by technological measures.

Duration of authors' rights and related rights. In deviation from the Copyright Directive 2006/116/EC amended by Directive 2011/77/2011[33] the Association Agreement sets forth that "the term of protection of cinematographic or audiovisual works shall expire not less than 70 years after…" (instead of—"shall expire 70 years after…") (Art. 163). Also, the rights of performers, of producers of the first fixation of a film and of broadcasting organisations "shall expire not less than 50 years after…" (instead of—"shall expire 50 years after…") (Art. 164). There are no provisions on the calculation of the term of protection when a work is published in volumes, parts, instalments, issues or episodes, as provided for in of Art. 1(5) of Directive 2006/116/EC as well substantive provisions of Arts. 3(2a)–3(2e) of Directive 2011/77/2011.

---

[29] See complete analysis in Kapitsa (n 22) 449–466.

[30] Parliament and Council Directive 2001/29/EC of 22 May 2001 on the Harmonisation of Certain Aspects of Copyright and Related Rights in the Information Society (2001) OJ L167 (InfoSoc Directive) 10.

[31] See Anna Shtefan, 'Copyright and Its Exceptions and Limitations in Ukraine' in this Volume.

[32] See Kostiantyn Zerov, 'Protection of Works Posted on the Internet Under Ukrainian Copyright Law' in this Volume.

[33] Parliament and Council Directive 2006/116/EC of 12 December 2006 on the Term of Protection of Copyright and Certain Related Rights (2006) OJ L372/12, as amended by Directive 2011/77/EU of 27 September 2011 (2011) OJ L265/1 (Copyright Directive).

Rental right and lending right. The Association Agreement does not incorporate the provisions of Art. 2(1); Arts. 3(4)–3(6); or Arts. 9(3) and 9(4) of Directive 2006/115/EC[34] on the specifics of granting distribution rights to authors and performers, exhaustion of rights etc.

Resale right. Article 190 of the Agreement includes the contents of only Art. 1 from Directive 2001/84/EC[35] concerning the resale right. However, a number of provisions in the Directive which are important for using the resale right were not included in the Agreement: works of art to which the resale right relates (Art. 2); principles and obligations of the parties to determine royalty rates at the legislative level (Art. 4 of the Directive contains respective royalty rates); calculation basis (Art. 5); determining a possibility for compulsory or optional collective management of the resale right (Art. 6); third-country nationals entitled to receive royalties (Art. 7). Moreover, Art. 190(1) of the Agreement refers to the resale right with respect to an "original work of art". However, the Ukrainian Law on Copyright and Related Rights (1994) 3792-XII does not define this term. Under the Directive, an "original work of art" to which the resale right is applied is different from and narrower than the respective definitions of a "work of fine art" and a "work of applied art" in Art. 1 of the Law. As a consequence, the Association Agreement does not appear to contribute to improving the resale right legislation in Ukraine, which has not been sufficiently developed in the country.

Satellite broadcasting and cable retransmission. Only two out of 12 informative articles of Directive 93/83/EEC[36] concerning satellite broadcasting and cable retransmission rights are provided in the Agreement (Art. 2, Art. 8 Directive and Arts. 191–192 Agreement).

Trade marks. Articles 193–200 of the Agreement contain some selective provisions of Directive 2008/95/EC.[37] New standards on trade marks provided in Directive 2015/2436[38] are not reflected in the Agreement. Nor are there such provisions of Directives 2008/95/EC, 2015/2436 as grounds for refusal or invalidity if the application for registration of the trade mark was made in bad faith; concerning trade marks including badges, emblems and escutcheons other than those covered by Art. 6*ter* Paris Convention; the clarification of the time when a trade mark has acquired a distinctive character for the purpose of registration; or limitation in consequence of acquiescence (Arts. 3(2)(c), 3(2)(d), 3(3), 9, Directive 2008/95/EC etc.).

Geographical indications. The approach taken in the Association Agreement to the protection of geographical indications differs from that provided in the 1995

---

[34] Parliament and Council Directive 2006/115/EC of 12 December 2006 on Rental Right and Lending Right and on Certain Rights Related to Copyright in the Field of Intellectual Property (2006) OJ L376/28.

[35] Parliament and Council Directive 2001/84/EC of 27 September 2001 on the Resale Right for the Benefit of the Author of an Original Work of Art (2001) OJ L272/32.

[36] Satellite Broadcasting and Cable Retransmission Directive.

[37] Parliament and Council Directive 2008/95/EC of 22 October 2008 to Approximate the Laws of the Member States Relating to Trade Marks (2008) OJ L299/25.

[38] Parliament and Council Directive (EU) 2015/2436 of 16 December 2015 to Approximate the Laws of the Member States Relating to Trade Marks (Recast) (2015) OJ L336/1.

Interim Agreement and the 1994 PCA. Under the Interim Agreement, Ukraine was to ensure the level of protection of geographical indications and designations of origin, as defined in Regulation (EEC) No. 2081/92.[39] The analysis of the Ukrainian legislation and the 2006 version of this Regulation (Regulation (EC) No. 510/2006[40]) revealed a number of provisions which should be incorporated into the Ukrainian legislation.[41] However, the Association Agreement (Arts. 201–211) does not include most provisions of substantive law regarding the protection of geographical indications, providing just a few of them and focussing on mutual recognition of geographical indications and cooperation. Moreover, the Association Agreement does not contain commitments for Ukraine to approximate its legislation to the Agricultural Products Regulation (EU) No. 1151/2012.[42]

Supplementary protection certificate. Article 220 in the Agreement does not set forth whether Ukraine must approximate its legislation to Regulation (EC) No. 469/2009,[43] Regulation (EC) No. 1610/96,[44] nor does it contain any provisions of those regulations except for the term of a further period of protection for a medicinal or plant protection product.

Plant varieties. The Agreement does not provide any direct standards requiring Ukraine to approximate its respective law to the EU legislation. Art. 228 "Plant varieties" just states that the parties shall co-operate to promote and reinforce the protection of plant varieties rights in accordance with the UPOV Convention, including the optional exception to the breeder's right. However, the analysis of the conformity of the Ukrainian Law on the Protection of Plant Variety Rights 1993, 3116-XII to the Plant Variety Regulation (EC) No. 2100/94[45] and other EU acts shows that there are a number of provisions that need to be transposed into the Ukrainian legislation.[46]

Enforcement of intellectual property rights. Some provisions of the Enforcement Directive are given in an abridged form. Other provisions of the Directive on such

---

[39] Council Regulation (EEC) No. 2081/92 of 14 July 1992 on the Protection of Geographical Indications and Designations of Origin for Agricultural Products and Foodstuffs (1992) OJ L208/1.

[40] Council Regulation (EC) No. 510/2006 of 20 March 2006 on the Protection of Geographical Indications and Designations of Origin for Agricultural Products and Foodstuffs (2006) OJ L93/12.

[41] State Department for Approximation of Legislation, 'Overview of the State of Adaptation of Ukrainian Legislation to Acquis Communautaire' (EU adaptation of legislation overview), (2007) 132–135. See also Anastasiia Kyrylenko, 'Why so Few Geographical Indications in Ukraine? Legal, Political and Socio-Economic Perspective' in this Volume for a detailed analysis of Ukrainian legislation on geographical indications.

[42] Parliament and Council Regulation (EU) No. 1151/2012 of 21 November 2012 on Quality Schemes for Agricultural Products and Foodstuffs (2012) OJ L343/1.

[43] Parliament and Council Regulation (EC) No. 469/2009 of 6 May 2009 Concerning the Supplementary Protection Certificate for Medicinal Products (2009) OJ L152/1.

[44] Parliament and Council Regulation (EC) No. 1610/96 of 23 July 1996 Concerning the Creation of a Supplementary Protection Certificate for Plant Protection Products (1996) OJ L198/30.

[45] Council Regulation (EC) No. 2100/94 of 27 July 1994 on Community Plant Variety Rights (1994) OJ L227/1.

[46] Yuriy Kapitsa, *Intellectual Property Law of the European Union and the Legislation of Ukraine* (Slovo 2006) 350–361.

issues as measures for preserving evidence, provisional and precautionary measures or corrective measures[47] are not included at all.

2.2.4 Further Challenges for Approximation of IP Legislation

A general challenge for approximating EU legislation is that nowadays some provisions of Chapter 9 are outdated. They do not reflect provisions of the Directives on the protection of trade marks ((EU) 2015/2436),[48] orphan works (2012/28/EU),[49] collective management (2014/26/EU),[50] trade secrets ((EU) 2016/943),[51] copyright and related rights in the Digital Single Market (2019/790)[52] etc. Indeed, the authority of the Association Council involves updating or amending the Annexes to the Association Agreement (Art. 463). However, such annexes are absent from Chapter 9, except for geographical indications. One can only guess what actions will be taken by the Council in this case.

In addition, the Agreement does not cover the mechanism for Ukraine's participating in the system of unitary patent protection and joining the European Patent Convention, which is the prerequisite for joining the EU, as well as bringing its legislation into line with the convention.

Furthermore, the EU legislation is one of those areas that are changing and developing rapidly. What will the Parties to the Agreement do if EU acts make changes which conflict with certain provisions of Chapter 9? Since the only way to make changes to the Agreement is to make amendments which are to be ratified by the EU Member States and Ukraine, it is obvious that amending the Agreement faces great difficulties, and it is the issue that should be addressed.

As regards possible positive prospects related to the expectations of direct effect of Chapter 9 "Intellectual property", it should be mentioned that the majority of provisions contain references to the integration of the provisions into the national

---

[47] Enforcement Directive, art 7(1), (2), art 7(2), (3), arts 9(4), (5), (6) and 10(3).

[48] Trade Mark Directive.

[49] Parliament and Council Directive 2012/28/EU of 25 October 2012 on Certain Permitted Uses of Orphan Works (2012) OJ L299/5.

[50] Parliament and Council Directive 2014/26/EU of 26 February 2014 on Collective Management of Copyright and Related Rights and Multi-territorial Licensing of Rights in Musical Works for Online Use in the Internal Market (2014) OJ L84/72 (Collective Management Directive). For further details on current reforms in this field, see Liubov Maidanyk, 'On the Reforms, Practice and Perspective of the Law on Collecting Societies in Ukraine' in this Volume.

[51] Parliament and Council Directive (EU) 2016/943 of 8 June 2016 on the Protection of Undisclosed Know-how and Business Information (Trade Secrets) Against Their Unlawful Acquisition, Use and Disclosure (2016) OJ L157/1 (Trade Secrets Directive); On the protection of trade secrets in Ukraine, see also Olga Bakalinska, 'Legal Mechanisms of Protection Against Unfair Competition in Ukraine—Prerequisites, Problems and Trends' in this Volume.

[52] Parliament and Council Directive (EU) 2019/790 of 17 April 2019 on Copyright and Related Rights in the Digital Single Market and amending Directives 96/9/EC and 2001/29/EC (2019) OJ L130/92.

legislation, which does not imply their direct effect.[53] Similar to the application of international treaties in the EU,[54] in Ukraine[55] the direct application of provisions of an international treaty is possible if those are formulated in the treaty as having direct effect. But this can be applied only to a small number of articles in Chapter 9.[56]

Furthermore, it is worth noting that the Partnership and Cooperation Agreement between the EU and Ukraine managed to avoid most of these drawbacks. The provisions in the Agreement on Ukraine's commitment to improve the protection of IP "in order to provide, by the end of the fifth year after the entry into force of the Agreement for a level of protection similar to that existing in the Community, including effective means of enforcing such rights", together with the Ukrainian Law on the National Programme of Approximation of Ukrainian Legislation to that of the European Union 2004, No. 1629-IV, allowed for addressing the problem of Ukrainian legislation approximation with new EU acts and required that the EU court rulings be taken into account during the legislative adaptation.[57]

Finally, another deficit is that the Association Agreement does not impose requirements that Chapter 9, as well as EU acts, in their implementation and application must be interpreted in conformity with the relevant rulings of the ECJ. However, especially the IP domain significantly relies on ECJ practice and national court jurisprudence as concerns a considerable number of provisions of EU directives and regulations including those reflected in Chapter 9. This issue is further discussed in the following section.

In sum, incorporating only certain selected provisions of EU acts in its Association Agreement with Ukraine as well as in its agreements with Moldova and Georgia (without including the countries' commitments to take into account the current EU acts and new EU acts as well as without the implementation mechanism and requirements to apply ECJ rulings) is an unfortunate legal decision. Ultimately, the selectiveness and incompleteness of the Agreement causes great difficulties in implementing and applying its intellectual property protection provisions in Ukraine.

[53] See on the issue of direct effect of the provisions of the Association Agreement also Roman Petrov, 'The EU–Ukraine Association Agreement as a General Framework of Contemporary EU–Ukraine Relations' in this Volume.

[54] ECJ C-12/86 *Meryem Demirel v Stadt Schwäbisch Gmünd* (1989) ECLI:EU:C:1987:400, para 14.

[55] In the resolution of the Plenum of the High Specialised Court of Ukraine for Civil and Criminal Cases No. 13, of 19 December 2014 on the Application by Courts of Ukraine of International Treaties in the Administration of Justice set forth that "when administering justice, the court may apply provisions of international treaties directly as part of the Ukrainian legislation if taking respective actions is within the court competence or if these are formulated as having direct effect in international treaties", para 14.

[56] For example, art 162, art 216, etc. It should be mentioned that the Supreme Court took a number of decisions about the application of provisions provided in the Association Agreement. One of them is about art 198 in the Agreement dealing with grounds for trade mark revocation. The decision is interesting because the Court refers to the direct effect of the provisions in art 198 although art 198 only states that "'the Parties shall provide'" for taking certain actions specified in the article. See Ukrainian Civil Court of Cassation of the Supreme Court, Order 87826668 (2020) 760/12081/17.

[57] It should be mentioned that the latter hardly ever took place, in fact.

3 Problem Applying ECJ Judgments When Interpreting EU Law in Associated Countries

The ECJ has passed a considerable number of judgments on the interpretation of provisions in the EU directives and regulations on IP. Such rulings are part of the *acquis* and are binding for all judicial and administrative authorities in the EU Member States.[58] They are especially important for filling regulatory gaps of certain EU acts. This is true e.g. for the Medicinal Products SPC Regulation (EC) No. 469/2009[59] and its predecessor, Regulation (EEC) No. 1768/92, with over 40 ECJ rulings on its interpretation. Also, Court interpretations are necessary for interpreting concepts laid down in the Database Directive 96/9/EC,[60] such as "database", "investment in ... the obtaining ... of the contents" of a database, "investment in ... the ... verification ... of the contents", "extraction" and "re-utilisation", as well as "substantial part, evaluated ... quantitatively, of the contents of [a] database".[61] Another example is the criterion "individual character" of a design based on Design Directive 98/71/EC,[62] which the Association Agreement has introduced. This criterion differs from the previous criteria of patentability for designs in Ukraine, and it is interpreted in the ECJ judgment C-345/13,[63] as well as rulings of national courts. There is no doubt that applying only EU IP directives and regulations without considering ECJ judgments when interpreting EU acts would increase the disharmony of legislation and would not meet the objectives of creating the European Single Market.

In fact, the Association Agreements of the EU with Ukraine, Moldova and Georgia do not include any provisions obliging those countries to apply ECJ IP judgments when implementing the Agreement or when national courts apply the Agreement and EU acts. This requirement is made only for financial services, telecommunication

---

[58] ECJ C-283/81 *Srl CILFIT and Lanificio di Gavardo SpA v Ministry of Health* (1982) ECLI:EU:C:1982:335; ECJ C-10/97 *Ministero delle Finanze v IN.CO.GE.90 Srl, Idelgard Srl, Iris90 Srl, Camed Srl, Pomezia Progetti Appalti Srl (PPA), Edilcam Srl, A. Cecchini & C. Srl, EMO Srl, Emoda Srl, Sappesi Srl, Ing. Luigi Martini Srl, Giacomo Srl and Mafar Srl.*(1998) ECLI:EU:C:1998:498.

[59] Parliament and Council Regulation (EC) No. 469/2009 of 6 May 2009 Concerning the Supplementary Protection Certificate for Medicinal Products (2009) OJ L152/1.

[60] Parliament and Council Directive 96/9/EC of 11 March 1996 on the Legal Protection of Databases (1996) OJ L77/20.

[61] ECJ C-203/02 *The British Horseracing Board Ltd and Others v William Hill Organization Ltd* (2004) ECLI:EU:C:2004:695; ECJ C-338/02 *Fixtures Marketing Ltd v Svenska Spel AB* (2004) ECLI:EU:C:2004:696; ECJ C-444/02 *Fixtures Marketing Ltd v Organismos prognostikon agonon podosfairou AE (OPAP)* (2004) ECLI:EU:C:2004:697; ECJ C-46/02 *Fixtures Marketing Ltd v Oy Veikkaus Ab* (2004) ECLI:EU:C:2004:694, etc.

[62] Parliament and Council Directive 98/71/EC of 13 October 1998 on the Legal Protection of Designs (1998) OJ L289/28 (Design Directive). For a detailed analysis of Design Protection in Ukraine see Anastasiia Kyrylenko, 'The Reformed Design Law in Ukraine: What is Right with EU Trade Agreements?' in this Volume.

[63] ECJ C-345/13 *Karen Millen Fashions Ltd v Dunnes Stores, Dunnes Stores (Limerick) Ltd* (2014) ECLI:EU:C:2014:2013.

services, postal and courier services and international maritime transport services (Art. 6, Annex XVII).[64]

While the Agreement provides for dispute settlement concerning the interpretation, implementation or good faith application of the Agreement (Art. 477) and separate procedures applying to some chapters[65] of Title IV (Art. 322),[66] this does not compensate for this deficit. The provisions of Arts. 322 and 477 apply to disputes of the parties to the Agreement, but they do not include any mechanism for receiving interpretations of EU law, which is necessary, for example, when there is litigation in Ukraine which requires the interpretation of EU law provisions transposed into the Ukrainian legislation. At the same time, the legal systems of Ukraine, Moldova and Georgia do not stipulate a direct application of ECJ judgments by national courts. As a result, when applying the implemented Agreement provisions, EU acts may run into great difficulties in associated countries where court practices may differ from the EU court practice of interpreting the implemented EU acts.

Moreover, the Agreements do not reflect the EU experience of taking into account ECJ judgments in creating the EEA and in the activities of the EFTA. One of the major issues when creating the EEA was determining requirements and mechanisms for considering ECJ judgments when implementing and applying EU acts. During the EEA negotiations the parties were certain that it was insufficient to make the national laws identical to EU acts in order to achieve the proper integration into the EU internal market. The EEA could be created only if the respective provisions of law in the EU and EEA countries were interpreted and applied in the same manner.[67] As a result, Art. 6 EEA Agreement[68] included the requirement that the provisions of the EEA Agreement as well as the acts adopted in application of the Treaty establishing the EEC and the Treaty establishing the ECSC, in their implementation and application, be interpreted in conformity with the relevant rulings of the ECJ handed down prior to the date of signature of the EEA Agreement (Art. 6). The Agreement sets out that in order to achieve a uniform interpretation of the provisions of the Agreement and Community legislation, the EEA Joint Committee shall keep under constant review the development of the case law of the European Communities and the EFTA Court

[64] However, the mechanism for realising the provisions of art 6 has not been developed yet (more than six years after the agreement was concluded) even for those areas.

[65] Chapter 3 (Technical Barriers to Trade), Chapter 4 (Sanitary and Phytosanitary Measures), Chapter 5 (Customs and Trade Facilitation), Chapter 6 (Establishment, Trade in Services and Electronic Commerce), Chapter 8 (Public Procurement) or Chapter 10 (Competition), or which otherwise imposes upon a Party an obligation defined by reference to a provision of EU law (art 322).

[66] Article 322 provides that where a dispute raises a question of interpretation of a provision of EU law, the arbitration panel shall not decide the question, but request the ECJ to give a ruling on the question. In such cases, the deadlines applying to the rulings of the arbitration panel are suspended until the ECJ has given its ruling. The ruling of the ECJ is binding on the arbitration panel.

[67] Halvard Haukeland Fredriksen 'The EEA and the Case-Law of the CJEU: Incorporation Without Participation?' in Erik Oddvar Eriksen and John Erik Fossum (eds), *The European Union's Non-Member—Independence under Hegemony?* (Routledge 2015) 102–117.

[68] Agreement on the European Economic Area (1994) OJ L1/3.

(Art. 105) and shall act so as to preserve the homogeneous interpretation of the Agreement (Art. 106).

Article 108 of the Agreement provides for the creation of a Court of Justice (EFTA Court), which is supposed to act in accordance with a separate agreement between the EFTA States. Pursuant to Art. 3(1) and (2) of the Agreement between the EFTA states on the establishment of the Surveillance Authority and a Court of Justice, "the Court shall pay due account to the principles laid down by the relevant rulings by the [ECJ] given after the date of signature of the EEA Agreement" when interpreting the Agreement and EU acts. The practice of the EFTA Court involves receiving requests from national courts to interpret certain provisions of EU acts. During the proceedings the Court receives written observations from the European Commission and the EFTA Surveillance Authority. In its judgments, the Court provides an analysis of the respective EU acts, EU court rulings and national legislation and interprets the provisions of EU acts.[69]

It should be mentioned that Ukraine has extensive experience of applying the judgments of the European Court of Human Rights in court proceedings. It is based on Ukraine's involvement in the European Convention on Human Rights, according to which the contracting parties undertake to abide by the final judgment of the Court in any case to which they are parties (Art. 46), as well as on the application of the Ukrainian Law on the Execution of Judgments and the Application of the Case-law of the European Court of Human Rights 2006, 3477-IV. Pursuant to Art. 17 of the Law, the Convention and the practice of the European Court of Human Rights must be used as legal sources in Ukrainian court proceedings.

In conclusion, as regards the use of ECJ judgments by the Ukrainian courts, the lack of resolution of that problem in the Association Agreement is a major obstacle to the effective application of EU acts in associated countries. It may also lead to the development of court practice different from that in the EU and a lowering of the level of protection of rights in certain areas (design protection, supplementary protection certificates, databases *sui generis* etc.) in addition to the fact that it will take many years to develop a national practice of applying the transposed EU standards in Ukrainian courts.

4 Law-Making Process Regarding IP in Ukraine and the EU *Acquis*

This section takes a closer look at the practical approach in law-making that Ukraine undertook to approximate its IP legislation to the EU *acquis*. The key question is what approaches were used in Ukraine in developing changes to laws, and to what extent the laws adopted in 2019–2020 reflect the EU acts addressed in the Association

---

69 See EFTA Court E-5/16 *Request by the Norwegian Board of Appeal for Industrial Property Rights in the case of Municipality of Oslo* (2017) and other judgments.

Agreement. In Ukraine, three legislative periods related to the approximation of IP law to EU law can be identified:

(a) 2001–2004: creating an institutional legislative approximation mechanism; carrying out comparative studies of the Ukrainian and EU laws; preparing proposals and plans concerning changes to the legislation.
(b) 2005–2018: submitting draft laws on legislative approximation to the Verkhovna Rada of Ukraine, which, though submitted by the Government (2010, 2012, 2016, 2017, 2018) and members of Parliament, they were rejected by Parliament or revoked by the Government. The only exception is the Ukrainian Law on Efficient Management of Property Rights of Right Holders in the Sphere of Copyright and Related Rights 2018, 2415-VIII, which implements the Collective Management Directive 2014/26/EU. After the Directive was adopted, interested groups of deputies submitted four alternative bills on collective management in 2017, which made the Government finally submit its respective draft law in December 2017.
(c) 2019–2020: adopting the package of laws on industrial property, aimed at taking into account EU acts.[70] 2021—submitting a draft law on copyright and related rights as well as four alternative bills,[71] which indicates different interests of their developers due primarily to their different views on collective management in Ukraine.

The lack of the legislative approximation methodology developed by the EU within the framework of the PCAs (see Sec. 2.1.2) resulted in searching a required organisational and legal mechanism in Ukraine by using the experience of associated countries of Central and Eastern Europe. In this respect, Poland's experience is particularly valuable. The complexity and the broad range of issues which emerged during legislative approximation in Poland prompted it to select a group of experts from academic centres and local and foreign law firms on a tender basis. The experts were supposed to identify the current acts of Poland and the EU in each of 23 branches of law, to make a detailed analysis of them, including the analysis of EU court rulings; to establish which changes must be made to the Polish legislation; and to draw up proposals regarding amendments to current regulations and adoption of new regulations. The research findings were published as reports complemented by the Polish translations of EU acts.[72]

---

[70] Ukrainian Law on Amendments to Certain Laws of Ukraine on Improving Protection of Rights to Topographies of Semiconductor Products 2019, 111-IX; Ukrainian Law on Amendments to Certain Laws of Ukraine Regarding the Improvement of the Legal Protection of Geographical Indications 2019, 123-IX; Ukrainian Law on Amendments to Certain Legislative Acts of Ukraine on Strengthening the Security and Protection of Rights to Trademarks and Industrial Designs and Combating Patent Abuse 2020, 815-IX; Ukrainian Law on Amendments to Certain Legislative Acts of Ukraine Regarding the Patent Law Reform 2020, 816-IX.

[71] Draft Laws of Ukraine dated 24 May 2021: No. 5552; 9 June 2021, No. 5552-1; 9 June 2021, No. 5552-2; 9 June 2021, No. 5552-3; 9 June 2021, No. 5552-4.

[72] Maciej Górka, 'Development of Legislation for EU Accession: The Example of Poland' (1998) 2 Ukrainian Legal Journal 26 (27–30).

Ukraine's example is of interest because the development of the legislative approximation mechanism was related to the initiatives of the public authorities.[73] In 2004, the Verkhovna Rada of Ukraine adopted the Ukrainian Law on the National Programme of Approximation of Ukrainian Legislation to that of the European Union 2004, No. 1629-IV. According to this law, legislative approximation primarily involves: determining a list of relevant EU legal acts; translating them into Ukrainian; conducting complex comparative research on the conformity of Ukrainian legislation to that of the EU; drafting recommendations on approximation of Ukrainian legislation to that of the EU; determining the list of law-making measures; and drafting laws and other legal acts. The organisational mechanism included the preparation of conclusions about the conformity of draft laws and by-laws with EU legislation and the planning of draft laws on the part of the Ministry of Justice, as well as action taken by the Inter-Agency Coordination Council on Adaptation of Legislation of Ukraine to EU Legislation, among others. The sources of the *acquis communautaire* included ECJ decisions in addition to primary law, directives and regulations.[74]

The Ukrainian experience of adapting legislation has revealed a number of issues regarding the scope of comparative research, its organization and objectives, and ways of presenting its findings, all of which indicate differences in approaches to doing it. However, the law does not specify the content and methodology for carrying out comparative studies, and this resulted in different views on them. In particular, the analysis of the comparative research into EU tax law, financial services, accounting and audits, customs regulations, customer rights protection, state procurement etc. conducted in Ukraine in 2003–2005 shows that the experts' approaches varied in the areas and scope of their studies.[75] The primary attention was devoted to the description of European legislation. The Ukrainian legislation, in contrast, was examined separately and in general terms and only in some cases was there a more detailed review of common and different characteristics of EU and Ukraine's respective regulations as well as some recommendations on how to improve the domestic law.

As to IP sphere the comparative studies were done by experts of the Centre for Intellectual Property Studies and Technology Transfer of NAS of Ukraine, the Ministry of Justice of Ukraine, the Center for European and Comparative Law and other organisations.

The analysis of the legislative adaptation carried out at the start of the research made it clear that it was impossible to review EU and Ukrainian IP laws separately and to discuss only some challenging issues which must be resolved based on the EU experience. It was not sufficient to analyse a specific EU act without evaluating its relevance based on the practice of applying it, or to analyse the provisions which were excluded from the draft act during the preparation stage but which, nevertheless, might be of interest for Ukraine. While EU acts were adopted for the purpose of legislative harmonisation, in certain areas of national IP legislation, approximation

[73] Irina Kravchuk and Mikhailo Parapan, *Harmonization of National Legal Systems with EU Law* (Slovo 2005).

[74] In reality, the attention was mostly focused on EU acts rather than judgments of the EU court.

[75] Kapitsa (n 22) 490–492.

was not realised, and EU harmonisation tools were not applied. Nevertheless, the issues that are not covered by EU acts may be important for Ukraine. In the course of the research great attention was paid to EU court judgments on the interpretation of EU acts.

As a result, the following approach to dealing with EU acts was suggested, which included clarifying issues for each area of intellectual property legislation:

- reasons for harmonisation;
- experience in protecting certain IP rights in EU Member States at the moment of adopting the harmonisation act, review of current international treaties in the EU Member States at the time;
- preparation of an act and its review by EU institutions (Green Papers, White Papers, the European Commission, European Parliament, Economic and Social Committee documents, analysis of different opinions at the time the respective act was adopted);
- reasons for making amendments to the EU act, its development through EU court rulings;
- findings of the analysis of approximation of EU Member States legislation with EU acts; shortcomings in regulation; existence of draft changes to the act, examination of the practice of applying it.

Then the provisions of the respective EU act, ernational treaties, court rulings and Ukrainian legislation were investigated, after which proposals were developed on how to change the respective domestic laws. In parallel with the research, more than 600 pages of EU acts and abstracts of EU court rulings were translated, meeting the uniform terminology standards. Two-level editing was done: by the expert who investigated the particular area and by the project manager. The 2004 research findings were submitted to the Ministry of Justice of Ukraine and other executive authorities, used in drafting intellectual property legal acts and published.[76] Unfortunately, due to the political changes and the procrastination of public authorities in submitting and adopting draft laws, the process of legislative approximation was delayed for over 15 years. As a result of the absence of exact timelines for the implementation of the Association Agreement concerning IP, the submission of draft laws to the Verkhovna Rada of Ukraine was repeatedly postponed.

The laws that passed in 2019–2020 took into account first of all provisions of Title IV, Chapter 9 "Intellectual property" of the Association Agreement and some EU acts. In sum, they ignored EU court judgments on the interpretation of provisions of EU acts as a whole, and they disregarded the provisions of EU acts adopted after the Association Agreement was concluded, such as the Trade Mark Directive (EU) 2015/2436 (basing changes on Directive 2008/95/EC) and the Trade Secrets Directive (EU) 2016/943. Also, the provisions of the adopted laws have substantial gaps compared with the EU acts and EU court rulings on designs and supplementary protection certificates. There is no legislative approximation to the Plant Variety

---

[76] Kapitsa (n 46).

Regulation (EC) No. 2100/94. A number of provisions in the Geographical Indications Regulation (EU) No. 1151/2012 were not taken into consideration; similarly, there is no description of the Regulation or any reference to it in the Agreement (including the commitments *ex officio* of Member States to provide administrative and judicial enforcement of geographical indications rights; protection of traditional specialties guaranteed; or optional quality terms). The Enforcement Directive was not fully implemented either. In light of these deficits, the following section discusses the challenges of the legislative approximation for selected intellectual property subject matter.

5 Challenges of Legislative Approximation for Some Intellectual Property Subject Matter

5.1 Unregistered Designs

The articles of the Association Agreement on unregistered designs (UD) (Arts. 212–218) neither contain important provisions of Art. 85(2) of the Regulation on Community Designs (EC) No. 6/2002,[77] nor do they consider the judicial practice of the EU court and EU Member States. This may result in the development of trolling in Ukraine and the violation of the rights of other persons with the help of UD rather than enhancing the protection of rights. In particular, the Ukrainian Law 2020, 815-IX, adopted in order to implement the Agreement,[78] contains no provision corresponding to Art. 85(2) of the Regulation. This provision, of primary importance for exercising UD rights, states that in proceedings in respect of an infringement action or an action for threatened infringement of a UD, the court shall treat the design as valid if the right holder produces proof that the design has been made available to the public and indicates what constitutes the individual character of the design. However, the defendant may contest its validity by way of a plea or with a counterclaim for a declaration of invalidity.

In addition, the Law has no substantive provision taking into account the ECJ judgment in case C-479/12 or rulings of national courts which have held that the holder of the protected design must bear the burden of proving that the contested use results from that design being copied.[79] This allows trolling to be used because the Law lacks provisions which mandate the court to assess the proof of the existence of

[77] Council Regulation (EC) No. 6/2002 of 12 December 2001 on Community designs (2001) OJ L3/1 (Community Designs Regulation).

[78] Ukrainian Law on Amendments to Certain Legislative Acts of Ukraine on Strengthening the Security and Protection of Rights to Trademarks and Industrial Designs and Combating Patent Abuse 2020, 815-IX.

[79] ECJ C-479/12 *H. Gautzsch Großhandel GmbH & Co. KG v Münchener Boulevard Möbel Joseph Duna GmbH* (2014) ECLI:EU:C:2014:75, para 56.

UD rights and require the right holder to provide evidence that the design has been copied by the third party.

As a result of such "implementation" of the Association Agreement, the UD holder can, for example, use the mechanism for providing proof[80] (in the EU it can be done in the framework of provisional and precautionary measures[81]) in order to limit the rights of other persons to a shape, drawing, trademark or registered design,[82] as well as the import of goods to Ukraine. This is due to a lack of judicial assessment of whether the right holder has proof that the conditions for making the design available to the public are met and whether it is indicated what constitutes the individual character of his design. Also it would be sufficient that the UD holder's claim statement indicates that in their opinion the other design is a copy, assuming that it is the defendant who must produce proof that the UD has not been copied.

It should be underlined that the EU approach is the exact opposite, and was developed *inter alia* by judicial practice. During court proceedings on the alleged infringement of UD rights by the third party:

(1) The plaintiff shall provide proof of making the design available to the public within the Community.[83]

(2) It shall be indicated what constitutes the individual character of his Community design.[84]

(3) Evidence shall be produced that the plaintiff is the person who has UD rights. In other words, it shall be proven that the person is the designer or his successor in title or the right to the Community design belongs to his employer.[85]

(4) Proof shall be given that the UD has been copied by the third party. This approach is *essential* for reducing the abuse of UD rights. In case C-479/12, for example, the ECJ ruled that "the holder of the protected design must bear the burden of proving that the contested use results from copying that design.[86]

As far as cases on invalid UD are concerned, it is the UD holder who must provide proof of UD novelty (Community Designs Regulation, Art. 5(1)) and individual character (Art. 6) and evidence that the design is not dictated by its technical function

---

[80] Code of Commercial Procedure of Ukraine, art 110; Code of Civil Procedure of Ukraine, art 116.

[81] Enforcement Directive, art 9.

[82] If the UD holder claims that UD rights emerged before registration applications for the respective industrial designs or trade marks filed by other persons.

[83] Community Designs Regulation, art 11(2); ECJ C-479/12 *H. Gautzsch Großhandel GmbH & Co. KG v Münchener Boulevard Möbel Joseph Duna GmbH* (2014) ECLI:EU:C:2014:7.

[84] Community Designs Regulation, art 85(2). ECJ C-345/13 *Karen Millen Fashions Ltd v Dunnes Stores and Dunnes Stores (Limerick) Ltd* (2014) ECLI:EU:C:2014:2013 (n 66). In particular, in the High Court of Ireland judgment in *Karen Millen Ltd. v Dunnes Stores & Anor* (2007) IEHC 449, it was indicated that the plaintiff, who claimed an unregistered design, was to bear the burden of proving that he had that right.

[85] Community Designs Regulation, art 14(3); German Federal Supreme Court (BGH), *Bolero-jäckchen* (2012) I ZR 23/12.

[86] *Gautsch v Duna*, para 44. See also rulings of national courts, e.g., Lithuania Court of Appeal, Order 2A-73-823/2018 (2018).

and is not a design of interconnection (Art. 8).[87] In contrast, Ukrainian Law 2020 815-IX does not impose on the right holder the duty of producing respective proof.[88]

5.2 Utility Models

The PCA agreements and the Association Agreements do not mention the practical value of using the experience of EU Member States in applying unharmonised IP legislation. The body of such legislation was substantial when PCAs were concluded with NIS in 1994–1996.[89] At present this experience is quite useful both in the domain referred by EU directives and regulations to the competence of Member States[90] and in areas where the legislation was not harmonised by 2021: utility models, trade names, computer-implemented inventions, certain areas of copyright and related rights, employee IP, IP agreements, criminal IP enforcement and others.

The failure to take into consideration unharmonised legislation of Member States in legislative approximation may lead to a situation in which the implemented standards of EU acts in third countries are surrounded by a network of legal standards that ignore the practice of EU Member States, which, as a result, may cause an overall decline in the efficiency of legislation. On the other hand, the failure to take into account trends in the development of unharmonised legislation in the EU may bring about a complicated search for optimal ways of regulating the respective relations in third countries, as can be illustrated by the example of utility models (UM).[91]

The practice of granting protection documents for UM in Ukraine reveals a much higher number of registered UM discoveries compared with that in EU Member States.[92] Resolving the UM legal protection problem in Ukraine assumed economic and political importance in 2004–2020 because of the spread of patent trolling, the circumvention of patented inventions through UM, the grant of many patents on well-known processes, devices and substances and, as a consequence, the decline in the level of patent protection of inventions in Ukraine and the reduction in possibilities

---

[87] See ECJ C-345/13 *Karen Millen Fashions Ltd v Dunnes Stores and Dunnes Stores (Limerick) Ltd* (2014), Opinion of Advocate General Wathelet ECLI:EU:C:2014:206, para 65, 83.

[88] Ukrainian Law on Amendments to Certain Legislative Acts of Ukraine on Strengthening the Security and Protection of Rights to Trademarks and Industrial Designs and Combating Patent Abuse 2020, 815-IX.

[89] Industrial designs, biotechnological inventions, IP enforcement, trade secrets, collective management organisations, specific areas of copyright and related rights, utility models, computer implemented inventions, trade names, etc.

[90] For instance, determination of specific incidents of exceptions and limitations according to the InfoSoc Directive, art 5.

[91] See also Leonid Tarasenko, '15.Legislative Reforms on Patents, Utility Models and Industrial Designs in Ukraine' in this Volume.

[92] In 2018, the percentage ratio of UM applications to invention applications was: Ukraine 426%; Portugal 8%; France 1.4%; Germany 12%; Austria 9%; Denmark 2%; Greece 2%; Spain 78%; Italy 13%; Finland 12%. Our calculations are based on WIPO data https://www.wipo.int/ipstats/en/statistics/country_profile/ accessed 10 July 2021.

to invest in using IP. It is related to the absence of the inventive step criterion (or another criterion of a non-obvious technological solution) as well as the absence of a substantive examination for the UM, which in addition to a device can cover (as in the case of inventions)—a process (method), substance, microorganism strain etc.

The Ukrainian judicial practice exposed the complexity or even impossibility of declaring the UM patent invalid in court proceedings, due to the absence of the inventive step criterion, which weakens the ability to counter trolling in court.[93]

Indeed, in Ukraine in 1993–2002, the UM subject matter was only defined as a "device capable of industrial application"[94] without any trolling or law application problems. The change to the UM subject matter was done to save the practice of granting declarative patents with a limited validity term (five years, 1993–2000; six years, 2000–2002) without examining them in terms of their novelty and inventive step. Declarative patents had been used as a temporary measure until the examination system was established in Ukraine. Meanwhile it was possible to apply for 20-year patents including examination with a five to six year approval period.

The practice of issuing declarative patents was often criticised as restraining innovative activities in the country and preventing investments in new technologies.[95] When the new Civil Code of Ukraine was adopted in 2003, these patents ceased to be issued but instead the subject matter of UM was expanded to become identical to an invention. A short approval period for UM patents (six to 12 months) caused a dramatic increase in the number of UM applications, which replaced the declarative patents, and a general mismatch between invention applications and UM ones, the latter numbering four times as many as the former.

As a result of criticism on the part of both experts and foreign companies, in 2020 the subject matter of the UM was narrowed down to a device and a method; however, there was still no inventive step.[96] Thus, the Law has not made significant changes concerning trolling. Despite the expansion of powers of the Chamber of Appeals regarding declaring UM rights invalid, it will still be impossible for the court to declare the UM rights invalid in cases where the UM is a new but obvious technical solution because there is no inventive step or other criterion of non-obvious technical solution established for UM.

---

[93] Explanatory note to the Ukrainian Draft Law on Amendments to Certain Legislative Acts of Ukraine Regarding the Patent Law Reform 2020, 816-IX.

[94] Ukrainian Law on Protection of Rights to Inventions and Utility Models 1993, 3687-XII, art 5(2).

[95] See Committee of the Verkhovna Rada of Ukraine on Science and Education (CSE), Decision of 4 April 2008 No. 14 on the Status of State Regulation and Management in the Field of Development, Legal Protection and Protection of Intellectual Property and Innovation in Ukraine; CSE Hearings on 'The Issues on the Industrial Property within the Innovation Economy of Ukraine: Effectiveness and Legislation and State Regulation' in 2009 and the Committee Chairman Volodymyr Polokhalo, *Intellectual Property in Formation of Innovative Economy of Ukraine: Challenges of Legislative Providing and State Regulation* (Parliamentary Publishing House on the Initiative of the Committee on Science and Education 2010) 226.

[96] Ukrainian Law on Amendments to Certain Legislative Acts of Ukraine Regarding the Patent Law Reform 2020, 816-IX.

Looking at other jurisdictions appears informative when discussing perspectives for Ukrainian legislation. The analysis of the practice of UM rights protection in 14 "old" EU Member States and Great Britain[97] shows that:

- there is no protection of UM rights in six territories (Luxembourg, Sweden, Great Britain, Belgium, the Netherlands, Ireland);
- there is an inventive step requirement in five countries (or the former lower degree of inventiveness has been made equal to the inventive step, as it is for inventions) (France, Spain, Germany, Austria, Denmark);
- in two countries, protection of rights is possible only for three-dimensional objects (Italy, Greece) and in Italy the lower inventive step level is used;
- in two countries (Finland, Spain) there is the lower inventive step level and exceptions from protection.

Indeed, the trend in some EU Member States is to raise requirements for UM rights protection. For example, the German Federal Supreme Court (BGH) ruled in the case *Demonstrationsschrank*, in 2006, that the same inventive step requirement shall be established for utility models as for inventions.[98] A similar approach is taken in Austria.

An interesting change in invention protection law has recently taken place in Spain. The Spanish Law on Patents (2015), 24/2015 sets out that if a UM patent is expected to be used for enforcement, a report shall be made on the prior art which would be made available to the public. In the event that the claim is filed before the submission of the report, it is possible to request the suspension of proceedings until the report is submitted.[99]

In this respect, three options to improve the protection of UM rights in Ukraine should be considered[100]:

- Option 1: Taking into account the experience of Luxembourg, Sweden, Great Britain, Belgium, the Netherlands and Ireland, *to cancel* the protection of rights to utility models in Ukraine.
- Option 2: To introduce the protection of rights to utility models only for three-dimensional objects in technology (but not processes, substances, compositions of substances or biological substances). Also, to provide an inventive step criterion for utility models. To make a substantive examination mandatory in terms of patentability conditions (novelty, inventive step, industrial application) when the UM rights are exercised for judicial protection in the courts, or for administrative protection by Antimonopoly Committee, or in the framework of customs actions.
- Option 3: Similar to option 2, to provide for the protection of utility models as a type of invention with the same patentability conditions.

[97] Yuriy Kapitsa, 'Utility Model Protection—Trends in the European Union and Challenges for Ukraine' (2020) 3 Journal of Theory and Practice of Intellectual Property 27 (33–35).

[98] X ZB 27/05, GRUR 842.

[99] Spanish Law on Patents (as amended by Law 6/2018 of 3 July 2018) 2015, 24/2015, art 148(3)(4).

[100] Kapitsa (n 97) 36–38.

These measures should raise the level of protection of inventions and utility models in Ukraine, promote investments in high-technology industry and stop the unfair applications and use of UM patents.

5.3 *Compensation for Infringement of Intellectual Property Rights*

As shown in the following, the direct transfer of certain provisions from the Association Agreement and the Enforcement Directive to the legislation of third countries may cause difficulties in compensating for damages when intellectual property rights are infringed, compared with the previous procedure.

Article 240 Association Agreement and Art. 13 Enforcement Directive state that the judicial authorities may, "in appropriate cases, set the damages as a lump sum on the basis of elements such as at least the amount of royalties or fees which would have been due if the infringer had requested authorisation to use the intellectual property right in question". The practice of applying the Directive indicates that in certain countries it is possible to demand increased damages for some infringements, especially concerning copyrights and related rights, which are calculated as double (or more) the amount of royalties (Austria, Belgium, the Czech Republic, Germany, Greece, Poland, Romania, Slovenia etc.).[101]

In 2001–2017, the Ukrainian Law on Copyright and Related Rights 1994, 3792-XII, Art. 52(2) stated that in the case of violation of the copyright and (or) related rights, it was possible to pay compensation, to be prescribed by the court, in an amount from 10 to 50,000 times the minimum wage, in lieu of damage compensation or income collection. The amount of compensation in this case was to be dependent on the extent of the infringement and (or) the defendant's intentions. Since the minimum wage rose every year,[102] the annual size of compensation greatly increased accordingly.

In 2018, within the framework of legislative approximation to the Association Agreement, the Law was amended. The provisions on minimum and maximum amount of compensation were removed and trends in the EU were taken into account, setting out that a court shall have the right to issue a resolution or award concerning

> payment of compensation determined by the court as a lump sum on the basis of such elements as doubled, and in case of intentional violation—as a triple amount of remuneration

---

[101] European Commission, 'Analysis of the Application of Directive 2004/48/EC of the European Parliament and the Council of 29 April 2004 on the Enforcement of Intellectual Property Rights in the Member States—Accompanying document to the Report COM (2010) 779 final' (Working Document) SEC (2010) 1589 final.

[102] In 2001—118 UAH. Since 1 January 2021—6,000 UAH.

> or commissions that would have been paid if the offender applied for permission to use the disputed copyright or related rights instead of indemnity or revenue collection.[103]

This resulted in a substantial decrease in the number of lawsuits on the violation of IP rights, the payment of compensations including those initiated by collective management organisations due to considerably lower amounts received by collective management organisations compared to the previous procedure and the absence of judicial practice of applying royalty rates.

Given the amount of minimum salaries in 2017 (3,200 UAH, or 120 USD[104]), paying damages ranging from 10 to 50,000 times the minimum wage meant the compensation paid for the improper use of, for instance, the recording of one song in a bar or a café ranged from 1,200 to 6 million USD, and in 2021 (minimum wages—6,000 UAH, or 211 USD[105]), from 2,110 to 10.55 million USD. The respective amount of damages for the improper use of several recordings could exceed the total income of a bar or a café.

There is no such compensation amount in either the EU or the US. Section 504 US Copyright Act states that the copyright owner may elect to recover,

> instead of actual damages and profits, an award of statutory damages for all infringements involved in the action, with respect to any one work, for which any one infringer is liable individually, or for which any two or more infringers are liable jointly and severally, in a sum of not less than 750 USD or more than 30,000 USD as the court considers just.[106]

As a result of the interested parties' lobbying to cancel the application of the provisions of the Association Agreement and the Enforcement Directive and to return to the previous procedure for setting the amount of compensation, two approaches to establishing the amount of damages were combined in the draft law dated 10 March 2020 and developed by the Ministry of Economy of Ukraine, which runs counter to the practice of applying the Directive. In addition to the approach based on the amount of royalties or fees, there is a possibility to pay compensation in the amount of up to 50,000 times the minimum subsistence income.[107] The recovery of the old

[103] Ukrainian Law on Efficient Management of Property Rights of Right Holders in the Sphere of Copyright and/or Related Rights 2018, 2415-VIII, para 6(2)(h) Section VI Final and Transitional provisions.

[104] 26.69 UAH per 1 USD at the exchange rate of the National Bank of Ukraine (NBU) as of 5 January 2017.

[105] 28.43 UAH per 1 USD at the NBU exchange rate as of 5 January 2021.

[106] According to Section 504(c)(2)—in a case where the copyright owner sustains the burden of proving, and the court finds, that infringement was committed willfully, the court in its discretion may increase the award of statutory damages to a sum of not more than 150,000 USD. In a case where the infringer sustains the burden of proving, and the court finds, that such infringer was not aware and had no reason to believe that his or her acts constituted an infringement of copyright, the court in its discretion may reduce the award of statutory damages to a sum of not less than 200 USD.

[107] Draft Ukrainian Law on Copyright and Related Rights 2020, art 57(3), published by the Ministry of Economy of Ukraine on 10 March 2020.

model was also provided for in a draft law submitted by a number of deputies in 2021.[108]

As a consequence of our and other experts' criticism of the unjustified amount of minimum and maximum levels of compensation and the simultaneous lobbying for the old model, a Draft Ukrainian Law on Copyright and Related Rights 2021, 5552–4 submitted by the Cabinet of Ministers to the Verkhovna Rada of Ukraine provided for a possibility to award damages in the amount ranging from two to 2,000 times the minimum subsistence income for working-age individuals, which makes the ceiling of compensation lower than before, in addition to the payment of compensation based on the amount of royalties. As of 1 January 2021, it set the limits of compensation from 4,540 UAH to 4.54 million UAH (80–80,000 USD) with a ceiling that is 2.6 times as much as that in the US.[109]

As can be seen, the Ukrainian practice shows the preservation of the previous approach to establishing the top and bottom compensation rates and the simultaneous existence of the approach based on the amount of royalties (fees). Receiving damages that greatly exceed the right holder's losses and the illegal income of the infringer is in fact unjust enrichment, which contradicts the spirit of the Enforcement Directive.

Furthermore, the example above illustrates the fact that the formal legislative approximation to the EU acts may cause significant difficulties in enforcing intellectual property rights. In our opinion, these drawbacks could be absent if, together with amendments to the law, indicative minimum royalty rates were set for a limited period which could be used by courts until there develops a practice of applying the real royalty rates.

Finally, if Ukrainian courts applied the provisions of Art. 240 of the Association Agreement on the payment of a lump sum as a direct effect standard and it were interpreted according to the EU judicial practice, the approach of paying compensations based on the amount of royalties could become the main approach in Ukraine.

6 Towards a Methodology of Approximation of Intellectual Property Legislation in Associated Countries and PCA Countries to That in the EU

So far, the analysis has identified and discussed the problems, causes and concrete examples related to the approximation of Ukrainian and other NIS IP legislation to the EU *acquis* in the last decades. Given the findings, this section aims to provide a methodological guidance to further improve approximation in the future.

The analysis of legislative approximation in NIS has allowed us to identify three possible approaches to legislative approximation in 1. the countries bound by "soft commitments" of the PCA or other agreements on legislative approximation, which

[108] Ukrainian Draft Law on Copyright and Related Rights 2021, 5552-3.

[109] Taking into account that the minimum subsistence income (2,270 UAH as of 1 January 2021) is lower than the minimum wage and that in the draft law the limits of compensation were reduced.

do not provide for accession to the EU, 2. the countries that have concluded association agreements with the EU creating a free trade area, and 3. EU candidate countries. As is shown above, both the PCA and the Association Agreements with Ukraine, Georgia and Moldova do not contain any mechanisms for approximating their IP legislation to that in the EU in an efficient manner.

6.1 Countries Bound by Approximation Requirements Without Wider Integration with the EU

The major factor constraining the legislative approximation is that it is unfeasible for PCA countries to introduce a fast mechanism for considering EU court rulings like that applied by EFTA countries. As a result, it does not seem reasonable to approximate the legislation to unclear provisions of the EU directives and regulations, which necessarily require EU court practice for their clarification. And even if the legislative approximation is achieved, PCA countries will constantly lag behind the Member States in their practice because they will not have taken EU court rulings into consideration.

How should these drawbacks be addressed when it comes to the further approximation of EU rules? It is suggested to apply a "feasibility" and "best practices" approach, which includes several measures:

(1) Determining the degree of legislative approximation in the country, based on the economic and political feasibility of a particular degree of approximation.
(2) Considering the process of preparing EU acts with the focus on the content of EU directives and regulations as a compromise between the Member States and the EU authorities. Determining whether the adopted provisions of directives and regulations are the best of those proposed, with the focus on the use of the best proposals and the experience of Member States rather than the adopted "compromise", "intermediary" and vague provisions.
(3) Assessing the conformity of EU acts with multilateral international treaties (WIPO etc.) concluded by NIS, the EU and EU Member-States, and with documents of international organisations, and in the case of non-conformity of EU acts with international acts, addressing the issue of how to apply certain provisions.
(4) Analysing the practice of implementing EU directives and regulations in the Member States. Determining the best implementation practices.
(5) Analysing unharmonised national EU Member States' laws in the respective area which reveal the best national practice in addition to the harmonised laws.
(6) Analysing the development of the EU legislation, including reasons for making amendments. Paying attention to inefficient and vague law standards.
(7) Studying the EU court interpretations of EU acts.
(8) Examining weaknesses in the regulation and draft amendments to the acts.
(9) Outlining prospects for the development of EU law.

(10) Determining the effectiveness of applying the directives (regulations) based on points 2–9 above.
(11) Determining institutional basis and organisational actions required to enforce EU acts.

The purpose of this approach is to prepare legislative proposals that consider only those provisions of EU acts and laws of the EU Member States that have demonstrated their efficient application, are clear and are not expected to be reviewed or changed in the near future. In addition, the best practices of implementing EU acts and EU court practice are used. In fact, some aspects of the approach mentioned above were used in NIS countries during the implementation of their PCA agreements.

However, the provisions of EU acts should not be implemented when (a) there is a positive national practice of applying existing national law in third countries and (b) introducing provisions of EU acts without taking into account EU court judgments may result in lowering the level of IP protection (e.g. preserving the extended term of a patented medicinal product, which is the practice of most NIS as well as in the US, Japan and other countries, instead of introducing a supplementary protection certificate for medicinal products; or when patentability criteria for industrial designs are preserved that are different from those in the EU but that work quite effectively in most NIS).

6.2 Countries with Association Agreements That Involved Creating a Free Trade Area

As regards the countries whose Association Agreements provide for creating a free trade area, the developers of such agreements should determine why the Association Agreements with Ukraine, Moldova and Georgia have their own requirements for each area of the Agreement without any mechanism for approximating intellectual property legislation instead of uniform requirements for their legislative approximation.

It is unacceptable that the Association Agreements ignore the issue of the EU court judgments to be taken into account in the implementation of their provisions or the provisions of EU acts because, as a result, it (a) imposes on the associated countries the provisions of EU acts that cannot be efficiently applied without EU court rulings; (b) makes the legislative practice in those countries constantly lag behind the EU; (c) makes it possible to create a judicial practice of applying provisions of the Agreements and EU acts in Ukraine, Georgia and Moldova that may differ from the ECJ interpretations.

The issues may be resolved by creating a sustainable mechanism for approximating the national IP legislation with that provided in the EU in Ukraine, Georgia and Moldova. It could include:

(1) The adoption by the Association Council of a document establishing a mechanism for approximating IP legislation with that in the EU. Similar to Annex

XVII to the Agreement on financial and other services, this document must provide:

- Ukraine's legislative approximation commitments to the adopted and future EU acts;
- EU commitment to informing Ukraine about new EU acts or changes to its legislation;
- a mechanism for setting a timeframe for implementing such acts;
- specifics of implementing provisions of EU regulations and directives;
- that intellectual property provisions of the Agreement and EU acts must be implemented and interpreted based on the respective ECJ rulings;
- a mechanism for assessing and monitoring EU acts;
- a list of EU acts with which Ukraine has not approximated its legislation.

(2) A mechanism for Ukrainian judicial agencies which will allow them to take into account ECJ judgments on the interpretation of EU acts when applying the legislation. For this purpose it is necessary:

- to make amendments to the Ukrainian Law on the Judiciary and the Status of Judges 2016, 1402-VIII establishing the powers of the Supreme Court (similar to the competence of EFTA Court) to interpret EU acts based on the ECJ rulings when applying provisions of EU acts and of the Agreement as transposed into the Ukrainian legislation;
- to provide other courts with a procedure for applying to the Supreme Court for interpretation;
- to issue a decision within the framework of the Association Agreement or, if necessary, conclude another agreement, similar to those realising the EEA Agreement and EFTA Surveillance and Court Agreement, which: introduces exchange of information between the ECJ and the Supreme Court on court rulings; provides the Supreme Court with a procedure for receiving written observations submitted on behalf of the authorised bodies of the Association Agreements and the European Commission; if necessary, interprets the EU law standards about which the ECJ has issued no rulings; and establishes a procedure whereby the Supreme Court can apply directly to the ECJ.

(3) Since it is insufficient to just formally transpose provisions of the Agreement and EU acts into national legislation in order to apply them in an efficient manner, it should also include proposed amendments to be made to the Ukrainian Law on the National Programme of Approximation of Ukrainian Legislation to that of the European Union (2004), 1629-IV and to by-laws on:

- determining the best legislative approximation practices in implementing EU acts in EU Member States and using them in preparing draft laws;
- providing for an obligatory analysis of unharmonised legislation of EU Member States and determining the best practices that should be taken into account in legislative approximation;

- establishing a mandatory procedure for listing EU court rulings on the interpretation of EU acts in the respective area of draft laws and providing information on their incorporation in these drafts in supporting documents to the bills (Explanatory notes and others) and in certificates on the conformity of draft laws to Ukraine's commitments to European integration and EU law.[110]

(4) An objective monitoring system of legislative approximation.

The analysis of the long-time activities of the ministries responsible for IP matters shows that they are unable to perform a critical analysis of their own performance in preparing draft laws, in terms of both their quality and the efficiency of their application. This kind of assessment has periodically been made in Ukraine via parliamentary hearings and hearings in the Verkhovna Rada Committee on Education, Science and Innovations.[111] In this respect it is essential to start preparing annual white papers on the protection of intellectual property rights in Ukraine, including the issues of its legislative approximation to that in the EU[112] within the framework of individual EU projects or via creating an independent commission in the respective Committee of the Verkhovna Rada of Ukraine.[113]

6.3 EU Candidate Countries

The European Council decision of 23 June 2022 granting the status of candidate country to Ukraine and Moldova actualises the question of ways the approximation should be carried out by candidate countries. Also, should approximation be based on Association Agreement provisions or differ from them?

Undoubtedly, the EU accession should not become a "legislative shock" for candidates, and the preparatory time should be used for both changing legislation and application practice in accordance with EU standards as well as taking into account other countries' accession to the EU.

It should be noted that Association Agreements with Central and Eastern Europe candidate countries envisaged higher approximation standards ("provide … for a level of protection similar to that existing in the Community") than the Association Agreement with Ukraine. As well, approximation was carried out in accordance with

[110] The Cabinet of Ministers of Ukraine Resolution No. 950 of 18 July 2007 on Regulations of the Cabinet of Ministers of Ukraine 2007, para 35, ruled that such notes shall be prepared for draft laws.

[111] For example: The Parliamentary Hearings on Intellectual Property—'Building an Effective Intellectual Property Protection System in Ukraine' dated 16 December 2019; Parliamentary Hearings and Committee of the Verkhovna Rada of Ukraine on Science and Education hearings dated 15 October 2014; 5 October 2009, 3 July 2009; 3 September 2008; 21 March 2007.

[112] The Committee of the Verkhovna Rada of Ukraine on Education, Science and Innovations has experience in preparing such papers.

[113] This commission could be made up of experts from scientific institutions, universities, professional associations and non-governmental organisations.

the European Commission "White Paper in Preparation of the Associated Countries of Central and Eastern Europe to Integration into the Internal Market of the Union" of 1995 with a list of EU acts, in accordance to which national legislation should be changed, and specific approximation tasks, including requirements for the effective operation of government bodies.

In addition, for Bulgaria and Romania, which joined the EU later, it was stipulated that they account for key ECJ rulings, which were specified by the ECJ, and a mechanism for the official translation of EU acts into the national language was implemented, with publication in the Official Journal of the EU (see Secs. 2.1.2, 3).

The current Association Agreements with Ukraine and Moldova are hardly to be considered the basis for IP approximation in a similar way due to the lack of obligations taking into account EU acts and ECJ practice and also due to the absence of requirements regarding IP state authorities' effectiveness.

If, during the accession, Ukraine and Moldova limit themselves to only considering the IP provisions of the Association Agreements, this may lead to the loss of significant time that could be used for the development of the EU-oriented national legal system. It will also require cardinal work to change the legislation in accordance with the EU acts and the practice of the ECJ after joining the EU. Relevant in this regard are:

1. Inclusion in the roadmap or other document that will determine the preparation of Ukraine and Moldova for their accession to the EU of activities indicated in para (1)–(3) of Sec. 6.2, including the requirements for approximation of legislation to the EU acts as they are, and not to individual extracts from EU acts referred to in the Association Agreements.
2. Determination by the EU authorities of a list of the most important ECJ rulings and transfer of these decisions to Ukraine and Moldova for consideration in the approximation of legislation.
3. Organisation of official translation into the national language of EU acts using European Commission translation guidelines, as well as professional legal editing. In this case, translations of various government bodies and organisations made earlier in Ukraine can be used. These translations must be published in the national electronic register of EU acts, and a system should be implemented to support their updating to current EU acts. Consideration should also be given to publishing said translations in the Official Journal of the EU.
4. It is important from our point of view that, before Ukraine joins the EU, the mechanism should be implemented for taking into account the decisions of the ECJ on the interpretation of the EU acts implemented in the legislation of Ukraine (see Secs. 3, 6.2.1(2)). This is new in comparison with other previous candidate countries. At the same time, the preparation for accession may take 10 years. On the one hand, this time should be used to prepare the judiciary for the application of the *acquis*. On the other hand, as noted earlier, taking into account only the provisions of the Association Agreement or only EU acts will not allow the effective application of Ukrainian IP legislation for the indicated 10 years.

Based on the above, it is necessary:

(1) to discuss and clarify the plans laid out in the European Commission Communication: "Making the most of the EU's innovative potential. An intellectual property action plan to support the EU's recovery and resilience" COM/2020/760 final, which states: "in the context of Free Trade Agreements (FTAs), the Commission will continue to seek ambitious IP chapters with high standards of protection, to ensure a level playing field for EU businesses and boost economic growth".[114] As can be seen, both the concept and the content of theses "ambitious IP chapters" require significant improvements and changes to the existing chapters on "Intellectual Property" in the Association Agreements with Ukraine, Georgia and Moldova, which do not contain a sustainable mechanism for approximating their IP legislation with that of the EU.

(2) The roadmap and other documents on Ukraine's accession to the EU should fully provide the mechanism for national IP legislation approximation to EU acts, which is absent in the Association Agreement, as well as taking into account ECJ judgements in this area.

7 Conclusion

The agreements concluded by the EU with Ukraine and also with other Newly Independent States (Interim, Partnership and Cooperation and Association Agreements) opened up new prospects for developing intellectual property legislation in these countries with a view to their approximation with the EU law. It should have contributed to raising the level of protection of IP rights in NIS, to promote the interests of right holders and the activities of European companies in NIS and vice versa and to provide conditions for creating free trade areas with Ukraine, Moldova and Georgia.

However, the European Union has not developed the methodology for approximating NIS legislation with that in the EU, as it did for the associated countries as candidates for accession to the EU. The major issue of legislative approximation distinctions between the EU candidate countries and NIS has not been resolved. As a consequence, the intellectual property provisions in the Partnership and Cooperation Agreements concluded between the EU and ten NIS, which require providing protection of IP rights similar to that in the EU within five years after the agreements came into effect, were not complied with.

Concluding the Association Agreements with Ukraine, Georgia and Moldova in 2014 was supposed to raise the economic interaction between the EU and these countries to a new level. However, the analysis of provisions in Chapter 9 Title IV "Intellectual property" in the Agreement and the *acquis* shows that some provisions of EU acts which were in force at the time of preparation of the Agreement were reflected to different extents in the chapter, while other important provisions were not

[114] European Commission, 'Making the Most of the EU's Innovative Potential—An Intellectual Property Action Plan to Support the EU's Recovery and Resilience' (Communication) COM (2020) 760 final, Section 6.

included at all. Moreover, the Association Agreement does not set out any general commitments for Ukraine to approximate its intellectual property legislation with the existing and future EU acts, unlike in other areas covered in the Agreement, as well with the ECJ judgments on the interpretation of EU acts.

As a result, a number of important provisions of EU acts as well as new EU acts were not taken into consideration when Ukrainian laws were amended in 2019–2020. In some areas the non-application of the entire *acquis* even created conditions conducive to abusing intellectual property rights and trolling rather than improving the protection of these rights. The lack of an instrument for taking into consideration the EU Court rulings makes the third countries constantly lag behind the EU practices and brings about great difficulties in applying laws in some cases. It should be pointed out that the Association Agreements with Ukraine, Georgia and Moldova differ greatly from the EEA Agreement and EFTA Surveillance and Court Agreement in the area of intellectual property; in the latter, an efficient instrument of legislative approximation is provided.

Based on the above analysis, it is essential to develop three approaches to legislative approximation: one for the countries that concluded the PCA or similar agreements which do not provide for a broader integration or accession to the EU, one for the countries that concluded association agreements with the EU creating a free trade area, and one for candidate countries.

In the latter case the experience of EEA countries should be fully used in legislative approximation and both the EU and Ukraine should take specific steps to create an efficient sustainable mechanism to approximate the Ukrainian intellectual property legislation to that in the EU. This should also include establishing commitments on the part of Ukraine to approximate its legislation to the adopted and future EU acts; setting up the EU's obligation to inform Ukraine about new EU acts and amendments to its legislation; and providing specifics of implementing EU regulations and directives and timelines for their implementation.

It is critically important to create an instrument for taking into account the ECJ judgments on the interpretation of EU acts to be used by Ukrainian judicial authorities when applying the provisions of the Agreement and the EU acts that have been transposed into the Ukrainian legislation. To this end it is necessary, first, to take into consideration the practice of implementing the EEA Agreement and the EFTA Surveillance and Court Agreement and, second, within the framework of the Association Agreement or, if necessary, in a separate document: (a) to introduce an exchange of information on the rulings of the ECJ and the Supreme Court; (b) to establish a procedure whereby the Supreme Court will receive written observations submitted on behalf of the authorised bodies of the Association Agreement and the European Commission so that the Court can make its decisions on the interpretation of the implemented EU acts; (c) in cases where it is necessary to interpret the provision of EU acts about which there are no respective EU Court judgments, to establish a mechanism whereby the Supreme Court can directly apply to the EU Court. Furthermore, it is worthwhile to make amendments to the Ukrainian Law on the Judiciary and the Status of Judges 2016 1402-VIII determining the powers of the Supreme Court (similar to the powers of the EFTA Court) (a) to interpret provisions of EU acts transposed into the Ukrainian legislation based on the EU Court rulings; (b) to establish a procedure whereby other courts can apply to the Supreme Court for receiving such interpretations.

References

Annual Reports of the International Intellectual Property Alliance https://www.iipa.org/

Committee of the Verkhovna Rada of Ukraine on Science and Education, Hearings 'Industrial Property in the Innovative Economy of Ukraine: Effective Application of Legislation and State Regulation' (2009) in Volodymyr Polokhalo (ed) *Intellectual property in formation of innovative economy of Ukraine: challenges of legislative providing and state regulation* (Parliament Publishing House 2010) [Комітет Верховної Ради України з Питань Науки і Освіти, Матеріали Слухань 'Промислова Власність в Інноваційній Економіці України: Ефективність Застосування Законодавства та Державного Регулювання' (2009) у Володимир Полохало (ред) Інтелектуальна Власність у Формуванні Інноваційної Економіки України: Проблеми Законодавчого Забезпечення та Державного Регулювання (Парламентське видавництво 2010)]

Committee of the Verkhovna Rada of Ukraine on Science and Education, Decision of April 4 2008 No. 14 'On the Status of State Regulation and Management in the Field of Development, Legal Protection and Protection of Intellectual property and Innovation in Ukraine' (2008) [Комітет Верховної Ради України з Питань Науки і Освіти, Рішення від 16 квітня 2008 No 14 'Про Стан Державного Регулювання і Управління у Сфері Розвитку, Правової Охорони і Захисту Інтелектуальної Власності та Інноваційної Діяльності в Україні' (2008)]

European Commission, 'Making the Most of the EU's Innovative Potential—An Intellectual Property Action Plan to Support the EU's Recovery and Resilience' (Communication) COM (2020) 760 final

European Commission, 'Comprehensive Monitoring Report on the State of Preparedness for EU Membership of Bulgaria and Romania' (Communication) COM (2005) 534 final

European Commission, 'Bulgaria 2005 Comprehensive Monitoring Report' (Report) SEC (2005) 1352 final

European Commission, 'Agenda 2000—Commission Opinion on Poland's Application for Membership of the European Union' (Opinion) COM(97)2002, 1997

European Commission, 'Preparation of the Associated Countries of Central and Eastern Europe to Integration into the Internal Market of the Union' (White Paper) COM (95) 163 final, 1995

Maciej Górka, 'Development of Legislation for EU Accession: The Example of Poland' (1998) 2 Ukrainian Legal Journal 26 [М. Горка, 'Розвиток Законодавства з Метою Вступу до ЄС: Приклад Польщі' (1998) 2 Журнал Український Правовий Часопис 26]

Halvard Haukeland Fredriksen 'The EEA and the Case-Law of the CJEU: Incorporation Without Participation?' in Erik Oddvar Eriksen and John Erik Fossum (eds), *The European Union's Non-Member—Independence under Hegemony?* (Routledge 2015) 102

Yuriy Kapitsa, 'Utility Model Protection—Trends in the European Union and Challenges for Ukraine' (2020) 3 Journal of Theory and Practice of Intellectual Property 27 [Юрій Капіца, 'Охорона прав на корисні моделі—тенденції в Європейському Союзі та виклики для України' (2020) 3 Журнал Теорія і практика інтелектуальної власності 27]

Yuriy Kapitsa, *Intellectual Property Rights of the European Union: Formation, Institutions, Directions of Development* (Academiperiodica 2017) [Юрій Капіца, 'Право Інтелектуальної Власності Європейського Союзу: Формування, Інститути, Напрями Розвитку' (Академперіодика 2017)]

Yuriy Kapitsa, 'Features of Harmonization of Legislation of the NIS Countries with the Legislation of the European Union in the Field of Intellectual Property Protection' (2011) 3 Journal The

Law of Ukraine 92 [Юрій Капіца, 'Особливості Гармонізації Законодавства Країн СНД із Законодавством Європейського Союзу у Сфері Охорони Інтелектуальної Власності' (2011) 3 Журнал Право України 92]

Yuriy Kapitsa, *Intellectual Property Law of the European Union and the Legislation of Ukraine* (Slovo 2006) [Юрій Капіца, *Право Інтелектуальної Власності Європейського Союзу та Законодавство України* (Слово 2006)]

Irina Kravchuk and Mikhailo Parapan, *Harmonization of National Legal Systems with EU Law* (Slovo 2005) [Ірина Кравчук та Михайло Парапан, 'Гармонізація національних правових систем з правом ЄС' (Слово 2005)]

Viktor Muraviov, 'Legal Mechanism of Implementation of the Association Agreement Between Ukraine and the European Union' (2015) 8 Journal Viche 7 [Віктор Муравйов, 'Правовий Механізм Реалізації Угоди про Асоціацію між Україною та Європейським Союзом' (2015) 8 Журнал Віче 7]

National Intellectual Property Strategy of Ukraine, The Proceedings of the Parliamentary Hearings in the Verkhovna Rada of Ukraine 'Building an Effective System of Intellectual Property Protection in Ukraine' 2019 (Verkhovna Rada of Ukraine, Committee on Economic Development, Parliamentary Publishing House 2019) [Матеріали парламентських слухань у Верховній Раді України 'Побудова Ефективної Системи Охорони Інтелектуальної Власності в Україні' 2019 (Верховна Рада України, Комітет з питань Економічного Розвитку, Парламентське видавництво 2019)]

State Department for Approximation of Legislation, 'Overview of the State of Adaptation of Ukrainian Legislation to Acquis Communautaire' (Nika 2007) [Державний Департамент Адаптації Законодавства, 'Огляд Стану Адаптації Законодавства України до Acquis Communautaire' (Nika 2007)]

Roman Petrov, 'EU–Ukraine Association Agreement's Effective Implementation Into the Legal Order of Ukraine: Challenges and Successes' in Ondrej Hamulák and Naděžda Sisková (eds.), *European Studies: The Review of European Law, Economics and Politics* (Wolters Kluwer 2019)

Eugene Stuart, Edoardo Fano, Linda Scales, Gerda Leonaviciene and Anna Lazareva, *Intellectual Property Law and Policy—Law Approximation to EU Standards in the Republic of Moldova* (Sinectica-Com 2010)

Guillaume Van der Loo, *The EU–Ukraine Association Agreement and Deep and Comprehensive Free Trade Area* (Brill—Nijhoff 2016)

Strategic Directions of the Intellectual Property Area Development in Ukraine

Olena Orliuk

Contents

Abstract This chapter is devoted to analysis of the National Strategy on Intellectual Property Area Development in Ukraine till 2025 (the National IP Strategy). The research is based on expert approaches, the World Intellectual Property Organization's guidelines, analysis of the international IP framework, and on activities of the state authorities within the context of development and implementation of the

O. Orliuk (✉)
Ukrainian National Office for Intellectual Property and Innovations, Kyiv, Ukraine
e-mail: olena.orliuk@knu.ua

H. Richter (ed.), *Competition and Intellectual Property Law in Ukraine*,
MPI Studies on Intellectual Property and Competition Law 31,
https://doi.org/10.1007/978-3-662-66101-7_13

National IP Strategy. The National IP Strategy puts special emphasis on the tasks facing the national legislator in the adoption of national legislation to fulfill Ukraine's obligations under the Association Agreement with the EU in the field of intellectual property. It underlines the need to promote the development of IP management, ensure the growth of innovative potential of research institutions, review the role of intellectual property in the activities of small and medium-sized enterprises (SMEs), and to enhance the functional potential and transparency of collective management organizations (CMOs). The demand of developing the security system for geographical indications, which should include practical methods for the registration, protection and promotion of national geographical indications in the EU market, based on the Association Agreement with EU, is pointed out. The agenda also includes actions against patent trolling as well as organizing campaigns to inform the public about the adverse effects of piracy and counterfeiting. The joint actions with the international community will continue within the WTO cooperation, considering the WHO's position to demonopolize the IP rights for the objects involved in counteracting the COVID-19 pandemic.

1 Introduction

1.1 European Integration and IP in Ukraine

By signing the Association Agreement with the European Union in 2014,[1] Ukraine has actively extended its path towards European integration, including in the field of intellectual property (IP). Approximately 100 pages of the Agreement are devoted to IP rights and their protection, harmonization and implementation of the provisions of European legislation in the legislation of Ukraine.

Moreover, Ukraine has recognized the active development of innovation and the digital economy. This aligns with the policies of the European Union in terms of developing the Digital Single Market and launching the Digital Europe 2025 Strategy, as well as the European Research and Innovation Area, and joining projects as a part of Horizon 2020 and Horizon Europe, etc. In addition, Ukraine, as a member of the Eastern Partnership, is actively studying the steps of the European Union to support the development of innovative and green economies, including social entrepreneurship, as well as the new EU Economic and Investment Plans for the Eastern Partnership countries. This is largely in line with the EU4Digital Eastern Partnership

[1] Association Agreement between the European Union and its Member States, of the one part, and Ukraine, of the other part (2014) OJ L161, (EU-Ukraine Association Agreement). For details see Roman Petrov, 'The EU–Ukraine Association Agreement as a General Framework of Contemporary EU–Ukraine Relations' and Yuriy Kapitsa, 'Association Agreements and Problems Approximating Intellectual Property Legislation of Third Countries with the EU Acquis: The Case of Ukraine' in this Volume.

Digital Economy and Society Development Program[2] launched in Ukraine by the European Union on 22 May 2019. This program aims at enhancing the benefits of the EU Digital Single Market for Ukraine and other Eastern Partnership countries in stimulating economic growth and job creation, improving people's lives and helping businesses. After all, supporting sustainable digital transformation is one of the five policy priorities identified by the European Commission in its proposal for the long-term political goals of the Eastern Partnership after 2020.[3]

Furthermore, despite the existing achievements in the field of IP in past decades, Ukraine continues to face a number of problems in this area: insufficient development of the results of intellectual creativity and innovative activity, that forms the basis of a competitive knowledge-based, digital economy; extremely low use by small and medium-sized enterprises (SMEs) of potential IP; an insufficient level of public administration in the field of IP protection, due to the incompleteness of institutional reform in this area; a low level of cooperation between state, professional and public institutions in the field of legal protection and protection of IP; the high level of piracy and counterfeiting, which poses an increased risk to the economic security of the country and the health of the domestic consumer; a lack of participation of IP rightholder in actions to protect IP rights, which significantly reduces the effectiveness of the measures to protect IP rights; pending process in setting up a specialized IP court; patent trolling; lack of transparency in the activities of organizations for collective management of copyright and related rights (CMOs); and the lack of a consistent IP policy in the science and education systems with a low level of culture in the IP field, etc. As a result, IP in Ukraine in the last years has been considered as one of the key factors in the country's economic, social and cultural development.

Given the broader circumstances, issues of economic and social development have become particularly acute in the face of the challenges posed by the global spread of the COVID-19 pandemic over the past two years. A special situation for Ukraine is found in the political challenges related to the prolongation of hostilities by the Russian Federation and the occupation of Crimea for the eighth year in a row. These and other factors negatively affect the country's economy, significantly reducing the level of its investment attractiveness and perception of stability in the eyes of both domestic and foreign investors, including respect for property rights and protection of IP rights.

At the same time, actions have been undertaken by the relevant authorities, including government institutions and international partners, to allow us to look forward with some optimism concerning the progress of Ukraine in developing a digital economy and innovation society, as well as the area of IP directly, which

[2] Peter Stano, 'Joint Communication: Eastern Partnership policy beyond 2020: Reinforcing Resilience—An Eastern Partnership that Delivers for All' *European Union External Action* (18 March 2020) https://eeas.europa.eu/headquarters/headquarters-homepage/76166/joint-communication-eastern-partnership-policy-beyond-2020-reinforcing-resilience-%E2%80%93-eastern_en accessed 13 June 2022.

[3] Peter Stano et al., 'Eastern Partnership: Commission Proposes New Policy Objectives for Beyond 2020' *European Commission* (18 March 2020) https://ec.europa.eu/commission/presscorner/detail/en/IP_20_452 accessed 13 June 2022.

is in the focus of this chapter. Moreover, Ukraine understands the complexity and multi-vector nature of the tasks its faces in the field of IP, which are not limited to legislative changes only.

1.2 Towards the National Strategy for IP

Understanding the importance of IP for the national economy, innovation and culture for the development of society as a whole prompted the Government of Ukraine in 2018 to begin steps to develop a draft "National Strategy for Intellectual Property of Ukraine for 2020–2025"[4] (hereinafter "the Strategy"). Important reasons for this include the increasing role of IP in the actions of government institutions involved in economic and cultural development, the rethinking of the role of IP in generating national income, as well as the active cooperation between Ukraine and the World Intellectual Property Organization (WIPO).

In fact, this is not the first attempt by Ukraine to put together a strategy for the development of the IP sphere. However, it is the first approach which is based on the study of international experience and national practices and methodologies proposed by WIPO which has allowed it to obtain the desired outcome, embodied in the relevant draft National Strategy. The development of the Strategy was preceded by the recognition of the need for its adoption at the level of acts of the parliament (Verkhovna Rada) of Ukraine as a result of parliamentary and committee readings on IP and innovation activity during the period 2014–2018, in the process of discussions at the meetings of the Intellectual Property Council initiated by the Cabinet of Ministers of Ukraine in 2019. The successful achievement of the draft Strategy document was also realized through the application of the WIPO guidelines,[5] aimed at providing a standard and integrated approach to policy, strategy, institutional reform and modernization of IP. The cooperation of representatives of the government of Ukraine with WIPO experts allowed consistent implementation of the main steps proposed by these guidelines.

The Strategy was developed on the basis of the National Intellectual Property Office on behalf of the Ministry of Economic Development and Trade of Ukraine with the assistance of WIPO in accordance with the Memorandum between the Ministry

[4] National Intellectual Property Office, 'National Intellectual Property Strategy of Ukraine for the Period 2020–2025' (2019) NIPO, 142 https://drive.google.com/file/d/1oqjabxZiTempwJjaZsO1NoLt7fvP_qxj/view accessed 13 June 2022. This draft has been authored by Petro Borovyk, Oleksandr Butnik-Siverskyi, Oleg Chernobai, Oleksandr Doroshenko, Mykhailo Dubinskyi, Igor Yegorov, Volodymyr Haustov, Yuriy Kapitsa, Oksana Kashyntseva, Ivan Kulchytskyi, Liubov Maidanyk, Bogdan Morklianyk, Viktor Moskalenko, Olena Orliuk, Bogdan Paduchak, Mykola Pototskiy, Mykola Skyba, Mykola Stefanchuk, Ruslan Stefanchuk, Olena Tverezenko etc., moderation and final editing Olena Orliuk.

[5] WIPO, 'Development Agenda Project DA_10_05: Development of National Intellectual Property Strategies National Intellectual Property (IP) Strategies—Meeting of Experts' *WIPO* (January 2012) https://www.wipo.int/meetings/en/details.jsp?meeting_id=25442 accessed 13 June 2022.

of Economic Development and Trade of Ukraine and WIPO in 2018–2019. Extensive consultations were conducted to assess the situation and existing issues along with the involvement of relevant public authorities, academia, non-governmental organizations, and civil society, followed by a comprehensive expert analysis of the current situation in this area.

As a result, together with WIPO experts[6] in the context of implementation of the Memorandum, the priority goals of the National IP Strategy as well as specific measures to achieve them were identified. This included meetings and interviews with several hundred business and innovation representatives, professionals form the IP and legal area, universities and scientific institutions, central executive bodies, judicial and law enforcement agencies, the state IP protection system, and non-governmental organizations.[7] Furthermore, a number of meetings and consultations with the National Team of Experts on IP Strategy preparation were held to determine the structure and objectives of the Strategy, which were subsequently approved by the National Intellectual Property Office. Thus, in Ukraine the steps towards drafting the Strategy defined by the WIPO guidelines were consistently implemented, namely: the IP assessment mission was carried out, the project team was formed, field research and data collection was conducted, national consultations were held, and the draft document was produced and reviewed.

The draft National Strategy for the Development of Intellectual Property was examined during national discussions and meetings with business, the IP professional community, the public sector, government and judiciary, etc., where were held in autumn 2019 in different regions of Ukraine.[8] The components of the Strategy were consistently disclosed and discussed. Conducting such discussions allowed the collection of broad feedback and making a number of changes to the developed document.

Furthermore, also analyzed and taken into account in the development of this Strategy is the following: recommendations on strategic goals for the direction of reforms, defined by Supplementary Agreement No. 1 between the government of Ukraine and the European Commission, acting on behalf of the European Union, to the Financing Agreement of the Framework Program for Support of the Agreements between Ukraine and the European Union of 15 August 2014[9] and measures

[6] Yuliya Samayeva, 'Intellectual Property—It is not About Laws, but Economic Development' *ZN'UA* (23 March 2019) https://www.nas.gov.ua/siaz/Ways_of_development_of_Ukrainian_science/article/19036.2.016.pdf accessed 26 October 2022

[7] Including during IV IP FORUM on 5 June 2019, IP LET FORUM on 20–21 June 2019 by IP Center of Ukraine.

[8] 'First Public Discussion of the Draft National Strategy in the Field of Intellectual Property discussion of the National Public Project in the Field of Intellectual' *Scientific Research Institute of Intellectual Property* http://ndiiv.org.ua/index.php/ua/rada-molodykh-vchenykh/novyny/309-vidbulosia-pershe-publichne-obhovorennia-proektu-natsionalnoi-stratehii-u-sferi-iv accessed 13 June 2022.

[9] Agreement between the Government of Ukraine and the European Commission, acting on behalf of the European Union, to the Agreement on the Financing of the Framework Program in Support of the

determined by the Government of Ukraine to implement the Association Agreement[10]; and WIPO expert recommendations, as well as WIPO recommendations on developing national IP strategies for transition economies.[11]

A common understanding was reached that the development and practice of the national system of legal protection of IP should be based on principles of serving the public interests in the sphere of IP, openness of the public administration to public control and ensuring its transparency, compliance of legislative efforts with Ukraine's international obligations, the European vector of development, compliance of the legal mechanism of legal protection of IP rights with the modern challenges of the information environment, and the development of innovation systems and increased innovation attractiveness of Ukraine. Accordingly, these factors form the strategy on the development of the national IP system and its compliance with international standards, which is a combination of political, institutional, technological, economic, legal, innovative, educational, scientific and cultural components.

The presentation of the draft National Strategy for the Development of Intellectual Property of Ukraine for the period 2020–2025 took place at parliamentary hearings on IP in the parliament of Ukraine on 16 December 2019.[12] The provisions of the Strategy were later presented during the Dialogue on Intellectual Property Rights between Ukraine and the EU on 18 November 2020.[13] Despite the lack of official approval of the project, in particular due to inconsistencies in the form of the document (as a government document or at the level of a decree of the President of Ukraine, taking into consideration the complexity of tasks and objectives), the actual implementation of the IP Strategy started in 2020. However, so far, it has not yet been officially adopted by parliament.

Agreements between Ukraine and the European Union of 15 August 2014 (2016) (ENPI/2013/024-446).

[10] Action Plan for the Implementation of the Association Agreement between the European Union and the European Atomic Energy Community and their Member States, of the other part, and Ukraine, of the other part. Approved by the Resolution of the Cabinet of Ministers of Ukraine No. 1106, 25 October 2017.

[11] World Intellectual Property Organization, 'Guidance for the Development of a National Intellectual Property Strategy in Countries in Transition: Prepared by the Division for Certain Countries in Europe and Asia' (Guidance Document).

[12] Parliamentary Hearings in the Verkhovna Rada on building an effective system of Intellectual Property Protection in Ukraine, 16 December 2019 https://static.rada.gov.ua/zakon/new/par_sl/sl161219.htm accessed 13 June 2022.

[13] Oleksandr Romanyshyn took part in the meeting of the Ukraine-EU Dialogue on Intellectual Property Rights, Ministry of Economic Development, Trade and Agriculture of Ukraine (19 November 2020) https://www.kmu.gov.ua/news/oleksandr-romanishin-vzyav-uchast-u-zasidanni-dialogu-z-prava-intelektualnoyi-vlasnosti-ukrayina-yes accessed 10 July 2022.

2 Setup of the Goals and Tasks of the National IP Strategy

Developing an innovation-oriented, digital economy in Ukraine cannot take place in the absence of an effective and capable national system of IP legal protection, which acts not only to protect and develop intellectual potential, but also to advance national producers' competitiveness. Over the last decade, the momentum for reform in Eastern Europe and the South Caucasus, including Ukraine, has stagnated, indicating a range of long-standing obstacles to economic diversification and innovation, according to a report by the UN Economic Commission for Europe.[14] Taking this into account, developing a strong system for protection and enforcement of IP rights acquires an additional role.

Ukraine is party to various international treaties and agreements in the field of IP, as well as a being member of the WTO since 2008[15] and is an associate member of the Eastern Partnership with the European Union. According to the Association Agreement, Ukraine is obliged to ensure adequate protection of IP rights and to promote the commercialization of IP by reducing significantly the level of piracy, counterfeiting and by eliminating patent trolling, as this directly affects the level of investment attractiveness of Ukraine.[16] In addition, policies should aim at building a balance of private and public interests, which characterizes the field of IP. The national system of IP and IP management should provide the maximum assistance.

Thus, the National Intellectual Property Strategy was prepared by an expert body based on the understanding of the key importance of IP in the development of innovation and the digital economy, as well as the tasks set by Ukraine for gradual integration into the European innovation and research space.

Ultimately *the vision* of the National IP Strategy is that IP ought to become a fundamental instrument for creating a friendly environment for innovation, inventiveness, creative activity and free competition, for the economic and cultural development of Ukraine, strengthening its scientific potential, thus raising the level of investment attractiveness of the country. It was determined that this strategic mission is dependent on the successful completion of legislative, institutional and judicial reforms in the IP area. This comprises the creation, protection, management, and commercialization of IP, maximizing IP potential, the creation of an effective system for protection of IP rights, support for invention, raising the level of education and culture and promoting knowledge in the field of IP, which in general would contribute to the development of a national competitive digital economy based on knowledge, innovation and creativity, and increase Ukraine's investment attractiveness.

The Strategy aims to develop a competitive national economy based on knowledge and innovation, and involves a set of formulated measures implemented by the Government, which include:

---

[14] United Nations Economic Commission for Europe, 'Sub-regional Innovation Policy Outlook 2020: Eastern Europe and the South Caucasus', ECE/CECI/26, 2020, 334.

[15] See Zvenyslava Opeida, 'Competition and International Trade: Complementing Trade Defense Policy with Effective Competition Policy in Ukraine' in this Volume.

[16] Art 80, 157 AA.

- Creation—promoting and encouraging the creation of objects of IP rights;
- Use—introduction of favorable conditions and mechanisms for the use of objects of IP rights in production, in the other branches of the economy;
- Management—developing effective state management in the field of IP through advancing the effectiveness of the state institutions in the system for protection of IP, the examination of applications and issuance of protection documents;
- Legislation—improvement of the legislation on the protection of IP rights;
- Protection of rights—improving mechanisms of protection of IP rights through strengthening protection;
- Culture and education—creating a high level of culture and education in the field of IP.

The proper use of IP provides an opportunity to achieve positive synergetic outcomes in various fields and stimulate creative activity, innovation, investment attractiveness and economic growth of Ukraine. This is due to the comprehensive and multifunctional character of IP and its presence in all spheres of economic, scientific, cultural and social life. In this context, it is necessary to implement a number of effective measures for the progressive integration of IP in all these spheres in Ukraine. For this purpose, the Strategy identified following common goals:

- Institutional development of the National Intellectual Property System as an integral part of creating conditions for the development of an innovative, digital economy in Ukraine;
- Improvement of the legal framework for IP, including its harmonization with EU legislation and the implementation of international treaties to which Ukraine is a party;
- Stimulation of invention and creativity, the promotion and development of a high culture in the field of IP, educational activities aimed at informing the general public about the role of IP and increasing interest in protecting and upholding IP rights, thus ensuring the national system of IP and national economy as a whole by highly skilled personnel;
- Infrastructure development and implementation of a consistent policy to promote the creation, protection and use of IP as a key tool in creating the conditions for the country's transition to an innovative model of economic growth with its focus on digitalization;
- Compliance with copyright protection challenges of the digital economy, improvement of organizations representing the interests of creators of IP and services in the field of IP;
- Improvement of the level of legal protection by the mechanisms of IP with respect to plant breeding achievements;
- Improvement and an increase of efficiency and coordination of activities of state bodies whose sphere of activity is related to the protection of IP rights, e.g. the judicial system;
- Development of effective infrastructure for preventing and combating counterfeiting and piracy;

- A significant increase in the effectiveness of IP rights mechanisms, including the active use of alternative means of resolving disputes in the field of IP;
- IP policy as an organic segment of national policies aimed at innovative, cultural development of the country, thereby increasing its innovative attractiveness;
- Development of international, regional and bilateral cooperation in the field of IP and integration of Ukraine into the European and international intellectual space;
- Improvement of management and the legal protection of IP rights in certain areas of the national economy which are of strategic importance.

3 Targets and Means to Achieve the Expected Results of the National IP Strategy

As mentioned above, the National IP Strategy in Ukraine aims to improve the economic performance of Ukraine by developing the IP system to increase the possibilities for innovators, creators, inventors, businessmen, researchers and educators to create, manage and protect their IP. The Strategy also intends to allow government to contribute to its experience in the administration and application of IP laws and rights. In addition to increasing domestic innovation, the Strategy aims to create a more attractive environment for domestic investment. Another important feature is to increase the general public's understanding of the role and importance of IP in the economic wellbeing of society.

To achieve this goal and the strategic objectives of the National IP Strategy, the expert body eventually developed specific measures and actions that found support in the process of long public discussions and presentation of the document in the relevant Ministry and the parliament of Ukraine. Taking into account the WIPO guidelines for the development of National IP Strategies, the experts conducted an in-depth analysis of the current state of the national IP system and identified existing problems. The analysis was performed on the following vectors: (1) IP in the economy of Ukraine; (2) trends in filing applications and obtaining protection certificates; (3) incentives for the creation and use of IP items; (4) legal principles for protection of IP rights in Ukraine; (5) the institutional framework of the IP protection system; (6) coordination of the functioning the IP protection system; (7) infrastructure that facilitates the creation and use of IP items; (8) IP rights protection; and (9) distribution of knowledge about IP, training and advanced training of IP specialists.

Based on the results of the expert study, a SWOT analysis (strengths, weaknesses, opportunities and threats) of the creation, protection, use of IP items, and the IP rights protection system was prepared. In addition, the problems that determine government actions in implementing the Strategy were outlined.

To achieve the strategic objectives, eight blocks were identified, a brief analysis of which is offered below. For each block, strategic objectives were defined and subdivisions were given for which the relevant objectives were also defined and specific successive steps were proposed to achieve such objectives. Solving the tasks within these areas is considered optimal at the current stage of economic, social and cultural development of Ukraine.

The Strategy also offers an assessment of the impact and costs of implementing the strategy, including the main indicators for monitoring the implementation of the provisions of the Strategy in terms of attracting IP outcomes to the innovation system, as well as procedures and reporting and monitoring. Three stages of the Strategy implementation are envisaged, and their main content is determined. The adoption of the Strategy involves the development and adoption of specific action plans for each stage.

3.1 Public Management, System of Protection and Legislation in the Field of IP

An effective governing body in the field of IP that has a proactive attitude makes it possible to achieve the objectives of the Strategy, namely the development of an optimal, high-quality and efficient national system of legal IP protection, capable of forming and implementing a transparent public model for overcoming existing challenges and risks, and offering effective tools form the IP field as incentives for the development of related economic and social factors.

Among the specific ways to achieve this goal, the following has been identified: first of all, the development of an effectively functioning National Intellectual Property Authority and the formation of its structure on the basis of the main functions of the national office determined by international practices, including examination of applications and provision of legal protection to IP items; quality control for examination of applications; consideration and arbitration of IP disputes; ensuring state registration of copyright rights; personnel management and business processes administration; international, state policy in the field of IP and legal issues; systematization and consolidation of IP protection methods; information and consulting and methodological and educational activities and support of innovations; maintaining records of IP items; development of automated systems, management of them and transition to the provision of services in a digital format; and administrative activities and resource management.

Specific measures to achieve the strategic objectives set should also include:

- Ensuring the transparency and publicity of National Intellectual Property Authority activities, implementing an effective mechanism for supervision of its activities, including the establishment of a Supervisory Board;
- Development and implementation of effective changes and an efficiency management system in the National Intellectual Property Authority with the purpose of retaining important personnel and ensuring a high level of personnel motivation;
- Conducting a competition for the head of the body in accordance with the requirements set by applicable law;

- Ensuring the Appeals Chamber's activities within the National Intellectual Property Authority operate according to the principles of legality, impartiality, independence, transparency, reliability, collegiality, and qualified staffing;
- Ensuring effective examination through qualitative improvement of the work of expert units management, their information and methodological support; updating of local acts aimed at ensuring the legal protection of industrial property objects; creation of methodological units capable of analyzing and generalizing results of the expertise, and developing guidelines for the experts;
- Provision of advanced training of experts to the level of the EPO's experts to ensure the reliable operation of the National Intellectual Property Authority as an International Searching Authority and International Preliminary Examining Authority, with mandatory involvement of EPO experience, etc.

In terms of legislative changes, it is worth noting the following objectives set for lawmakers in order to improve national legislation and fulfill Ukraine's obligations under the Association Agreement with the EU. In particular, the Strategy identifies the following strategic goals in the field of industrial property. First, Ukraine should increase its investment attractiveness through state-guaranteed, reliable and quickly obtainable high-quality legal protection of inventions. This would stimulate the interest of Ukrainian inventors in obtaining legal protection for inventions in Ukraine and abroad, achieving a reasonable ratio of patented technical solutions with a high level of inventive creativity as well as those which are essentially minor improvements and do not require significant creative contribution. Second, Ukraine should improve the investment climate and eliminate the barrier to free competition in the form of "patent trolling" through raising the standards of legal protection of industrial design closer to the European level.

After all, Ukraine currently has available resources, including human capital assets, which allow it to increase significantly existing indicators in international rankings, to increase its innovation and inventive level, providing a further boost to industrial development based on innovation and technology. In 2019, Ukraine joined the small group of countries that achieved high performance of their innovations (being in the lower middle-income countries); at the same time, Ukraine left the top 50, coming in at place 53.[17] In 2020, Ukraine improved this ranking by eight points, coming in at place 45.[18] The country has achieved better results in the field of innovative production than innovative resources. Instead, in 2021 as a result of economic losses from the COVID-19 pandemic, Ukraine took the 49th place, entering the TOP-3 countries of the lower-middle income economic group.[19]

---

[17] Soumitra Dutta et al., 'Global Innovation Index 2019: Creating Healthy Lives – The Future of Medical Innovation' (Report) 2020.

[18] Soumitra Dutta et al., 'Global Innovation Index 2020: Who Will Finance Innovation?' (Report) 2020.

[19] Soumitra Dutta et al., 'Global Innovation Index 2021: Tracking Innovation through the COVID-19 Crisis' (Report) 2021.

According to the rating Doing Business 2019 from the World Bank, Ukraine ranked 71st out of 190 countries for ease of doing business (in 2018—76th).[20] According to these data, Ukraine's position is relatively good, given the tendency to improve results, but the state of development and state support for innovative development of SMEs is not very attractive. At the same time, in 2020 Ukraine rose to the 64th place[21] in the ranking. Ukraine's expectations in climbing higher in the ratings were not met, as in August 2020 the World Bank temporarily suspended the publication of the Doing Business rating. The value of the overall index of Ukraine relative to the averages of the EU countries was 27%. Thus, an assessment of the innovative development of the national economy shows that Ukraine is still an "emerging innovator" in the group of countries.[22]

In 2011 the results of the EU project "Improving Innovation Strategies, Policies and Regulation in Ukraine" were presented.[23] In 2013, the United Nations Economic Commission for Europe conducted an assessment of the state of innovation in Ukraine based on a methodology that has been applied to some other post-Soviet countries.[24] The report presented by renowned international experts included not only an analysis of the situation in the innovation field, but also specific recommendations for improving the innovation situation in Ukraine. The latest thorough review of Ukraine's innovation sector, prepared by foreign experts as representatives World Bank, was presented in December 2017.[25] The World Bank experts noted negative tendencies in the innovation sphere of Ukraine, observed in 2014–2016. Their recommendations echoed largely the recommendations of previous reports prepared by independent foreign experts.

Considering these and many other factors, the developers of the Strategy have identified five goals regarding IP:

(1) To return to Ukraine's patents the authority and status of one of the most important indicators of economic innovation;
(2) Setting up the state IP legal protection system to prevent weak patents from being granted;
(3) Consideration of the possibility to introduce a special regime for granting patents for inventions in such important sectors of the Ukrainian economy as the pharmaceutical industry, medicine and the agricultural sector through improving

[20] World Bank Group, 'Doing Business 2019: Training for Reform' (Report) 2019.

[21] World Bank Group, 'Doing Business 2020: Comparing Business Regulation in 190 Economies' (Report) 2020.

[22] Lucia Caudet, '2019 Innovation Scoreboard 2019: The Innovation Performance of the EU and its Regions is Increasing', *European Commission* (17 June 2019) https://ec.europa.eu/commission/presscorner/detail/en/IP_19_2991 accessed 13 June 2022.

[23] European Commission, 'Innovation Policy: European Experience and Recommendations for Ukraine' 2011.

[24] United Nations Economic Commission for Europe 'Innovation Performance Review: Ukraine' (Review) ECE/CECI/16, 2013, 126.

[25] World Bank, 'Innovation and Entrepreneurship Ecosystem Diagnostic: Ukraine' (Report), 2017, 58.

the quality of patent examination in these areas with appropriate regulatory and methodological support;
(4) Conceptual and methodological decision on granting patents for inventions related to information technology, so that the IT sector could receive a reasonable means of patent protection;
(5) Providing information support to key industries (in particular, national security and defense, energy saving, ecology).

In terms of the protection of trademark rights, it was necessary to establish proper protection of trademark rights in Ukraine, taking into account the requirements of the Association Agreement and best practices and legislation of EU countries in this area. This includes shortening timeframe for processing trademark applications and improving the quality of expertise. For Ukraine this object of legal protection is almost the only one that shows a constant tendency towards increased registrations.

In turn, in order to ensure the quality of protection of geographical indications (GIs),[26] strategic objectives that have been identified are: first, introducing in Ukraine a system similar to that in Europe by adopting specific laws on GIs for agricultural products, wines and spirits; and second, the fulfillment of obligations under the Association Agreement and further harmonization with European legislation in the field of ensuring legal protection of GIs.

The need to review the timing of the examination and the issuance of security documents was also stressed. After all, it was found that the average term of consideration of applications in Ukrpatent for inventions prior to the grant of a patent increased from 24.5 months in 2014 to 27 months in 2018, and for trademarks similarly from 11.9 months to 16.8 months.[27] And this trend continues.

Regarding the direction "National legislation, compliance with international obligations, EU legislation, development of legislation", a significant factor in improving the legislation of Ukraine in the field of IP is the influence of international treaties signed by Ukraine. This includes the fulfillment of obligations under the WTO's Agreement on Trade-Related Aspects of Intellectual Property Rights (TRIPS) as well as agreements signed within the framework of WIPO. An urgent issue at this time is the implementation of changes in Ukrainian legislation in the field of IP in accordance with the requirements of the Association Agreement between Ukraine and the European Union, which should bring Ukrainian legislation in the field of IP into correspondence with EU standards and ensure the functioning of a free trade area between Ukraine and the EU regarding the establishment and the use of IP rights. The six specific measures to achieve these objectives are:

(1) The introduction of a sustainable mechanism for approximation of national legislation to EU legislation in the field of IP, with the adoption by the Association Council of the relevant mechanism, which includes: (a) Ukraine's commitment to approximation of legislation, including to future EU acts; (b) a list of EU

[26] For details, see Anastasiia Kyrylenko, 'Why so Few Geographical Indications in Ukraine? Legal, Political and Socio-Economic Perspective' in this Volume.

[27] State Enterprise Ukrainian Institute of Intellectual Property 'Industrial Property in Numbers. Indicators of Activity in the Field of Intellectual Property for 2018, Ukrpatent 2019, 64.

acts and timing for their implementation; (c) the EU's commitment to inform Ukraine about changes in existing and new EU acts; (d) consideration of unique aspects of the EU directives and regulations in the legislation of Ukraine; (f) a mechanism for evaluating the implementation of EU acts; and (g) the impact of their implementation as well as the application of the CJEU's interpretation of the provisions of the EU acts;

(2) Determining the appropriateness of joining new multilateral treaties of WIPO, including the Beijing Treaty on Audiovisual Performances, and the Marrakesh Treaty to Facilitate Access to Published Works for Persons Who Are Blind, Visually Impaired or Otherwise Print Disabled;
(3) Ensuring the coherence of laws regarding certain items of IP rights and the Civil Code of Ukraine and other laws, and unification of terminology in the process of implementation of measures on the implementation of the Association Agreement;
(4) Counteracting unfair use of rights to utility models and industrial designs and limiting patent trolling at the legislative level through: (i) enacting in national legislation regarding industrial designs the right to act on any unauthorized use of an unregistered industrial design; (ii) development of instruments of legal protection of an unregistered industrial design;
(5) Development of measures for the implementation of copyright and related rights protection in the digital environment;
(6) Improvement in the regulation of the protection of trade secrets and know-how regarding undisclosed know-how and business information (trade secrets) against their unlawful acquisition, use and disclosure, etc.

3.2 Generation of IP

This section defined as strategic objectives the achievement of compliance with the main components of the innovation system of Ukraine with respect to the requirements of developing an innovatively competitive and non-industrial-developed economy of Ukraine, and to provide high economic growth rates and raise living standards.

Particular attention focused on the necessity of providing incentives for inventive activity and patenting in priority areas. These include: (i) the technological development of industry on the basis of the 5th and 6th technological paradigm—Industry 4.0; (ii) overcoming the main obstacle encountered by Ukrainian enterprises, establishments and institutions, i.e. the lack of financial resources for innovative activity; and (iii) assistance of the state system of legal IP protection regarding the measures defined by the Strategy for development of sphere of innovative activities in Ukraine for the period till 2030, etc.

3.2.1 Research Funding, Development and Innovation

In the area of "Research funding, development and innovation" it was emphasized to increase the share of R&D funding in public and private sector spending in response to global trends in innovative systems development, EU policy and Ukraine's internal needs.

Furthermore, the need to actively involve the SME sector in innovation and the creation of IP was recognized to create favorable conditions for innovative development of SMEs. This includes stimulating the investment and innovation activity of SMEs; promoting the use of objects of IP rights by SMEs in production activities, conducting operations, services accomplishment, promotion of crated IP items in domestic and foreign markets; and ensuring access of SMEs to financial, information and other resources.

Strategic goals have been set to increase the innovative and intellectual level of the education and science sectors such as: increasing the capacity of higher education and scientific institutions in the creation and use of object of IP rights; implementation of innovation activities; technology transfer on the basis of adopted IP policy; providing highly professional human resources; development of an effective infrastructure to support innovation, technology transfer, use of IP items, created in universities and research institutions; the introduction of effective financial, tax and credit instruments aimed at the commercialization of objects of IP, research results and their use by enterprises. To achieve these goals, the need for the following was identified:

- Development and adoption of the recommendations concerning provisions on the structural unit for transfer of technology, innovation activity and IP of higher education and scientific institutions, with the details of issues concerning professional staffing and proper financing;
- Adoption of recommendations concerning IP policy for universities and research institutions, taking into account the Model Law on Intellectual Property Policy for Universities and Research Establishments developed by WIPO, and the European Commission's Communication "On the Management of Intellectual Property Rights and the Code of Practice for Universities and Other State Research Institutions";
- Organizing and conducting training in the regions of Ukraine concerning application of recommendations and introducing consulting support for the adoption of recommendations by universities and research institutions, etc.

Special attention is paid to such areas as: patent databases, patent and market information, technology information; use of artificial intelligence systems; development of advisory services, patent information centers and the creation and use of objects of IP. With regards to patents, the need was determined to create conditions for providing users in Ukraine with patent and market information, as well as services for the effective processing applications for inventions and utility models and other industrial property and implementation of activities for their commercialization. In this regard, specific measures include, in particular:

- Ensuring the completeness and quality of information provided by the Patent Database currently maintained by the Ukrpatent, and the creation of a special department for quality control of databases;
- Examining the question whether the patent information currently maintained by the Ukrainian patent office Ukrpatent should be included in WIPO's Patentscope Information System, following the example of patent offices in many EU countries, the USA, Canada, etc.;
- Establishment of information synchronization between the databases of inventions and useful models of Ukrpatent and Espacenet for the purpose of carrying out qualitative patent-related research in the use of international patent information;
- Completion of the improvement of standards DSTU 3574-97 (Patent form) and DSTU 3575-97 (Patent studies), which have been in operation since 2000, and the adoption of appropriate changes;
- Development new instruments of patent analytics with respect to patent landscapes, etc.

3.2.2 Education

Considerable attention is paid in the Strategy to the issues of education in the field of IP, training professional personnel and advanced training (education in area of IP, improvement skills). The analysis was conducted in terms of secondary and higher education, obtaining appropriate qualifications in the field of IP (in particular, patent attorney), advanced training, and extending research in this area.

According to the results of the analysis of educational programs taught in Ukrainian universities, the need was determined to provide high-quality higher education in IP based on an interdisciplinary approach. The level of knowledge in IP should be raised within the context of acquiring appropriate competences in other specialties in order to increase competitive human capital assets for the purpose of the high-tech, innovative development of the country. In addition, conditions for self-realization and creativity of the personality should be created, thus ensuring the needs of the society, the labor market and the state in qualified personnel.

The necessity is highlighted of constant activity in retraining and improvement of experts' qualifications in the issues of IP, management of innovative activity for departments involved in the transfer of technologies, innovative activity and IP in state authorities, higher education and scientific institutions, other establishments and organizations, methodological and personnel support, taking into account the role in the development of a national IP system and the development of a national innovation system, the creation of conditions for the professional provision of innovative, digital, creative development of Ukraine.

At the same time, it is emphasized that an understanding of IP should form starting in childhood. In particular, the expediency of spreading knowledge and information in the field of IP was recognized for secondary education as a vital component in the development of a culture of IP. Such a culture of IP would contribute to the overall stable functioning and strengthening of the national IP system; increasing respect for IP in order to encourage young people to appreciate their creative potential, and thus engage in intellectual, creative activity, develop the creativity of the nation, and create innovative products that will have national and/or international recognition.

Appropriate specific measures and successive steps have been identified to achieve these objectives. In particular, inclusion of the IP issue into national educational concepts and strategies was proposed. Teaching of IP-related knowledge should be introduced through the education system at all stages of school education within the New Ukrainian School. An audit should be carried out of school textbooks and teaching materials for the purpose of incorporating knowledge of IP into different areas of education and at different stages of processing. Measures should be implemented aimed at increasing the interest and level of awareness of young pupils in the importance of IP in solving urgent problems of society (artificial intelligence, Big Data, eco-security and climate change, implementation of "green" innovations, biotechnology, IT, IP and public health, traditional knowledge, etc.) and others.

For the purpose of public awareness, workers in certain industry schools, etc. of the importance of issues concerning the protection of IP, the need of expanding IP knowledge was stressed aimed at forming a high level of culture and education of Ukrainian society in this field. The role of the public in the functioning the national IP legal protection system should be increased.

Among the measures provided were the development of educational materials (booklets, cartoons, etc.) for preschool children and young children; the introduction of the course "Fundamentals of Intellectual Property" in the school curriculum in order to install in the minds of coming generations the principles of respect for the results of intellectual activity and creators, respect for IP rights; an increase in the availability of education in the field of IP and the development of business education; the establishment of university coordination centers under the relevant WIPO program at leading universities of Ukraine; organizing and conducting summer schools on IP under the auspices of WIPO at national universities; ensuring participation of representatives of Ukraine in vocational training and other training programs organized by the WIPO Academy, in accordance with the WIPO Program, etc.

3.3 Using of Intellectual Property, Technology Transfer

One of Ukraine's basic problems in the field of IP with respect to a sufficiently high level of inventive activity is the low level of commercialization of IP. The analysis identified weaknesses and suggests a number of areas that are considered the most relevant ones at the current stage.

Thus, in the direction of "Commercialization of IP. Problem issues: universities, research institutions" the following strategic objectives were set: the formation of an effective system of commercialization created in higher educational institutions, scientific institutions' items of IP rights, their use in industry, and an efficient technology transfer system; the adoption by higher education and research institutions of IP policy with a component on the transfer of knowledge, implementation through the development of recommendations, training on this policy towards practical activities; providing universities and scientific institutions with qualified personnel, who will conduct technology transfer and the commercialization of objects of IP.

The goals and steps in the commercialization of IP rights by enterprises, as well as the SME sector, were also identified in order to achieve positive dynamics of innovation activity of domestic enterprises.

Furthermore, it was stressed that there is a need to apply in Ukraine the positive experience of IP insurance gained in the world, in particular by the introduction of insurance products on the insurance market in Ukraine that cover losses related to violation of IP rights; thereby, increasing confidence in the insurance market for the payment of insurance indemnities in general and in the introduction of IP insurance in particular.

A separate area had to do with the introduction funds through state support for the commercialization of research results, technology transfer, innovation activities (universities, research institutions, industry, SMEs).

In order to develop the infrastructure for commercialization of IP, technology transfer and the use of R&D results, the need of eliminating existing barriers (legal, managerial, financial) was identified at all stages of commercialization of research results, technology transfer, innovation activities carried out by institutions of higher education and research institutions. The business sector should be engaged at the level of business associations, technological platforms, clusters to prioritize the scientific and technological development of Ukraine with the justification of choosing the areas where Ukraine can improve its competitive position in world markets. Innovative culture in the SME environment should be developed, which would stimulate the more active creation, protection and use of objects of IP. There should be an increase in the level of capacity of the subjects of innovative infrastructure in institutions of higher education and scientific institutions, and an increase in the level of awareness and consciousness of Ukrainian citizens and political establishment on the importance of the innovative way of developing the country's economy as a key factor in raising the level of competitiveness of the country and citizens' living standards.

Moreover, the Strategy stressed the need for: change of national standards for assessing IP rights aimed at the improving determination of the real value of intellectual resources of enterprises, as well as universities, research institutions, SMEs, taking into account the unique challenges of developing the information-intellectual economy; adaptation of the accounting system to the new information needs of internal and external users; deepening modernization of the methodology and accounting system in the information provision of sectoral and general management; elimination of discrepancies between national and international standards regarding the procedure for identifying intangible assets, criteria for their control, future economic benefits, cost reductions, which are taken into account when determining the tax base.

Special attention was paid to issues on improvement of the national tax system based on the baseline principles of taxation, in particular, efficiency and stability, which regulates and reproduces the features of IP and technology transfer.

In order to solve the problems in the direction of IP commercialization, the need of increasing quality of management was emphasized in the field of IP management and IP commercialization, which should facilitate the implementation of tasks connected with formation of the IP market, improving competitiveness of enterprises.

3.4 *Development of Creative Industries: Copyright and Related Rights*

The Strategy emphasizes that according to the annual report of the International Intellectual Property Alliance (IIPA), analysis of problems at the legislative and enforceable levels of copyright and related rights gives grounds for recommending leaving Ukraine in the so-called "priority watch list" in 2019.[28] In addition, Ukraine has been mentioned in List 301 since 1997, causing both economic and reputational losses.[29] This situation is due to a number of unresolved issues in the field of copyright and related rights. Legislative gaps relate to copyright and related rights in the information society using modern internet technologies, collective management and the use of unlicensed software. Despite the positive developments on these issues, a considerable number of legislative loopholes and obstacles remain with regard to the practical application of copyright and related rights protection mechanisms. There is a great need to develop additional legislative provisions in order to encourage the development of legal markets for online books, video games, movies and music, taking into account the rights of Ukrainian and foreign rights holders.

It was determined that the direction for development of national legislation is the continuation of the implementation of the Association Agreement provisions, also considering other relevant European approaches in the field of copyright and related rights,[30] in particular paying more attention to the issue of internet technologies, copyright and related rights in the digital market. A number of specific measures aimed at achieving the set objectives were identified.

The Strategy also emphasized that European integration and the rapid development of the information society require appropriate changes in the role of the authorized body of the state authority in the field of copyright and related rights in relation to such issues as: record-keeping of orphan works and out-of-commerce works; digitalization of the procedure for registration of author's copyright rights and copyright contracts; providing public access to the above-mentioned register of works; ensuring the possibility of resolving disputes in the field of collective management through alternative dispute resolution (ADR) procedures (arbitration, mediation).

[28] Office of the United States Trade Representative, '2019 Special 301 Report' (Report) 2019.

[29] Office of the United States Trade Representative, 'USTR Announces Results of Special 301 Annual Review' (Report) 1997.

[30] For details, see Anna Shtefan, 'Copyright and Its Exceptions and Limitations in Ukraine' and Kostiantyn Zerov, 'Protection of Works Posted on the Internet Under Ukrainian Copyright Law' in this Volume.

Regarding the application of the legislation, the need was emphasized to improve the level of protection in respect of copyright and related rights in the information society using modern internet technologies, as well as stopping offenses in this area. The following ways to achieve these objectives were identified:

- Implementation of activities aimed at stopping the spread of internet piracy;
- Improvement of national legislation on the protection of IP rights for items placed on the internet, increasing the number of objects of copyright and related rights protection in the digital environment;
- Further implementation of a roadmap towards the legalization of software in the public and private sectors;
- The expansion of cases of the free use of objects of copyright and related rights in order to maintain a balance of interests between society and users and taking into account European legislation;
- Improvement of the national legislation of the mechanism of compensation for violation of copyright and related rights;
- Regulating the protection of copyright and related rights while digitizing national cultural heritage and providing the community with digitized works, taking into account EU experience in the field of orphan works protection; protection of out-of-commerce works; the use of digitized copies of works in the public domain; and the creation and operation of digital libraries;
- Introduction of a mechanism for payment to authors and performers of just remuneration for the use of their works and other objects, if the previously agreed remuneration in the licensing or exclusive property transfer rights agreements proves to be disproportionately low compared to all subsequent relevant proceeds and other proceeds from the use of the works, objects, etc.

With regard to the development of the scope of collective management,[31] taking into account the negative practice that has developed in Ukraine in the last decade, strategic objectives have been set such as the creation of an optimal, high-quality and efficient non-state system of collective management of property rights of copyright and related rights capable of forming, implementing a transparent public model for overcoming existing challenges and risks. In addition, effective forms of collective management have should be proposed that will ensure a fair balance of interests, not only between different categories of rights holders and, further, between individual right holders in each of these categories, but also between the rights holders and the users as a whole. Collective management should be perceived not as a business, but as an important social mission to represent the property interests of the international community of authors, performers, producers of videograms and phonograms in the country.

Significant attention was paid to the issues concerning the definition of the economic impact of industries based on the use of objects of copyright and related rights, in particular in terms of improvement of the national system of monitoring

[31] For details, see Liubov Maidanyk, 'On the Reforms, Practice and Perspective of the Law on Collecting Societies in Ukraine' in this Volume.

industries based on objects of copyright and related rights and the impact of culture on the development of the country.

3.5 Protection of Rights on Plant Varieties and Animal Species

The following five main objectives were defined in this block:

(1) Increasing the technological effectiveness and the quality of examination of plant and animal variety, taking into account changes and updates in the selection and directions of the use of varieties;
(2) Harmonization of state policy on the use of plant varieties in economic activities in accordance with EU and international practice;
(3) Ensuring compliance of the organizational structure and personnel resources in the competent body of the administration to perform functions for the protection of rights in plant varieties, as the basic component of the mechanism of public administration in this area;
(4) Settlement of the procedural order for the examination of a variety with the extension of the applicant's rights;
(5) Establishing accountability of the subjects involved in the mechanism for performing the functions of the examination of the application, the conditions of interaction with the applicants, audit of the examination.

A separate area concerns the resolution of issues related to: (i) ensuring the legal protection of breeds of animals as objects of IP rights by creating legislative, institutional and enforcement mechanisms; (ii) the development of industrial production and the resumption of large livestock complexes with the introduction of innovation; and (iii) the selection and livestock breeding by farmers' households.

3.6 IP Protection

3.6.1 General Issues

There is no doubt that the existence of effective mechanisms for the protection against infringement of IP rights, the prosecution of perpetrators, as well as the possibility of taking preventive measures to prevent the violation of these rights are key factors that motivate individuals and companies to create and register objects of industrial property. As Ukraine aims to create a favorable business climate and attract investment, forming an innovative business environment and, in terms of the fulfillment of obligations under international treaties, the implementation of the Association Agreement with the EU, and the TRIPS Agreement, IP rights issues are of particular urgency. The provisions of Chapter 9 ("Intellectual Property") in the Association

Agreement supplement and clarify the rights and obligations of the Parties under the TRIPS Agreement[32] and other international treaties in the field of IP. Along with national strategic acts, in particular the Ukraine 2020 Sustainable Development Strategy, the reform of IP protection was included in the security sector.

The Strategy paid significant attention to the protection of IP rights both at the level of improving national legislation and at the level of law enforcement, including the effectiveness of procedures carried out by administrative, customs, law enforcement and judicial authorities.

National experts collected statistical data and conducted an analytical study both in terms of infringement of IP rights and in terms of litigation, as well as the application of measures of administrative, civil, economic and criminal liability. Experts also relied on European experience. After all, according to the EU Intellectual Property Office (EUIPO) the annual losses caused by counterfeiting and piracy in some sectors of the EU economy reach up to 60 billion EUR.[33] The updated in 2019 analysis shows that total losses are equivalent to 7.4% of total EU sales in 11 surveyed sectors of economy; moreover, up to 468,000 jobs are lost in these areas within the EU.[34]

Accordingly, the Strategy emphasizes among the objectives such points as significant increase of efficiency of judicial protection of IP rights, harmonization of IPR norms through the standards of the Association Agreement, accelerating the process of implementation of European approaches in order to build an effective IPR protection mechanism in Ukraine.

Specific measures to achieve the objectives include, in particular: introduction of a real mechanism for compensation of losses to the right holder and/or seeking compensation instead of indemnification for violations of IP rights; the introduction of an effective mechanism for the implementation of the right holders' right to terminate the violation of their rights on the internet; the introduction of a fast and effective mechanism of protection against "patent trolling"; improvement of national procedural legislation with the purpose of effective operation of the newly created superior specialized court in the implementation of judicial protection of IP rights; ensuring timely recording of evidence, means of securing a claim; improving the evidentiary quality of expert opinions; elimination of the state monopoly in expert activity; and resolving the issue of the relation between the Convention norms in terms of human rights and access to information, the right to health care, etc.

The Strategy also emphasized the need for creation of an effectively integrated institutional and adequately staffed system of criminal legal protection of IP rights

---

[32] Agreement on Trade-Related Aspects of Intellectual Property Rights, World Trade Organization.

[33] 'EUR 60 Billion Lost Every Year Across the EU due to Counterfeiting in 13 Key Economic Sectors' *European Union Intellectual Property Office* (June 2018) https://euipo.europa.eu/tunnel-web/secure/webdav/guest/document_library/observatory/docs/Press_releases/Spring_campaign_Press_release_final_EN_UK.pdf accessed 13 June 2022.

[34] European Union Intellectual Property Office, '2019 Status Report on IPR Infringement: Why IP Rights are Important, IPR Infringement and the Fight Against Counterfeiting' (Report), 2019 https://euipo.europa.eu/tunnel-web/secure/webdav/guest/document_library/observatory/documents/reports/2019_Status_Report_on_IPR_infringement/2019_Status_Report_on_IPR_infringement_en.pdf accessed June 13 2022.

in Ukraine, constructed taking into account the requirements of the Association Agreement and the best practices worldwide in this area.

3.6.2 Court System of IPRs Protection

Particular attention was paid to directly improving the judiciary in terms of its involvement in the protection of IP rights. It was considered extremely relevant to enhance the image of Ukraine regarding the proper and effective judicial protection of IP rights through increasing confidence in the judiciary in the field of IP. Also pointed out among the strategic objectives was: the adaptation of the rules of the current legislation on the judicial protection of IP rights to the requirements of the Association Agreement; ensuring the equal and correct application by courts of all instances of both procedural law and substantive law in the field of IP; predictability and stability of court decisions; the efficiency of the judicial authorities in protecting the right holders' rights; and improving the procedural aspects of the enforcement of litigation in the field of IP. This should be facilitated, first of all, by the completion of measures for the formation of the judiciary of the High Court of Intellectual Property and the commencement of its activities.[35] After all, this process has been going on since 2017.[36]

3.6.3 Customs IPR Protection

The Strategy also emphasizes the need of ensuring effective and transparent customs procedures related to the protection of IP rights. It should be noted that the State Customs Service of Ukraine provides publication of information on IPR objects registered in the Customs register of IP rights of Ukraine, and weekly updates of such information on its official website. As of 15 July 2019, a total of 4,072 IP rights have been submitted. During the period from 19 November 2020 to 14 January 2022, 647 items were entered into the register, mostly trade marks.[37] The customs notification procedure for intellectual property, despite the large number of objects registered there, it is not effective. Due to these reasons, customs procedures could be improved through digitalization and the transition to electronic document management in the operating of the customs register of IP rights and the development of an electronic system of operative exchange of information (using the latest digital technologies, software online resource) between the right-holding companies (or their representatives) and customs authorities.

[35] For details see Anna Shtefan and Olga Gurgula, 'The New Intellectual Property Court in Ukraine: Its Creation and Exclusive Jurisdiction' in this Volume.

[36] 'The Higher Qualification Commission of Judges Admitted to the Competition 219 Candidates for Judges of the Supreme Court of Intellectual Property' *Sudova Vlada Ukrainy* (21 March 2018) https://court.gov.ua/archive/451698/ accessed 13 June 2022.

[37] State Customs Service of Ukraine, Customs Register of Intellectual Property Rights https://cabinet.customs.gov.ua/reestrs404 accessed 13 June 2022.

3.6.4 Other IPR Protection Areas

In terms of improving the protection of IPRs under competition law, a number of measures have been developed to achieve systematic harmonization of legislation in the field of IP protection and competition legislation through increasing the involvement of the AMCU in protecting IP rights.[38]

The developers of the Strategy also concluded that it is expedient to create a specialized arbitration court and/or international commercial arbitration or, at least, the establishment of a relevant unit in one of the permanent arbitral tribunals or international commercial arbitration. This can be realized by, for example, developing the activities of the International Commercial Arbitration Court of Ukraine of the Specialized Board for the examination of foreign economic, and conducting training of profile arbitrators in the field of IP. The need of setting up a specialized mediation center(s) was also emphasized as an effective way of resolving IP disputes through the identification and training profile mediators in the field of IP.

3.7 *State Strategies, Programs and Concepts for the Development of Various Sectors of the Economy and IP*

Block 7 is devoted to the analysis of the coordination of state strategies, programs and concepts for the development of various sectors of the economy, and issues of creation, protection and use of IP. It covers promoting progressive, inclusive and sustainable economic growth, full and productive employment and decent job opportunities for all. This is supported by the creation of sustainable infrastructure, the promotion of comprehensive and sustainable industrialization as well as innovation, etc. as defined by the Sustainable Development Goals of Ukraine until 2030.[39] These goals are derived from the global goals of sustainable development to 2030 proclaimed by the resolution of the United Nations General Assembly of 25 September 2015.[40] They take into account the results of an adaptation to the specifics of Ukraine's development, and have been adopted to ensure Ukraine's national interests in sustainable development economy, civil society and the state to achieve an increase in the level and quality of life of the population, respect for constitutional rights and the freedoms of human beings and citizens.

---

[38] On the competition and IP law interface in Ukraine, see Olga Gurgula, 'The Intersection Between Intellectual Property and Competition Laws in the Pharmaceutical Sector: A Ukrainian Perspective' in this Volume.

[39] Decree of the President of Ukraine No. 722/2019 on the Sustainable Development Goals of Ukraine for the Period up to 2030 https://www.president.gov.ua/documents/7222019-29825 accessed 26 October 2022.

[40] United Nations, 'Resolution Adopted by the General Assembly on 25 September 2015' A/RES/70/1, 2015.

The formation in Ukraine of a highly developed, socially oriented economy based on knowledge and innovation was also defined by the "Sustainable Development Strategy Ukraine 2020",[41] and meets the relevant provisions of the Action Plan for the implementation of the Association Agreement between Ukraine and the EU.[42] It takes into consideration the strategy for development of the sphere of innovative activity for the period until 2030. Directions and methods to resolve problems include legal issues related to the protection and use of state-owned IP objects, created with the use of state budget funds.

In addition, the objects of analysis were the long-term strategy for the development of Ukrainian culture,[2] and the strategy for the development of SMEs in Ukraine for the period up to 2020.[43]

Special attention in this block was paid to the issue of geographical indications.[44] It was emphasized that GIs are related to rural development, but these are not included in the Strategy for promoting private investment in agriculture for the period up to 2023. The Ukrainian agricultural sector has an undervalued production and export potential, which can make a significant contribution to the economic growth of the country as a whole and the development of rural areas in particular. According to World Bank experts, a 30% increase in agricultural productivity can contribute to GDP growth of 4% over five years and 12.5% over 10 years.[45] Since GIs just add value to agricultural products, GI protection is a necessary component of rural development and therefore needs to be modified. The regions where goods are manufactured using GIs attract a significant number of tourists from other countries and can serve the development of the tourism business in Ukraine. This is not included in the 2026 Tourism and Resorts Development Strategy.[46] This strategy requires alignment with the IP Strategy.

3.8 *Specific Scopes and IP Issues*

Block 8 of the Strategy is devoted to the analysis of certain areas and the use of IP among them, namely:

---

[41] Sustainable Development Strategy "Ukraine 2020", approved by the Presidential Decree of 5 January 2015 No. 5/2015.

[42] Action Plan for the Implementation of the Association Agreement between Ukraine and European Union, Government Resolution of 25 October 2017 No. 1106.

[43] Strategy for Small and Medium-sized Enterprise Development in Ukraine until 2020, approved by the Decree of the Cabinet of Ministers of 24 May 2017 No. 504-r.

[44] For details see Anastasiia Kyrylenko, 'Why so Few Geographical Indications in Ukraine? Legal, Political and Socio-Economic Perspective' in this Volume.

[45] Cabinet of Ministers of Ukraine, Order from 5 July 2019, No. 595-r on Approval of the Strategy to Promote Private Investment in Agriculture until 2023.

[46] Cabinet of Ministers of Ukraine, Order from 16 March 2017, No. 168-r, on Approval of the Strategy for the Development Strategy for the Development of Tourism and Resorts for the Period up to 2026.

Pharmaceuticals and problems of IP: Strategic goals are the development of a legal protection system of IP in the sphere of pharmaceuticals in Ukraine, which should: contribute to balance the interests of society, the right to life and health and the patent holder's property interests; respond to international best practices and based on strict criteria of patentability, prepared by the UNDP and WHO; ensure the fair use of patent rights and fair competition in the medicines market; reduce the financial burden on the state budget while providing medicines for the population; and promote the development of the national pharmaceutical industry.

Agriculture and IP issues: Strategic goals are the formation of an innovative model of agricultural development that will allow for the long-term securing advancement of the industry, sustainable economic growth, which will contribute to an increase in the annual growth of gross agricultural products, increase of labor productivity, and a high level of competitiveness.

The sphere of defense and IP: Strategic goals are the modernization and outstripping development of the defense-industrial complex of Ukraine, increasing its production capacity, developing globally competitive weapons and equipment using IP objects, importing substitution and increase of own production of critical components and materials, support of perspective, practically directed research and development works in the field of state defense order (SDO).

Traditional knowledge and traditional cultural expressions: Strategic goals are introduction of the legal protection of traditional knowledge (TK) and traditional cultural expressions (TCEs) in Ukraine by the mechanisms of IP.

4 Current Issues on the Reformation of the IP Area in Ukraine in the Process of the National IP Strategy Implementation

The introduction of this chapter showed the factors of Ukraine's policy to improve the protection and enforcement of IP rights were taken into account when launching a large-scale reform of IP laws in 2016. This reform not only aimed to adopt updated special legislation implementing the EU and relevant European standards in this area (which was implemented in the field of industrial property in late 2019–2020), but also initiated the implementation of deep institutional reform, especially at the level of executive and judicial authorities.

Some positive steps were taken in the field of IP during the years 2017–2018. In 2017 in connection with the adoption of the Law of Ukraine[47] "On State Support for Cinematography in Ukraine", several important changes were made to other laws of Ukraine regarding the protection of copyright and related rights on the internet,

[47] Ukrainian Law on State Support for Cinematography in Ukraine 2017, 1977-VIII.

in particular, to the Law "On Copyright and Related Rights", the Code of Administrative Offenses, the Criminal Code of Ukraine. Also, in 2017 amendments[48] were adopted supplementing the provisions of the procedural legislation of Ukraine on the High Court of Intellectual Property. In 2018 a separate law was adopted to streamline collective management organizations (CMOs)[49] taking into account the specific remarks of international experts and the provisions of Directive 2014/26/EC "On collective management of copyright and related rights and multi-territorial licensing of rights in musical works for online use in the internal market". However, Ukrainian legislation on copyright and related rights remains inconsistent with the Association Agreement. The parliament of Ukraine is considering several alternative versions of the draft law "On Copyright and Related Rights". Its adoption is expected in 2022.

The adoption by the parliament of Ukraine of the Law "On Amendments to the Law of Ukraine on Effective Management of Property Rights of Copyright Holders and (or) Related Rights to ensure income collection from the rights of collective management organizations" should be considered a positive factor contributing to solving problems in the sphere of UCO activity.[50]

Ukraine's fulfillment of its obligations under the Association Agreement in terms of customs procedures was implemented by adopting the amendments to the Customs Code of Ukraine in 2019.[51]

In the field of industrial property,[52] the following laws of Ukraine were adopted in 2019–2020 to fulfill the obligations under the Association Agreement to harmonize the provisions of legislative acts of Ukraine in the field of industrial property: on the composition of semiconductor products[53]; on GIs[3]; and on combating patent abuse.[54] At the same time, it should be noted that bylaws in the field of industrial property remain inconsistent with the provisions of relevant laws, which complicates the acquisition and exercise of property rights in such items.

---

[48] Ukrainian Law on Amendments to the Code of Commercial Procedure of Ukraine, the Civil Procedure Code of Ukraine, the Code of Administrative Judiciary of Ukraine and other legislative Acts 2017, 2147-VIII.

[49] Ukrainian Law on the Effective Management of Property Rights of Copyright Holders in the Sphere of Copyright and (or) Related Rights 2018, 2415-VIII.

[50] Ukrainian Draft Law on Effective Management of Property Rights of Rights Holders in the Field of Copyright and (or) Related Rights 2021, No. 1960-IX.

[51] Ukrainian Law on Amendments to the Customs Code of Ukraine Concerning the Protection of Intellectual Property Rights at Movement of the Goods Across Customs Border of Ukraine 2019, 202-IX.

[52] For details, see Leonid Tarasenko, 'Legislative Reforms on Patents, Utility Models and Industrial Designs in Ukraine' in this Volume.

[53] Ukrainian Law on Amendments to Certain Legislative Acts of Ukraine on Improving the Protection of Rights to the Topographies of Semiconductor Products 2019, 111-IX.

[54] Ukrainian Law on Amendments to Certain Legislative Acts of Ukraine Concerning Strengthening the Protection and Protection of Rights to Trademarks and Industrial Designs and Combating Patent Abuse 2020, 815-IX; Ukrainian Law on Amendments to Some Legislative Acts of Ukraine Concerning the Reform of Patent Legislation 2020, 816-IX.

In addition to European integration, Ukraine faces the issue of expanding its participation in the development of international initiatives in the field of IP protection within WIPO, the WTO, as well as consideration of the expediency of accession to the European Patent Convention and new multilateral international treaties (e.g. the Beijing Treaty on Audiovisual Performances, and the Marrakesh Treaty to Facilitate Access to Published Works for Persons Who Are Blind, Visually Impaired or Otherwise Print Disabled).

A significant embodiment of the step-by-step solution of the tasks set by the reform was the adoption on 16 June 2020 of Law on National Intellectual Property Authority.[55] Under the new law, the NIPA was created as a special organization that is responsible for protecting the rights to not only industrial property, but also copyright and related rights. Further, under special decision of Cabinet of Ministers of Ukraine,[56] the functions of the NIPA were entrusted to the state enterprise "Ukrainian Institute of Intellectual Property" (Ukrpatent). It should be noted that the adoption of this law has actually completed a four-year period of institutional reform of the IP sector in Ukraine.[57] Along with the reform of the collective management system, the establishment of the NIPA was one of the main reforms to be carried out in accordance with the Sustainable Development Strategy "Ukraine 2020", the Concept of Reforming the State Intellectual Property Legal Protection System in Ukraine[58] and the Action Plan on the Implementation of the Concept of Reforming the State System of Legal Protection of IP in Ukraine. At the same time, Ukrpatent does not fully perform the functions of the NIPA; there was no formation of management and governing bodies or supervisory bodies of the NIPA, etc. Therefore, institutional reform in the field of IP has not yet been implemented, as provided for by the Strategy and national legislation.

The legislative initiative of parliament members to submit to the parliament of Ukraine draft laws on amendments to some legislative acts of Ukraine to strengthen the protection of IP rights[59] should be taken as a positive step towards protection of IP rights, as well as the Supreme Court of Intellectual Property.[60] The adoption of the latter, along with the resumption of the operating the High Qualifications Commission of Judges in Ukraine, should launch the Court's IP operation.

It should be noted that the need to improve national legislation in the field of IP protection was emphasized by international and domestic experts of the Technical

---

[55] Ukrainian Law on Amendments to Some Legislative Acts of Ukraine on the Establishment of a National Intellectual Property Authority 2020, 703-IX.

[56] Cabinet of Ministers of Ukraine, Order from 13 October 2020, No. 1267-r on the National Intellectual Property Authority.

[57] Olena Orliuk and Nataliia Korogod 'Improvement of Intellectual Property Management in Ukraine' (2020) 6 Theory and Practice of Intellectual Property Journal 171.

[58] Cabinet of Ministers of Ukraine, Order from 1 June 2016, No. 402 on Approval of the Concept of Reforming the State System of Legal Protection of Intellectual Property in Ukraine.

[59] Ukrainian Draft Law, No. 6464; Ukrainian Draft Law, No. 6464-1.

[60] Ukrainan Draft Law, No. 6487.

Assistance Project for the establishment of the High Court of Intellectual Property,[61] implemented by the Queen Mary University Center for Commercial Law in London with the support of the Ministry of Foreign Affairs and Development of the United Kingdom and the British Embassy in Kyiv.[62] The study involved a specially created International Council of Experts, chaired by Lord Newberger, former President of the Supreme Court of the United Kingdom. In addition, well-known international and Ukrainian judges and experts (including the author of this experiment)[63] became members of the international expert council.

Kyiv National University, named after Taras Shevchenko, is active in the field of IP education programs. It offers several master's degree programs in this field, a profile department of IP and information law, as well as a research and educational center on IP. In addition, in 2021 the University adopted a relevant act on IP policy. The Research Institute of Intellectual Property of the National Academy of Legal Sciences of Ukraine plays a leading part in the country in the direction of conducting significant research in the field of IP, training scientific personnel and expert processes. It was on its basis that the draft Strategy was largely developed, draft laws on the implementation of the Association Agreement were drafted into national legislation, a draft IP policy for universities and research institutions was prepared, a framework for the Court's IP was formed, and other projects were developed which are aimed at developing National IP System of Ukraine.

These facts suggest that Ukraine is successfully implementing the first stage of the National Strategy for the Development of Intellectual Property (despite its lack of formal approval), primarily in terms of changes in national legislation in the field of IP.

5 Conclusion

The evolution of the world economy is closely linked to the widespread use of intellectual resources, in which IP will be the main driving force for the current millennium. Going side by side with scientific and technological progress, IP is gaining global importance by increasing its relevance for key and fundamental policies such as food, health, labor, trade, culture, the environment, investment and scientific and technical transformations. The more important IP becomes for economic development and the creation of material goods, the more urgent are the issues on quality legal protection of IP. These include its effective commercialization, the effective protection of IP

[61] For details, see Anna Shtefan and Olga Gurgula, 'The New Intellectual Property Court in Ukraine: Its Creation and Exclusive Jurisdiction' in this Volume.

[62] See CCLS QMUL 'Ukraine DFID/FCO IP Court Project: The Final Report' (September 2020).

[63] Queen Mary University of London, 'FCDO Ukraine IP Court Project: UK Technical Assistance Project to Support the Establishment and Operation of the High Intellectual Property Court in Ukraine' (Final Report and Recommendation), 2020.

rights, creation of an effective system of awareness and public awareness in the field of IP, which should contribute to social and economic development of the country.

The development of the national system of IP should be considered in its complex context. It cannot be reduced to the adoption of amendments to national legislation, the effective operating relevant Ministry of Economy of Ukraine, or Ukrpatent's functions as a national IP authority. The development of the national IP system directly affects the implementation of the strategies adopted in recent years regarding innovation, digitalization, sustainable development, roadmaps for the implementation of sustainable development strategies until 2030, and the roadmap for entry into the European Research Area and more.

Implementation of the Strategy aims at expanding international cooperation in the field of IP, developing and strengthening links with WIPO; the International Union for the Protection of New Varieties of Plants; the United Nations Educational, Scientific and Cultural Organization; the United Nations Economic Commission for Europe; the European Patent Office; and with specialized agencies from different countries, including the European Union. The development of the Strategy has taken into account the progressive approaches to IP rights enshrined in "The Europe 2020 Strategy", which identified goals and strategic priorities of the EU, designed to consolidate European competitiveness on a global scale, particularly in the development of the Innovation Union, the European Research Area, and in the process of implementing the Digital Agenda for Europe. Steps envisaged by the Strategy are aimed at ensuring the integration of Ukraine into the international and European intellectual space, taking into account the national interests of Ukraine.

Therefore, the adoption of the National Strategy for the Development of Intellectual Property, developed in Ukraine by the National Expert Corps with the support of WIPO, is considered urgent. The in-depth and comprehensive analysis of the current situation in the field of national economy, policies and IP, set out in the Strategy provided a basis for identifying strengths and weaknesses of the national IP system, which depend on internal factors, and identified opportunities and threats, which may adversely affect its development, depending on external factors.

These problems can be solved on the basis of the package of strategic objectives proposed in the Strategy and ways to achieve them, and the priorities and measures to implement the strategic vision of the National Intellectual Property System are the main tool for economic, social and cultural development of Ukraine. Achieving these objectives will require the involvement and great efforts of all participants in the National Intellectual Property System, defined in the Strategy, on the basis of specific action plans approved by the government and supported by other branches on the national level. Working in its favor is that this Strategy defines a comprehensive, multidisciplinary and well-considered approach to issues related to the field of IP, based on a high degree of interagency, interdisciplinary and cross-sectoral cooperation at all levels, aimed at strengthening the National Intellectual Property System, while taking into account the European vector of development of Ukraine and international treaty obligations in the field of IP.

The New Intellectual Property Court in Ukraine: Its Creation and Exclusive Jurisdiction

Anna Shtefan and Olga Gurgula

Contents

Abstract Ukraine has set out to establish a new specialised IP Court. The creation of this IP Court is an important element of current reforms that are aimed at improving the operation of the Ukrainian judicial system. It is believed that the new Court will improve IP enforcement by decreasing the duration of court proceedings and simultaneously increasing the quality of decisions in IP cases. While the creation of the IP Court is generally considered to be highly desirable, certain issues in the set-up and operation of this Court may reduce the effectiveness of the judicial process in IP cases and require clarifications and/or adjustments. Among such matters is the

A. Shtefan (✉)
Copyright and Related Rights Department, Intellectual Property Scientific Research Institute of the National Academy of Legal Sciences of Ukraine, Kyiv, Ukraine
e-mail: anna_shtefan@ukr.net

O. Gurgula
Brunel Law School, Brunel University London, London, UK
e-mail: Olga.Gurgula@brunel.ac.uk

H. Richter (ed.), *Competition and Intellectual Property Law in Ukraine*,
MPI Studies on Intellectual Property and Competition Law 31,
https://doi.org/10.1007/978-3-662-66101-7_14

exclusive jurisdiction of the IP Court and a potential overlap with the jurisdiction of the administrative courts and other state authorities. This chapter will outline the developments leading to the establishment of the IP Court. It will also discuss certain examples of a potential collision between the jurisdictions of the IP Court and the administrative courts, and will provide suggestions on how this could be rectified.

1 A Global Trend Towards Increasing the Judicial Specialisation in the Field of IP

In the knowledge-based economy the role of intellectual property (IP) is becoming increasingly important.[1] During recent decades the protection of IP has undergone significant transformations. These include the broadening of the types of products and technologies that can be protected by IP rights on the one hand, and on the other a policy shift towards harmonisation of standards for protection and enforcement at the international level.[2] The latter includes the adoption of the Agreement on Trade-Related Aspects of Intellectual Property Rights (TRIPS),[3] which marked the beginning of a new era for the protection of IP at a global level. As world trade increases, the protection of IP and its effective enforcement becomes more important.[4] If the IP owners are not able to enforce their rights in a speedy and cost-effective manner with a predictable outcome the value and benefits of such rights are significantly undermined and their effect on economic growth reduced.[5] The creation of well-functioning IP enforcement mechanisms is considered to be of paramount importance because they help to facilitate an environment in which IP can fulfil its role of stimulating innovation, providing equitable benefits for both owners and users of IP.[6]

[1] This chapter draws on some of the findings and conclusions of a recently completed project funded by the UK Government and conducted by the Centre for Commercial Law Studies (QMUL) on the creation and functioning of a new IP court in Ukraine. The authors of this chapter formed part of the team of experts that prepared the project's report, which provided recommendations to the Ukrainian Government on possible ways to improve the legal framework related to the establishment and operation of this new IP court. The full report on this project and its findings can be found here: CCLS QMUL 'Ukraine DFID/FCO IP Court Project: The Final Report' (September 2020).

[2] World Bank, 'Intellectual Property Rights and Economic Development' (WDP 412, Discussion Paper) 2000.

[3] WTO Agreement on Trade-Related Intellectual Property Rights, Marrakesh Agreement Establishing the World Trade Organization, Annex 1C, 15 April 1994.

[4] International Bar Association, 'International Survey of Specialised Intellectual Property Courts and Tribunals' (2007) 3.

[5] See Advisory Council on Intellectual Property, 'Should the Jurisdiction of the Federal Magistrates Service be Extended to Include Patent, Trademark and Design Matters?' (2003) 2 https://www.ipaustralia.gov.au/sites/default/files/final_report_extending_jurisdiction_of_federal_magistrates.pdf?acsf_files_redirect accessed 6 November 2021.

[6] WIPO, 'Building Respect for Intellectual Property' https://www.wipo.int/enforcement/en/ accessed 6 November 2021.

The creation of a robust IP enforcement system—an essential element of which is an effective judicial system—has therefore been one of the key policy goals in many jurisdictions.[7] The benefits of introducing specialised IP judiciary are increasingly acknowledged worldwide because of the economic significance and the legal complexities associated with IP rights due to constant technological advancement. Many countries have either already established[8] or have been considering the introduction of various forms of a specialised judiciary,[9] including the UK, Germany, France, the Netherlands and the US.[10] A study on specialised IP judiciary found that their creation promotes greater understanding of, and familiarity with, IP related issues and "reduces judicial errors and lowers litigation costs, potentially resulting in greater consistency and increased predictability of case outcomes".[11] It also signals to the stakeholders that the government considers IP to be an important area for protection.[12]

In Ukraine, the creation of a specialised IP court (the High Court of Intellectual Property Rights (IP Court)) is a salient element of the ongoing judicial reform that is aimed at improving the operation of the judicial system in general, as well as the functioning of the IP enforcement system. The improvement forms part of Ukraine's international obligations. In particular, Ukraine is a party to a number of bilateral and multilateral international treaties which regulate the protection of IP rights,[13] including the TRIPS Agreement.[14] Under these various international instruments

[7] European Commission, 'A Balanced IP Enforcement System Responding to Today's Societal Challenges' (Communication), COM(2017) 707 final; European Commission 'Making the Most of the EU's Innovative Potential: An Intellectual Property Action Plan to Support the EU's Recovery and Resilience' (Communication), COM(2020) 760 final; United Kingdom Intellectual Property Office, 'Protecting Creativity, Supporting Innovation: IP Enforcement 2020' (Strategy on IP Enforcement) 2016.

[8] International Chamber of Commerce, 'Adjudicating Intellectual Property Disputes' (Report) ICC 2016.

[9] Kazakhstan, for example discusses the establishment of a specialised IP judiciary in its IP Strategy 2021–2025; See Kazakhstan Government Decree on the Approval of the IP Concept for the Development of Intellectual Property in the Republic of Kazakhstan in 2021–2025 https://legalacts.egov.kz/npa/view?id=5772344 accessed 6 November 2021.

[10] See Final Report (n 1).

[11] International Intellectual Property Institute and United States Patent and Trademark Office, 'Study on Specialized Intellectual Property Courts' IIPI and USPTO 2012, 1.

[12] Ibid 6.

[13] For example, Bern Convention for the Protection of Literary and Artistic Works (1886) on 31 May 1995, which entered into force for Ukraine on 25 October 1995; Madrid Agreement Concerning the International Registration of Marks (25 December 1991); Paris Convention for the Protection of Industrial Property (25 December 1991); Patent Cooperation Treaty (25 December 1991). For a detailed list of all IP related Ukrainian laws and international treaties see https://www.wipo.int/wipolex/en/profile.jsp?code=ua accessed 6 November 2021. For more details, see Yuriy Kapitsa, 'Association Agreements and Problems Approximating Intellectual Property Legislation of Third Countries with the EU Acquis: The Case of Ukraine' in this Volume.

[14] Ukraine joined the Agreement on Trade-Related Aspects of Intellectual Property Rights (1994) on 16 May 2008.

Ukraine is obliged to provide efficient protection and enforcement of IP rights within its territory. For example, under Art. 41(1) TRIPS, members have undertaken to

> [...] ensure that enforcement procedures [...] are available under their law to permit effective action against any act of infringement of intellectual property rights covered by this Agreement, including expeditious remedies to prevent infringements and remedies which constitute a deterrent to further infringements.

Under a more recent international treaty—namely the Association Agreement signed between Ukraine and the European Union[15]—Ukraine has undertaken to provide "[...] measures, procedures and remedies necessary to ensure the enforcement of intellectual property rights".[16]

While none of its international obligations of ensuring efficient protection and enforcement of IP rights requires Ukraine to establish a specialised IP court in order to fulfil these obligations,[17] the establishment of such a court has been viewed as being an effective way of improving the IP enforcement system.[18] It was received positively by Ukrainian legal professionals as well as the academic community and is expected to become an effective and valuable tool for IP rights holders.[19] In particular, it is believed that the creation of a specialised IP court will improve the IP enforcement system in Ukraine by decreasing the duration of court proceedings and simultaneously increasing the quality of decisions in IP cases.[20] This, it is hoped, will be achieved, inter alia, by selecting and training skilled judges within specific areas of IP specialisation, as well as by developing a uniform and consistent judicial

[15] Association Agreement between the European Union and its Member States, of the one part, and Ukraine, of the other part (2014) OJ L161/3 (EU–Ukraine Association Agreement), in which Chap. 9 "Intellectual Property" contains a comprehensive list of substantive provisions on various types of intellectual property, as well as procedural provisions on IP enforcement.

[16] EU–Ukraine Association Agreement, art 230.

[17] See, for example, TRIPs, art 41(5), according to which "[i]t is understood that this Part does not create any obligation to put in place a judicial system for the enforcement of intellectual property rights distinct from that for the enforcement of law in general, nor does it affect the capacity of Members to enforce their law in general".

[18] See e.g. Mykola Pototsky and Mariya Zakharenko, 'A Specialised Court that Considers Disputes Related to Intellectual Property in Ukraine: A Mistake or Necessity?' (2014) Legal Bulletin 204 (discussing whether the creation of a specialised IP court will make the IP protection system in Ukraine more effective).

[19] Tetiana Pashkovska, 'The Intellectual Property High Court is on the Finish Line' (2017) *Yurydychna Gazeta* http://yur-gazeta.com/publications/actual/vishchiy-intelektualniy-sud-na-finishniy-pryamiy.html accessed 6 November 2021.

[20] The decision to create a specialised IP court in Ukraine was also an issue of intense debate. Some experts emphasised that "the policy choice to create such a court should be based on an informed and transparent analysis of the situation in the country." See Democracy Reporting International 'Ukraine's New Intellectual Property High Court: Implications for the Justice System' (29 May 2018) https://democracy-reporting.org/en/office/ukraine/news/ukraines-new-high-intellectual-property-court-implications-for-the-justice-system accessed 6 November 2021. They argue that this standard was not sufficiently met in Ukraine because the policy choice to establish the IP Court was not supported by convincing evidence and was not preceded by a broad public discussion and consultation with regards to the advantages and disadvantages of creating such specialised court. They also note that "[t]he explanatory note to the Law On the Judiciary and Status of Judges justifies

practice. Although the new IP court is not yet operational its launch remains high on the agenda in Ukraine, and it is expected to start functioning in the near future.

This chapter will discuss how the new IP Court in Ukraine was created, including the developments that had led to it. It will then examine certain matters regarding the exclusive jurisdiction of the IP Court. Specifically, it will analyse a number of issues that may lead to an overlap between the jurisdiction of the IP Court and jurisdictions of the administrative courts and other state authorities. It will also provide recommendations on how to resolve these overlaps to achieve a better judicial certainty.

2 Creation of the IP Court in Ukraine

2.1 Developments Leading to the Establishment of the IP Court

Disputes concerning IP rights can be very complex. This is because they require not only the knowledge of specific legal norms related to an IP right in question, but also often necessitate a deep understanding of technical aspects of IP protected products (e.g. disputes over pharmaceutical or computer-implemented inventions). In Ukraine such disputes have been traditionally considered by three different types of courts: commercial, civil and administrative. While it provides a number of options for resolving IP disputes the system has a significant disadvantage, namely that it routinely generates confusion as to the jurisdiction of those courts in IP disputes. It also frequently results in lengthy judicial processes and divergent court practices when considering identical IP issues. In addition, different courts and procedures, as well as uneven levels of expertise of judges, often lead to unpredictable and inconsistent outcomes in IP disputes.[21] Therefore, the legal community has long argued that the creation of IP specialisation is necessary to overcome these problems.[22]

---

the creation of the court by referring generally to the positive experience of other European countries with intellectual property courts, without explaining further the details of these experiences and why they are relevant for Ukraine" (Ibid).

[21] This problem, for example, was acknowledged in Ukrainian Parliament Decree on the Recommendations to the Parliamentary hearings "Protection of intellectual property in Ukraine: problems of legislative framework and its enforcement" 2007, 1243-V ("[…] it is necessary to take further steps in relation to implementing IP specialisation in courts. It is therefore necessary to resolve the problem of the appropriate identification of courts' jurisdiction relating to specific categories of cases. Not all the courts of civil jurisdiction have implemented sufficient specialisation and training of judges to ensure effective IP dispute resolution").

[22] Svitlana Parkhomchuk, 'Ways of Introducing Bodies of Patent Jurisdiction into the Ukrainian Judicial System' (2012) 2 Problems of Civil and Commercial Law in Ukraine; National Strategy for the Development of the Sphere of Intellectual Property in Ukraine for the Period up to 2020, 2014 (unofficial text) https://uba.ua/documents/ip-strategy28082014.pdf accessed 6 November 2021.

The idea of a specialised IP court was first officially advanced in the 2001 Presidential Decree on measures relating to the protection of intellectual property in Ukraine.[23] In particular, the possibility of creating a specialised patent court was to be analysed as part of a range of measures aimed at strengthening IP protection.[24] This had been preceded by the designation of Ukraine as a "Priority Foreign Country" under the US Special 301 Report.[25] This list of countries contains the worst IP offenders with inadequate IP laws. Ukraine was included in this list because of its "persistent failure to take effective action against significant levels of optical media piracy and to implement adequate and effective intellectual property laws".[26] Due to this the US recording industry estimated it was losing over 200 million USD annually.[27]

At the same time, ideas advancing IP specialisation in the Ukrainian courts had started to take shape in the form of judicial training in the early 2000s. The aim of this was to provide a uniform IP background to the judges operating in different courts. While only a small fraction of judges received such training it nevertheless had a positive effect on the quality of decisions, and this was particularly in evidence in the commercial courts. Further steps were taken in 2003 when specialised judicial chambers were created in the High Commercial Court of Ukraine (the cassation instance at that time), including the creation of a chamber to consider IP related disputes.[28]

The discussions regarding IP specialisation have also included suggestions that such cases should belong to the jurisdiction of only one type of court to enhance the effectiveness and quality of IP adjudication.[29] As statistically most of the IP cases were considered by commercial courts,[30] the suggestions centred on the idea that IP

---

[23] Ukrainian President Decree on measures relating to the protection of intellectual property in Ukraine 2001, 285/2001.

[24] There is no information on further developments in this regard from the 2001 Decree. However, the need for the creation of a specialised IP court was also stated in the Concept of the development of the state system of IP protection during 2009–2014, approved by the Board of the State Department of Intellectual Property; Protocol No. 11, 11 March 2009.

[25] USTR 'Ukraine Designated as Priority Foreign Country Under Special 301' (2001) https://ustr.gov/archive/Document_Library/Press_Releases/2001/March/Ukraine_Designated_as_Priority_Foreign_Country_Under_Special_301.html accessed 6 November 2021.

[26] Roman Kuybida and Roman Smalyuk, 'Where did the IP Court Come from and where did it Disappear?' (2019) *Reanimation Reform Package* https://rpr.org.ua/news/zvidky-vziavsia-i-kudy-znyk-ip-sud/ accessed 6 November 2021.

[27] USTR (n 25) accessed 6 November 2021.

[28] Order of the High Commercial Court on the Establishment of the Judicial Chambers in the High Commercial Court of Ukraine 2003, N18.

[29] Yuriy Neclesa, 'Problems of Realisation of the Patent Justice in Ukraine' (2018) 3 Comparative-analytical Law 115.

[30] For example, in 2016, out of 997 IP related lawsuits 647 were filed with commercial courts. See Nina Kucheruk, 'IP High court: Who? When? Where?' (18 October 2017) *Yurydychna Gazeta* http://yur-gazeta.com/publications/practice/sudova-praktika/vishchiy-ipsud-hto-de-koli.html accessed 6 November 2021.

disputes should fall within the jurisdiction of these courts.[31] This idea gained ground and formed part of the 2007 recommendations for the improvement of IP protection to be considered by the Parliament.[32] In particular, as a result of the Parliamentary hearings it was decided to look at the possibility of transferring IP disputes to the jurisdiction of the commercial courts due to the higher level of IP expertise of the commercial court judges.[33] This has eventually resulted in the establishment of the IP Court within the system of the commercial courts, as well as the development of the IP Court's procedural rules within the general rules of the Commercial Procedural Code (CPC) applied by the commercial courts.

As a consequence, over the last decade the discussion on how to improve the quality of IP disputes can be divided into two main choices: the establishment of a separate IP court, or the introduction of IP chambers within the local and appellate courts. Eventually, the first—namely the establishment of a separate IP court—was adopted.[34]

2.2 *Judicial Reform in Ukraine and the Establishment of the IP Court*

On 2 June 2016 the Parliament of Ukraine adopted two laws which set the current judicial reform in train. The first introduced changes to the provisions related to justice within the Constitution of Ukraine.[35] The second law—the Law on the Judicial System and the Status of Judges (the Law on the Judicial System)—amended the judicial system itself.[36] These laws began a root and branch transformation of the Ukrainian judicial system and the administration of justice generally. The new Law on the Judicial System is a major overhaul of Ukraine's judiciary. Among other things it introduces major changes to the structure and jurisdiction of the Supreme Court and creates two new specialised courts, including the IP Court. The latter, under the

---

[31] Neclesa, 'Problems of Realisation of the Patent Justice in Ukraine' (n 29).

[32] This problem, for example, was acknowledged in Ukrainian Parliament Decree on the Recommendations to the Parliamentary hearings "Protection of Intellectual Property in Ukraine: Problems of Legislative Framework and its Enforcement" 2007, 1243-V.

[33] Ibid recommendation 3. The allocation of IP cases within the jurisdiction of the commercial courts was also actively discussed by the legal community. See e.g. the discussion during the round table held by the Ukrainian Bar Association 'Patent Court: Pros and Cons' (27 October 2015) http://vgsu.arbitr.gov.ua/news/1851/ accessed 6 November 2021.

[34] While the legal community had diverse views as to whether the creation of a separate IP court was justified, and whether the establishment of a more in-depth specialisation within the current judicial system was the optimal means of facilitating this, the majority of IP professionals, academics and members of the Parliament supported the creation of a court. See e.g. Pashkovska, *Yurydychna Gazeta* (n 19) accessed 6 November 2021.

[35] Ukrainian Law on the Amendments to the Constitution of Ukraine (Regarding Justice) 2016, 1401-VIII.

[36] Ukrainian Law on the System of Justice and the Status of Judges 2016, 1402-VIII (hereinafter Law on the Judicial System).

Law on the Judicial System, was to be established within 12 months of the date when the Law came into force, i.e. September 2017.

In September 2017 the President issued a decree which established the new IP Court.[37] Further, the number of judges was agreed upon.[38] It was decided that the number of judges in the IP Court will be 21 at the first instance[39] and nine at the Appellate Chamber.[40] On 30 September 2017, the High Qualifications Commission of Judges (which is responsible for the selection of the judiciary) announced the start of competition for the positions of first instance IP judges for the Court.[41] The competition for the nine positions at the Appellate Chamber was launched in October 2018.[42] Finally, on 13 February 2020, the new entity, the IP Court, was officially registered.[43] However, even though the IP Court has been formally established, as of the time of writing it is still not operational.[44]

3 Some Issues Regarding the Jurisdiction of the IP Court That Require Clarification

3.1 Jurisdiction of the IP Court Under the Commercial Procedural Code

One of the main reasons for creating the IP Court in Ukraine is to accumulate all IP disputes (except for criminal cases) within one court, which would be heard by judges with sufficient knowledge and experience in this field to ensure high quality of IP adjudication. The jurisdiction of the IP Court is defined in Art. 20(2) CPC. This provision covers a wide scope of IP and unfair competition disputes. In particular, it stipulates that the IP Court will consider the following categories of cases:

(1) disputes concerning the rights to an invention, utility model, industrial design, trademark (sign for goods and services), commercial name and other intellectual property rights, including the right of prior use;

---

[37] Ukrainian President Decree on the establishment of the High Court of Intellectual Property 2017, 299/217.

[38] Ukrainian State Court Administration Order on the Establishment of the Quantity of Judges in the IP High Court, approved by the Decision of the High Judicial Council (2017) 3065/0/15-17.

[39] Ibid.

[40] Upon the Petition by Head of the State Judicial Administration of Ukraine 2018, 8-13462/1820.

[41] Decision of the High Qualification Commission of Judges 2017, 98/зп-17.

[42] See Announcement of the High Qualifications Commission of Judges 2017, 929.

[43] Judicial Authority in Ukraine, 'The High IP Court has Been Registered' (2020) https://court.gov.ua/press/news/889183/ accessed 6 November 2021.

[44] Final and Transitional Provisions of the Law on the Judicial System, art 15s. XII.

(2) disputes concerning the registration of IP rights, invalidation, extension of IP, annulment of patents, certificates, other acts that certify or on the basis of which such rights arise, or which violate such rights or the related lawful interests;
(3) cases concerning the recognition of a trademark as well known;
(4) disputes concerning the rights of an author and related rights, including disputes concerning collective management of the author's property rights and related rights;
(5) disputes regarding the entering into, modification, termination and execution of an agreement with respect to the exercise of IP rights and commercial concessions;
(6) disputes concerning protection against unfair competition in relation to: unlawful use of signs or goods of another manufacturer; copying of the appearance of the product; collection, disclosure and use of trade secrets; appeal against decisions of the Antimonopoly Committee of Ukraine on issues specified in this subsection.

At first glance, the list of cases that fall under the jurisdiction of the IP Court covers all possible IP disputes. Moreover, the wording of this provision, i.e. that the IP Court "considers cases related to the IPRs, *in particular* [...]" (emphasis added), means that the list of cases specified in the CPC is not exhaustive. This implies that the IP Court may consider cases that are not specifically mentioned in the CPC if these cases are IP-related.

At the same time, cases which are not explicitly mentioned in this provision may risk being considered as falling under the jurisdiction of other courts. This includes cases in which one of the parties is a state authority. Under the Code of Administrative Proceedings any public law dispute related to decisions, actions or inactions of a state authority falls within the exclusive jurisdiction of the administrative courts.[45] Even if the decisions, actions or omissions of a state authority are related to IP, the public law nature of the dispute comes to the fore. It should be noted, however, that since the IP Court is not yet operational and the discussed provisions have not yet been applied, this analysis is currently theoretical. It may be possible that when the IP Court begins to function it will consider all IP-related cases. However, we believe that it is important to clarify any potential gaps in the jurisdiction of the IP Court to avoid any confusion in determining which court has the authority to hear a particular case. The following sections will discuss cases that are not explicitly mentioned in the CPC and which would be appropriate to refer to the IP Court. The clarification regarding such cases and inclusion of them to the list of disputes that fall within the jurisdiction of the IP Court would help to ensure high quality adjudication in all IP cases.

[45] Code of Administrative Procedings, art 19(1).

3.2 IP-Related Administrative Cases Which Should Be Considered by the IP Court Rather than the Administrative Courts

There are a number of IP-related administrative cases that require an in-depth knowledge of IP law. These cases are currently heard by the administrative courts and are not likely to be referred to the IP Court once it is operational unless explicitly mentioned in the CPC. This is due to the fact that, as mentioned above, such disputes have a public law nature as they arise from public relations, involving a state body and concerning its activities. Since these disputes fall under the exclusive jurisdiction of the administrative courts the fact that it is also IP-related would not be a sufficiently valid reason for the dispute to be referred to the IP Court. However, IP-related disputes of this kind often require the court to analyse the object of the dispute, the scope of rights of the rightsholder, the compliance with the procedure for registration of IP rights and other aspects that require knowledge in the field of IP. Unlike the judges of the IP Court, administrative court judges usually do not have any special training and necessary qualifications to properly assess such matters. This therefore significantly complicates the case analysis undertaken by administrative court judges and can lead to erroneous decisions. Therefore, it may be more appropriate for such disputes to be considered by the IP Court.

3.2.1 Customs-Related Disputes That Involve IP Rights

This category of disputes concerns challenges against the decisions of customs authorities which currently fall within the jurisdiction of the administrative courts. One type of these involves disputes where the customs authority has already cleared goods, and the IP right holder has subsequently detected that such goods may infringe their IP rights. The analysis in such cases is centred on the assessment of goods cleared by the customs authority and whether they infringe the rightsholder's IP rights. In other words the dispute does not relate to the goods clearance procedure or the powers of the customs authority. The main issue that the court must consider in this dispute is whether the IP right in question has been infringed, and this requires knowledge of IP law.

Another category relates to the registration of the objects of IP rights in the customs register. This is a special procedure aimed at preventing goods that may infringe upon IP rights being imported into or exported from Ukraine's territory. The rightsholder who has a reason to believe that their IP rights are being (or may be) infringed by the movement of goods across the customs border of Ukraine has the right to apply for registration of such an IP protected object in the customs register.[46] After registration of the object in this customs register of the objects of IP rights, the customs authorities

[46] Customs Code of Ukraine 2012, 4495-VI, art 398(2).

shall take measures to ensure the protection of these IP rights.[47] In particular, if a third party submits a customs clearance declaration for goods suspected of infringing IP rights included in the register the customs authorities may temporarily suspend the customs clearance of such goods.[48]

In cases where the inclusion of a certain object of IP rights in the customs register is refused, the rightsholder may appeal in court. Since the appeal in such a case will be against the customs authority's decision—meaning that the nature of the dispute would be public—such a dispute would fall under the jurisdiction of the administrative courts. However, as with the previous category of cases, the adjudication of such disputes requires a detailed analysis of the relevant IP rights. In particular, the court would need to assess the object with respect to which the registration was requested; whether any patents and trademark certificates that support the registration exist; whether there is any other rightsholder who challenges these patents and trademark certificates; and whether there are sufficient grounds for the refusal to include a protected object on the register, etc. Such cases require a thorough analysis of IP-related matters, as well as an in-depth understanding of IP law.

Some cases in this category can be rather complex. For example, in 2018 the Dnipropetrovsk District Administrative Court considered a dispute related to a registered design. In particular, the owner of a design "Humana" (No. 29851, issued in 2015) requested the customs authority to include this design in the customs register of IP rights under the section "baby food packaged for retail sale". The request was rejected by the customs authority, which explained that this design was registered under Class 32 "graphic symbols and logos, textural patterns, ornaments" and that the scope of legal protection provided under this registered design covers only logos and does not cover any other goods including baby food packaged for retail sale. The owner of the design appealed the decision and the court therefore had to establish the scope of protection by the registered design, namely whether it applies to baby food packaged for retail sale. During the hearing, the customs authority, acting as the defendant, also informed the court that in accordance with the international registration in 2007 the trademark "HUMANA" was protected in Ukraine, including in relation to baby food. Moreover, while this case was pending, the owner of that trademark filed a lawsuit in the civil court to invalidate the design "Humana" (No. 29851), which was later invalidated by the civil court. The administrative court rejected the design owner's lawsuit on these grounds.[49] However, had the design not been challenged, the administrative court would have needed to examine it to determine the scope of protection it provided, and establish whether the refusal to include the design in the customs register was correct. Therefore, this dispute was based on IP law rather than the customs procedures. As a result, if the assessment of a case requires knowledge and application of IP law, such a case may be more appropriate to refer to the IP Court rather than administrative courts.

---

[47] Ibid art 398(5).

[48] Ibid art 399.

[49] Dnipropetrovsk District Administrative Court, Decision 72707259 (2018) 804/576/16.

3.2.2 Tax-Related Disputes Concerning IP Rights

In Ukraine, all tax disputes fall under the jurisdiction of the administrative courts. However, in some cases tax issues are closely intertwined with IP law and it is the latter that becomes primary for resolving the dispute. This applies, for example, to cases concerning royalties. The Tax Code defines royalty as a payment received as a remuneration for the use or granting of the right to use the object of IP rights.[50] Under Ukrainian law royalty payment transactions are not subject to a value added tax (VAT).[51] This means that a company that receives a royalty is not required to pay VAT on the amount of that royalty. However, disputes on whether the payment is a royalty often arise when a company receives or pays a fee, but, as a result of a tax audit, the tax authority decides that this payment is not a royalty, and therefore requires the company to pay VAT. The company may consequently challenge this decision before the court. While (as was mentioned above) these are considered to be tax disputes, the primary matters are not tax issues but those related to IP rights. The court would need to determine whether the object of the payment is IP protected; whether the actual use of this object relates to the type of use covered by the royalty; and whether the recipient of the royalty owns IP rights that protect this object. In such disputes, knowledge of tax law would be secondary since resolving this case requires knowledge of IP law and not tax law. The Tax Code contains certain additional rules related to royalties. An example of one of these rules is that royalties do not include payment for the right to distribute copies of software products without the right to reproduce them.[52] However, even in this case, the court must analyze the contract in order to determine the content of the rights under the contract. Only after establishing all the issues related to IP rights will the court be able to conclude whether the payment is a royalty and, accordingly, is exempt from payment of VAT.

Judicial practice in Ukraine contains a significant number of cases which require the administrative courts to analyse tax disputes related to IP while having limited or no knowledge of it. This lack of knowledge of IP often leads to the administrative courts failing to resolve the dispute correctly. An example of this is related to the supply of software products.[53] A company supplied software products by selling household appliances with the activation key for such software. After the audit the tax authority decided that the remuneration for such operations should be subject to VAT because the company was selling an activation key for a software product, and not the software product itself. The first instance administrative court noted that while transactions that involve the supply of software products for which the IP ownership is transferred are subject to VAT exemption, in this case there was no transfer of ownership to consumers. What was actually transferred was the right to use the IP object. Also, it was found that the fiscal receipts indicated the name of the product sold as an "activation key" rather than a "software product". Therefore,

---

[50] Tax Code of Ukraine 2010, 2755-VI, art 14(1)(225).

[51] Ibid art 196(1)(6).

[52] Ibid art 14(1)(225).

[53] Dnipropetrovsk Administrative Court of Appeal, Decision 72890364 (2018) 804/4301/17.

the court concluded that these transactions were subject to VAT. At the appeal, the Administrative Court of Appeals reached an opposite conclusion and decided that the electronic activation key is an integral component of a software product and ensures its functionality. Therefore, the fact that only the "activation code" was sold, was not supported by evidence. The court found that despite the name of a supplied product was incorrectly identified in fiscal receipts (an "activation key" instead of a "software product"), the activation key is an integral component of the application program which provides the use of the functionality of certain versions of the program. It is therefore a software product in the meaning of the Tax Code of Ukraine and so not subject to VAT.[54]

This example makes it clear that in such cases IP law issues are crucial when determining the merits of a case. It is true that the royalty disputes are diverse and may involve issues relating to other aspects of tax law. However, if the crux of a tax dispute is an IP right, it may be very difficult for the court to arrive at a correct conclusion without knowledge of IP law. Therefore, such cases are more suited to be considered by the IP Court rather than the administrative courts.

3.3 IP-Related Disputes that Require Clarification

Certain IP-related cases require further clarification regarding their jurisdiction, as some potentially may fall within the jurisdiction of the administrative courts, while others may fall within the jurisdiction of the civil courts. In addition, some cases that potentially fall within the jurisdiction of the IP Court raise questions as to the exact procedure under which they should be considered. Although the CPC clearly regulates the procedure for hearing disputes in the first, appeal and cassation instances, for some cases the law is silent about the applicable procedure.

3.3.1 Disputes Related to the Refusal to Register IP Rights

The jurisdiction of the IP Court under Art. 20(2)(2) CPC covers a wide range of disputes related to registration of IP rights.[55] This provision does not mention appeals on the refusal to register an IP right, however. Appeals on the refusal to register an IP right may be covered by the phrase "disputes concerning registration [...] of IP rights". Where registration is refused, however, this provision can also be construed as not including such disputes, as the registration has not occurred and there is therefore no dispute concerning registration as such. The lack of reference to such a dispute may therefore create confusion as to which court should consider such cases. Under the Code of Administrative Proceedings these cases have fallen within the jurisdiction

---

[54] Dnipropetrovsk Administrative Court of Appeal, Decision 72890364 (2018) 804/4301/17.

[55] E.g. disputes concerning third party challenges on the registration of an IP right based on its violation of their own IP right.

of the administrative courts on the grounds of being appeals on decisions, actions or inaction of state authorities.[56] As the CPC does not explicitly mention such cases they may be considered as remaining formally within the jurisdiction of the administrative courts.[57]

In fact, the administrative courts have handled such disputes for many years. However, in May 2019, in a case related to an appeal upon the refusal to register a trademark, the Grand Chamber of the Supreme Court concluded that such disputes (including in relation to other IP rights) concern IP rights and should therefore not be considered under administrative proceedings. The Court emphasised that it is incorrect to extend the jurisdiction of administrative courts to a dispute only because the defendant in such a case was a state authority and its decision was being appealed. What should determine whether a case falls under the administrative jurisdiction is its essence (i.e. content, or nature). Public law disputes which are considered by the administrative courts are disputes between the parties to a public law relationship. However, since the essence of this case is IP and not public law related, it should not be considered by the administrative courts.[58] The Court then determined the jurisdiction based on the type of the party to the dispute, i.e. the dispute fell within the jurisdiction of the commercial court because the plaintiff in this particular case was a private enterprise.[59] According to the current rules such a dispute would be heard in the civil court if the plaintiff is a natural person. This is the current practice of establishing a jurisdiction in such cases.[60]

The conclusions of the Supreme Court on what should be regarded as a public law dispute raise an interesting issue. On the one hand, in May 2019 the registration of IP rights could be considered to be administrative services which were provided by a specifically authorised state body. Under this approach, disputes concerning such services fell under the definition of a public law dispute in accordance with the Code of Administrative Proceedings.[61] On the other hand, the approach changed in June 2020. It is now considered that actions related to the protection of IP rights are not administrative services.[62] This therefore means that, at present, disputes related to the registration of IP rights should not be covered by the jurisdiction of the administrative courts.

[56] Ukrainian Code of Administrative Proceedings, art 19(1).

[57] See e.g. Decision of the District Administrative Court of Kyiv (2018) regarding the annulment of the decision on the refusal to register a trade mark under the application for the registration m201409130 and the obligation to undertake such registration of a trade mark 826/4752/16; Kyiv Appellate Administrative Court, Decision (2018) 826/15329/16 on the annulment of the state registration of a trade mark.

[58] Supreme Court, the Grand Chamber, Order 82420761 (2019) 826/15263/18.

[59] Ibid.

[60] See e.g. Pechersk District Court of Kyiv, Decision 95704237 (2021) 757/45469/20-ц, in which the dispute related to an appeal on the refusal to grant a patent to a natural person was considered by the civil court.

[61] Ukrainian Code of Administrative Proceedings, art 4(1), (2).

[62] Ukrainian Law on the Amendments to Some Laws of Ukraine on the Establishment of a National Intellectual Property Authority 2020, 703-IX, art 9.

This decision by the Supreme Court seems to resolve the confusion regarding the jurisdiction of such cases, and once the IP Court becomes fully operational they will fall under its jurisdiction. However, even after the Supreme Court's decision the administrative courts continue to hear disputes regarding appeals against the refusal to register IP rights. For example, in September 2020, one such dispute was heard and decided on the merits by the first instance administrative court.[63] When appealed, the Administrative Court of Appeals reversed this decision, following the Supreme Court's position mentioned above. However, it indicated that the disputes concerning the protection of IP rights are civil law disputes and should be considered by the civil court.[64] Such a finding has further muddied the waters in the discussion on the jurisdiction of such disputes. In both the cases discussed above the plaintiffs were legal entities, while the defendant was an entity that has the power to register IP rights. No natural person was a party to these disputes, which would trigger the jurisdiction of the civil courts. Thus, while the Supreme Court ruled that the dispute over the refusal to register IP rights fell within the jurisdiction of the commercial court, the Administrative Court of Appeals drew attention to the civil nature of the dispute and referred it to the jurisdiction of the civil courts. The latter case is currently under cassation in the Grand Chamber of the Supreme Court.[65] This raises the question on whether the court will confirm its conclusions that the commercial courts should consider such cases, or come to a different conclusion. This, however, makes it potentially possible that competition between the IP Court and the civil courts over this type of dispute may arise. To avoid this, it would be advisable to supplement the CPC with a provision stating that disputes on appealing the refusal to register IP rights should be heard by the IP Court.

3.3.2 Recognition of a Trademark as Well Known

In Ukraine, the recognition of a trademark as well known may be conducted in two types of proceedings. Article 25 Law on Trademarks defines that such a recognition may be performed either by the Appellate Chamber of the National Authority for Intellectual Property (Appellate Chamber) or the court.[66] An out-of-court recognition can be done upon the request of a trademark owner before the Appellate Chamber, who must provide evidence demonstrating that the trademark is well known with respect to particular goods or services.[67] The law establishes a detailed procedure for this type of recognition.[68] The procedure includes a list of possible evidence

[63] District Administrative Court of Kyiv, Decision 92041356 (2020) 640/22143/19.

[64] Administrative Court of Appeals, Order 95611071 (2021) 640/22143/19.

[65] Grand Chamber of the Supreme Court, Order 97506809 (2021) 640/22143/19.

[66] Ukrainian Law on the Protection of Right for Signs on Goods and Services 1993, N 3689-XII.

[67] Regulations of the Appellate Chamber of the National Authority for Intellectual Property, approved by the order of the Ministry of Economic Development, Trade and Agriculture of Ukraine 2021, 610/36232, Chapter IV.

[68] Ibid.

which may prove the intensity and duration of the trademark use on the territory of Ukraine, as well as other factors confirming that the trademark is particularly famous.

At the same time, according to Art. 20 CPC, the IP Court may also recognise a trademark as well known.[69] However, the CPC does not define the procedure for such recognition by the IP Court. In cases where there is a dispute between the parties, the recognition of a trademark as well known by the IP Court would be conducted under the general rules of procedure that govern the adjudication of commercial disputes. However, if an IP owner were to petition the IP Court to recognise a trademark as well known in cases where there is no dispute, the general procedure for considering disputes between the parties would not apply. Similarly, the procedure developed by the Appellate Chamber would not apply either. As a result, it is unclear under what procedure such recognition should be performed in cases where there is no dispute.

It may be the case that the drafters of the new CPC intended that the recognition of a trademark as well known by the IP Court would take place only in a proceeding when there is a dispute about the use of a trademark. In such a case, the lawsuit for recognising the trade mark as well known would need to be filed together with the claim to prohibit the defendant from using the trademark in dispute and, depending on the circumstances, to perform some other actions (for example, to compensate damages). However, in such a case the dispute would relate to the protection of trademark rights. This is covered by a separate provision in the CPC, namely, Art. 20(2)(1). The recognition of a trademark as well known is not an independent category of cases where there is no dispute. As a result, the absence of a separate procedure for recognition of a trademark as well known in the CPC may force its owner to contrive a dispute in order to get their trade mark recognised as well known in the IP Court.

To avoid these challenges for the trademark rightsholders, it may be advisable to clearly define the jurisdiction of the IP Court and the Appellate Chamber, so that the former would consider cases on the recognition of trademarks as well known where there is a dispute between the parties, while the latter would consider cases where there is no such dispute. Finally, the appeals against the decisions of the Appellate Chamber would then fall within the jurisdiction of the IP Court, which should be included in Art. 20 CPC.

3.3.3 Overlapping Jurisdiction Between the IP Court and the Civil Courts

There is also a type of dispute in which the jurisdiction of the IP Court and the civil courts could potentially coincide. In commercial litigation there is a special type of proceeding in the form of a court order[70] which is designed to recover a debt under a contract if such a debt does not exceed 100 times the living wage.[71] This procedure is convenient because it allows the debt to be recovered in an expeditious

[69] Commercial Procedural Code, art 20(2)(3).

[70] Commercial Procedural Code, arts 147–160.

[71] In 2021, one hundred subsistence minimums for employable persons were about 7,900 EUR.

manner without a lengthy trial. The court considers such an application for a debt recovery within five days of its receipt without conducting a hearing with the participation of the applicant and the debtor.[72] The procedure in the form of a court order can be applied to all contracts, including those that involve IP rights (e.g. license agreements).

At the same time, a certain category of IP rightsholders cannot take advantage of this simplified procedure because the CPC puts the limit on who can use it. The parties to this procedure may only be legal entities and natural persons with entrepreneur status.[73] An entrepreneurial status is a formal legal status that can be obtained by individuals by means of state registration.[74] It allows a natural person to conduct commercial (business) activities without establishing a legal entity. However, this status is not mandatory. The author or inventor may own and license their IP rights as a natural person without any registration. A natural person may also use the rights under a contract concluded with another rightsholder. Due to the limitations in the CPC, however, the creditor will not be able to use the procedure in the form of a court order to recover a debt under such a contract because they do not meet the requirements envisaged in the CPC. The only recourse available to such individuals is to rely on the general procedure in the IP Court. However, resolving a dispute under the general procedure may take several months as compared with five days under the court order proceedings. This therefore provides unequal opportunities to different types of plaintiffs, limiting their right to judicial protection without any reasonable justification. It should be noted that the Civil Procedural Code that applies to disputes between natural persons contains a similar proceeding in the form of a court order.[75] However, it is not clear whether a creditor would be able to apply for a debt recovery with the civil court if a dispute would relate to the execution of a contract in the field of IP law. The latter types of contracts under Art. 20(2)(5) CPC are within the competence of the IP Court. Moreover, it may be possible for the civil court to refuse to consider such an application because it does not fall within its jurisdiction. This may lead to a situation in which the creditor in such cases would not be able to use the court order proceedings either in the IP Court, or in the civil courts. This gap should be resolved as otherwise this would violate the fundamental principles of equal access to justice.

[72] Commercial Procedural Code, art 154(1).

[73] Ibid art 147(3).

[74] Ukrainian Law on the State Registration of Legal Entities, Natural Persons-Entrepreneurs and Civil Organisations 2003, 755-IV.

[75] Civil Procedural Code, arts 160–173 (such proceedings originally emerged in civil litigation, where they proved to be effective and were later adopted in commercial litigation).

4 Conclusions

The establishment and effective operation of an IP court is a policy-driven decision aimed at encouraging innovation, facilitating investment and guaranteeing the protection of the IP rightsholders' interests. The creation of a specialised IP court in Ukraine is an important element of the current judicial reform that is aimed at improving the operation of its judicial system and enhancing the system of IP protection and enforcement as part of the country's international obligations. Despite some positive changes in the area of IP protection and enforcement during the last decade, Ukraine still remains part of the USTR 301 Report under "Priority Watch List".[76] It is therefore believed that the establishment of the specialised IP Court in Ukraine will improve protection by creating high quality jurisprudence, signaling to individuals and businesses that their investments in IP will be effectively protected. Such a result can be seen from the operation of IP judiciary in other mature jurisdictions, such as the UK, France, Germany, the Netherlands and the US, which consistently increase the specialisation of their judiciaries in the field of IP. This, in turn, positively influences the quality of IP jurisprudence in these jurisdictions.

For the IP Court to successfully function its jurisdiction must be clearly defined. As discussed in this Chapter, however, there are certain gaps in the scope of its jurisdiction that may lead to overlaps with other courts and state authorities. In particular, the analysis of customs and tax disputes involving an IP element demonstrated that it would be more appropriate for such cases to be considered by the IP Court rather than the administrative courts, as it is currently the case. This is because for such cases the application of IP law is key to resolving the dispute, while the customs border procedures or tax law are secondary. Similarly, the procedures for recognising a trademark as well known, and for appeals against the decisions on the refusal to register an IP right, should be clarified. Finally, to avoid the overlaps between the jurisdiction of the IP Court and the civil courts (or inability to use any of these courts altogether) natural persons should be allowed to use the simplified proceeding in the form of a court order for small debt recoveries. We believe that the clarifications of these gaps in the exclusive jurisdiction of the new IP Court in Ukraine will contribute to the efficient functioning of this Court, as well as the IP enforcement system in general.

References

Advisory Council on Intellectual Property, 'Should the Jurisdiction of the Federal Magistrates Service be Extended to Include Patent, Trademark and Design Matters?' (2003) 2 https://www.ipaustralia.gov.au/sites/default/files/final_report_extending_jurisdiction_of_federal_magistrates.pdf?acsf_files_redirect

[76] See USTR '2021 Special 301 Report', USTR 2021, 59 (the Report 2021 specifically mentions the creation of the new IP court, i.e. "Progress continues, albeit slowly, to establish a fully functional specialized Intellectual Property High Court, legislatively enacted in 2017").

Democracy Reporting International 'Ukraine's New Intellectual Property High Court: Implications for the Justice System' (2018) https://democracy-reporting.org/en/office/ukraine/news/ukraines-new-high-intellectual-property-court-implications-for-the-justice-system

European Commission 'Making the Most of the EU's Innovative Potential. An Intellectual Property Action Plan to Support the EU's Recovery and Resilience' (Communication) COM(2020) 760 final

European Commission, 'A Balanced IP Enforcement System Responding to Today's Societal Challenges' (Communication) COM(2017) 707 final

International Bar Association, 'International Survey of Specialised Intellectual Property Courts and Tribunals' (2007) 3

International Chamber of Commerce, 'Adjudicating Intellectual Property Disputes' (Report) ICC 2016

International Intellectual Property Institute and United States Patent and Trademark Office, 'Study on Specialized Intellectual Property Courts' IIPI and USPTO 2012

Judicial Authority in Ukraine, 'The High IP Court has been Registered' (2020) https://court.gov.ua/press/news/889183/ [Судова Влада України, 'Зареєстровано Вищий Суд з Питань Інтелектуальної Власності' (2020)]

Nina Kucheruk, 'IP High court: Who? When? Where?' (18 October 2017) *Yurydychna Gazeta* http://yur-gazeta.com/publications/practice/sudova-praktika/vishchiy-ipsud-hto-de-koli.html [Ніна Кучерук, 'Вищий IP-суд: Хто, Де, Коли?' (18 жовтня 2017) *Юридична Газета*]

Roman Kuybida and Roman Smalyuk, 'Where Did the IP Court Come From and Where Did it Disappear?' (2019) Reanimation Reform Package https://rpr.org.ua/news/zvidky-vziavsia-i-kudy-znyk-ip-sud/ [Роман Куйбіда та Роман Смалюк, 'Звідки Взявся і Куди Зник IP-Суд?' (2019) Реанімаційний Пакет Реформ]

National Strategy for the Development of the Sphere of Intellectual Property in Ukraine for the Period up to 2020, 2014 (unofficial text) https://uba.ua/documents/ip-strategy28082014.pdf [Національна Стратегія Розвитку Сфери Інтелектуальної Власності в Україні на Період до 2020 Року, 2014 (неофіційний текст)]

Yuriy Neclesa, 'Problems of Realisation of the Patent Justice in Ukraine' (2018) 3 Comparative-analytical law 114 [Юрій Неклеса, 'Проблеми Реалізації Патентної Юстиції в Україні' (2018) 3 Порівняльно-Аналітичне Право 114]

Svitlana Parkhomchuk, 'Ways of Introducing Bodies of Patent Jurisdiction into the Ukrainian Judicial System' (2012) Problems of Civil and Commercial Law in Ukraine [Світланаа Пархомчук, 'Шляхи Впровадження в Судову Систему України Органів Патентної Юрисдикції' (2012) Проблеми Цивільного та Підприємницького Права в Україні]

Tetiana Pashkovska, 'The Intellectual Property High Court is on the Finish Line' (2017) *Yurydychna Gazeta* http://yur-gazeta.com/publications/actual/vishchiy-intelektualniy-sud-na-finishniy-pryamiy.html [Тетяна Пашковська, 'Вищий «Інтелектуальний» Суд: на Фінішній Прямій' (2017) *Юридична Газета*]

Mykola Pototsky and Mariya Zakharenko, 'A Specialised Court that Considers Disputes Related to Intellectual Property in Ukraine: a Mistake or Necessity?' (2014) 3 Legal Bulletin 201 [Микола Потоцький та Марія Захаренко, 'Спеціалізований Суд із Розгляду Справ у Сфері Інтелектуальної Власності в Україні: Помилка чи Необхідність?' (2014) 3 Юридичний Вісник 201]

The announcement of the High Qualifications Commission of Judges 2017 [Оголошення Вищої Кваліфікаційної Комісії Суддів 2017]

Ukraine DFID/FCO IP Court Project: the Final Report (2020) Centre for the Commercial Legal Studies, Queen Mary University of London ('Final Report') https://www.qmul.ac.uk/media/qmul/media/2019/Report_QM_10.28_ENG.pdf.

Ukrainian Bar Association, 'Patent Court: Pros and Cons' (2015) http://vgsu.arbitr.gov.ua/news/1851/ [Асоціація Правників України, 'Патентний суд: За та Проти' (2015)]

United Kingdom Intellectual Property Office, 'Protecting Creativity, Supporting Innovation: IP Enforcement 2020' (Strategy on IP Enforcement) 2016

United States Trade Representative, '2021 Special 301 Report', USTR 2021
United States Trade Representative, 'Ukraine Designated as Priority Foreign Country Under Special 301' (2001) https://ustr.gov/archive/Document_Library/Press_Releases/2001/March/Ukraine_Designated_as_Priority_Foreign_Country_Under_Special_301.html
World Bank, 'Intellectual Property Rights and Economic Development' (WDP 412, Discussion Paper)
World Intellectual Property Organization, 'Building Respect for Intellectual Property' https://www.wipo.int/enforcement/en/

Legislative Reforms on Patents, Utility Models and Industrial Designs in Ukraine

Leonid Tarasenko

Contents

L. Tarasenko (✉)
Intellectual Property, Information and Corporate Law Department, Ivan Franko National University of Lviv, Lviv, Ukraine
e-mail: leonid.tarasenko@lnu.edu.ua

H. Richter (ed.), *Competition and Intellectual Property Law in Ukraine*,
MPI Studies on Intellectual Property and Competition Law 31,
https://doi.org/10.1007/978-3-662-66101-7_15

Abstract This chapter is devoted to the characteristics of Ukrainian patent law, which regulates the relationship of granting, exercise, termination and protection of intellectual property rights to inventions, utility models and industrial designs. The questions are of high current relevance, due to the implementation of the last Ukrainian patent law reform, which took place in 2020. The chapter elaborates the history and characteristics of the current state of legal regulation and identifies associated problems and the prospects for improvement. It focuses on the main innovations of patent legislation on inventions, utility models and industrial designs, including the procedure for granting and exercising exclusive rights. Furthermore, it describes of the status of the National Intellectual Property Authority and discusses its role in protecting industrial property rights.

1 Relevance

Inventions, utility models and industrial designs are objects of patent law that need proper legal protection. In 2020, a comprehensive reform of industrial property law took place in Ukraine, including a reform of patent law. Prior to 2020, the most recent changes to the laws governing patent relations were made in 2012. Reforming industrial property law in Ukraine is one of the stages in the implementation of the Association Agreement concluded between Ukraine and the EU, in which a significant part of the provisions relate to the reform of intellectual property law.[1] While considering the reform of patent law in 2020, this chapter covers the following issues: the formation and development of industrial property law in Ukraine; objects of patent law (what may or may not be protected by law as an invention, a utility model or an industrial design); the conditions for granting legal protection to inventions, utility models and industrial designs; the exercise and protection of intellectual property rights in objects of patent law, including the introduction of out-of-court procedure for protection of patent rights (post grant opposition). This chapter also analyses the legal status of the national intellectual property body as a national patent office.

[1] See Yuriy Kapitsa, 'Association Agreements and Problems Approximating Intellectual Property Legislation of Third Countries with the EU Acquis: The Case of Ukraine' in this Volume.

2 Objects of Patent Law: Legal Nature and Significance

Traditionally in Ukraine, as in the EU Member States, inventions and utility models are the results of an intellectual and creative activity of people in any field of technology, while industrial designs are the result of an intellectual and creative activity of people in the field of artistic creation. Thus, Ukrainian legislation clearly distinguishes between an invention (and utility model) and an industrial design as separate objects of industrial property law, which have their own legal nature. In accordance with the legislation of Ukraine, industrial design is not considered a copyright object but is rather classified as an object of patent law. This is reflected in the provisions of the Civil Code of Ukraine, which in a separate part of the article on the objects of intellectual property rights includes inventions, utility models and industrial designs.

Inventions and utility models are primarily technical solutions aimed at protecting technology and innovations. Patents therefore play an important role in confirming the intellectual property rights of the owners of these technological and innovation solutions. The law interprets a patent as a document, which indicates the priority, authorship and intellectual property rights to the invention (utility model).[2] Analysing the convergence of the provisions of national Ukrainian legislation and theories of intellectual property rights, it is worth noting that in Ukraine today patent laws reflect the theory of exclusive rights (independence of intellectual property from property rights), but not proprietary theory (belonging of intellectual property to the property rights). Although in judicial practice sometimes there are court decisions which recognize the ownership of certain intellectual property.

The absolute number of patents for inventions and utility models and certificates (patents) for industrial designs is relatively small in Ukraine when compared with the EU and the US. Statistical indicators for the last few years show the following number of granted patents (certificates) in Ukraine: *inventions* in 2019—2,200 patents, in 2020—2,200 patents, in 2021—2,400 patents; *utility models* in 2019—8,400 patents, in 2020—6,400 patents, in 2021—4,500 patents; *industrial designs* in 2019—2,600 patents, in 2020—2,000 patents (certificates), and in 2021—1,900 certificates.[3] Ukraine is not among the leading countries in the number of patents granted for inventions (and the gap is significant—the number of patents granted annually in the first five countries amounts to several hundred thousand[4]), but in terms of utility model patents, Ukraine ranks comparably high. This can be explained by the different legal regimes of utility models in different countries, which affects the possibility of patenting them.[5] However, this does not mean that the invention and development of designs in Ukraine are at a low level. There may be various reasons for the small

[2] Ukrainian Law on Protection of Rights to Inventions and Utility Models 1994, 3687-XII, art 1.

[3] 'Statistics of Ukrpatent' Ukrpatent 2021 https://ukrpatent.org/uk/articles/statistics accessed 31 December 2021.

[4] 'Intellectual Property Statistics' WIPO 2021 https://www.wipo.int/ipstats/en/ accessed 31 December 2021.

[5] Draft National Intellectual Property Strategy of Ukraine for the Period 2020–2025 https://drive.google.com/file/d/1oqjabxZiTempwJjaZsO1NoLt7fvP_qxj/view accessed 31 December 2021.

number of granted patent certificates, including, for example, the ignorance of inventors or designers about the provisions of patent law, an unwillingness to patent, and a lack of financial capacity to patent and/or further commercialize the use of patents.[6] In Ukraine, there is a declining trend in the registration of patent law objects due to the shortcomings of the patent system in Ukraine as a whole. According to the draft of National Strategy for the Development of Intellectual Property in Ukraine for the period 2020–2025,[7] Ukraine has weak patents that monopolized a certain part of the market in certain areas of the economy. This enables patent trolling (the unfair use of patent rights) which virtually deprives the important and dynamic information technology (IT) industry of the ability to use patent protection. A patent is often perceived by inventors not as a security document, but as a necessity, because the absence of a patent is a sign of inferiority in the eyes of potential investors.[8] In the scientific literature some authors rightly emphasize that measures to strengthen inventive activity should be introduced straight away. These could include new financial and tax mechanisms to support the creation and use of patent law objects; improved legal protection of patent law objects created at the expense of the budget; the addressing of problems concerning the commercialization of objects of inventive activity; improvement of the system of payment of fees for obtaining security documents; and the introduction of training for specialists in innovation, technology transfer and intellectual property.[9] Of course, the quality of legal regulation should also assist inventors and designers in patenting their technical and design solutions. Therefore, the reform of patent law that took place in 2020 is important in solving the problems in the field of invention mentioned above.

The following sections will discuss the formation and development of patent law in Ukraine from 1991 to the present (Sec. 3); the content of industrial property reform 2020 (Sec. 4.1); the legal status of the National Intellectual Property Authority (NIPA) (Sec. 4.2); legal regulation of inventions and utility models (Sec. 4.3); and the legal regulation of industrial designs (Sec. 4.4). Finally, the chapter will draw a conclusion (Sec. 5).

3 Development of Industrial Property Regulation After 1991

The patent legislation of Ukraine went through several stages of development that were determined by the specific historical periods that Ukraine lived through:

(1) 1991–2004—the establishment of national industrial property law.

---

[6] See more about the development of inventive activity: Yuriy Kapitsa et al., *Inventive Activity in Academic Organisations* (Logos 2021).

[7] See Olena Orluik, 'Strategic Directions of the Intellectual Property Area Development in Ukraine' in this Volume.

[8] Draft National Intellectual Property Strategy of Ukraine for the period 2020–2025 (n 5).

[9] See more Kapitsa et al. (n 6) 56.

(2) 2004–2014—the development of national patent legislation.
(3) 2014 to now—the harmonization of national patent legislation with EU law and improvement of legislation, considering the development of the digital environment.

3.1 *Period 1991–2004*

The first stage of the development of patent law is characterized by the fact that national legislation on the legal protection of inventions, utility models and industrial designs began to be established. The role and significance of the objects of patent law were grossly underestimated during the existence of the USSR.[10] Legal regulation was incomplete because market relations were absent at that time and patent rights mainly belonged to state enterprises (and indeed actually to the state). Patents were used by the state and were not usually in civil circulation due to the lack of a market economy. Almost all patentees had the status of employees, and the inventions or utility models had a legal regime of service inventions in which all property rights belonged to the enterprises. After Ukraine attained independence its transition to the market economy led to the retention of many state-owned enterprises and the "exit" of patents to the capital market, something that is widely acknowledged.[11]

The first Ukrainian laws on industrial property—the Ukrainian Law on the protection of rights to inventions and utility models and on protection of rights to industrial designs—were adopted only in December 1993. With their adoption the objects of patent law received legal regulation and their legal regime was defined. Of course, it would not be correct to state that no legislative regulation of patent relations existed before 1993. Numerous provisions of the Civil Code of the Ukrainian Soviet Socialist Republic (the main act of the civil legislation) were in force. But the number of these rules was insignificant, so they only enshrined the main principles of the regulation of patent relations. It is noteworthy that the Civil Code of the Ukrainian Soviet Socialist Republic regulated certain aspects of the creation and use of inventions, utility models and industrial designs. But these norms were not enough for the proper definition of their legal. These rules could serve only as the basic principles of legal regulation.

In 1994–1995, several bylaws were passed giving detail to the laws of 1993. Among them were rules for drawing up and filing an application for a Ukrainian patent for an invention and utility model; instructions for preparing a description of a patent for an invention or utility model for publication; and rules for drawing up and filing an application for a Ukrainian patent for an industrial design, etc. These acts

[10] Michael Hoseh, 'The USSR Patent System' (1960) 4 Patent, Trademark and Copyright Journal of Research and Education 220; Betsy Ancker-Johnson, 'Technology Exchange with the USSR: Patents and Licenses' (1974) 17(4) Research Management Journal 14.

[11] Igor Yegorov, 'Post-Soviet Science: Difficulties in the Transformation of the R&D Systems in Russia and Ukraine' (2009) 38(4) Research Policy Journal 600; Elena Tverytnykova and Maryna Gutnyk, 'The Patent-license System of Ukraine in the Second Half of the XX Century' (2020) 29(2) Journal Studies in the History and Philosophy of Science and Technology 76.

were adopted by the State Patent Office (National Patent Office of Ukraine) and were important because they defined the patenting procedure and set the requirements for the application, the rules for filing and the procedure for reviewing applications. It is impossible and impractical in the law to delve into the procedural aspects of patenting. Therefore, this procedure should be provided for in the bylaws.

In 2000 the legislation on inventions, utility models and industrial designs was updated with the Law of Ukraine on the Protection of the Rights to inventions and utility models being published in a new edition. These legislative amendments became the basis of the legal regulation of relations with respect to the acquisition, exercise and protection of rights to inventions and utility models. This version of the law (with subsequent amendments and additions) is still in force today. Generally speaking, legislators had already carried out an effective reform of the part of the legislation on industrial property. These changes can be considered as historic for the following reasons.

First, the activity and legal status of the Ukrainian Institute of Intellectual Property (Ukrpatent, the examination institution for patent applications) and the Institution/Ustanova (the Central State Executive Body) were separated. Prior to the adoption of these changes, the State Patent Office was the only body examining patent applications and granting patents for inventions, utility models and industrial designs. However, the new legislative approach divided these functions between two subjects. The State Patent Office (now Ukrpatent) has been accepting and examining applications since 2000. Consideration of applications includes formal, qualification examination. Based on its examinations, the Ukrpatent issues a positive or negative opinion on the possibility of granting a patent. However, the actual granting of patents has been the competence of the Institution. Throughout the years 2000–2020 the functions of the Institution were performed by the Ministry of Education and Science, by the Ministry of Economy and by the State Service for Intellectual Property. Such a legislative approach does not correspond to European state systems of legal protection of industrial property.

Second, several amendments to the law on invention and utility model patents were made. In particular, the definitions of "invention" and "utility model" were amended, the law was supplemented by the possibility of granting a declarative patent for the invention for six years, and the period of validity of the patent for the utility model was amended. Thus, up to the year 2000 the utility model was regarded as a constructive execution of the product. These legislative amendments proposed a single definition of an invention and utility model produced by the intellectual activity of a person in any field of technology. The possibility of granting a declaratory patent for an invention (as a kind of patent) established by this law is debatable.[12] In particular, a declarative patent for an invention was granted by the patent office after a formal examination, which contributed to the rapid patenting of the technology.

---

[12] Leonid Tarasenko, 'Patent Law' in Oleksandra Yavorska et al., *Intellectual Law of Ukraine* (Textbooks and Manuals 2016) 219 (609); Olena Orliuk et al., *Intellectual Property Law* (In Yure 2007) 350; Olena Kharytonova, *Intellectual Property Law* (Yurinkom Inter 2015) 544; Eugene Grekov, 'Legal Regulation of Patenting Treatments in Ukraine and the World: Current Status and Prospects' (2013) 1 Bulletin of the Academy of Legal Sciences of Ukraine 114.

Furthermore, the patentee could challenge the commercial viability of the patented technology, and if the patent was found to work and be capable of generating revenue, it could be converted from a declaratory patent to a full patent (by filing an application for a qualifying examination and deciding on the grant of a patent by the patent office). These legal provisions were amended in 2020 by the law, which substantially reformed the national legislation.[13]

Considering this stage, one may note that national legislation on industrial property in general (and patent law in particular) has been established and developed. The adopted laws laid the foundation for more than ten years for the legal regulation of patent relations.

3.2 *Period 2004–2014*

The start of second stage in the development of the national Ukrainian patent legislation was the adoption of the Civil Code of Ukraine, which had a significant impact on the establishment of the legal regime of inventions, utility models and industrial designs.

The Code included the fourth book of "Intellectual Property Law" which determined in detail the basic legal rules to protect all industrial property objects (patent rights objects, the means of individualization, the commercial secret, the rationalization proposal, etc.). Special attention should be paid to the general provisions on intellectual property, which had been specifically highlighted in national legislation for the first time.[14] Among them are important rules on the relationship between intellectual property rights and property rights; personal non-property (moral) and intellectual property rights; the distribution of rights to intellectual property, created in connection with the employment contract or to order; and on ways to protect intellectual property rights.

Regarding patent law, one may note the expansion of the list of utility model objects—the process was added as a patent object as a utility model. This led to the development of patent trolling, as the decision to expand the objects of the utility model was wrong and led to the weakening of patent protection of inventions in Ukraine as a whole, as through the utility model well-known processes and devices (i.e. obvious technical solutions) were patented.[15]

It was expected that in the future the special legislation in the field of patents and industrial designs would be brought in compliance with the provisions of the Civil Code of Ukraine. Currently this has happened only partially. Thus, there is still a tension between the Law of Ukraine on the protection of rights to Inventions and

---

[13] See Sec. 4.3.4 in this chapter.

[14] Civil Code of Ukraine 2003, 1089-IX, art 35.

[15] See more Kapitsa et al. (n 6) 23–25.

utility models and the Civil Code of Ukraine on the ownership of property patent rights in the case of a service invention.[16]

Subsequently, after the entry into force of the Civil Code of Ukraine, the legislation on industrial property developed rather slowly. During 2004–2014, very few amendments were made to most laws. On the one hand, this testified to a more-or-less appropriate legal framework for the functioning of patents and industrial designs. On the other hand there was a certain stagnation in the improvement of legal regulation, as public relations developed much faster than the rule of law. Objectively, it must be said that in ten years the state has failed to properly improve the legal framework (which is the basis of innovation).[17] It is, first and foremost, about stimulating invention and development of start-ups. Thus, in 2006 the Law of Ukraine on State Regulation of Activities in the Field of Technology Transfer was adopted. This, among other things, was aimed at "ensuring the effective use of scientific, technical and intellectual potential of Ukraine, manufacturability, protection of property rights to domestic technologies".[18] This law was not as effective as it should have been. The inventive process in Ukraine remained low, without proper support from the state. Statistics from Ukrpatent show that the number of applications for inventions gradually decreased between 2005 and 2014 from about 6000 in 2005 to 4800 in 2014 applications per year.[19] The number of applications for utility models in the same years balanced within 8000–9000 annually.[20] For the same period the same figures are hundreds of times higher in the EU and the US than in Ukraine.[21]

Therefore, the second period (2004–2014) can be described as a stage of stagnation in the development of national legislation on patents and industrial designs. Although the Civil Code of Ukraine was initially adopted as a basis for legal regulation and for further reform and improvement of laws in this area, these norms were not sufficient for the proper regulation of research relations. Only certain point changes can be characterized positively. In particular, the Law of Ukraine "On Protection of Industrial Designs" (2012) updated a number of legislative provisions on the procedure for examination of applications. The legislation on patents and industrial designs has hardly improved in the past ten years. When one considers that technical progress is based on new innovative technological solutions (patents), it's clear that this lack of progress has hindered efforts to attract investment to Ukraine, has stifled growth of innovative industrial production and has discouraged the development of start-ups in Ukraine.[22]

---

[16] The Civil Code of Ukraine states that these rights belong jointly to the employer and employee – but the special law states that these rights belong only to the employer as a person which has the right to file an application and the right to register a service invention (utility model).

[17] Draft National Intellectual Property Strategy of Ukraine for the period 2020–2025 (n 5).

[18] Ukrainian Law on State Regulation of Activities in the Field of Technology Transfer 2006, 143-V.

[19] Ukrpatent 2021 (n 3) accessed 31 December 2021.

[20] Ibid.

[21] Draft National Intellectual Property Strategy of Ukraine for the period 2020–2025 (n 5).

[22] Ibid.

During the second stage, no attention was paid to certain trends in patents, namely the development of the market for technology and innovation and the gradual decline of the already small number of applications for inventions, utility models and industrial designs.

3.3 Since 2014

The third stage can be described as the harmonization of national legislation on patents and industrial designs with EU law, along with the impact of digitalization on the development of legislation on patents and industrial designs.

A separate chapter in the EU–Ukraine Association Agreement (Association Agreement) is devoted to the regulation of intellectual property relations. Ukraine has undertaken to bring its national legislation in line with the provisions of the Association Agreement which pays a lot of attention to patents and industrial designs.[23] The purpose of improving national legislation in the field of industrial property is to strengthen its commercial component. It is a question of expansion of cooperation between Ukraine and the EU countries concerning commercial use of innovative products and other products of creative activity.

In 2016, the Government approved the "Concept of reforming the state system of legal protection of intellectual property in Ukraine".[24] It stressed the need to address the main problems in intellectual property sphere in general law (and particularly in patent law). These were the inability of the state to ensure the development of intellectual property as an important element of the national innovation system and the basis of innovative economy; the lack of significant progress in adapting the regulatory framework to modern economic conditions (the presence of "patent trolling", internet piracy, dissatisfaction with the needs of the IT industry, military-industrial and agro-industrial complexes, etc.); and the complicated system of state management in intellectual property sphere (the presence of Ukrpatent as an expert institution in the field of industrial property and authorities that grant patent documents—patents, certificates, etc.).

In 2019, the Draft of National Intellectual Property Strategy of Ukraine for the period 2020–2025 was developed.[25] Although this document was interpreted as a project, it played a significant role in the actual reform of intellectual property legislation. The basic principles of reforming the legislation on patents and industrial designs, which were described in the Draft National IP Strategy, were further reflected in the adopted laws in 2020.

In addition, at the third stage of reforming the legislation on patents and industrial designs, attention should be paid to the development of digital technologies and their

[23] EU–Ukraine Association Agreement 2014, art 212–222.

[24] Order of the Cabinet of Ministers of Ukraine 402-r of 1 June 2016 on the Concept of reforming the state system of legal protection of intellectual property in Ukraine.

[25] Draft National Intellectual Property Strategy of Ukraine for the period 2020–2025 (n 5).

impact on industrial property.[26] Society has been rapidly developing in the information and IT sphere in recent years. Access the internet is becoming a basic right. As people "live" in the digital environment, so industrial property develops new technologies and begins to be actively used on the internet and other digital technologies. Thus, the objects of patent law—especially inventions and utility models—often include technologies related to the digital environment (i.e. start-ups of a technological nature). The above-mentioned "computer implemented inventions" (inventions based on a computer program) are also becoming widespread. The procedure for acquiring intellectual property rights to such objects needs to be improved. Ways of using such objects may also have features due to the specifics of the digital environment and the internet. In fact, the above outlines the future steps necessary to improve the legal regulation of the use of patents and industrial designs. In addition, the issue of patentability of computer programs is still unresolved. Given the rapid development of the IT industry in Ukraine and the large number of relevant developments produced by IT specialists (each technical solution is based on programming), stagnation in the relevant legal field is unhelpful.

4 Reform of Industrial Property Law in 2020

4.1 Context of the Reform

Legislation in the sphere of industrial property needed to be significantly updated because public relations regarding the invention are developing rapidly. The lack of a proper legal basis created preconditions for numerous abuses and violations of the rights and interests of investors and right holders, especially through patent trolling and the lack of a statutory mechanism for revoking declaratory patents by the patent office (rather than invalidating them in court), real compensation for damages caused by actions infringing the rights to patents and industrial designs, etc.[27]

2020 was a turning point in the reform of industrial property, when three main legislative acts were adopted. These were on the establishment of a national intellectual property body; on strengthening the protection of rights to trademarks and industrial designs and the fight against patent abuse; and on the reform of patent

[26] See Gennady Androschuk, 'Trends in the Development of Artificial Intelligence Technology: Economic and Legal Aspect' (2019) 3 Journal of Theory and Practice of Intellectual Property 84; Igor Yakubivsky, 'Objects of Patent Law' (2021) 43 Journal Rule of Law 112; Oleksandra Yavorska et al., *IT law* (Levada 2017) 276–296.

[27] Roman Shishka, 'Countering Patent Trolling in Ukraine' (2017) 23 Journal of Civilization 73; Gennady Androschuk, 'Patent Trolling Against Innovations: State, Tendencies, Threats' (2013) 1 Journal Law and Innovation Society http://nbuv.gov.ua/UJRN/pric_2013_1_3 accessed 31 December 2021; Leonid Tarasenko, 'Protection of Intellectual Property Rights to Inventions (Utility Models) and Industrial Designs' (2016) 7 Journal Wroclaw-Lviv Legal Journals 247.

law.[28] These laws are an important regulator of patent relations as they contribute to the provision of adequate legal protection to inventions, utility models and industrial designs. Of course, not all problematic aspects of patents and industrial designs have been resolved (in terms of damages, recovery of compensation, inventions based on a computer program, etc. and some legislation needs to be specified at the level of bylaws (for example on the activities of the NIPA Chamber of Appeals). But the reform of patent law has taken place, and this is positively reflected in various aspects of patent law, particularly the acquisition of patent rights, and their exercise and protection.

The main issues of the patent law reform are as follows:

- The state system of legal protection of intellectual property has been changed (it now includes the Ministry of Economy of Ukraine, the National Intellectual Property Authority, other state enterprises and institutions operating in the field of intellectual property).
- The NIPA was established, the functions of which were later entrusted to Ukrpatent.[29]
- The concepts of the objects of invention, utility model and industrial design were newly defined and cannot be protected as objects of patent law.
- The final refusal of declaratory patents for inventions was accepted.
- The name of the protection document of an industrial design was changed (becoming a certificate rather than a patent).
- The conditions for granting legal protection to industrial designs have been improved by determining the conditions for protection (novelty and originality).
- Industrial designs were divided into registered and unregistered categories.
- The terms of validity of property rights to an industrial design have been changed.
- A mechanism to combat the so-called "evergreen patents" by improving the legal characteristics of the inventive step in the field of pharmaceuticals was introduced.
- The term of additional protection of rights to inventions in the field of pharmaceuticals was established (by introducing the Supplementary protection certificate).
- The electronic submission of applications for registration of inventions, utility models and industrial designs was introduced.
- Applicants can now divide their application for invention, utility model and industrial design.
- The content of the rights of the patent owner for an invention, the object of which is biological material or the process of obtaining biological material, has been improved.

[28] Ukrainian Law on Amendments to some Laws of Ukraine on the Establishment of a National Intellectual Property Body 2020, 703-IX; Ukrainian Law on Amendments to Some Laws of Ukraine Concerning Strengthening the Protection of Rights to Trademarks and Industrial Designs and Combating Patent Abuse 2020, 815-IX; Ukrainian Law on Amendments to Some Laws of Ukraine on Patent Law Reform 2020, 816-IX.

[29] Order of the Cabinet of Ministers of Ukraine 1267-r of 13 October 2020 on National Intellectual Property Body.

- The content of intellectual property rights to registered industrial designs and the granting of such rights to holders of unregistered industrial designs have been improved.
- The "Bolar" provision has been implemented in national legislation.
- Legal provisions on judicial protection of patent rights have been improved.
- A pre-grant opposition procedure was introduced.
- The procedure for out-of-court appeals against the decision of the NIPA on the application for registration of an invention, utility model, or industrial design to the NIPA Chamber of Appeals was improved.
- An out-of-court procedure for invalidating the rights to an invention, utility model, or industrial design was introduced to combat patent trolling (the post-grant opposition procedure).

4.2 Establishment of the National Intellectual Property Authority

The first part of patent law reform legislation is the Law of Ukraine which established a national patent office—the NIPA.[30] One may note the urgent need for this institution, because it is the NIPA, as mentioned above, that exercises all the powers to provide legal protection to the objects of patent law, as well as has the authority to protect such rights and to combat patent trolling.

The disadvantage of the legislative technique is that the legal status of NIPA is not defined in a separate law, but in an overarching law which has amended several legislative acts.[31] All these acts introduced the same legal provisions: the definition of NIPA; its powers (specifying the powers of each intellectual property objects in each special law); the legal status and competence of the governing bodies of NIPA (head of NIPA, supervisory board); the competence of the Chamber of Appeals; guarantees of independence of the Chamber of Appeals and experts of NIPA; and the legal status of the attestation and appellate commission of NIPA. Therefore, it was more expedient to adopt a law on NIPA rather than duplicating the rules on the legal status of NIPA, its structure, competence, etc. in several laws of intellectual property legislation. At the same time, these legislative changes should be positively assessed in substance, as Ukraine now has a fully-fledged patent office, as in the EU, the US, etc.

[30] Ukrainian Law on Amendments to some Laws of Ukraine on the Establishment of a National Intellectual Property Body 2020, 703-IX.

[31] Ukrainian Law on Protection of Rights to Inventions and Utility Models 1994, 3687-XII; Ukrainian Law on Protection of Rights to Industrial Designs 1994, 3688-XII; Ukrainian Law on Protection of Rights to Marks for Goods and Services 1994, 3689-XII; Ukrainian Law on Protection of Rights to Layout of Semiconductor Products, 1998, 621/97-BP; Ukrainian Law on Legal Protection of Geographical Indications 1999, 752-XIV; Ukrainian Law on Copyright and Related rights 1994, 3792-XII.

The NIPA is a state organization that is a part of the state system of legal protection of intellectual property, appointed at the national level by the Cabinet of Ministers of Ukraine.[32] The NIPA exercises its powers in the field of intellectual property in accordance with the law and has the right to represent Ukraine in international and regional organizations. It is authorized to accept applications for the registration of patent law objects; conduct examinations (preliminary, formal, qualification); and make decisions based on the results of applications, state registration of inventions, utility models and industrial designs, and to grant patents and certificates for them. It is also responsible for the invalidation of rights to inventions, utility models and industrial designs, and the maintenance of state registers of all intellectual property, along with international cooperation in the field of legal protection of intellectual property and representation of Ukraine's interests in the protection of intellectual property rights in the World Intellectual Property Organization and other international organizations in accordance with the law.

The legal status of the NIPA's Chamber of Appeals has also been reformed by expanding its powers and changing its competence, including in the fight against patent trolling. The NIPA Chamber of Appeals is a collegial body composed of experienced intellectual property professionals. The Chamber of Appeals considers objections to the NIPA's decisions on the acquisition of industrial property rights, looks at applications for invalidation of industrial property rights in whole or in part, at applications for recognition of a trademark well known in Ukraine, and other issues related to it competences in accordance with the law. The NIPA is also responsible for the training, certification and registration of patent attorneys. Some of these powers (e.g. issuance of patents, certificates, activities of the Chamber of Appeals, etc.) were taken away from the Ministry of Economy of Ukraine, which now exercises only the powers of the central executive body in the field of intellectual property.

Ukraine has completed the transition to a two-tier system of legal protection of intellectual property in which the central place is given to the NIPA. This is fully in line with the experience of foreign state systems of legal protection of intellectual property. For example, the European Patent Office operates in the EU, and examines both applications and grants European patents. The UK also has an Intellectual Property Office which performs the same functions, as does the United States Patent and Trademark Office. International experience in the operation of patent offices demonstrates the merit of combining the functions of the examining and the registering institution in granting patents.[33]

[32] Ukrainian Law on Protection of Rights to Inventions and Utility Models 1994, 3687-XII, art 1(2).

[33] Gennady Androschuk, 'The Patent System in the World Economy: Development Scenarios' (2010) 3 Journal of Theory and Practice of Intellectual Property 10; Gennady Androschuk and Lyudmyla Rabotyagova, 'US Patent System Reform: An Analysis of Change' (2017) 3(3) Journal Science, Technology, Innovation 61; Vadym Barsky, *On the Nature of the Powers of the State Enterprise Ukrainian Institute of Intellectual Property '(Ukrpatent)'* (OLDI-PLUS 2021) 87; Olena Orliuk and Natalia Korogod, 'Improvement of Intellectual Property Management in Ukraine' (2020) 6 Journal of Theory and Practice of Intellectual Property 169.

4.3 Legal Protection of Inventions and Utility Models

4.3.1 General Characteristics

The Law of Ukraine "On Amendments to Certain Legislative Acts of Ukraine Concerning the Reform of Patent Legislation" is aimed at the improvement of the legal protection of inventions and utility models. It was adopted to implement the requirements of Arts. 219–223 Association Agreement as well as the provisions of Directive 98/44/EU on the legal protection of biotechnological inventions, Regulation (EU) 469/2009 on supplementary protection certificates for medical devices and other regulatory EU acts in the field of patents to harmonize the requirements of current legislation of Ukraine "On the Protection of Rights to Inventions and Utility Models with EU law.

This law introduced significant changes and amendments to the Law of Ukraine "On the Protection of Rights to Inventions and Utility Models". These changes are extremely important and necessary, as they do not blindly copy the provisions of the legislation of many EU countries, but instead try to comprehensively solve the problems of legal regulation that existed and did not contribute to the spread of innovation and other new technologies. In particular, the law provides for the final waiver of the declaratory patent for an invention (without checking the criterion of "inventive step"); updated the list of objects that are granted legal protection as utility models; improved the conditions for granting legal protection to inventions and utility models, including the ban on the issuance of so-called "evergreen" patents; and provided legal mechanisms to combat patent trolling, among other things.

As of today, the legal protection of inventions and utility models is characterized as follows: the law provides one definition of the concepts of invention and utility model, according to which they are the result of intellectual, creative human activity in any field of technology. The differences between the invention and the utility model are further contained in the list of objects that can be protected as a utility model, in the simplified procedure for consideration of the application for state registration of the utility model (examination of the application consists of preliminary and formal examination). Moreover, utility model rights may be declared invalid totally or in part during the entire term of the property rights to the utility model and after their termination, etc. There are two varieties of invention (utility model), namely service and secret.

4.3.2 Legal Regime of the Invention and Utility Model

The invention and utility model as objects of industrial property law of Ukraine have both common and distinctive features. Common to them both are the conditions for granting legal protection (except for the lack of inventive step in the utility model); the subject composition of right holders; the rights and responsibilities of the patent owner; and the methods and procedures for the protection of rights. Distinctive features are a wider list of objects that can be patented as inventions; the procedure for patenting (in terms of qualifying examination of an application for an invention; the possibility of further objections to the registration of inventions—"pre grant opposition"); limited time of "post grant opposition" to invalidate the rights to the invention; the possibility of extending the validity of property rights to the invention (supplementary protection certificate); and a patent for an invention is strong, while a patent for a utility model is weak (due to failure to qualify for a utility model application). The law also establishes the features of legal protection of inventions in the field of biotechnology.

The list of objects of the invention is wider than the list of objects of the utility model. In particular, the object of the invention may be a product or a process (method). The product can be a device, substance, strain of micro-organism, cell culture of plants and animals, and so on.[34] Instead, a utility model can be either a device (as one type of product) or a process (method). This legislative approach is debatable, as in the scientific literature and in the draft National Intellectual Property Strategy of Ukraine for the period 2020–2025 it was proposed to define only a device as an object of a utility model.[35] Indeed, there are three main approaches to determining the legal regime of utility models in the world: the waiver of protection of utility model rights in general; the introduction of inventive step requirements for utility models; and the protection of only three-dimensional objects as utility models. The EU countries also practice the exclusion from the legal protection of the utility model's methods, drugs and compositions, and chemicals.[36] These trends have been generally taken into account and reflected in the law (namely in the patent law reform of 2020), and are also supported by scholars.[37] In particular, after the reform of patent law, legal protection does not apply to the following objects (i.e. they cannot be patented as inventions or utility models): biological processes of reproduction of plants and animals; surgical or therapeutic treatments; diagnostic methods; human cloning processes; and products or a processes involving natural biological material, etc. But these exceptions apply to both inventions and utility models. Instead, the process (method) can be protected both as an invention and as a utility model. This approach, which is reflected in the law, deserves criticism because, as we see from European experience, it needs to be adjusted—method should be removed from the list of utility models, or inventive step added to the patentability of the utility model.

---

[34] The object of the invention, the legal protection of which is provided in accordance with the law, may be a product (device, substance, strain of a microorganism, culture of plant and animal cells, etc.), or a process, method (Ukrainian Law on Protection of Rights to Inventions and Utility Models 1994, 3687-XII, art 6(2)).

[35] Draft National Intellectual Property Strategy of Ukraine for the period 2020–2025 (n 5).

[36] Yuriy Kapitsa, 'Utility Models Protection – Trends in the European Union and Challenges for Ukraine' (2020) 3 Journal of Theory and Practice of Intellectual Property 27 (33).

[37] A patent cannot guarantee the proven therapeutic effect or safety of a particular method of diagnosis or treatment, because the indicators may change during the clinical application of the present invention. See more Oksana Kashyntseva, 'Human Rights and Patenting of Methods of Human Diagnosis and Treatment in the Context of Health Care Reform' (2014) 4 Journal of Theory and Practice of Intellectual Property.

The Ukrainian reform of patent law (2020) did not reflect any approach to the utility model implemented in the EU. Analysing the European experience of legal protection of utility models, it seems that the abandonment of utility models is premature, and therefore it seems appropriate to narrow the list of objects of utility models (leaving only the device), and the introduction of an inventive step criterion. However, the legislative changes in 2020 rightly removed from the list of objects of the invention and utility model) a new application of a known product or process.

4.3.3 Terms of Legal Protection

Article 6 Law of Ukraine "On the Protection of Rights to Inventions and Utility Models" defines the conditions for their legal protection which include two components: (1) consistency of the invention or utility model to public order and generally accepted principles of morality; and (2) compliance of the invention or utility model with the conditions of patentability.

This law does not contain an interpretation of public order and generally accepted principles of morality. In determining whether an invention or utility model contradicts public order, one should consider the explanations contained in the Recommendations on certain issues of examination of the application compiled by Ukrpatent. Clause 7.2 of these Recommendations contains a list of cases that are interpreted as a violation of public order and moral principles of society: harm to life and health of humans or animals; damage to plants; causing significant damage to the environment as a result of commercial use of the invention or utility model (for example in the process of human cloning, the use of human embryos for industrial or commercial purposes, etc.).[38] Contravention of the moral principles of society means a violation of ethical norms, rules of conduct in society based on traditional spiritual and cultural values, ideas of goodness, honour, dignity, public duty, conscience and justice.[39] Therefore, inventions and utility models cannot be protected if they relate to pornographic products, or products that promote war, national and religious enmity, fascism, disrespect for national and religious shrines, drug addiction, substance abuse, alcoholism, smoking, and so on.

The conditions of patentability are classic and do not differ from the conditions established by foreign—primarily European—legislation.[40]

---

[38] Order of Ukrpatent 91 of 7 April 2014 on Methodological Recommendations on Certain Issues of Examination of the Application for Invention (Utility Model). See also Tetyana Komarova, 'The Patentability of Biotechnological Inventions in the EU: The Ukrainian Context' in this Volume.

[39] Ukrainian Law on Protection of Public Morality 2003, 1296-IV.

[40] An invention is patentable if it is new, has an inventive step and is industrially applicable, utility model is patentable if it is new and industrially applicable (Ukrainian Law on Protection of Rights to Inventions and Utility Models 1994, 3687-XII, art 7(1), 7(2)). Therefore, traditionally the inventive step is unique to the invention.

Novelty

Novelty is equally inherent in both the invention and the utility model. Novelty means that the invention or utility model should not be part of the already known prior technology. The state of the technology includes all information that has become publicly available in the world before the date of application to the NIPA or, if priority is claimed, before the date of its priority. The prior technology also includes the content of any application for state registration in Ukraine of an invention or utility model. Public information is information about other inventions and utility models, applications for inventions and utility models in Ukraine and abroad, and information about technical solutions and innovations used in the world by any person. With the development of the digital environment, a lot of information that can affect the novelty is contained on the internet (including information about technical solutions, their images, videos on the application of various technical solutions, etc.).[41]

The novelty is checked by NIPA at the stage of qualification examination by conducting a patent search. The applicant may, when filing an application, attach a patent search report carried out by the competent International Searching Authority. In this case, for the second time, a full patent search is no longer conducted, and only applications filed with the NIPA are checked. Patent search is important given that it is based on the formula of the invention and its description and drawings, as well as possible permissible changes of the formula of the invention using the patent information base of NIPA. Conducting a patent search before filing an application allows a person to know whether the product or process that they have invented is actually an invention, because the applicant learns about a registered invention or utility model and its formula which may fully or partially coincide with the applicant's formula.

An Inventive Step

The patent law reform of 2020 significantly changed the understanding of the inventive step. Inventive step means the non-obviousness of a technical solution for a specialist in a particular field, a new technical solution should not explicitly follow from the prior technology.[42]

The person skilled in the technology, who has special, in-depth knowledge of the prior technology, can make their own reasonable conclusions about the possible consequences of the application of certain technical processes. Therefore, the inventive step as a condition for the patentability of the invention is a "breakthrough" on

---

[41] If the inventor (or the person who received from the inventor directly or indirectly such information) discloses information about the invention (utility model) within six months before the date of application to the NIPA, it will not affect the novelty (Ukrainian Law on Protection of Rights to Inventions and Utility Models 1994, 3687-XII, art 7(6)).

[42] An invention has an inventive step if it is not obvious to a person skilled in the technology, and it does not follow explicitly from the prior technology (Ukrainian Law on Protection of Rights to Inventions and Utility Models 1994, 3687-XII, art 7(7)).

the scientific and technical level in a field of knowledge. In particular, in order to combat evergreen patents, the following was introduced (and successfully tested in EU countries): a development that clearly follows from the prior technology can be recognized as a new form of the prior technology drug, including salts, esters, ethers, compositions, combinations and other derivatives, polymorphs, metabolites, pure forms, particle sizes, and isomers (if they do not differ significantly in efficiency).[43] This provision is important to eliminate the monopoly on the production of certain drugs that use the same active ingredient but change the excipients. In this case, prior to the adoption of these legislative changes, it was permissible to permanently patent new forms of the drug known from the prior technology which led to an unfair patent monopoly. This was because until October 2020 in Ukraine patents were granted for drugs that had long passed into the public domain in the EU or the US. Now such a practice will be considered unacceptable.[44] These changes are fully consistent with the provisions of TRIPS Agreement, in particular Art. 8 TRIPS (which shows the need to prevent the abuse of intellectual property rights and to prevent the use of practices that disproportionately restrict trade or adversely affect technology transfer).[45]

Industrial Applicability

Industrial applicability as a condition of patentability of both the invention and the utility model indicates the possibility of using the protected object in industry or in another field of activity.[46] The description and the formula should describe the means and methods by which it is possible to implement the invention or utility model in the form as it is described in the independent paragraph of the formula. Therefore, for anyone (but usually for a specialist) it should be a clear design of the technical solution, which is described in the application materials (in the description and the formula). This is a potential opportunity for industrial reproduction of a product or process that reflects the essence of the invention or utility model, and hence the usefulness for society, which is manifested in the future use of the invented product or process in various industries. This feature also characterizes its suitability for industrial use.

The novelty and industrial suitability of the utility model are not checked at the stage of application review by the NIPA, as these actions are performed only at the stage of qualification examination, which is not inherent for the utility model. Therefore, the utility model is presumed to have novelty and industrial applicability, but this conclusion can be revoked either by the NIPA (if any interested person

---

[43] Ukrainian Law on Amendments to Some Laws of Ukraine on Patent Law Reform 2020, 816-IX.

[44] Oksana Kashyntseva, 'Key Points of the Ukrainian Patent Reform in the Health Care Sphere' (2018) 3 Journal of Theory and Practice of Intellectual Property 46 (47).

[45] See Oksana Kashyntseva, 'Patent Law and Access to Medicines in Ukraine' in this Volume.

[46] Ukrainian Law on Protection of Rights to Inventions and Utility Models 1994, 3687-XII, art 7(8).

applies to the NIPA Chamber of Appeals with an application for invalidation of a utility model patent by out of court procedure)[47] or by a court.

The conditions for the patentability of a utility model should be reviewed in the light of the European experience in legal protection. It is sensible to provide in the law either a real verification of novelty (i.e. introduction of qualification examination in this part), and/or, as mentioned above, it is expedient to introduce inventive step as a condition of patentability. This will make the utility model patent strong and make patent trolling impossible. Such positions are supported by the scientific community.[48]

4.3.4 Patent

Priority, authorship and intellectual property rights for the invention or utility model is certified by a patent. The patent does not certify the ownership of the invention or utility model, but it confirms that its owner has intellectual property rights. The patent reform of 2020 made significant changes to the law which now provides for the following types of patents:

- Invention patent granted for a period of 20 years following a formal qualification examination (if the application is founded on an international application, the term of intellectual property rights for the invention is calculated from the date of filing the international application);
- Utility model patent, which is granted for a period of 10 years based on a formal examination.

A subtype of these patents is a patent for a secret invention (utility model).[49]

The patent law reform of 2020 finally abolished the possibility of granting a declaratory patent for an invention, which was granted for a period of six years based on the results of only a formal examination of the application for an invention. Since 2004, the Civil Code of Ukraine has not provided for declaratory patents.[50]

---

[47] Any person may submit to the NIPA Chamber of Appeals a substantiated application for invalidation of the rights to an invention (utility model) in whole or in part on the grounds of non-compliance of the invention (utility model) with the patentability conditions specified by law (Ukrainian Law on Protection of Rights to Inventions and Utility Models 1994, 3687-XII, art 33-1(1)).

[48] Kapitsa, 'Utility Models Protection—Trends in the European Union and Challenges for Ukraine' (n 36) 27 (33).

[49] A patent for a secret invention (utility model) is valid for the period of determining its degree of, but not longer than the statutory term of intellectual property rights to the invention or utility model in general (Ukrainian Law on Protection of Rights to Inventions and Utility Models 1994, 3687-XII, art 6(8)). The possibility of granting a patent for a secret utility model is a debatable issue. The draft National Strategy for the Development of Intellectual Property in Ukraine for the period 2020–2025 noted the improvement of the national patent law in relation to the acquisition and realization of property rights for secret inventions (utility models), and considered the option to abandon them in general.

[50] The declaratory patent for an invention was granted without a qualification examination; instead an examination for local novelty was conducted (there was done only verification of patents for

At the same time, the special law on the protection of rights to inventions and utility models was not unified with the norms of the Civil Code of Ukraine. The 2020 reform eliminated these inconsistencies. This legislative approach is to be welcomed because the invention is a technical solution tested by the patent office which must objectively meet the conditions of patentability. Therefore, NIPA must necessarily check the novelty, inventive step and industrial applicability of the invention, which is possible only at the stage of qualification examination. If the applicant does not want to submit their technical solution to a qualifying examination, it is advisable to apply for a utility model, which is a weaker object of patent law (due to the presumption of its compliance with patentability).

A patent for an invention or utility model traditionally only covers the territory of Ukraine as the state that granted the patent.[51] To obtain legal protection abroad, one must go through the procedure of obtaining a patent in the appropriate country (alternatively it is possible to file an international application for an invention with legal protection in several countries simultaneously under the PCT Agreement).

The law provides for the possibility of establishing for the owner of a patent for a medicinal product or an active pharmaceutical ingredient of a medicinal product, etc. a period of additional protection equal to the period between the date of filing an application to NIPA and the date of obtaining the first permit of the competent authority.[52] In any case the term of additional protection may not exceed five years. The extension of property patent rights is certified by a supplementary protection certificate. This approach is fully in line with European practice of establishing an additional term for the rights of inventions in the pharmaceutical field.

4.3.5 Subjects of Rights to Inventions and Utility Models

The inventor, employer or assignee of the inventor or employer has the right to register an invention or utility model.[53]

The primary subject who has the right to obtain a patent for an invention or utility model is the inventor as an individual. The inventor is a person whose intellectual, creative activity created the invention or utility model.[54] Individuals who did not make a personal creative contribution to its creation but only provided the inventor/inventors with technical, organizational, or material assistance in its creation

inventions and utility models granted in Ukraine and verification of previously filed applications for inventions and utility models in Ukraine).

[51] Patents applied for in the various countries of the Union by nationals of countries of the Union shall be independent of patents obtained for the same invention in other countries, whether members of the Union or not (Paris Convention for the Protection of Industrial Property (as amended on September 28, 1979), art 4bis (1).

[52] Ukrainian Law on Protection of Rights to Inventions and Utility Models 1994, 3687-XII, art 27-1.

[53] Ibid art 8–10.

[54] Ibid art 1(13).

and/or the registration of the application, are not recognized as inventors. Also, artificial intelligence, the legal personality of which is not defined in the patent legislation of Ukraine, cannot be recognized as an inventor.[55]

A legal entity cannot be an inventor under any circumstances, but it can be the applicant as the employer or assignee of the inventor.[56]

Inventors who have jointly created an invention or utility model have the same rights to register unless otherwise provided by contract between them.[57] The contract is the regulator of relations between several inventors. This agreement refers to both the right to file an application for an invention (utility model) and the future exercise of patent rights. The legislative changes of 2020 provided an opportunity to change the applicant during the registration of. In particular, in the case of revision of the terms of the agreement about inventors, at the joint request of persons named in the application as inventors and persons who are inventors but not listed in the application as inventors, NIPA amends the relevant application documents.

Service Invention

The right to register an service invention (utility model) has the employer of the inventor, unless otherwise provided by contract between them (labour or civil law contract).[58] This rule is not consistent with the provisions Civil Code of Ukraine, according to which the intellectual property rights to the object created in connection with the implementation of the employment agreement (contract) belong to the employee who created the object and the employer jointly, unless otherwise provided by this Code or contract.[59] Therefore, the Civil Code of Ukraine imperatively emphasizes that exceptions to the rule regarding the ownership of property rights to an official invention may be established either by the Code or by a contract.

Special legislation on inventions and utility models may not establish an exception to this rule. Only a contract, and the law does not specify which one (obviously labour or civil law contract), can transfer all intellectual property rights for an invention or utility model to the employer.[60]

---

[55] This issue is very controversial. See more about artificial intelligence as a subject of IP law: Gennady Androschuk, 'Artificial Intelligence: Economics, Intellectual Property, Threats' (2021) 3 Journal of Theory and Practice of Intellectual Property 45; Tetyana Katkova, 'Artificial Intelligence in Ukraine: Legal Aspects' (2020) 6 Journal Law and Society 46; Elizaveta Tymoshenko, 'Artificial Intelligence as a Subject of Intellectual Property Rights' (2020) 4 Journal of Kyiv University of Law 328.

[56] Ukrainian Law on Protection of Rights to Inventions and Utility Models 1994, 3687-XII, arts 9, 10.

[57] Ibid art 8(2).

[58] Ukrainian Law on Protection of Rights to Inventions and Utility Models 1994, 3687-XII, art 9.

[59] Civil Code of Ukraine 2003, 1089-IX, art 429(2).

[60] Such a legislative approach is imperfect. There are several models in foreign practice of service inventions (utility models), according to which employers acquire the rights to them. Therefore, in our opinion, it is expedient to change the legal regime of service inventions (utility models),

The current patent legislation stipulates that after an employee creates a technical solution that could potentially be an invention (utility model), the employer has the right to take one of the following actions within four months: (1) apply to the NIPA for state registration of the invention or utility model; (2) transfer the right to such registration to another person; or (3) decide to preserve the service invention or utility model as confidential information. An important guarantee for the employee is the rule that obliges the employer within the same period to enter into a written agreement with the inventor on the amount and terms of payment of remuneration in accordance with the economic value involved. If the employer has not used the above opportunities, the right to register a service invention or utility model passes to the inventor.[61]

In summary, the legal regime of service inventions (utility models) in Ukraine needs significant adjustment. First of all, the law should clearly define the concept of a service invention (utility model). It should identify cases when the invention (utility model) can be considered as a service invention (taking into account the possibility of creating a service invention (utility model) during the employment contract or after its termination, or the same when several employers apply for registration of rights to it, etc.), who the applicant may be, who owns the intellectual property rights, the features of the payment of remuneration to the inventor, etc. It should not be forgotten that it is the employer who directs the employee to carry out certain activities, teaches them (internships, training, etc.), gives them official tasks, creates the conditions for invention, pays wages, coordinates their inventive activities, and so on. Of course, the creation of each service invention is accompanied by its own characteristics, but it is necessary at the legal level to eliminate the legal vacuum regarding the legal regime of the service invention (utility model), giving the employer intellectual property rights.

Successors

The assignee of the inventor or employer also has the right to obtain a patent. Succession can occur by inheritance (for the inventor) or by contract. The condition for filing an application by the heir of the inventor is the acceptance of the inheritance and registration of rights to it. The document confirming the registration of inheritance rights, including the rights to file an application for an invention (utility model), is a

providing both the right to apply and property rights that will follow from the state registration of an invention (utility model) to the employer. Of course, in practice, this problem is solved by contractual regulation (in the employment contract, the employee usually transfers all the rights associated with the invention, a utility model that can potentially be created, including the right to apply). But this does not solve the gap in legal regulation. In addition, the law now emphasizes that the Civil Code of Ukraine has priority in regulating intellectual property relations. This approach is incorrect, as intellectual property is not a part of civil law, but a complex branch of legislation. Therefore, a special law on inventions (utility models) should determine the rules governing these relations.

[61] Ukrainian Law on Protection of Rights to Inventions and Utility Models 1994, 3687-XII, art 8(4).

Certificate of Inheritance, granted after the expiration of six months from the date of its opening.[62] At the same time, there is a gap in the law regarding the inheritance of the right to file an application for an invention (utility model). The notary may refuse to grant a Certificate of Inheritance for such an object as an invention (utility model) if the testator has not yet acquired the intellectual property right to it. A document certifying the intellectual property right to an invention (utility model) is a patent, so a person is not considered as an inventor before receiving it, and they do not have intellectual property rights in the invention, or utility model. Therefore, the testator is not considered as an inventor (this status is not confirmed by a patent).[63] The inheritance clearly includes the right to design an invention (utility model). However, this right cannot be confirmed by any document, the submission of which is required by the Rules for drawing up and submitting an application for an invention and an application for a utility model.

After creating an object that can be registered as an invention (utility model), its author has the right to apply (registration of the invention). This right may be transferred to other persons under the contract.

4.3.6 Patenting Procedure

Submission of Application

The possibility to file an application in electronic form is an innovation that was introduced under the Reforms of patent law (2020),[64] and there is now a right to choose either the paper or electronic application form. For applications submitted in electronic form, electronic record-keeping is carried out in accordance with the legislation in the field of electronic documents and electronic document management. The applicant must be identified by a qualified electronic signature.

The application for an invention or utility model must relate to one or a group of inventions related to a single inventive concept (i.e. the requirement of unity of invention or utility model). The application is drawn up in the Ukrainian language and must contain an application for state registration, a description and formula, drawings (if they are referenced in the description), and an abstract.[65]

The inventor has the right to demand that he not be mentioned as the inventor in any publication of the NIPA, in particular in the information about the application or the state registration of the invention or utility model.[66] However their name will

---

[62] Civil Code of Ukraine 2003, 1089-IX, art 1298.

[63] Ibid art 1218.

[64] Ukrainian Law on Protection of Rights to Inventions and Utility Models 1994, 3687-XII, art 12(1).

[65] Ibid art 12(5).

[66] Ibid art 12(1).

be written in the patent, something that is fully in line with the requirements of the Paris Convention for the Protection of Industrial Property.[67]

Important elements of the application for the invention or utility model are the description and formula of invention.[68] The description is intended to disclose its technical essence. It must be set out so clearly and completely that it can be implemented by a specialist in the specified field of science and technology. The essence of the invention or utility model is the most important part of the description, because it is expressed by a set of essential features sufficient to achieve the technical result. Signs are significant if they affect the technical result that can be achieved and are in causal connection with the specified result. The invention discloses a technical result that can be achieved by it, and is a description of a technical solution to a specific problem that may be useful in a particular field of technology.

The formula is a conclusion that follows the description. The formula should express its essence, be based on the description and be stated in a given order clearly and concisely. The formula should be short and clear, but it should also contain all the essential features of the invention or utility model, due to which it is possible to achieve the technical result specified by the applicant. If the formula is not based on a description, this is the basis for invalidating the patent rights in court or by the Chamber of Appeals. The formula is a very important component of the patent application, as it is intended to determine the scope of legal protection granted by the patent. The formula should characterize the invention or utility model in the same terms as the description. Features in the formula are set out in such a way as to ensure the possibility of their identification and the unambiguous understanding of their content by a skilled person based on the prior technology.

Examination of the Application and Granting of a Patent

The reform of patent legislation in 2020 also affected the procedure for examining the application. For a utility model this consists of a preliminary examination and a formal examination, and applications for an invention are additionally subject to a qualification examination. The procedure for conducting these examinations is defined in the Rules for consideration of applications for inventions and applications for utility models.[69] These Rules have been in force since 2002 and have not been amended. Therefore, the Rules are subject to update in connection with changes in patent law, as well as in connection with the need to bring them to a more modern state corresponding to the realities of today.

---

[67] Paris Convention for Protection of Industrial Property (as amended on September 28, 1979), art 4ter.

[68] Ukrainian Law on Protection of Rights to Inventions and Utility Models 1994, 3687-XII, art 12(7), 12(8).

[69] Order of the Ministry of Education and Science of Ukraine 197 of 15 March 2003 on the Rules of Consideration of the Application for Invention and Utility Model.

All the above types of examinations are conducted by the NIPA. The results of the examination of the application are generally reflected in the reasoned conclusion of the examination. Based on this conclusion the NIPA decides to accept or refuse the state registration of the invention or utility model, and then informs the applicant.

Preliminary examination of the application aims to determine whether the invention or utility model should not be disclosed because it contains information that is a state secret (for example, inventions intended for use in defence and national security). A state expert on secrets should be involved in this process.

Formal expertise performs several functions that are especially important for the utility model, because the NIPA's decision on the state registration of the utility model is based on the results of this examination. The formal examination determines whether the invention or utility model can be registered as such. The NIPA checks whether a potential invention or utility model is a technical solution. It should be emphasized that the examination ends here, and if the utility model is found to be a technical solution, the NIPA will grant a patent for it. Terms of patentability are not checked.

After the application is received by the NIPA, the application materials are considered to be confidential information. The NIPA publishes information about the application for an invention only after 18 months from the date of its submission.[70] This allows the interested person to submit to the NIPA: (1) an objection to the application (the so-called "pre-grant opposition" procedure) on the grounds of non-compliance of the invention with the conditions of legal protection (the deadline for filing such an objection is limited—the objection can only be filed within six months after publication of the application); (2) a request for an information search on the basis of formula of invention, taking into account the description and drawings; and (3) comments on the compliance of the claimed invention to the conditions of legal protection.[71] The results of the objection, request or comments are reflected in the final conclusion of the examination of the application and the NIPA does not decide on objections separately.

Qualification examination is aimed at verifying a potential invention under the terms of patentability, and is conducted either at the request of the applicant (filed within three years from the date of filing) or at the request of another person (filed after the publication of information on the invention, but not later than three years from date of application).[72] If the applicant (inventor) does not submit such an application for a qualification examination within the specified period, the application is considered withdrawn. The applicant may withdraw the application at any time without giving a reason.[73]

The applicant in the process of qualification examination of the application for an invention has the right to make changes to the formula, which cannot go beyond the

[70] Ukrainian Law on Protection of Rights to Inventions and Utility Models 1994, 3687-XII, art 16(16).

[71] Ibid art 16(17), 16(18).

[72] Ibid art 16(19).

[73] Ibid art 17.

technical essence of the invention and increase the scope of rights compared with the original formula of invention published by the NIPA.[74]

An important guarantee for the future owner of the patent for an invention is to provide the applicant with temporary legal protection of the future invention in the scope of the formula of invention from the date of publication of the application. In particular, temporary legal protection after the state registration of an invention allows the patent owner to claim damages from a person who illegally used the invention.[75] But the patent owner must prove the fact that the infringing person is aware of the existence of the published application. In this regard, the applicant (future patent owner) must send a written notice to the potential infringer indicating the application number (registration of the invention), the essence (claims) of the invention, and must indicate already published information about the application for an invention used without the applicant's permission.

Based on the above examinations of the application the NIPA decides on the state registration of the invention or utility model—provided that it meets the conditions for granting legal protection—and publishes information about it in the Industrial Property Bulletin. The NIPA should then publish a description of the patent within three months, which should include a formula and a description of the invention or utility model, as well as a drawing referenced in the description. Within a month after the state registration the NIPA grants a patent to the applicant. In connection with the simplified procedure for granting a patent for a utility model, there is a rule according to which a patent for a utility model is granted under the responsibility of its owner for compliance with the conditions of patentability.[76] The NIPA does not bear any responsibility for possible non-compliance with the conditions provided by legal protection and a utility model patent is of a declarative nature in law.

If the NIPA has taken a negative decision for the applicant and refused the state the applicant has the right to appeal to the NIPA Chamber of Appeals or in court within two months by filing an objection against the decision.[77] The NIPA Chamber of Appeals considers the objection within two months and makes a motivated decision to satisfy (fully or partially) the objection, or to refuse to satisfy it. In case of satisfaction of the objection due to violation of the procedure of examination, the application is returned to the NIPA for re-examination.

The decision of the Chamber of Appeals may be appealed in court within two months from the date of receipt of the decision.[78] Remarkably, this is a reduced term of judicial appeal against the decision of the Chamber of Appeals when compared with the general limitation period of three years.

---

[74] Ibid art 16(21).

[75] Ibid art 21.

[76] Ibid art 22.

[77] Ibid art 24(1).

[78] Ibid art 24(9).

4.3.7 Patent Owner Rights

After the state registration of the invention or utility model the applicant becomes the owner of the patent and receives the traditional exclusive patent rights: the right to use it, and the right to allow and prohibit third parties from using it.

Using of the invention or utility model traditionally involves:

- the manufacture of a product using a patented invention or utility model, the use of such a product, offering it for sale, including via the internet, and the sale, import and other introduction into civil circulation or storage of the product for these purposes[79];
- the application of the process protected by the patent, or its proposal for use in Ukraine, if the person proposing this process knows that its use is prohibited without the consent of the patent owner, or that this is already obvious.[80]

It is important that the product is considered to be manufactured using a patented invention or utility model if each feature is included in the independent claim of formula, or a feature equivalent to it.[81] The process protected by the patent is considered to be applied if each feature included in the independent claim of formula or an equivalent is used. This fact can be established only by conducting a forensic examination. Unfortunately, there is only a small number of forensic experts in Ukraine who perform this type of examination (about 20). In this case, the essential features of the formula of the invention or utility model are not directly identified in the claims of formula, and their definition is the prerogative of the forensic expert, who at their discretion interprets certain features as essential, groups them, and so on.

The law establishes a presumption of guilt of a manufacturer of similar products where there is a suspicion that they are counterfeit and produced in violation of patent rights.[82] In particular, any product, the manufacturing process of which is protected by a patent, is considered to be manufactured using this process in the absence of evidence to the contrary, provided that at least one of two requirements is met. These are:

- the product manufactured using the process protected by the patent is new;
- there is reason to believe that this product is manufactured using this process and the patent owner is unable by reasonable effort to determine the process used in the manufacture of this product.

In this case, the burden of proof that the process of making a product identical to that produced by the process protected by the patent differs from the latter rests with the person in respect of whom there are reasonable grounds to believe that it

[79] Each of these actions (manufacture, use, sale, advertising, etc.) is an independent infringement of patent rights if it is committed by a third party without the consent of the patent owner.

[80] Ukrainian Law on Protection of Rights to Inventions and Utility Models 1994, 3687-XII, art 28(2).

[81] Ibid art 28(2).

[82] Ibid art 28(2).

infringes the rights of the patent owner. However, this presumption applies only to such an object of the invention (utility model) as a process and does not apply to the product itself.

The Plenum of the High Commercial Court of Ukraine ruled on some issues relating to dispute-resolution practice concerning property rights. It stated that the patent owner does not have to prove the fact of manufacture to another person who is using the patented process. Instead, the burden of proof lies with that other person.

The basic principle that ensures the patenting of inventions is that any person who uses a patented invention without the permission of the patent owner commits illegal acts (except as expressly provided by applicable law).[83]

The Supreme Court also repeatedly draws attention to the application of the presumption of guilt of the infringer of patent rights.[84]

4.3.8 Use in Digital Environment

Inventions and utility models can be used in the digital environment, particularly on the internet. However, such use is quite limited because the object of the invention or utility model is a certain technical solution that usually cannot be used online. The legislation of Ukraine on inventions and utility models contains only one direct rule on their use on the internet: use of the invention or utility model on the internet is possible by offering for sale a particular product.[85] The object of an invention or utility model is a product or process (i.e. method), but only a product can be offered for sale on the internet. At the same time, intellectual property rights to an invention or utility model which is a method of obtaining a product also applies to a product directly obtained by this method. The law does not disclose the concept of "offer for sale" of the product. In our opinion this concept includes a direct offer of the website owner or the owner of the account to sell a particular product, as well as advertising this product for sale (including advertising by intermediaries, dealers, etc.). The use of inventions and utility models on the internet is also possible through the direct application of a particular product using the internet. These are "computer implemented inventions" that are used in the digital environment, and which are part of certain software. There is no special legal regulation of these relations in Ukraine. The use of inventions and utility models in the digital environment therefore requires a proper legal framework because this is an example when public relations are developing faster than the relevant legislation.

---

[83] Resolution of the Plenum of the High Commercial Court of Ukraine on some issues of dispute resolution practice related to the protection of intellectual property rights 2012, art, 83(1).

[84] Ukrainian Supreme Court 84,274,330 (2019) 757/39433/16; Ukrainian Supreme Court 85,743,549 (2019) 2018/17264/2012; Ukrainian Supreme Court 98,267,364 (2021) 2–3659/11.

[85] Ukrainian Law on Protection of Rights to Inventions and Utility Models 1994, 3687-XII, art 28(2).

4.3.9 Restriction of the Rights of the Patent Owner

The patent owner may allow third-party use of the invention or utility model by concluding license agreements (i.e. granting an exclusive or non-exclusive license).[86] At the same time, in cases provided by law, inventions and utility models may be used without the consent of the patent owner based on a compulsory license. Such use is treated as a restriction of the rights of the patent owner. In particular, the law provides for the possibility of granting compulsory licenses in the following cases: (1) non-use or insufficient use of the invention or utility model for three years; (2) granting of dependent and cross-license; and (3) granting of a license for public needs.[87] The institution of a compulsory license is necessary, but the legal regulation of these relations is imperfect. For example, in the first and second case the decision to grant a compulsory license is made by a court, and in the third case by the government. Instead, the positive practice of the EU countries[88] should be adopted by giving these powers to the NIPA (on the issuance of compulsory licenses in all the above cases). In the event of a compulsory licensing dispute, it should be considered by the High Court on Intellectual Property (after it starts functioning).[89] It is also necessary to change the concept of public interest as a basis for granting a compulsory license. The public interest should include the health needs of the population, the interests of national security (as provided by the patent law of Portugal and Spain), the country's economic interests (as in Germany, Portugal, France, Poland, Spain, etc.) and the cessation of anti-competitive practices by the patent owner (as in France, Spain, etc.).[90]

4.3.10 Actions that Are not Considered Infringement of Patent Rights

The patent law reform of 2020 has updated the list of actions that are not recognized as infringement of patent rights.[91] These are the right of the previous user without commercial purpose (fair use of technical solution identical to the claimed invention or utility model before the filing date in the interests of its activities); use for scientific purposes or experiments; use in extraordinary circumstances (natural disaster,

[86] Ibid art 28(7).

[87] Ibid art 30.

[88] Compulsory government licenses under the law of most EU countries are issued by the national patent office (in particular, Portugal, Spain, Poland, Hungary, Sweden, etc.). In some countries, such licenses may be issued by a court (Germany, France). However, it should be noted that this is not a general court, but a specialized court—a patent court, which hears disputes exclusively over industrial property.

[89] As of today, the Ukrainian Draft Law on High Court on Intellectual Property 2021, 6487 has been submitted to the parliament. See Anna Shtefan and Olga Gurgula, 'The New Intellectual Property Court in Ukraine: Its Creation and Exclusive Jurisdiction' in this Volume.

[90] Spanish Law on Patents 2015; Industrial Property Code of Portugal 2018; Intellectual Property Code of France 1992; German Patent Act 1936; Polish Act on Industrial Property 2000.

[91] Ukrainian Law on Protection of Rights to Inventions and Utility Models 1994, 3687-XII, art 31.

catastrophe, epidemic, etc.) with the notification of the patent owner as soon as it becomes practically possible with the payment of appropriate compensation; and the introduction into commercial circulation of a product manufactured with the use of a patented invention or utility model by any person who has purchased it without infringing the rights of the patent owner.

New rules in actions that do not infringe the rights arising from the patent cover commercial use of the invention or utility model by any person who lawfully purchased a product manufactured using it and who could not know that the product was manufactured in violation of the rights of the patent owner. In this case, the use of such the product should be terminated at the request of the patent owner or a license agreement should be concluded with them.[92]

The national patent law also reflected the Bolar provisions. In particular, the importation into the territory of Ukraine in the manner prescribed by law the goods manufactured using the invention or utility model for research and/or its use in research conducted to prepare and submit information for drug registration is not recognized infringement of the rights arising from the patent.[93] This means that during the validity of the patent a third party can use a generic drug which is protected by a valid patent, but only in the process of research in preparation to enter the market of medicines after the expiration of a competitor's patent. This legal provision allows significant preparations for the registration of a medicinal product that will be treated as a generic. After the expiration of the patent, the generic drug can immediately enter the market, which will reduce the cost of these drugs for the consumer.

In addition, manufacture of a product or medicinal product containing a product using the patented invention and other actions for the use of the invention are not recognized as infringements of additional protection of rights to inventions if they are necessary for the manufacture of a product or medicinal product containing a product for export to third countries.[94]

4.3.11 Patent Invalidation

The patent law reform of 2020 introduced several innovations regarding the invalidation of rights to inventions and utility models. Instead of invalidating a patent the invalidation of the rights to an invention or utility model was introduced.[95] Judicial practice has so far not adopted legislative changes, as courts continue to invalidate patents, not rights.

Invalidation of rights to an invention or utility model is possible in or out of court. The grounds for invalidation in court are: non-compliance with the conditions of patentability; the presence in the formula of features that were not in the application; violation of the procedure for patenting in foreign countries; and state registration as a

[92] Ibid art 31(4).

[93] Ibid art 31(5).

[94] Ibid art 31(6).

[95] Ibid art 33.

result of filing an application in violation of the rights of others.[96] The most common reason for invalidating a patent is the inconsistency of the invention or utility model with the conditions of patentability (in particular, the lack of novelty). This fact can be proved in court by providing a conclusion of a forensic expert or the conclusion of the NIPA on inconsistency with the conditions of patentability. Rights to an invention or utility model declared invalid in whole or in part in court are considered invalid from the date of publication of information on the state registration.

Court establish the presence or absence of novelty as of the date of filing the application.[97] The question of the lack of novelty should be decided while taking into account the same criteria for verifying novelty as the question of its existence.[98] Criteria for checking the novelty and requirements for the formula and the procedure (content) of the examination are essentially determined by the Rules of consideration of the application for invention and application for utility model approved by the order of the Ministry of Education and Science of Ukraine from 15 March 2002 No. 197. The conclusion as to the conformity of the invention with the conditions of patentability may not contradict the provisions of these Rules.

The right to file a lawsuit for invalidation of a patent for an invention or utility model lies with any interested person, not necessarily the owner of another patent (which opposes the granting of the defendant's patent).[99]

When recognizing the rights to an invention (utility model) as invalid in whole or in part in court, NIPA informs about it in the Bulletin "Industrial Property."

4.3.12 Post-Grant Opposition

One innovation in the 2020 reform of patent law is the introduction of an out-of-court procedure for recognizing the rights to an invention (utility model) invalid (known as a "post-grant opposition" procedure).

In the EU post-grant opposition procedures are commonly used in the fight against unscrupulous applicants who patent well-known technical solutions (i.e. patent trolling). As stated above, Ukraine only introduced such a procedure in 2020.[100] Out-of-court recognition of the invalidity of rights to an invention or utility model is carried out by the NIPA Chamber of Appeals. Any person may apply to the Chamber of Appeals with such a statement. The basis for invalidation of rights is the inconsistency of the invention or utility model with the conditions of patentability. In contrast to the grounds for invalidation of rights in-court, it has to be noted that there is only one ground for invalidation of rights out-of-court.

[96] Ibid art 33(1).

[97] Ukrainian Supreme Court 83,876,293 (2019) 910/6996/18.

[98] Ukrainian Supreme Court 98,367,498 (2021) 910/19256/16, Ukrainian Supreme Court 98,361,184 (2021) 910/2318/16.

[99] Ukrainian Supreme Court 86,503,966 (2019) 910/13040/17.

[100] Ukrainian Law on Amendments to Some Laws of Ukraine on Patent Law Reform 2020, 816-IX.

The law sets a deadline for filing an application for invalidation of rights to an invention—within nine months from the date of publication of information on the state registration of the invention.[101] However, an application for invalidation of utility model rights may be filed for the entire term of the property rights and even after their termination.[102] The parties to the case are the person who filed the application and the patent owner, who have equal rights to provide evidence. The adversarial principle applies to the proceedings—each party must prove the circumstances to which it refers as the basis of its claims or objections. The term of consideration is four months (but can be extended for an additional two months).[103] The Chamber of Appeals can decide to invalidate the rights to the utility model in whole or in part, or to refuse to satisfy such a statement. This decision must be approved by order of the NIPA.

4.3.13 Unresolved Issue: Remedies

Patent law reform has not affected ways to protect patent rights. The most common remedies are the cessation of infringement of patent rights and compensation for damages caused by such infringement. Liability for infringement of patent rights in the form of damages may arise only in the simultaneous presence of the following conditions: (1) the fact of illegal conduct of the defendant; (2) damage caused to the subject of intellectual property rights; (3) a causal link between the wrongful conduct of the person and the damage caused; and (4) the fault of the person who caused the damage. It is the plaintiff (patent owner) who must prove the existence of the first three conditions.[104] Therefore, when proving the fact of violation, it is very difficult to recover damages from the violator, as it is often difficult to calculate the specific amount of damage and prove the causal link between the wrongdoing and the damage. The Civil Code of Ukraine allows the right holder to choose such a method of protection as recovery of compensation instead of damages.[105] The Law of Ukraine "On the Protection of Rights to Inventions and Utility Models" also contains a provision that courts should resolve disputes about compensation in accordance with their competence. However, to properly regulate the mechanism of recovery of compensation, the law should provide for the conditions for recovery of compensation and its amount, etc. Such legislative changes may provide holders of patents for utility models with the opportunity not only to terminate the infringed right, but also to recover property damages.

---

[101] Ukrainian Law on Protection of Rights to Inventions and Utility Models 1994, 3687-XII, art 33-1(2).

[102] Ibid art 33-1(3).

[103] Ibid art 33-1(9).

[104] Resolution of the Plenum of the Supreme Commercial Court of Ukraine 2012 on some issues of dispute resolution practice related to the protection of intellectual property rights.

[105] Civil Code of Ukraine 2003, 1089-IX, art 432.

4.4 *Legal Protection of Industrial Designs*

4.4.1 The Main Changes

The Law of Ukraine "On Amendments to Certain Legislative Acts of Ukraine Concerning Strengthening the Protection and Protection of Rights to Trademarks and Industrial Designs and Combating Patent Abuse" is the third law adopted within the framework patent law reforms.[106] This law improves the legal regulation of trademarks and industrial designs and aims to reform the legislation on industrial property in general.[107]

The main legislative changes concerning the legal protection of industrial designs are as follows: changed conditions of protection (supplemented by an individual nature condition); the division of industrial designs into types (registered, unregistered); the creation of the opportunity to submit an application in electronic form; the increase of the maximum validity of rights to no more than 25 years; the type of security document required became a certificate instead of a patent; and the establishment of an out-of-court procedure for revoking the certificate by appealing to the NIPA Chamber of Appeals (combating "patent trolling").

4.4.2 Object of Industrial Design

Industrial design is an important result of the intellectual, creative activity of the person in the field of art designing. The reform of patent legislation has changed the quality of legal regulation of legal protection of industrial designs, bringing it closer to EU standards.

An industrial design is the appearance of a product or part thereof.[108] Appearance is determined by lines, contours, colour, shape, texture and/or the material of the product, and/or its finish.

The law stipulates that the following may not receive legal protection as industrial designs: objects of unstable shape made of liquid, gaseous, loose, or similar substances; the result of intellectual, creative activity in the field of artistic design, embodied or applied in a product that is part of a composite product and is invisible during normal use of the product; features of the appearance of the product due solely to its technical functions; and features of the appearance of the product, the size and shape of which must be accurately reproduced in order for one product to

---

[106] Ukrainian Law on Amendments to some Laws of Ukraine Concerning Strengthening the Protection of Rights to Trademarks and Industrial Designs and Combating Patent Abuse 2020, 815-IX.

[107] See Anastasiia Kyrylenko, 'The Reformed Design Law in Ukraine: What is Right with EU Trade Agreements?' in this Volume.

[108] Ukrainian Law on Protection of Rights to Industrial Designs 1994, 3688-XII, art 5(2).

be mechanically connected to another product or located inside, around or in front of another product so that each product can perform its function.[109]

4.4.3 Certificate and Validity

Acquisition of rights to a registered industrial design is confirmed by a certificate, which provides an image of the industrial design. Given the fact that before the entry into force of the Law "On Amendments to Some Laws of Ukraine Concerning Strengthening the Protection of Rights to Trademarks and Industrial Designs and Combating Patent Abuse", the patent office granted patents, as of today, the rights to industrial designs are certified by both Patents and Certificates granted from August 2020. Prior to the entry into force of the Law "On Amendments to some Laws of Ukraine Concerning Strengthening the Protection of Rights to Trademarks and Industrial Designs and Combating Patent Abuse",[110] the Patent Office issued patents for industrial designs. As of today, the rights to industrial designs are certified by Certificates issued since August 2020. Therefore, as of today, protection documents for industrial designs are patents (issued before August 2020) and certificates (issued since August 2020). Acquisition of the right to industrial design, which has an international registration, does not require a certificate.

The law sets the validity of property rights to registered and unregistered industrial design. The 2020 reform of patent law changed the validity of property rights to an industrial design. Generally this period is five years from the date of filing the application to the NIPA. This period may be extended several times for additional five-year periods, but the total validity period may not exceed 25 years from the date of application.[111]

The term of legal protection of an unregistered industrial design is three years from the date of its bringing to the public notice on the territory of Ukraine.[112] An unregistered industrial design shall be deemed to have been made public if it has been published, exhibited, used in trade or otherwise made public in such a way that, in the ordinary course of business, such measures may, for objective reasons, become known in circles which specialize in the relevant field and operate in Ukraine. An industrial design disclosed to a third party under explicit or implicit conditions of confidentiality shall not be deemed to have been made public.[113] This approach is in line with the experience of EU legal regulation. There is currently no law enforcement practice in Ukraine to protect rights to unregistered industrial designs.[114]

---

[109] Ibid art 5(3).

[110] Ukrainian Law on Amendments to some Laws of Ukraine Concerning Strengthening the Protection of Rights to Trademarks and Industrial Designs and Combating Patent Abuse 2020, 815-IX.

[111] Ukrainian Law on Protection of Rights to Industrial Designs 1994, 3688-XII, art 5(5).

[112] Ibid art 5(6).

[113] Ibid art 6(2).

[114] See more about protection of the rights to unregistered industrial designs: Oleksandr Doroshenko and Lyudmyla Rabotyahova, 'New Institute of Intellectual Property Law in Ukraine—Unregistered

The scope of legal protection provided for a registered industrial design is determined by the image of the industrial design entered in the state register. The novelty is that the image of the industrial design, and not the list of its essential features (as provided by law) determines the scope of legal protection. This approach is quite justified, as the essential features of an industrial design are an evaluative concept that can be interpreted differently by the rights holder, infringer, expert, judge, etc. The Law strengthened the scope of legal protection of an industrial design by stipulating that any other industrial design that does not give an informed user a distinct general impression will be considered identical to the industrial design to which the rights are protected.[115] Industrial designs are also considered to be identical if their essential features differ only in minor details.[116] Of course, the question of identity and the question of the general impression of the informed user should be proved by the conclusion of the forensic examination.

To determine the scope of legal protection the degree of freedom of the author is considered—limiting the author's ability to develop solutions to the appearance of a product for a particular purpose related to the functional features of the product.

4.4.4 Conditions for Granting Legal Protection

The conditions for granting legal protection to an industrial design are to some extent similar to the conditions for granting legal protection to inventions and utility models. In particular, the industrial design must not contradict public order, generally accepted principles of morality and must meet the criteria of protection, which the law distinguishes as novelty and individual character.

The novelty of the industrial design is manifested in the fact that there is no identical industrial design that has been made public before the date of submission of the application to the NIPA (for a registered industrial design) or before the date of public communication (for an unregistered industrial design).[117] In establishing the novelty, patents (certificates) valid for industrial designs in Ukraine and other countries of the world, applications to the relevant patent offices, and any publicly available data on the design of products used in Ukraine and abroad are taken into account.

An industrial design shall be deemed to have an individual character if the general impression it makes on an informed user differs from the general impression made on such user by any other industrial design communicated to the public.[118] Individual

---

Industrial Design' (2020) 4 Journal Theory and Practice of Intellectual Property 42; Yuriy Kapitsa, 'Unregistered Industrial Design: Features of Protection of Rights in the European Union and the Problems of Trolling in Ukraine' (2020) 5 Journal Theory and Practice of Intellectual Property 60; Nina Samolovova, 'Unregistered Industrial Design in the Fashion Industry' (2021) 3 Journal Theory and Practice of Intellectual Property 11.

[115] Ukrainian Law on Protection of Rights to Industrial Designs 1994, 3688-XII, art 6(3).

[116] Ibid art 6(2).

[117] Ibid art 6(2).

[118] Ibid art 6(3).

character is a new criterion of protection, which gives the industrial design a distinctiveness among other industrial designs (both registered and unregistered). This is an important criterion that complements the novelty, and together with it forms the scope of legal protection.[119]

4.4.5 Types of Industrial Designs

The reform of patent legislation in 2020 divided registered and unregistered industrial designs.[120] A registered industrial design is an industrial design, information on which is entered in the Register of Industrial Designs and for which a certificate has been granted, or which has been granted legal protection in Ukraine in accordance with an international agreement. An unregistered industrial design is an industrial design that has been made public in the manner prescribed by law, but which has not been entered in the Register of Industrial Designs. This innovation is an important one as the product design is not always protected as a registered industrial design. Instead, it will effectively protect common product designs that for some reason have not been registered as industrial designs.

The law establishes certain differences in the exercise of rights to registered and to unregistered industrial designs. In particular, the owner of a registered industrial design has exclusive rights to use the industrial design themselves, or to permit or prohibit its use by third parties.[121] The use of an industrial design is taken to mean the manufacture of a product using a registered industrial design; the use of such a product; offers for sale, including via the Internet; sale, import, export and other introduction into civil circulation; or storage of such product in pursuit of these purposes.[122]

The general impression of the informed user on the appearance of the registered industrial design and on another similar product is the main criterion for establishing the fact of use of the industrial design by another person.[123]

The owner of an unregistered industrial design which has been made public shall have the right to prohibit its copying and use, provided that such use is the result of copying an unregistered industrial design. The law provides that an industrial design is not considered the result of copying if it is created by the author's independent work, which can be considered unfamiliar with the industrial design brought to public notice by its owner.[124] Therefore, if a third party proves that they have created a product that mimics the appearance of an unregistered industrial design without being aware of the rights to such an unregistered industrial design, their actions

[119] See Anastasiia Kyrylenko, 'The Reformed Design Law in Ukraine: What is Right with EU Trade Agreements?' in this Volume.

[120] Ukrainian Law on Protection of Rights to Industrial Designs 1994, 3688-XII, art 5(4).

[121] Ibid art 20(2).

[122] Ibid art 20(2).

[123] Ibid art 20(2).

[124] Ibid art 20(9).

will not be considered an infringement of the industrial design. Such an exception does not apply to a registered industrial design. Therefore, any third-party use of a product copying a registered industrial design will be considered as a violation whether that third party knew or did not know about the existence of the industrial design certificate, and the certificate holder will have the right to prohibit such use.

4.4.6 Patenting

The author, employer or assignees of the author or employer have the right to register an industrial design. The right to register the industrial design passes to the author if the employer does not apply to the NIPA within four months from the date of receipt of this notice.

The author is always a person whose creative work has created an industrial design. The connection of the industrial design with copyright is important. Where appropriate, a layout or sketch of an industrial design which is the object of copyright is usually initially created. In these cases the product itself can also be protected as an industrial design and as a work of applied art. There is no norm in the law on the ratio of industrial design rights and copyrights to the layout, sketch, etc. The only way to protect copyright (if the author of the layout, sketch, etc. believes that the industrial design is a reproduction of his copyright object) is the requirement to invalidate the industrial design rights due to state registration of the industrial design in violation of the rights of others, in particular copyright. If a dispute arises between the author of the layout or sketch, etc. (copyright subject) and the owner of the unregistered industrial design, the method of protection may be the termination of the infringing action if the fact of reproduction of the copyright object in the unregistered industrial design can be proved.

The application for registration of an industrial design may be submitted in paper or electronic form, the method of submission being chosen by the applicant. The application must contain an application for state registration of an industrial design; a set of images of the product (the product itself or in the form of its layout or drawing) which give a complete picture of its appearance; a description of the industrial design; and drawings (if necessary).[125] The materials of the application are subject to examination, which is conducted by the NIPA. The examiners determine whether the submitted design (object) belongs to the objects that can be registered as an industrial design, whether it contradicts public order and generally accepted principles of morality.[126] Conditions of protection (novelty, individual character) are not checked. Therefore, the examination is a formal one. The results of the examination are reflected in the conclusion based on whether the NIPA decides to register the industrial design or to refuse on the state registration of the industrial design. State registration of an industrial design is carried out under the responsibility of its owner for compliance of the industrial design with the criteria of protection. Therefore, by

[125] Ibid art 11(4).

[126] Ibid art 14(8).

its legal nature, a certificate granted to the author of an industrial design (or another applicant) is declaratory as the applicant declares that the industrial design meets the requirements for protection.

If an application for an industrial design certificate is refused, the applicant may appeal the decision of the NIPA either in—or out-of-court within two months (in the latter case to the NIPA Chamber of Appeals by filing an objection against the decision).[127] The decision of the Chamber of Appeals may also be appealed by the applicant in court within two months of its adoption.[128]

4.4.7 Actions that Are not Considered as Infringements of Industrial Design Rights

Actions that are not considered as infringements of industrial design rights are almost identical to actions on inventions and utility models, namely non-commercial use, the right of the previous user, for scientific purposes, in extraordinary circumstances, and so on.[129] The principle of exhaustion of the right to a registered industrial design also applies.[130] The introduction into civil circulation of a product manufactured using a registered industrial design, after the introduction of this product into civil circulation by the owner of an industrial design or its special permit is not recognized as a violation of industrial design rights.

4.4.8 Invalidation of the Certificate

Industrial design rights may be declared invalid in- or out-of-court with the court procedure applied only to the invalidation of rights to a registered industrial design. There is no corresponding norm in the law regarding the unregistered industrial design. On the other hand, the provisions of the law on invalidation of industrial design rights out of court (by appealing to the Chamber of Appeals) do not specify whether it is a registered or unregistered industrial design. We believe that the rights to both registered and unregistered industrial designs may be declared invalid in court. This conclusion is based on the universality of the right to go to court to protect the violated rights.

The grounds for invalidating the rights to a registered industrial design in court are[131] non-compliance of the industrial design with the conditions for granting legal protection; the presence in the image of an industrial design of features that were not provided by the application; and state registration of an industrial design in violation of the rights of others.

[127] Ibid art 19(1).
[128] Ibid art 19(9).
[129] Ibid art 22(1), 22(2).
[130] Ibid art 22(3).
[131] Ibid art 25(1).

The law stipulates that such a claim may be filed by an interested person during the entire term of validity of property rights to an industrial design and after their termination.[132] Nevertheless, when applying to the court, one should take into account the statute of limitations, which in this case is three years from the moment when the person learned or could learn about the violation of his right or about the person who violated it.

The out-of-court procedure for invalidation of industrial design rights consists in the submission by any person to the NIPA Chamber of Appeals of a substantiated application for invalidation of industrial design rights in full or in part based on non-compliance of the industrial design with the conditions of legal protection. An important aspect is that such a statement can be filed throughout the term of validity of property rights to an industrial design and after their termination. The procedure and principles of consideration of such an application are identical to those in a similar procedure for invalidation of utility model rights.[133] The term for consideration of the application by the NIPA Chamber of Appeals is three months.[134] Based on the results of consideration of the application, the Chamber of Appeals makes a reasoned decision, approved by the order of the NIPA, to invalidate the rights to the industrial design in whole or in part, or refuses to satisfy the application.

We note the importance of the out of court procedure for revocation of a certificate for an industrial design in the framework of the procedure "post grant opposition". This is an effective mechanism for combating patent trolling, which also applies to industrial designs (registration as industrial designs of well-known product designs).

5 Conclusions

Patent legislation in Ukraine was significantly updated in 2020 when national law was harmonized with EU law and the provisions of the EU–Ukraine Association Agreement were implemented into domestic law. Intellectual property, in our opinion, is not a part of civil law, but a complex branch of law which includes civil law, competition law, administrative law, and procedural features of cases and rules from other branches of law regulating intellectual property relations. Therefore, special legislation on inventions, utility models and industrial designs should determine the features of the regulation of patent relations.

It is important to start the functioning of the national patent office (the NIPA), which has comprehensive powers to accept and review applications for patent objects, to grant patents, certificates, to invalidate patents and certificates. In addition, the NIPA acts as an international patent searching body.

Significant changes have been made to the legislation of Ukraine regarding inventions. These changes (particularly revoked treatment and diagnostic methods)

[132] Ibid art 25(2).

[133] Ibid art 25-1.

[134] Ibid art 25-1(7).

affected the object of the invention revoked declaratory patents, prevented the granting of "evergreen patents" in the field of pharmaceuticals, identified features of inventions in biotechnology, and introduced the provision of "Bolar". Given the opportunity to obtain a supplementary protection certificate, the procedure for conducting the examination of the application was improved and the procedures "pre-grant opposition" and "post grant opposition" were introduced.

The reform of patent law has redefined the legal regime of utility models, narrowing the list of objects that can be protected as such. A mechanism for revoking patents that do not meet the conditions for patentability (combating patent trolling) has also been introduced. At the same time, the utility model as an object of patent law needs further improvement, as utility model patents should continue to be considered as weak in Ukraine due to non-verification of the utility model for compliance with patentability conditions and lack of inventive step.

Another unresolved problem relating to the patent law reform is the real recovery of damages caused to rights holders because of the infringement of their rights, which can be solved by introducing compensatory protection mechanisms (introduction of compensation for infringement of patent rights).

The legal regime of service inventions and utility models in Ukraine needs to be significantly adjusted. The law should clearly define the concepts of service invention and utility model, and cases where they can be considered official. This should take into the possibility of creating a service invention (utility model) during the employment contract, after its termination, or—where several employers apply for registration of rights to it—determine the features of the payment of remuneration to the inventor.

Industrial designs as objects of legal protection have also undergone significant positive changes. These changes affected patent objects; types of industrial design ("unregistered industrial design introduced"); and security documents (certificate instead of patent). They also changed the validity of rights to industrial designs by reducing the validity of the certificate to 5 years, but increased the total validity to 25 years taking into account the possibility of extending the validity of the certificate); improved the provisions on the exercise of rights to industrial designs; and introduced a procedure for revocation of the certificate ("post grant opposition").

The reform of patent legislation in 2020 has brought Ukraine closer to EU standards in the field of industrial property and improved mechanisms for acquiring, exercising and protecting patent rights.

References

Betsy Ancker-Johnson, 'Technology Exchange with the USSR: Patents and Licenses' (1974) 17.4 Research Management Journal 14

Gennady Androschuk, 'Artificial Intelligence: Economics, Intellectual Property, Threats' (2021) 3 Journal of Theory and Practice of Intellectual Property 45 [Геннадій Андрощук, 'Штучний Інтелект: Економіка, Інтелектуальна Власність, Загрози' (2021) 3 Теорія і Практика Інтелектуальної Власності 45]

Gennady Androschuk, 'Trends in the Development of Artificial Intelligence Technology: Economic and Legal Aspect' (2019) 3 Journal of Theory and Practice of Intellectual Property 84 [Геннадій Андрощук 'Тенденції Розвитку Технології Штучного Інтелекту: Економіко-Правовий Аспект' (2019) 3 Теорія і Практика Інтелектуальної Власності 84]

Gennady Androschuk and Lyudmyla Rabotyagova, 'U.S. Patent System Reform: An Analysis of Change' (2017) 3(3) Journal Science, Technology, Innovation 61 [Геннадій Андрощук та Людмила Работягова, 'Реформа Патентної Системи США: Аналіз Змін' (2017) 3(3) Наука, Технології, Інновації 61]

Gennady Androschuk, 'Patent Trolling Against Innovations: State, Tendencies, Threats' (2013) 1 *Journal Law and Innovation Society* http://nbuv.gov.ua/UJRN/pric_2013_1_3 [Геннадій Андрощук 'Патентний Тролінг Проти Інновацій: Стан, Тенденції, Загрози' (2013) 1 *Право та Інноваційне Суспільство*]

Gennady Androschuk, 'The Patent System in the World Economy: Development Scenarios' (2010) 4 Journal of Theory and Practice of Intellectual Property 36 [Геннадій Андрощук 'Патентна Система у Світовій Економіці: Сценарії Розвитку' (2010) 4 Теорія і Практика Інтелектуальної Власності 36]

Vadym Barsky, *On the nature of the powers of the state enterprise Ukrainian Institute of Intellectual Property '(Ukrpatent)'* (OLDI-PLUS 2021) [Вадим Барський, *Щодо Природи Повноважень Державного Підприємства Український Інститут Інтелектуальної Власності '(Укрпатент)'* (Олді Плюс 2021)]

Oleksandr Doroshenko and Lyudmyla Rabotyahova, 'New Institute of Intellectual Property Law in Ukraine—Unregistered Industrial Design' (2020) 4 Journal Theory and Practice of Intellectual Property 42 [Олександр Дорошенко та Людмила Работягова, 'Новий Інститут Права Інтелектуальної Власності і Україні—Незареєстрований Промисловий Зразок' (2020) 4 Теорія і Практика Інтелектуальної Власності 42]

Draft National Intellectual Property Strategy of Ukraine for the period 2020–2025 https://drive.google.com/file/d/1oqjabxZiTempwJjaZsO1NoLt7fvP_qxj/view

Eugene Grekov, 'Legal Regulation of Patenting Treatments in Ukraine and the World: Current Status and Prospects' (2013) 1 Bulletin of the Academy of Legal Sciences of Ukraine 114 [Євген Греков, 'Правове Регулювання Патентування Способів Лікування в Україні та Світі: Сучасний Стан і Перспективи Розвитку' (2013) 1 Вісник Академії Правових Наук України 114]

Michael Hoseh, 'The USSR Patent System' (1960) 4 Patent, Trademark and Copyright Journal of Research and Education 220

'Intellectual Property Statistics' WIPO 2021 https://www.wipo.int/ipstats/en/

Yuriy Kapitsa, T G Kossko, D S Makhnovskyi, I I Khomenko, N I Aralova, M P Turov, *Inventive Activity in Academic Organisations* (Logos 2021) [Юрій Капіца та інші, *Винахідницька Діяльність у Наукових Установах* (Логос 2021)]

Yuriy Kapitsa, 'Unregistered Industrial Design: Features of Protection of Rights in the European Union and the Problems of Trolling in Ukraine' (2020) 5 Journal Theory and Practice of Intellectual Property 60 [Юрій Капіца, 'Незареєстрований Промисловий Зразок: Особливості Захисту Прав в Європейському Союзі та Проблеми Тролінгу в Україні' (2020) 5 Теорія і Практика Інтелектуальної Власності 60]

Yuriy Kapitsa, 'Utility Models Protection—Trends in the European Union and Challenges for Ukraine' (2020) 3 Journal of Theory and Practice of Intellectual Property 27 [Юрій Капіца, 'Охорона Прав на Корисні Моделі: Тенденції у Європейському Союзі та Виклики для України' (2020) 3 Теорія і Практика Інтелектуальної Власності 27]

Oksana Kashyntseva, 'Key Points of the Ukrainian Patent Reform in the Health Care Sphere' (2018) 3 Journal of Theory and Practice of Intellectual Property 46 [Оксана Кашинцева, 'Ключові Положення Української Патентної Реформи в Сфері Охорони Здоров'я' (2018) 3 Теорія і Практика Інтелектуальної Власності 46]

Oksana Kashyntseva, 'Human Rights and Patenting of Methods of Human Diagnosis and Treatment in the Context of health Care Reform' (2014) 4 Journal of Theory and Practice of Intellectual Property 5 [Оксана Кашинцева, 'Права Людини та Патентування Методів Діагностики та

Лікування Людини в Контексті Реформування Сфери Охорони Здоров'я' (2014) 4 Теорія і Практика Інтелектуальної Власності 5]

Tetyana Katkova, 'Artificial Intelligence in Ukraine: Legal Aspects' (2020) 6 Journal Law and Society 46 [Тетяна Каткова, 'Штучний Інтелект в Україні: Правові Аспекти' (2020) 6 Право і Суспільство 46]

Olena Kharytonova, Serhiy Vasyliovych Kivalov, Kharitonov Evgeny Olegovich, Kateryna Georgievna Nekit, *Intellectual Property Law* (Yurinkom Inter 2015) [Олена Харитонова та інші, *Право Інтелектуальної Власності* (Юрінком Інтер 2015)]

Olena Orliuk and Natalia Korogod, 'Improvement of Intellectual Property Management in Ukraine' (2020) 6 Journal of Theory and Practice of Intellectual Property 169 [Олена Орлюк і Наталія Корогод, 'Удосконалення Системи Управління Інтелектуальною Власністю в Україні' (2020) 6 Теорія і Практика Інтелектуальної Власності 169]

Olena Orliuk and O D Sviatotsky, *Intellectual Property Law* (InYure 2007) [Олена Орлюк та інші, *Право Інтелектуальної Власності* (ІнЮре 2007)]

Ninaa Samolovova, 'Unregistered Industrial Design in the Fashion Industry' (2021) 3 Journal Theory and Practice of Intellectual Property 11 [Ніна Самоловова, 'Незареєстрований Промисловий Зразок в Індустрії Моди' (2021) 3 Теорія і Практика Інтелектуальної Власності 11]

Roman Shishka, 'Countering Patent Trolling in Ukraine' (2017) 23 Journal of Civilization 73 [Роман Шишка, 'Протидія Патентному Тролінгу в Україні' (2017) 23 Часопис Цивілістики 73]

'Statistics of Ukrpatent' *Ukrpatent* (2021) https://ukrpatent.org/uk/articles/statistics ['Статистика Укрпатенту' *Укрпатент* (2021)]

Leonid Tarasenko, 'Protection of Intellectual Property Rights to Inventions (utility models) and Industrial Designs' (2016) 7 Journal Wroclawsko-Lwowskie zeszyty prawnicze 247 [Леонід Тарасенко, 'Захист Прав Інтелектуальної Власності на Винаходи (Корисні Моделі) і Промислові Зразки' (2016) 7 Вроцлавсько-Львівський Юридичний Вісник 247]

Leonid Tarasenko, 'Patent Law' in Yuliya Glado, *Intellectual Law of Ukraine* (Textbooks and Manuals 2016) 219

Elena Tverytnykova and Maryna Gutnyk, 'The Patent-license System of Ukraine in the Second Half of the XX Century' (2020) 29(2) Journal Studies in the History and Philosophy of Science and Technology 76 [Олена Тверитникова і Марина Гутник, 'Патентно-Ліцензійна Система України у Другій Половині XX Ст' (2020) 29 (2) Дослідження з Історії і Філософії Науки і Техніки 76]

Elizaveta Tymoshenko, 'Artificial Intelligence as a Subject of Intellectual Property Rights' (2020) 4 Journal of Kyiv University of Law 328 [Єлизавета Тимошенко, 'Штучний Інтелект як Суб'єкт Права Інтелектуальної Власності' (2020) 4 Часопис Київського Університету Права 328]

Igor Yakubivsky, 'Objects of Patent Law' (2021) 43 Journal Rule of Law 112 [Ігор Якубівський, 'Об'єкти Патентного Права' (2021) 43 Правова Держава 112]

Oleksandra Yavorska, *IT Law* (Levada 2017) [Олександра Яворська та інші, *IT Право* (Левада 2017)]

Igor Yegorov, 'Post-Soviet Science: Difficulties in the Transformation of the R&D Systems in Russia and Ukraine' (2009) 38(4) Research Policy Journal 600

Patent Law and Access to Medicines in Ukraine

Oksana Kashyntseva

Contents

Abstract This chapter is devoted to aspects of the impact of intellectual property on the market of medicines through the prism of the balance of private and public interests. It describes Ukraine's path to reform in the field of intellectual property (IP) in the context of expanding access to medicines and presents a review of the social and legal factors that accelerated patent reform in medicine and pharmacy. Novelties in legislation are reviewed from the standpoint of their deferred impact on the market of medicines and the rapid effect of the reform. The events of the COVID-19 pandemic, which caused rapid changes in the spirit of IP, which culminated in proposals for its liberalization, influenced the preparation of this material. Calls for exemptions from IP rights concerning the objects used to counter the pandemic are heard even more often within the framework of the TRIPS Council at WTO events. In the current Ukrainian legislation, most of the norms that provide for IP exemptions in the interests of society to protect public health are declarative in nature and do not provide a legal mechanism for their implementation. Unfortunately, the patent reform did not implement all IP exemptions, and compulsory licensing and government use should be drafted by the government of Ukraine. It should be noted that during the preparation of this material the task force involving the WHO and World Bank

O. Kashyntseva (✉)
Department of Intellectual Property Rights and Human Rights in Healthcare, Intellectual Property Scientific Research Institute of the National Academy of Legal Sciences of Ukraine, Kyiv, Ukraine
e-mail: kashyntseva@ukr.net

H. Richter (ed.), *Competition and Intellectual Property Law in Ukraine*,
MPI Studies on Intellectual Property and Competition Law 31,
https://doi.org/10.1007/978-3-662-66101-7_16

experts as well as leading Ukrainian experts began its work at the Ministry of Health of Ukraine with the aim of developing the Health Care Reform Strategy until 2030, "Access to Medicines" being part of it. Among others, it will include provisions on IP and access to treatment.

1 Introduction

The modern concept of IP law in the field of pharmacy up until 2020 (when the COVID-19 pandemic was announced by WHO) can be conditionally divided into two periods: the first period started in the mid-1970s with the beginning of the era of drug patenting and lasted until the 1990s,[1] when messages on the need for certain IP exemptions from IP rights in medicines for poor and developing countries started to be heard at the international policy level. These messages were characteristic of the second period. In March 2020, when WHO declared the beginning of the COVID-19 pandemic and announced at the same time solidarity clinical trials in the field of treatment and prevention of COVID, a third period can be said to have begun. This is a time when access to treatment has become the key to the survival of the human population. The spirit of the rule of law and the absolute value of human life can no longer allow human deaths in an amount commensurate with the Spanish flu pandemic of the early twentieth century.

All three periods can be attributed to socioeconomic factors. The *first period* was due to the rapid development of biomedicine, which required and still requires significant financial and human resources that only business could provide. But in accordance with market laws, business is supposed to ensure profit and minimize the risks from scientific failure. Hence the absolute priority of IP property rights and lobbying for the adoption of relevant norms in international legal regulation.

In 1994, during the Uruguay Round of the General Agreement on Tariffs and Trade, the Agreement on Trade-Related Aspects of Intellectual Property Rights (TRIPS Agreement) was adopted. The Agreement sets minimum standards for the legal protection of intellectual property rights and thus unifies approaches to the protection of rights to inventions in the field of pharmacy. Although the main purpose of the TRIPS Agreement was to strike a balance between the rights of patent holders (in this case pharmaceutical companies) and the public interest in the availability of medicines, some analysts argue that the Agreement was the result of active lobbying in favor of large pharmaceutical companies and that it formalized pro-business approaches in regulating IP legal protection in the field of medicines on the international level.[2]

---

[1] It is the period when international law (TRIPS) determined the minimum standards of patent protection.

[2] John Braithwaite and Peter Drahos, 'Hegemony Based on Knowledge: The Role of Intellectual Property', in Jianfu Chen and Gordon Walker (eds), Balancing Act: Law, Policy and Politics in Globalisation and Global Trade (The Federation Press, Sydney 2004) 204–223.

Such a business-centric model of financing biomedicine and pharmacy facilitated scientific breakthroughs for some period of time. However, this model could only evolve up to the historical moment when property rights were absolutized, after which it started contradicting fundamental human rights—the right to life and health. The second period was a strong manifestation of this situation when we had lost the balance.

The *second period* was due to the onset of the HIV-AIDS, hepatitis and tuberculosis epidemics. The dynamism of people, their rapid migration and the development of human rights in action (refugees were being granted asylum more and more; developed countries were accepting migrants from third-world countries) posed a challenge: either poor countries, which had already begun to drown in epidemics, would be given access to treatment, or one could expect pandemics of these dangerous diseases. And the greatest obstacle to the implementation of the strategy to prevent the spread of infectious diseases from third-world countries was IP. A 20-year patent monopoly on medicines also meant a monopoly on prices. The lack of competition in the face of fierce demand led to excessively high prices, unaffordable for the budgets of developing countries and even more so for the budgets of poor countries. At this stage, there appeared the 2004 Doha Declaration on the TRIPS Agreement and Public Health.

And finally, the *third period*, our contemporary time. This is a period of rethinking IP rights, a period to begin an international dialogue both within the framework of the UN and within the WTO. The COVID-19 pandemic has caused a re-evaluation of patent protection for inventions in the field of pharmacy, gradually transforming it from an end in itself into an instrument for ensuring a fair balance between the property rights of patent holders and the right to health.

Ukraine existed within this global context at all three stages. Because of its powerful generic pharmaceutical industry inherited from the Soviet era, which was transferred into private hands and multiplied by modern technologies; because it has a developing economy, an epidemic of HIV-AIDS, hepatitis and tuberculosis, a rapid increase in cancer after the Chernobyl disaster and military aggression on the eastern borders; and because of its desire to be a recipient of high technologies in pharmacy, Ukraine is ready to become a center for contract manufacturing of medicines, compete with leading generic companies and be a competitive player in the market of generics. Everything that has prevented Ukraine from doing this earlier and what has already been done with a view to the future will be discussed below.

2 Political and Legal Background of Patent Protection in the Health Care System in Ukraine

Today Ukraine is a member of major international organizations in the field of intellectual property, in particular the World Trade Organization (WTO). In 2008 it signed the Agreement on Trade-Related Aspects of the Intellectual Property Rights

(TRIPS). In addition to the intellectual property standards set by the TRIPS Agreement, Ukraine undertook further international obligations on the protection of intellectual property rights by signing free trade agreements with the European Free-Trade Association (EFTA) and the EU. These provisions, called the TRIPS-plus provisions, indicate that they are above the standard of protection set out in the TRIPS Agreement. Such additional provisions include, among others: data exclusivity, patent term extension and measures of enforcement of patent protection. In 2014 Ukraine signed the EU–Ukraine Association Agreement and undertook obligations to partially harmonize its national regulations related to the circulation of medicines with European Union standards. Moreover, Ukrainian legislation contains several TRIPS-plus provisions, i.e. patent linkage and overly burdensome preconditions for compulsory licensing, which Ukrainian legislators have introduced on their own initiative without any international obligations.

A number of the TRIPS-plus provisions that were incorporated into the EU–Ukraine Association Agreement in 2014 without their due adaptation to Ukrainian interests could potentially become extremely difficult barriers on the way to the expansion of access to essential medicines.[3] Such provisions are: data exclusivity and patent term extensions. The patent linkage is a so-called "old TRIPS-plus" provision and was implemented by the Ukrainian legislature on "their own initiative" in 2011; it led to the absence of marketing authorization in the Ukrainian market for several generic drugs to treat hepatitis C, cancer and other diseases.

The national legislation harmonization process has become an excellent opportunity to advocate for the inclusion of the TRIPS-flexibilities and mitigate the existing TRIPS-plus provisions in the patent law of Ukraine. The TRIPS-flexibilities include the following provisions: exhaustion of rights (parallel imports), patentable subject matter definition, research and experimental use exception, regulatory (Bolar) exception, compulsory licensing, public, non-commercial use (government use), patent oppositions and certain provisions in the competition law and implementation of transition periods.

Some of the above provisions have already been implemented in national patent law; some legislative changes are still ahead. The inclusion of the provisions listed above allows for the balance of strong intellectual property rights protection and the needs of public health to save the lives of the most vulnerable members of society. Patent system reform is the solution to a balanced approach to IP protection and access to medicines. The *strategic goal* of patent reform is to implement European standards in the health care sector in a manner that will expand the access to treatment and medications by balancing intellectual property protection with the public interest. The *social purpose* of patent reform was and is to ensure access to essential medicines by opening the market to cheaper generic medicines, which was determined in the state strategy for implementing the policy of providing the population

[3] Sergiy Kondratyuk, 'Best Practices of Implementation of Public Health Related Flexible Provisions of the WTO TRIPS Agreement in Belarus, Georgia, Moldova and Ukraine and Steps Forward for Advocacy', *East Europe and Central Asia Union of PLWH* http://ecuo.org/en/best-practices-on-flexible-provisions-of-the-wto-trips-agrement/.

with medical supplies for the period up to 2025.[4] The COVID-19 pandemic now poses new challenges to us.

One of the most burning issues for Ukraine was the issue of patent trolling[5] due to the imperfections of the national patent system, which prompted the Intellectual Property Research Institute of the National Academy of Legal Sciences of Ukraine, together with the charitable Organization "100% Life", to conduct research from 2018 to 2020 with the goal of identifying the share of evergreening patents for medicines in Ukraine.[6] Comparing the prices of medicines in Ukraine to the prices of the nearest neighbors revealed much higher prices in Ukraine.[7]

In many cases the reason for this is that Ukrainian legislation allows pharmaceutical companies to obtain so-called evergreening patents, which provide them with a monopoly on the import (production) of drugs. "Evergreening patents" is a term used with reference to patents for pharmaceutical products to indicate the artificial continuation of the exclusive rights guaranteed by a patent for an active substance of a pharmaceutical by filing a new application and obtaining a new patent for various additional forms and new properties of the active substance, as well as diagnostic, therapeutic and surgical methods of treatment for humans and animals that use the specified active substance. Thus, pharmaceutical companies artificially extend the monopoly on a drug in Ukraine due to patents that formally meet the requirements of the law but in practice do not have significant advantages over existing counterparts.

International organizations, in particular the World Health Organization (WHO) and the United Nations Development Program (UNDP), pay their attention to the dangerous influence of evergreening patents. International organizations have developed two important documents with recommendations for improving intellectual property law: Guidelines for the examination of pharmaceutical patents (January 2007), developed with the support of WHO, UNCTAD and ICTSD, and Guidelines for the examination of patent applications relating to drugs (June 2016), developed with the support of UNDP.

These documents of international organizations became the basis for conducting research on the availability and percentage of evergreening patents in the Ukrainian market of pharmaceuticals. To determine whether a patent or an application for an invention belongs to the category of evergreening patents, it is necessary to first classify the object (or objects) of patenting. The object of the patent may be a substance presented as an individual chemical compound or composition or a new application

[4] Cabinet of Ministers of Ukraine Resolution 2018/1022/ of 5 December 2018 on the State strategy for the implementation of state policy of providing the population with medical supplies for the period up to 2025.

[5] Here we should note that patent trolling is a broad legal category and includes both the use of imperfections of the patent system to obtain derivative patents with low innovation, and the abuse of procedural rights to delay the relevant cases in court.

[6] Petrenko Sergey et al., 'Report: Evergreening Patents in Ukraine' (Report), 2020 https://network.org.ua/wp-content/uploads/2020/12/Report-eng-curves-1-1.pdf.

[7] Petro Ivasiuk, 'The Same Drugs in Ukraine are Several Times More Expensive than Abroad' UNN (10 August 2018) https://www.unn.com.ua/uk/news/1746240-odni-y-ti-zh-liki-v-ukrayini-v-razi-dorozhche-nizh-za-kordonom.

of a known substance, or the object may be a method of application of the substance or its preparation or production of intermediates, etc.

Thus, in the aforementioned study we characterized individual chemical compounds and characterized the compositions. We also analysed the patents and patent applications with characteristics of "evergreening" that belong to the category of "secondary" patents/patent applications, because they are essentially based on the primary patent, which protects or protected a particular innovative chemical compound. At the same time, it should be borne in mind that not every "secondary" patent is automatically "evergreening". In order to determine whether a patent for an individual chemical compound or composition based on it is "evergreening", it is recommended to test the claimed chemical according to the following criteria, taking into account the presence/absence of differences in technical results.

As the number of biotechnological drugs entering the Ukrainian market grows every year, this study could not escape their attention. The approach to the analysis of patents for biotechnology inventions is generally similar to the approach in the guidelines applicable to other inventions for chemical compounds, substances, compositions, etc. There is no separate methodology that would apply to biotechnological objects yet.

For the study, it was also important what problems accompanied a particular drug during its use and how they were solved or not solved, which could be found in scientific publications in open and accessible sources. This information was used in the analysis of evergreening, including for biotechnology objects.

Based on these criteria, the researchers analysed 132 patents on pharmaceutical products presented in Ukrainian market. The study was based on the patented single-source medicines, whose share exceeded 100,000 USD in centralized procurement in 2017, as well as drugs whose share in hospital and pharmacy procurements exceeded 50 million UAH in 2017.

Additionally, the study included some medicines where the presence of a patent was or had been an obstacle to access to treatment. These included drugs that had been purchased from one manufacturer for a long time due to a patent monopoly, drugs that were either not purchased (had not been purchased for a long time) or whose procurement in the future was questionable due to the existence of patent monopolies, and so on.

Thus, the following result was obtained: during the five years preceding the start of this study, 3,350 patent applications were filed in these areas and 2,303 patents were issued. According to the analysis, 60 patents can be assigned to the category of "evergreening", while the remaining 72 patents cannot.

Finally, slightly more than 45% of the analysed patents fall into this category, and this has become the starting point and the last argument to persuade the MPs to carry out patent reform in Ukraine.[8]

---

[8] Team of authors providing the study, scientific editing by Oksana Kashyntseva, 'Intellectual Property and Ensuring Access to Treatment in a Pandemic: Scientific and Practical Publication', Research Institute of Intellectual Property of the National Academy of Law Sciences of Ukraine (Interservice 2021) (214).

3 The Outline of Patent Law in the Sphere of Pharmacy in Ukraine

It took more than ten years before the Law of Ukraine "On Amendments to Certain Legislative Acts of Ukraine (Regarding the Reform of Patent Legislation)" was adopted on 21 July 2020 (hereinafter—the Law on Patent Reform). The lack of political will to pursue a protectionist policy towards the national manufacturer and the interests of patients hampered the adoption of previous draft initiatives in the field of patent legislation in the Verkhovna Rada of Ukraine of previous convocations. Today, for the first time in Ukraine, we face the phenomenon of "pharmaceutical nationalism", which arose in the pandemic both on national and international levels. Ever since the governments of countries with strong branded and generic pharmaceutical industries have taken the position of prioritizing the national supply of drugs for the treatment of COVID-19, national drug production has become the basis of the state's biological security in Ukraine. And the patent reform carried out by the Ukrainian Parliament in the first pandemic summer—21 July 2020—now looks even more far-sighted.

But have we achieved all the desired goals for Ukraine with the adopted changes, and when will the national manufacturer and the domestic patient feel their positive effects?

We divide the legal changes introduced by the Law on Patent Reform into the following groups:

The first group contains legal changes whose legal consequences come immediately with the adoption of the Law on Patent Reform. These also include changes that provide for the adoption of relevant bylaws for their implementation. *Inter alia*:

- introduction of the possibility to appeal the submitted applications (pre-grant opposition);
- exclusion of therapeutic and surgical treatments from patentable objects;
- introduction of mitigated additional protection of inventions related to medicines;
- introduction of the Bolar exemption into national legislation.

The second group contains legal changes whose legal consequences are delayed in time: these are changes in the patentability of medicines in terms of new therapeutic effect and new forms of known substances, if they do not lead to improved therapeutic effect. The success of these changes depends on the development of the draft rules for expert examination of the application for inventions relating to medicinal products. The rules should be a tool to guarantee the provision of legal protection for truly innovative products and to protect against abuse through a patent monopoly.

The third group contains legal changes that were laid down at the level of draft law initiatives but are not yet reflected in the final text of the law. However, the government of Ukraine continues to work on relevant regulations. These include: compulsory licensing of inventions relating to medicinal products and the use of inventions relating to medicinal products without the consent of the patent owner in extraordinary circumstances, as well as exemptions from IP rights to objects relating to the diagnosis, treatment and prevention of COVID-19.

Let us focus on the legal consequences whose impact can be felt immediately and which contribute to the establishment of healthy competition in the market. One is the opportunity to appeal filed applications for inventions for compliance with their inventive step without the need to wait for the grant of such patents. Such a possibility exists in EU law as a pre-grant opposition. This legal instrument is extremely effective both for preventing the abuse of patent rights and for assisting in the process of expert examination at Ukrpatent. Any persons who believe that the grant of a patent may infringe their rights or legally protected interests, from the moment of publication of information about the application, may read the arguments of both the applicant and the person who objects to the grant of such a patent. It should be noted that the very fact of the introduction of the option to appeal applications into the national legislation prompted the withdrawal of some applications from Ukrpatent immediately after the adoption of the said law in the first reading. Meanwhile, while the other provisions of the draft law were discussed between the first and second readings, the issue of *pre-grant opposition* was raised by supporters of maintaining the status quo in patent law, but it was closed by the argument of the effectiveness of *pre-grant opposition* in EU practice.

Non-controversial provisions also include new provisions under the Patent Reform Law which exclude therapeutic and surgical treatments from legal protection, similar to EU law. By implementing the TRIPS-plus provision in the national legislation with the aim to achieve the strategically important goal of WTO membership, the legislator at the same time made the Ukrainian patient and the national pharmaceutical manufacturer hostage to the imbalance of patent legislation.

According to our study of the data of the Ukrainian Patent Office in the period of 2000–2015, the share of national patents in the field of medical technologies is near 9.85% (in medicines 5.5%) of all patents in all fields of technology in Ukraine. In comparison, for European countries in the same period, the share of patents granted in the field of medical technologies in relation to other sectors of technologies is much lower.[9] However, this statistical information does not reflect the real situation in Ukrainian health care. It reflects the gaps in the national patent legislation, which allows weak patents to be granted in the field of medicine and pharmacy.[10]

Provisions with rapid legal implications also include the supplementary legal protection of medical inventions developed in accordance with best international practices and the Bolar exemption. Since the last two legislative novelties are crucial for the formation of healthy competition in the market of medicines in Ukraine, we will describe them in separate sections.

[9] Oksana Kashyntseva, 'National Patent Reform in the Sphere of Health Care Basing on a Rule of Law' (2015) Legislation Reform.

[10] Oksana Kashyntseva, 'QUO VADIS: Ukrainian Patent Reform in the Frame of EU Ukraine Association Agreement' (2018) Social and Legal Sciences.

4 Supplementary Protection of Medical Inventions

The introduction of supplementary legal protection for inventions in the field of medicine aims to balance the property interests of the patent owner and the interests of society, which on the one hand wants to obtain an effective and safe drug and introduce additional administrative procedures for marketing authorization which delay its sale and the profit of the patent owner in a certain market, and on the other hand wants to get rid of the monopoly and let drug prices dictate as soon as possible.

We can agree that both desires of the society are quite valid, but let's try to assess the situation from the standpoint of the patent owner. He begins the final stage of clinical trials, usually when a patent for a drug has already been granted. However, it is not yet possible to take advantage of a patent monopoly due to clinical trials, in which companies need to prove the safety and efficacy of the drug and go through relevant administrative procedures to bring the drug to market. The testing period for new pharmaceuticals takes up to 12 years from the date of invention/discovery and filing of the patent application for the invention, thus reducing the effective life of the patent to eight years.[11]

To remedy this injustice, Regulation (EC) No. 469/2009 of 6 May 2009 "On the introduction of a supplementary protection certificate for medicinal products" (hereinafter Regulation (EC) No. 469/2009)[12] introduced the possibility to extend a patent (over 20 years) for another five to ten years on average to compensate for lost years of patent protection.

Back in 2000, the Law of Ukraine "On the Protection of Rights to Inventions and Utility Models" was supplemented with a provision stating that the term of a patent for an invention, the object of which is a medicinal product, animal protection product, plant protection product, etc. and which requires marketing authorization from the competent authority, may be extended at the request of the patent owner for a period equal to the period between the date of filing the application and the date of receipt of such authorization, but not more than five years.

As we can see, this norm did not provide for any restrictions on the object of additional protection and did not contain a reference either to the basic patent (active pharmaceutical substance and its use) or to the first registration on the market of a medicinal product. Such uncertainty with more precise criteria has made it possible to provide additional protection not only for the main patent but also for all secondary patents, which protect the same medicinal product through the same mechanisms for the registration of evergreening patents. In many cases, this ensures additional protection for the drug for a period exceeding five years, as it was five years for all secondary patents before the reform, which proposed to calculate the real period

---

[11] Commission of the European Communities, 'Proposal for a Council Regulation Concerning the Creation of a Supplementary Protection Certificate for Medicinal Products' (Proposal) COM/90/101FINAL, § 2.

[12] Regulation No. 2009/469 of the European Parliament and of the Council (EC) of 6 May 2009 concerning the supplementary protection certificate for medicinal products (Codified Version) (2009) OJ L152 (1–10).

before the obtained patent and marketing authorization and only in case the company comes to the Ukrainian market during the first year from the first appearance in the world (Art. 27-1 Law Protection of Rights to Inventions and Utility Models).

The application of the EU Regulation has shaped the relevant case law at the level of EU Member States. In developing amendments to the patent legislation regarding the SPC, Ukraine used the experience of European case law described below.

The cases described below are classified into respective categories based on their analysis: clarification of the term of the first marketing authorization for the use of the medicinal product and the time from which the 15-year term of the supplementary certificate is calculated; clarification of the concept of a "medicinal product"; clarification of what exactly is considered to be a basic patent, as well as the subjects that are entitled to receive such additional protection.[13]

Thus, the European Court of Justice in a number of decisions clarified the concept of a "medicinal product". In particular, the Court reviewed the cases including only one form of the medicinal product (for example, injections) in the marketing authorization; and the question was raised whether in this case the effect of SPC extends to other forms of medicinal product use (tablets, suspensions, etc.).

In the case C-392/97 1999, the European Court of Justice stated that if a product in the form specified in the marketing authorization is protected by a valid basic patent, the supplementary protection certificate may be extended to the form of the medicinal product specified in the basic patent.[14]

Interestingly, the European Court of Justice has made a decision that the provisions of the Regulation should also apply to other products having characteristics similar to a medicinal product, such as cosmetics, if they are the subject of patent protection.[15] However, in these cases, the decisions of the European Court of Justice extend the scope of the certificate as compared to the method and scope of application of the drugs specified in the first marketing authorization.

In 2011, the European Court of Justice heard two strategic cases, Case C-322/10 (*Medeva*) and C-422/10 (*Georgetown*), concerning the interpretation of Art. 3 Regulation (EC) 469/2009, which determines the conditions for obtaining SPC.[16] The *Medeva* case concerned a case in which a patent was granted for two active pharmaceutical ingrediencies. At the same time, authorization was granted for use of a combination of these substances to manufacture a vaccine against *Bordetella pertussis*. However, the vaccine also contained other active ingredients that acted in parallel against diphtheria and tetanus. The UK Patent Office and the courts have refused to grant the certificate due to non-compliance of the drug with the basic patent.

---

[13] Yuriy Kapitsa, 'Certificates of Additional Protection of EU Medicines and Continuation of Legal Protection of Inventions in Ukraine' (2016) Theory and Practice of Intellectual Property 49.

[14] Judgement of the Court (Fifth Chamber) of 16 September 1999 C-392/97 (1999).

[15] Handelsgericht Wien, Austria, Opinion *Advocate General Cosmas* C-77/97, *Osterreichische Unilever GmbH v. Smithkline Beecham Markenartikel GmbH* (1998).

[16] Court of Appeal (England & Wales) United Kingdom, Judgment of the Court (Fourth Chamber), *Medeva BV v Comptroller General of Patents, Designs and Trade Marks* (2011) C-322/10.

In the *Georgetown University* case, marketing authorization was granted to a combination of APIs for which a patent had previously been granted. However, when the university applied for certificates for individual APIs listed in the authorization and in the patent, it got a refusal due to the inconsistency of applications and the authorization.

One of the strategic decisions of the European Court of Justice in 2015 was whether a supplementary protection certificate could be granted if a substance protected by a basic patent (*Protein D*) and a marketing authorization described the substance as a "carrier" for active ingredients (*Pneumococcal polysaccharides*), i.e. as an adjuvant that enhances their effect. However, it was significant for the court that this enhancement effect was not mentioned in the first marketing authorization. The court took the position that the issuance of SPC for API as an adjuvant not defined as such in the first marketing authorization was unlawful (Case C 631/13).[17]

One of the latest cases clarified the answer to the preliminary ruling filed by the High Court of Justice (England and Wales), Chancery Division (Patents Court) (United Kingdom), related to Art. 3(a) Regulation (EC) No. 469/2009 of the European Parliament and of the Council of 6 May 2009 concerning the supplementary protection certificate for medicinal products.[18]

According to the Court, said article must be interpreted as meaning that a product composed of several active ingredients with a combined effect is "protected by a basic patent in force" within the meaning of that provision where, even if the combination of active ingredients of which that product is composed is not expressly mentioned in the claims of the basic patent, those claims relate necessarily and specifically to that combination.

For that purpose, from the point of view of a person skilled in the art and on the basis of the prior art at the filing date or priority date of the basic patent: the combination of those active ingredients must necessarily, in light of the description and drawings of that patent, fall under the invention covered by that patent, and each of those active ingredients must be specifically identifiable, in light of all the information disclosed by that patent.[19]

This decision supplements the ECJ's extensive case law on Art. 3a, including the *Medeva* and *Eli Lilly/HGS* cases. In the *Medeva* case in 2011, the Court concluded that Art. 3a must be interpreted as precluding the competent industrial property office of a Member State from granting an SPC relating to active ingredients which are not specified in the wording of the claims of the basic patent relied on in support of the application for such a certificate. Two years later, the ECJ added in *Eli Lilly/HGS* that when the active ingredient is covered by a functional formula in the claims of a patent issued by the European Patents Office, Art. 3(a) SPC Regulation does not, in

[17] Trevor Cook, 'The Court of Justice Recasts the EU Patent Term Extension System' (2014) 19 Journal of Intellectual Property Rights (144).

[18] England and Wales High Court of C-121/17, *Teva UK Ltd, Accord Healthcare Ltd, Lupin Ltd, Lupin (Europe) Ltd, Generics (UK) trading as 'Mylan' v Gilead Sciences Inc*, (2017).

[19] ECJ, (Decision) C-121/17 *Teva UK Ltd, Accord Healthcare Ltd, Lupin Ltd, Lupin (Europe) Ltd, Generics (UK) trading as 'Mylan' v Gilead Sciences Inc, C 121/17*, decision about art 3(a) of the Supplementary Protection Certificate (SPC) Regulation (2018).

principle, preclude the grant of an SPC for that active ingredient, on condition that it is possible to reach the conclusion on the basis of those claims that the claims relate, implicitly but necessarily and specifically, to the active ingredient in question. The main contribution of this case law relates to products composed of several active ingredients with a combined effect. According to the ECJ, each of those active ingredients must be specifically identifiable, in light of all the information disclosed by that patent.

So, how did Ukraine make use of the EU experiences? With the entry into force of the Law of Ukraine "On Amendments to Certain Legislative Acts of Ukraine on the Reform of Patent Legislation",[20] a new approach to providing additional protection to inventions in the field of pharmacy was proposed. The Ukrainian Law introduces a formula for calculating the term of such protection: it limits the scope of protection and sets requirements for the application procedure. Thus, according to current Ukrainian legislation, the term of additional protection of the invention is equal to the period between the date of filing the application with the patent authority and the date of obtaining the patent owner's first authorization from the competent authority reduced by five years.

In addition, according to the first part of Art. 27-1 Law of Ukraine "On Protection of Rights to Inventions and Utility Models", additional protection may be granted only to an invention whose object is an active pharmaceutical ingredient of a medicinal product, the process of obtaining a medicinal product or the use of a medicinal product. From now on, the rights to additional protection are limited to a product (active pharmaceutical ingredient or a set of active pharmaceutical ingredients of a medicinal product), permitted for circulation in Ukraine by the relevant competent authority under Ukrainian law, and its respective use as a medicinal product. Besides, supplementary protection may be granted only if the application for authorization of a medicinal product that was claimed for additional protection with the aim to introduce it into civil circulation in Ukraine was filed within one year from the date of submission of such application for the first time in any country.

This approach will significantly limit the number of decisions on supplementary protection and will do away with the practice of extending the validity of all secondary patents that protect a medicinal product.

An important novelty that will have a positive impact on the availability of generic medicines is the implementation of the provisions of Regulation (EU) 2019/933 of the European Parliament and of the Council on supplementary protection certificates for medicinal products on the so-called manufacturing and storage waivers.[21] In accordance with Part 6 of Art. c27-1 Law of Ukraine "On Protection of Rights to Inventions and Utility Models", the use of the invention during the period of additional protection is not recognized as a violation of the rights in an invention if it is used for:

---

[20] Ukrainian Law on Amendments to Certain Legislative Acts of Ukraine Concerning the Reform of Patent Legislation 2020, 816-IX.

[21] This provision was lobbied for by a national manufacturer with experience in contract drug production up to 2004.

- manufacture of a product or medicinal product containing a product using a patented invention for export to third countries, as well as other actions recognized as the use of the invention, if they are necessary for the manufacture of a product or medicinal product containing the product for export to third countries;
- manufacture of a product or medicinal product containing the product using the patented invention not earlier than six months before the expiration of the additional protection period for storage in order to put into circulation after the expiration of the additional protection period, as well as other actions recognized as the use of the invention, if they are necessary for the manufacture of a product or medicinal product containing the product and its storage not earlier than the specified period.

This norm is aimed at enabling the earliest release of generic versions of drugs on the national market and at the development of a national pharmaceutical manufacturer, which will now be able to start production of the medicinal product for export much earlier.

These changes to the national legislation in the field of additional protection of inventions create undoubtedly more favorable conditions for increasing the availability of medicines in Ukraine compared to the regime that existed before 2020. However, as these changes bring a radically new approach, different from the previous practice of extending the patent, it is extremely important to develop detailed, clear bylaws for their effective application, giving the possibility to eliminate any inconsistencies that could raise questions from the expert when considering the relevant applications.

Thus, in the study of the impact of TRIPS-plus provisions on access to medicines, the reviewed data demonstrate that the economic effect of additional protection of inventions is extremely negative as far as the availability of medicines is concerned. During the period of additional monopoly, which averages four years and six months for the drug, the state overpays 62–87.5% on the purchase of one drug. On the purchase of a mere four drugs considered in the study of evergreening patents in the Ukrainian market, in the absence of additional protection, the state could have saved almost 95 million UAH.[22]

The provision of additional protection for inventions in the field of pharmacy is an obligation of Ukraine under the Association Agreement, and therefore, despite the negative effect of the regime on the availability of medicines, this norm cannot be excluded from national legislation. However, we hope that the safeguards available in the new version of the Law of Ukraine "On Protection of Rights to Inventions and Utility Models" will provide an opportunity in the future to mitigate the harmful consequences of the regime to a certain extent and ensure the interests of the population in access to treatment.

[22] Anastasiia Homeniuk, 'Study of the Impact of TRIPS-plus Provisions on the Availability of Medicines in Ukraine' https://network.org.ua/wp-content/uploads/2020/12/Doslidzhennya-vplyvu-polozhen-TRIPS-1-2-1.pdf accessed 2 April 2022.

5 Bolar Exemption in the Ukrainian Pharmaceutical Market

Lawful importation of goods manufactured using the invention (utility model) for research and/or use of the invention (utility model) in research conducted to prepare and submit information for registration of a medicinal product is no longer recognized as an infringement of the rights arising from the patent (Art. 31(5) Law of Ukraine "On Protection of the Right to Inventions and Utility Models"). A similar provision is contained, in particular, in Directive 2001/83/EC of the European Parliament and of the Council of 6 November 2001 on the Community code relating to medicinal products for human use (hereinafter—Directive 2001/83/EC).

The opponents, including representatives of the originator manufacturers, accuse the legislator of violating the exclusivity of pharmaceutical dossier data, citing the norm of Art. 222 Association Agreement between Ukraine and the EU. On the other hand, the intellectual property experts involved in the development of this provision do not see any violations here and set out the following arguments.

On the market, the drug is protected by patent law and the right to protect information on the data of the pharmaceutical (registration) dossier—data exclusivity which was implemented into the Ukrainian legislation under the demand of TRIPS before Ukraine possessed membership in WTO.

It is important that both legal institutions complement each other. For example, after the expiration of patent rights (valid for 20 years plus five years of additional legal protection), the countdown of five years of data exclusivity begins from the moment of filing an application for the first registration of an original drug with the State Expert Center at the Ministry of Health of Ukraine (hereinafter SEC MH of Ukraine). Therefore, in practice, even after the expiration of patent rights, the exclusivity of the data does not allow the generic drug to enter the market, as it will not be registered before the expiration of the five-year term of their protection.

Thus, the amendments introduced by the law to Art. 31 Law of Ukraine "On Protection of Rights to Inventions" and Art. 9 Law of Ukraine "On Medicinal Products" apply only when both the patent and the exclusivity of data have exhausted themselves in Ukraine.

These novelties do not violate the provisions of Art. 222 Association Agreement between Ukraine and the EU, as they are guarded by the provisions of the same Art. 9 Law of Ukraine "On Medicinal Products", according to which the information contained in the application for state registration of medicinal products and its annexes, in accordance with the provisions of this law and other regulations of Ukraine, is subject to state protection against disclosure and unfair commercial use.

So what are the illegal actions specified by Art. 222 Association Agreement between Ukraine and the EU? The first is disclosure, and the second unfair commercial use.

Responding to the question on disclosure, let's mention that when applying for a generic drug registration, the applicant refers to the publicly available information of the original product dossier, which is always published on the relevant FDA or

EMA resources or by other regulatory authorities responsible for the registration of medicinal products. The application is also accompanied by bioequivalence studies conducted by the manufacturer of a generic. Therefore, the applicant's reference to the information contained in the dossier of the original medicinal product in its published part and its use for review by the experts carrying out their professional activities cannot be considered its disclosure, let alone unfair commercial use.

The case law of the European Court of Justice is valuable for us when we need to determine the coordinates of the proposed changes in light of European integration processes. The court clearly demonstrated its position in the case *PTC Therapeutics International v EMA*[23] and in the case *MSD Animal Health Innovation and Intervet International v EMA*.[24] It is stated in these cases that the widest possible public access to documents available in the institutions, bodies and offices of the Union shall be really encouraged. An exception to this principle may be used to protect commercial interests only if the holder/applicant of the marketing authorization proves that the disclosure of the documents may pose a risk of specific harm to the commercial interests of the persons concerned. The above-mentioned cases give grounds to conclude that certain information cannot be considered confidential due to its disclosure and publication. Of course, those cases did not deal with either the Bolar exception or test data exclusivity as such but concerned primarily the presumption of confidentiality under Regulation 1049/2001/EC.

Thus, according to the amendments made by the law to the Ukrainian legislation, the entry of a generic medicinal product on the market is possible only on the day after the expiration of patent protection or data exclusivity, or both protection regimes at the same time. Before the patent reform, which will take place the day after the termination of these legal protection regimes, we have the possibility only to begin studies and, having received positive results, to submit an application to the SEC MOH of Ukraine. If the result is negative, then one can continue research, improve production, etc. Therefore, the release of a generic drug is delayed for years due to the inability to be ready to enter the market the day after the fall of the market monopoly ensured by the patent and the exclusivity of the originator data.

6 The Instruments of IP Law to Ensure Access to Medicines

International intellectual property law, in particular the TRIPS Agreement, contains an effective set of legal instruments to ensure access to medicines. In accordance with international practice, flexible provisions of the TRIPS Agreement have been used as per the provisions of the Doha Declaration on the TRIPS Agreement and

[23] General Court (Second Chamber), (Judgment) T-818/15 *PTC Therapeutics International v. EMA* (2018).

[24] General Court (Second Chamber), (Judgment) T-729/15 *MSD Animal Health Innovation and Internet International v. EMA* (2018).

public health in low-income and developing countries. Now, the pandemic has significantly affected the ability to utilize these tools. The Doha Declaration on the TRIPS Agreement and Public Health (in its para. 6) recognized that developing countries with insufficient or no manufacturing capacity in the pharmaceutical sector could face difficulties in making effective use of compulsory licensing under the TRIPS Agreement. The WTO's decision of 30 August 2003 set up a system intended to overcome these difficulties. Article 219 "Patent and Public Health" of the Association Agreement between EU and Ukraine also states the priority of the Doha Declaration for the public health sphere.

We finalized this chapter in the second year of the COVID-19 pandemic, and it has had a lasting impact on content and personal attitude of the author towards the balance between IP and access to medicines. The Director-General of the WHO issued a statement mentioning that "the world is on the brink of a catastrophic moral failure" due to unequal international distribution of COVID-19 vaccines, and that these actions would only prolong the pandemic and the restrictions needed to contain it.[25] As a result, human tragedies and economic unrest have prompted the international community to reconsider its approach to the formation of intellectual property policy in the field of medicines, which is moving towards "pharmaceutical nationalism".[26] The statement of the Biden administration regarding the possible waiver of international patent protection for vaccines against COVID-19 is also historic. The USA stated that it would begin participating in WTO negotiations on conditions for intellectual property exclusion, for disclosure of patents and dossiers on vaccine manufacture, which should make the latter widely available and allow low-income countries to use biosimilars.[27]

In the pandemic, we see trends towards the liberalization of intellectual property rights in the field of medicine through the definition of special intellectual property rights in health care. *Sui generis* trends are also reflected in the Association Agreement between Ukraine and the EU, which contains the provision "Patents and Public Health" (Art. 219).

No doubt, the COVID-19 pandemic has become a catalyst for global trends towards the liberalization of intellectual property rights in the field of medicine. Issues of liberalization of intellectual property began to be considered not only from the standpoint of providing treatment to poor countries, but also from the standpoint

---

[25] World Health Organization, 'WHO Director-General's Opening Remarks at 148th Session of the Executive Board', *World Health Organization* (18 January 2021) https://www.who.int/director-general/speeches/detail/who-director-general-s-opening-remarks-at-148th-session-of-the-executive-board accessed 2 April 2022.

[26] 'Vaccine Nationalism Means that Poor Countries will be Left Behind' *The Economist* (28 January 2021) www.economist.com/graphic-detail/2021/01/28/vaccine-nationalism-means-that-poor-countries-will-be-left-behind accessed 2 April 2022.

[27] Nathaniel Weixel, 'Biden backs COVID-19 Vaccine Patent Waivers', *The Hill* (5 May 2021) https://thehill.com/policy/healthcare/551992-biden-backs-covid-19-vaccine-patent-waivers accessed 2 April 2022.

of the common good. Today, the spirit of IP law seems to be changing: strong protection of innovation and access to treatment no longer compete, but are potentially complementary.

Let us have a look at the standpoint of the governments of Germany and France as the economically strongest Europeans countries. In Germany, the "Law on the Protection of the Population in the Event of an Epidemic Situation of National Importance" entered into force. The law provides, *inter alia*, for amendments to the Patent Law, according to which the Federal Ministry of Health has the right to authorize the use of relevant patents to ensure the manufacture and supply of pharmaceuticals or medical products. In 2020, France adopted the Emergency Law No. 2020-290 to combat the COVID-19 epidemic, which introduced Art. 3131-15 to the French Public Health Code. This provision allows the prime minister to order the requisition of all goods and services necessary to fight the health disaster, to temporarily control the price of products and, if necessary, to take any measures to ensure that patients are provided with appropriate drugs to deal with the health disaster.[28]

It is beneficial for Ukraine to learn from the experience of Canada, both in terms of facilitating negotiations with major vaccine manufacturers to establish national drug production and in terms of developing legislation in the field of compulsory licensing.[29]

Of course, voluntary licenses from patent owners, which provide for the full transfer of technology and not just patent disclosure, are the most effective tool for the national production of biosimilars. However, international experience shows that pharmaceutical companies hold back the issuance of compulsory licenses. Therefore, our government's biosecurity portfolio should include an effective tool for compulsory licensing or emergency use of biosimilars and generic drugs by the government. In fact, this is provided by Art. 5 Paris Convention for the Protection of Industrial Property of 1883 (hereinafter: the Paris Convention) [6], which states that each country of the Union has the right to take legislative measures to issue compulsory licenses to prevent abuses that may arise as a result of the exercise of an exclusive right granted by a patent.

Article 31 TRIPS Agreement provides for the right to use a patent without the permission of the patent owner by the government of the member state or by a third party with the permission of the government in case of emergency in the country or in other circumstances of extreme necessity.

---

[28] Jordana Sanft et al., 'Governmental Use of Patented Inventions During a Pandemic: A Global Survey' *Norton Rose Fullbright* (16 April 2020) https://www.nortonrosefulbright.com/-/media/files/nrf/nrfweb/knowledge-pdfs/governmental-use-of-patented-inventions-during-a-pandemic-guide.pdf accessed 2 April 2022.

[29] 'Backgrounder—Government of Canada Investments in COVID-19 Vaccines, Therapeutics and Biomanufacturing Capacity' (2 February 2021) https://www.canada.ca/en/innovation-science-economic-development/news/2021/02/backgrounder--government-of-canada-investments-in-covid-19-vaccines-and-biomanufacturing-capacity.html accessed 2 April 2022.

Article 219 Association Agreement between Ukraine and the EU states that the parties recognize the importance of the Doha Declaration. In interpreting and exercising the rights and obligations under Chap. 9 "Intellectual Property", the parties shall ensure compliance with the Doha Declaration.

It is important that the legal grounds for governments to use the compulsory licensing mechanism under subparagraph (b) of para. 5 Doha Declaration are determined by each country at its own discretion. Some examples of possible grounds are set out in Art. 31 TRIPS Agreement, such as:

- public non-commercial use;
- use in case of emergency in the country or other circumstances of extreme necessity;
- use to prevent anti-competitive practices;
- interdependence of patents.

Besides, the Paris Convention allows compulsory licensing in case of non-use or insufficient use of the invention. For example, the long-term non-use of patented drugs for COVID-19 in Ukraine may in the future (supposedly due to the unwillingness to spend on obtaining a registration certificate for a medicinal product) be grounds for compulsory licensing and manufacture or supply of a generic version of such a drug or biosimilar, if it concerns a biological medicinal product. The recent situation of the lack of vaccines and the downtime of production facilities that were ready to manufacture the vaccines gives another example of the fact that the patent owner is not too accustomed to socially responsible behavior in the world… even in a pandemic, when millions of deaths are caused by the lack of access to drugs.[30]

Practice shows that the pre-pandemic world practice demonstrates that the application of compulsory licensing mechanisms in health care allows us to conclude that the first two grounds are widely used in developing and low-income countries.

In contrast, in the EU, the most common reason for compulsory licensing in health care, again in the pre-pandemic era, was to prevent anti-competitive practices. Unfortunately, such a practice does not exist in Ukraine at all due to the lack of legal grounds. The pandemic also dictated its rules for EU countries, which quickly changed their legislation to expand the use of compulsory licensing and emergency use.

Ukraine has to take into account the EU experience. The development of relevant provisions in competition law is currently among the legislator's priorities, especially given that the prevention and/or correction of anti-competitive practices impeding access to medicines is one of the important flexible provisions of the TRIPS Agreement. Thus, the interpretation of the provision with respect to anti-competitive practices is included in Art. 8(2), Art. 31(1)(k) and Art. 40 TRIPS Agreement. It is noteworthy that the TRIPS Agreement does not contain a definition

[30] Christopher Rowland et al., 'Drug Companies Defend Vaccine Monopolies in Face of Global Outcry' *The Washington Post* (20 March 2021) https://www.washingtonpost.com/business/2021/03/20/covid-vaccine-global-shortages accessed 2 April 2022.

of anti-competitive behavior and thus leaves the WTO members free to determine anti-competitive actions and develop their own policy towards them.

The issuance of compulsory licenses under Art. 31 (1)(k) TRIPS Agreement as a remedy for anti-competitive practices, as opposed to compulsory licenses under Art. 31 (1)(b) TRIPS Agreement, does not require prior negotiations with the patent owner. There is not even a requirement about the notification of the patent owner, as in the case with the government use of the patent.

In accordance with Art. 31 (1)(k) TRIPS Agreement, the need to remedy anti-competitive practices may be taken into account in determining the amount of compensation to the patent owner. This means that in particularly serious cases of anti-competitive practices compensation may not be paid at all. In practice, anti-monopoly authorities also resort to imposing fines on violators, which is another deterrent to anti-competitive behavior.

So, the TRIPS Agreement does not limit the possibility to determine the grounds for compulsory licensing at the level of national legislation, but requires them to be properly enshrined at the level of national law (Art. 31 TRIPS).

According to Art. 31 TRIPS Agreement, there are several possible scenarios for the use of patented inventions without the permission of the right holder, depending on the initiator of the compulsory license:

- use at the initiative *of a third party* with the permission of the government;
- government use or use by the government-authorized contractor at the initiative of the government in the case of public non-commercial use.

Today, countries have gone much further and raised the issue of expanding the mechanisms of intellectual property rights in order to gain access to what is so far the only way to overcome the pandemic—exemptions for IP rights to vaccines.

Analysis of TRIPS Council papers, which provide the arguments of the countries advocating for temporary exemption from intellectual property rights for the objects used for diagnosis, therapy and prevention of COVID-19, gives us grounds to conclude that such measures should be introduced in order to provide mankind with vaccines as soon as possible, as well as to develop domestic production of vaccines and medicines as a component of the biological safety of the given countries.[31]

Observing global trends, we understand that countries are getting ready to produce medicines in emergencies. Voluntary licensing issues are raised by the Technology Access Partnership TAP, administered by UN Technology Bank or through the Open COVID Pledge Initiative. However, so far we do not see any significant progress in this direction. We are witnessing a tense situation with regard to access to COVID-19 prevention technologies.

The analytical report "Accelerating COVID-19 Vaccine Production via Involuntary Technology Transfer" presented by South Center is extremely valuable to us. It states that "currently discussed proposals at the WTO related to increasing the

[31] World Trade Organization, 'Waiver from Certain Provisions of the TRIPS Agreement for the Prevention, Containment and Treatment of Covid-19, Communication from India and South Africa', IP/C/W/669, 2020.

production of COVID-19 vaccines, including the EU proposal to clarify the use of compulsory licensing and the submission by South Africa and India on the intellectual property (IP) waiver, require complementary mechanisms to rapidly improve the production of COVID-19 vaccines that are urgently needed today".[32]

However, the governments opposing the waiver argue that current WTO rules already allow countries to apply for "compulsory licensing" to override IP during emergencies.

And it is important to note here that compulsory licensing provides access to a patent, but under conditions that are not always possible to achieve. As noted, TRIPS Art. 31 requires negotiations with the patent owner, but as of October 2021, in most cases such negotiations were unsuccessful. In addition, the disclosure of a patent for vaccines is totally insufficient without the transfer of access to know-how and technology in general. Therefore, in order to overcome the limited access to vaccines two proposals were submitted to the WTO: the first one concerns the interpretation of the flexible provisions of the TRIPS Agreement, and the second the possibility of disclosing not only the patent but also the technology.

As for the first proposal, it concerns the clarification for a uniform interpretation of the TRIPS Agreement flexible provisions, agreed in Marrakesh back in 1994 and foresightedly detailed in 2017. Today, in a pandemic, they can be used to introduce IP rights exemptions in the form of compulsory licensing.[33] South Africa and India were the first to step up with the initiative to temporarily waive IP rights in the TRIPS Agreement[34]; the EU joined the discussion later on and now it is partially supported by the US.[35]

As for the second key proposal, it concerns the disclosure and transfer of know-how. The urgency of expanding access to such knowledge through C-TAP is the key to accelerating the release of vaccines in the required amounts, which will allow us to vaccinate a critical number of people to stop the mutation of the virus. However, at the time of writing, negotiations on such a transfer have failed. For example, negotiations between Biolyse (Canada's powerful cancer drug manufacturer), which can produce two million doses a month, and Johnson & Johnson (J&J) were unsuccessful. J&J refused to license its technology to Biolyse.[36]

Representatives of some law schools mention that it is currently acknowledged that there are no specific provisions in international and national IP laws, similar to

---

[32] Olga Gurgula, 'Accelerating COVID-19 Vaccine Production via Involuntary Technology Transfer' (2021) South Centre Policy Brief No. 102.

[33] World Trade Organization, 'Agreement on Trade-Related Intellectual Property Rights (as amended on 23 January 2017): Marrakesh Agreement Establishing the World Trade Organization, Annex 1C, 15 April 1994', *WTO* (2017) https://www.wto.org/english/docs_e/legal_e/31bis_trips_01_e.htm accessed 2 April 2022.

[34] IP/C/W/669, 2020.

[35] Weixel, *The Hill* (n 27) https://thehill.com/policy/healthcare/551992-biden-backs-covid-19-vaccine-patent-waivers accessed 2 April 2022.

[36] Arianna Schouten, 'Canada Based Biolyse Pharma Seeks to Manufacture COVID-19 Vaccines for Low Income Countries, may test Canada's Compulsory Licensing for Export Law' *Knowledge Ecology International* (12 March 2021) https://www.keionline.org/35587 accessed 2 April 2022.

the compulsory licensing mechanism developed for patents, that would allow access to trade secrets held by pharmaceutical companies if they are not willing to share this information voluntarily.[37] In legal literature we find the statements: "Unlike patents, regulatory entities do not grant or confirm trade secrets; rather, one has a trade secret by keeping valuable information secret. Trade secrets are not meant to be shared unless the owner authorizes it and then, usually, under a requirement of secrecy by the authorized party. Thus, the core trade secret legal action is one for misappropriation of it by a former employee/competitor through commercial espionage or sloppy trade secret management."[38]

Instead, it seems legitimate to consider the provisions of Art. 73 "Security Exceptions" of the TRIPS Agreement as possible grounds for disclosure and use of know-how in a pandemic. However, the application of this norm at the level of national legislation also requires appropriate changes in national legislation. It also seems that the principles of the TRIPS Agreement contained in Art. 8 allow us to use trade secrets for public health purposes.

In conclusion, it should be mentioned that although it is extremely important for Ukraine to be able to use the flexible provisions of the TRIPS Agreement both for the production of vaccines and over time for the production of specific COVID treatment medicines, the government should have in mind the need to clarify the production capacities of the national manufacturers in order to enable the production of such vaccines and medicines exclusively for the national market, at least in the first stage, as the priority is to meet the needs of the national patient. And, of course, compulsory know-how licenses (trade secrets) should contain provisions limiting the time and number of doses produced, similar to compulsory licenses for inventions.

7 Conclusions

As we can see, Ukraine is a country with intellectual property legislation that is fully in line with international IP law. By providing proper legal protection to inventions in the field of pharmacy, Ukraine is trying to grant quality protection documents that would have value in the market of IP objects. At the same time, as a member of the WTO, Ukraine seeks to maximize the benefits for the development of the national economy in a global context. And this shapes a new challenge—pharmaceutical nationalism. Today, no country can feel safe if it is unable to provide its population with critical medicines under certain emergencies. This right should be exercised through the compulsory licensing of inventions for medicinal products, through the use of inventions by the government in the public interest, but most effectively through

[37] Gurgula, 'Accelerating COVID-19 Vaccine Production via Involuntary Technology Transfer' (n 32).

[38] David S Levine, 'Covid-19 Trade Secrets and Information Access: An Overview' (2021) *InfoJustice*.

voluntary licenses. At the same time, legislation, industry and human resources have to be prepared for these challenges.

The world should come out as a winner from this pandemic. We have to change the spirit of IP law in the field of pharmacy; we need we need to begin prioritizing the development of sectors of national economies in favor of the development of local generic pharmaceutical production. And we have to get closer to the formation of a new ethics—the ethics of socially responsible business focused on people and society. However, the balance of private and public interests in IP can be ensured not only by legislation that meets international standards, but also by an effective judicial system. In Ukraine, this should be ensured by a specialized court—the Court of Intellectual Property.

References

'Backgrounder—Government of Canada investments in COVID-19 Vaccines, Therapeutics and Biomanufacturing Capacity' *Innovation, Science and Economic Development Canada* (2 February 2021) https://www.canada.ca/en/innovation-science-economic-development/news/2021/02/backgrounder--government-of-canada-investments-in-covid-19-vaccines-and-biomanufacturing-capacity.html

John Braithwaite and Peter Drahos, 'Hegemony Based on Knowledge: The Role of Intellectual Property', in Jianfu Chen and Gordon Walker (eds), *Balancing Act: Law, Policy and Politics in Globalisation and Global Trade* (The Federation Press, Sydney 2004)

Trevor Cook, 'The Court of Justice Recasts the EU Patent Term Extension System' (2014) 19 Journal of Intellectual Property Rights 141

Olga Gurgula, 'Accelerating COVID-19 Vaccine Production via Involuntary Technology Transfer' (2021) South Centre Policy Brief No. 102

Anastasiia Homeniuk, 'Study of the Impact of TRIPS-plus Provisions on the Availability of Medicines in Ukraine' https://network.org.ua/wp-content/uploads/2020/12/Doslidzhennya-vplyvu-polozhen-TRIPS-1-2-1.pdf [Анастасія Гоменюк, 'Дослідження впливу положень ТРІПС-плюс на доступність лікарських засобів в Україні']

Petro Ivasiuk, 'The Same Drugs in Ukraine are Several Times More Expensive than Abroad' *UNN* (10 August 2018) https://www.unn.com.ua/uk/news/1746240-odni-y-ti-zh-liki-v-ukrayini-v-razi-dorozhche-nizh-za-kordonom [Петро Івасюк, 'Одні й ті ж ліки в Україні в рази дорожче, ніж за кордоном' *УНН* (10 серпня 2018)]

Yuriy Kapitsa, 'Certificates of Additional Protection of EU Medicines and Continuation of Legal Protection of Inventions in Ukraine', (2016) 5 Theory and Practice of Intellectual Property 49 [Юрій Капіца, 'Сертифікати Додаткової Охорони Лікарських Засобів ЄС та Продовження Правової Охорони Винаходів в України', Теорія і Практика Інтелектуальної Власності 5 (2016) 49]

Oksana Kashyntseva, 'QUO VADIS: Ukrainian Patent Reform in the Frame of EU Ukraine Association Agreement' (2018) Social and Legal Sciences

Oksana Kashyntseva, 'National Patent Reform in the Sphere of Health Care Basing on a Rule of Law (2015) Legislation Reform

Sergiy Kondratyuk, 'Best Practices of Implementation of Public Health Related Flexible Provisions of the WTO TRIPS Agreement in Belarus, Georgia, Moldova and Ukraine and Steps Forward for Advocacy', (2015) East Europe and Central Asia Union of PLWH https://ecuo.org/en/best-practices-on-flexible-provisions-of-the-wto-trips-agrement/

David S Levine, 'Covid-19 Trade Secrets and Information Access: An Overview' (2021) InfoJustice

References

Centre for Commercial Law Studies and Queen Mary University of London, FCDO Ukraine—IP Court Project' (Final Report) 2020

Draft on the National Strategy for the Development of Intellectual Property of Ukraine for the Period 2020–2025 (2019) NIPO, 142 https://drive.google.com/file/d/1oqjabxZiTempwJjaZsO1NoLt7fvP_qxj/view [Проект Національної Стратегії Розвитку Сфери Інтелектуальної Власності України на Період 2020–2025 роки (2019) НОІВ, 142]

Soumitra Dutta, Bruno Lanvin, and Sacha Wunsch-Vincent, *Global Innovation Index 2019: Creating Healthy Lives—The Future of Medical Innovation,* (Cornell University, INSEAD, and the World Intellectual Property Organization 2019)

European Commission, *Innovation Policy: European Experience and Recommendations for Ukraine* (Phoenix 2011) [Європейська Комісія, *Інноваційна політика: Європейський досвід та рекомендації для України* У 3-х томах (Фенікс 2011)]

Olena Orliuk and Nataliia Korogod 'Improvement of Intellectual Property Management in Ukraine' (2020) 6 Theory and Practice of Intellectual Property Journal 169 [Олена Орлюк та Наталія Корогод 'Удосконалення Системи Управління Інтелектуальною Власністю в Україні' (2020) 6 Теорія і Практика Інтелектуальної Власності 169]

Parliamentary Hearings of Ukraine, 'Building an Effective Intellectual Property Protection System in Ukraine' *Verkhovna Rada of Ukraine* (16 December 2019) [Парламентські слухання України, 'Побудова Ефективної Системи Захисту Інтелектуальної Власності в Україні' *Верховна Рада України* (16 грудня 2019)]

Yuliya Samayeva, 'Intellectual Property—WB, 2017, 58it is Not About Laws, but Economic Development' *ZN'UA* (23 March 2019) https://www.nas.gov.ua/siaz/Ways_of_development_of_Ukrainian_science/article/19036.2.016.pdf [Юлія Самаєва, 'Інтелектуальна Власність — це не про Закони, це про Розвиток Економіки' ZN'UA (23 березня 2019)]

State Enterprise Ukrainian Institute of Intellectual Property 'Industrial Property in Numbers. Indicators of activity in the field of Intellectual Property for 2018', Ukrpatent 2019 [Державне Підприємство Український Інститут Інтелектуальної Власності 'Промислова Власність у Цифрах. Показники Діяльності у Сфері Інтелектуальної Власності за 2018 рік', Укрпатент 2019]

United Nations Economic Commission for Europe 'Innovation Performance Review of Ukraine', UNECE, 2013, 126

World Bank, 'Ukraine: Innovation and Entrepreneurship Ecosystem Diagnostic' (2017), 58, WB, 2017, 58 https://openknowledge.worldbank.org/handle/10986/28831

Christopher Rowland, Emily Rauhala and Miriam Berger, 'Drug Companies Defend Vaccine Monopolies in Face of Global Outcry' *The Washington Post* (20 March 2021) https://www.washingtonpost.com/business/2021/03/20/covid-vaccine-global-shortages

Jordana Sanft, Chelsea Nimmo and Colin Hyslop, 'Governmental Use of Patented Inventions during a Pandemic: A Global Survey' *Norton Rose Fullbright* (16 April 2020) https://www.nortonrosefulbright.com/-/media/files/nrf/nrfweb/knowledge-pdfs/governmental-use-of-patented-inventions-during-a-pandemic-guide.pdf

Arianna Schouten, 'Canada Based Biolyse Pharma Seeks to Manufacture COVID-19 Vaccines for Low Income Countries, may Test Canada's Compulsory Licensing for Export Law' *Knowledge Ecology International* (12 March 2021) https://www.keionline.org/35587

Petrenko Sergey, Zhikharev Alexander and Trofymenko Mykyta, 'Report: Evergreening Patents in Ukraine' (Report), 2020 https://network.org.ua/wp-content/uploads/2020/12/Report-eng-curves-1-1.pdf

Team of authors providing the study, scientific editing by Oksana Kashyntseva, 'Intellectual Property and Ensuring Access to Treatment in a Pandemic: Scientific and Practical Publication', *Research Institute of Intellectual Property of the National Academy of Law Sciences of Ukraine* (Interservice 2021) [колектив авторів; за науковою редакцією Оксани Кашинцевої, 'Інтелектуальна Власність та Забезпечення Доступу до Лікування в Умовах Пандемії: Науково-Практичне Видання, *НДІ Інтелектуальної Власності НАПрН України* (Інтерсервіс 2021)]

'Vaccine Nationalism Means that Poor Countries will be Left Behind' *The Economist* (28 January 2021) www.economist.com/graphic-detail/2021/01/28/vaccine-nationalism-means-that-poor-countries-will-be-left-behind

Nathaniel Weixel, 'Biden backs COVID-19 Vaccine Patent Waivers', *The Hill,* (5 May 2021) https://thehill.com/policy/healthcare/551992-biden-backs-covid-19-vaccine-patent-waivers

World Health Organization, 'WHO Director-General's Opening Remarks at 148th Session of the Executive Board', *World Health Organization* (18 January 2021) https://www.who.int/director-general/speeches/detail/who-director-general-s-opening-remarks-at-148th-session-of-the-executive-board

World Trade Organization, 'Waiver from Certain Provisions of the TRIPS Agreement for the Prevention, Containment and Treatment of Covid-19: Communication from India and South Africa', IP/C/W/669, 2020

World Trade Organization, 'Agreement on Trade-Related Intellectual Property Rights (as amended on 23 January 2017): Marrakesh Agreement Establishing the World Trade Organization, Annex 1C, 15 April 1994', *WTO* (2017) https://www.wto.org/english/docs_e/legal_e/31bis_trips_01_e.htm

The Patentability of Biotechnological Inventions in the EU: The Ukrainian Context

Tetyana Komarova

Contents

Abstract The problems of bioengineering development and the use of its results in medicine have become extremely important due to the powerful development of modern technologies and their capabilities. At the same time, this issue cannot be attributed purely to the field of medicine, as it is also closely related to the ethical, social, economic and, of course, legal spheres. If we talk about the legal side of the issue, it is impossible not to touch on the topic of patenting the results of bioengineering. Patenting the results of bioengineering has begun to form a new vector in scientific research. If earlier the scientific study of cells of organisms, including human ones, was based on openness and access of the whole scientific community to its course and results, now it has become a commercialised and monetised domain. The difficulty in understanding this issue is compounded by the fact that the use of living cells in research remains an area in which there is no consensus among states. This chapter aims to identify the spheres in which it is forbidden to patent

The chapter is a significantly expanded and updated version of a previously published article by the author: Tetyana Komarova, 'The Patentability of Biotechnological Inventions in the EU: The Impact on Therapeutic Practice' (2020) 73 Wiadomosci Lekarskie 1747.

T. Komarova (✉)
Department of European Union Law, Yaroslav Mudryi National Law University, Kharkiv, Ukraine
e-mail: t.v.komarova@nlu.edu.ua

H. Richter (ed.), *Competition and Intellectual Property Law in Ukraine*,
MPI Studies on Intellectual Property and Competition Law 31,
https://doi.org/10.1007/978-3-662-66101-7_17

the results of medical research and as a consequence there is no legal protection of biotechnological inventions. It focuses on Ukrainian and European legislation and their comparison because Ukraine must study the European experience and practice of patenting the results of bioengineering, as the Association Agreement makes European standards in this area part of its legal system. Moreover, the chapter outlines some trends in the development of legal regulation of bioengineering. All these questions are important in the light of the development of the Ukrainian market for biotechnological developments (according to the Annual Report of the National Intellectual Property Office of Ukraine, in the period 2016–2020 1208 applications for inventions in the field of "biotechnology" were submitted).

1 Ukraine's Path to Europeanisation of Its Legal System

Ukraine has declared its desire to integrate into the legal space of the European Union. This is one of the strategic directions of Ukraine's state policy, which is confirmed by the adoption of the Law of Ukraine "On the National Program for Adaptation of Ukrainian Legislation to European Union Legislation 2004 and the signing of the Association Agreement between Ukraine and the European Union", which makes it possible to move from partnership and cooperation to association in the political and economic spheres.[1] Many Ukrainian regulations enshrine Ukraine's obligation of approximation of its national legislation to the *acquis communautaire* or the EU *acquis*. Moreover, in 2019, the Ukrainian Constitution was supplemented by provisions fixing the irreversible course of the state to achieve the criteria of full membership in the EU. It should be noted that few European countries have introduced similar provisions into their constitutional legislation.[2]

The main goal of the Association Agreement between Ukraine and the EU is to promote the implementation of the Association Agreement by creating a suitable environment in which the goals of political and economic integration can be achieved and by setting a list of priorities for joint sectoral work. The success of such an Association Agreement's implementation largely depends on the understanding of the EU legal system, the principles and mechanisms of its functioning. In this context, it is essential from a practical point of view to analyse Ukraine's achievements on its path to European integration and to identify those sectors in which Ukrainian legislation still needs to harmonise.

One of such priority sectors is the regulation of intellectual property. Bringing intellectual property in line with EU standards has been of interest to both Ukraine and the EU since the 1994 Partnership and Cooperation Agreement between Ukraine

[1] For details on the Association Agreement and approximation in the field of IP, see Roman Petrov, 'The EU–Ukraine Association Agreement as a General Framework of Contemporary EU–Ukraine Relations' and Yuriy Kapitsa, 'Association Agreements and Problems Approximating Intellectual Property Legislation of Third Countries with the EU Acquis: The Case of Ukraine' in this Volume.

[2] For example, Bulgaria, Croatia, Hungary, Romania, Montenegro.

and the European Communities (PCA). Ukraine's ratification of the Agreement on Trade-Related Aspects of Intellectual Property Rights of 15 April 1994 (TRIPS) and the accession to the WTO in 2008[3] also exacerbated the need to secure intellectual property rights to the common standards applicable at the international level and implemented in all signatory states. The purpose of the TRIPS Agreement is to promote technological innovation and the transfer and dissemination of technology such that they are mutually advantageous to producers and users of technological knowledge, conducive to social and economic welfare, and reflective of a balance of rights and obligation.[4]

The PCA was the first shy step of the Ukrainian legal system toward European integration. It was not very successful, which can be explained by the fact that the PCA imposed on Ukraine mostly soft commitments without setting clear deadlines for the approximation of its legal system to international standards in a wide range of spheres. The intellectual property sphere was the only one in which the PCA fixed that Ukraine shall continue to improve the protection of intellectual, industrial and commercial property rights in order to provide, by the end of the fifth year after the entry into force of the Agreement, for a level of protection similar to that existing in the Community, including effective means of enforcing such rights.[5] Moreover, paragraph 1 of Annex III lists the multilateral conventions on intellectual, industrial and commercial property rights to which Ukraine shall accede.[6]

Thanks to the PCA, Ukraine ratified some international legal acts, and thus some progress was made in approaching global standards of intellectual property protection. However, the Ukrainian legal system in this sphere was still weak and imperfect. Legislative innovations were mainly related to increasing the responsibility for infringement of intellectual property, rather than building a system of legal acts and effective institutions that would strengthen the existence of intellectual property as a value of Ukrainian society.[7] Even the fact that Ukraine ignored the implementation of the European Community's directives and regulations which were listed in the

[3] See also Zvenyslava Opeida, 'Competition and International Trade: Complementing Trade Defense Policy with Effective Competition Policy in Ukraine' in this Volume.

[4] Agreement on Trade-related Aspects of Intellectual Property Rights 1994, art 7.

[5] Partnership and Cooperation Agreement between the European Communities and their Member States, of the one part, and Ukraine, of the other part (1998) OJ L49/3 (Partnership and Cooperation Agreement), art 50.

[6] Art 50 concerned: Berne Convention for the Protection of Literary and Artistic Works 1971; Rome Convention for the Protection of Performers, Producers of Phonograms and Broadcasting Organizations 1961; Protocol Relating to the Madrid Agreement Concerning the International Registration of Marks 1989; Nice Agreement concerning the International Classification of Goods and Services for the Purposes of the Registration of Marks 1977, amended 1979; Budapest Treaty on the International Recognition of the Deposit of Microorganisms for the Purposes of Patent Procedures 1977, modified in 1980; International Convention for the Protection of New Varieties of Plants 1978.

[7] Regarding the adaptation of Ukrainian legislation to international standards of that time, see Yuriy Kapitsa, 'Status and Directions of Adaptation of Ukrainian Legislation in the Field of Intellectual Property Protection to EU legislation' (2005) 1 Law of Ukraine 66–70; Doris Long et al., *Protection of Intellectual Property Rights: Norms of International and National Law and Their Law Enforcement* – A Practical Guide ("K.I.S." 2007).

Interim Agreement on trade and trade-related matters[8] (which was obligatory before the PCA came into force) confirms the ineffectiveness of the mechanisms of implementation and control over implementation of the PCA and the fact that Ukraine was not ready for deep integration.

Further changes are related to the entry into force on 1 September 2017 of the Association Agreement, which marked the beginning of a new crucial stage in the "Europeanisation" of Ukraine's legal system. Unlike the PCA, the Association Agreement imposes on Ukraine specific and clear obligations on approximation of its legislation to EU law. This enabled large-scale legislative reforms, which made a certain amount of EU law part of Ukrainian legislation.[9] Thus, even the case law of Ukraine indicates the possibility of direct application of the provisions of the Association Agreement.[10]

Particular attention in the Association Agreement is paid to intellectual property, particularly Chap. 9 of Sec. IV. But Ukrainian obligations in the sphere of intellectual property have some peculiarities. All obligations are fixed in the body of the Agreement (Chap. 9 of Sec. IV) without providing any list of EU legislation which should be implemented by Ukraine (the exception is the list related to geographical indications[11]). In comparison with other areas there are no special annexes to the Agreement concerning intellectual property. For example, in the sphere of energy cooperation, special annexes provide lists of EU legislation and fix the obligation of Ukraine to approximate its legislation to the EU's within the stipulated timeframes.[12] Moreover, Ukraine is obliged to inform the European Commission about all registered draft laws concerning energy and obtain the Commission's legal opinions in order to be taken

[8] Interim Agreement on Trade and Trade-related Matters between the European Community, the European Coal and Steel Community and the European Atomic Energy Community, of the one party, and Ukraine, of the other part (1995) OJ L311(Interim Agreement on Trade and Trade-related Matters), Annex III, art 18.

[9] For Ukraine's progress in implementing the Association Agreement, see https://pulse.kmu.gov.ua accessed 26 October 2022. For the stage of progress in the implementation of the Association Agreement in the part related to intellectual property, see https://pulse.kmu.gov.ua/ua/direction/intelektualna-vlasnist accessed 26 October 2022.

[10] It is a question of large-scale application by the Supreme Court of the primacy of the Association Agreement over the Ukrainian legislation, which was first applied in the Ukrainian Supreme Court, Decision No. 910/14972/17 *Zentiva k.s. v. MEDT and Alliance of Beauty* (2018), which concerns Association Agreement, art 198. Concerning Europeanisation of Ukrainian judiciaries, see Roman Petrov and Paul Kalinichenko, 'The Europeanization of Third Country Judiciaries Through the Application of the EU Acquis: The Cases of Russia and Ukraine' (2011) 60(2) International and Comparative Law Quarterly 325. See also Roman Petrov, 'The EU–Ukraine Association Agreement as a General Framework of Contemporary EU–Ukraine Relations' and Yuriy Kapitsa, 'Association Agreements and Problems Approximating Intellectual Property Legislation of Third Countries with the EU Acquis: The Case of Ukraine' in this Volume.

[11] Association Agreement, Geographical Indications–Legislation of the Parties and Elements for Registration and Control, Annex XXVII-A to Chapter 9 Title IV; See also Anastasiia Kyrylenko, 'Why so Few Geographical Indications in Ukraine? Legal, Political and Socio-Economic Perspective' in this Volume.

[12] Association Agreement, Energy Cooperation, Including Nuclear Issues, Annex XXVII-B to Chapter 1 Title V.

into account during decision-making.[13] The Government of Ukraine may consult the European Commission as regards the compatibility with the EU *acquis* of any proposal for an act implementing the legislation in the energy sector, and the Parties shall exchange information through the secretaries of the Association Council.

Another example is Art. 264 Association Agreement, which provides that Art. 262 (competition law), Art. 263(3) (transparency of financial relations between public and private actors) and Art. 263(4) (compensation to entities of general economic interest) will be interpreted "using as sources of interpretation the criteria arising from the application of Arts. 106, 107 and 93 Treaty on the Functioning of the European Union, including the relevant jurisprudence of the Court of Justice of the European Union, as well as relevant secondary legislation, frameworks, guidelines and other administrative acts in force in the European Union".[14]

But in the case of intellectual property there are no such mechanisms, which explains that some rules of the Association Agreement are already outdated.[15] What poses an even bigger problem are the lively changes in the EU intellectual property legislation and the huge amount of advancing EU case law in this area. The Association Agreement does not provide any mechanisms and possibilities for Ukraine to take into account new EU legal acts and developments in the sphere of intellectual property.[16]

It should be underlined that the Court of Justice of the EU has adopted a so-called integration-oriented approach, implying that the provisions of the bilateral legal instruments should be interpreted "so far as possible" in correspondence with similar provisions under EU law.[17]

Such a situation generates a lot of open-ended questions concerning the boundaries of Ukrainian obligations to improve its legislation in the sphere of intellectual property. Such a situation leads, as Yuriy Kapitsa says, "to the need for a comprehensive comparative study of Ukrainian and EU legislation in the sphere of intellectual property, preparation of proposals for changes in legislation, development of the methodology of such a study to clarify the feasibility and effectiveness of adaptation of legislation for countries that do not envisage accession to the EU in the near future".[18]

---

[13] Association Agreement, Energy Cooperation, Including Nuclear Issues, Annex XXVII-A to Chapter 1 Title V.

[14] On the Association Agreement and competition law, see Kseniia Smyrnova, 'The "Europeanization" of Competition Law in Ukraine' in this Volume.

[15] For example, concerning new Unitary Patent System.

[16] See also Yuriy Kapitsa, 'Association Agreements and Problems Approximating Intellectual Property Legislation of Third Countries with the EU Acquis: The Case of Ukraine' in this Volume.

[17] See Marc Maresceau, 'Turkey: A Candidate State Destined to Join the Union', in Nic Niamh Shuibhne and Laurence W Gormley (eds), *From Single Market to Economic Union. Essays in Honour of John A Usher* (Oxford University Press, 2012) 315 (323).

[18] Yuriy Kapitsa, 'Conducting Comparative Studies of the Law of Ukraine and the European Union: Questions of Methodology' (2006) 9 Bulletin of the Ministry of Justice of Ukraine 56.

2 Patentability of Biotechnological Inventions Under the Ukrainian Association Agreement

The subject of this chapter is the approximation of Ukrainian legislation in the field of biotechnology to EU standards and the protection of intellectual property rights that relate to biotechnology. In particular, this covers patenting biotechnology, which is one of the effective legal instruments for intellectual property rights that provides the patent owner's exclusive rights for commercial use of the invention. One can agree with some authors who underline that the "protection provided to intellectual property by the laws of Ukraine contributes to increasing the number of inventions and innovation proposals, increasing investment, development of research activities that lead to technical progress, improving the quality of industrial products, improving the cultural level of citizens".[19]

The importance of this issue is emphasised by the fact that a separate article of the Association Agreement addresses this area, namely Art. 221 "Protection of Biotechnological Inventions". This provision reflects EU law. In particular, Art. 221(1) Association Agreement establishes that:

> Parties shall protect biotechnological inventions under national patent law. They shall, if necessary, adjust their patent law to take account of the provisions of this Agreement. This Article shall be without prejudice to the obligations of the Parties pursuant to international agreements, and in particular the TRIPS Agreement and the Convention on Biological Diversity of 1992.

Article 221(2) reveals the basic concepts such as "biological material" and "microbiological process", stating that:

> (a) 'biological material' means any material containing genetic information and capable of reproducing itself or being reproduced in a biological system;
> (b) 'microbiological process' means any process involving or performed upon or resulting in microbiological material.

A list of items that may or may not be patented is also included. It states that inventions which are new, which involve an inventive step and which are susceptible of industrial application shall be patentable even if they concern a product consisting of or containing biological material or a process by means of which biological material is produced, processed or used. Biological material which is isolated from its natural environment or produced by means of a technical process may be the subject of an invention even if it previously occurred in nature. An element isolated from the human body or otherwise produced by means of a technical process, including the sequence or partial sequence of a gene, may constitute a patentable invention, even if the structure of that element is identical to that of a natural element. The industrial

[19] Pavlo Tsybulov, *Fundamentals of Intellectual Property* (Institute of Intellectual Property and Law 2002) 52. Also see: Lubov Fedulova and Ludmila Tsybuldka, 'Trends in the Formation of the Latest Technological Structure in the World Economy: The Role of Intellectual Property Management' (2011) 12 Ukraine Economy 23 (24).

application of a sequence or a partial sequence of a gene must be disclosed in the patent application.[20]

The following shall not be patentable: Plant and animal varieties; essentially biological processes for the production of plants or animals; the human body, at the various stages of its formation and development, and the simple discovery of one of its elements, including the sequence or partial sequence of a gene.[21] Inventions shall be considered unpatentable where their commercial exploitation would be contrary to public policy or public morality; however, exploitation shall not be thus deemed contrary merely because it is prohibited by law or regulation. In particular, the following shall be considered unpatentable: Processes for cloning human beings; processes for modifying the germ line genetic identity of human beings; uses of human embryos for industrial or commercial purposes; processes for modifying the genetic identity of animals which are likely to cause them suffering without any substantial medical benefit to man or animal, and also animals resulting from such processes.[22]

Thus, these provisions of Art. 221 Association Agreement repeat the provisions of Arts. 2, 3, 4, 5, 6 Directive 98/44 of the European Parliament and the Council of the EU on the legal protection of biotechnological inventions. Such construction of the Association Agreement and the duplication of the provisions of the Directive in it has made part of the EU legislation an integral part of the national legal system of Ukraine.[23] This phenomenon is remarkable because it constitutes a form of extraterritorial application of EU law in third countries that are not Members of the Union. Of course, this does not imply an extraterritorial effect of EU law in the literal sense, because the legal basis for the application of these norms is an international agreement, which upon ratification by a third state becomes an integral part of its legal system.[24] However, in promoting cooperation with third countries, the EU often incorporates the rules of its secondary law into the provisions of relevant international treaties, thus ensuring harmonisation with the legal systems of its partners, which in fact constitutes a territorial extension of the EU law. The Court of Justice of the EU in the case of *Boukhalfa* explicitly stated that, as a general rule, the founding treaties and secondary EU law operate in the territory of its Member States, but do

---

[20] Association Agreement, art 221(3).

[21] Association Agreement, art 221(4).

[22] Association Agreement, art 221(5).

[23] On the transposition of the European Union into the legal systems of third countries, see Roman Petrov, *Transposition of the European Union Acquis into the Legal Systems of the Third Countries* (Istina 2012). On the legislative methodology of approximation, see Yuriy Kapitsa, 'Association Agreements and Problems Approximating Intellectual Property Legislation of Third Countries with the EU Acquis: The Case of Ukraine' in this Volume.

[24] See Vyktor Muravyov, 'Extraterritorial Action of European Union Law in the Legal Systems of Third Countries and Association Agreements' (2013) 117(1) Current Issues of International Relations 61–73; Ludmyla Falalieieva, 'Human Rights and Extraterritorial Application of the EU Law: Evolution of Jurisdictional Models Application Practice' (2017) 1(46) Journal of International Relations of KNU 91–98.

not exclude the possibility of EU law being applied outside of its territory.[25] An example of such is the international treaties of the EU and especially the Association Agreement, which is an “advanced” type of EU international agreement.

At the same time, in order to interpret such norms of EU law incorporated in the Association Agreement, it appears necessary to refer to the practice of interpretation of these norms by the European Union, namely the practice of the Court of Justice of the EU (CJEU), which is the monopolist in interpreting EU law.[26] Despite the fact that some scholars question the possibility of use of the CJEU’s practice without clear empowerment of this by Chap. 9 of Sec. IV of the Association Agreement,[27] our strong belief is that it is the only way to make approximation effective.

It should be acknowledged that this is a challenge for Ukraine’s law enforcement practice, as it requires appropriate competencies and awareness of EU law. That is why for the successful application of the above-mentioned norms of the Association Agreement and further approximation of the Ukrainian legal system, it is crucial to study the genesis of the adoption and practice of the application of Directive 98/44, which formed the basis of Art. 221 Association Agreement.

But the main challenge is that the Association Agreement does not provide any mechanism of quick and effective response to changes and developments of EU intellectual property legislation. This is problematic because intellectual property is a highly dynamic sphere, especially if we are talking about its development by the EU judiciary. To solve this issue, legal instruments guaranteeing the homogenous interpretation and application of rules in this area should exist. In this regard, Yuriy Kapitsa has argued that due to long legislative procedures in Ukraine, it would be better to give the leading role in harmonisation to the Supreme Court. He proposes to give the Supreme Court the jurisdiction to give clarifications on the Association Agreement or EU acts which are implemented in Ukrainian laws, and also to provide rules for clarification requests of Ukrainian courts to the Supreme Court.[28]

3 Patentability of Biotechnological Inventions Under EU Law

What is the stage of the patentability of biotechnological inventions under EU law? One of the first and illustrative cases of patenting the results of mammalian research was the case of the so-called Oncomouse or Harvard mouse, which was a transgenic mouse developed for cancer research at Harvard University. Applications for a patent

[25] ECJ C-214/94 *Ingrid Boukhalfa v. Bundesrepublik Deutschland* (1996) EU:C:1996:174.

[26] On the role of the Court Justice of the EU in the interpretation and development of EU law, see Tetyana Komarova, *Court of Justice of the European Union: Development of the Judicial System and Practice of Interpretation of EU Law: Monograph* (Law 2018).

[27] Yuriy Kapitsa, *European Union Intellectual Property Law: Formulation, Institutes, Directions of Development* (Academperiodyka 2017) 445.

[28] Ibid 466.

for the invention of the Oncomouse were filed in the United States, Europe and Canada. In Canada, the patent was granted, although it was accompanied by a high-profile lawsuit that reached the Supreme Court of Canada. In Europe, a patent for this invention was issued in 1985 by the European Patent Office, although 20 years later, this decision was challenged precisely because of the ethical and moral side of this process and its contradictions of public order (*ordre public*). Nevertheless, the competent European authorities did not find grounds for revoking the patent, as the 1973 European Patent Convention excludes the patentability of animal species but does not exclude the patentability of the animals themselves. Only in 2006 was the patent revoked due to non-payment of registration fees and certain shortcomings in the patenting process.

In 1984, the US Patent and Trademark Office also granted a patent for the Harvard mouse, but much attention was paid to the fact that the invention does not contain human cells or human embryonic cells. This can be interpreted to mean that the Office drew attention to the problem of patenting inventions related to the genetic modification of human cells.

It is clear that the development of genetic engineering is also associated with the use of human biomaterials, which raises an even greater layer of ethical concerns. The European Union, as a powerful supranational entity with broad competences granted by its Member States, could not stay away from these pressing issues. Thus, the EU has taken many measures (both organisational and institutional) to develop legal and ethical standards for biomedicine. For example, a special independent advisory body to the European Commission, the European Group on Ethics in Science and New Technologies (EGE), was set up in 1991 to advise EU institutions on bioethics and ethics in science. Also, in 1998, the European Parliament and the Council of the EU adopted Directive 98/44 on the legal protection of biotechnological inventions, which provided some answers to questions that arose in practice.[29] The need for such a Directive was due to the extraordinary growth of bioengineering research in Europe and, at the same time, the uncertainty of researchers about the possibility of patent protection of their scientific results, as the 1973 European Patent Convention did not provide precise answers to many questions.

As the EU positions itself as a democratic player in the international arena, it is significant that the adoption of the Directive was preceded by more than ten years of negotiations with all stakeholders. And, first of all, these negotiations concerned the ethical side of the possibility of patentability of biotechnological inventions.[30] Thus, the most active participants in these negotiations were the European Parliament as a representative of the people of Europe, who advocated the dominance of ethics over

[29] Parliament and Council Directive 98/44/EC of 6 July 1998 on the Legal Protection of Biotechnological Inventions (1998) OJ L213/13, 13–21.

[30] For the discussion of the society and scientists concerning legal protection of biotechnology, see Jens Hillebrand, 'Legal Protection of Biotechnological Inventions: Preconditions, Content, Scope and Prospects for the Future' (2003) 3 Intellectual Property 42; Yuriy Kapitsa and Karina Shakhbazian, 'Protection of the Rights to Inventions in the Field of Biotechnology in the European Union and Under the Legislation of Ukraine' (2005) 1(26) Theory and Practice of Intellectual Property 19.

economic interests, and the EGE, which also insisted on this approach. Greenpeace also submitted its position that the possibility of patenting inventions related to genetic engineering is a commercialisation of the human body and therefore has a negative implication.

Directive 98/44 in its Art. 5 enshrined that:

> 1. The human body, at the various stages of its formation and development, and the simple discovery of one of its elements, including the sequence or partial sequence of a gene, cannot constitute patentable inventions. 2. An element isolated from the human body or otherwise produced by means of a technical process, including the sequence or partial sequence of a gene, may constitute a patentable invention, even if the structure of that element is identical to that of a natural element.

In addition Art. 6 Directive established that inventions shall be considered unpatentable where their commercial exploitation would be contrary to public policy (*ordre public*) or morality. This norm is generally accepted.[31] In particular, non-patentable are: Human cloning processes, human germline genetic modification processes, use of human embryos for industrial or commercial purposes, processes of altering the genetic identity of animals that may cause their suffering without any significant medical benefit to humans or animals, and also animals that are the result of such processes. On the basis of the Directive, the European Patent Organization in 1999 included the grounds for non-patentability of inventions in the Implementing Regulations to the European Patent Convention.[32]

In response to the adoption of Directive 98/44, the Netherlands brought an action against the European Parliament and the Council for annulment, claiming that it violated human dignity.[33] The Netherlands' claim was also supported by Italy and Norway. The Court of Justice in 2001 ruled that the Directive is not contrary to EU law, as elements of the human body cannot be patented per se. Only inventions that combine a natural element with a technical process that allows the natural element to be isolated or manufactured for industrial use can be the subject of patent protection.

Thus, a part of the human body may be part of a product that is patentable but in no way by itself. This difference also applies to work on human gene sequences or partial sequences. The result of such work can be the basis for the grant of a patent only if the application is accompanied by a description of the original method of sequential actions that led to the invention as well as an explanation of industrial application. Thus, the protection provided by the Directive applies only to the results of inventive, scientific or technical work and extends to biological data that exist in their natural state and can be applied in industry.

Unfortunately, this decision of the Court of Justice did not answer many questions, as there were still inconsistencies with the provision of Recital 42 of the Directive, which states that the uses of human embryos for industrial or commercial purposes

---

[31] Yan Min, 'Morality—An Equivocal Area in the Patent System' (2012) 34(4) European Intellectual Property Review 261 (263).

[32] Implementing Regulations to the European Patent Convention, rules 28–29.

[33] ECJ C-377/98 *Kingdom of the Netherlands v. European Parliament and* Council of the European Union (2001) EU:C:2001:523.

must be excluded from patentability. Still, at the same time, such exclusion does not affect inventions for therapeutic or diagnostic purposes which are applied to the human embryo and are helpful to it.

The inconsistency concerns the fact that there is no unified definition of such a term as "human embryo". Due to different national laws in Europe, there is a significant difference in how this term is understood in the EU Member States. Thus, in the UK, an embryo is a live fetus whose fertilisation process is complete (when two cells have emerged), including the egg during fertilisation. In Spain, a distinction is made between pre-embryonic, embryonic and fetal conditions. Up to 14 days, the set of cells is considered a pre-embryo; from 14 days to 2.5 months, an embryo; and after that, a fetus. In Germany, an embryo is a fertilised human egg that can develop from the moment the cell nuclei fuse. Providing a uniform definition of the embryo is a somewhat controversial issue, as it is difficult to say whether this can be attributed to the EU competence.

The wording of the Directive also completely ignores the fact that modern reproductive medicine has the ability to manipulate human eggs and sperm in a way that is not regarded as cloning or as an intervention in the human embryo, and therefore patent applications for the use of human germ cells under the Directive may be granted as patents for parts of the human body. The possibility of patenting the results of such activities clearly hinders the activities of doctors and limits the access of both doctors and bioengineering developers to the information they may need to save patients' lives.

An example of this is the patents of the American company Myriad for the so-called breast cancer gene (BRCA1), which is considered responsible for the hereditary form of breast cancer. These patents have also been validated and obtained in Europe, and their subjects are, for example: Gene sequences for the breast cancer gene in all variations and mutations, encoded proteins, use of gene sequences for diagnosis, use of gene sequences for therapy, use of gene sequences for testing new drugs and all cells into which the gene can be transferred. The company that first patented the gene sequence may prohibit the use of this information by other entities and thus block medical practices and developments in this area. In this regard, in 1997, the Senate Committee of the German Research Group (DFG) expressed its position that the patentability of such processes affects the freedom of choice of doctors, and the exclusion of the possibility of obtaining patents is ethically justified.

A rather significant step in the interpretation of the Directive was the CJEU ruling in 2011 in the *Brüstle* case, which concerned the interpretation of Art. 6(2) Directive.[34] The circumstances of the case were that in 1997 the German neurologist Brüstle applied for a patent for the invention of isolation and purification of neuronal cells taken from embryonic stem cells. It has been claimed that the present invention can be used for therapeutic purposes, for example in the fight against Parkinson's disease. Greenpeace appealed the patent, and the German Federal Patent Court annulled the patent, which Dr. Brüstle challenged in the German Federal Court. In 2010 the Federal Patent Court of Germany in turn sent a preliminary request to

[34] ECJ C-34/10 *Oliver Brüstle v. Greenpeace eV.* (2011) EU:C:2011:669.

the Court of Justice for an interpretation of Art. 6(2)(c) Directive regarding the part that prohibits the "uses of human embryos for industrial and commercial purposes". In its judgment, the Court of Justice stated that the patenting of human embryonic stem cells violates the right to human dignity.

The Court of Justice has ruled that the definition of "embryo" should be interpreted autonomously and uniformly in relation to all EU Member States. The lack of a single definition of the human embryo poses a risk to the authors of some biotechnological inventions seeking to patent them in the Member States that have the narrowest concept of the human embryo and are the most liberal in terms of patenting, while in the other Member States these inventions cannot be patented. This situation will negatively affect the smooth functioning of the EU internal market. The Court emphasised that, although the concept of the human embryo is a very sensitive social issue in many Member States, reflecting traditions and value systems, it should provide an appropriate definition, limiting itself to a legal interpretation of the Directive's provisions.

Considering that the Directive provides that the human body at different stages of its formation and development cannot be a patented invention, the Court has given a very broad interpretation of the definition of embryo. Accordingly, any human ovum must, once fertilised, be regarded as a "human embryo" within the meaning and for the purposes of Art. 6(2)(c) Directive since such fertilisation is the beginning of the process of human development. Also, a "human embryo" is an unfertilised human egg into which a cell nucleus has been transplanted from a mature human cell, as well as any unfertilised human egg whose division and further development is stimulated by parthenogenesis. That is, an embryo is any human egg that divides and is able to begin the process of human development.

It has become significant for the scientific medical community that the prohibition of the use of human embryos also extends to such patenting for scientific purposes. The use of human embryos in inventions could be patentable only for therapeutic or diagnostic purposes. Moreover, the invention of embryonic stem cells could not be patented since the embryo is destroyed to extract them, which is also contrary to the right to human dignity.

The decision provoked a stormy reaction among the EU Member States because, as noted above, there are significant differences between states regarding the definition of "embryo". The European Court of Human Rights also spoke about this, emphasising that a broad consensus has not yet been reached on this issue, and the limits of the state's discretion on this issue should be quite wide.[35] The scientific community also reacted violently to the ruling of the Court of Justice and even sent letters to the Court explaining that stem cells could be taken not from viable embryos,

---

[35] ECtHR *H v Norway* 17,004/90 (1992); ECtHR *Vo v France* 53,924/00 (2004); ECtHR Evans v United Kingdom 6339/05 (2006). See Richard M Schwartz and Timo Minssen, *'Life After Myriad: The Uncertain Future of Patenting Biomedical Innovation and Personalised Medicine in an International Context' (2015) 3 Intellectual Property Quarterly 189; An Baeyens and Tom Goffin, 'European Court of Justice: ECJ 2015/2, International Stem Cell Corp v. Comptroller General of Patents, Designs and Trade Marks, Case C-364/13' (2015) 22 (2) European Journal of Health Law 141.*

but from biomaterial that is intended for disposal.[36] The Court of Justice took responsibility and entered the territory, which had not been entered before. No judicial body has tried to harmonise and propose a single European standard for approaching the timing of the beginning of human life.[37]

The result of this decision of the Court of Justice is obvious—a significant slowdown in scientific progress in the field of genetic engineering, which is aimed at drug development. Indeed, the Directive does not prohibit the use of human embryos in the context of scientific research, as it regulates only the issue of patenting biotechnological inventions. But it is clear that for scientists and medical practitioners, patenting their invention is logical and facilitates their work. Therefore, in this sense, the decision of the Court of Justice clearly does not promote the development of research of stem cells in the EU, as each time they have to prove the existence of therapeutic or diagnostic objectives of the research. In practice, this is a rather difficult task, which will result in many laboratories moving their facilities outside the EU, for example to China or the United States.[38] Moreover, in the United States, there is no morality clause in patent law, and all attempts to limit the patentability of bioengineering inventions at the legislative level have failed,[39] so the field for research and legal protection of its results is more attractive to medical scientists.

Further development took place with the Court of Justice ruling in 2014 in the case of *International Stem Cell Corporation*, where the International Stem Cell Corporation wanted to patent in the UK the invention of a process in which a human egg is activated by various chemical and electrical methods and can grow into a blastocyst phase (approximately 200–300 cells after cell division), but is unable to develop further because it lacks the parental DNA needed to form the placenta. Based on the *Brüstle* decision, the present invention is not patentable as it also falls under the too broad definition of "embryo" given by the Court of Justice.

But in its *International Stem Cell Corporation* decision, the Court of Justice clarified that an "embryo" can be considered an unfertilised human egg, the division and further development of which is stimulated by parthenogenesis, if it "has the inherent ability to develop into a human".[40] And here, the crucial thing is not the beginning of the process of cell proliferation but the cells' ability to become a human.

---

[36] See Katerina Sideri, *Bioproperty, Biomedicine and Deliberative Governance: Patents as Discourse on Life* (Routledge 2014) 79, 80; Austin Smith, 'No to Ban on Stem-Cell Patents' (2011) 472(7344) Nature 418.

[37] See Andrea Faeh, 'Judicial Activism, the Biotech Directive and its Institutional Implications – is the CJEU Acting as a Legislator or a Court when Defining the "Human Embryo"?' (2015) 4 European Law Review 613.

[38] See Alice Yuen-Ting Wong and Aurdlie Mahalatchimy, 'Human Stem Cells Patents – Emerging Issues and Challenges in Europe, United States, China, and Japan' (2018) 21(5–6) The Journal of World Intellectual Property 326.

[39] Anna Nordberg and Timo Minssen, 'A 'Ray of Hope' for European Stem Cell Patents or 'Out of the Smog into the Fog'?: An Analysis of Recent European Case Law and How It Compares to the US' (2016) 47(2) International Review of Intellectual Property and Competition Law 138 (160).

[40] ECJ C-364/13 *International Stem Cell Corporation v. Comptroller General of Patents, Designs and Trade Mark* (2012) EU:C:2014:2451, para 28.

National courts should decide the question of when this possibility arises, and it is they who may prohibit the patenting of relevant inventions in matters of *public order* and *morality*. It is clear that it is not possible to achieve a uniform attitude of the courts of all Member States, as this position will depend on the traditions of each EU Member State. It can be predicted that, for example, in Poland, the courts will be inclined to deny the patenting of inventions of processes related to parthenogenesis, and in more liberal states on this issue—to allow it. Such different approaches can lead to a violation of the freedoms of the EU common market. By the way, in the UK, the competent authority, after a preliminary ruling by the Court of Justice, granted a patent to the International Stem Cell Corporation.

After the decision in the case of *International Stem Cell Corporation* it can be stated that the role of courts in matters of ethics and morality has become quite significant.[41] In this regard, the process of harmonisation of judicial activities within the EU needs considerable attention, as medicine is an area covered by EU freedoms. This was brought to the attention of the European Commission in 2018 as well, and it addressed a formal request to the EGE, which is currently developing a conclusion on the ethics of gene editing. This conclusion will analyse the ethical, societal, fundamental rights of genome editing programs in humans, animals and plants, as well as a set of policy recommendations for the EU Member States. These recommendations will harmonise (namely, harmonise, not unify) the approaches of doctors/researchers on these issues. European researchers have repeatedly drawn attention to this.[42]

4 Comparison and Implications

4.1 Overview on the Regulatory Frame in Ukraine

When comparing the provisions of Ukrainian to EU legislation in the field of biotechnology and biotechnological patenting, it becomes clear that Ukraine has not yet done its homework in total, and there are currently some differences in legal regulation.

[41] See Fruzsina Molnár-Gábor, 'Science, Ethics, and Patents: Ethically-motivated Barriers to the Patenting of the Results of Human Embryonic Stem Cell Research' in Christine Hauskeller, Arne Manzeschke and Anja Pichl (eds), *The Matrix of Stem Cell Research: An Approach of Rethinking Science in Society* (Routledge 2019) 50–67; Enrico Bonadio, 'Biotech Patents and Morality after Brüstle' (2012) 34(10) European Intellectual Property Review 433; H P Brack, 'Post Brüstle Developments in EU Biotech Patent Law at the CJEU' (2016) 1(16) Epi Information.

[42] Rob Aerts, 'The Unitary Patent and the Biotechnology Directive: Is Uniform Protection of Biotechnological Inventions Ensured?' (2014) 36(9) European Intellectual Property Review 584; Aisling McMahon, 'An Institutional Examination of the Implications of the Unitary Patent Package for the Morality Provisions: A Fragmented Future Too Far?' (2017) 48(1) International Review of Intellectual Property and Competition Law 42.

Ukraine has a sizeable regulatory array for the regulation of biotechnology, in particular the Constitution of Ukraine,[43] Book 4 of the Civil Code of Ukraine,[44] the Law of Ukraine "On the Protection of Rights to Inventions and Utility Models 1993",[45] the Law of Ukraine "On the Protection of Rights to Industrial Designs 1993",[46] Law of Ukraine "On the Protection of Rights to Marks for Goods and Services 1993",[47] Law of Ukraine "On the Protection against Unfair Competition 1996"[48] as well as the existence of a huge body of bylaws.[49] These regulations were extensively amended in 2020 in connection with the implementation of the Association Agreement,[50] but still did not fully take into account the specifics of intellectual property in biotechnology—a point with which many Ukrainian scientists agree.[51] The main problem is the lack of a specialised act on biotechnology in the Ukrainian legislation in the field of intellectual property protection and the lack of a system in a large legislative array. This is not an easy task, considering that several Ukrainian scholars agree that Ukrainian intellectual property law is quite contradictive.[52]

Article 6 Law on the Protection of Rights to Inventions and Utility Models states that legal protection is provided to the invention (utility model), which does not contradict public order or generally accepted moral principles and meets the conditions of patentability, and the object of the invention may be a product or process.[53] The act provides an open list of what can be a product: Device, substance, a strain of microorganism, cell culture of plants and animals and so on.

The Order of the Ministry of Education and Science on approval of the Rules for drawing up and submitting an application for an invention for applications for a utility model sample 2001 expands the list of examples of products that are the object of the invention and mentions device, mechanism, system (complex) interacting devices,

[43] Constitution of Ukraine 1996, 254к/96-ВР, art 141.

[44] Civil Code of Ukraine 2003, 435-IV.

[45] Ukrainian Law on Protection of Rights to Inventions and Utility Models 1993, 3687-XII.

[46] Ukrainian Law on Protection of the Rights to Industrial Designs 1993, 3688-XII.

[47] Ukrainian Law on Protection of Trademark Rights for Goods and Services 1993, 3689-XII.

[48] Ukrainian Law on Protection from Unfair Competition 1996, 236/96-ВР.

[49] Ukraine traditionally maintains a two-tier system of legislation in the field of intellectual property law. It still continues legal tradition of placement of norms on intellectual property law in the system of civil law.

[50] Ukrainian Law on Amendments to Certain Legislative Acts of Ukraine Concerning the Reform 2020, 816-IX.

[51] Iryna Kuzmych, 'Legislative Convergence on Patenting of Intellectual Property on Biotechnologies' (2020) 3 Law Review of Kyiv University of Law 259 (259); Andryi Olefir 'On the Issues of Legal Protections of Biotechnologies' (2015) 1 The Theory and Practice of Intellectual Property 71(74) (the author analyzed contradictions which were not harmonized in 2020).

[52] Olena Orliuk, 'Intellectual Property in Ukraine: Experience, Legislation, Problems, Prospects' (2011) 3 Law of Ukraine 20 (17); Katerina Horbachova, et al., 'National Strategy for the Development of Intellectual Property in Ukraine in the Context of Ensuring Compliance with International Obligations' (2020) 3 Legal Scientific Electronic Journal 88 (90).

[53] See also Leonid Tarasenko, 'Legislative Reforms on Patents, Utility Models and Industrial Designs in Ukraine' in this Volume.

structure, product, substance, microorganism strain, plant and animal cell culture and other biological material, including transgenic plants and animals, data, measurement of parameters, diagnosis, treatment and process management which is the object of technology. The object of a utility model, the legal protection of which is provided under this Law, may be a device or process (method).

4.2 The Challenge to Define the Concept of "Biotechnology" and Its Relation with Intellectual Property

However, Ukrainian legislation does not contain an interpretation of the concept of "biotechnology", despite the fact that this phenomenon requires a balanced legal regulation. Legal certainty could stimulate the activities related to the use of biotechnology and its involvement in industry. It can be done by correct, well-grounded legal regulation of all aspects of biotechnology and direct definition of biotechnology. This definition should contain the necessary and sufficient features that would cover the section of this phenomenon, which is of practical importance for the socio-economic situation in the country.

Only in some bylaws can one find attempts to define biotechnology, but these definitions are not complex, and they are sectoral in nature. For example, the Resolution of the Cabinet of Ministers of Ukraine "On Approval of the State Program of Industrial Development for 2003–2011" stated that: "biotechnology provides for the production of biostimulators of plant growth, organo-mineral fertilizers of complex action, the latest technologies for antibiotics, immunobiological drugs, including immunoglobulin of various species, and animal protection products".[54] However, in the strict sense this is not a definition but rather an attempt to make a list of targets of production activities. Moreover, this list is not exhaustive and does not cover the full range of industrial development activity.

The next act which seeks to define "biotechnology" is the Order of the Ministry of Health of Ukraine "On Approval of Methodical Guidelines" "Medico-biological researches of production strains of microorganisms and toxicological and hygienic assessment of microbial drugs, determining their safety and justification of hygienic standards and regulations", which defines biotechnology as the technology of product production using living cells of organisms (microorganisms, plants, animals).[55] This definition is also not complex and does not set a proper legal framework.

These examples show that Ukraine lacks a unified, systematic approach to understanding biotechnology. Without a full-fledged definition on the legislative level it is

[54] Resolution of the Cabinet of Ministers of Ukraine of 28 July 2003, No. 1174 on Approval of the State Program of Industrial Development for 2003–2011.

[55] Order of the Ministry of Health of Ukraine of 26 October 1004, No. 521 "On approval of methodical guidelines 'Medico-biological researches of production strains of microorganisms and toxicological and hygienic assessment of microbial drugs, determining their safety and justification of hygienic standards and regulations'".

hard to develop the biotechnological market, and harmonisation with international standards becomes very difficult.

Of course, we should not forget that in 1994 Ukraine ratified the Convention on biodiversity, which contains a definition of biotechnology which states that: "'Biotechnology' means any technological application that uses biological systems, living organisms, or derivatives thereof, to make or modify products or processes for specific use".[56] In accordance with Art. 9 Ukrainian Constitution, this Convention became the integral part of Ukrainian legislation, but it is preferable to develop the definition in a separate legal act. Moreover, it is necessary to develop a national strategy and plan for the development of biotechnology in Ukraine, which should be based on an expert assessment of current legislation, assistance in conducting activities and research necessary for the growth of the biotechnology cluster in Ukraine.[57]

Actually, the first step was taken: The protection of intellectual property was included in the National Economic Strategy of Ukraine until 2030 as a priority sphere. The Strategy states that Ukraine is characterised by an insufficient level of intellectual property protection. According to the component "Protection of intellectual property rights" of the Global Competitiveness Index 2019, Ukraine received only 3.4 out of 7 points, ranking 118th in the world—much lower than other post-socialist countries.[58] Additionally a draft of the Strategy for the development of intellectual property was developed to promote and strengthen the effective creation, development, management and protection of intellectual property at the national level.[59]

Another positive step is that on 18 August 2021, the Cabinet of Ministers of Ukraine adopted a Resolution on approval of the procedure for the use of funds provided in the state budget for the creation of biocluster "Biosafety and development of biotechnological technologies". It is planned that the cluster will start its work on the basis of the Center for Public Health, but it is necessary to engage academia and business in its research and activities. Only the deep cooperation of state, academia, business and international partners will create proper system for this biocluster.

Academics also try to help by developing research in the biotechnological sphere. Realising the gap in Ukraine's legal techniques, academics elaborate on rather complex definitions of biotechnology. For example, Olefir A notes:

> Biotechnology is a system of methods and techniques for using living organisms and biological processes in production, which involves the manufacture of products containing substances of biological origin derived from biological sources (cells of microorganisms,

---

[56] United Nations Convention on Biological Diversity 1993, art 2.

[57] On the strategic directions of biotechnological sphere development of leading countries, see Tetyana Iukhnovska and Tetyana Gruzdova, 'Strategic Directions for Development of the Biotechnology Sector in Some World Countries: Guidelines for Ukraine' (2015) 2(53) Ukrainian Society 50.

[58] Resolution of the Cabinet of Ministers of Ukraine of 3 March 2021, No. 179 on Approval of the National Economic Strategy for the Period up to 2030.

[59] On details of the National IP Strategy of Ukraine, see Olena Orliuk, 'Strategic Directions of the Intellectual Property Area Development in Ukraine' in this Volume.

> animals and plants, products of their vital activity), using technical devices based on the use of genetic engineering and hybrid technologies. Other features of biotechnology include the following: 1) application mainly in such areas of production as pharmaceuticals, medicine, agriculture, food, energy, environmental protection; 2) the content of technology consists of inventions, plant varieties and trade secrets, while patent protection is not a mandatory attribute of biotechnology; 3) it may contain one object of property rights, several objects of intellectual property rights, several technologies in the structure of one (single technology); 4) may have both intangible and tangible forms; 5) the subject is a biological material, in particular, isolated by technical means from their own natural environment; a product consisting of or containing biological material; biological processes of creation, processing of such material, its isolation from the natural environment and analysis.[60]

This definition characterises biotechnology both as an object of legal protection and as a priority sphere of economic development. It could be used by the legislator because it considers main features of biotechnology such as: The presence of a living organism or element, a production purpose and focus on transformation, creation of new properties in existing materials, products, raw materials involved in further technological or production processes.

4.3 The Law on Protection of Rights to Inventions and Utility Models (2020) in Light of the Association Agreement

Another shortcoming which was overcome in 2020 by drafting the Law on Protection of Rights to Inventions and Utility Models[61] was the difference between the provisions of the Association Agreement and the Ukrainian legislation. For example, the Ukrainian Law on Protection of Rights to Inventions and Utility Models before 2020 referred to a product or process involving natural biological material biotechnology as an object of inventions as well as of utility models. At the same time, the provisions of the Association Agreement, which, as noted above, were borrowed from Directive 1998/44, only refer to the object of inventions.[62] The difference between the invention and the utility model lies in the degree of inventive step, which shows that the innovation of the invention is not obvious.[63] Moreover, when assessing the novelty of a utility model, information on the open use of devices with a similar purpose abroad is not included; when issuing a security document for a utility model, the examination should not verify the compliance of the intellectual property object with such conditions of patentability as novelty and industrial suitability. However, there are no differences in the scope of rights granted to the patent owner of the invention and

[60] Olefir 'On the Issues of Legal Protections of Biotechnologies' (n 51) 71(73 and 74).

[61] For a complex review of reform 2020, see Leonid Tarasenko, 'Patent Legislation Reform (2020): Main Innovations of Inventions (Utility Models)' (2021) 73 Visnyk of the Lviv University Series Law 67.

[62] Association Agreement, art 221 (1).

[63] See also Leonid Tarasenko, 'Legislative Reforms on Patents, Utility Models and Industrial Designs in Ukraine' in this Volume.

the owner of the utility model. A patent for both an invention and a utility model give its owner exclusive rights to use the object. The only difference is in the protection period.[64] At the same time, a simpler procedure for obtaining a patent for a utility model made it more attractive in Ukraine, and as a result it was used for "patent trolling". The practice of European states shows that for these reasons a lot of them waived the protection of utility model rights; some states introduced the "inventive step" as a requirement for utility models or limited the object of the protection only to three-dimensional objects. In most states biotechnological inventions could not be protected as a utility model. The Ukrainian legislator took this into account in 2020 and removed a new application of a product or process from the objects of the invention and utility model. It was included that only a device (and this is just one type of product) or a process (method) can be the object of a utility model. The substance, the strain of the microorganism, the cell culture of the plant and the animal cannot be the object of a utility model. After that it is clear that the product or the process which relates to biological material could not be protected as a utility model because of its nature.

Significant are the changes that were made in 2020 to Art. 6(1) Ukrainian Law on Protection of Rights to Inventions and Utility Models regarding the requirement that the invention (utility model), in order to be patented, must not contradict public order or generally accepted principles of morality and must meet the conditions of patentability. Previously, the patent system only formally interacted with morality and it was very rare that ethical principles needed to be taken into account when granting a patent.[65] Only with the development of biotechnology has this situation changed. Ethics, morality and law became interrelated components and are extremely important for society's acceptance of inventions created by genetic engineering.[66]

It should be noted that Art. 6(1) crystallised in this form only in 2020 and so far has been subject to modification several times. In the first edition of 1994, the Law established the requirement that the invention (utility model) not contradict "public interests". Later, in 2003, this requirement was replaced by compliance with "public order" and in 2012 with compliance with "principles of humanity and morality". The changes of 2020 were clearly dictated by the provisions of the Association Agreement and focused on universally recognised principles of morality. Earlier, when considering the case of the *International Stem Cell Corporation*, we already concluded that unification is not possible at this stage, and the answer will depend on the cultural characteristics of each country.[67]

However, as Ukraine now refers to "universally recognised principles of morality", the competent authorities should closely monitor the development of European and

---

[64] Under the changes of 2020 it is 20 years for the invention and 10 years for the utility model.

[65] Oleksandr Slobodian, 'Features of Patenting Biotechnological Inventions in the European Patent Office' (2013) 1 Chronicles of Kyiv Institute of Law 225 (228).

[66] Olena Ponomarova, 'Experience of EU Countries on Ethical Aspects of Patenting Biotechnologies in the Field of Medicine and Pharmacy' (2021) 2 Theory and Practice of Intellectual Property 23 (24).

[67] See Janne Rothmar Herrmann and Malene Rowlandson, 'The Role of Ethics and Morality in EU Law' (2008) 5(6) Journal of International Biotechnology Law 241.

world practice (for example, the practice of the European Patent Office), as the Association Agreement itself provides only an approximate list of cases that would be contrary to public morality[68]: processes for cloning human beings; processes for modifying the germ line genetic identity of human beings; uses of human embryos for industrial or commercial purposes; processes for modifying the genetic identity of animals which are likely to cause them suffering without any substantial medical benefit to man or animal, and also animals resulting from such processes.[69]

Another problematic issue is the discrepancy between the provisions of the Association Agreement and the Ukrainian legislation on the grounds of the non-patentability of objects. The Ukrainian Law on the Protection of Rights to Inventions and Utility Models contains a broader list of objects that are not subject to patenting. Article 6(3) Law "On the Protection of Rights to Inventions and Utility Models" stipulates that such biotechnological objects as:

> [P]lant varieties and animal breeds are not subject to legal protection; basically biological processes of reproduction of plants and animals that do not belong to non-biological and microbiological processes, as well as the products of such processes; human cloning processes; processes of change through the germ line of human genetic identity; use of human embryos for industrial or commercial purposes; processes of changing the genetic identity of animals that may cause their suffering without any significant medical benefit to humans or animals, as well as animals bred as a result of such a process; the human body at different stages of its formation and development, as well as the simple detection of one of its elements, in particular the sequence or part of the gene sequence; a product or process involving a plant or animal whose use is restricted to a particular plant variety or animal breed; a product or process which relates to natural biological material which is not separated from its natural environment or which is not the product of a technical process.

In contrast, Art. 221(4) and Art. 221(5) Association Agreement enshrine the following as not patentable:

> plant and animal varieties; essentially biological processes for the production of plants or animals; the human body, at the various stages of its formation and development, and the simple discovery of one of its elements, including the sequence or partial sequence of a gene;
>
> (a) processes for cloning human beings;
>
> (b) processes for modifying the germ line genetic identity of human beings;
>
> (c) uses of human embryos for industrial or commercial purposes;
>
> (d) processes for modifying the genetic identity of animals which are likely to cause them suffering without any substantial medical benefit to man or animal, and also animals resulting from such processes.

If we compare these provisions, it becomes clear that the provisions of the Association Agreement provide greater discretion for patent authorities when it comes to refusing to patent biological processes because it is rather difficult to assess the condition of "essentially biological processes" for the production of plants or animals.

---

[68] Association Agreement, art 221(5).

[69] TRIPS, art 27, provides that members may exclude from patentability inventions, the prevention within their territory of the commercial exploitation of which is necessary to protect ordre public or morality, including to protect human, animal or plant life or health or to avoid serious prejudice to the environment.

5 Conclusion

Despite great progress in the harmonisation of intellectual property law to European and international standards in 2020, there are still several factors in Ukraine that may lead to violations of intellectual property protection in the field of biotechnology. These include the imperfection of Ukrainian patent law, which does not take into account the peculiarities of biotechnological intellectual property, the imperfection of the administrative and legal mechanism of protection and enforcement of intellectual property rights in biotechnology and the low level of institutional capacity and inefficient use of scientific potential in the development of biotechnology and intellectual property.

However, as for the priority of the Europeanisation of Ukrainian intellectual property law, the main problem is not even the imperfection of the legal mechanisms for its protection and enforcement or contradictions between different legal acts, but rather the specifics of our obligations in this sphere under the Association Agreement. Chap. 9 of Sec. IV "Intellectual Property" of the Association Agreement does not provide an effective mechanism for implementation of the IP EU *acquis*. First of all, it will be effective to have special lists of EU legislation for approximation to the Ukrainian legal system within the stipulated timeframes. Moreover, this list should be flexible in order to account for all changes in EU legislation and case law of the CJEU. Without such a mechanism it is impossible to interpret the Association Agreement effectively and harmonise Ukrainian intellectual property law with EU standards. Right now, we have an open-ended question on the boundaries of Ukrainian obligations to improve its legislation in the sphere of intellectual property.

This question is a general problem of Association Agreement implementation, not only in the sphere of intellectual property. For a long time, Ukrainian scholars have discussed the necessity of adoption of a special law on the implementation of the Association Agreement which would help to unify approaches on the approximation of the Ukrainian legal system. Right now, many doctrinal conclusions concerning this question have been drawn, but we need a resolution on a high level. For example, the adoption in 2006 of the Law of Ukraine "On the Execution of Judgments and Application of the Case Law of the European Court of Human Rights" crucially helped to resolve several problematic issues with the application of the ECHR and ECtHR's decisions in Ukraine.

Definitely a special legal act on biotechnology should be adopted in Ukraine, because despite the huge number of legal acts on intellectual property, there is no unified, systematic approach to the understanding of biotechnology. Without a full-fledged legal definition, it is hard to develop the biotechnological market and achieve harmonisation with international standards.

All these steps in the development of biotechnology in Ukraine, in our opinion and the opinion of other scholars,[70] significantly depend on the intensification of cooperation between research institutions, government and businesses, which should

[70] Olha Poliakova and Viktoriia Shlykova, 'The Patenting of Biotechnological Developments in Ukraine: Trends and Structure' (2017) 2 The Problems of the Economy 124 (128).

be a priority of state science and technology policy and the key to successful European integration processes.

References

Rob Aerts, 'The Unitary Patent and the Biotechnology Directive: Is Uniform Protection of Biotechnological Inventions Ensured?' (2014) 36(9) European Intellectual Property Review 584

An Baeyens and Tom Goffin, 'European Court of Justice: ECJ 2015/2, International Stem Cell Corp v. Comptroller General of Patents, Designs and Trade Marks, Case C-364/13' (2015) 22(2) European Journal of Health Law 141

Enrico Bonadio, 'Biotech Patents and Morality after Brüstle' (2012) 34(10) European Intellectual Property Review 433

H P Brack, 'Post Brüstle Developments in EU Biotech Patent Law at the CJEU' (2016) 1(16) Epi Information 20

Andrea Faeh, 'Judicial Activism, the Biotech Directive and its Institutional Implications—is the CJEU Acting as a Legislator or a Court when Defining the "Human Embryo"?' (2015) 4 European Law Review 613

Ludmyla Falalieieva, 'Human Rights and Extraterritorial Application of the EU Law: Evolution of Jurisdictional Models Application Practice' (2017) 1(46) Journal of International Relations of KNU 91 [Людмила Фалалєєва, 'Права Людини та Екстериторіальна Дія Права ЄС: Еволюція Практики Застосування Юрисдикцій' (2017) 1(46) Вісник Міжнародних Відносин 91]

Lubov Fedulova and Ludmila Tsybuldka, 'Trends in the Formation of the Latest Technological Structure in the World Economy: The Role of Intellectual Property Management' (2011) 12 Ukraine Economy 23 [Любов Федулова та Людмила Цибульська, 'Тенденції Становлення Новітнього Технологічного Укладу у Світовій Економіці: Роль Управління Інтелектуальною Власністю' (2011) 12 Економіка України 23]

Jens Hillebrand, 'Legal Protection of Biotechnological Inventions: Preconditions, Content, Scope and Prospects for the Future' (2003) 3 Intellectual Property 42 [Дженс Гілленбранд, 'Правовий Захист Біотехнологічних Винаходів: Передумови, Зміст, Обсяг та Перспективи на Майбутнье' (2003) 3 Інтелектуальна Власність 42]

Katerina Horbachova, Volodimir Nejevelo and Iryna Haihan, 'National Strategy for the Development of Intellectual Property in Ukraine in the Context of Ensuring Compliance with International Obligations' (2020) 3 Legal Scientific Electronic Journal 88 [Катерина Горбачова, Володимир Нежевело та Шрина Хайхан, 'Національна Стратегія Розвитку Сфери Інтелектуальної Власності в Україні в Контексті Забезпечення Виконання Міжнародних Зобов'язань' (2020) 3 Юридичний Науковий Електронний Журнал 88]

Tetyana Iukhnovska and Tetyana Gruzdova, 'Strategic Directions for Development of the Biotechnology Sector in Some World Countries: Guidelines for Ukraine' (2015) 2(53) Ukrainian Society 50 [Тетяна Юхновська та Тетяна Груздова, 'Стратегические Направления Развития Биотехнологической Сферы Некоторых Стран Мира: Ориентиры для Украины' (2015) 2(53) Український Соціум 50]

Yuriy Kapitsa, *European Union Intellectual Property Law: Formulation, Institutes, Directions of Development* (Academperiodyka 2017) [Юрій Капіца, *Право Інтелектуальної Власності Європейського Союзу: Формування, Інститути, Напрями Розвитку* (Академперіодика 2017)]

Yuriy Kapitsa, 'Conducting Comparative Studies of the Law of Ukraine and the European Union: Questions of Methodology' (2006) 9 Bulletin of the Ministry of Justice of Ukraine 56 [Юрій Капіца, 'Проведення Порівняльних Досліджень Права України та Європейського Союзу: Питання Методології' (2006) 9 Бюлетень Міністерства юстиції України 56]

Yuriy Kapitsa, 'Status and Directions of Adaptation of Ukrainian Legislation in the Field of Intellectual Property Protection to EU Legislation' (2005) 1 Law of Ukraine 66 [Юрій Капіца, 'Стан та Напрями Адаптації Законодавства України у Сфері Охорони Інтелектуальної Власності до Законодавства ЄС' (2005) 1 Право України 66]

Yuriy Kapitsa and Karina Shakhbazian, 'Protection of the Rights to Inventions in the Field of Biotechnology in the European Union and Under the Legislation of Ukraine' (2005) 1(26) Theory and Practice of Intellectual Property 19 [Юрій Капіца та Карина Шахбазян, 'Охорона Прав на Винаходи у Галузі Біотехнологій в Європейському Союзу та за Законодавством України' (2005) 1(26) Теорія і Практика Інтелектуальної Власності 19]

Tetyana Komarova, *Court of Justice of the European Union: Development of the Judicial System and Practice of Interpretation of EU law: Monograph* (Law 2018) [Тетяна Комарова, *Суд Європейського Союзу: Розвиток Судової Системи та Практики Тлумачення Права ЄС: Монографія* (Право 2018)].

Iryna Kuzmych, 'Legislative Convergence on Patenting of Intellectual Property on Biotechnologies' (2020) 3 Law Review of Kyiv University of Law 259 [Ірина Кузмич, 'Законодавча Конвергенція щодо Патентування Об'єктів Інтелектуальної Власності на Біотехнології' (2020) 3 Часопис Київського Університету Права 259]

Doris Long, Patricia Ray, V Zharov, T Sheveleva and I Vasilenko Drobiazko, *Protection of Intellectual Property Rights: Norms of International and National Law and their Law Enforcement*—A Practical Guide ("K.I.S." 2007) [Доріс Лонг, Патріціа Рей, В. Жаров та ін., *Захист Прав Інтелектуальної Власності: Норми Міжнародного і Національного Законодавства та їх Правозастосування* ("К.І.С." 2007)]

Marc Maresceau, 'Turkey: A Candidate State Destined to Join the Union', in Nic Niamh Shuibhne and Laurence W Gormley (eds), *From Single Market to Economic Union: Essays in Honour of John A Usher* (Oxford University Press 2012)

Aisling McMahon, 'An Institutional Examination of the Implications of the Unitary Patent Package for the Morality Provisions: A Fragmented Future Too Far?' (2017) 48(1) International Review of Intellectual Property and Competition Law 42

Yan Min, 'Morality—An Equivocal Area in the Patent System' (2012) 34(4) European Intellectual Property Review 261

Fruzsina Molnár-Gábor, 'Science, Ethics, and Patents: Ethically-motivated Barriers to the Patenting of the Results of Human Embryonic Stem Cell Research' in Christine Hauskeller, Arne Manzeschke and Anja Pichl (eds), *The Matrix of Stem Cell Research: An Approach of Rethinking Science in Society* (Routledge 2019)

Vyktor Muravyov, 'Extraterritorial Action of European Union Law in the Legal Systems of Third Countries and Association Agreements' (2013) 117(1) Current Issues of International Relations 61 [Віктор Муравйов, 'Екстратериторіальна Дія Права Європейського Союзу у Правопорядках Третіх Країн і Угоди про Асоціацію' (2013) 117(1) Актуальні Проблеми Міжнародних Відносин 61]

Anna Nordberg and Timo Minssen, 'A 'Ray of Hope' for European Stem Cell Patents or 'Out of the Smog into the Fog'?: An Analysis of Recent European Case Law and How it Compares to the US' (2016) 47(2) International Review of Intellectual Property and Competition Law 138

Andryi Olefir 'On the Issues of Legal Protections of Biotechologies' (2015) 1 The Theory and Practice of Intellectual Property 71 [Андрій Олефір, 'До Проблеми Правової Охорони Біотехнологій' (2015) 1 Теорія і Практика Інтелектуальної Власності 71]

Olena Orliuk, 'Intellectual Property in Ukraine: Experience, Legislation, Problems, Prospects' (2011) 3 Law of Ukraine 20 [Олена Орлюк, 'Інтелектуальна Власність в Україні: Досвід, Законодавство, Проблеми, Перспективи" (2011) 3 Право України 20]

Roman Petrov, *Transposition of the European Union Acquis into the Legal Systems of the Third Countries* (Istina 2012)

Roman Petrov and Paul Kalinichenko, 'The Europeanization of Third Country Judiciaries Through the Application of the EU Acquis: The Cases of Russia and Ukraine' (2011) 60(2) International and Comparative Law Quarterly 325

Olha Poliakova and Viktoriia Shlykova, 'The Patenting of Biotechnological Developments in Ukraine: Trends and Structure' (2017) 2 The Problems of the Economy 124 [Ольга Полякова та Вікторія Шликова 'Патентування Біотехнологічних Розробок в Україні: Тенденції та Структура' (2017) 2 Проблеми Економіки 124]

Olena Ponomarova, 'Experience of EU Countries on Ethical Aspects of Patenting Biotechnologies in the Field of Medicine and Pharmacy' (2021) 2 Theory and Practice of Intellectual Property 23 [Олена Пономарьова, 'Досвід Країн ЄС щодо Етичних Аспектів Патентування Біотехнологій у Сфері Медицини і Фармації' (2021) 2 Теорія і Практика Інтелектуальної Власності 23]

Janne Rothmar Herrmann and Malene Rowlandson, 'The Role of Ethics and Morality in EU Law' (2008) 5(6) Journal of International Biotechnology Law 241

Richard M Schwartz and Timo Minssen, 'Life After Myriad: The Uncertain Future of Patenting Biomedical Innovation and Personalised Medicine in an International Context' (2015) 3 Intellectual Property Quarterly 189

Katerina Sideri, *Bioproperty, Biomedicine and Deliberative Governance: Patents as Discourse on Life* (Routledge 2014)

Austin Smith, 'No to Ban on Stem-cell Patents' (2011) 472 (7344) Nature 418

Oleksandr Slobodian, 'Features of Patenting Biotechnological Inventions in the European Patent Office' (2013) 1 Chronicles of Kyiv Institute of Law 225 [Олександр Слободян, 'Особливості Патентування Біотехнологічних Винаходів у Європейському Патентному Відомстві' (2013) 1 Часопис Київського Університету Права 225]

Leonid Tarasenko, 'Patent Legislation Reform (2020): Main Innovations of Inventions (Utility Models)' (2021) 73 Visnyk of the Lviv University Series Law 67 [Леонід Тарасенко, 'Реформа Патентного Законодавства (2020): Основні Новації щодо Винаходів (Корисних Моделей)" (2021) 73 Вісник Львівського Університету Серія Юридична 67]

Pavlo Tsybulov, *Fundamentals of Intellectual Property* (Institute of Intellectual Property and Law 2002) [Павло Цибульов, *Основи Інтелектуальної Власності* (Інститут Інтелектуальної Власності і Права 2002)]

Alice Yuen-Ting Wong and Aurélie Mahalatchimy, 'Human Stem Cells Patents—Emerging Issues and Challenges in Europe, United States, China, and Japan' (2018) 21(5–6) The Journal of World Intellectual Property 326

The Reformed Design Law in Ukraine: What is Right with EU Trade Agreements?

Anastasiia Kyrylenko

Contents

Abstract This chapter will examine the recent legal reform of Ukrainian design law against the background of the discussion concerning the adverse effect of European Union law on third countries' legal order, which is being particularly pursued in European scholarly circles. The author will trace the positive impact of the EU norms on Ukrainian design legislation. This positive impact is namely achieved through the introduction of new registrability requirements modelled on the EU system. The author will further examine how Ukrainian policy-makers fill legal gaps in the definitions and interpretation of those notions that are not covered in the EU–Ukraine Association Agreement, namely those that are not included in the letter of the law but have been developed within ECJ judicial practice (e.g. freedom of the designer,

This Chapter, written between April and October 2021, looks at EU trade agreements through the prism of the EU–Ukraine Association Agreement (AA). Negotiated along with EU–Georgia and EU–Moldova AAs in early 2010s, the EU–Ukraine AA extensively regulated trade relationships with Ukraine, a non-candidate country. On 23 June 2022, the European Council decided to grant the status of candidate country to Ukraine and to the Republic of Moldova. While a new chapter in EU–Ukraine policy is about to open, this Chapter's conclusions are relevant both for Ukraine, and for other third countries, with whom the EU has a privileged relationship.

A. Kyrylenko (✉)
Global Innovation Law and Policy, University of Alicante, Alicante, Spain
e-mail: anastasiia.kyrylenko@ua.es

H. Richter (ed.), *Competition and Intellectual Property Law in Ukraine*,
MPI Studies on Intellectual Property and Competition Law 31,
https://doi.org/10.1007/978-3-662-66101-7_18

informed user). Lastly, the author will discuss the practicalities and difficulties of the export of norms from the EU to third countries, particularly complicated in areas where there is a gap between codified norms and the actual judicial practice of the ECJ.

1 Introduction

In the mid-2000s, the European Union (EU) adopted several policy documents[1] that marked a policy shift in its approach to trade agreements with third countries, including intellectual property (IP) norms. The 2004 "Strategy for the Enforcement of IPR (Intellectual Property Rights) in Third Countries" invited the EU to revisit its approach to the IP norms negotiated as part of the trade agreements to include provisions on civil and border enforcement modelled upon the EU's own *acquis* acts.[2] This line of action was repeated and further reinforced in the 2014 IPR Strategy.[3] In parallel to the IP-specific strategies, the 2006 Global Europe Communication called upon the EU to conclude trade agreements which would be comprehensive and ambitious in their scope.[4]

These documents opened the phase of EU trade agreements with exhaustive chapters on IP rights. By doing so, the EU joined the so-called IP *demandeurs* countries, i.e., countries that strongly require their trade partners to adhere to certain IP standards.[5] Although the policy documents originally prioritised enforcement and geographical indications,[6] the EU's trade agreements soon expanded to other areas, including copyright[7] and the protection of undisclosed know-how and business information.[8] Examples of such comprehensive agreements include the EU–South Korea free trade agreement, the EU's Association Agreements (AA) with Georgia, Moldova

---

[1] European Commission, 'Strategy for the Enforcement of Intellectual Property Rights in Third Countries' 2005/C 129/03; European Commission, 'Global Europe: Competing in the World—A Contribution to the EU's Growth and Jobs Strategy' (Communication) COM(2006) 567 final.

[2] 2005/C 129/03, 5–6.

[3] European Commission, 'Trade, Growth and Intellectual Property—Strategy for the Protection and Enforcement of Intellectual Property Rights in Third Countries' (Communication) COM(2014) 389 final, para 3.5.

[4] COM(2006) 567 final, para 4.2.

[5] E.g. the US or Canada.

[6] See 2005/C 129/03, 5–6 regarding civil and border enforcement. Regarding geographical indications, Dev S Gangjee, 'Generecide: The Death of a Geographical Indication?' in Dev S Gangjee (ed) *Research Handbook on Intellectual Property and Geographical Indications* (Edward Elgar Publishing 2016) 508(516) quotes a policy document by DG Agri, which stipulates that "a satisfactory GI Chapter is a 'must have' for the EU [new generation agreements]".

[7] For instance, Trade Agreement between the European Union and its Member States, of the one part, and Colombia and Peru, of the other part and the accession of Ecuador, art 223 regulates the resale right for the benefit of the author of an original work of art.

[8] See Agreement between the European Union and Japan for Economic Partnership (EU–Japan Economic Partnership Agreement), arts 14.36–14.37; EU–Vietnam Trade Agreement, art 12.41.

and Ukraine, and the EU–Canada Comprehensive and Trade Agreement, to name just a few.

Since its early beginnings, the EU's new external IP policy has been extensively criticised in scholarly circles.[9] Frequently voiced criticism has addressed the lack of a tailor-made approach (mainly due to the use of legal transplants from the EU IP *acquis*) that would reflect the partner's level of development[10]; an asymmetry in bargaining strength between the EU and its partners, which invites third countries to accept any provision put forward by the EU[11]; the erosion of policy space through the inclusion of TRIPS (Agreement on Trade-Related Aspects of Intellectual Property Rights)-plus and TRIPS-extra norms into the bilateral trade agreements[12]; or the use of norms that would primarily favour the interests of right holders to the detriment of other societal groups.[13]

These efforts, together with similar criticism of US external IP policy, culminated in a seminal publication in which leading academics in this field of research drafted the "Principles for Intellectual Property Provisions in Bilateral and Regional

---

[9] Leading publications on the matter include contributions to Josef Drexl et al. (eds), *EU Bilateral Trade Agreements and Intellectual Property: For Better or Worse?* (Springer 2014); Anselm Kamperman Sanders, 'The EU and Its IP Policies' in Pedro Roffe and Xavier Seuba (eds), *The ACTA and the Plurilateral Enforcement Agenda* (Cambridge University Press 2014) 259; Thomas Jaeger, 'The EU Approach to IP Protection in Partnership Agreements' in Christoph Antons and Reto M Hilty (eds), *Intellectual Property and Free Trade Agreements in the Asia–Pacific Region* (Springer 2015) 171(171–210); Anke Moerland, 'Do Developing Countries Have a Say? Bilateral and Regional Intellectual Property Negotiations with the EU' (2017) 48 International Review of Intellectual Property and Competition Law 760(760–783); Xavier Seuba and Elena Dan, 'The European Foreign Policy for Intellectual Property Enforcement' in Josef Drexl and Anselm Kamperman Sanders (eds), *The Innovation Society and Intellectual Property* (Edward Elgar Publishing 2019) 160(160–187).

[10] Henning Grosse Ruse-Khan, 'Principles for Intellectual Property Provisions in Bilateral and Regional Agreements' (2013) 44 International Review of Intellectual Property and Competition Law 878(882); Xavier Seuba, 'The Relevance of the Principles for Intellectual Property Provisions in Bilateral and Regional Agreements vis-à-vis European Preferential Trade Agreements' (2013) 44 International Review of Intellectual Property and Competition Law 943(944); Souheir Nadde-Phlix, 'IP Protection in EU Free Trade Agreements vis-à-vis IP Negotiations in the WTO' in Josef Drexl et al. (eds), *EU Bilateral Trade Agreements and Intellectual Property: For Better or Worse?* (Springer 2014) 133(136); Xavier Seuba, *The Global Regime for the Enforcement of Intellectual Property Rights* (Cambridge University Press 2017) 170.

[11] Pedro Roffe, 'Intellectual Property Chapters in Free Trade Agreements: Their Significance and Systemic Implications' in Josef Drexl et al. (eds), *EU Bilateral Trade Agreements and Intellectual Property: For Better or Worse?* (Springer 2014) 17(23); Carlos M Correa, 'High Costs, Negligible Benefits from Intellectual Property Provisions in FTAs' (2013) 44 International Review of Intellectual Property and Competition Law 902(902); Moerland, 'Do Developing Countries Have a Say?' (n 9) 760(763).

[12] Ruse-Khan, 'Principles for Intellectual Property Provisions' (n 10) 878(881); Moerland, 'Do Developing Countries Have a Say?' (n 9) 760(773–774).

[13] Roffe, 'Intellectual Property Chapters in Free Trade Agreements' in Drexl et al. (n 11) 17(24–26); Seuba, 'The Relevance of the Principles' (n 10) 122–126 and 192–193.

Agreements" (Max Planck Institute for Innovation and Competition Law (MPI) Principles).[14] These principles are aimed at guiding third countries in the do's and don'ts of negotiating IP norms with IP demanding countries. Although the MPI Principles and other academic publications mostly addressed these issues in EU trade agreements generally, some also more specifically targeted the approaches adopted in the EU–Ukraine AA.[15]

In the case of Ukraine, this EU "predisposition" to include IP *acquis* norms is further reinforced by the fact that EU–Ukraine relations (including the AA) fall under the auspices of the European Neighbourhood Policy (ENP).[16] Launched by the EU, the ENP targets the EU's southern[17] and eastern[18] neighbours. Within this policy, legislative approximation (i.e. implementation of EU law in the national laws of the neighbouring countries) is one of the two core elements.[19] Although the approximation objective[20] is relevant to all sectors and fields of bilateral cooperation, its applicability to IP norms presents an interesting angle for academic discussion.[21]

At the same time, within Ukraine the IP provisions under the EU–Ukraine AA were welcomed in Ukrainian academic publications.[22] The Agreement, and more

---

[14] Grosse Ruse-Khan, 'Principles for Intellectual Property Provisions' (n 10) 878(878–883).

[15] Seuba and Dan, 'The European foreign Policy for Intellectual Property Enforcement' in Drexl and Kamperman Sanders (n 9) 160(160–187).

[16] European Commission, 'Wider Europe—Neighbourhood: A New Framework for Relations with our Eastern and Southern Neighbours' (Communication) COM(2003) 104 final. For a legal and policy background to the ENP, see contributions to Dieter Mahncke and Sieglinde Gstöhl (eds), *Europe's Near Abroad: Promises and Prospects of the EU's Neighbourhood Policy* (P.I.E. Peter Lang 2008); Roman Petrov and Peter Van Esluwege (eds), *Legislative Approximation and Application of EU Law in the Eastern Neighbourhood of the European Union* (Routledge 2014); Sieglinde Gstöhl (eds), *The European Neighbourhood Policy in a Comparative Perspective: Models, challenges, lessons* (Routledge 2016); Tobias Schumacher et al. (eds), *The Routledge Handbook on the European Neighbourhood Policy* (Routledge 2018); Stefan Lorenzmeier et al. (eds), *EU External Relations Law: Shared Competences and Shared Values in Agreements Between the EU and its Eastern Neighbourhood* (Springer 2021).

[17] Algeria, Egypt, Israel, Jordan, Lebanon, Libya, Morocco, Palestine, Syria, and Tunisia.

[18] Armenia, Azerbaijan, Belarus, Georgia, Moldova, and Ukraine.

[19] Together with preferential treatment for trade. COM (2003) 104 final, para 2.

[20] EU–Ukraine AA, art 1, also the "progressive approximation" of Ukrainian legislation to that of the EU as one of the Agreement's main objectives.

[21] See also Yuriy Kapitsa, 'Association Agreements and Problems Approximating Intellectual Property Legislation of Third Countries with the EU Acquis: The Case of Ukraine' in this Volume.

[22] See Olena Kadetova, *EU–Ukraine Association Agreement in the System of Sources of Intellectual Property Law* (Yurinkom Inter 2019) 110–143; Olena Kadetova, 'To the Questionnaire of Characteristics and Ways of Development of Legislation in the Field of Intellectual Property in Ukraine' (2018) 1 Theory and Practice of Intellectual Property 88(88–97); Volodymyr Kryvolapchuk, Svitlana Ful, 'Legal Protection of Geographical Indications in the Context of the Association Agreement between Ukraine and the EU' (2018) 3 Theory and Practice of Intellectual Property 51(51–59); Yuriy Dehtiarenko, 'Current and Problem Issues of Ukrainian Legislation in the Field of Protection of a Variety of Plants in the Context of the Agreement on Association with the EU' (2018) 5 Theory and Practice of Intellectual Property 75(75–82). See also Yuriy Kapitsa, *European Union Intellectual Property Law: Formation, Institutes, Directions of Development* (Akademperiodyka, 2nd ed. 2020) 465–466, discussing how the EU–Ukraine Association Agreement fails to provide a mechanism

generally the EU IP *acquis*, were often seen as the best possible direction for the national legislative efforts or at least a good reference point. The main criticism made of the Agreement was that it did not include *all* possible *acquis* IP acts, and instead would only partially include norms in the EU IP law at the time of the drafting of the Agreement.[23] The implementation of EU IP *acquis* has also been perceived as a priority by the Ukrainian legislator,[24] even when such *acquis* is not included in the scope of the AA.[25]

Written at the crossroad of these two academic schools, this chapter considers how the norms on designs included in Arts. 212–218 EU–Ukraine AA impacted the Ukrainian system of industrial design protection.

The underlying analysis focuses on designs for two main reasons. First, design protection is rarely regulated in bilateral agreements, including those concluded by the EU. When compared with the few other EU trade agreements in which design protection is regulated, the EU–Ukraine AA stands out as being the most demanding and exhaustive.[26] Second, within Ukraine design rights as regulated prior to the implementation of the AA were known to be one of the most problematic due to their abusive use by right holders, a phenomenon referred to in Ukraine as "(design) patent trolling".[27] Norms such as individual character or exclusion from protection for functional features may well become a solution to the problem.

---

for updating Ukraine's obligations where new IP *acquis* acts are adopted in the EU. See also, in this volume, Roman Petrov, 'The EU–Ukraine Association Agreement as a General Framework of Contemporary EU–Ukraine Relations' and Yuriy Kapitsa, 'Association Agreements and Problems Approximating Intellectual Property Legislation of Third Countries with the EU Acquis: The Case of Ukraine' in this Volume.

[23] Yuriy Kapitsa, 'Reform of National Legislation for the Protection of Intellectual Property under the Association Agreement between Ukraine and the European Union' (2016) 11 Law of Ukraine 118 (118–123).

[24] Decree of the Cabinet of Ministers of Ukraine on the approval of the conceptual foundation for reforming the state system of intellectual property protection of Ukraine 2016, 402-p. Implementation of the EU–Ukraine Association Agreement is referred to as one of the reform's main priorities.

[25] One example to illustrate this statement is the Ukrainian Draft Law on Copyright and Related Rights 2021, 5552, art 60. Article 60 implements norms on the use of protected content by online content-sharing service providers, regulated in Parliament and Council Directive 2019/790/EU of 17 April 2019 on copyright and related rights in the Digital Single Market (2019) OJ L130/92 (DSM Directive), art 17. Despite not being bound to it by bilateral obligations, Ukraine plans to implement it *voluntarily*. At the same time, at the time of writing most EU Member States have not yet implemented the DSM Directive.

[26] See the analysis in Natalia Kapyrina, 'Design Rights in EU PTAs: Where Does Such Internalization Lead?' (2019) 53(4) Journal of World Trade 647 (647–677).

[27] "Patent trolling" is used to refer to situations of abusive registrations, where commonly known objects (e.g. clothes hangers or matches) are registered as designs and then used to block importations of such goods at the Ukrainian border. See Oleksandr Chernadchuk, 'Patent Trolling as a Type of Infringement of Intellectual Property Rights' (2019) 41(2) Scientific Journal of the International Humanitarian University 38 (38–41).

Hence, after the background to the research has been presented in Secs. 1 and 2 follows with a discussion of what was included in the design norms of the EU–Ukraine AA, and, what is more important, what was left out as compared to the *acquis* design norms that existed at the time of the negotiations. Section 3, in turn, investigates how these norms were implemented into Ukrainian design legislation and the potential pitfalls that occurred as the result of implementation. Finally, Sec. 4 of the chapter provides the reader with conclusions and recommendations both as to the content of EU trade agreements with other third countries and as to the implementation process for such countries.

2 Design Norms in the EU–Ukraine Association Agreement

2.1 What Was Included

As briefly advanced above, the EU tends to include IP provisions modelled on its own *acquis* in trade agreements with third countries. In the case of Armenia, Georgia, Moldova, and Ukraine, this policy is further reinforced by the overarching objective of legislative approximation as part of the ENP. At the same time, as this sec. will show, even within the ENP none of the other trade agreements with ENP countries is as exhaustive with regard to designs as the Ukrainian agreement.

Section 4 "Designs" of the Agreement consists of seven articles, which are closely modelled on Regulation No. 6/2002 on Community Designs,[28] without directly referring to the Regulation itself.

Section 4 first introduces the core definitions, as also found in Art. 3 Design Regulation, covering the notions "design", "product", and "complex product". In this regard, the EU–Ukraine agreement is the only one of the EU trade agreements in which these definitions are included.[29]

Article 213 of the Agreement regulates the requirements for design protection, namely "novelty" and, what is most important, "individual character", as provided in Arts. 4–6 Design Regulation. This is also unprecedented in the ENP region, as equivalent provisions in other agreements are loosely based on the TRIPS requirement and stipulate that designs shall be new and original.[30] The definition of individual character refers to notions known to EU lawyers—but alien to their Ukrainian counterparts—such as the "informed user", "freedom of the designer" or "overall impression".

---

[28] Council Regulation (EC) 6/2002 of 12 December 2001 on Community Designs (2001) OJ L3/1 (Design Regulation); Parliament and Council Directive 98/71/EC of 13 October 1998 on the legal protection of designs (1998) OJ L289/28 (Design Directive) includes provisions similar to those of the Design Regulation. The Design Directive is not chosen as the point of reference because it does not include norms on unregistered designs, unlike the EU–Ukraine Association Agreement.

[29] Kapyrina, 'Design Rights in EU PTAs' (n 26) 647 (657).

[30] See EU–Armenia CEPA, art 242(1); EU–Georgia AA art 181(1); EU–Moldova AA art 308(1).

A common feature of all four ENP agreements is the provisions on the protection of component parts in complex products, as also found in Art. 4(2) Design Regulation. These provisions exclude from design protection component parts of complex products where such component parts do not remain visible during normal use.[31]

The EU–Ukraine agreement also mandates Ukraine to exclude from protection features of the design that are solely dictated by its technical function, and the must-fit features.[32] In EU design law, the equivalent norms are found in Art. 8(1),(2) Design Regulation; they are meant to prevent excessive protection for functional features and to preserve the downstream market.[33] Kapyrina sees the practice of including these norms in EU trade agreements as "an important safeguard for preserving interoperability".[34] The EU–Ukraine agreement does not, however, include the so-called "Lego exception",[35] found in Art. 8(3) Design Regulation, whereby a design serving the purpose of allowing the multiple assembly or connection of mutually interchangeable products within a modular system would still be eligible for protection.

The EU–Ukraine agreement provides for an obligation to protect unregistered designs as a separate IP right, following the EU model of unregistered Community designs (UCD). This is in sharp contrast to the agreements with Moldova[36] and Armenia,[37] where the parties are allowed to choose legal means for the protection of unregistered designs (e.g. through unfair competition law), while the agreement with Georgia remains silent on this point.

Article 218 EU–Ukraine AA further provides for the mandatory cumulation of design and copyright rights, textually reproducing the equivalent provision in Art. 96(2) Design Regulation. The parties are nevertheless allowed to define the extent and the conditions of such cumulative protection, including the level of originality required.

Other TRIPS-plus norms in the EU–Ukraine agreement include the extension of the term of protection to 25 years,[38] a list of invalidity grounds,[39] a list of exceptions to design rights, including acts done privately and for non-commercial purposes, acts done for experimental purposes, an exception for teaching,[40] and an exclusion from

[31] EU–Ukraine AA, art 213(2).

[32] EU–Ukraine AA, art 217(3–4).

[33] Graeme B Dinwoodie and Jens Schovsbo, 'Design Protection for Products That are "Dictated by Function"' in Anette Kur et al. (eds), *The EU Design Approach: A Global Appraisal* (Edward Elgar Publishing 2018) 142 (142, 153–154); Uma Suthersanen, 'Excluding Designs (and Shape Marks): Where Is the EU Court of Justice Going?' (2019) 50 International Review of Intellectual Property and Competition Law 157 (157–160).

[34] Kapyrina, 'Design Rights in EU PTAs' (n 26) 647 (662).

[35] Dinwoodie and Schovsbo, 'Design Protection for Products That are "Dictated by Function"' in Kur et al. (n 33) 142 (145, 154).

[36] EU–Ukraine AA, art 309.

[37] EU–Ukraine AA, art 243.

[38] EU–Ukraine AA, art 214(1).

[39] EU–Ukraine AA, art 215.

[40] EU–Ukraine AA, art 217(1).

protection for designs that are contrary to public policy or to accepted principles of morality.[41]

2.2 *What Was Omitted*

2.2.1 Within Regulation (EC) No. 6/2002

As explained above, the EU–Ukraine AA includes design norms modelled upon (certain provisions of) the Design Regulation rather than including an obligation to implement the Design Regulation as a whole. Other Chapters of the AA include long lists of EU Directives and Regulations[42] that Ukraine has to implement into its national legislation. Far from advocating the inclusion of EU IP Directives and Regulations into trade agreements with third countries as a whole,[43] this sec. will instead look into which provisions of the Design Regulation were omitted and, potentially, the reasons why.

The most notable omission in the EU–Ukraine AA is the provisions regulating the protection of spare parts. Under Art. 110 Design Regulation, design protection for a component part of a complex product is waived where it is necessary for the purpose of the repair of that complex product so as to restore its original appearance ("repair" clause). This provision allows the avoidance of restrictions of competition in the spare parts market which is of utmost importance for suppliers of aftermarket spare parts, namely in the automotive industry.[44] In Joined Cases *Acacia* (2017), the Court of Justice of the European Union (ECJ) confirmed that the purpose of the "repair" clause is to avoid the creation of captive markets in certain spare parts and to protect a consumer from being indefinitely tied to a given manufacturer.[45] In contrast, EU Member States (MS) were unable to achieve a compromise to include similar norms in the Design Directive.[46] Article 14 Design Directive thus includes

---

[41] EU–Ukraine AA, art 217(5).

[42] This is, for instance, the case of Chapter 5 "Customs and Trade Facilitation" and Chapter 6 "Establishment, Trade in Services and Electronic Commerce" of Title IV, EU–Ukraine AA.

[43] In fact, the decision to include only certain provisions of relevant IP *acquis* rather than a legal act as a whole may well be the EU's response to the criticism, explained above, that the EU adopts a "one-size-fits-all" approach to all third countries, disregarding their level of development and the appropriateness of the suggested legal framework.

[44] Josef Drexl, 'Counterfeiting and the Spare Parts Issue' in Christophe Geiger (ed), *Criminal Enforcement of Intellectual Property—A Handbook of Contemporary Research* (Edward Elgar 2012) 369(369, 378–380).

[45] ECJ Joined Cases C-397/16 and C-435/16 *Acacia* (2017) EU:C:2017:992, para 50. See also Dana Beldiman et al., 'Spare Parts and Design Protection—Different Approaches to a Common Problem: Recent Developments from the EU and US Perspective' (2020) 69(7) GRUR International 673(678/680); EGC T-525/13 *H&M Hennes & Mauritz v. OHMI—Yves Saint Laurent (Sacs à main)* (2015) EU:T:2015:617, para 21.

[46] Annette Kur et al., 'The EU Design Approach—a Global Appraisal' in Annette Kur et al. (eds), *The EU Design Approach: A Global Appraisal* (Edward Elgar 2018) 251 (268).

the so-called "freeze-plus" provisions, whereby EU MS can either maintain in force existing legal provisions for design protection of spare parts, or introduce changes only if the purpose is to liberalise the market for such parts. This lack of agreement at the level of EU MS (rather than it being due to development or policy erosion concerns) explains the omission of a "repair" clause in the EU–Ukraine AA. The "repair" clause is not included because it would ruin the existing status quo under the Design Directive, as any such provision would also become binding on EU MS.[47]

Another notable absence in the EU–Ukraine AA is a provision equivalent to Art. 8(3) Design Regulation. This provision, sometimes referred to as the "Lego exception",[48] allows for the protection of designs serving the purpose of allowing the multiple assembly or connection of mutually interchangeable products within a modular system. Article 8(3) acts as an exception to the exclusion from protection of "must-fit" features regulated in Art. 8(2).[49] Within the EU, the Lego exception is criticised for the lack of justification of a privileged approach to modular systems[50] and for an uncertainty in scope.[51] This might explain why the EU decided not to include an equivalent provision in the EU–Ukraine AA.

Surprisingly, the EU–Ukraine AA does not include a provision equivalent to that under Art. 4(3) Design Regulation. Under Art. 4(2)(a) Design Regulation, as also found in Art. 213(2)(a) EU–Ukraine AA, a component part of a complex product would be eligible for protection only if it remains visible during normal use of the complex product. The definition of what such "normal use" is (e.g. "use by the end user, excluding maintenance, servicing or repair work") is provided in Art. 4(3) Design Regulation, but is omitted in the EU–Ukraine AA. This is even more remarkable, as other ENP agreements do include equivalent provisions.[52]

---

[47] Council Decision 2014/295/EU of 17 March 2014 on the signing, on behalf of the European Union, and provisional application of the Association Agreement between the European Union and the European Atomic Energy Community and their Member States, of the one part, and Ukraine, of the other part, as regards the Preamble, art 1, and Titles I, II and VII thereof (2014) OJ L161/1 (Council Decision on EU–Ukraine AA); Guillaume Van der Loo, *The EU-Ukraine Association Agreement and Deep and Comprehensive Free Trade Agreement: A New Legal Instrument for EU Integration Without Membership* (Brill 2016) 196–197. Council Decision on EU–Ukraine AA, art 5 precludes the agreement's direct effect in the EU itself. However, Van der Loo maintains that a unilateral Council Decision may not be interpreted as precluding the direct effect of provisions of a bilateral agreement, as consent to such preclusion was not given by both Parties.

[48] Dinwoodie and Schovsbo, 'Design Approach for Products That are "Dictated by Function"' in Kur et al. (n 33) 142 (154–155). Kur and Levin disagree with this theory, stating that a similar approach is also found in German judicial practice. See Annette Kur and Marianne Levin, 'The Design Approach Revisited: Background and Meaning' in Annette Kur et al. (eds), *The EU Design Approach: A Global Appraisal* (Edward Elgar Publishing 2018) 1 (12).

[49] EGC T-515/19 *Lego/EUIPO—Delta Sport Handelskontor* (2021) EU:T:2021:155, para 33.

[50] Oliver Ruhl and Jan Tolkmitt, *Gemeinschaftsgeschmacksmuster* (Carl Heymanns Verlag 2019) art 8, para 73.

[51] Dinwoodie and Schovsbo, 'Design Approach for Products That are "Dictated by Function"' in Kur et al. (n 33) 142 (154).

[52] See EU–Armenia CEPA, art 242(3); EU–Georgia AA, art 181(3); EU–Moldova AA, art 308(3).

At procedural level, norms are excluded that concern the presumption of validity of both registered and unregistered designs equivalent to Art. 85 Design Regulation. Article 85 states that registered Community designs shall be treated by courts as valid, and unregistered Community designs shall be treated as valid if the right holder proves that such unregistered design meets the requirements for protection.

In addition to the substantive and procedural norms described above, the EU–Ukraine AA also leaves out the Regulation's recitals. Within the EU, recitals are often instrumental for interpreting substantive provisions. For instance, the assessment of individual character as elaborated by the General Court[53] and reflected in the European Union Intellectual Property Office's Guidelines, is based on the criteria found in Recital 14. The fact that a design shall not have an aesthetic quality, which is a cornerstone element of EU design law,[54] is also only stipulated in Recital 10. However, these and other recitals are not included in the EU–Ukraine AA.

2.2.2 Within a Broader System of EU Design Law

Within a broader system of EU design law, the interpretative judgments of the ECJ are another area which is not included in the EU–Ukraine AA. Unlike the Chapters on electronic commerce,[55] public procurement[56] or competition,[57] the Chapter on intellectual property does not make any reference to the ECJ judicial practice as a source of interpretation for the norms included therein. This could be attributed to an unease among the EU's negotiators themselves as to how the EU is impacting third countries' IP laws and how this leads to the erosion of policy space in these countries.

---

[53] EGC T-525/13 *H&M Hennes & Mauritz v OHMI—Yves Saint Laurent (Sacs à main)* (2015) EU:T:2015:617, para 21.

[54] ECJ C-395/16 *DOCERAM* (2018) EU:C:2018:172, Opinion of Advocate General Saugmandsgaard, paras 25–27. Before the adoption of the Design Directive, certain EU MS (e.g. UK) did require designs to have ornamental or aesthetic value. A design feature was considered functional if it did not have ornamental or aesthetic value. This approach lies at the base of the causative theory in the examination of functional features. See also Lavinia Brancusi, 'Designs Dictated by their Technical Function' in Gordian Hasselblatt (ed), *Community Design Regulation* (Hart Publishing 2015) 125 (138–139).

[55] Under EU–Ukraine AA, art 6 to Annex XVII to Chapter 6 "Establishment, Trade in Services and Electronic Commerce", where relevant provisions of Chapter 6 are identical in substance to corresponding rules of the Treaty on the Functioning of the European Union and to acts adopted pursuant thereto (e.g. Directive 2000/31/EC), "those provisions shall, in their implementation and application, be interpreted in conformity with the relevant rulings of the Court of Justice of the European Union".

[56] Under EU–Ukraine AA, art 153, "due account shall be taken of the corresponding case law of the European Court of Justice" during the legislative approximation in the area of public procurement.

[57] Under EU–Ukraine AA, art 264, "the relevant jurisprudence of the Court of Justice of the European Union" shall be used as a source interpretation for norms on state aid.

Within the EU, the ECJ's judicial activism and its role in the interpretation of EU IP *acquis* is vividly discussed in academic circles.[58] When addressing the harmonising decisions of the ECJ, Levin states that the Court "ultimately determines the rules of the game".[59] Cassier and Strowel refer to the ECJ as a policy-maker and a "co-legislator", which "completes the unachieved work of the European legislator" in areas where Member States were unable to reach a compromise on the exact meaning of norms.[60]

Indeed, the interpretation of enigmatic concepts of EU design law, such as "informed user"[61] or "features of appearance of a product which are solely dictated by its technical function",[62] is complicated unless the ECJ interpretative judicial practice is consulted.

In the landmark judgment *PepsiCO* (2011),[63] the ECJ provided the definition of "informed user", a legal fiction that is used during the examination of a design's individual character. ECJ defined the informed user as:

> lying somewhere between [...] the average consumer, applicable in trade mark matters, who need not have any specific knowledge and who, as a rule, makes no direct comparison between the trade marks in conflict, and the sectoral expert, who is an expert with detailed technical expertise.[64]

This definition is now a cornerstone in both invalidity and infringement design proceedings in the EU.[65]

In another landmark case, *DOCERAM* (2018),[66] the ECJ offered useful guidance as to how features "solely dictated by a technical function" shall be defined. Between two opposing theories, that of "multiplicity of forms" and that of "causality",[67] the

---

[58] Marianne Levin, 'The harmonising decisions from Luxembourg' in Annette Kur et al. (eds), *The EU Design Approach: A Global Appraisal* (Edward Elgar Publishing 2018) 49; Alain Strowel and Kim Hee-Eun, 'The Balancing Impact of General EU Law on European Intellectual Property Jurisprudence' in Ansgar Ohly and Justine Pila (eds), *The Europeanization of Intellectual Property Law: Towards a European Legal Methodology* (Oxford University Press 2013) 121; Vincent Cassiers and Alain Strowel, 'Intellectual Property Law Made by the Court of Justice of the European Union' in Christophe Geiger et al. (eds), *Intellectual Property and the Judiciary* (Edward Elgar Publishing 2019) 175. On the ECJ's judicial activism in copyright cases, see also Eleonora Rosati, *Copyright and the Court of Justice of the European Union* (Oxford University Press 2019).

[59] Levin, 'The harmonising decisions from Luxembourg' in Kur et al. (n 58) 49 (50).

[60] Cassiers and Strowel, 'Intellectual Property Law Made by the Court of Justice of the European Union' in Geiger et al. (n 58) 175 (178, 197).

[61] Design Regulation, art 6.

[62] Design Regulation, art 8(1).

[63] ECJ C-281/10 P *PepsiCo v. Grupo Promer Mon Graphic* (2011) EU:C:2011:679.

[64] Ibid para 53.

[65] On the application of this concept in national EU MS case law, see Estelle Derclaye, 'EU Design Law: Transitioning Towards Coherence? Fifteen Years of National Case Law' in Niklas Bruun et al. (eds), *Transition and Coherence in Intellectual Property Law* (Cambridge University Press 2021) 56.

[66] ECJ C-395/16 *DOCERAM* (2018) EU:C:2018:172.

[67] For explanations on both theories, ECJ C-395/16 *DOCERAM* (2018) EU:C:2018:172, Opinion of Advocate General Saugmandsgaard, paras 19–22. See also the analysis in Tobias Endrich,

ECJ introduced an autonomous approach to interpretation. On the one hand, the ECJ approach in *DOCERAM* suggests basing the analysis on whether the technical function is the only factor which determines the features of the appearance of the product[68] (i.e. the Court indicates the approach used in the causality theory). On the other hand, although "the existence of alternative designs [is not] decisive",[69] the Court points out that the existence of alternative designs is one of the factors to be taken into account in the analysis (i.e. the Court applies the approaches used in the multiplicity of forms theory).[70]

Other cases that are important from an interpretative perspective include Joined Cases *Easy Sanitary Solutions* (2017), on whether in invalidity proceedings it has to be proven that an informed user effectively knew of an earlier design[71]; or *H. Gautzsch Grosshandel* (2014), on the interpretation of "circles specialised in the sector concerned" pursuant to Art. 7 Design Regulation.[72] This list continues expanding.[73]

For a non-EU country such as Ukraine, the implementation of EU *acquis* norms that are actively interpreted by the ECJ, represents an additional effort in deciding on whether and how such interpretative case law shall be reflected in the country's national legal order.

'Pinning Down Functionality in EU Design Law—A Comment on the CJEU's *DOCERAM* Judgment (C-395/16)' 14(2) Journal of Intellectual Property Law & Practice (2019) 156 (156–167); Suthersanen, 'Excluding Designs (and Shape Marks)' (n 33) 157 (157–160); Uma Suthersanen and Marc D Mimler, 'An Autonomous EU Functionality Doctrine for Shape Exclusions' 69(6) GRUR International (2020) 567 (567–577).

[68] ECJ C-395/16 *DOCERAM* (2018) EU:C:2018:172, para 32.

[69] Ibid.

[70] Ibid para 37.

[71] ECJ Joined Cases C-361/15 P and C-405/15 P *Easy Sanitary Solutions v. Group Nivelles and EUIPO* (2017) EU:C:2017:720.

[72] ECJ C-479/12 *H. Gautzsch Grosshandel* (2014) EU:C:2014:75.

[73] At the moment of writing, a preliminary reference is pending before the ECJ as to whether, in order to be protected as an unregistered Community design, the appearance of a part of the product must be made available separately from the whole product, or whether the making available of the design of that product in its entirety is sufficient. See also ECJ C-123/20 *Ferrari SpA v. Mansory Design & Holding GmbH, WH,* Opinion of Advocate General Saugmandsgaard.

3 Ukranian First-Take on EU-Modelled Design Law

3.1 Law 815-IX, Amending Ukrainian Design Law

In July 2020, Ukraine implemented amendments[74] required by the EU–Ukraine AA into its Design Law.[75] The reformed design law allows the tracing of the impact of EU IP norm-export on the Ukrainian design system at legislative level. This will be done in the sec. below. However, the Ukrainian specificities present two caveats:

The first amendments to the Design Law were adopted in July 2020, and entered into force in August 2020. However, at the moment of writing, no relevant design cases under the 2020 Law could be detected, neither at judicial[76] nor at administrative level.[77] This significantly limits any discussion on the impact of the EU–Ukraine AA on the Ukrainian design system.

The second one applies broadly to the analysis of IP provisions in trade agreements. Any evaluation of their impact on national systems requires first a definition of what a "positive" or a "negative" IP provision is. In this regard, Trimble observes that such definition is challenging, as "no single IP law is ideal for all countries at all times".[78] Moreover, even an initially sound provision may cause challenges because of an inappropriate implementation, especially in the case of legal transplants.[79] Also, different groups of stakeholders will perceive a given IP provision differently.[80] Nevertheless, within the realm of international law, academics concur that national IP laws should respond to internal challenges rather than external pressure[81]; the resulting norms should achieve a broader balance rather than favour one

---

[74] Ukrainian Law on Amendments to Certain Legislative Acts of Ukraine to Raise Protection and Enforcement of Trade marks and Designs and to Fight Patent Trolling 2020, 815-IX.

[75] Ukrainian Law on Protection of Rights to Designs 1994, 3770-XII ("Design Law").

[76] The legal database "Unified State Register of Judicial Decisions" allows search by applicable legal norms, including those from the 2020 Design law.

[77] Industrial Designs (2020) https://ukrpatent.org/uk/articles/ap-industrial-design accessed 13 September 2021.

[78] Marketa Trimble, 'Unjustly Vilified TRIPS-Plus?: Intellectual Property Law in Free Trade Agreements' American University Law Review 1 (22).

[79] Henning Grosse Ruse-Khan, 'From TRIPS to FTAs and Back: Re-Conceptualising the Role of a Multilateral IP Framework in a TRIPS-plus work' in Fabian Amtenbrink, Denise Prévost and Ramses A Wessel (eds), *Netherlands Yearbook of International Law 2017* (Springer 2018) 57(64); Roffe, 'Intellectual Property Chapters in Free Trade Agreements' in Drexl et al. (n 11) 17(22); Moerland, 'Do Developing Countries Have a Say?' (n 9) 760 (765).

[80] Trimble, 'Unjustly Vilified TRIPS-Plus?' (n 78) 1 (23).

[81] Grosse Ruse-Khan, 'Principles for Intellectual Property Provisions' (n 10) 878 (879–880).

particular group of stakeholders.[82] It is through this lens that Ukrainian Design Law will be addressed below.[83]

The most radical change in the Ukrainian design system is the introduction of "individual character" as an additional protection requirement alongside novelty. Under Art. 6(3) Design Law,

> a design shall be considered to have individual character if the overall impression it produces on the informed user differs from the overall impression produced on such a user by any design which has been made available to the public.

This definition is taken word-for-word from Art. 213(4) EU–Ukraine AA and from equivalent provisions of the EU Design Regulation.

This additional step narrows the scope of protection for designs as compared to systems where the only requirement for registration is novelty. Under previous Ukrainian law, "abusive" registrations[84] were possible for such objects as toilet paper,[85] boxes of matches,[86] barbeque sticks,[87] or tyres.[88] Moreover, these designs were registered in the Ukraine's register for customs enforcement of IP and used by their holders to prevent the importation of basic household goods into the territory of Ukraine.[89] With the introduction of individual character, such simplistic designs that do not result from the designer's innovation[90] can be quickly invalidated.

Another example of the balanced approach to design protection are norms on functional designs. Article 5(3) Design Law, as amended in 2020, excludes from design protection features that are solely dictated by technical functions, and "must-fit" features. These provisions of Ukrainian law are modelled on exclusions foreseen under Art. 8 EU Design Regulation to prevent technological innovation being hampered by granting design protection.[91] The previous registration system in

---

[82] The need for a balanced approach to IP provisions in trade agreements is also recognised in the European Commission's policy documents. See COM (2014) 389 final, para 2.2.

[83] The 2020 Law also introduced other amendments, such as administrative invalidity proceedings for designs, which are not discussed further because their introduction is not due to the implementation of the AA. Note, however, that the European Commission plans to introduce mandatory administrative proceedings for invalidating a national design right. See also European Commission, 'Commission Staff Working Document—Evaluation of EU legislation on design protection' SWD (2020) 264 final, 47–49.

[84] The term "abusive" is used in inverted commas, as such registrations were completely legal as per the requirements of the Ukrainian Design Law prior to 2020.

[85] Ukrainian designs, registered under No. 26706, No. 26707, No. 26708, No. 26709, No. 26710.

[86] Ukrainian design, registered under No. 26905.

[87] Ukrainian design, registered under No. 27154.

[88] Ukrainian designs, registered under No. 28140, No. 28141, No. 28142, No. 28143, No. 28144. On the registration of a carbonizer under previous design law, see Ganna Yudina, 'Concept of Industrial Design in Ukraine and EU' (2014) 5 Theory and Practice of Intellectual Property 57 (61).

[89] Chernadchuk, 'Patent Trolling as a Type of Infringement of Intellectual Property Rights' (n 27) 38 (38–41).

[90] Under Recital 7 Design Regulation, the purpose of enhanced protection for designs is to encourage innovation and the development of new products and investment in their production.

[91] Design Regulation, recital 10.

Ukraine was prone to accept designs that would otherwise be recognised as merely functional.[92] These norms are an example of TRIPS-plus provisions aimed at safeguarding the broader societal interests.[93] Equivalent norms in EU design law serve to prevent the monopolisation of downstream markets, preserve interoperability[94] and safeguard “fair and profitable competition for all Community undertakings”.[95]

Within the same reform, Ukraine implemented the so-called “Lego exception”, allowing protection for designs serving the purpose of allowing the multiple assembly or connection of mutually interchangeable products within a modular system.[96] Ukraine was not required to do this by the EU–Ukraine AA and implemented the norm voluntarily. As mentioned above, the equivalent norm in the EU law is criticised in academic circles.[97] The Lego exception has also a very limited applicability inside the EU itself.[98] This approach to implementation illustrates how Ukraine perceives EU *acquis* norms as its maximum legislative aim,[99] as well as a possible lack of awareness on the negative aspects of certain EU norms.

Other balance-oriented provisions implemented through the EU–Ukraine AA include the introduction of the requirement to conform with the public order and morality principle.[100]

The EU–Ukraine AA also introduced norms that favour the interests of right holders. One example of such a norm is the increase of the duration of design rights from 15 to 25 years,[101] as mandated by Art. 214 AA. Ukrainian Design Law now also foresees protection for partial designs,[102] as per Art. 212 AA, which according to Kapyrina is beneficial to right holders from sectors such as the automotive industry that participate in incremental innovation in an already competitive scenery.[103]

---

[92] As an example, the database of Ukrainian designs includes carbonizers, motorcycle carburettors, carburettors for scooters, or internal combustion engine carburettors.

[93] Kapyrina, ‘Design Rights in EU PTAs’ (n 26) 647 (662).

[94] For features dictated solely by a technical function, Dinwoodie and Schovsbo, ‘Design Protection for Products that are “Dictated by Function”’ in Kur et al. (n 33) 142 (142). For must-fit features, Dinwoodie and Schovsbo, ‘Design Protection for Products that are “Dictated by Function”’ in Kur et al. (n 33) 142 (153); Kapyrina, ‘Design Rights in EU PTAs’ (n 26) 647 (662).

[95] ECJ C-395/16 *DOCERAM* (2018) EU:C:2018:172, Opinion of Advocate General Saugmandsgaard, para 38.

[96] Design Law, art 5(3).

[97] See Sec. 2.2.1. See also Oliver Ruhl and Jan Tolkmitt, *Gemeinschaftsgeschmacksmuster* (Carl Heymanns Verlag 2019) art 8, para 73.

[98] At the moment of writing, only one case in which Design Regulation, art 8(3) was applied has reached the General Court. See EGC T-515/19 *Lego/EUIPO—Delta Sport Handelskontor* (2021) EU:T:2021:155.

[99] See also footnote 25.

[100] Design law, art 5(1). Kapyrina finds that such provisions in EU trade agreements are favourable to the interests of developing countries. See Kapyrina, ‘Design Rights in EU PTAs’ (n 26) 647 (669).

[101] Design Law, art 5(4).

[102] Design Law, art 5(2).

[103] See Kapyrina, ‘Design Rights in EU PTAs’ (n 26) 647 (666).

Another example is the introduction of unregistered design rights, previously unknown in the Ukrainian legal order. Under Art. 5(6) Design Law, an unregistered design shall be protected for a period of three years as from the date on which the design was first made available to the public within the territory of Ukraine.

Within the EU, a justification for the introduction of this right is provided in Recital 16 Design Regulation. This Recital refers to some of the industry sectors that "produce large numbers of designs for products frequently having a short market life where protection without the burden of registration formalities is an advantage and the duration of protection is of lesser significance".

According to Kur and Levin, protection for unregistered designs was "the most innovative feature" of the draft Design Regulation prepared by the Max Planck Institute in the early 90s.[104] Unregistered design rights were introduced in the EU on the basis of earlier research by Marianne Levin, who, after analysing various national systems of design protection, reached the conclusion that copying was the most widespread challenge for the fashion industry.[105] At the same time, neither EU nor Ukrainian law limit the scope of unregistered designs to any particular industry. Moreover, inside Ukraine, right holders have not been active in relying on this new right, including in the fashion industry. This could be attributed to a lack of awareness of the advantages of the unregistered design rights.

3.2 Filling Legislative Gaps by Means of the Guidelines: A Good yet Temporary Solution

The implementing exercise has revealed itself to be more complicated in areas where EU norms are constructed through judicial activism.[106] Ukrainian policy-makers refrained from defining in the Design Law those norms that had not been defined in the AA. At the administrative level, some legal gaps can be resolved through the Guidelines for Design Examination.[107] They are to be adopted through an order of the Ukrainian Ministry of the Economy and applied by the Patent Office during examination and invalidity proceedings.

[104] Kur and Levin, 'The Design Approach Revisited' in Kur et al. (n 48) 1 (20).

[105] Ibid. Note that the automotive industry also relies on unregistered design rights in the EU. See ECJ C-123/20 *Ferrari* (2021) EU:C:2021:628, Opinion of Advocate General Saugmandsgaard.

[106] See Sec. 2.2.2.

[107] Ukrainian Draft Order of the Ministry of Economy of Ukraine on Approving Rules for Drafting and Submitting Applications for Designs and on Examination of Applications for Designs and for International Registration of Designs 2021.

The Guidelines introduce definitions for such notions as "informed user" and "freedom of the designer", mostly inspired by the relevant ECJ case-law.[108] Nevertheless, as predicted by Kapyrina,[109] the implementation of complex notions that are not settled in EU design law may also lead to further divergences in third countries. The approach chosen by Ukrainian policy-makers for the examination of functional features is modelled on the "causality" theory. Nevertheless, additional approaches are introduced. Under para 7.5 Guidelines, where features are visible during the normal use of the product, these features are in most cases necessary for the functioning of the product but are not dictated solely by the technical function of the product, but also possess esthetical qualities. This method, unfound in equivalent EU practice, offers a fresh perspective on functional features.

At judicial level, the interpretation issue remains. The aforementioned Guidelines do not have binding force for the judiciary. The Grand Chamber of the Supreme Court admits the use of ECJ case law as a persuasive source of law to ensure a harmonious interpretation of Ukrainian legislation with settled standards of the EU's legal system; nevertheless, it underlines the fact that ECJ case law is a source of law only within the EU itself.[110] Several lower-instance courts have invoked ECJ cases in trade mark-related cases.[111]

Nevertheless, Ukrainian courts are required to be cautious when applying interpretative judicial practice of the ECJ, and this for several reasons.[112] First, most of the ECJ practice in the field of IP is not accessible in Ukrainian, which might create a language barrier for the judiciary.[113] Moreover, the application of foreign law concepts requires a thorough training of local practitioners. Most importantly,

[108] "Informed user", as defined under Guidelines, para 2.5, is modelled on ECJ C-281/10 P *PepsiCo v. Grupo Promer Mon Graphic* (2011) EU:C:2011:679, para 53. "Freedom of the designer", as defined under Guidelines, para 2.6, is modelled on EGC T-9/07 *Grupo Promer Mon Graphic v. OHMI- PepsiCo* (2010) EU:T:2010:96, paras 67, 72.

[109] Kapyrina, 'Design Rights in EU PTAs' (n 26) 647 (668).

[110] Grand Chamber of the Supreme Court, Order 80,783,425 (2019) 9901/636/18. For a broader perspective on the ECJ impact on Ukrainian judiciary see Roman Petrov, 'The Impact of the Court of Justice of the European Union on the Legal System of Ukraine' in Arie Reich and Hans-W Micklitz, *The Impact of the European Court of Justice on Neighbouring Countries* (OUP 2020) 189 (193–198).

[111] Petchers'kij District Court of Kyiv, Order 93,843,068 (2020) 757/19365/19-ц; Northern Commercial Court of Appeal 82,158,234 (2019) 910/13209/18. Note that, in this same case, the Supreme Court did not rely on ECJ case law as a persuasive source of law. See Supreme Court 83,783,100 Order (2019) 910/13209/18.

[112] For an alternative view, see Yuriy Kapitsa, 'Association Agreements and Problems Approximating Intellectual Property Legislation of Third Countries with the EU Acquis: The Case of Ukraine' in this Volume.

[113] This unlike the Republic of Moldova, which, due to close linguistic ties with Romania, can access all the relevant jurisprudence translated into Romanian. See Plenum of the Supreme Court of the Republic of Moldova on the Application of Certain Provisions of Copyright and Related Rights Law, No. 1, from April 25, 2016, which requires Moldovan courts to apply ECJ case-law to interpret communication to the public, exceptions and limitation to copyright law. See also Plenum of the Supreme Court of the Republic of Moldova on the application of certain provisions of trade mark law, No. 1, from February 6, 2017, which required Moldovan courts to apply ECJ case-law to

Ukrainian courts do not have a tradition of teleological interpretation and tend to interpret law literally. The application of approaches found in ECJ case law may thus become complicated for the Ukrainian judiciary.

4 Conclusion and Recommendations

For several years now, IP norms in trade agreements between developed and developing countries have drawn the attention of scholars worldwide. This chapter has discussed one example of such an export of norms, that of substantive design law in the EU–Ukraine AA. The fact that other areas such as geographical indications or enforcement provisions have already been actively debated by scholars made the analysis of design norms even more urgent.

Although IP demanding countries should be cautious with the export of norms, this chapter has shown that TRIPS-plus features (the object of much criticism) may also have a positive impact on third countries' legal order: they potentially bring a more balanced approach to IP norm-setting. In the case of Ukraine, implementing EU design norms allowed the issue of abusive registrations to be overcome, an issue which has long haunted Ukrainian policy-makers and practitioners alike.

The analysis has also highlighted the fact that, while the export of norms remains the EU's preferred policy option, not all the body of EU IP law is fit for such export. Where excessively vague and obscure norms are included (often as the result of complicated negotiations within the EU itself), such norms require additional interpretation from the ECJ, which is later not included in the EU trade agreements. This calls for an additional effort on the part of third countries during the implementation stage.

Of course, not every element of Ukraine's experience is subject to extrapolation to other third countries. Ukraine has a long-standing history of *acquis* implementation, including in the area of IP,[114] which made some of its experiences unique and the implementation exercise less radical. Nevertheless, the analysis of design norms has shown the importance of informed implementation on the part of third countries, i.e., a thorough knowledge of what lies behind the EU IP norms that the country is to implement.

---

interpret the distinctiveness of slogans, similarity of marks, scope of trade mark rights, exhaustion of trade marks.

[114] 98/149/EC, ECSC, Euratom: Council and Commission Decision of 26 January 1998 on the conclusion of the Partnership and Cooperation Agreement between the European Communities and their Member States, of the one part, and Ukraine, of the other part, OJ L49, 19.2.1998, 1–2. See also Yuriy Kapitsa, 'Association Agreements and Problems Approximating Intellectual Property Legislation of Third Countries with the EU Acquis: The Case of Ukraine' in this Volume.

References

Dana Beldiman, Constantin Blanke-Rosser and Anna Tischner, 'Spare Parts and Design Protection – Different Approaches to a Common Problem. Recent Developments from the EU and US Perspective' (2020) 69(7) GRUR International 673

Lavinia Brancusi, 'Designs Dictated by their Rechnical Function' in Gordian Hasselblatt (ed), *Community Design Regulation* (Hart Publishing 1st edn. 2015) 125

Vincent Cassiers and Alain Strowel, 'Intellectual Property Law made by the Court of Justice of the European Union' in Christophe Geiger, Craig Allen Nard and Xavier Seuba (eds), *Intellectual Property and the Judiciary* (Edward Elgar Publishing 2019) 175

Carlos M Correa, 'High Costs, Negligible Benefits from Intellectual Property Provisions in FTAs' (2013) 44 International Review of Intellectual Property and Competition Law 902

Oleksandr Chernadchuk, 'Patent Trolling as a Type of Infringement of Intellectual Property Rights' (2019) 41(2) Scientific Journal of the International Humanitarian University 38 [Олександр Чернадчук, 'Патентний Тролінг як Вид Порушення Прав на Об'єкти Інтелектуальної Власності' (2019) 41(2) Науковий Вісник Міжнародного Гуманітарного Університету 38]

Yuriy Dehtiarenko, 'Current and Problem Issues of Ukrainian Legislation in the Field of Protection of a Variety of Plants in the Context of the Agreement on Association with the EU' (2018) 5 Theory and Practice of Intellectual Property 75 [Юрій Дегтяренко, 'Актуальні та Проблемні Питання Законодавства України у Сфері Охорони Сортів Рослин у Співвідношенні з Угодою про Асоціацію з ЄС' (2018) 5 Теорія і Практика Інтелектуальної Власності 75]

Estelle Derclaye, 'EU Design Law: Transitioning Towards Coherence? Fifteen Years of National Case Law' in Niklas Bruun, Graeme B. Dinwoodie, Marianne Levin and Anshar Ohly (eds), *Transition and Coherence in Intellectual Property Law* (Cambridge University Press 2021) 56

Graeme Dinwoodie and Jens Schovsbo, 'Design Protection for Products That are "Dictated by Function"' in Anette Kur, Marianne Levin and Jens Schovsbo (eds), *The EU Design Approach: A Global Appraisal* (Edward Elgar Publishing 2018) 142

Josef Drexl, Henning Grosse Ruse-Khan and Souheir Nadde-Phlix (eds), *EU Bilateral Trade Agreements and Intellectual Property: For Better or Worse?* (Springer 2014)

Josef Drexl, 'Counterfeiting and the Spare Parts Issue' in Christophe Geiger (ed), *Criminal Enforcement of Intellectual Property - A Handbook of Contemporary Research* (Edward Elgar 2012) 369

Tobias Endrich, 'Pinning Down Functionality in EU Design Law – A Comment on the CJEU's *DOCERAM* Judgment (C-395/16)' 14(2) Journal of Intellectual Property Law & Practice (2019) 156

European Commission, 'Commission Staff Working Document – Evaluation of EU legislation on design protection' SWD(2020) 264 final

European Commission, 'Trade, Growth and Intellectual Property – Strategy for the Protection and Enforcement of Intellectual Property Rights in Third Countries' (Communication) COM(2014) 389 final

European Commission, 'Global Europe: Competing in the World - A Contribution to the EU's Growth and Jobs Strategy' (Communication) COM(2006) 567 final

European Commission, 'Strategy for the Enforcement of Intellectual Property Rights in Third Countries' 2005/C 129/03

European Commission, 'Wider Europe – Neighbourhood: A New Framework for Relations with our Eastern and Southern Neighbours' (Communication) COM(2003) 104 final

Dev S Gangjee, 'Generecide: The Death of a Geographical Indication?' in Dev S Gangjee (ed) *Research Handbook on Intellectual Property and Geographical Indications* (Edward Elgar Publishing 2016) 508

Henning Grosse Ruse-Khan, 'From TRIPS to FTAs and Back: Re-Conceptualising the Role of a Multilateral IP Framework in a TRIPS-plus work' in Fabian Amtenbrink, Denise Prévost, Ramses A. Wessel (eds), *Netherlands Yearbook of International Law 2017* (Springer 2018) 57

Henning Grosse Ruse-Khan, 'Principles for Intellectual Property Provisions in Bilateral and Regional Agreements' (2013) 44 International Review of Intellectual Property and Competition Law 878

Sieglinde Gstöhl (ed) *The European Neighbourhood Policy in a Comparative Perspective: Models, challenges, lessons* (Routledge 2016)

Thomas Jaeger, 'The EU Approach to IP Protection in Partnership Agreements' in Christoph Antons and Reto M Hilty (eds), *Intellectual Property and Free Trade Agreements in the Asia-Pacific Region* (Springer 2015) 171

Olena Kadetova, *EU/Ukraine Association Agreement in the System of Sources of Intellectual Property Law* (Yurinkom Inter 2019) [Олена Кадєтова, *Угода про Асоціацію України з Європейським Союзом в Системі Джерел Права Інтелектуальної Власності* (Юрінком Інтер 2019)]

Olena Kadetova, 'To the Questionnaire of Characteristics and Ways of dDvelopment of Legislation in the Field of Sntellectual Property in Ukraine' (2018) 1 Theory and Practice of Intellectual Property 88 [Олена Кадєтова, 'До Питання про Характеристику та Шляхи Розвитку Законодавству у Сфері Інтелектуальної Власності в Україні' (2018) 1 Теорія і Практика Інтелектуальної Власності 38]

Anselm Kamperman Sanders, 'The EU and Its IP Policies' in Pedro Roffe and Xavier Seuba (eds), *The ACTA and the Plurilateral Enforcement Agenda* (Cambridge University Press 2014) 259

Yuriy Kapitsa, *European Union Intellectual Property Law: Formation, Institutes, Directions of Development* (Akademperiodyka 2nd edn. 2020) [Юрій Капіца, *Право Інтелектуальної Власності Європейського Союзу: Формування, інститути, Напрями Розвитку* (Академперіодика 2 вид. 2020)]

Yuriy Kapitsa, 'Reform of National Legislation for the Protection of Intellectual Property under the Association Agreement between Ukraine and the European Union' (2016) 11 Law of Ukraine 118 [Юрій Капіца, 'Реформування Національного Законодавства з Охорони Інтелектуальної Власності Відповідно до Угоди про Асоціацію між Україною та Європейським Союзом' (2016) 11 Право України 118]

Natalia Kapyrina, 'Design Rights in EU PTAs: Where Does Such Internalization Lead?' (2019) 53(4) Journal of World Trade 647

Volodymyr Kryvolapchuk and Svitlana Ful, 'Legal Protection of Geographical Sndications in the Context of the Association Agreement Between Ukraine and the EU' (2018) 3 Theory and Practice of Intellectual Property 51 [Володимир Криволапчук та Світлана Филь, 'Правова Охорона Географічних Зазначень у Контексті Угоди про Асоціацію між Україною та ЄС' (2018) 3 Теорія і Практика Інтелектуальної Власності 51]

Annette Kur, Marianne Levin and Jens Schovsbo, 'The EU Design Approach – a Global Appraisal' in Annette Kur (ed), *The EU Design Approach: A Global Appraisal* (Edward Elgar 2018) 251

Marianne Levin, 'The Harmonising Decisions from Luxembourg' in Annette Kur, Marianne Levin and Jens Schovsbo (eds), *The EU Design Approach: A Global Appraisal* (Edward Elgar Publishing 2018) 49

Stefan Lorenzmeier, Roman Petrov and Christoph Vedder (eds), *EU External Relations Law: Shared Competences and Shared Values in Agreements Between the EU and its Eastern Neighbourhood* (Springer 2021)

Dieter Mahncke and Sieglinde Gstöhl (eds), *Europe's Near Abroad: Promises and Prospects of the EU's Neighbourhood Policy* (P.I.E. Peter Lang 2008)

Anke Moerland, 'Do Developing Countries Have a Say? Bilateral and Regional Intellectual Property Negotiations with the EU' (2017) 48 International Review of Intellectual Property and Competition Law 760

Souheir Nadde-Phlix, 'IP Protection in EU Free Trade Agreements vis-à-vis IP Negotiations in the WTO' in Josef Drexl, Henning Grosse Ruse-Khan and Souheir Nadde-Phlix (eds), *EU Bilateral Trade Agreements and Intellectual Property: For Better or Worse?* (Springer 2014) 133

Why so Few Geographical Indications in Ukraine? Legal, Political and Socio-Economic Perspective

Anastasiia Kyrylenko

Contents

Abstract In September 2017, the EU–Ukraine Association Agreement entered into force, and with it, some 3,000 geographical indications (GIs) from the EU received protection in Ukraine. In turn, only two Ukrainian GIs were filed by Ukrainian authorities for protection in the EU. This chapter looks into the reasons behind such a low number of registered GIs in Ukraine, from a legal, political and socio-economic perspective. This is achieved mainly through historical research, which is complemented by a comparative perspective from other countries in the Central and Eastern Europe region, as well as discussion with local policy-makers. Although many causes are uncovered throughout this chapter, recent developments of the GI system in Ukraine also show that many of them can be surmounted, provided there is sufficient interest and support.

This Chapter was written between September and December 2021. It aimed at analysing how historical developments, such as the imitative character of agriculture in Tsarist Russia or the Soviet collectivisation, impacted modern-day GIs in Ukraine. While I tried to base my analysis on robust research, conclusions such as "population resettlement leads to a loss of GI knowledge" seemed distant. As I prepare this Chapter for print, Russian full-scale invasion continues, Ukrainian population is once again forced to resettle and territories, where PDO "Melitopol cherry" and PDO "Kherson watermelon" are produced, remain occupied.

A. Kyrylenko (✉)
Global Innovation Law and Policy, University of Alicante, Alicante, Spain
e-mail: anastasiia.kyrylenko@ua.es

H. Richter (ed.), *Competition and Intellectual Property Law in Ukraine*,
MPI Studies on Intellectual Property and Competition Law 31,
https://doi.org/10.1007/978-3-662-66101-7_19

1 Introduction

In September 2017, the EU–Ukraine Association Agreement entered into force, and with it, some 3,000 geographical indications (GIs) from the EU received protection in Ukraine under a system of mutual recognition of GIs.[1] In turn, Ukraine filed only two GIs for protection in the EU ("Soniachna Dolyna" and "Novyj Svit", both for wines[2]), even though a *sui generis* GI law in Ukraine was first adopted in 1999,[3] and a first GI was registered back in 2007.

It was such a low number of Ukrainian GI registrations, included under the EU–Ukraine Association Agreement, that motivated this research. If one looks into the history of Ukrainian wine-making (wine being the prototype of the EU GI system[4]), the historical parallels with the EU system is striking: Ukraine (then part of the Russian Empire) suffered a phylloxera crisis in end of nineteenth century,[5] struggled to recover from it with a Wine Purity law,[6] and discussed the adoption of *terroir*-based systems as a possible solution.[7] In Southern Ukraine—part of the Black Sea wine belt, along with Moldova, southern Russia, Georgia, and Armenia[8]—the geographical conditions also resembled those of Western European vineyards.[9] However, despite having a long-standing vinicultural tradition, as well as a predominantly agricultural

---

[1] Association Agreement between the European Union and its Member States, of one part, and Ukraine, of the other part (2014) OJ L161/3 (the EU–Ukraine Association Agreement), art 202.

[2] Also spelled as "Soniachna Dolina" and "Novy Svet". At the moment of negotiations, Ukraine had a total of 19 GIs, with most of them registered for mineral waters and ineligible for protection as per EU standards.

[3] Ukrainian Law on Indications of Origin 1999, No. 752-IX.

[4] Dev Gangjee, *Relocating the Law of Geographical Indications* (Cambridge University Press 2012) 78, 124, 127.

[5] Stephen V Bittner, *Whites and Reds: A History of Wine in the Lands of Tsar and Commissar* (Oxford University Press 2021) 60–85; On the phylloxera crisis in France and its role in the creation of *sui generis* protection, see Andrea Zappalaglio, *The Transformation of EU Geographical Indications Law: The Present, Past and Future of the Origin Link* (Routledge 2021) 35–36; Gangjee (n 4) 93–96; Bittner (n 5) 66 observes that the south of the Russian Empire (nowadays, Southern Ukraine and Moldova) was actively cooperating with southern France in their fight against phylloxera.

[6] See Bittner (n 5) 27 discussing how the absence of formal protection for *terroir* was a central component of the wine-making crisis, after which the 1914 Russian Wine Purity law was adopted. On a similar French Law from 1905, see Gangjee (n 4) 98–102; Zappalaglio (n 5) 36–37.

[7] Bittner (n 5) 28–29 discusses the work of Mikhail Konstantinovich Ballas, a Russian Empire wine researcher, who in 1903 "despite using the term [*terroir*] only twice [...] described something that resembled the ways *terroir* would come to be understood in the latter half of the twentieth century". The importance of developing local GIs and taking *terroir* into account was also the main message of Lev Golytsin during his speech at the First congress of winegrowers and winemakers of Russia in 1902. This is discussed in Sec. 3.2.1 below.

[8] Bittner (n 5) 181.

[9] See Bittner (n 5) 38 and 57 explaining how the geography and patterns of winemaking in southern Ukraine resemble those of Western Europe, such as Bordeaux.

economy[10] (agriculture being another industry commonly rich in GIs), Ukraine never developed into a fully-fledged GI system in Ukraine.

This chapter thus intends to discuss the reasons behind that. The analysis covers the time-period from early twentieth century, when the local winemakers started looking at the French Appellation d'Origine Contrôlée (*AOC*) system as a post-phylloxera solution, until 2017, when the EU–Ukraine Association Agreement entered into force, and with it a new chapter in the history of Ukrainian GIs opened. Although the reasons behind a low number of local GIs in Central and Eastern European countries[11] have generally caught only a limited interest among GI scholars, findings from research available laid the foundation for this chapter. They include a lack of capacitated public institutions,[12] Soviet-type economic planning,[13] traumas of collectivisation,[14] and population resettlement in the Soviet Union and its satellite states.[15] These are complemented by a research of historical analyses, cited extensively throughout the chapter, as well as by discussions with local policy-makers, to receive their first-hand experience. The reasons identified are presented from a legal, political and socio-economic perspective.

2 Legal and Political Perspective

2.1 Absence of an International Framework to Which Ukraine Could Gravitate Before the PCA with the EU

Political and legal factors which foster the creation of a protection system for GIs (and other IP rights, for that matter) mainly include international and bilateral agreements which oblige a country to implement a specific regime. Here Ukraine has only relatively recently faced the gravitational force of a *sui generis* protection system for GIs, that of the European Union.

---

[10] According to the World Bank data from 2018, 71.3% of Ukraine's land area is agricultural land. In Europe, Ukraine is only surpassed by the United Kingdom (71.7%); major EU agricultural countries, Spain and France, account for 52.4 and 52.3% of land area respectively.

[11] For an overview of GI systems and statistics in the EU Member States which joined after 2004, see Zappalaglio (n 5) 148–155; On Croatia, see Alexander Wirsig and Wolfgang Heisrath, 'Welcome to the Club? The Significance of Protected Geographical Indications and Designations of Origin in Europe, With Special Consideration of the Croatian Situation' (2020) 55 Hrvatski Croatian: International Symposium on Agriculture 109 (112).

[12] Wirsig and Heisrath, 'Welcome to the Club?' (n 11) 109 (113).

[13] Anna Kapala, 'Protection of Geographical Indications of Agricultural Products and Foodstuffs in International Law' (2007) 1 Agricultural Law Review 150 (150–165).

[14] Anastasiya Shtaltovna and Hart N Feuer, 'Modern Resilience of Georgian Wine: Geographical Indications and International Exposure' in Alessandro Bonanno et al. (eds), *Geographical Indication and Global Agri-Food Development and Democratization* (Routledge 2020) 134 (142).

[15] Zappalaglio (n 5) 154.

Bilaterally, the EU is currently the main driving force behind the introduction of *sui generis* GI systems in third countries, mostly through conclusion of trade agreements. The EU's "new generation"[16] trade agreements are unimaginable without an extensive series of provisions on geographical indications.[17] In this respect Engelhardt cites officials from the Directorate-General for Agriculture and Rural Development (DG AGRI), who state that "a satisfactory GI Chapter is a "must have" for the EU" in a trade agreement.[18] Such exhaustive norms generally include lists of EU GIs to be protected in the partner country, the extension of protection under Art. 23 TRIPS to all categories of products (what is known as the "GI extension"), and provisions requiring the "un-genericis[ing]" of certain GIs, which had become generic in the partner country.[19] Polemics are not uncommon, especially in trade negotiations between Old World and New World countries.[20] At the same time, geographical indications have only a limited harmonisation internationally, mainly due to the Old World/New World dichotomy.[21] *Sui generis* protection for GIs was first introduced internationally[22] with the adoption of Lisbon Agreement for the Protection of Appellations of Origin in 1958. Influenced by the French system of

---

[16] "New generation" trade agreements are those comprehensive trade agreements negotiated after 2006.

[17] Tim Engelhardt, 'Geographical Indications Under Recent EU Trade Agreements' (2015) 46(7) International Review of Intellectual Property and Competition Law 783 (787); Liam Sunner, 'How the European Union is Expanding the Protection Levels Afforded to Geographical Indications as Part of its Global Trade Policy' (2021) 16 Journal of Intellectual Property Law and Practice 341 (341–347).

[18] Engelhardt, 'Geographical Indications Under Recent EU Trade Agreements' (n 17) 783 (787).

[19] Ibid.

[20] In scholarly literature, Old World countries mainly refer to the European Union, especially Western European countries; New World countries include the US, Canada, Australia, New Zealand, as well as several Latin American countries; Bernard O'Connor, 'The European Union and the United States: Conflicting Agendas on Geographical Indications—What's Happening in Asia?' (2014) 9(2) Global Trade and Customs Journal 66 (66–69); Jill E Hobbs, 'A Protectionist Bargain?: Agriculture in the European Union—Canada Trade Agreement' (2015) 49(3) Journal World Trade 437 (437–456); Benjamin Farrand, 'Two Continents, Divided by Deep Philosophical Waters?: Why Geographical Indications Pose a Challenge to the Completion of the TTIP' (2017) 7(2) European Journal of Risk Regulation 269 (269–273).

[21] Daniel J Gervais and Matthew Slider, 'The Geneva Act of the Lisbon Agreement: Controversial Negotiations and Controversial Results' in William van Caenegem and Jen Cleary (eds), *The Importance of Place: Geographical Indications as a Tool for Local and Regional Development* (Springer 2017) 15 (15–16); Anna G Micara, 'The Geneva Act of the Lisbon Agreement for the Protection of Appellations of Origin and Their International Registration: An Assessment of a Controversial Agreement' (2016) 47 International Review of Intellectual Property and Competition 673 (674); O'Connor, 'The European Union and the United States: Conflicting Agendas on Geographical Indications' (n 20) 66 (66–69).

[22] The Paris Convention for the Protection of Industrial Property of 1883 did require protection for indications of source and appellations of origins under arts 1(2) and 10 bis, but only against unfair competition and not as a *sui generis system*.

Appellation d'Origine (AO),[23] the Lisbon Agreement requires its members to protect geographical indications under a *sui generis* system, i.e. protection through unfair competition or consumer protection laws is not sufficient. This requirement, scholars believe,[24] explains why the Lisbon Agreement had such a low level of participation.

The Soviet Union, of which Ukraine was part for the majority of the twentieth century, never joined the Lisbon agreement.[25] Similarly, only few of the Soviet Union's satellite states, belonging to what was known as the Eastern Bloc, signed the Lisbon Agreement prior to 1991.[26] The Soviet Union was also reluctant to join other international treaties in the field of intellectual property, including the Berne Convention.[27] In the meantime, Soviet Ukraine became one of the world's leading makers of "Soviet Champagne", produced in Crimea and Eastern Ukraine using the *méthode champenoise* and mainly destined for export.[28]

It was not until mid-1990s that Ukraine came under the EU's (then, the European Communities') external policy on GIs. First, the Partnership and Cooperation Agreement (the PCA),[29] which was signed in 1995 between the European Communities and Ukraine, required Ukraine to "[...] provide [...] a level protection similar to that existing in the Community" for intellectual and industrial property rights (Art. 50). The predominant reading of this clause was that to do so Ukraine had to implement IP-related *acquis* acts. Soon after, Ukraine adopted its first *sui generis* GI law.[30]

Ukraine's obligations on GIs under the PCA were part of the EU's more general policy to export its legislation in trade-related areas to post-Soviet states, where such legislation was mostly missing, due to the socialist past. Adopting the EU model, the European Commission later claimed, 'reduce[s] the invention costs of political and economic costs of reform'.[31] Nevertheless, due to a soft nature obligation under the

[23] Bernard O'Connor, *The Law of Geographical Indications* (Cameron May 2004) 37; Micara, 'The Geneva Act of the Lisbon Agreement for the Protection of Appellations of Origin and Their International Registration' (n 21) 673 (676).

[24] O'Connor (n 23) 39; Daniel J Gervais, 'Reinventing Lisbon: The Case for a Protocol to the Lisbon Agreement (Geographical Indications)' (2010) 11 Chicago Journal of International Law 67 (79).

[25] As of end of 2021, Ukraine has not expressed any intention to sign the Lisbon Agreement.

[26] Czechoslovakia joined the Lisbon Agreement in 1966, Hungary in 1967, and Bulgaria in 1975. See Zappalaglio (n 5) 150 concerning the EU's new member states joining the Lisbon Agreement.

[27] See Budylin, discussing how the USSR and the US were reluctant to join the Berne Convention. The USSR did sign the Paris Convention, in 1965; Serhei Budylin, 'Winnie-the-Pooh Joins the WTO: Copyright Issues for "Old" Foreign Works' (2014) 1 Journal of the Intellectual Property Court 48 (48–66).

[28] Bittner (n 5) 177–189. According to Bittner, in 1979 Ukraine exported 4.9 million of bottles of Soviet Champagne, including to Western Europe. Overall, 75% of Soviet Champagne, produced in Ukraine, was exported.

[29] Council and Commission Decision 98/149/EC of 26 January 1998 on the conclusion of the Partnership and Cooperation Agreement between the European Communities and their Member States, of the one part, and Ukraine, of the other part (1998) OJ L49/1 (Cooperation Agreement).

[30] Ukrainian Law on Indications of Origin 1999, No. 752-IX.

[31] European Commission, 'Taking Stock of the European Neighbourhood Policy (ENP) Implementation of the European Neighbourhood Policy in 2009 Sectoral Progress Report' COM(2010) 207 final, para 6.

PCA (including the diplomatic model of the dispute-settlement system),[32] Ukraine was less inclined to fully comply with its approximation obligations.

In 2008, Ukraine joined the WTO, which required the implementing of the TRIPS Agreement, including its Section 3 on Geographical Indications. Several amendments were introduced that same year,[33] but GI protection remained mostly unsolicited by Ukrainian producers: between 2007, when the first Ukrainian GI was filed, and 2014 only 14 Ukrainian GIs were registered, mainly for mineral waters. Moreover, early versions of the Ukrainian GI law allowed single individuals (and not only associations of producers) to register their brands as GIs.[34] Due to this, almost all Ukrainian GIs from the early years were mere individual brands, rather than geographical names.[35]

The EU–Ukraine Association Agreement (the AA), signed in 2014 and in force since 2017, opened a new chapter in Ukrainian GI system, both internally and as part of bilateral relations with the EU. Articles 201–211 AA require the mutual recognition by the Parties of a long list of GIs, predominantly originating from the EU. As in the EU mineral waters have not been covered by GI protection since Regulation (EC) No. 692/2003,[36] only two Ukrainian GIs could be filed for reciprocal protection in the EU. Moreover, under Art. 405 AA Ukraine had to approximate its national legislation to Regulation (EC) No. 510/2006 on agricultural products and foodstuffs, Regulation (EC) No. 110/2008, Regulation (EC) No. 509/2006 on spirit drinks, and Regulation (EC) No. 479/2008 on wines.

Legislative reform,[37] together with an increased interest on the side of policy-makers and EU-funded technical assistance, has brought a boom in the registration of Ukrainian GIs. Since the entry into force of the newest GI law, several traditional GIs have been "uncovered" and registered in Ukraine, including "Hutsul Sheep Bryndzya" for cheese and "Melitopol Cherry". Of the five newer GIs, three are immediately available for protection in the EU (being agricultural products) and two more

---

[32] Diplomatic model, as opposed to a quasi-judicial model, relies on consultations and diplomatic negotiations, with a limited possibility to have recourse to legal adjudication. See Ignacio Garcia Bercero, 'Dispute Settlement in European Union Free Trade Agreements: Lessons Learned?' in Lorand Bartels and Federico Ortino (eds), *Regional Trade Agreements and the WTO Legal System* (Oxford 2006) 383 (389–393).

[33] Ukrainian Law on Introduction of Amendments to Certain Laws of Ukraine in the Sphere of Intellectual Property, in order to implement requirements related to Ukraine's entry into the WTO 2008, 254-VI.

[34] This was amended by Ukrainian Law on Geographical Indications 2019, 123-IX. Currently, if a single individual or legal entity applies for GI protection, several reservations exist.

[35] This is, for instance, the case with "Myrhorodska", the first Ukrainian GI, which is also registered as trade mark.

[36] Council Regulation (EC) No. 692/2003 of 8 April 2003 Amending Regulation (EEC) No. 2081/92 on the Protection of Geographical Indications and Designations of Origin for Agricultural Products and Foodstuffs (2003) OJ L99/1.

[37] Ukrainian Law on Geographical Indications 2019, 123-IX; Anastasiia Kyrylenko, 'Use It or Lose It? Ukraine Amends Its Law on GIs' (2020) 15 Journal of Intellectual Property Law and Practice 17 (17–18).

can be registered when the EU expands its GI scheme to non-agricultural products. Several more potential Ukrainian GIs remain in the pipeline, such as "Kherson watermelon" and "Transcarpathian honey".

2.2 *Protection Under Trade Mark and Consumer Protection Law*

2.2.1 Before the Disintegration of the Soviet Union

As already mentioned above, *sui generis* GI protection is not the only model for protecting geographical indications in a broader sense. Other possible models include protection under collective or certification trade marks, under unfair competition law, or under consumer protection law. During Soviet Union times, certain of the functions nowadays attributed to GIs (e.g. protection of a product's quality) were fulfilled by trade mark and consumer protection law.

The Soviet Union started regulating trade marks with the 1922 Decree "On Trade marks", issued by the Council of People's Commissars of the Russian Soviet Federative Socialist Republic.[38] The decree laid down norms, common to trade mark legislation of that time, such as absolute grounds for refusal of registration for generic or deceptive signs (Art. 4). The 1922 Decree was replaced in 1926 and 1936 by successive Decree on Trade marks.[39] The 1936 Decree required all Soviet enterprises to mark their products with what were known as "production marks", which had to indicate the enterprise's name, location, the state standard according to which the product was produced, and several other items.[40] The 1962 Trade Mark Order was another important milestone, as it brought standards closer to Western ones, by expanding protection to services and allowing foreigners to register trade marks in the Soviet Union.[41] The last trade mark reform before the Soviet Union's dissolution occurred

---

[38] The Soviet Union's Regulation of the Council of People's Commissars of the Russian Soviet Federative Socialist Republic on Trade Marks 1922; For the history of Soviet trade mark law, see Oleg Gorodov, The Right to Means of Individualization: Trademarks, Service Marks, Appellations of Origin, Brand Names, Commercial Designations (Wolters Kluwer 2006) 20–27; Uwe Bohnet, *Trade Mark Law in the People's Republic of China and Russia: A Comparative Legal Study Taking into Account the Development of German Law* (Carls Heymanns Verlag 1996) 23–28; A Vida, 'The Law of Industrial Property in the Peoples' Democracies and the Soviet Union' (1964) 12 International and Compliance Law Quarterly 280 (280–286); Joseph M Lightman, 'The USSR Trademark System and East–West Trade' (1966) 10(1) Patent, Trademark and Copyright Journal of Research and Education 11 (11–32); Jonathan Cohen and Serge Bauer, 'The New Trademark Law in the Soviet Union' (1991) 81(4) Trademark Reporter 397 (397–407); Cay Hober, 'Protection of Foreign Trademarks in the Soviet Union' (1979) 14(3) Texas International Law Journal 367 (367–388).

[39] Gorodov (n 38) 21–22.

[40] Gorodov (n 38) 22; Lightman, 'The USSR Trademark System' (n 38) 11 (15).

[41] Gorodov (n 38) 23–24.

with the 1974 Trade Mark Order, aimed at implementing the Paris Convention and the Nice agreement.[42]

However, Soviet trade mark legislation was different from its Western counterparts in many other ways. In the Soviet Union private enterprises were mostly illegal until mid-1980s and all production was run by the state; Soviet trade marks served to identify state-owned factories, and were not granted to individuals until the 1962 Law,[43] nor were they used as a competitive tool.[44]

As a consequence, the functions of trade marks also differed.[45] The function of guaranteeing the origin of the marked goods or services, labelled as essential trade mark function by the European Court of Justice (ECJ) in 1978,[46] was not applicable under Soviet Union legislation. Instead, trade marks served as quality control symbols,[47] a role similar to the one currently fulfilled by the EU's quality schemes.[48] Vida explains that the quality function fulfilled two roles: that of assuring consumers that trade-marked goods were of a certain quality; and that of fastening responsibility of defaulting enterprises in cases of bad quality.[49] For instance, under Art. 23 Trade Mark Law of 1962, as amended in 1965, a trade mark licence could only be granted, provided that the licence agreement required the licensee to maintain the quality of the goods. The approach gradually changed after 1965, after the Soviet Union joined the Paris Convention and undertook several reforms of its trade mark law.[50]

In parallel, certain functions, which are now fulfilled by the GI protection, were covered by the consumer protection law, which standardised the production of products, including foodstuffs and alcohol. GOSTs,[51] adopted by the State Committee of the USSR on standards, included lengthy requirements, which were called specifications and prescribed how certain categories of goods had to be produced. This included GOST 13918-88 "Soviet Champagne", GOST 7208-84 "Wines" (including port, sherry and madeira) or GOST 7616-55 "Milk, dairy products and dairy cans" (including "Moscow cheese" and "Holland cheese"). GOSTs were mandatory for

42 Gorodov (n 38) 25.

43 Cohen and Bauer, 'The New Trademark Law in the Soviet' (n 38) 397 (400).

44 Lightman, 'The USSR Trademark System' (n 38) 11 (15–16); Vida, 'The Law of Industrial Property in the Peoples' Democracies and the Soviet Union' (n 38) 280 (285).

45 Vida, 'The Law of Industrial Property in the Peoples' Democracies and the Soviet Union' (n 38) 280 (285).

46 ECJ C-102/77 *Hoffmann-La Roche/Centrafarm* (1978) ECLI:EU:C:1978:108, para 14.

47 Lightman, 'The USSR Trademark System' (n 38) 11 (15–16); Vida, 'The Law of Industrial Property in the Peoples' Democracies and the Soviet Union' (n 38) 280 (284); Hober, 'Protection of Foreign Trademarks in the Soviet Union' (n 38) 367 (367).

48 Parliament and Council Regulation (EU) No 1151/2012 of 21 November 2012 on quality schemes for agricultural products and foodstuffs (2012) OJ L343/1, Recitals 2 and 3.

49 Vida, 'The Law of Industrial Property in the Peoples' Democracies and the Soviet Union' (n 38) 280 (284).

50 Hober, 'Protection of Foreign Trademarks in the Soviet Union' (n 38) 367 (367).

51 Acronym from Russian, standing for State Pan-Soviet Standard. Before 1940, GOSTs were labelled as OSTs.

production across the Soviet Union, notwithstanding where exactly Moscow cheese was to be produced.

Soviet trade mark and consumer protection norms, together with the Soviet Union's policy of collectivisation and industrialisation of agriculture,[52] deferred interest in introducing a *sui generis* GI regime in Ukraine until late 1990s.

2.2.2 Between 1991 and 1999

On the eve of the Soviet Union's final disintegration, a new Soviet Trade Mark Law was passed in July 1991.[53] It was praised by contemporary scholars for its comprehensive character.[54] The Law was meant to enter into force on 1 January 1992, but was abandoned when the Soviet Union was dissolved.[55] Following the principle of continued application of Soviet laws until relevant Ukrainian legislation had been adopted,[56] the 1974 Soviet Trade Mark Law was applied for more several years. However, the 1991 law was used as baseline when post-Soviet trade mark legislation was developed.[57] The first Ukrainian Trade Mark Law was adopted several years after Ukraine regained its independence, in 1993.[58] Under Art. 6(2) 1993 Trade Mark Law, geographically descriptive elements could be included in a trade mark, as non-protectable elements, where they were not dominant elements in such sign. These norms were taken over from the 1991 Soviet Trade Mark Law.[59]

In turn, the first Ukrainian law with a *sui generis* GI system was adopted in 1999.[60] The system of "qualified geographical indications", introduced by the 1999 GI Law, was partially modelled upon the EU's Protected Designation of Origin (PDO) and Protected Geographical Indications (PGI), albeit through more complex wording. Both agricultural and non-agricultural products have been eligible for GI protection since the 1999 law. The first Ukrainian GI was registered, for a mineral water named "Myrhorodska", in 2007.

Before the 1999 GI Law came into force many products that had potential as GIs were registered as trade marks by producers, who saw a market opportunity. This

[52] See Sec. 3.1.1.

[53] Cohen and Bauer, 'The New Trademark Law in the Soviet' (n 38) 397 (397).

[54] Cohen and Bauer, 'The New Trademark Law in the Soviet' (n 38) 397 (399).

[55] Bohnet (n 38) 27.

[56] Ukrainian Regulation on Procedure for Temporary Application at the Territory of Ukraine of Certain Legislative Act of the USSR 1991, 46.

[57] Bohnet (n 38) 28.

[58] Ukrainian Law on Protection of Rights to Trademarks for Goods and Services 1994, 3689-XII.

[59] Bohnet (n 38) 28; Cohen and Bauer, 'The New Trademark Law in the Soviet' (n 38) 397 (400).

[60] Ukrainian Law on Protection of Rights to Indicate the Origin of Goods 1999, No 752-IX.

includes "Carpathian tea",[61] "Ukrainian spotykach" (a traditional fruit liquor)[62] and "Poltava honey".[63] Where these or similar trade marks are still in force, a GI registration may be denied, under a Ukrainian provision on relative grounds for refusal, which is similar to Art. 6(4) Regulation (EU) No 1151/2012.[64] These registrations might have closed the opportunities for development of local geographical indications, which could only be registered from January 2000 onwards.[65]

3 Socio-Economic Perspective

3.1 Adverse Soviet Union's Policies

While GIs quality schemes were developing in Western Europe with the objective of preserving traditional family farming and small-sized agricultural enterprises,[66] the Soviet Union of the 1920s to the 1950s was focused on transforming itself from an agricultural to an industrialised power. This was done through a series of policies, including forced collectivisation of small farms, industrialisation, and forced population resettlement. These policies were not conducive (to say the least) to the preservation of traditional production methods among Ukrainian farmers and producers.

---

[61] Figurative trademark "Карпатський чай", No. 25634, filed on 14 October 1999, registered on 17 June 2002. Currently in force.

[62] Figurative trademark "Спотикач український", No. 17952, filed on 5 August 1998, registered on 15 February 2001. Currently in force.

[63] Word trademark "Полтавський мед", No. 48702, filed on 24 December 2002, registered on 15 March 2005. Not in force.

[64] Regulation (EU) No. 1151/2012 of the European Parliament and of the Council of 21 November 2012 on Quality Schemes for Agricultural Products and Foodstuffs (2012) OJ L343/1(Regulation on GIs). Under Ukrainian Law on protection of Rights to Geographical Indications 2000, 2188-III, art 8(1)(f), an indication shall be denied registration as a GI if it "is identical or similar so that it can be confused with a trademark, the rights to which are recognized in Ukraine, if, given the reputation, renown and duration of use of this trademark, such legal protection may mislead consumers as to the true identity of the product".

[65] I thank the participants of the Max Planck Institute's workshop in Kyiv, in October 2021, for bringing up this argument during the discussion of the draft Chapter. While this argument was brought up by those, who had been involved in the formation of Ukrainian IP system in the 1990s, other policy-makers, with whom I discussed this article, do not necessary agree with this reasoning.

[66] Zappalaglio (n 5) 107–111 explains how the history of EU GI policy cannot be divorced from the history of Common Agricultural Policy (CAP), which was based on family farms and small agricultural enterprises.

3.1.1 Forced Collectivisation and Industrialisation

In late 1920s, the Soviet Union introduced two policies which had a disastrous impact on small farms in Ukraine: collectivisation and industrialisation.

Collectivisation aimed to replace small private farming with collectively-owned and state-owned farms, to increase food production for local consumption and agricultural exports by concentrating farmers in larger producing units. Collectivisation was meant to provide resources for a rapid industrialisation of the Soviet economy, introduced to transform it from agricultural-based to heavy industry-based. Moreover, family-based farming was seen as a sign of the bourgeoisie, who were oppressed in Soviet times.[67] It was not until Perestroika in the 1980s that the importance of family-based farming for the overall economy was rediscovered.[68]

The two policies combined disrupted small farming in Ukraine, which had already been hit by civil war in late 1910s and expropriations in early years of Soviet rule.[69] Industrialisation also brought changes in the pattern of employment: the Soviet urban population doubled in 1926–1939, while non-agricultural employment (in sectors such as industry, construction and transport) trebled during those years.[70]

In parallel to collectivisation[71] and industrialisation, the Soviet Union also imposed, in late 1920s, the policy of "dekulakisation", i.e. elimination of certain categories of farmers through requisition of food, property expropriation, forced resettlement, or execution.[72] "Kulak" was a term used in Soviet propaganda to denote wealthier small farmers. Different criteria were employed by Soviet authorities to define a "kulak": those who used hired labour; those who owned livestock; or those who possessed a bigger farming area per family (notwithstanding the number of family members).[73] Kulaks were treated as enemies of the state, hostile to the Soviet vision of economic development. Few reliable statistics are available on the toll of dekulakisation. To illustrate the extent of the impact of dekulakisation one may

---

[67] Katja Bruisch, 'The Soviet Village Revisited: Household Farming and the Changing Image of Socialism in the Late Soviet Period' (2016) 57 Cahiers du Monde Russe 81 (81).

[68] Ibid.

[69] Bittner (n 5) 18 affirms that Russian Revolution, civil war and expropriation in early Soviet years were disastrous for winemaking. He adds, on page 117, that the vast majority of winemakers were small-scale growers and private farmers.

[70] Stephen G Wheatcroft and Robert W Davies, 'Soviet Industrialization Reconsidered: Some Preliminary Conclusions about Economic Development between 1926 and 1941' (1986) 39(2) The Economic History Review 264 (273). According to the 1926 and 1937 Soviet Censuses of Ukraine, urban population specifically in Ukraine grew from 18.1 to 33.61%. This excludes the territory of Western Ukraine, which became part of the Soviet Union between 1939 and 1944. See statistics and analysis in Omelian Rudnytskyi et al., 'Demography of a Man-made Human Catastrophe: The Case of Massive Famine in Ukraine 1932–1933' (2015) 42 Canadian Studies in Population 53 (56–57).

[71] Conquest suggests treating dekulakisation and collectivisation as two aspects of the same policy. Robert Conquest, *The Harvest of Sorrow: Soviet Collectivisation and the Terror—Famine* (Oxford University Press 1986) 117.

[72] Pavel Polian, *Against Their Will: The History and Geography of Forced Migrations in the USSR* (Central European University Press 2004) 70–84.

[73] Conquest (n 71) 74–76.

look into statistics provided by Pavel Polian: in 1929–1930 some 100,000 kulaks were deported from Ukraine.[74] To fight the farmers' opposition to collectivisation and dekulakisation Soviet authorities used mass starvation and mass executions.[75] Collectivisation and dekulakisation were also conducted in the post-war Western Ukraine and the Baltics countries, after they were annexed by the Soviet Union during the Second World War.[76]

As the result of agricultural collectivisation and industrialisation, food and alcohol production were centralised in collectively-owned and state-owned farms. Centuries-old traditions of small farming were lost in Ukraine.[77] Origin link, inherent to the EU GI system, was also lost, as products which had traditionally originated from certain regions of the Soviet Union were now produced in centrally-controlled factories across the Soviet Union. The example of "Khvanchkara" Georgian wine is telling. The name "Khvanchkara", protected in Georgia as a GI since 2005, stems from an eponymous village in northern Georgia.[78] However, during Soviet times both factories in Georgia and the Interrepublic Wine Factory in Moscow were producing Khvanchkara wine.[79] This, Bittner notes, precluded the development of a sense of terroir.[80] Similar negative impacts of the centrally-controlled economy on GI development was observed in Poland.[81] Another long-term consequence of collectivisation, suggested by Georgian researchers, may be the reluctance of modern-day farmers to set-up cooperative-like structures, necessary for the establishment of a GI.[82] In parallel to that, the implementation of industrialisation policy, according to

---

[74] Polian (n 72) 70–75. This excludes the territory ofWestern Ukraine, which became part of the Soviet Union between 1939 and 1944.

[75] Conquest (n 71); Rudnytskyi et al., 'Demography of a Man-made Human Catastrophe: The Case of Massive Famine in Ukraine 1932–1933' (n 70) 53 (56–57).

[76] Emily Baran, 'It takes a Village: Collectivization in the Postwar Ukrainian Borderlands' (2018) 60(3–4)) Canadian Slavonic Papers 529 (537); David Feest, 'The Collectivization of Agriculture in the Baltic Soviet Republics, 1944–1953' in Constantin Iordachi and Arnd Bauerkamper (eds), *The Collectivization of Agriculture in Communist Eastern Europe: Comparison and Entanglements* (Central European University Press 2014) 79 (80).

[77] The absence of family farming until early 1990s was also brought up as one of the main reasons behind the lack of Ukrainian GIs in conversations with several stakeholders.

[78] PDO "Khvanchkara" was the first protected GI in Georgia, registered since 14 July 2005. According to the product specifications, Khvanchkara received its current name in 1930s, prior to that it was labelled as "Kipiani" wine and written mentions of it exist since mid-nineteenth century. Khvanchkara is also protected in the EU, under Annex XVII-D to EU–Georgia Association Agreement.

[79] Wine labels from Tbilisi and Moscow factories, used in 1980s, are available at https://flb.ru/upload/2019/06/3-1-khvachkara-tbilis-rozliv.jpeg and https://flb.ru/upload/2019/06/3-2-khvanchkara-N20-msk_rozliv-1980.jpeg accessed 12 November 2021. Along the same lines, Bittner (n 5) 237 describes how "grape must from across the Soviet Union was shipped by train car for processing at the world's largest winery, the Interrepublic Wine Factory in Moscow".

[80] Bittner (n 5) 172–173.

[81] Kapala (n 13) 110.

[82] Shtaltovna and Feuer (n 14) 142 cite "the fresh trauma of forced collectivization" as one of the reasons why the Georgian system of GIs is less successful than its Western European counterpart.

certain scholars, has generally a negative impact on the development of local GIs as opposed to countries where traditional (artisanal) production methods are favoured.[83]

3.1.2 Forced Population Resettlement

Together with forced collectivisation and industrialisation, the Soviet Union pursued a policy of forced population resettlement from the early 1930s to the 1950s. Mass resettlement included deportation due to ethnicity (such as the total deportation of Crimean Tatars in May 1944)[84] or class (such as the deportation of kulaks),[85] resettlement to repopulate territories which had been vacated due to purges, and labour force transfer to distant parts of the USSR.[86]

Forced resettlement occurred throughout the territory of Ukraine as part of the dekulakisation campaign. Repression affected not only small farmers but also specialists, such as winemakers.[87] However, this chapter is not the place to discuss in detail the actual numbers of victims of repression, or the reasons behind that, but rather how such repression affected the formation of geographical indications in Ukraine.

Once again, the first obvious impact is the loss of traditional practices, which were not passed to the following generations. Polian notes that when selecting where to deport small farmers to the Soviets had "the tendency to ignore the natural and climatic conditions (and therefore traditional skills of the deported kulaks)".[88] Other consequences can be deduced from observing the development of GI systems in the

[83] Kindstedt maintains that the difference in the number of GI-protected cheeses between southern Europe and northern Europe is because countries such as England, the Netherlands and Denmark opted for industrialised cheese making, while countries such as France, Italy, Spain and Greece preserved traditional production methods. However, an economic study by Filippi and Triboulet shows that protecting a product under a GI quality scheme may paradoxically lead to industrialisation of production methods, as GI producers face demands from the market to reduce production costs and increase supply. See Paul Kindstedt, *Cheese and Culture: A History of Cheese and its Place in Western Civilization* (Chelsea Green Publishing 2012) 214–216; Maryline Filippi and Pierre Triboulet, 'Traditional Products and Industrialization Processes: The Coherence of Geographical Indications' in Artur Cristóvão (ed), *Farming and Rural Systems Research and Extension: European Farming and Society in Search of a New Social Contract – Learning to Manage Change* (2004) 69–82.

[84] According to different estimates between 187,500 and 191,000 Crimean Tatars were deported from the Crimea, and many of them died before reaching their final destination. See estimates in Brian Glyn Williams, 'The Hidden Ethnic Cleansing of Muslims in the Soviet Union: The Exile and Repatriation of the Crimean Tartars' (2002) 37 Journal of Contemporary History 323 (334–335); Greta Lynn Uehling, *The Crimean Tatars' Deportation and Return* (Palgrave Macmillan 2004) 3–4.

[85] According to different estimates between 2,500,000 and 5,000,000 Ukrainian kulaks were deported in 1930 and 1931, many of them died before reaching their final destination. See estimates in Conquest (n 71) 126–127, 142–143.

[86] Polian (n 72) 57–69.

[87] Bittner (n 5) 152–155 traces the biographies of the victims of repression in the wine industry in the 1930s.

[88] Polian (n 72) 73.

countries of Central Europe, as forced resettlement also took place in the annexed territories of Poland, the Baltic republics, Romania and Finland.[89]

As Zappalaglio observes in this regard, countries in Central Europe are more actively using Traditional Specialities Guaranteed (TSGs) than those in Southern Europe, which have a strong preference for PDOs and PGIs.[90] TSGs are a quality scheme, which is not linked to a specific geographical area. An interview conducted by Zappalaglio with a senior Polish official explains that this interest in TSGs might be due to the forced resettlement of population in Poland, which caused certain traditions to expand beyond a specific region, thus losing its original link necessary for a GI.[91] A similar situation can be seen in Finland, as demonstrated by the specifications to the Finnish "Kalakukko" TSG.[92] While specifications to current Ukrainian GIs do not echo a similar issue, massive resettlement of population from Ukraine during the Soviet era could not have failed to have a negative impact on the preservation of the origin link.

Ukraine is yet to introduce TSGs in its legislation,[93] though Ukrainian policy-makers have already identified several eligible products, such as bortsch, Kyiv-style cutlet and Poltava dumplings.[94] It remains to be seen whether TSGs will succeed to the extent that they do in Central Europe.

3.2 *Consumers' Preferences and Price Premium*

Two additional explanations for the low number of local GIs arise from a review of the literature and conversations with local stakeholders: the unwillingness of local consumers to pay more for premium products[95]; and industry's tendency to imitate

[89] Polian (n 72) 115–123. Auvo Kostiainen, 'Genocide in Soviet Karelia: Stalin's Terror and the Finns of Soviet Karelia' (1996) 21 Scandinavian Journal of History 331 (331–342).

[90] Zappalaglio (n 5) 151–155.

[91] Basing his words on the interview, Zappalaglio elaborates that "[i]n fact, the Soviet occupation of the country led to the dislodgement of different communities and the standardisation of many elements of the Polish national heritage, including the production of some traditional foodstuffs. [...] Poland was indeed aware of the existence of different traditional productions. It could not, however, locate them in a specific place anymore". See Zappalaglio (n 5) 154–155.

[92] Zappalaglio gives the example of the Finnish "Kalakukko" TSG, the specifications for which state that "[a]fter the Second World War, part of Karelia passed to what was then the Soviet Union, and the population of the region was moved to other parts of Finland. Thus the art and tradition of making kalakukko spread throughout Finland." See Zappalaglio (n 5) 154–155. However, the specifications of Ukrainian GIs do not make specific reference to the Soviet Union policies or the impact of population resettlement.

[93] Ukrainian Draft Law on Peculiarities of Legal Protection of Geographical Indications to Agricultural Products and Food Products, Protection of Rights and Application of Quality Schemes, including Traditional Guaranteed Features for Agricultural Products and Food Products 2021, 5616.

[94] Impact Assessment of Ukrainian Draft Law 2021, 5616. See https://www.me.gov.ua/Documents/Download?id=5780c80f-a99b-4284-98ef-07800d4bebb5 accessed 8 November 2021.

[95] This reason was brought up in a discussion with a local policy-maker.

products from Western Europe in response to consumers' preferences.[96] Confirming or refuting these would require robust economic or social science research, which are beyond the scope of this chapter. However, both reasons are briefly discussed below, so as to offer avenues for future research in this area.

3.2.1 The Imitative Character of Local Industry in Response to Consumers' Preferences

In 1902, Lev Golytsin, a leading Russian[97] winemaker of Tsarist times, spoke at the first congress of winegrowers and winemakers of the Russian Empire, held in Moscow. In parallel to similar developments in Western Europe,[98] Russian winemakers were searching for ways for their industry to recover from phylloxera.[99]

One problem, said Golytsin, was the use of additives in winemaking, such as grain alcohol and beetroot sugar. This, according to Golytsin, would replace the vine culture with a culture of beetroot and potato, "and become the second phylloxera".[100] Winemakers' efforts to preserve the quality of Russian wine culminated in the 1914 Wine Purity law.[101]

But Golytsin also saw a different way of overcoming the crisis: that of developing local GIs to replace the widespread labelling under French "champagne"[102] or "cognac".[103] The upper classes, Golytsin said, had a habit for foreign wines, "and as a

[96] Bittner (n 5) 170–172.

[97] The term "Russian" is used here with reference to Russian Empire, which in 1902 included almost all modern-day Ukrainian territories, with the exception of parts of Western Ukraine. Lev Golytsin (1845–1915) was the founder of winemaking in Crimea and the pioneer of production of sparkling wine in Crimea and in Abrau-Durso (now Krasnodar region, Russia). The name of Golytsin's winemaking estate, Novyj Svit, is a registered Ukrainian PDO for sparkling wines.

[98] Gangjee (n 4) 93–96 and Zappalaglio (n 5) 35–36 explain how the phylloxera crisis pushed for the development of Appellation d'Origine Contrôlée (AOC) system in France.

[99] Regarding the context of the first congress of winegrowers and winemakers of Russia, see Bittner (n 5) 98–104.

[100] The full text of Golytsin's speech is available at https://nashevino.ru/blog/knowledge/poslanie-l-s-golicyna-nashi-gody accessed 29 November 2021.

[101] Stephen V Bittner, 'A Problem of Taste: An American Connoisseur's Travels through the Soviet Union's Black Sea Vineyards and Wineries' (2018) 19(2) Kritika: Explorations in Russian and Eurasian History 305 (305).

[102] It is interesting to observe that, back in 1902, Golytsin was even using the term "sparkling wine", rather than "champagne", when describing, which types of wines are characteristic of which area in Russian Empire.

See Lev Golytsin, 'Typology of Russian wines in 1902,' Speech in the Section "Winemaking" of the All-Russian Congress of Winegrowers and Winemakers, Moscow, 1902. The speech is available at https://nashevino.ru/blog/history/tipologiya-vin-rossii-v-1902-g accessed 29 November 2021.

[103] Bittner (n 5) 96 includes an 1894 picture of a "wine and cognac display case" of the trading house Vladimir Vishniakov, produced at the southern shore of Crimea.

result, winegrowers and winemakers introduced a foreign nomenclature, which must be eliminated by creating Russian types of wine", different for each region.[104]

As already discussed above, Soviet authorities, who soon after that congress took power, had no interest in developing Soviet GIs. Instead, local food and wines were labelled as "Soviet Champagne", "Crimean Sherry", "Crimean port"[105] and Soviet "Holland cheese".[106] The Soviet wine industry, Bittner concluded, was, just like its Tsarist predecessor, deeply imitative of Western European traditions.[107]

In the same vein, Alison K. Smith, extensively quoting historical sources, relates the efforts to imitate Western European cheeses in Tsarist Russia in the eighteenth and nineteenth centuries.[108] Swiss experts were brought in to transfer their knowledge and contemporary authors published guides on how to imitate Roquefort, Parmesan and Brie, among others.[109] More than a century later, the European Union reclaimed these names through the EU–Ukraine Association Agreement.

3.2.2 Unwillingness to Pay Price Premium for a GI Protected Product

Geographical indications often come with a price premium. According to a recent study, commissioned by the European Commission, the sales value of EU GI products was on average 2.07 times higher than the sales value of comparable standard products without a GI label.[110] This, in turn, requires consumers being willing to pay a price premium,[111] and a certain purchasing power within the country of consumption. For instance, when studying the profiles and motives of GI buyers with regard to

[104] The full text of Golytsin's speech is available at https://nashevino.ru/blog/knowledge/poslanie-l-s-golicyna-nashi-gody accessed 29 November 2021.

[105] Anatolii Avidzba et al., 'On the Names of Ukrainian Wine Products with Geographical Indications of Other Countries' (2011) 2 Magaratch: Vine Growing and Wine Making 26 (26–28). In this article, the authors defend that certain naming, such as champagne, shall be preserved as they became generic in Ukraine. See also Bittner (n 5) 171.

[106] Soviet state standard for milk and dairy products, GOST 7616–55, 1972.

[107] Bittner (n 5) 172.

[108] Alison K Smith, 'From Gruyères to Gatchina: The Meaning of Cheese in Tsarist Russia' (2021) Food, Culture and Society 1 (2–15). Smith believes that the efforts to imitate Western European cheeses were unsuccessful because of a different *terroir.*

[109] Ibid.

[110] The European Commission, 'Study on Economic Value of EU Quality Schemes, Geographical Indications (GIs) and Traditional Specialities Guaranteed (TSGs)' Final Report, 2021, 102. To the opposite, Loureiro and McCluskey conclude, when studying PGI "Gallician Veal", that GI quality schemes do not automatically mean a price premium, it is more dependent on the product's quality. See Maria Luz Loureiro and Jill J McCluskey, 'Assessing Consumer Response to Protected Geographical Identification Labelling' (2000) 16(3) Agribusiness 309 (309–320). The European Commission study, at 26, also recognises that EU GIs include products with low-price premium, for instance regional wine and fresh meat.

[111] For a literature review of economic studies on consumers' willingness to pay for geographical indications, see Cerkia Bramley et al., 'The Economics of Geographical Indications: Towards a Conceptual Framework for Geographical Indication Research in Developing Countries' in World Intellectual Property Organization (ed) *The Economics of Intellectual Property: Suggestions for*

the Greek "Zagora" PDO, Fotopoulus and Krystallis observe that buyers of Zagora apples "belong to upper social and income groups".[112] Ukraine, a country with the lowest GDP per capita in Europe,[113] may have only few "indication-of-origins fans", as Fotopouls and Krystallis call this group of consumers.

Poverty as a negative factor for the development of GIs in Ukraine was brought up throughout twentieth century. Golytsin, in his speech in 1902 which was mentioned above, stated that the general economic crisis was affecting the wine-making industry.[114] Bittner, building on his research of winemaking in Tsarist Crimea, observes that local consumers of early twentieth century did not show "a willingness to pay a premium for Crimean terroir".[115] Similarly, Mayner A. Amerine, a US vinicultural scientist, made several research trips to the Soviet Union in the 1960s and 1970s. Critical of the quality of Soviet wine, Amerine concluded that it was not a problem of terroir, but of the population's poverty.[116]

Researchers have yet to study the development of Ukrainian GIs from an economic perspective.[117] However, certain indirect indicators may point to the correctness of this assumption. For instance, the export statistics of Champagne (a French PDO) show that the consumption in Ukraine is at the levels of Cyprus, Lebanon or the Dominican Republic,[118] which may be indicative of how affordable premium products are for middle-income Ukrainian consumers.

4 Perspectives

In this chapter I have discussed the causes behind such a low number of registered geographical indications in modern-day Ukraine. The analysis covered the period from the early twentieth century, when similar systems started emerging in Western Europe, until 2017, when the EU–Ukraine Association Agreement entered into force.

Further Research in Developing Countries and Countries with Economies in Transition (WIPO 2009) 109 (124–127).

[112] Christos Fotopoulos and Athanasios Krystallis, 'Quality Labels as a Marketing Advantage: The Case of the "PDO Zagora" Apples in the Greek Market' (2003) 37(10) European Journal of Marketing 1350 (1370).

[113] According to the World Bank data from 2020.

[114] The full text of Golytsins speech is available at https://nashevino.ru/blog/knowledge/poslanie-l-s-golicyna-nashi-gody accessed 29 November 2021.

[115] Bittner (n 5) 108.

[116] Bittner (n 5) 183.

[117] One of the few pieces of research available on the issue is Anatolii Kucher et al., 'Consumer Willingness to Pay a Price Premium for Ecological Goods: A Case Study from Ukraine' (2019) 7 Environmental and Socio-economic Studies 38 (38–49).

[118] In 2019 155,939 75 cl bottles were sold in Ukraine, 148,053 in Cyprus, 158,189 in Lebanon, and 145,721 in the Dominican Republic. See statistics in https://www.champagne.fr/assets/files/economie/2019/bulletin_exp%C3%A9ditions_2019.pdf accessed 29 November 2021.

These reasons, already elaborated on above, include an absence, up until the mid-1990s, of a "model" system, such as the one currently exported by the EU: protection of names, potentially registerable as GIs, through trade mark and consumer law. There also was a loss of historical memory, through Soviet policies of forced collectivisation, industrialisation and forced resettlement.

This chapter is primarily focused on the Ukrainian GI system. However, many of its conclusions are applicable to two other Eastern European countries with strong vinicultural and agricultural economies: Georgia and Moldova. Those two countries were also parts of the Russian Empire and then of the Soviet Union, thus having a shared legal tradition with Ukraine. After regaining their independence, both countries introduced *sui generis* GI laws,[119] modelled upon the EU system. Similarly to Ukraine, in 2014 Georgia and Moldova signed Association Agreements with the EU. However, differences also exist: while many other regions of the then Russian Empire were imitating Western European products, Georgia focused on forging its own identity, at least in wine production,[120] which led to a significant number of local GI registrations.[121] This offers avenues for further research concerning the influence of factors beyond merely legal ones on the development of local GI systems.

Returning to the Ukrainian setting, more recent developments show that despite a complicated history, the GI system in Ukraine is not doomed to failure. At the governmental level, further development of the GI system is included in major policy documents, such as the National Economic Strategy 2030.[122] In parallel, a boom in GI registration is taking place and traditional products are being rediscovered. Five new GIs have been registered since the legal reforms of 2019.[123]

Most of these registrations were driven by EU-funded technical assistance. Between 2017 and 2020 the EU financed a project the objective of which was supporting the development of the GI system in Ukraine.[124] The project aimed both

---

[119] The Moldovan Law on the Protection of Geographical Indications, Appellations of Origin and Traditional Specialities Guaranteed 2008, 66-XVI. The Georgian Law on the Appellation of Origin and Geographical Indication of Goods 1999, 2108-llc.

[120] Georgia is sometimes referred to as the "cradle of wine". For a history of Georgian winemaking, see Shtaltovna and Hart (n 14); Bittner (n 5) 47–49.

[121] Georgia registered 18 Georgian GIs for wines in the European Union when signing the EU–Georgia Association Agreement in 2014. As of early 2022, there are 38 Georgian GIs, mainly for wines and cheeses, which were added through an update of Annexes to the EU–Georgia Association Agreement.

In comparison, Moldova filed no local GIs when signing the EU–Moldova Association agreement, but has added six GIs at later stages, all for wines and spirits.

[122] Strategic objectives 9(4)(7) and 14(2)(5).

[123] These are the "Hutsul Sheep Bryndzya" PDO, the "Hutsul Cow Bryndzya" PDO, the "Melitopol Cherry" PDO, the "Krolevetsk Towels" PGI and the "Petrykivka painting" PGI.

[124] Support to the Development of a Geographical Indications System in Ukraine EuropeAid/138706/DH/SER/UA *European Commission International Cooperation and Development* (7 February 2017) https://webgate.ec.europa.eu/europeaid/online-services/index.cfm?ADSSChck=1520868685908&do=publi.detPUB&page=1&aoref=138706&searchtype=QS&orderbyad=Asc&orderby=ref&nbPubliList=15&userlanguage=en accessed 8 November 2021.

at the identification and registration of Ukrainian GIs (with three successful registrations),[125] as well as at rebranding Ukrainian products that are imitating EU GIs, which are to be phased-out under the EU–Ukraine Association Agreement.[126] The EU provides similar support to other countries under the Eastern Neighbourhood Policy.[127]

This shows how certain deficiencies, such as lack of familiarisation or lack of public capacity, may be compensated for, including through EU-funded technical assistance.

References

Anatolii Avidzba, Anatolii Yalanetskiy, Irina Matchina, Viktor Zagorouiko and Daria Volynkina, 'On the Names of Ukrainian Wine Products with Geographical Indications of Other Countries' (2011) 2 Magaratch: Vine Growing and Wine Making 26 [Анатолий Авидзба, Анатолий Яланецкий, Ирина Матчина, Виктор Загоруйко и Дарья Волынкина, 'О наименованиях винодельческой продукции украинского производства, содержащих географические указания других стран' (2011) 2]

Emily Baran, 'It Takes a Village: Collectivization in the Postwar Ukrainian Borderlands' (2018) 60(3–4) Canadian Slavonic Papers 529

Stephen V Bittner, *Whites and Reds: A History of Wine in the Lands of Tsar and Commissar* (Oxford University Press 2021)

Stephen V Bittner, 'A Problem of Taste: An American Connoisseur's Travels Through the Soviet Union's Black Sea Vinyeards and Wineries' (2018) 19(2) Kritika: Explorations in Russian and Eurasian History 305

Uwe Bohnet and Katja Bruisch, 'The Soviet Village Revisited: Household Farming and the Changing Image of Socialism in the Late Soviet Period' (2016) 57(1) Cahiers du Monde Russe 81, *Trade Mark Law in the People's Republic of China and Russia: A Comparative Legal Study Taking into Account the Development of German Law* (Carls Heymanns Verlag 1996) [Uwe Bohnet, *Das Markenrecht in der Volksrepublic China und Russland: Eine Rechtsvergleichende Studie Unter Berücksichtigung der Deutschen Rechtsentwicklung* (Carls Heymanns Verlag 1996)]

---

[125] The "Hutsul Sheep Bryndzya" PDO, the "Hutsul Cow Bryndzya" PDO and the "Melitopol Cherry" PDO, registered with the assistance of the project; the "Kherson Watermelon" PDO, the "Transcarpathian Honey" PDO and the "Dniester Walnut" PGI, identified as part of the project's activities.

[126] Such as the "Feta" PDO. Ukrainian producers of Feta-style cheese are renaming their product as "Nabil".

[127] For example, in 2017 the EU financed a study on the identification of Moldovan products potentially registrable as geographical indications or traditional specialities guaranteed. Sixty-seven such products were identified. On the results of the study, see Anatolie Fala, 'The Results of the Study to Identify Traditional Products and Handicrafts that can be Promoted under Geographical Indications in the Republic of Moldova' (2018) 4 Intellectus 47 (47–63). In Armenia the EU has been implementing, since February 2021, a 3 million EUR technical assistance project, which, inter alia, aims at phasing-out the use of name "cognac" by Armenian authorities and at finding a new name to replace it. See the minutes to the Third Meeting of the EU–Armenia Partnership Committee in Trade configuration, available at https://trade.ec.europa.eu/doclib/docs/2021/june/tradoc_159632.pdf accessed 19 February 2022.

Cerkia Bramley, Estelle Biénabe and Johann Kirsten, 'The Economics of Geographical Indications: Towards a Conceptual Framework for Geographical Indication Research in Developing Countries' in World Intellectual Property Organization (ed) *The Economics of Intellectual Property: Suggestions for Further Research in Developing Countries and Countries with Economies in Transition* (WIPO 2009) 109

Serhei Budylin, 'Winnie-the-Pooh Joins the WTO: Copyright Issues for "Old" Foreign Works' (2014) 1 Journal of the Intellectual Property Court 48 [Сергей Будылин, 'Винни-Пух вступает в ВТО. Проблема авторских прав на «старые» иностранные произведения' (2014) 1 Журнал Суда по интеллектуальным правам 48]

Jonathan Cohen and Serge Bauer, 'The New Trademark Law in the Soviet Union' (1991) 81(4) Trademark Reporter 397

Robert Conquest, *The Harvest of Sorrow: Soviet Collectivisation and the Terror— Famine* (Oxford University Press 1986)

Tim Engelhardt, 'Geographical Indications Under Recent EU Trade Agreements' (2015) 46(7) International Review of Intellectual Property and Competition Law 783

European Commission, 'Study on Economic Value of EU Quality Schemes, Geographical Indications (GIs) and Traditional Specialities Guaranteed (TSGs)' Final Report, 2021

European Commission, 'Communication from the Commission to the European Parliament and the Council— Taking stock of the European Neighbourhood Policy' COM(2010)207 final

Anatolie Fala, 'The Results of the Study to Identify Traditional Products and Handicrafts that can be Promoted under Geographical Indications in the Republic of Moldova' (2018) 4 Intellectus 47 [Anatolie Fala, 'Rezultatele Studiului de Identificare a Produselor Tradiţionale şi Obiectelor de Meşteşugărit şi Artizanat ce Pot fi Promovate Sub Indicaţii Geografice în Republica Moldova' (2018) 4 Intellectus 47]

Benjamin Farrand, 'Two Continents, Divided by Deep Philosophical Waters?: Why Geographical Indications Pose a Challenge to the Completion of the TTIP' (2017) 7(2) European Journal of Risk Regulation 269

David Feest, 'The Collectivization of Agriculture in the Baltic Soviet Republics, 1944–1953' in Constantin Iordachi and Arnd Bauerkamper (eds), *The Collectivization of Agriculture in Communist Eastern Europe: Comparison and Entanglements* (Central European University Press 2014) 79

Maryline Filippi and Pierre Triboulet, 'Traditional Products and Industrialization Processes: The Coherence of Geographical Indications' in Artur Cristóvão (ed), *Farming and Rural Systems Research and Extension: European Farming and Society in Search of a New Social Contract—Learning to Manage Change* (2004) 69

Christos Fotopoulos and Athanasios Krystallis, 'Quality Labels as a Marketing Advantage: The Case of the "PDO Zagora" Apples in the Greek Market' (2003) 37(10) European Journal of Marketing 1350

Dev Gangjee, *Relocating the Law of Geographical Indications* (Cambridge University Press 2012)

Ignacio Garcia Bercero, 'Dispute Settlement in European Union Free Trade Agreements: Lessons Learned?' in Lorand Bartels and Federico Ortino (eds), *Regional Trade Agreements and the WTO Legal System* (Oxford 2006) 383

Daniel J Gervais and Matthew Slider, 'The Geneva Act of the Lisbon Agreement: Controversial Negotiations and Controversial Results' in William van Caenegem and Jen Cleary (eds), *The Importance of Place: Geographical Indications as a Tool for Local and Regional Development* (Springer 2017) 15

Daniel J Gervais, 'Reinventing Lisbon: The Case for a Protocol to the Lisbon Agreement (Geographical Indications)' (2010) 11 Chicago Journal of International Law 67

Brian Glyn Williams, 'The Hidden Ethnic Cleansing of Muslims in the Soviet Union: The Exile and Repatriation of the Crimean Tartars' (2002) 37(3) Journal of Contemporary History 323

Lev Golytsin, 'Speech in the First All-Russian Congress of Winegrowers and Winemakers' (30 November 2015) *HB* https://nashevino.ru/blog/knowledge/poslanie-l-s-golicyna-nashi-gody [Лев Голицын, 'Речь Л. С. Голицына на Первом съезде виноделов России' (2015)]

Lev Golytsin, 'Typology of Russian Wines in 1902', Speech in the Section "Winemaking" of the All-Russian Congress of Winegrowers and Winemakers, Moscow (24 August 2015) https://nashevino.ru/blog/history/tipologiya-vin-rossii-v-1902-g [Лев Голицын, 'Типология вин России в 1902 г.', Выступление в секции "Виноделие" Всероссийского Съезда Iноградарей и Виноделов, Москва (24 августа 2015)]

Oleg Gorodov, *The Right to Means of Individualization: Trademarks, Service Marks, Appellations of Origin, Brand Names, Commercial Designations* (Wolters Kluwer 2006) [Олег Городов, *Право на Средства Индивидуализации: Товарные Знаки, Знаки Обслуживания, Наименования Происхождения Товаров, Фирменные Наименования, Коммерческие Обозначения* (Волтерс Клувер 2006)]

Jill E Hobbs, 'A Protectionist Bargain?: Agriculture in the European Union— Canada Trade Agreement' (2015) 49(3) Journal World Trade 437

Cay Hober, 'Protection of Foreign Trademarks in the Soviet Union' (1979) 14(3) Texas International Law Journal 367

Anna Kapala, 'Protection of Geographical Indications of Agricultural Products and Foodstuffs in International Law' (2007) 1 Agricultural Law Review 150 [Anna Kapala, 'Ochrona Oznaczeń Geograficznych Produktów Rolnych i Srodków Spożywczych w Prawie Międzynarodowym' (2007) 1 Przegląd Prawa Rolnego 150]

Paul Kindstedt, *Cheese and Culture: A History of Cheese and its Place in Western Civilization* (Chelsea Green Publishing 2012)

Auvo Kostiainen, 'Genocide in Soviet Karelia: Stalin's Terror and the Finns of Soviet Karelia' (1996) 21(4) Scandinavian Journal of History 331

Anatolii Kucher, Maria Heldak, Lesia Kucher, Olha Fedorchenko and Yuliia Yurchenko, 'Consumer Willingness to Pay a Price Premium for Ecological Goods: A Case Study From Ukraine' (2019) 7(1) Environmental and Socio-economic Studies 38

Anastasiia Kyrylenko, 'Use It or Lose It? Ukraine Amends Its Law on GIs' (2020) 15(1) Journal of Intellectual Property Law and Practice 17

Joseph M Lightman, 'The USSR Trademark System and East-West Trade' (1966) 10(1) Patent, Trademark and Copyright Journal of Research and Education 11

Maria Luz Loureiro and Jill J McCluskey, 'Assessing Consumer Response to Protected Geographical Identification Labelling' (2000) 16(3) Agribusiness 309

Greta Lynn Uehling, *The Crimean Tatars' Deportation and Return* (Palgrave Macmillan 2004)

Anna G Micara, 'The Geneva Act of the Lisbon Agreement for the Protection of Appellations of Origin and Their International Registration: An Assessment of a Controversial Agreement' (2016) 47(6) International Review of Intellectual Property and Competition Law 673

Bernard O'Connor, 'The European Union and the United States: Conflicting Agendas on Geographical Indications— What's Happening in Asia?' (2014) 9(2) Global Trade and Customs Journal 66

Bernard O'Connor, *The Law of Geographical Indications* (Cameron May 2004) 37

Pavel Polian, *Against Their Will: The History and Geography of Forced Migrations in the USSR* (Central European University Press 2004)

Omelian Rudnytskyi, Nataliia Levchuk, Oleh Wolowyna, Pavlo Schevchuk and Alla Kovbasiuk, "Demography of a Man-made Human Catastrophe: The Case of Massive Famine in Ukraine 1932–1933" (2015) 42(1–2) Canadian Population Society 53

Anastasiya Shtaltovna and Hart N Feuer, "Modern Resilience of Georgian Wine: Geographical Indications and International Exposure" in Alessandro Bonanno, Kae Sekine and Hart N Feuer (eds), *Geographical Indication and Global Agri-Food: Development and Democratization* (Routledge 2020) 134

Alison K Smith, "From Gruyères to Gatchina: The Meaning of Cheese in Tsarist Russia" (2021) Food, Culture and Society 1

Liam Sunner, "How the European Union is Expanding the Protection Levels Afforded to Geographical Indications as Part of its Global Trade Policy" (2021) 16(4–5) Journal of Intellectual Property Law and Practice 341

A Vida, "The Law of Industrial Property in the Peoples' Democracies and the Soviet Union" (1964) 12 International and Compliance Law Quarterly 280

Stephen G Wheatcroft, Robert W Davies and John M Cooper, "Soviet Industrialization Reconsidered: Some Preliminary Conclusions about Economic Development between 1926 and 1941" (1986) 39(2) The Economic History Review 264

Alexander Wirsig and Wolfgang Heisrath, "Welcome to the Club? The Significance of Protected Geographical Indications and Designations of Origin in Europe, with Special Consideration of the Croatian Situation" (2020) 55(15) Hrvatski Croatian: International Symposium on Agriculture 109

Andrea Zappalaglio, *The Transformation of EU Geographical Indications Law: The Present, Past and Future of the Origin Link* (Routledge 2021)

Copyright and Its Exceptions and Limitations in Ukraine

Anna Shtefan

Contents

A. Shtefan (✉)
Copyright and Related Rights Department, Intellectual Property Scientific Research Institute of the National Academy of Legal Sciences of Ukraine, Kyiv, Ukraine
e-mail: anna_shtefan@ukr.net

H. Richter (ed.), *Competition and Intellectual Property Law in Ukraine*,
MPI Studies on Intellectual Property and Competition Law 31,
https://doi.org/10.1007/978-3-662-66101-7_20

Abstract This chapter outlines the main provisions of the copyright law of Ukraine in the light of the Berne Convention for the Protection of Literary and Artistic Works, WIPO models, EU legislation and TRIPS. On this basis, the chapter enquires deeper into the peculiarities of exceptions and limitations as a mechanism for balancing the interests of the author and society. As a member of the Berne Convention, Ukraine applies the three-step test to copyright exceptions and limitations. At the same time, each type of free use of works has its own specific conditions which determine the scope and characteristics of the lawful free use of works: for some exceptions and limitations, the use of works must be exclusively non-commercial; in other cases, the possibility of obtaining a commercial benefit is irrelevant. Some types of copyright exceptions and limitations that are provided for in the legislation of EU Member States do not yet apply in Ukraine, although they are mentioned in the EU–Ukraine Association Agreement. The study of the types of free use of works allows one to characterize the system of copyright exceptions and limitations, the rules of their application, and their further development in Ukrainian copyright law.

1 Introduction: The Basis of Ukrainian Copyright

1.1 Legislation in the Field of Copyright and Related Rights in Ukraine

Copyright law of modern Ukraine was formed and continues to develop under the influence of international agreements and European legal regulation. Leading world standards and the latest legal trends in this sphere serve as a guideline of what changes should be made in legislation so that it covers all legal relations involved in the creation and use of works. In addition to a voluntary desire to improve domestic legislation, Ukraine has certain obligations under the Association Agreement with the EU.[1] As defined in the Association Agreement, Ukraine will carry out gradual approximation of its legislation to EU law.[2] Supplementing domestic legislation with provisions of European law is one of the most important aspects of the European integration process. It will also contribute to the further development and modernization of copyright law in Ukraine.

[1] Association Agreement between the European Union and its Member States, of the one part, and Ukraine, of the other part (2014) OJ L161/3 (EU–Ukraine Association Agreement).

[2] Ibid art 474.

The Ukrainian copyright system comprises two basic laws: the Civil Code of Ukraine (Civil Code)[3] and the Law of Ukraine "On Copyright and Related Rights" (Law on Copyright).[4] In addition, there are a number of laws that regulate certain areas of creation and use of works. This applies in particular to architecture, theaters, publishers, and the media. Such laws contain separate rules related to copyright but in general these rules do not go beyond the basic principles of regulation provided for in the Civil Code and the Law on Copyright.

As for the Civil Code, it contains the main provisions on copyright. When it was being developed, the Civil Code was not intended to cover all aspects of legal regulation in this sphere, but only to express the essence and conceptual principles of copyright. That is why in many cases the provisions of the Civil Code directly refer to other legislative acts. For example, when listing the ways of using works, the Civil Code directly mentions some of them and notes that other actions, established by the law, also constitute the use of a work.[5]

The sphere of copyright is the most fully and comprehensively covered by the Law on Copyright. Its first edition was adopted in late 1993 after Ukraine, having restored independence in 1991, sought to abandon the remnants of the Soviet regulation which did not correspond to the existing trends in the field of copyright at that time. Ukraine acceded to the Berne Convention in 1995,[6] and the first edition of the Law on Copyright was based on the main provisions of the convention and took them into account. That is, at the time of Ukraine's accession to the Berne Union, the Law on Copyright already reproduced all the rules established by the convention on copyright protection, its exceptions and limitations, and the term of its duration. Subsequently, Ukraine joined the World Intellectual Property Organization Copyright Treaty (2001)[7] and the Treaty on the Establishment of the World Trade Organization (2008),[8] which made the TRIPS Agreement binding for Ukraine. However, even before the accession to these agreements in 2001, a new edition of the Law on Copyright was adopted[9] which contained all the main provisions of these agreements. After significant changes in 2001, the Law on Copyright was amended several times, influenced in part by international treaties of which Ukraine is not yet a member. This applies, in particular, to copyright exceptions and limitations for visually impaired persons based on the provisions of the Marrakesh Treaty to Facilitate Access to Published Works for Persons Who Are Blind, Visually Impaired, or

[3] Civil Code of Ukraine 2003, 435-IV, art 444.

[4] Ukrainian Law on Copyright and Related Rights 1993, 3792-XII, arts 21–25.

[5] Civil Code, art 441(2).

[6] Ukrainian Law on Ukraine's accession to the Berne Convention for the Protection of Literary and Artistic Works 1995, 189/95-BP.

[7] Ukrainian Law on Ukraine's accession to the World Intellectual Property Organization Copyright Treaty 2001, 2733-III.

[8] Ukrainian Law on Ratification of the Protocol on Ukraine's accession to the World Trade Organization 2008, 250-VI.

[9] Ukrainian Law on Amendments to the Law of Ukraine on Copyright and Related Rights 2001, 2627-III.

Otherwise Print Disabled (Marrakesh Treaty).[10] Ukraine has not yet acceded to the Marrakesh Treaty but it has already improved exceptions and limitations for persons who, due to visual or dyslexic impairment, cannot perceive printed and visual information. Thus, in the field of copyright, Ukraine strives to ensure that its domestic legislation is as consistent as possible with the world level of legal regulation.

In May 2021 a copyright reform began in Ukraine when the Parliament registered a new edition of the draft Law on Copyright.[11] Less than a month later, four more alternative bills that also propose a new edition of the Law on Copyright were registered.[12] Each of these documents seeks to modernize the field of copyright including expanding the list of copyright exceptions and limitations. However, the authors of the bills proposed different approaches to the legal regulation of many copyright aspects, as well as certain exceptions and limitations. In July 2021, a roundtable discussion was held with leading copyright experts and bill proponents on the key issues of the bills.[13] During the discussion, the experts were unanimous in their opinion that all of the bills needed improvement by combining them into one general document in which the existing deficiencies will be eliminated. The working group that would perform this function was not formed. However, on 1 July 2022, Bill 5552-1 was adopted as a basis and is expected to be adopted in its entirety as a new edition of the Law on Copyright in the near future.

It should be noted that the current copyright exceptions and limitations are contained in the provisions of all the bills without substantive changes. As for the new exceptions and limitations proposed to be introduced in the Ukrainian legislation, in some cases the relevant provisions of the bills contain different rules. All these aspects will be considered further, although before analyzing the Ukrainian system of free use of works, it is reasonable to briefly describe the peculiarities of copyright in Ukraine.

1.2 Main Provisions of Copyright and Related Rights in Ukraine

In general, Ukraine's copyright is very close to the basic provisions of European law. This applies to all conceptually important aspects that determine the conditions and the scope for legal protection of works and rights of the authors.

[10] Marrakesh Treaty to Facilitate Access to Published Works for Persons Who Are Blind, Visually Impaired, or Otherwise Print Disabled (2013).

[11] Ukrainian Draft Law on Copyright and Related Rights 2021, 5552.

[12] Ukrainian Draft Law on Copyright and Related Rights 2021, 5552-1; Ukrainian Draft Law on Copyright and Related Rights 2021, 5552-2; Ukrainian Draft Law on Copyright and Related Rights 2021, 5552-3; Ukrainian Draft Law on Copyright and Related Rights 2021, 5552-4.

[13] Ukrainian National Bar Association: Discussion on Copyright and Related Rights: Key Draft Laws *UNBA* (16 July 2021) https://unba.org.ua/events/2080-diskusiya-na-temu-%C2%ABavtorske-pravo-ta-sumizhni-prava-klyuchovi-zakonoproekti%C2%BB.html accessed 9 December 2021.

Copyright protects works, the list of which is inexhaustible.[14] Any object that is the result of creativity has the potential to obtain copyright protection even if this object is not mentioned in the law. The legal protection occurs automatically due to the fact of creation of the work and does not require any formalities.[15] State registration of works is not mandatory[16] and in no way affects the emergence of copyright or the scope of legal protection.

The primary subject of copyright is the author of the work—a natural person whose creative labor has resulted in the creation of the work.[17] In the case of a work created in the performance of official duties or under a custom contract, copyright does not accrue directly to the employer or customer but can only be transferred to them.[18] Therefore, the primary subject, irrespective of the motives and conditions of creation, is always the author of the work. The emergence of copyright directly from a legal entity is not provided for in Ukraine but copyright may be transferred to other individuals or legal entities, in particular, by inheritance or contract.[19]

In Ukraine there is a presumption of authorship: in the absence of evidence of others, the person mentioned as the author on the original or a copy of the work is considered to be the author.[20] The presumption of authorship gives grounds to consider the person whose name is inscribed on the work or its reproduction as the author even if there is no other evidence of authorship of this person. Thus, the mere notation of an individual as the author of a work is sufficient to consider him or her to be the author.

The author is guaranteed a complex of non-property rights, i.e., the right to be recognized as the author of the work,[21] to have the author's name noted in connection with the use of the work,[22] to have a pseudonym noted in connection with the use of the work,[23] to be anonymous in connection with the use of the work,[24] and to inviolability of the work.[25] The non-property rights of the author are protected indefinitely.[26] As for proprietary rights, they consist in the author's right to use the work independently,

---

[14] Ukrainian Law on Copyright and Related Rights 1993, 3792-XII, art 8(1).

[15] Ibid art 11(2).

[16] Ibid art 11(5).

[17] Ibid art 11(1), 1(1)(1).

[18] Civil Code, arts 429(2), 430(2).

[19] Ukrainian Law on Copyright and Related Rights 1993, 3792-XII, art 7(1).

[20] Ibid art 11(1).

[21] Civil Code, art 423(1)(1).

[22] Civil Code, art 423(1)(1), Ukrainian Law on Copyright and Related Rights 1993, 3792-XII, art 14(1)(1).

[23] Civil Code, art 438(1)(3), Ukrainian Law on Copyright and Related Rights 1993, 3792-XII, art 14(1)(3).

[24] Civil Code, art 438(1)(2), Ukrainian Law on Copyright and Related Rights 1993, 3792-XII, art 14(1)(2).

[25] Civil Code, art 439, Ukrainian Law on Copyright and Related Rights 1993, 3792-XII, art 14(1)(4).

[26] Ukrainian Law on Copyright and Related Rights 1993, 3792-XII, art 28(10).

as well as to allow or prohibit the use of the work by others.[27] The ways of using a work are given in the legislation in the form of an open list[28]; therefore, if there are new types of information or ways to distribute or store information that can be applied to works, such types of use automatically fall within the scope of the law. In Ukraine, there is the resale right (droit de suite), which gives authors the opportunity to receive a share of the amount of sales of the original work of art or the original manuscript of a literary work.[29] Also, in addition to the exceptions and limitations provided by law, the author has the right to payment of remuneration for each use of the work.[30]

As a general rule, property rights are protected throughout the life of the author and 70 years after the author's death[31] but there are some special ways of calculating the term of legal protection which are applied in appropriate cases. In particular, if the work is co-authored, the copyright is valid for the life of the co-authors and 70 years after the death of the last surviving co-author.[32]

Related rights in Ukraine are protected separately from copyright. No formalities are required for the emergence and exercise of related rights; they arise due to the fact of performance of the work, production of the phonogram, or publication of the broadcasting program.[33] Subjects of related rights are vested with non-property rights associated with the indication of their name in connection with the use of the relevant objects,[34] and proprietary rights determining the impact on the use of subject matter of related rights.[35] The term of related rights is 50 years from the date of the first recording of the performance,[36] the date of the first publication of the phonogram or its first recording if the phonogram was not published within that period,[37] or the date of the first communication to the public of the broadcasting program.[38]

In case of non-recognition, non-compliance or infringement of copyright or related rights, the author or another right holder has ample opportunities for protection which can be carried out in civil, commercial, administrative or criminal proceedings.[39] At the same time, in Ukraine there is an extrajudicial procedure for terminating violations of copyright and related rights on the Internet[40] that allows an author or

[27] Ibid art 15(1).

[28] Ibid art 15(3).

[29] Civil Code, art 448.

[30] Ukrainian Law on Copyright and Related Rights 1993, 3792-XII, art 15(5).

[31] Ibid art 28(2).

[32] Ibid art 28(4).

[33] Ibid art 37(2).

[34] Ibid art 38.

[35] Ibid arts 39, 40, 41.

[36] Ibid art 44(1).

[37] Ibid art 44(2).

[38] Ibid art 44(3).

[39] See Anna Shtefan and Olga Gurgula, 'The New Intellectual Property Court in Ukraine: Its Creation and Exclusive Jurisdiction' in this Volume.

[40] Ukrainian Law on Copyright and Related Rights 1993, 3792-XII, art 52(1).

other rights holder to apply to the owner of the site and (or) the web page on which the work is used, or to the hosting provider with a request to stop the violation. As a result, access to the work or subject matter of related rights may be terminated but blocking of the website in general is not allowed.

1.3 Peculiarities of Ukrainian Regulation of Copyright and Related Rights

Despite the significant similarity of Ukrainian copyright law with the basic principles of European legal regulation, Ukraine has some rules that differ from EU law or do not exist in Europe. These include the following.

First, in Ukraine there is a presumption of the creative nature of the work. It is interesting to note that this presumption is not established by law; it was introduced in the resolutions of the Plenum of the Supreme Court of Ukraine.[41] According to this presumption, the result of intellectual activity is presumed to have been produced by creative labor, unless proven otherwise.[42] That is, the author does not have to prove in any way that a work is creative and therefore protected by copyright. As long as no one disputes the existence of a creative contribution to the production of a work this work is considered to be a result of creative activity. This approach is very convenient for authors but at the same time, the presumption of creativity generates a lot of abuse when a non-conscientious person demands recognition of copyright in one existing word or phrase or object that is the result of purely technical work, and other interested parties have to specifically prove that this object is not creative.

Second, Ukrainian law recognizes that the interview is an object of co-authorship, and its authors are the person who gave the interview and the person who conducted it. Publication of the interview recordings is allowed only with the interviewee's consent.[43] This position is very debatable. While a journalist or other person who prepares and conducts an interview does make a creative effort to create an interview, the person who answers the question actually shares some information or expresses his or her own opinion. It seems to be a mistaken belief to consider this to be creativity

[41] In the past, the Supreme Court had the power to issue special acts, such as Plenum resolutions, which clarify issues of judicial practice, namely how courts should apply the law in certain categories of cases. Such resolutions are not regulations but courts are required to apply them. In 2010, the Ukrainian Law on Judicial System and the Status of Judges, 2453-VI abolished this authority. The new Ukrainian Law on Judicial System and the Status of Judges 2016, 1402-VIII also does not provide for such a power for the Supreme Court. However, existing Plenum resolutions which have not been overturned by the Supreme Court itself remain in force and must be taken into account by the courts.

[42] Resolution of the Plenum of the Supreme Court of Ukraine of June 4, 2010 No. 5 On the application by courts of the rules of the legislation in cases of protection of copyright and related rights, para 18. This resolution was adopted one month before the Supreme Court lost the power to issue such acts.

[43] Ukrainian Law on Copyright and Related Rights 1993, 3792-XII, art 13(3).

and to protect the copyright of simple statements on the merits of questions. The co-sponsorship of the interview was enshrined in the very first edition of the Law on Copyright when Ukraine had already abandoned the censorship and other interference with the media that had prevailed in Soviet times. However, it is possible that in this way the state has decided to establish a certain control over the media and other interview organizers, who must obtain separate permission to distribute the interview from the person who has already agreed to give the interview. If the interview is live, the interviewee cannot influence the distribution of the interview, edit it, add something that was not said, or, on the contrary, delete a part of the answer. When it comes to publishing an interview recording, the interviewee can not only insist on making changes to the content of the interview but can even prohibit its publication. This seems rather paradoxical but the rule of co-authoring an interview still exists.

Third, there is an extended list of authors of audiovisual works in Ukraine. These include the director and producer, the author of the script and (or) texts and dialogues, the author of a musical work specially created for audiovisual work with or without text, the art director, the cameraman, and the director of photography.[44] The authorship of such persons is recognized if their contribution to the audiovisual work is creative. However, by virtue of the presumption of creativity, even an ordinary cameraman who was not involved in the direction but only set up cameras on location can claim to be considered an author. Usually these issues are regulated by a contract, which determines what functions a person performs when creating an audiovisual work and whether such functions are creative in nature. Also, in the case of a dispute, the affiliation or non-affiliation of a person to the authors of an audiovisual work may be established by a court.

Fourth, the law protects not only the audiovisual work, but also the videogram, which is a subject matter of related rights. A videogram is a video recording of the performance of a work or any moving images, with or without sound, except for recording that is part of an audiovisual work.[45] A videogram differs from an audiovisual work in that it is a simple video recording of something where the person making the recording does not affect the course of events but only records them. Legal protection of videograms in the context of the scope of rights and the validity of the rights is analogous to the legal protection of phonograms. If a videogram is included in an audiovisual work (for example, a separate recording of dawn, traffic on the street, etc.), it loses the status of an independent subject matter of related rights and is considered a part of the audiovisual work.

Some differences between Ukrainian law and EU law relate to copyright exceptions and limitations. For the most part, this is reflected in the fact that some European rules are not provided for in the Ukrainian legislation. There are also cases where certain exceptions and limitations which are provided for both in the EU and in Ukraine are regulated somewhat differently.

[44] Ibid art 17(1).

[45] Ibid art 1(1)(11).

2 The Purpose and Basic Rules of Copyright Exceptions and Limitations

2.1 The Need to Balance Interests as a Basis for Exceptions and Limitations

The main purpose of copyright is to establish a regime of protection of rights and regulation of relations involved in the creation and use of works. Therefore, copyright is primarily focused on ensuring the interests of authors and other rights holders, leaving them the exclusive prerogative to use the works and decide their future fate during the period of their legal protection. At the same time, seeking ways to strengthen the safeguards of observance and protection of the rights and interests of authors, copyright also tries to take into account the interests of society.

The difficulty in solving this problem is related to the fact that the interests of authors and society often do not coincide. The authors strive to have full control over their works, to determine who will use them when and how and how much these users will pay for it. The authors' position is quite understandable because in a certain sense the work is the result of the investment of time and creative effort, as well as the cost of the materials and equipment necessary to create the work. The author should be able not only to recover these costs but also to benefit economically from the use of the work to satisfy his or her other needs. The author's right to protection of his moral and material interests is provided by the Universal Declaration of Human Rights (UDHR).[46] The Constitution of Ukraine guarantees the right to own, use and dispose of the results of one's intellectual creative activity[47] and the protection of moral and material interests arising in connection with various types of intellectual activity,[48] and nothing can deprive the author of these rights.

At the same time, other rights are guaranteed in a democratic state. The realization of these rights would be impossible if the work were under the absolute power of the author. Numerous areas of social life require free access to works in order for it to function and develop properly, so copyright must leave room for other interests besides those of the author. Science, culture and art must be open to others; every member of society must be able to freely participate in them to gain intellectual, aesthetic and spiritual pleasure from the works. As the UDHR declares, everyone has the right freely to participate in the cultural life of the community, to enjoy the arts and to share in scientific advancement and its benefits.[49] The development of society is inconceivable without acquiring new knowledge and deepening it, so the legal protection of works should not interfere with the possibility of using them for teaching and research. The same applies to information the free dissemination of which is guaranteed to both citizens and the media. Therefore, copyright should not

---

[46] United Nations Universal Declaration of Human Rights 1948, art 27(2).

[47] Constitution of Ukraine 1996, 254к/96-ВР, art 41(1).

[48] Ibid art 54(1).

[49] Universal Declaration of Human Rights, art 27(1).

be left out of the most important and significant interests of society. Thus, copyright should provide a balance of interests with a dual purpose: "To protect the interest of the public and protect the interests of authors".[50]

Balancing the interests of the author and society is carried out through cases that allow the use of the work without the permission of the author. Ukrainian law uses several terms for such cases: exceptions and limitations,[51] limitations on proprietary rights,[52] lawful use of the work without the consent of the author,[53] free use of the work.[54] All of these terms indicate cases where the proprietary rights of the author are limited in some way,[55] including when the use of copyrighted work is carried out without the author's permission. Free use of works cases "are not covered by the author's exclusive rights",[56] that is, they narrow the scope of copyright because they "restrict the exercise of rights".[57] Such cases are also commonly referred to as non-contractual use of works since no agreement is reached between the author and the user. Establishment of such exceptions and limitations is aimed at satisfying those needs and interests that have primary public importance.

The legislation of Ukraine provides for exceptions and limitations in the interests of various user groups, in particular: authors who create scientific, analytical, or critical works; persons who have dyslexia or are vision impaired; mass media; libraries and archives; persons and organizations engaged in educational activities; specially authorized state bodies that carry out judicial and administrative procedures. At the same time, it has pointed out that "of particular interest to many copyright scholars, there are almost no exceptions or limitations that cover what Jessica Litman has called "lawful personal use" of copyrighted works. Exceptions and limitations instead tend to be directed at public uses of high social value".[58] Indeed, in Ukraine, for individuals who are not authors, journalists, teachers or persons with visual impairments, the regime of exceptions and restrictions provides only the right to reproduce certain types of works for personal purposes. This can be perceived as insufficient care of the state for the needs of such persons who might wish to use the works freely in other

---

[50] Michael B Gunlocks, 'A Balance of Interests: The Concordance of Copyright Law and Moral Rights in the Worldwide Economy' (2001) 11(3) Fordham Intellectual Property, Media and Entertainment Law 601(603).

[51] Civil Code, art 424(2).

[52] Ukrainian Law on Copyright and Related Rights 1993, 3792-XII, art 15(6).

[53] Civil Code, art 426(3), 444.

[54] Ukrainian Law on Copyright and Related Rights 1993, 3792-XII, art 21.

[55] Limitations on proprietary rights may also apply to other cases, such as the exhaustion of proprietary rights to copies of a work lawfully introduced into civil circulation (Law on Copyright, art 15(7)) or the limited term of copyright protection (Law on Copyright, art 28).

[56] Komzuk Leonid, 'The Content of Copyright' in Olena Orliuk (ed.), *Fundamentals of Intellectual Property* (Interservise 2016) 136.

[57] Yevgen Michurin, 'Approaches to the Formation of the Concept of Limitations of Proprietary Rights of Individuals' (2007) 2 Forum of Law, 151 (156).

[58] Julie E Cohen, 'Copyright and Creativity' in Brian Fitzgerald and Benedict Atkinson (eds), *Copyright Future, Copyright Freedom: Marking the 40th Anniversary of the Commencement of Australia's Copyright Act 1968* (Sydney University Press 2011) 134 (136).

ways as well. However, the purpose of exceptions and limitations is not to satisfy all potential interests of users. The balance of interests, as James Boyle correctly points out, "is highly context dependent"[59] so it cannot be perfectly accurate. The purpose of copyright is to ensure a relationship in which society can fully develop and authors can freely exercise their rights.

It is worth noting that "the definition of an exception in any legal system presupposes a situation where what is "excepted" would otherwise be within the scope of the rule".[60] Exceptions and limitations take place when a certain rule established by law operates under a special regime. A special regime provides for a different way of applying the rule but it does not function permanently or instead of the main regime, but rather applies in certain cases and within certain limits. Exceptions and limitations are a legal compromise that must be reached in order for both parties, the author and society, to obtain the maximum possible positive result. The UDHR quite rightly states that everyone shall be subject only to such limitations as are determined by law solely for the purpose of securing due recognition and respect for the rights and freedoms of others and of meeting the just requirements of morality, public order and the general welfare in a democratic society.[61]

2.2 *Three-Step-Test for Exceptions and Limitations*

In Ukraine, all exceptions and limitations are established according to the three-step test of the Berne Convention for the Protection of Literary and Artistic Works[62] (the Berne Convention). This test is implemented in the Law on Copyright.[63]

The Berne Convention provides that it shall be a matter for domestic legislation in the state parties to permit the reproduction of such works in certain special cases, provided that such reproduction does not conflict with a normal exploitation of the work and does not unreasonably prejudice the legitimate interests of the author.[64] This provision contains three basic requirements[65] that the free use of works should satisfy:

---

[59] James Boyle, 'A Manifesto on WIPO and the Future of Intellectual Property' (2004) 9(2) Duke Law and Technology Review, 1 (8).

[60] Maurizio Borghi, 'Exceptions as Users' Rights in EU Copyright Law' (2020) CIPPM Jean Monnet Working Papers 6/2020.

[61] Universal Declaration of Human Rights, art 29(2).

[62] Berne Convention for the Protection of Literary and Artistic Works, Paris Act of July 24, 1971, as amended on September 28, 1979.

[63] Ukrainian Law on Copyright and Related Rights 1993, 3792-XII, art 15(6).

[64] Berne Convention, art 9(2).

[65] For more information about the three-step-test see: Annette Kur, 'Of Oceans, Islands, and Inland Water—How Much Room for Exceptions and Limitations Under the Three-Step Test?' (2009) 8(3) Richmond Journal of Global Law and Business; Christophe Geiger et al., 'The Three-Step Test Revisited: How to Use the Test's Flexibility in National Copyright Law' (2014) 29(3) American University International Law Review; Daniel J Gervais, 'Making Copyright Whole: A Principled

(1) The free use of a work should be restricted to certain special cases. The scope and limits of the free use of works are not determined accidentally or at one's individual discretion but are envisaged by the law that establishes a clear list of cases when such use is permissible and lawful;
(2) The free use of a work should not conflict with its normal use. The use of the work by the copyright holder and the free use of the work by third parties must be carried out in different ways. There should be no competition between the author or other copyright holder and third parties regarding use the work;
(3) The free use of a work should not unreasonably prejudice the legitimate interests of the author. Only extremely important public interests may outweigh the copyright and require such free use of the work when this would harm the interests of the author. However, as a general rule, the free use of a work should not give rise to any obstacles to or other negative effects on the possibility of the exploitation of the work by the author. An author may not be deprived of the possibility of obtaining economic benefit from the use of his or her work for the reason that the benefit is already received by another person acting within the limits of copyright.[66]

Thus, exceptions and limitations must be proportionate and shaped in such a way as not to interfere with the normal exercise of authors' rights. Cases of free use of works in no way affect the content and scope of copyright. They are additional rules that apply regardless of the use of the work by the author or other copyright holder and do not complicate this use. This is directly stated in the Constitution of Ukraine: every citizen has the right to the results of their intellectual and creative activity; no one may use or distribute them without consent except as provided by law.[67]

The free use of a work does not mean something limitless and absolute; it is only a certain degree of freedom which, however, must comply with the frameworks established by law. Each exception and limitation has its own conditions of use, and the user has no right to deviate from them. If the user does not comply with the terms of use of the work and does not follow the requirements established by law, such actions will be classified as a violation of the rights of the author or other right holder.

The requirements that must be met in applying each specific exception and limitation vary. Free use usually includes the requirement that the name of the author and the source of the borrowing be mentioned but in some cases there are no such requirements. For most exceptions and limitations, it does not matter whether the user receives a direct or indirect commercial benefit from the use of the work. However, there are cases when the lack of commercial purpose is one of the conditions for the free use of the work. Therefore, if the user seeks to derive economic benefit from

---

Approach to Copyright Exceptions and Limitations' (2008) 5(1) University of Ottawa Law and Technology Journal 1 (23–39); Martin Senftleben, *Copyright, Limitations and the Three-step Test: An Analysis of the Three-Step Test in International and EC Copyright Law* (Kluwer Law International 2004).

[66] Anna Shtefan, 'Freedom of Panorama: The EU Experience' (2019) 11(2) European Journal of Legal Studies 13 (21–22).

[67] Constitution of Ukraine, art 54(2).

such use of the work, it is necessary to have the appropriate permission from the author or other copyright holder although the same non-commercial use of the work is subject to exceptions and limitations. The volume and scope of use which must be observed are also very important. Since these conditions are individual for each case, it is reasonable to consider them in more detail in the analysis of the main exceptions and limitations provided by the Ukrainian legislation.

3 Existing Exceptions and Limitations Under Ukrainian Copyright Law

Exceptions and limitations are mentioned in the Civil Code[68] but it refers directly to other provisions of the law. A complete list of such cases is set out in the Law on Copyright.[69] This list is exhaustive so any other use of a work not expressly provided by the law does not constitute free use of a work.

Without the consent of the author and without payment of remuneration, the use of works is allowed in the following cases:

(1) citing for critical, polemical, scientific, or informational purposes[70];
(2) inclusion of literary and artistic works as illustrations in publications, broadcasts, sound recordings, or videos of an educational nature[71];
(3) use of works on current economic, political, religious and social issues[72];
(4) use of works seen or heard during current events to highlight these events[73];
(5) reproduction of works in catalogs of public exhibitions, auctions, fairs[74];
(6) publishing works in special formats for persons with visual impairments and dyslexia[75];
(7) reproduction of works for judicial and administrative proceedings[76];
(8) public performance of musical works during official and religious ceremonies or funerals[77];
(9) reproduction of publicly proclaimed speeches and other similar works[78];
(10) use of works to create parodies, caricatures or potpourri,[79]

---

[68] Civil Code of Ukraine, art 444.
[69] Ukrainian Law on Copyright and Related Rights 1993, 3792-XII, arts 21–25.
[70] Ibid art 21(1)(1).
[71] Ibid art 21(1)(2).
[72] Ibid art 21(1)(3).
[73] Ibid art 21(1)(4).
[74] Ibid art 21(1)(5).
[75] Ibid art 21(1)(6).
[76] Ibid art 21(1)(7).
[77] Ibid art 21(1)(8).
[78] Ibid art 21(1)(9).
[79] Ibid art 21(1)(9–1).

(11) adaptation of audiovisual works for persons with visual impairments and dyslexia[80];
(12) reproduction of excerpts of works for educational purposes[81];
(13) reproduction, modification and decompilation of computer programs[82];
(14) reproduction of works for personal use.[83]

Without the author's permission but with payment of remuneration, such use of works is allowed:

(1) reprographic reproduction of works by libraries and archives[84];
    reprographic reproduction of works by educational institutions for classroom teaching[85];
(2) reproduction of audiovisual works and performances recorded in phonograms and videograms.[86]

In these cases, the remuneration is paid through collective management organizations.[87] The entities that are charged a fee for reproduction are manufacturers and (or) importers of digital, analog and other equipment and material media with which it is possible to carry out such reproduction. The amount of remuneration is determined as a percentage of the cost of such equipment and material carriers.[88]

In the following, exceptions and limitations designed to serve the most important public interests will be discussed. These include education, teaching, dissemination of information, personal use, and ensuring the interests of persons with visual impairments and dyslexia. It will also be determined what conditions must be met for the free use of works and what existing shortcomings should be corrected in order to make the regime of exceptions and limitations more effective.

[80] Ibid art 21(1)(11).

[81] Ibid art 23(1)(1).

[82] Ibid art 24.

[83] Ibid art 25.

[84] Ibid art 22.

[85] Ibid art 23(1)(2).

[86] Ibid art 25(2).

[87] See Liubov Maidanyk, 'On the Reforms, Practice and Perspective of the Law on Collecting Societies in Ukraine' in this Volume.

[88] Ukrainian Law on Effective Management of Property Rights of Copyright and (or) Related Rights Holders 2018, 2415-VIII, art 23.

3.1 Exceptions and Limitations Established to Ensure the Dissemination of Information

3.1.1 Citation

The citation rule provides for the use of brief excerpts from works to the extent justified by the intended purpose, including quoting articles from newspapers and magazines in the form of press reviews, if this is required by the critical, polemical, scientific, or informational nature of the work in which the quotations are included.[89] A citation is a relatively short excerpt from a literary, scientific or any other published work that is used with a mandatory reference to its author and sources of borrowing by another person in her or his works in order to make her or his statements clearer or to refer to another author's views in an authentic wording.[90] Citation serves the individual interests of authors and the realization of their right to freedom of expression and also promotes the development of science and culture and the free dissemination of information.

The law does not contain specific conditions regarding the amount of work that can be used as a quotation. This is determined by the user on the basis of the purposes and needs of the quotation. The main requirements that must be observed are prior lawful publication of the work used and the indication of the author and the source of borrowing. If the work has not been published or has been published illegally, it may not be cited. Without indication of the author and the source of borrowing, the use of a fragment of a work is considered copyright infringement even if the use has no commercial purpose.

Sometimes in practice, when a fragment of a TV program is quoted, the user may believe that leaving the TV channel's logo is enough for the use to be legitimate. However, information that does not contain the name of the author cannot be regarded as satisfying the legal requirements. For example, a Ukrainian TV channel while creating its programs used 19 short excerpts from another TV channel's programs. After broadcasting these programs, the TV channel-rights holder appealed to the court for copyright protection. The defendant argued that the presence of a logo on the excerpts used properly reflects the source of borrowing, so the right to cite was exercised in good faith. The court did not agree with this argument and decided that there was an illegal rebroadcasting of used excerpts.[91] This conclusion is absolutely correct since the law does not provide for the option to independently determine whether to indicate the author's name when citing.

---

[89] Ukrainian Law on Copyright and Related Rights 1993, 3792-XII, art 21(1)(1).

[90] Ibid art 1(1)(60).

[91] Commercial Court of Kyiv, Decision 41871014 (2014) 910/21872/14.

3.1.2 Use of Works on Current Economic, Political, Religious and Social Issues

This exception permits the free use of articles, speeches, lectures, performances, and other works in their entirety as long as the conditions established by law are satisfied[92]:

(1) The subject matter of the work concerns current economic, political, religious, or social issues. These areas are important and usually arouse great public interest, so the law assumes that the dissemination of such information should be free. Works related to the problems of the economy, politics, religion or society as a whole, not to current issues in these areas, as well as works on other topics may not be used within the scope of this exception.
(2) Prior publication or communication to the public of the work being used.
(3) The author has not prohibited reproduction, public performance or communication of a work to the public. Apart from the fact that free use of works in Ukraine is carried out according to the general rule "use is allowed if it is specifically allowed", there is an additional rule for this exception: "use is allowed if it is not specifically prohibited by the author". The reservation of such prohibition may be made in any way chosen by the author, but it must be clearly understood and refer to a particular work. In Ukraine there has been no practice of application of such prohibitions so far, but every author can take advantage of this opportunity.

This exception may apply to a variety of materials, including social media posts. In particular, the courts of the Kherson region considered the case of the reproduction of a publication from a social media page about the events during the city council session. The publication was reproduced on the website of a local newspaper with the name of the author and the address of the site where the primary source is located. The author of the publication provided a set of arguments in support of the fact that such use was unlawful. The court of the first instance found the claim groundless. The Court of Appeal supported this decision and pointed out that the publication dealt with current political issues and there was no indication of special conditions for its use or an outright prohibition on its use.[93] Thus, the purpose of informing about current events that relate to issues important to society justifies the free use of various materials about those events, not just traditional works such as articles published in the press.

3.1.3 Use of Works Seen or Heard During Current Events to Highlight These Events

One of the main activities of the media is to inform the public about events taking place in the country and the world. Their course is often directly related to the subject

[92] Ukrainian Law on Copyright and Related Rights 1993, 3792-XII, art 21(1)(3).
[93] Kherson Court of Appeal, Decision 89368012 (2020) 661/2040/19.

matter of copyright. When covering events in the field of culture and art—opening of a museum exposition, exhibition of works of fine art, premiere of a play, etc.—the works in relation to which the event is held are one of the main elements of a news report or article. In addition, news coverage often indirectly touches on works that are located or performed at the venue of particular events. In all these cases, the media, which are guaranteed their freedom to operate and their freedom to disseminate any information, have the right to freely reproduce, publicly report or make available to the public works in accordance with such requirements[94]:

(1) The use of works is carried out in order to highlight current events. The use of the works must be targeted and directly related to the event being reported.
(2) Works are seen or heard during current events. Notification of an event may not be accompanied by the use of works that are in no way related to that event. These can only be works that are shown, demonstrated or performed at the place where the event takes place or are otherwise related to the event.
(3) The scope of use is justified by the informational purpose. The free use of a work is allowed only insofar as it is connected with the coverage of an event. Certain types of works such as photographs, paintings, sculptures or works of architecture, due to their nature, usually cannot be used in part. Musical works, choreographic and dramatic performances, audiovisual and other works the performance or demonstration of which lasts over time must be used only in fragments. The determination of the duration of such fragments is left to the user and is determined by the information needs.

Under the same conditions, the works can be used by means of cinematography, for example, to create biographical, documentary or scientific films, and by means of photography.

3.1.4 Use of Public Speeches and Other Similar Works

Exceptions for the purpose of dissemination of information also include free reproduction in newspapers and other periodicals, broadcasting and communication to the public of public speeches, messages, reports and other similar works.[95] The law does not specify the notion of public proclamation of a work. Based on the content of the legislative definitions of public performance, public demonstration, etc., given in Art. 1 of the Law on Copyright, public may be considered to be the use of a work which occurs in a place where persons not belonging to the same family and close acquaintances of that family are present or may be present. The use of publicly proclaimed works must have an informational purpose and the scope of use must correspond to this purpose.

[94] Ukrainian Law on Copyright and Related Rights 1993, 3792-XII, art 21(1)(4).
[95] Ibid art 21(1)(9).

3.2 *Free Use of Works for Educational Purposes*

3.2.1 The Inclusion of Literary and Artistic Works as Illustrations in Periodicals, Broadcasts, Sound Recordings, or Videos of an Educational Nature

The use of literary and artistic works as illustrations in journals or magazines, broadcasts and recordings is allowed with the indication of the name of the author and the source of borrowing, when a periodical (or broadcast or recording) is purely educational,[96] such as a textbook, handbook, or anthology.[97] If a periodical (broadcast, recording) is informational, entertaining, or of any other character not directly intended for teaching, permission must be obtained to include works or fragments thereof in such a publication.

It should be noted that in Ukrainian jurisprudence there is sometimes a misinterpretation of the scope of this exception. In one example, an artist discovered that her drawing had been reworked into an embroidery scheme and the scheme was posted in a magazine that publishes embroidery schemes for various patterns and images. The author did not authorize the reprocessing and publication of her drawing and appealed the unlawful use. Rivne local court considered that there was a permitted free use of the work for educational purposes, because the drawing was used to teach embroidery.[98] The Court of Appeal of Rivne region cancelled this decision and satisfied the artist's claims.[99] The Supreme Court supported the opinion of the Court of Appeal.[100] The court of first instance did not pay attention to the fact that the magazine which publishes schemes for embroidery is an informational and not an educational one. That is, the court interpreted the provision of the law too broadly and applied it incorrectly. This exception does not cover any publication from which one can learn something, but only educational periodicals as such.

This exception differs from citation in two aspects.

First, when using works in educational publications, broadcasts and recordings, the amount of use can be much greater than when quoting. Some objects, such as photographs, poems, short essays, etc., may be reproduced in full if they are for educational purposes and do not conflict with the general principles of the free use of works.

Second, unlike citations, the use of works or fragments of them in publications, broadcasts, and educational recordings is not related to research, substantiation of one's opinion, analysis of existing approaches, and so on. The use of works in such cases is intended both for the study of the works themselves, in particular, literature, and to illustrate other materials that are the subject of the discipline.

---

[96] Ibid art 21(1)(2).

[97] Ukrainian National Standard, Main Types 2015, 3017:2015, point 4.9.4.

[98] Rivne Local Court, Decision 68369277 (2017) 569/12278/16-ц.

[99] Court of Appeal of Rivne Region, Decision 70569535 (2017) 569/12278/16-ц.

[100] Supreme Court, Order 90168860 (2020) 569/12278/16-ц.

3.2.2 Reproduction of Copies of a Work for Study

Achieving a teaching goal is often associated with the need to reproduce copies of works. Reproduction of works is interpreted in law as the making of copies of a work in material form, as well as the recording in material or electronic form of sounds and (or) moving images.[101] That is, if the work has a static form (text, photograph, etc.), it can be reproduced only by making a material copy. Works whose form of expression is audiovisual (moving image) can be reproduced in electronic form.

The Law on Copyright provides for three cases where the reproduction of copies of a work for educational purposes may be carried out without the permission of the author.

First, it is permitted to reproduce excerpts from published written and audiovisual works as illustrations for teaching purposes.[102] This rule applies to two kinds of works: written works, which can be artistic, scholarly, journalistic, or any other kind, and audiovisual works, which can also be of any kind. The subject of reproduction is the part of the work that is directly related to the study of a specific subject, a particular topic of the discipline.

Second, libraries and archives whose activities are not aimed directly or indirectly at making a profit may freely reproduce works under the following conditions[103]:

(1) reproduction is made by reprographic means, covering photocopying or other similar means except for records in electronic, optical or other computer-readable form[104];
(2) reproduction is carried out at the request of a natural person;
(3) the object of reproduction is a single published article or other small work or excerpt from a written work (except computer programs and databases), with or without illustrations;
(4) one copy of the reproduced work is made;
(5) the library or archive has sufficient grounds to believe that this copy will be used for the purpose of education, training or private research.

Third, educational institutions are free to reproduce published articles, other small works, or excerpts from written works with or without illustrations,[105] in compliance with the following requirements:

(1) reproduction is reprographic;
(2) reproduction is carried out for classroom studies;
(3) reproduction of the work is an isolated incident and is not systematic in nature;
(4) the volume of reproduction corresponds to the educational purpose.

[101] Ukrainian Law on Copyright and Related Rights 1993, 3792-XII, art 1(1)(12).
[102] Ibid art 23(1)(1).
[103] Ibid art 22(1)(1).
[104] Ibid art 1(1)(49).
[105] Ibid art 23(1)(2).

In fact, this exception covers the creation by an educational institution of a single reprographic copy or photocopy of a work or a fragment of a work for classroom use. In this regard, it was rightly noted that "if teachers are allowed to extract reasonable amounts of the copyright work, they then should be allowed to reproduce more than one copy because they often have more than one student in the class—they cannot ask all their students to share only one copy".[106] Indeed, the practical value of using a single reprographic copy in such cases is quite questionable. If the whole class needs to get acquainted with it, such a gradual individual acquaintance can take up the whole lesson or a significant part of it. This is inefficient for teaching so it is not surprising that in practice teachers do not comply with the condition of single reproduction and produce as many copies as necessary to ensure a normal learning process in the classroom.

In addition, this exception, which was revised in 2003, applies only to classroom teaching, while distance education remains outside it. This problem will be considered in more detail later when the issue of exceptions and limitations that should be added to Ukrainian legislation is investigated.

3.3 Ensuring the Interests of Persons with Visual Impairments and Dyslexia

One of the most important tasks of a civilized society is to provide access to works for people who, due to blindness, visual impairment or dyslexia, cannot read the printed text. Such people have the right to education, cultural, spiritual, and other development, as well as access to information on an equal basis with everyone else. To realize these rights there are special types of adaptation of the formats of works so that people with visual impairment or dyslexia can perceive information by hearing or touch with the help of relief-dot font.

For a long time in Ukraine, only the reproduction and publication of works in Braille was allowed as part of the free use of works. In 2015, under the influence of the Marrakesh Treaty, Ukrainian legislation was supplemented by several new provisions.

In addition to publishing works in relief-dot font, it is also permitted to publish audio works with special digital formatting and markup for easy navigation.[107] Such works may be distributed to visually impaired and dyslexic persons, as well as provided to the library funds of specialized libraries, libraries of educational institutions and rehabilitation centers for the visually impaired, public organizations of the

[106] Nhan T T Dinh, 'Promoting Innovation and Development by Rethinking the Role of Copyright Limitations and Exceptions in Vietnam' (2016) Faculty of Law Queensland University of Technology.

[107] Ukrainian Law on Copyright and Related Rights 1993, 3792-XII, art 21(1)(6).

blind, and enterprises, institutions, or organizations where people with visual impairment disabilities work. Distribution of works in these formats should not directly or indirectly lead to the achievement of a commercial goal.

Also to ensure the interests of people with visual impairments and dyslexia it is allowed to adapt existing and creating audiovisual works through the use of audio description.[108] Such adaptation consists in creation in video production of a separate soundtrack with a description of the character, subject, setting, or action.[109] The Law on Copyright does not provide for the absence of a commercial purpose in the distribution of audiovisual works with audio description. Therefore, the use of such works may be intended to generate income, in particular from the sale of copies of the work or tickets to a cinema screening.

3.4 *Free Reproduction of Works for Personal Purposes (Private Use)*

The main part of the users of the works are individuals who are interested in being able to meet their aesthetic and spiritual needs, develop their hobbies or otherwise enjoy culture and art. The Law on Copyright allows individuals to freely reproduce lawfully published works for personal or family use.[110]

The concept of personal goals has no interpretation in the law. Something that concerns a person's personality, her or his inner world or inner self can be considered personal. Personal goals do not relate to the realization of a person in professional or entrepreneurial activities, do not serve to meet social or domestic needs but relate exclusively to individuals, their worldview, cultural and spiritual development.

As for the family, it is defined as being created on the basis of marriage, blood consanguinity, adoption, as well as on other grounds not prohibited by law and not contrary to the moral principles of society.[111] A family consists of persons who live together, share a common household, and have mutual rights and responsibilities. Spouses are also considered a family if, for reasons of study, work, medical treatment, need to care for parents, children, and for other justifiable reasons, the wife and husband do not live together. A child belongs to the family of his or her parents even if he or she does not live with them.[112]

It should be noted that this exception is designed for voluntary and conscientious compliance with the above requirements. In practice, it is almost impossible to determine whether a reproduced copy has been passed on to another person who does not belong to the family.

---

[108] Ibid art 21(1)(11).

[109] Ibid art 1(1)(3).

[110] Ibid art 25(1).

[111] Family Code of Ukraine 2002, 2947-III, art 3(4).

[112] Ibid art 3(2).

4 Prospective Exceptions and Limitations for Further Development of Ukrainian Copyright Law

The previous section mentioned all cases of free use of works in Ukraine. And although they cover a wide range of public interests, in the EU exceptions and limitations apply to some other areas that are not taken into account in the Law on Copyright. In addition to the gaps already mentioned in the previous section, there are a number of other provisions that need to be implemented in Ukrainian legislation. Due to the conclusion of the Association Agreement, the system of exceptions and limitations that exists in the EU is a guideline for further improvement of this system in Ukraine.

The Association Agreement contains provisions only on some individual cases of free use of works. A much larger list of such cases is given in Directive 2001/29/EC on the harmonisation of certain aspects of copyright and related rights in the information society (InfoSoc Directive).[113] In addition, some exceptions and limitations are provided in the Directive 2019/790/EU on copyright and related rights in the Digital Single Market (Digital Single Market Directive).[114] This study will focus on the exceptions and limitations that Ukraine is required to implement under the Association Agreement. Some other provisions of EU law which should be provided in the legislation of Ukraine to increase the level of public interest in the free use of works will also be considered.

4.1 Copyright Exceptions and Limitations Ukraine Is Required to Implement Under the Association Agreement

Many of the exceptions and limitations set out in the Association Agreement are already provided for in the Law on Copyright: private use,[115] use of short excerpts in connection with the reporting of current events,[116] use solely for the purposes of teaching or scientific research,[117] and reproduction and decompilation of computer programs.[118] The Association Agreement mentions three more cases of free use of works that do not yet exist in the Law on Copyright.

[113] Parliament and Council Directive 2001/29/EC of 22 May 2001 on the Harmonisation of Certain Aspects of Copyright and Related Rights in the Information Society OJ L167.

[114] Parliament and Council Directive 2019/790/EU of 17 April 2019 on Copyright and Related Rights in the Digital Single Market and Amending Directives 96/9/EC and 2001/29/EC OJ L130, arts 3–6.

[115] EU–Ukraine Association Agreement, art 172(1)(a).

[116] Ibid art 172(1)(b).

[117] Ibid art 172(1)(d).

[118] Ibid arts 183, 184.

4.1.1 Ephemeral Fixation by a Broadcasting Organisation by Means of Its Own Facilities and for Its Own Broadcasts

This provision follows from the InfoSoc Directive, which, among exceptions and limitations to the reproduction right, provides for ephemeral recordings of works and that the preservation of these recordings in official archives may be permitted on the grounds of their exceptional documentary character.[119] Ukrainian law does not contain such an exception but there is another rule that obliges broadcasting organizations to record all their broadcasts.

Television and radio organizations must record all broadcasts that they have broadcast or rebroadcast or that a third party has on their behalf broadcast or retransmitted in full and unaltered form (telecommunications operator) and keep such recordings for 14 days from the date of distribution.[120] If within this period a complaint is received regarding the content of a certain program, its record is kept until the complaint is considered and a decision on it is made.[121]

That is, the recording of any program should be carried out and kept for at least 14 days from the date of distribution regardless of whether the program is of documentary nature and whether any work is reproduced within this program. Formally, the broadcasting organization achieves the same result in the form of recording and storage of programs which is provided as an exception for ephemeral fixation of works. At the same time, the creation and storage of broadcast records under current Ukrainian law is not a right that would correspond to the interests of broadcasters but an obligation that must be fulfilled in the interests of others. This is often related to refutation of inaccurate information and protection of honor, dignity and business reputation. It also applies to cases of distribution of banned content, and then the recording of the program will serve as evidence that the broadcaster has committed a violation of the law. It is easy to see that there is no question of the rights of the broadcaster itself, as the program recordings are actually needed to be used against the broadcaster in order to protect the rights and interests of others. Thus, the provisions on the compulsory recording and retention of transmissions do not replace an exception which would give the broadcasting organization the right to make ephemeral records of works.

The inclusion of this exception in the Law on Copyright is proposed in four of the five bills mentioned in Sec. 1.1, and in all cases it is worded in the same way as in the InfoSoc Directive. This suggests that in the near future the ephemeral fixation by a broadcasting organisation will appear in the Ukrainian system of exceptions and limitations in full compliance with the European regulation.

---

[119] InfoSoc Directive, art 5(2)(d).

[120] Ukrainian Law on Television and Radio Broadcasting, art 48(4).

[121] Ibid art 48(5).

4.1.2 Transient or Incidental Reproductions Which Are an Integral and Essential Part of a Technological Process

The application of this exception, first established in the InfoSoc Directive,[122] is limited by certain criteria. As the CJEU specified, an act of reproduction may be exempted only if it satisfies five conditions, that is, if the act is temporary; it is transient or incidental; it is an integral and essential part of a technological process; the sole purpose of that process is to enable a transmission in a network between third parties by an intermediary or a lawful use of a work or protected subject matter; and the act does not have any independent economic significance.[123]

The need for this exception is explained by the fact that "similar to other industrial users of copyright such as Internet/network service providers, broadcasters also engage in temporary, technical and incidental reproductions that are ancillary to the broadcast".[124] Such reproduction as an essential part of a technological process is not expressed in the purposeful use of works and is not associated with any benefit. This is an integral part of the notification process, which is purely technical. Since broadcasting organizations cannot avoid transient or incidental reproduction in the course of their main activities and it is not aimed at generating revenue, it is quite true that in the EU such actions belong to the cases of free use of works.

There are no such rules in Ukrainian legislation yet. Nevertheless, four of the five bills discussed in Sec. 1.1 provide for this exception as it is expressed in the InfoSoc Directive. Since the settlement of this issue is part of Ukraine's obligations under the Association Agreement, the new Law on Copyright should contain a provision allowing for free transient or incidental reproduction when it is an integral and essential part of a technological process and is carried out without a commercial purpose.

4.1.3 Exceptions Related to Databases

Exceptions to restricted acts relating to databases have existed in the EU since the adoption of Directive 96/9/EC on the legal protection of databases[125] and its implementation in the domestic law of the Member States. Ukrainian law does not contain any special rules related to the free use of databases. Like all other works, they may be subject to some general exceptions and limitations; however, this is insufficient compared to the rules specifically provided for databases in the EU.

---

[122] InfoSoc Directive, art 5(1).

[123] ECJ C-527/15 *Stichting Brein v. Jack Frederik Wullems* (2017) EU:C:2017:300, para 60.

[124] Canadian Association of Broadcasters, 'Copyright Consultations 2009' *Canadian Association of Broadcasters* https://www.cab-acr.ca/french/copyright/pdf/2009_copyright_submission.pdf accessed 9 December 2021.

[125] Parliament and Council Directive 96/9/EC of 11 March 1996 on the Legal Protection of Databases (1996) OJ L77.

The Association Agreement provides for several exceptions and limitations related to databases.

It allows, first, performance by the lawful user of a database or a copy thereof of any of the following acts:

(a) temporary or permanent reproduction by any means and in any form, in whole or in part;
(b) translation, adaptation, arrangement and any other alteration;
(c) any form of distribution to the public of the database or copies thereof;
(d) any communication, display or performance to the public;
(e) any reproduction, distribution, communication, display or performance to the public of the results of the acts referred to in subparagraph (b)

which is necessary for purposes of access to the contents of the database and normal use of the contents by the lawful user shall not require the authorisation of the author of the database. Where the lawful user is authorised to use only part of the database, this provision shall apply only to that part.[126]

The need for this rule may be explained by the fact that a legitimate user of the database or its copy should be able to access and use the content that the database contains. Such an opportunity should be granted without obtaining a separate authorisation, without any agreement with the author of the database or another right holder.[127] Ukrainian law does not provide for similar rules for the free use of databases.

Second, the Association Agreement contains a list of some other cases where the use of databases may take place without the consent of the author or other copyright holder:

(1) reproduction for private purposes of a non-electronic database.[128] As mentioned in the previous section, free reproduction of works for private use is allowed in Ukraine.[129] The provisions of the Law on Copyright do not specify databases; therefore, reproduction for personal use may cover electronic databases. This is inconsistent with the European approach, which associates reproduction for personal use exclusively with non-electronic databases. To resolve this inconsistency, the law should explicitly state that this exception does not apply to electronic databases;
(2) use for the sole purpose of illustration for teaching or scientific research, as long as the source is indicated and to the extent justified by the non-commercial purpose to be achieved.[130] Ukrainian law does not mention databases among the exceptions and limitations concerning the use of works for educational or teaching purposes. On the contrary, the law directly states that literary and

[126] EU–Ukraine Association Agreement, art 189(1).

[127] Anna Shtefan, 'Copyright Exceptions and Limitations in the EU–Ukraine Association Agreement' (2019) 5 Theory and Practice of Intellectual Property, 5 (12).

[128] EU–Ukraine Association Agreement, art 189(2)(a).

[129] Ukrainian Law on Copyright and Related Rights 1993, 3792-XII, art 25(1).

[130] EU–Ukraine Association Agreement, art 189(2)(b).

artistic works,[131] written and audiovisual works,[132] and published articles and other small works[133] may be used for education. Moreover, if reproductions are carried out by libraries and archives, they are not allowed to reproduce databases even if it is necessary for scientific research or educational purposes, as this is expressly prohibited by law.[134] The use of databases for teaching or scientific research can be done by citation, because in this case the list of works is not limited to their individual types.[135] However, this is not enough in comparison with the rules in force in the EU, where the educational or scientific purpose is provided with wider opportunities for the use of works. Therefore, the Law on Copyright should be supplemented with provisions that would allow the reproduction of databases when such reproduction is for scientific or educational purposes;

(3) use for purposes of public security or an administrative or judicial procedure.[136] Reproduction of works for judicial or administrative proceedings to the extent justified by the purpose of these proceedings is one of the types of free use of works in Ukraine.[137] The list of works that can be used under this exception is not limited, and therefore databases also fall under it. At the same time, Ukrainian legislation does not provide for the use of works for the purposes of public security. This is a significant gap, as, unlike most other types of works, databases can contain information that is needed to ensure public safety. This indicates that this part of the Law on Copyright needs to be clarified and improved.

All of the bills proposing a new edition of the Law on Copyright specified in Sec. 1.1 contain an article on the free use of databases. They all reproduce a provision of the Association Agreement which, in turn, is based on the provisions of Directive 96/9/EC. Thus, this exception would be fully consistent with the approach that applies in the EU.

4.2 Copyright Exceptions and Limitations That Should Be Included in the Ukrainian Legislation to Better Ensure the Interests of Society

There are some exceptions and limitations the implementation of which is not part of Ukraine's obligations under international agreements. However, taking such cases into account in Ukrainian legislation will be very useful as they have either already

[131] Ukrainian Law on Copyright and Related Rights 1993, 3792-XII, art 21(1)(2).

[132] Ibid art 23(1)(1).

[133] Ibid arts 22(1)(1), 23(1)(2).

[134] Ibid art 22(1)(1).

[135] Ibid art 21(1)(1).

[136] EU–Ukraine Association Agreement, art 189(2)(c).

[137] Ukrainian Law on Copyright and Related Rights 1993, 3792-XII, art 21(1), (7).

proved to be widely used in practice or they represent the modern needs of society. Providing for such cases will contribute to the development of a system of exceptions and limitations in Ukraine and increase the level of ensuring the interests of society.

The first of such exceptions is the freedom of panorama, the rule that allows individuals to create images of artistic works which are permanently located in public places—by taking photographs, video, drawing, etc.—and to use such images without the consent of the author.[138] This rule comes from the InfoSoc Directive, which sets the possibility to provide for exceptions or limitations to the exclusive reproduction right of works, such as works of architecture or sculpture, located permanently in public places.[139] In Ukraine, the use of images of works permanently located in public places may be carried out by the media when covering current events,[140] as well as by publishers of works, broadcasts and recordings of educational character when the works are illustrations in such publications.[141] However, these cases do not cover all uses that fall under the rule of freedom of panorama. In particular, many Ukrainians regularly take photos of various works located on the streets, in parks, squares, etc., and share such photos on social networks and other websites. Many of these works are protected by copyright but no one applies to the author for permission to take a picture of the work and use it in this way. The right to reproduce a work for personal purposes does not cover the freedom of panorama because the use of photographs of works is public; other Internet users can share them on their pages. This does not correspond to the reproduction of the work solely for personal purposes or for the family, which is a prerequisite for private use in Ukraine.[142] Even in the case of a panoramic photograph of a city depicting many works of architecture, formally, using such a photograph without the permission of the copyright holders may be considered a copyright infringement. In European countries, the issue of freedom of panorama is resolved differently: in some, the use of images of works can have any purpose, while others stipulate a purely non-commercial purpose; the author may or may not be remunerated.[143] It will be useful for Ukraine to study the experience of Member States, which will allow it to choose the model of freedom of panorama that is best aligned with the Ukrainian legal system and takes into account the interests of both the author and the users.

The second exception that is necessary in Ukrainian legislation is the possibility of free use of works for individuals who are unable, due to a physical disability, to hold or manipulate a book or to focus or move their eyes to the extent normally necessary for reading, as provided by the Marrakesh Treaty.[144] Currently in Ukraine, works in accessible formats can be distributed only among blind, visually impaired

---

[138] Shtefan, 'Freedom of Panorama: The EU Experience' (n 66) 13 (14).

[139] InfoSoc Directive, art 5(3)(h).

[140] Ukrainian Law on Copyright and Related Rights 1993, 3792-XII, 21(1)(4).

[141] Ibid art 21(1)(2).

[142] Ibid art 25(1).

[143] Shtefan, 'Freedom of Panorama: The EU Experience' (n 66) 13 (17–20).

[144] Marrakesh Treaty to Facilitate Access to Published Works for Persons Who Are Blind, Visually Impaired, or Otherwise Print Disabled (2013), art 2(2)(d).

and dyslexic persons.[145] The rule of Ukrainian legislation does not apply to persons who have normal vision but due to the peculiarities of their physical condition cannot read printed works. This significantly hinders the access of such persons to education, information, culture, and art, which places them in a very vulnerable position compared to other members of society. It is also advisable to work on the establishment of exceptions and limitations aimed at ensuring the interests of people with hearing impairments such as the creation of subtitles in audiovisual works and television programs. Although there are no such exceptions at the international level, people with hearing impairments also have significant barriers to accessing information and art and cannot exercise their rights to the same extent as people without hearing impairments. This shows that the interests of a certain part of Ukrainian society still remain outside the balance of interests which it is one of the goals of copyright to ensure. Therefore, this part of the Ukrainian legislation needs significant improvement.

The third exception is the use of works for distance learning. The need to include this exception in the system of Ukrainian exceptions and limitations has already been confirmed in practice. As noted above, in Ukraine only reprographic reproduction of certain types of works for classroom activities is allowed.[146] For distance learning, which takes place using online platforms, it is also necessary to reproduce and provide students with some materials, but this possibility is not mentioned in the law. This issue became especially relevant in 2020–2021, when due to the COVID-19 pandemic educational institutions were forced to conduct most lessons, lectures, and practical classes online. If it was necessary to send students learning materials in electronic form, teachers did so, despite the fact that in such cases, free reproduction of works is not allowed. Regardless of the COVID-19 pandemic, distance learning has developed significantly in recent years, but Ukrainian legislation still does not reflect the needs of society related to such learning, although providing pupils and students with the text of a reproduced work in electronic format is essentially similar to providing a paper copy. This leads to the conclusion that the exception for the reproduction of copies of works for teaching needs to be updated. To achieve this goal, it will be useful to study the experience of the legal regulation of the use of works for online learning in the EU, in particular the provisions of the Digital Single Market Directive and the results of its implementation in the legislation of the Member States.

These examples do not exhaust the list of exceptions and limitations which should be supplemented by Ukrainian legislation. There are other rules in the EU that can be useful to consider in order for the Ukrainian system of exceptions and limitations to meet the needs of a wider range of users. This would improve the balance of interests of authors and society and contribute to the deepening of European integration processes in Ukraine.

---

[145] Ukrainian Law on Copyright and Related Rights 1993, 3792-XII, 21(1)(6).

[146] Ibid art 23(1)(2).

5 Conclusion

In Ukraine, copyright is developing quite actively. As a result of this development the legal regulation of relations connected with creation and use of works is improving. An important role in this process is played by the system of exceptions and limitations which ensure public access to education, science, culture, art, information, aesthetic and spiritual needs. As shown in this study, the Ukrainian legislation contains a long list of cases in which the use of the work is allowed without the consent of the author. However, some of these rules need to be reviewed and updated to meet today's needs, as has already been confirmed in practice. In addition, a number of exceptions and limitations that exist in the EU are still not taken into account in the Ukrainian legislation. This creates certain gaps in the system of exceptions and limitations and keeps the interests of certain groups of users outside of this system. Consequently, it negatively affects the balance of interests sought by copyright law. Thus, the issues of free use of works require further research and development of specific proposals to improve the Ukrainian legislation in this area.

References

Maurizio Borghi, 'Exceptions as Users' Rights in EU Copyright Law' (2020) CIPPM Jean Monnet Working Papers 6/2020

James Boyle, 'A Manifesto on WIPO and the Future of Intellectual Property' (2004) 9(2) Duke Law and Technology Review 1

Canadian Association of Broadcasters, 'Copyright Consultations 2009' *Canadian Association of Broadcasters* (2009) https://www.cab-acr.ca/french/copyright/pdf/2009_copyright_submission.pdf

Julie E Cohen, 'Copyright and Creativity' in Brian Fitzgerald and Benedict Atkinson (eds), *Copyright Future, Copyright Freedom: Marking the 40th Anniversary of the Commencement of Australia's Copyright Act 1968* (Sydney University Press 2011) 134

Nhan T Dinh, 'Promoting Innovation and Development by Rethinking the Role of Copyright Limitations and Exceptions in Vietnam' (2016) Faculty of Law Queensland University of Technology

Christophe Geiger, Daniel J Gervais and Martin Senftleben, 'The Three-Step-Test Revisited: How to Use the Test's Flexibility in National Copyright Law' (2014) 29(3) American University International Law Review 581

Daniel J Gervais, 'Making Copyright Whole: A Principled Approach to Copyright Exceptions and Limitations' (2008) 5(1&2) University of Ottawa Law and Technology Journal 1

Michael B Gunlicks, 'A Balance of Interests: the Concordance of Copyright Law and Moral Rights in the Worldwide Economy' (2001) 11(3) Fordham Intellectual Property, Media and Entertainment Law 601

Annette Kur, 'Of Oceans, Islands, and Inland Water—How Much Room for Exceptions and Limitations Under the Three-Step Test?' (2009) 8(3) Richmond Journal of Global Law and Business 287

Yevgen Michurin, 'Approaches to the Formation of the Concept of Limitations of Proprietary Rights of Individuals' (2007) 2 Forum of Law 151 [Євген Мічурін, 'Підходи до Формування Поняття Обмежень Майнових Прав Фізичних Осіб' (2007) 2 Форум Права 151]

Martin R F Senftleben, *Copyright, Limitations and the Three-step Test: An Analysis of the Three-Step Test in International and EC Copyright Law* (Kluwer Law International 2004)

Anna Shtefan, 'Copyright Exceptions and Limitations in the EU–Ukraine Association Agreement' (2019) 5 Theory and Practice of Intellectual Property 5 [Anna Shtefan, 'Copyright Exceptions and Limitations in the EU–Ukraine Association Agreement' (2019) 5 Теорія і Практика Інтелектуальної Власності 5]

Anna Shtefan, 'Freedom of Panorama: The EU Experience' (2019) 11(2) European Journal of Legal Studies

Olena Orliuk (ed), *Fundamentals of Intellectual Property* (Interservise 2016) [Олена Орлюк (ред.), *Основи Інтелектуальної Власності* (Інтерсервіс 2016)]

Protection of Works Posted on the Internet Under Ukrainian Copyright Law

Kostiantyn Zerov

Contents

Abstract This chapter examines copyright protection and enforcement regarding works posted on the internet in light of the current Ukrainian and EU case-law practice. Along with the process of using a copyrighted work on the internet, the chapter focuses on four legal issues. First, the "making available of a work to the public" is discussed. This should be defined as a type of communication to the public in such a way that members of the public may access this work from a place and at a time individually chosen by them. Unlike current Ukrainian legislation,

Parts of Section 5 are a translation of the article Kostiantyn Zerov and Anna Shtefan, 'Termination of Copyright and Related Rights Infringements on the Internet: a Review of Legislative Novelties' (2017) 3 Theory and Practice of Intellectual Property journal 18 (19–23)". The author is grateful for Anna Shtefan for consenting to including it here.

K. Zerov (✉)
Intellectual Property and Information Law Department of the Educational, Scientific Institute of Law, Taras Shevchenko National University of Kyiv, Kyiv, Ukraine
e-mail: zerov@knu.ua

H. Richter (ed.), *Competition and Intellectual Property Law in Ukraine*,
MPI Studies on Intellectual Property and Competition Law 31,
https://doi.org/10.1007/978-3-662-66101-7_21

this interpretation corresponds with the provisions of the WIPO Copyright Treaty and the EU–Ukraine Association Agreement. The chapter goes on to examine the key issue of exhaustion of rights for works uploaded to the internet and provides reasons why exhaustion should not apply to posting works on the internet. Thirdly, the chapter analyzes copyright infringement types susceptible to taking place on the internet. In particular, it discusses the conditions under which the act of placing hyperlinks/framing/hotlinking to other websites and objects can be considered as the use of a work and, therefore, as copyright infringement. Finally, the chapter describes copyright enforcement for works posted on the internet by extrajudicial measures, including the Ukrainian version of the "notice and takedown" procedure.

1 Introduction

The constant development of the internet and its spread to all spheres of human life has posed many essential copyright issues. In March 2017, a legal mechanism appeared in Ukraine to help protect and enforce the copyright of works posted on the internet. In addition, the Association Agreement between Ukraine and the EU (Association Agreement) entered into force on 1 September 2017.[1] Chapter 9 of Title IV of the Association Agreement contains provisions on achieving an appropriate and adequate level of protection of intellectual property rights, including copyright. Ukrainian copyright legislation and case-law practice should adapt to these new standards.

Without proper understanding on both the theoretical level and the level of law enforcement practice of such new standards as "rules of the game", the Ukrainian legislator could take the wrong approach when passing the long-awaited reform of copyright and related rights.

This chapter outlines and discusses the provisions of the Ukrainian legislation in comparison with European standards. It includes an analysis of the legal regime of works posted on the internet in connection with economic rights that cover posting of work on the internet and the applicability of the copyright exhaustion doctrine to works placed on the internet in Ukraine; actions that can be considered as copyright infringement that relate to works posted on the internet (including scenarios of hyperlinking and framing); and the legal analysis of the procedure for termination of infringement on the internet in Ukraine as an example of non-jurisdictional enforcement of copyright.

[1] Association Agreement between the European Union and its Member States, of the one part, and Ukraine, of the other part OJ L161 (Association Agreement).

2 Rights and Stages of Using a Copyrighted Work on the Internet

2.1 Lack of a Consistent Approach in Ukraine

To determine whether there has been an infringement of copyright in posting work on the internet, it is necessary to examine the legality of such posting through the prism of how the works are used.

There is no doubt that posting a work on the internet constitutes its use. It would therefore require the copyright holder's permission, unless statutory restrictions on property copyright apply. Article 15 Ukrainian Law "On Copyright and Related Rights"[2] and Art. 441 Civil Code of Ukraine[3] provide an non-exhaustive list of independent ways of using the work. Posting the work on the internet as a separate way of using the work is not mentioned.

Particular attention should be paid to this issue when the person who posted the work does not own the entire volume of property rights (e.g. a licensee).

The Civil Code of Ukraine in Art. 1109(6) unambiguously states the following: "the rights to use the object of intellectual property rights and the methods of its use, not defined in the license agreement, are considered not granted to the licensee". Thus, the licensee may violate the copyright by placing the work on the network if the license agreement does not specify the full range of rights necessary to post the work on the network according to a certain scenario of use.

Ukrainian case law has not yet developed a straightforward approach to using works on the internet. In its Resolution on the application by courts of the law in cases of protection of copyright and related rights the Plenum of the Supreme Court of Ukraine states: "posting of works on the internet in a form accessible to public use is the making of works available to the public in such a way that its representatives can access the works from anywhere and at any time of their choice".[4] In contrast, the Plenum of the Supreme Economic Court of Ukraine recognizes the posting of works on the internet in a form available for public use as a reproduction of the work.[5] Furthermore, the case law shows that some Ukrainian courts interpret the posting of the work on the internet as a public broadcast of the work.[6]

Given these diverging court interpretations, clarity is needed to determine the legal regime of works posted on the internet. For this purpose it is necessary to analyze the rightsholder's intellectual property rights (methods of using a work, namely the

[2] Ukrainian Law on Copyright and Related Rights 1994, 3792-XII, art 15.

[3] Civil Code of Ukraine 2004, 435-IV, art 441.

[4] Supreme Court of Ukraine, Resolution of the Plenum on the application by courts of the law in cases of protection of copyright and related rights 4 June 2010 No. 5, para 31.

[5] Supreme Economic Court of Ukraine, Resolution of the Plenum on some issues of dispute resolution practice related to the protection of intellectual property rights 17 October 2012 No. 12, para 46.

[6] Podilskyi District Court of Kyiv City, Decision 47686172 (2015) 758/4012/15-c; Holosiivskyi District Court of Kyiv City, Decision 24651132 (2012) 2601/7669/12.

right of reproduction and the right to make the work available to the public) with particular reference to the stages of such use on the internet.

2.2 Right of Reproduction

Historically, the first form of use of a work (and still one of the main forms) was its reproduction. According to the Ukrainian Law "On Copyright and Related Rights", a reproduction constitutes the manufacturing of one or more specimens of work in any material form, as well as recording thereof for temporary or permanent storage in electronic (including digital), optical, or other computer-readable forms.[7] However, as the main act of civil legislation, the Civil Code of Ukraine does not contain a bounding reference to a "specimen" of the work.[8] Similarly, according to Art. 173 Association Agreement, the right to reproduce a work includes direct or indirect, temporary or permanent reproduction by any means and in any form, in whole or in part.[9]

Considering the nature of the circulation of the work in digital form, it is advisable that uploading, storing the work in digital form, and saving a copy of the work on the end user's device is a reproduction of a copy of the work, not a specimen stored in the person who posted the work on the internet. The legislation of Ukraine knows the concept of "copy of the work". The material form (specimen) is only one of the possible types of such a copy, which cannot be posted on the internet because a specimen is a copy of the work made in material rather than digital form.

In general, the approach of Ukrainian legislators to the application of the right of reproduction to works expressed in digital form is fully harmonized with established world practice, namely with the agreed statement to Art. 1(4) WIPO Copyright Treaty, under which "the reproduction right and the exceptions to that rightfully apply in the digital environment [...]".[10]

This right of reproduction with the use of the work on the internet includes the following logical stages:

- initial input (uploading) of the work in digital form on the internet;
- temporary acts of reproduction, which are transient or incidental and an integral and essential part of a technological process. Temporary reproductions, according to the provisions of Ukrainian legislation, are not included in cases of free use of the work with the name of the author, in contrast to the provisions of Art.

[7] Ukrainian Law on Copyright and Related Rights 1994, 3792-XII, art 1.

[8] Civil Code of Ukraine 2004, 435-IV, art 441.

[9] EU–Ukraine Association Agreement, art 173.

[10] Agreed statements concerning the WIPO Copyright Treaty (1996) https://wipolex.wipo.int/en/text/295456 accessed 1 October 2021.

5(1) Directive 2001/29/EC,[11] which under certain conditions allow free temporary reproduction. Instead, the provisions on short-term reproductions must be implemented in Ukrainian law under Art. 175 Association Agreements[12];
- saving a copy of a work in digital form on the recipient's (end-users) device is also a reproduction, but another person will make such reproduction.

Thus the right of reproduction is applicable and necessary for the lawful posting of a copy of a work on the internet, despite a certain inconsistency of the internal Ukrainian legislation. At the same time, in order to qualify the actions of a person who uploads a copy of a work on the internet as a potential copyright infringement, only the first stage of reproduction is legally significant, namely the initial input (uploading) of the work in digital form on the internet. The remaining cases of the reproduction of the work on the network can be considered in the context of the specificity of the liability of other persons (internet intermediaries and end-users, respectively).

2.3 *Right to Make the Work Available to the Public and Right to Broadcasting of Work*

The second right to use on the internet is the right to make the work available to the public. According to Art. 1 Ukrainian Law "On Copyright and Related Rights", this right is considered as a sub-part of the right to distribute the work. However, Art. 15 of the same law considers making available as an independent right.[13] However, it can be argued that this approach is erroneous.

The WIPO Copyright Treaty (WCT), which was adopted in 1996,[14] distinguishes between two distinct rights of use of works. The first is the "right to distribution" (Art. 6). According to the agreed statement to this article it consists exclusively of fixed copies that can be put into circulation as tangible objects. The other is the "right of communication to the public"[15] (Art. 8), part of which is an "interactive" making available right through which members of the public may access works from a place and at a time individually chosen by them. This division is also typical for EU Member States (Art. 3, 4 Directive 2001/29/EC[16]), and it is also reflected in Art. 174 Association Agreement.[17]

[11] Parliament and of the Council Directive 2001/29/EC of 22 May 2001 on the harmonisation of certain aspects of copyright and related rights in the information society (2001) OJ L167 (InfoSoc Directive), art 5(1).

[12] Association Agreement, art 175.

[13] Ukrainian Law on Copyright and Related Rights 1994, 3792-XII, art 1, 15.

[14] WIPO Copyright Treaty (WCT) (1996).

[15] WIPO Copyright Treaty (WCT) (1996), art 8.

[16] InfoSoc Directive, arts 3, 4.

[17] Association Agreement, art 178.

It needs to be noted here that the concept of "communication to the public" remains undefined by EU Directives. As a consequence, "in parallel to the EU policy and legislative agenda, the construction of the EU copyright framework owes a great deal to the role undertaken by the CJEU".[18] Some scholars of Court of Justice of the European Union (CJEU) practice assume that the communication to the public must be analyzed in two phases.

> The first phase concerns the initial interpretation [...] characterized by traditional analogue thinking, given that the reasoning used in the cases focused on traditional modes of broadcasting and retransmission. The second phase or the Internet phase began with Svensson[19] and is distinguishable because of its Internet Aspect.[20]

The second phase implications will be referred in the Sec. 4.3 of this chapter.

According to CJEU case-law the right of communication to the public combines two cumulative elements: an "act of *communication*", and a "communication to the *public*". "The concept of communication must be construed broadly, as referring to any transmission of the protected works, irrespective of the technical means or process used".[21] When someone uses a specific technical means different from that of the original communication, retransmission must be considered a "communication". However, a mere technical means to ensure or improve reception of the original transmission in its catchment area does not constitute a "communication". Ukrainian legislation and case-law practice do not have any interpretation of this concept yet.

Regarding the second cumulative element, Ukrainian legislation does not contain an interpretation of the concept of "public". However, concerning other uses—namely public performance, public demonstration, and public display—Ukrainian law uses the construction "persons who do not belong to the family or close acquaintances of this family". In general, it is seen that the same approach is possible for the making available rights defined in the encyclopedic literature, namely the Dictionary of the Ukrainian language, the "public" means certain circles of viewers and readers.[22] Even though dictionaries are not legal acts, Ukrainian courts often refer to dictionaries and encyclopedias to interpret common terms in certain categories of cases. Therefore, in the event of a relevant dispute, it is very likely that a court may look to this or another well-known dictionary to interpret a particular term (in this case, the term "public") that is not available at the legislative level.

European case law has developed an approach, according to which "public" means

> an indefinite number of potential recipients (i.e., regardless of whether they take advantage of this opportunity), which, in turn, requires a fairly large number of people. The criterion

---

[18] Eleonora Rosati, *Copyright and the Court of Justice of the European Union* (Oxford University Press 2019) 18.

[19] ECJ C-466/12 *Nils Svensson and Others v. Retriever Sverige AB* (2014) ECLI:EU:C:2014:76.

[20] Justin Koo, *The Right of Communication to the Public in EU Copyright Law* (Hart Publishing, 2019) 47.

[21] ECJ C-403/08 *Football Association Premier League Ltd and Others v. QC Leisure and Others* and C-429/08 *Karen Murphy v. Media Protection Services Ltd* (2011) ECLI:EU:C:2011:631, para 193.

[22] Ukrainian Dictionary (1976) Volume 7, 723.

of a 'sufficiently large number of persons' determines that the concept of 'public' implies a certain *de minimis* threshold, which excludes groups of persons from the concept which are too small or insignificant.[23]

At the same time, it is necessary to consider the total number of users who have already gained access, and will do so in the future. "It does not matter whether access to the work was provided "one on one" if, at the same time, the total number of such users could be significant".[24]

At present, the Ukrainian legislation defines another independent way (i.e. not as a part of communication to the public) of using the work—the broadcast. This is defined as over-the-air transmission of works, performances, sounds and/or images, broadcast organization programmes, performances or any sounds and/or images fixed on phonograms (videograms) and so on, where the said transmission can be received by an unlimited number of persons in various places located at a distance from the place of transmission where the images or sounds cannot be received without it. Transmissions take place via radio waves (or laser beams, gamma rays, etc.) including via satellite or remote transmission by wires or any type of surface or underground/underwater cable (conductor, fiber optic or other) in the form of signals. These include encoded signals if the public receives a means of decoding them from or with the consent of a broadcast organization.

In other words, this economic right refers by default to "classic" linear broadcasting (TV and radio). However, is it possible on the internet? In cases where the interactive mode of communication is absent (for example, the user can not choose where to start watching an audiovisual work but only has the right to connect to a continuous existing data stream), it is evident that a "making available" right is inappropriate. Such cases—which are rare—can generally be considered as independent broadcasting right under current Ukrainian legislation.

2.4 *Actual Scenarios of Using a Work on the Internet*

A brief analysis was made of the ways in which the work is used on the internet concluded that it was impossible to use work on the internet exclusively within one right of use. Each work goes through certain stages of use, the order of which should be noted. Zjatyckyj, Terletsky, and Leontiev believe that,

---

[23] ECJ C-135/10 *Società Consortile Fonografici (SCF) v. Marco Del Corso* (2012) ECLI:EU:C:2012:140, para 86.

[24] ECJ C-89/04 *Mediakabel BV v. Commissariaat voor de Media* (2005) ECLI:EU:C:2005:348, para 30; ECJ C-192/04 *Lagardère Active Broadcast v. Société pour la perception de la rémunération équitable (SPRE) and Gesellschaft zur Verwertung von Leistungsschutzrechten mbH (GVL)* (2005) ECLI:EU:C:2005:475, para 31; ECJ C-306/05 *Sociedad General de Autores y Editores de España (SGAE) v. Rafael Hoteles SA* (2006) ECLI:EU:C:2006:764, para 37; ECJ C-607/11 *ITV Broadcasting Ltd and Others v. TVCatchUp Ltd* (2013) ECLI:EU:C:2013:147, paras 32–34.

> with some simplification, three stages of using the work on the internet are distinguished. These are recording (uploading) the work on the server (the right to reproduction); accessing of the work on the internet (the right of making available); an appearance on the user's device (the right to reproduction of the work).[25]

However, this does not appear convincing because using a work on the internet may not begin with the uploading of the work to a separate server. A person can share access to objects already on specific hardware (for example, by creating his own File Transfer Protocol server or sharing files via Peer-to-Peer [P2P] networks). In this case, the initial reproduction of the work can be done before the initial posting (uploading) of the work and without violation of copyright.

In addition, these scholars have considered only one way to post works on the internet, namely by uploading the work to a specific server. However, technological development has given impetus to new ways of posting works on the internet. This necessitates the determination of the peculiarities of the legal regime of protection of such works. This diversity is manifested in the different order of actions for the work, which is presented in digital form (and hence the rights of its use), and therefore, in our opinion, excludes the possibility of a separate universal scheme of the order of use of works posted on the internet. Other ways to post works on the internet include the following:

- Using software that includes multiple transmission of the work among users (P2P-exchange). If the file is exchanged via P2P, reproduction is made simultaneously with the making available to the public;
- Cloud-based file syncing, which involves works in digital form being updated in a separate hardware directory and simultaneously uploaded to the cloud server (reproduction), and—optionally—to other users' hardware (also reproduction). The files in this directory are also usually available through the cloud service website and various software applications (making them available to the public);
- Representing the work on-demand and interactive presentation of the work on request. This group also includes Catch-Up TV—a technology that allows users to watch an audiovisual work or program (broadcast) sometime after the initial broadcast—and Time-Shifting technology, which allows users to stop watching an audiovisual work or program (broadcast) and later resume watching from that place (reproduction).[26]

2.5 Conclusion

Thus, the posting of a work on the internet may be covered by several economic rights, depending on the actual scenario of use: (a) right of reproduction; (b) right to

[25] Sergey Zjatyckyj, Konstantyn Leont'ev and Vasiliy Terleckij, 'Copyright on the Internet: Three Stages of One Process' (2001) 8 Intellectual Property 5 (7).

[26] Kostiantyn Zerov, *Features of Copyright Protection for Works Posted on the Internet* (Interservis 2018) 35.

make the work available; or (c) right to the broadcasting of work. At the same time, each scenario of the use of the work should be considered individually.

3 Exhaustion of Copyright for Works Posted on the Internet

The issue of copyright exhaustion cannot be overlooked when considering the posting of works on the internet. The essence of the concept of exhaustion of rights is that the rightsholder at the time of the first sale loses his right to control the further distribution of such work and gathering additional benefits for such future distribution.

In the EU the issue of exhaustion of copyright for works posted on the internet can be found in two Directives. According to the provisions of Art. 3(3) Directive 2001/29/EC (Art. 174(3) of the Association Agreement, respectively), an act of communication to the public cannot lead to the exhaustion of rights.[27] But at the same time, under provisions of Art. 4(2) Directive 2009/24/EC of the European Parliament and of the Council of 23 April 2009 on the legal protection of computer programs, "[t]he first sale in the Community of a copy of a program by the rightholder or with his consent shall exhaust the distribution right within the Community of that copy, with the exception of the right to control further rental of the program or a copy thereof".[28] The understanding of this provision in connection to the internet was established by the CJEU in *UsedSoft GmbH v. Oracle*. The CJEU stated that copyright

> is exhausted if the copyright holder who has authorised, even free of charge, the downloading of that copy from the Internet onto a data carrier has also conferred, in return for payment of a fee intended to enable him to obtain a remuneration corresponding to the economic value of the copy of the work of which he is the proprietor, a right to use that copy for an unlimited period.[29]

In contrast to the EU Member States practice, in Ukraine there is no legislative division of the applicability of the concept of exhaustion of rights depending on certain objects (e.g. computer programs) and no legal obligations to implement the provisions of Art. 4(2) Directive 2009/24/EC are bounded under the Association Agreement. The provisions on the exhaustion of copyright in Ukraine are placed in Art. 15(7) Ukrainian Law "On Copyright and Related Rights", namely

> if specimens [i.e. copies made in any material form] of a lawfully published work are lawfully put into civil circulation by their first sale in Ukraine, then their re-entry into circulation by

[27] InfoSoc Directive, art 3.

[28] Parliament and of the Council Directive 2009/24/EC of 23 April 2009 on the Legal Protection of Computer Programs OJ L111, 16–22, art 4(2).

[29] ECJ C-128/11 *UsedSoft GmbH v. Oracle International Corp.*, (2012) ECLI:EU:C:2012:407, para 89.

sale, gift, etc. without the consent of the author (or another person who has the copyright) and without payment of royalties is granted.[30]

It is necessary to note several factors when analysing this norm. First, as defined in Art. 15(7) Ukrainian Law "On Copyright and Related Rights", the exhaustion of copyright refers to specimens of works—i.e. the material form of their expression—which cannot be applied to the internet. Second, the exhaustion of rights relates exclusively to distribution right and cannot be applied to other rights. Third, saving a copy of a work in digital form on the end user's device is a reproduction of another object—namely a copy of the work on another medium—and not a copy of the work stored by the person who initially posted the work on the internet.

In this manner, the official position of the Supreme Economic Court of Ukraine, which indicates that "the exhaustion of rights applies only to copies of the work, which are expressed in material form; in other forms of expression of the work, the exhaustion of the right may not occur, in particular, the right to distribute the work on the internet"[31] corresponds to the factors outlined above and is seen as a proper solution within the issue of exhaustion of copyright for works posted on the internet.

4 Types of Copyright Infringement for Works Posted on the Internet

Article 50 Ukrainian Law "On Copyright and Related Rights" provides a de-facto list of possible copyright infringements:

a) actions by any person that infringe the personal non-proprietary rights of copyright and (or) related rights holders stipulated in Articles 14 and 38 of this Law, and their proprietary rights specified in Articles 15, 17, 27, 39, 40–41 of this Law, subject to the proprietary rights restrictions stipulated in Articles 21 through 25, 42, and 43 of this Law as well as abuse by officials of the organization of collective management of official position, which led to non-payment or improper distribution and payment of remuneration to copyright holders;

b) piracy in the field of copyright and (or) related rights—publication, reproduction, import into the customs territory of Ukraine, export from the customs territory of Ukraine and distribution of counterfeit specimens of works (including computer programs and databases), phonograms, videograms, illegal publication of programs of broadcasting organizations, camcorders, cardsharing, as well as Internet piracy, i.e. committing any actions that are recognized as an infringement of copyright and (or) related rights using the Internet in accordance with this article;

c) plagiarism—promulgation (publication), in full or in part, of another person's work under the name of a person who is not the author of this work;

d) importation into the customs territory of Ukraine, without permission of the persons holding the copyright and (or) related rights of specimens of works (including computer software and databases), phonograms, videograms, and broadcast programs;

[30] Ukrainian Law on Copyright and Related Rights 1994, 3792-XII, arts 1, 15.

[31] Supreme Economic Court of Ukraine, Resolution of the Plenum on some issues of dispute resolution practice related to the protection of intellectual property rights of 17 October 2012 No. 12, para 40.

e) actions that pose a threat of infringement of copyright and (or) related rights;

f) any actions for the intentional circumvention of technical means of protection of copyright and (or) related rights, in particular the production, distribution, importation for distribution and use of means of such circumvention;

g) forging, altering, or eliminating rights-management information, in particular rights-management information in electronic form, without the permission of the copyright and (or) related rights holders or the persons implementing such management;

h) the distribution, importation into the customs territory of Ukraine for distribution purposes, and broadcast of objects of copyright and (or) related rights from which rights-management information, in particular, that in electronic form, has been eliminated or altered without the permission of the copyright and (or) related rights holders.

i) camcording, cardsharing.[32]

However, not all of them may relate to works posted on the internet. For example, objectively, specimens of works cannot be imported into the customs territory of Ukraine without the permission of the relevant persons, as this type of copyright infringement applies only to tangible objects. Nevertheless, the essence of copyright infringement on works posted on the internet is the same as in the real (analogue) world—infringement of economic and/or personal non-economic copyright.

This section will consider a brief analysis of certain types of actions related to works posted on the internet, which can be considered a violation of copyright in Ukraine.

4.1 Internet Piracy

Ukrainian legislation in Art. 50 Ukrainian Law "On Copyright and Related Rights" recognizes one of the types of copyright infringement as "piracy", namely the

> publication, reproduction, import into the customs territory of Ukraine, export from the customs territory of Ukraine, and distribution of counterfeit copies of works (including computer programs and databases, phonograms, videograms, illegal publication of programs of broadcasting organizations, camcording, card sharing).[33]

Separately, in this article lawmakers identify "internet piracy" as the commission of any action that under *this article* is recognized as a violation of copyright and/or related rights using the internet. The use of the wording "of this article" rather than "paragraph or part of this article" is surprising. However, they are, by their nature, independent types of copyright infringement regardless of the form of expression of the work. Such an "extended" interpretation of the concept of piracy may lead to plagiarism or infringement of personal non-economic rights also being qualified as internet piracy.

Thus, the definition of "internet piracy" appears erroneous. Moreover, the very term "piracy" concerning works posted on the internet is to some extent duplicate

[32] Ukrainian Law on Copyright and Related Rights 1994, 3792-XII, Art. 50.

[33] Ibid.

and redundant. The current Ukrainian legislation has sufficient legal grounds to classify the illegal posting of the work on the internet as a violation of copyright. Thus, Art. 50(a) Ukrainian Law "On Copyright and Related Rights" recognizes copyright infringement as the commission by any person of actions that violate the personal non-economic rights and/or economic rights of copyright subjects, subject to the restrictions provided by law.[34] Therefore, actions on the illegal use of works, particularly posting them on the internet, should be classified as copyright infringement under paragraph "a" of Art. 50 Ukrainian Law "On Copyright and Related Rights", not as piracy. At the same time, this problem is purely theoretical. It refers to issues of legal technique, since the Ukrainian legislation does not provide distinctions or guidance as to the possibility of applying different methods of enforcement of the rights, as well as the amount of compensation or damages to be paid by the infringer when copyright infringement was committed under paragraph "a" or "b" or any other of Art. 50 Ukrainian Law "On Copyright and Related Rights".

4.2 Means of Copyright Infringement

The possibility of applying the Ukrainian concept of "single ongoing copyright infringement" concerning works posted on the internet deserves further attention. This concept was developed by the Ukrainian case law[35] regarding "analogue" cases. Following para 51-2 of the Resolution of the Plenum of the Supreme Economic Court of Ukraine in 2012 No. 12, "each fact of illegal use of copyright objects, including repeated use of the same object, constitutes an independent violation".[36] Uploading a particular work on the network can constitute its use by a copyright infringer in two ways: (a) by reproducing it—uploading the work to the server; and (b) direct placement—communication of the work to the general public. Copies of the work made when viewing the website or downloading the work (reproduction) will be made by other entities and end-users. We think that it is quite plausible that a similar approach will be used in the "internet" cases because the potential number of such reproductions (number of views or downloads by end-users) may indicate the estimated amount of damages to the rightsholder and the possible amount of income received by the infringer, but not on the number of facts of copyright infringement by the person who initially posted the work on the internet.

Riordan concisely sums up the role of copyright amid the various interests involved in internet intermediate liability when stating that the rights which copyright

[34] Ibid.

[35] Supreme Economic Court of Ukraine, Decision 57169375 (2016) 916/4567/14.

[36] Supreme Economic Court of Ukraine, Resolution of the Plenum on some issues of dispute resolution practice related to the protection of intellectual property rights of 17 October 2012 No. 12, para 51-2.

> confers embody the basic tension between encouraging optimal creation and consumption of works; their boundaries reflect delicate compromises between creators, consumers, disseminators, and many other interest groups. These conflicts are exemplified in the enforcement of copyright against internet intermediaries.[37]

It should be also noted, that in contrast to common law countries, Ukrainian civil copyright legislation does not distinguish between direct and indirect copyright infringement. Some safe harbours for internet intermediaries are stated in Art. 9 Ukrainian Law "On E-commerce".[38] However, in cases when the hosting service provider or the website or webpage owner does not take timely actions under Art. 52-1 Ukrainian Law "On Copyright and Related Rights"[39] (i.e. has been informed about a takedown notice and has the ability to supervise the actions of a direct infringer such as web blocking or deleting information etc.), and indirectly causes negative consequences to the rightsholder, they bear the same amount of civil liability for copyright infringements committed using the internet as a person who directly infringes copyright.

In addition, such persons will be legally liable if:

> a) the owner of a webpage has, within a period of three months, notwithstanding the cease-and-desist applications received and granted, allowed at least two cases of use on one or more webpages of which he is the owner, of the same copyright and/or related rights object on the same website;
>
> b) the owner of a webpage that is not the owner of the website has, within a period of 3 months, despite the received and granted cease and desist notices, allowed at least two uses of the same copyright and (or) related rights on the same website.[40]

4.3 Hyperlinking

The functioning of the internet generates new legal issues that are inextricably linked to its use but are not explicitly defined as copyright infringement. Therefore, one urgently needs to enquire not only into the types of copyright infringements defined in Art. 50 Ukrainian Law "On Copyright and Related Rights" but also into specific actions that occur when posting works on the internet. This includes the possibility of their qualification as copyright infringement while striking a fair balance between the interests of right holders to protect their works and the right of individuals to freedom of expression under the current legislation of Ukraine and the Association Agreement.

One of the essential and integral aspects of the functioning of the internet is the addressing between different websites and objects that are located on them. Such addressing is carried out through hyperlinks which have many forms and carry out various functions. In particular, they can refer to the websites on which the work is

---

[37] Jaani Riordan, *The Liability of Internet Intermediaries* (Oxford University Press 2016) 6.01.

[38] Ukrainian Law on E-commerce 2015, 675-VIII, art 9.

[39] Ukrainian Law on Copyright and Related Rights 1994, 3792-XII, art 52-1.

[40] Ukrainian Law on Copyright and Related Rights 1994, 3792-XII, art 52-1(15).

placed lawfully in addition to websites on which the work is placed with copyright infringement. Therefore hyperlinks themselves remain completely technologically neutral and do not create new copies of the work itself.

In general, how to qualify the actions of a person who posted a hyperlink remains unresolved in Ukraine. In the context of approximating Ukrainian legislation to EU standards, it is appropriate to conduct such qualification by accounting for the recent practice of the CJEU on the interpretation of Art. 3 Directive 2001/29/EC (provisions which are identical to Art. 174 Association Agreement) in *Svensson*[41] and *GS Media*.[42] This should hold true at least in so far as this does not conflict with the applicable legal regulation in Ukraine. The following three scenarios illustrate how to reconcile the standard under the EU case law with Ukrainian law.

In the first scenario, the initial communication of the work to the public is lawful, and the work posted on the internet is available without restriction to an indefinite number of potential users. In this case, users who know the appropriate address can use hyperlinks (i.e. the same technical means as in the case of the initial submission to the public—the internet) to access the work from "anywhere" (the internet) in addition to, for example simply entering the appropriate address within the browser. Such potential users are the public, covered by the permission of the copyright holder to use his work, and therefore the placement of hyperlinks to such works is not a new (secondary) submission to the public and does not require the permission of the copyright holder and is not copyright infringement.

In the second scenario, the initial communication of the work to the public is lawful, but access to the work is limited (for example, through the registration of paid access [subscription]). Persons who were not taken into account by the copyright holder within the limits of granting permission for the initial disclosure of the work to the public will also receive it. Such placement of a hyperlink, allowing access to the work despite these technical limitations, may well be further qualified as actions for conscious circumvention of technical means under paragraph "e" of Art. 50 Ukrainian Law "On Copyright and Related Rights".

In the third scenario, the initial communication of the work to the public was illegal. The CJEU, taking into account its precedent practice and the provisions of the EU directives, which are not reflected in the text of the Association Agreement in the case of *GS Media*, has identified two additional independent criteria for qualifying actions to place hyperlinks to an illegal source.

The first criterion is the awareness of the nature of the actions of the user who posted such a hyperlink. If the issue of qualifying actions for the placement of hyperlinks is applied to the approach (according to which all without exception hyperlinks would be recognized as the use of the work), internet users would be obliged to determine whether the work on the website ("sources") was posted illegally or not. Arbitration like this significantly affects the balance of interests of society and rightsholders and restricts the right of individuals to freedom of expression.

---

[41] ECJ C-466/12 *Nils Svensson and Others v. Retriever Sverige AB* (2014) ECLI:EU:C:2014:76.

[42] ECJ C-160/15 *GS Media BV v. Sanoma Media Netherlands BV and Others* (2015) ECLI:EU:C:2016:644.

Accordingly, the action of posting such a hyperlink should not be recognized as a communication to the public if the user did not know that the hyperlink refers to an illegal source. However, if it is established that the user knew or should have known that the hyperlink provided access to a work that was illegally posted on the internet (for example, given the fact that the copyright holder has notified such user), the provision of such a hyperlink should constitute a communication to the public.[43] It is possible to apply this criterion under Ukrainian law because the Plenum of the Supreme Economic Court of Ukraine has stated that "copyright enforcement is granted only against any *deliberate* unauthorized use by another person protected work (except for cases of free use of works provided by law)".[44]

The second criterion relates to the profitability placing of the hyperlink.

> When the posting of a hyperlink to a work that is freely available on another website is carried out by a person who, in so doing, does not pursue a profit, to take account of the fact that that person does not know and cannot reasonably know, that that work had been published on the Internet without the consent of the copyright holder.[45]

On the other hand, however,

> when the posting of hyperlinks is carried out for profit, it can be expected that the person who posted such a link carries out the necessary checks to ensure that the work concerned is not illegally published on the website to which those hyperlinks lead so that it must be presumed that that posting has occurred with the full knowledge of the protected nature of that work and the possible lack of consent to publication on the Internet by the copyright holder. In such circumstances, and in so far as that rebuttable presumption is not rebutted, the act of posting a hyperlink to a work that was illegally placed on the Internet constitutes a 'communication to the public'.[46]

Without appropriate changes to the law this economic approach is not compatible with current Ukrainian copyright law enforcement practice. Neither the Civil Code of Ukraine nor Ukrainian Law "On Copyright and Related Rights" (unlike, for example, the Ukrainian Law "On Trademark Protection") recognizes copyright infringement depending on the nature of the use of the work, i.e. whether it is commercial or non-commercial (except for some specific copyright limitations).

Therefore, it is vital to reflect the above *GS Media*'s approach at the legislative level in order to harmonize Ukrainian legislation with EU standards.

---

[43] ECJ C-160/15 *GS Media BV v. Sanoma Media Netherlands BV and Others* (2015) ECLI:EU:C:2016:644, para 49.

[44] Supreme Economic Court of Ukraine, Resolution of the Plenum on some issues of dispute resolution practice related to the protection of intellectual property rights of 1 October 2012 No. 12, para 55.

[45] ECJ C-160/15 *GS Media BV v. Sanoma Media Netherlands BV and Others* (2015) ECLI:EU:C:2016:644, para 47.

[46] Ibid para 51.

4.4 Framing, Hotlinking, and Other Technological Means

However, hyperlinks are not the only way to address the internet. If hyperlinks redirect a user from one website to another, the use of hotlink, framing, and embed technologies, based on hyperlinks, have the opposite function. These redirect content from another website/source server while the user stays on the same website. From a technical point of view, these technologies (like hyperlinks) create neither a new or derived work, nor copies of the work, but refer to an already existing work to which they facilitate access.

As of September 2021, there is no specific legislation on framing and hotlinking on the internet in Ukraine. The approaches of Ukrainian and European case-law practice regarding hotlinking, framing, and inclusion in the structure of the website of works from other websites are different.

Thus, paragraph 46 of the resolution of the Plenum of the Supreme Economic Court of Ukraine, on some issues of dispute resolution related to the protection of intellectual property rights No. 12 from 17 October 2012, states that:

> in itself, the fact of posting on the defendant's website work or object of related rights, identical to the plaintiff's object of intellectual property, indicates the fact of violation of such rights, provided that the potential infringer has not submitted evidence to the court to confirm the legality of his post on the website of the disputed work. *Reproduction of such an object from another site without confirmation of the legality of the use of the work cannot be grounds for release from liability.*[47]

Thus, according to the Supreme Economic Court of Ukraine, the use of hotlinking, framing, and embedding of works in digital form using internet markup tags may refer to the *reproduction* of the work and does not release the person (the website owner) from liability in case of illegal posting of these objects on other websites.

The CJEU used a different approach and addressed the qualification of framing actions in Case C-348/13 *BestWater International*. The Court found that if a

> protected work, freely available on an internet site, is inserted into another internet site by means of a link using the 'framing' technique, such as that used in the case in the main proceedings, [it] cannot be classified as 'communication to the public' since the work at issue is not transmitted to a new public or communicated a specific technical method different from that of the original communication.[48]

The inclusion of works that are publicly available on, for example, YouTube (or another website) in the structure of the website is not a violation of copyright under the same conditions and restrictions as in the case of posting hyperlinks to them.

However, as has already been shown above, these actions are not a reproduction but a communication of a work to the public. Reproduction of the work occurs only

---

[47] Supreme Economic Court of Ukraine, Resolution of the Plenum on some issues of dispute resolution practice related to the protection of intellectual property rights of 17 October 2012 No. 12, para 46 (italicization by author).

[48] ECJ C-348/13 *BestWater International GmbH v. Michael Mebes and Stefan Potsch* (2014) ECLI:EU:C:2014:2315, para 20.

on the website—on the side of the "source"—when a file is recorded on the server and on the end-user's side when viewing or downloading a file. Thus, we believe that the approach of Ukrainian judicial practice should be changed and harmonized with European standards.

5 Non-Jurisdictional Enforcement of Copyright for Works Posted on the Internet

The appropriate level of protection of rights in the event of their violation and bringing the infringer to justice is one of the indicators of the level of development of the legal system in the state. Copyright enforcement is carried out within the appropriate form of enforcement. Forms of copyright enforcement are divided into jurisdictional and non-jurisdictional. With jurisdictional enforcement a person whose copyright has been infringed applies to a court or the competent public authorities. For the enforcement of copyright, judicial enforcement is the most relevant form of jurisdictional enforcement. In these cases jurisdiction and commercial courts hear disputes concerning copyright enforcement in works posted on the internet, and this will continue until the Supreme Court of Intellectual Property has started its work.[49]

However, the jurisdictional enforcement requires time, from the filing a claim or a suit to the entering into force of a state body's decision. The non-jurisdictional form of enforcement provides the rightsholders with the opportunity to react more quickly to the violation (and with fewer costs incurred).

Copyright enforcement for works posted on the internet is characterized by a pre-trial appeal of the copyright holder either directly to the person who infringed copyright or to the relevant intermediary service provider with a statement to stop infringing his copyright and terminating access to the relevant works. Notices of cessation of violations in the United States are called "notice and takedown", and the most well-known of them is the procedure Sec. 512(c)(3) of the Digital Millennium Copyright Act in the USA.

In 2017, Art. 52-1 Ukrainian Law "On Copyright and Related Rights" established the Ukrainian version of the "notice and takedown procedure",[50] namely the Procedure to terminate infringements of copyright and/or related rights using the internet However, this Procedure is far from ideal, as some of its characteristics illustrate:

The Procedure may be applied only to a limited list of objects: audiovisual works, musical works, computer programs, videograms, phonograms, programs of broadcasting organizations. The possibility of filing a claim for termination of infringements concerning other copyright objects, which may also be presented in digital form and posted on the internet, has remained outside the scope of legal regulation.

---

[49] See Anna Shtefan and Olga Gurgula 'The New Intellectual Property Court in Ukraine: Its Creation and Exclusive Jurisdiction' in this Volume.

[50] Ukrainian Law on Copyright and Related Rights 1994, 3792-XII, art 52-1.

The Procedure is applicable only in cases of violation of economic rights. At the same time, with the posting of the object on the internet, personal non-economic rights may also be violated.

Contact with the owner of the website and/or webpage is the right, not the duty of the subject of copyright. This indicates the optional nature of the Procedure application and the absence of restrictions for the person using other methods and techniques that correspond to the essence of the non-jurisdictional form of protection.

Within the Procedure framework, the applicant shall apply for termination of the violation only through the representation of an attorney at law. In this case, the attorney at law must confirm in connection with the applicant's documents that the applicant has the right to terminate the violation of which a claim is made. This wording seems incorrect for several reasons. First, establishing the presence or absence of certain rights of a particular person is the exclusive competence of the court. The attorney at law may conclude that there are grounds to consider the applicant a subject of copyright and/or related rights. However, this conclusion does not give rise to legal consequences and will not bind any third parties. Second, copyright does not require state registration or any other formalities, so the primary subject of copyright and/or related rights may not have any document relating to the creation of the work or otherwise confirm the fact of creation of this object by this person. The application for termination of the infringement should contain only a reasoned statement that the applicant has intellectual property rights to the object of copyright and (or) related rights specified in the application, concerning the grounds for such rights and their validity; there is no requirement for documentary evidence of these facts. However, the Procedure establishes that the attorney at law should send the relevant application only after they have checked the documents provided by the applicant to confirm the fact that the applicant has the right to terminate the violation of which a request is made. This provision conflicts with the principle of automatic protection of the work.

Assuming that the implementation of the Procedure is a right of the person concerned and not an obligation, this in no way limits the possibility of filing claims for termination of copyright and/or related rights without the involvement of an attorney at law for all objects of copyright and related right.

It is seen that the wording regarding the term of copyright in the application needs to be improved. As a general rule, economic copyright rights are valid for the life of the author and 70 years after his or her death. If the applicant is the author, they cannot objectively know the term of the property rights to his works. This also applies to cases where the economic rights to the work have been alienated for the entire period of their legal protection in favour of another person, but the author of the work has not yet died.

The law de facto stipulates that the leading criterion in the application of the Procedure is the availability of posted electronic (digital) information from the territory of Ukraine. The application of the Procedure is not limited by territorial affiliation, which makes it possible to apply for a cessation of the infringement to persons in another jurisdiction, which is generally in line with the European approach. However, if such an approach is justified and effective within the jurisdictional form of protection due to the possibility of applying a web-blocking injunction addressed to providers of intermediate access (with the further theoretical possibility of enforcement of a Ukrainian court decision in a foreign jurisdiction), then within the non-jurisdictional form of protection concerning foreign elements it is possible only to send a statement to terminate the violation without the prospect of applying to them the provisions of the Ukrainian Procedure.

The established obligation of website owners and providers of hosting services without binding to the territory to post information about themselves in free access on their websites and (or) in public databases of records on domain names (WHOIS) is rather declarative. Moreover, from the standpoint of legislative technique, the attribution of this provision to the norm governing the cessation of copyright and/or related rights on the internet is impractical. The obligation of website owners and hosting providers to post information about themselves is not related directly with the implementation by the subject of copyright.

In Art. 52-2(2)(2) Ukrainian Law "On Copyright and Related Rights" stated that the hosting service provider is not liable for infringement of copyright and/or related rights, provided it meets the Procedure requirements for termination of infringement of copyright and/or related rights using the internet. According to Art. 9(4)(3) Law of Ukraine "On E-commerce",

> [a] provider of intermediate services in the information field, which provides permanent storage of information at the request of the recipient of hosting services, is not responsible for the content of transmitted or received information stored at the request of the recipient and for damage as a result of using the results of such services, provided that he has no information about the illegal activity or facts or circumstances indicating that the activity shows signs of illegal activity, or about claims for damages from such illegal activity, and the supplier after receiving such information take swift action to eliminate the possibility of access to or termination of access to information, including following the requirements of copyright and related rights legislation.[51]

Ukraine's legislation does not stipulate that the hosting service provider must obtain that information about illegal activities only within the limits of Art. 52-1 Ukrainian Law "On Copyright and Related Rights". Thus, it is seen that the rules of Art. 52-1(15) and of Art. 52-2(2)(2) Ukrainian Law "On Copyright and Related Rights" may be applied in limited cases.

The application of the Procedure in no way regulates the legal relationship regarding the termination of copyright violation with the use of software applications.

The timeframes for responses provided by the Procedure are unsuitable for LIVE broadcasts that can last only a few hours.

Under the Procedure, web blocking applies exclusively to electronic (digital) information specified in the application for termination of the violation. If access to electronic (digital) information cannot be prevented for technical reasons, the website owner or hosting service provider can prevent access to a webpage containing relevant electronic (digital) information.[52] When applying web blocking, it is necessary to

[51] Ukrainian Law on E-commerce 2015, 675-VIII, art 9(4).

[52] Ukrainian Law on Copyright and Related Rights 1994, 3792-XII, art 52-1(13).

assume that copyright and/or related rights are violated not by the very existence of the webpage but by the posting of a separate object on the internet in digital form. Other objects, the blocking of access to which may violate the rights and interests of third parties, may be lawfully posted on the website at the same time. Therefore, only in cases where access to a work or object of related rights posted without the permission of the relevant entity cannot be prevented for technical reasons (i.e. use of protocol HTTPS) should web-blocking be applied to the webpage as a whole.

In general, the termination of copyright infringements using the internet under the Procedure depends on the conduct of the website (or webpage) owner and the scope of the information about the website owner to the extent that allows him to apply for termination of the infringement and consists of stages, the order and content of which are defined in Art. 52-1 Ukrainian Law "On Copyright and Related Rights".

It should be noted that the implementation of the stages of the Procedure may be quite confusing for the average rightsholder. Given that the use of the Procedure is voluntary, the use of "traditional" cease and desist letters regarding an infringement on the internet in Ukraine is still quite common.

In addition, it is common for websites owners to develop their own simplified local regulations—procedures for dealing with complaints about copyright infringement. For example, such procedures can be found in Google, Facebook, YouTube, OLX, etc. When registering in the listed resources, users join these provisions. After the application of the rightsholder, the representatives of the website consider the specified requirement in specific terms and decide on the removal of the disputable work or rejection of the complaint. Furthermore, the user who posted the disputed work has the opportunity to appeal such a decision".

Thus, we believe that the Ukrainian Procedure requires significant improvement (like adding personal non-economic rights support and applying to all copyrighted works). At the same time, since there is no such procedure within the EU as such, perhaps it is the EU that should take a closer look at the Ukrainian version of the procedure in order to develop uniform rules for EU Member States.

6 Conclusion

Thus, based on a brief overview of the provisions of the Ukrainian legislation in comparison with European standards, the following points have been established.

The posting of work on the internet, depending on the actual scenario of use, may be covered by several economic rights: (a) right of reproduction; (b) right to make the work available; or (c) right to broadcasting of work. At the same time, each scenario of use of the work should be considered individually.

The copyright exhaustion doctrine does not apply to works placed on the internet in Ukraine, regardless of the type of work.

Ukrainian legislation provides a wide list of actions that can be considered as copyright infringement. Not all of them may relate to works posted on the internet, in addition, the wording of some infringements raises questions about the level of legislative technique. In addition, despite such a broad list, the civil legislation of Ukraine does not provide for the specifics of the amount of liability depending on the type of infringement.

Regarding hyperlinking and framing, the current Ukrainian legislation and judicial practice only partially meet European standards. For example, economic criteria, established in *GS Media*, is not acceptable for current Ukrainian copyright law enforcement practice without making appropriate changes to the law. Neither the Civil Code of Ukraine nor Ukrainian Law "On Copyright and Related Rights" (unlike, for example, the Ukrainian Law "On Trademark Protection") recognizes copyright infringement depending on the nature of the use of the work (commercial/non-commercial (except for some specific copyright limitations). Therefore, urgent reflection about the above GS-media approach is required at the legislative level in order to harmonize Ukrainian legislation with EU standards.

The long-awaited establishment of the Procedure for termination of infringement on the internet has improved the situation with the level of copyright protection in Ukraine. However, the Ukrainian procedure requires significant improvements (like adding personal non-economic rights support and applying to all copyrighted works). At the same time, since there is no such procedure within the EU as such, perhaps it is the EU that should take a closer look at the Ukrainian version of the procedure in order to develop uniform unified rules for the EU Members.

References

Justin Koo, *The Right of Communication to the Public in EU Copyright Law* (Hart publishing 2019)

Jaani Riordan, *The Liability of Internet Intermediaries* (Oxford University Press 2016)

Eleonora Rosati, *Copyright and the Court of Justice of the European Union* (Oxford University Press 2019)

Ukrainian Dictionary (1976) Volume 7 [Словник Української Мови (1976) Частина 7]

Kostiantyn Zerov, *Features of Copyright Protection for Works Posted on the Internet* (Interservis 2018) [Костянтин Зеров, *Особливості Захисту Авторських Прав на Твори, Розміщені в Мережі Інтернет* (Інтерсервіс 2018)]

Kostiantyn Zerov and Anna Shtefan, 'Termination of Copyright and Related Rights Infringements on the Internet: a Review of Legislative Novelties' (2017) 3 Theory and Practice of Intellectual Property journal 18 [Зеров Костянтин та Анна Штефан, 'Припинення Порушень Авторського Права і Суміжних Прав у Мережі Інтернет: Огляд Законодавчих Новел' (2017) 3 Теорія і Практика Інтелектуальної Власності 18]

Sergey Zjatyckyj, Konstantyn Leont'ev and Vasiliy Terleckij ' Copyright on the Internet: Three Stages of One Process' (2001) 8 Yntellektualjnaja Sobstvennost 5 [Сергей Зятицкий, Константин Леонтьев, Василий Терлецкий 'Авторское Право в Интернете: Три Стадии Одного Процесса' (2001) 8 Интеллектуальная Собственность 5]

Legal Framework for Output Based on Artificial Intelligence: Ukraine's Place on the Global Search Path

Kateryna Militsyna

Contents

Abstract This chapter outlines the Ukrainian discussion on providing a legal framework for output based on artificial intelligence (AI) with a view to identifying its place and embedding it in the global debate. To this end, the author briefly sets out a common theoretical basis together with practical insights of copyrightability requirements under Ukrainian copyright law and then proceeds to examine output based on AI against them. This assessment reveals the particularities of scholarly approaches to treating such output in Ukraine and other jurisdictions. While the threshold of human involvement sufficient for a work to obtain copyright protection is yet to be clarified, the Ukrainian academic sector generally considers that Ukrainian copyright law does not protect a considerable part of output based on AI. Further, the more sophisticated AI systems in creative industries will become, the more output based on AI will be non-copyrightable. Under these circumstances, Ukrainian scholarly circles have actively embarked on a search for a legal framework for such output.

K. Militsyna (✉)
Private International Law Department of the Educational and Scientific Institute of International Relations, Taras Shevchenko National University of Kyiv, Kyiv, Ukraine
e-mail: mpp.militsyna@clouds.iir.edu.ua

H. Richter (ed.), *Competition and Intellectual Property Law in Ukraine*,
MPI Studies on Intellectual Property and Competition Law 31,
https://doi.org/10.1007/978-3-662-66101-7_22

The chapter offers an overview of ideas put forward in this regard and puts them in an international context. Particular attention is paid to the initiative on introducing a new *sui generis* right for non-original computer-generated objects as the only proposal that has so far made its way to the legislative initiative level. By shedding light on the Ukrainian ideas, the chapter shows the way for future considerations and perspectives.

1 Introduction

Like other countries, Ukraine has been trying in recent years to make itself more attractive for AI-related projects and to support the development of AI systems. In 2019, the Expert Committee on the Development of Artificial Intelligence was set up under the Ministry of Digital Transformation of Ukraine to increase the country's competitiveness in the field of AI.[1] In 2020, the Cabinet of Ministers of Ukraine approved the Concept for the development of artificial intelligence (AI) in Ukraine, declaring the development of AI technologies as one of the priority areas of scientific and technological research.[2] Laws were passed[3] in 2021 to launch Diia.City, which is a unique legal regime for IT businesses.[4] The regime provides special tax conditions for its residents and introduces new concepts (gig contracts and gig specialists) into the Ukrainian legal system. To become a resident of Diia.City, a legal entity must meet certain criteria, among them a requirement for certain activities[5] within the field of IT. They do not explicitly mention the development of AI systems, but the list is broad enough to allow AI-related companies to become residents.[6]

Considering that such actions aim to fuel an *already strong* interest in the field of AI, it comes as no surprise that, like many countries, the development of AI systems has become a trend in Ukraine in recent years. Modern Ukrainian AI-based projects include both established superstars and rising stars. Reface, a face-swapping app that

---

[1] The Expert Committee on the Development of Artificial Intelligence under the Ministry of Digital Transformation of Ukraine http://ai.org.ua/index.html accessed 16 June 2022. The website disclaimer states that it is an unofficial test website that informally covers the work of the Committee.

[2] Decree of the Cabinet of Ministers of Ukraine on the approval of the Concept for the development of artificial intelligence in Ukraine 2020, 1556-p.

[3] Ukrainian Law on Stimulating the Development of the Digital Economy in Ukraine 2021, 1667-IX; Ukrainian Law on Amending the Tax Code of Ukraine and Other Ukrainian Laws to Stimulate the Development of the Digital Economy in Ukraine 2021, 1946-IX.

[4] Diia.City https://city.diia.gov.ua/ accessed 17 June 2022.

[5] Ukrainian Law on Stimulating the Development of the Digital Economy in Ukraine 2021, 1667-IX, art 5.

[6] The following companies related to using, developing and/or promoting AI systems have already become Diia.City residents: Reface, Roosh, Deus Robots, etc. See Diia.City Registry https://city.diia.gov.ua/en/registry/resident accessed 17 June 2022, providing an open and free access registry of Diia.City residents.

uses AI-powered deepfake technology, is one example of a high-profile project.[7] In 2020, the app went viral and entered the App Store and Google Play top charts.[8] Meanwhile, other Ukrainian AI-based start-ups are also gaining momentum. These include Elai.io, a text-to-video platform that allows users to save resources on filming content by turning their texts into customised videos in a few clicks.[9] Harmix serves as another example of a promising Ukrainian project. This platform is designed to select the right music for users' videos.[10] As the chapter examines issues relating to finding a legal framework for output based on AI,[11] these examples cover AI applications in creative industries, but certainly the interest in developing AI systems in Ukraine goes far beyond the creative sector.

Although each of the above projects provides for a different degree of user involvement, it seems that they all share the ambition to enable a user to achieve the desired result in a few clicks. The more successful such AI-powered projects are in pursuing this goal, the less room there remains for human creativity and the more challenges AI systems raise for copyright law. AI systems pose no threat to copyright law if they remain a tool in human hands, so determining the point at which AI becomes no longer a tool and the extent of human involvement sufficient for a work to be eligible for copyright protection is one of the perplexing questions.[12]

The answer depends on the state-of-the-art of AI systems in general as well as on the field of their application and technical aspects of a specific AI system. For the time being, it is generally accepted that modern AI systems remain narrow,[13] i.e. constrained to the tasks they were designed to perform. However, AI systems have diverse fields of application and differ in functioning. Admitting their narrowness is

---

[7] Reface https://hey.reface.ai/ accessed 12 July 2022.

[8] See Natasha Lomas, 'Reface Grabs $5.5 M Seed Led by A16z to Stoke its Viral Face-Swap Video App' *TechCrunch* (8 December 2020) https://tcrn.ch/33QdRAI accessed 12 July 2022.

[9] Elai.io https://elai.io/ accessed 12 July 2022.

[10] Harmix https://www.harmix.ai/ accessed 12 July 2022.

[11] For the purposes of this chapter, output based on AI encompasses both AI-assisted and AI-generated output.

[12] See P Bernt Hugenholtz and João P Quintais, 'Copyright and Artificial Creation: Does EU Copyright Law Protect AI-Assisted Output?' (2021) 52 International Review of Intellectual Property and Competition Law 1190 (1201).

[13] See Katherine B Forrest, 'Copyright Law and Artificial Intelligence: Emerging Issues' in Theodore F Claypoole (ed), *The Law of Artificial Intelligence and Smart Machines: Understanding A.I. and the Legal Impact* (American Bar Association 2019) 347 (352); Nadia Banteka, 'Artificially Intelligent Persons' (2021) 58(3) Houston Law Review 537 (543); Warren E Agin, 'A History of Artificial Intelligence' in Theodore F Claypoole (ed), *The Law of Artificial Intelligence and Smart Machines: Understanding A.I. and the Legal Impact* (American Bar Association 2019) 3(23–24). See also See Anna Shtefan, 'Creativity and Artificial Intelligence: A View from the Perspective of Copyright' (2021) 16(7) Journal of Intellectual Property Law and Practice 720 (727); Kostiantyn Zerov, 'Review of the Theoretical Approaches Regarding the Legal Protection of Objects Generated by Artificial Intelligence Systems in the Field of Copyright and Related Rights' (2021) 6 Theory and Practice of Intellectual Property 25 (26). Regarding state-of-the-art of modern AI systems, Joseph Straus, 'Artificial Intelligence—Challenges and Chances for Europe' (2020) 29(1) European Review 142(143) also recognises their narrowness but at the same time considers that AI is approaching general human-level intelligence.

not enough to establish a single threshold of human guidance required for work-like objects based on AI to receive copyright protection. This makes the issue highly case dependent.[14] Despite the common vision in this respect, scholarly approaches regarding the search for a legal framework for output based on AI differ between Ukraine and other jurisdictions. This, in turn, influences the various initiatives that are put forward as proposals for a regime.

To examine these issues, this chapter is structured as follows. Section 2 provides a common theoretical basis together with practical insights of copyrightability requirements under Ukrainian copyright law. In Sec. 3 we apply them to output based on AI to test whether it is subject to copyright protection. Section 4 offers an overview of ideas discussed in Ukrainian scholarly circles about providing a legal framework for output based on AI. Section 5 analyses draft provisions on a *sui generis* right for non-original computer-generated objects as the only proposal that has so far made its way to the legislative initiative level. Finally, Sec. 6 presents the conclusions.

2 Copyrightability Requirements Under Ukrainian Copyright Law

2.1 *List of Requirements*

Ukrainian copyright law distinguishes between basic and additional requirements for copyright protection. While compliance with the additional requirements broadens the scope of protection, meeting the basic requirements determines the eligibility of a work for copyright protection.[15] The latter criteria include originality and fixation requirements, referred to in Ukrainian copyright law as "creative efforts" and "objective form of expression" respectively. It is generally accepted that Ukrainian copyright law does not impose any other conditions for protection.[16] However, since Ukrainian copyright law provides for an explicit definition of "author" that must be satisfied for a work to qualify for copyright protection, this leads the author of the chapter to infer that there is another condition—the requirement of "authorship".

Hence, Ukrainian copyright law establishes three basic requirements for copyright protection: (i) authorship, (ii) originality, and (iii) fixation. Except where the law provides otherwise, these criteria are cumulative. Below we will briefly outline them

[14] See Josef Drexl et al., 'Artificial Intelligence and Intellectual Property Law—Position Statement of the Max Planck Institute for Innovation and Competition of 9 April 2021 on the Current Debate', (2021) No. 21–10 Max Planck Institute for Innovation and Competition, para III (21).

[15] See Olena Shtefan, 'The Concept of the Object of Copyright and the Criteria for its Protection' (2006) 6 Theory and Practice of Intellectual Property 3 (3–4).

[16] See Anna Shtefan, *Copyright and Related Rights: Peculiarities of Legal Protection, Enforcement and Defence* (Intellectual Property Research Institute of National Academy of Law Sciences of Ukraine, Ltd. NVP Interservice 2017) 11–12.

in Ukrainian copyright law, which will allow us to shed light on the question of the copyrightability of output based on AI under Ukrainian law.

2.2 Authorship

According to the Ukrainian Law "On Copyright and Related Rights", an author is an individual who created a work with his creative efforts.[17] From this we can conclude that, first, an author endows a work with own creativity, and second, an author is equated with a human being. There is also a presumption of authorship under which, unless proven otherwise, the person indicated as the author on the original or a copy of the work shall be deemed the author.[18]

The EU–Ukraine Association Agreement (AA), which is part of Ukrainian legislation,[19] might present in its Arts. 181 and 187 on computer programmes and databases an exception to the rule that the author is always a human being. This is not clear, due to the terminological differences between the texts of these articles in Ukrainian and in the EU languages the AA has been authenticated in.

The texts of Arts. 181(1) and 187(1) EU–Ukraine AA in all languages, except Ukrainian, refer to the authorship of computer programmes and databases respectively. The articles allow a legal person designated as the right holder by legislation to be an author, where the legislation of the Parties to the AA so permits.[20]

However, the Ukrainian text of these articles employs the term "subject" instead of "author".[21] While both terms exist in Ukrainian copyright law, they differ in scope. Subjects of copyright law include authors of works as well as other natural and legal persons who have acquired the rights under law or transaction.[22] Ukrainian copyright law makes a distinction between primary and secondary subjects in this respect. The author is the primary subject of copyright law, and the other persons listed in the

[17] Ukrainian Law on Copyright and Related Rights 1994, 3792-XII, srt 1(1)(1). As the law does not have an official English version of its text, the author wishes to note that she is using its English translation from the Database "Laws of Ukraine" in this chapter.

[18] Civil Code of Ukraine, art 435(1); Ukrainian Law on Copyright and Related Rights 1994, 3792-XII, art 11(1)(2). See also Anna Shtefan, 'Copyright and Its Exceptions and Limitations in Ukraine' in this Volume.

[19] Olha Kronda, 'Application of the Association Agreement between Ukraine and the European Union in the Field of Intellectual Property' (2018) 53 Uzhhorod National University Herald. Series: Law 105(106–107).

[20] EU–Ukraine AA, arts 181, 187. See the authentic texts of the EU–Ukraine AA in all languages except Ukrainian.

[21] EU–Ukraine AA, arts 181, 187. See the authentic text of the EU–Ukraine AA in Ukrainian.

[22] Ukrainian Law on Copyright and Related Rights 1994, 3792-XII, art 7. In this case the author deviates from the translation of the law available at the Database "Laws of Ukraine" and provides her own to make the translation closer to the original text of the article. One further note should be taken of the fact that the law's translation from the Database "Laws of Ukraine" uses the term "copyright holders" for subjects of copyright law. While this term is not a direct translation, it may better convey the meaning of the subject to a reader.

law are secondary ones.[23] This leads us to conclude that the concept of "subject" is broader than the concept of "author", meaning every author is a subject, but not every subject is an author.

The terminological dilemma stemming from the translation is complicated by the fact that the EU–Ukraine AA has no prevailing language clause, each text being equally authentic.[24] Accordingly, the question arises as to how such a dispute over the text of the EU–Ukraine AA in different languages will be resolved if it occurs.

As Ukraine is a party to the Vienna Convention on the Law of Treaties (Vienna Convention), Part III Sec. 3 Vienna Convention serves to assist in resolving such cases. Moreover, Ukrainian judicial practice has confirmed that where there is a conflict between equally authentic texts of an international treaty, the relevant provisions of the Vienna Convention shall apply.[25]

It follows from Art. 1 EU–Ukraine AA that one of its aims is to promote gradual rapprochement between the Parties.[26] It is also important to consider this provision together with the Preamble of the EU–Ukraine AA, where one of its paragraphs makes the political association and economic integration of Ukraine with the European Union dependent on progress in achieving convergence with the EU in political, economic and legal areas.[27] In the author's opinion, these provisions, together with the other ones that are essential in determining the object and purpose of the EU–Ukraine AA, can be used to interpret its provisions in a manner prescribed by the Vienna Convention.[28] Based on this rapprochement objective and given that Arts. 181(1) and 187(1) EU–Ukraine AA "stem" from Art. 2(1) Computer Programs Directive[29] and Art. 4(1) Database Directive[30] accordingly, it seems quite logical that if a dispute over the terms "author" or "subject" materialise, the choice ought to be made in favour of the "author".

However, the resolution of this terminological dilemma is not so clear from a judicial practice perspective. This is due to the rule earlier articulated by Ukrainian judicial practice according to which if there is an officially published text of a treaty in Ukrainian language, the courts are obliged to use this text.[31]

---

[23] Civil Code of Ukraine, art 435; Ukrainian Law on Copyright and Related Rights 1994, 3792-XII, art 11(1).

[24] EU–Ukraine AA, art 485.

[25] Resolution of the Plenum of the High Specialized Court of Ukraine for Civil and Criminal Cases on the application of treaties of Ukraine by the courts in the administration of justice 2014, v0013740-14, para 6.

[26] EU–Ukraine AA, art 1(2)(a).

[27] EU–Ukraine AA, preamble.

[28] Vienna Convention on the Law of Treaties, arts 31–33.

[29] Parliament and Council Directive 2009/24/EC of 23 April 2009 on the legal protection of computer programs (2009) OJ L111/16 (Computer Programs Directive), art 2(1).

[30] Parliament and Council Directive 96/9/EC of 11 March 1996 on the legal protection of databases (1996) OJ L77/20 (Database Directive), art 4(1).

[31] Resolution of the Plenum of the High Specialized Court of Ukraine for Civil and Criminal Cases on the application of treaties of Ukraine by the courts in the administration of justice 2014, v0013740-14, para 6. Although the above rule is not enshrined in legislation and is derived from a

Moreover, the question of differences in the text of the EU–Ukraine AA in different languages has ceased to be of mere theoretical interest, since it has already been raised in *Zentiva*, the landmark judgment on the direct effect of the EU–Ukraine AA provisions. Referring briefly to the issue of differences in the English version of the EU–Ukraine AA, the Commercial Cassation Court of the Supreme Court backed the decision to use the official text of the EU–Ukraine AA in Ukrainian.[32]

It is also worth noting that under Ukrainian law there is a procedure for correcting such translation errors,[33] but, unfortunately, its flaws cast great doubt on its viability.[34]

The above circumstances make it difficult to provide an unequivocal prediction as to how the terminological dilemma around "subject" and "author" will be resolved, should such a dispute arise. In any case, since Ukrainian copyright law itself puts an equal sign between an author and a human being, this problem concerns only the recognition of author's copyright status acquired under the legislation of a Party to the AA.

2.3 *Originality*

Except for certain works,[35] Ukrainian copyright law does not explicitly provide for originality as a requirement for copyright protection. Nevertheless, such a requirement does exist.[36] This conclusion is mainly based on the definition of "author" already referred to in the chapter. It appears from the definition that the work must be the result of the author's *creative efforts*[37] which leads to considering such efforts as a general criterion for all works to qualify for copyright protection. While there

source of judicial practice that was applicable prior to the judicial reform which became effective at the end of 2017, Ukrainian courts tend to continue following this rule. See Anna Shtefan, 'Some Issues of Application of the Association Agreement as the Source of Copyright of Ukraine' (2019) 1 Theory and Practice of Intellectual Property 5 (9–10) writing about this rule in more detail. For an alternative view, see Anastasiia Kyrylenko, 'Direct Effect in Ukraine of IPR Provisions from the EU–Ukraine Free Trade Agreement: A Principled Approach to the *Zentiva* case' (2019) 14(9) Journal of Intellectual Property Law and Practice 716 (720), who, in addressing the direct effect of treaties in Ukraine, adds that the Resolution in question, which sets out the respective rules, is no longer considered as relevant to a commercial lawsuit by the Commercial Chamber of the Supreme Court.

[32] Ukrainian Commercial Court of Cassation of the Supreme Court 75,399,206 (2018) 910/14972/17.

[33] Resolution of the Cabinet of Ministers of Ukraine on the approval of the procedure of the official translation of multilateral international treaties of Ukraine into Ukrainian 2006, 353.

[34] See Shtefan, 'Some Issues of Application of the Association Agreement as the Source of Copyright of Ukraine' (n 31) 5 (12–13).

[35] Ukrainian Law on Copyright and Related Rights 1994, 3792-XII, arts 9, 10(1)(e).

[36] See Liubov Maidanyk, 'The Concept of Originality of the Work in Copyright Law: Experience of the EU, Ukraine and Other Foreign Countries' (2018) 10 Entrepreneurship, Economy and Law 32 (32).

[37] Ukrainian Law on Copyright and Related Rights 1994, 3792-XII, art 1(1)(1).

is a lack of clarity on the relationship between "originality" and "creative efforts" and their meaning,[38] Ukrainian judicial practice often equates these concepts.[39] We will use the general term "originality" throughout this chapter, but with the caveat that the wording and essence of this criterion in Ukrainian copyright law is subject to debate.[40]

Draft laws that have been submitted as part of the ongoing copyright reform also address this issue. Despite different approaches, four out of five draft laws propose to expressly indicate originality as a requirement for all works.[41] Of all the legislative proposals, Draft Laws 5552-1 and 5552-4 are the most "demanding" on this point. They provide a definition of originality requiring a work to be the result of an author's own intellectual creation, as well as to reflect the creative choices made by the author at the time of its creation.[42]

Although traditionally Ukraine belongs to civil law countries,[43] it is quite common to seek answers to emerging issues in judicial practice which plays a significant role in filling legal gaps.[44] In the case of the originality requirement, Ukrainian judicial practice is comparatively limited and gives little guidance on its interpretation. The reason the judicial practice is not extensive in this regard may lie in the following

---

[38] The uncertainty comes, among other things, from the use of the term "originality" in relation to certain works and the term "creative efforts" in the definition of an author.

[39] See Ilarion Tomarov, 'Presumption of Works' Originality: is There a Need for It or Not?' *LegalShift* (22 March 2019) http://www.legalshift.com.ua/?p=1332 accessed 17 June 2022.

[40] Ibid, arguing that "creative efforts" standard is concerned with evaluating the creativity of the process (the author's efforts and probably intentions), while "originality" standard is aimed at evaluating the creativity of the result. By asking whether the author's intentions matter if the result is original, and, conversely, whether the efforts matter if the result is non-original, he makes his view clear that originality is a characteristic of a work and not process. See also Shtefan, 'Creativity and Artificial Intelligence' (n 13) 720 (721) who, in considering creativity in copyright law as a symbiosis of process and result, writes that the focus is still on the result. From a broader perspective, this discussion constitutes part of a global theoretical debate about subjective and objective standards of originality. See the outline of international debate in Tianxiang He, 'The Sentimental Fools and the Fictitious Authors: Rethinking the Copyright Issues of AI-Generated Contents in China' (2019) 27(2) Asia Pacific Law Review 218 (222–224).

[41] Ukrainian Draft Law on Copyright and Related Rights 2021, 5552; Ukrainian Draft Law on Copyright and Related Rights 2021, 5552-1; Ukrainian Draft Law on Copyright and Related Rights 2021, 5552-2; Ukrainian Draft Law on Copyright and Related Rights 2021, 5552-4.

[42] Ukrainian Draft Law on Copyright and Related Rights 2021, 5552-1, art 1(1)(41); Ukrainian Draft Law on Copyright and Related Rights 2021, 5552-1, art 1(1)(30).

[43] The drafters were inspired by the studies of Friedrich Carl von Savigny in developing the modern Civil Code of Ukraine which took the pandect (or German) system as the basis of its structure. See Anatolii Dovgert, 'The Doctrine of Private International Law in Ukraine at the Turn of the Century' (2020) 6 Law of Ukraine 13 (33–34).

[44] While judicial practice of the courts of first and appellate instances may be illustrative for understanding the prospects of a case at the relevant stages, judicial practice derived from the conclusions on the application of legal norms set forth in rulings of the Supreme Court is of the most importance. This is due to the legislative provisions according to which such conclusions shall be taken into account by other courts when applying such legal norms as well as shall be binding on all power holders which apply in their activities a regulatory act containing the relevant legal norm. See Ukrainian Law on the Judiciary and the Status of Judges 2016, 1402-VIII, art 13(5), (6).

factors. Firstly, by invoking the lack of the special knowledge required to establish whether a work is original or not, Ukrainian courts tend to "delegate" this issue and rely on forensic examinations and expert studies in this regard.[45] Under such circumstances, the court's role shifts from interpreting the requirement of originality and assessing whether the work fulfils it, to evaluating the expert conclusion as evidence in the case. Secondly, there is a presumption of originality in Ukrainian copyright law and the result of the intellectual activity shall be deemed to have been performed with creative efforts until proven otherwise.[46] This means that the burden of proof shifts to the person who wishes to challenge the originality of the work and, consequently, its copyright eligibility. Since Ukrainian courts are inclined to appoint forensic examinations in such cases, this makes the litigation process even more time-consuming, costly, and thus effectively inaccessible to those who may have claims. As a result many disputes are not taken to court.

Therefore, while the "creative efforts" standard with its implied emphasis on the process can be seen as an attempt to establish a high threshold of originality, the existing presumption of originality largely negates its relevance, making such a threshold in fact very low. Only those disputes that make it to a court have a chance of applying the high standard which is also conditioned upon the expert conclusion. All these factors, coupled with the presumption of authorship and the procedure of copyright registration in Ukraine—which only involves reviewing an application against formal criteria—contribute to abusive behaviour in enforcing copyrights.[47]

2.4 *Fixation*

An objective form of expression is mentioned in Art. 3 Ukrainian Law "On Copyright and Related Rights". Since Art. 3 establishes the scope of the law and refers to the works covered by it,[48] its interpretation leads us to conclude that fixation constitutes

[45] See Maidanyk, 'The Concept of Originality of the Work in Copyright Law' (n 36) 32 (33).

[46] Resolution of the Plenum of the Supreme Commercial Court of Ukraine on some issues of dispute resolution practice related to the protection of intellectual property rights 2012, v0012600-12, para 25; Resolution of the Supreme Court of Ukraine on the application of the legislation on copyright and related rights by the courts 2010, v0005700-10, para 18.

[47] Although there is no requirement for copyright registration, the registration procedure is quite popular among those wishing to abuse the rights and those wishing to protect themselves against such abuses in the future, because the registration gives a person an evidentiary advantage in the event of a legal dispute. See Oleksandra Javorska, 'Presumption of Creative Nature of the Work, Resulted in the Object of Intellectual Property Law: Theory and Practice of Application' (2017) 23 Časopis civìlìstiki 78 (79). See also Anna Shtefan, 'Copyright and Its Exceptions and Limitations in Ukraine' in this Volume briefly describing how the presumption of originality serves as a source of a lot of abuse.

[48] Ukrainian Law on Copyright and Related Rights 1994, 3792-XII, art 3.

a copyrightability requirement. However, the law does not elaborate on its essence.[49] It is generally acknowledged in Ukrainian academic circles that the objective form of expression requires a work to be real and exist independently of the author's consciousness so that it can be perceivable to the senses.[50] The question whether Ukrainian copyright law limits the senses by which works can be perceived remains unclear. Analysis of the list of works stated in Ukrainian Law "On Copyright and Related Rights"[51] suggests that the senses are limited to sight and hearing, but judicial practice has neither confirmed nor refuted this assumption.[52]

3 Copyrightability of Output Based on AI

Human-created works and output based on AI share the form of expression,[53] which often makes it difficult to distinguish one from the other in the absence of information on involvement of AI systems and object's origin.[54] Therefore, the fixation requirement generally poses no obstacle to copyrightability of output based on AI. Yet where output based on AI is assessed against originality and authorship requirements, the answer is less straightforward.

If output based on AI is examined against the originality requirement under Ukrainian copyright law, then, based on the existing presumption of originality, it will meet the said criterion by default. The compliance with this requirement may be challenged in court. Under these circumstances, the party disputing this fact will bear the burden of proof. As mentioned earlier, in such cases Ukrainian courts usually appoint forensic examinations, which makes the matter case- and even expert-dependent. As a general rule, an expert will be asked whether the object under examination is the result of creative efforts according to the information provided in the case file.[55] It is important that (a) the assessment of creative efforts takes into account whether the work reflects the author's personality, and (b) an author, in turn, is equated with

---

[49] See Liubov Maidanyk, 'Notion and Boundaries of Objective Form of Expression of a Work: Analyze of European and Ukrainian Approaches' (2019) 1 Theory and Practice of Intellectual Property 94 (94).

[50] See Shtefan (n 16) 12, 46.

[51] Ukrainian Law on Copyright and Related Rights 1994, 3792-XII, art 8.

[52] See Maidanyk, 'Notion and Boundaries of Objective Form of Expression of a Work' (n 49) 94 (95).

[53] See Shtefan, 'Creativity and Artificial Intelligence' (n 13) 720 (720).

[54] See Stefan Scheuerer, 'Artificial Intelligence and Unfair Competition—Unveiling an Underestimated Building Block of the AI Regulation Landscape' (2021) 70(9) GRUR International 834 (837).

[55] Scientific and methodological recommendations on the preparation and appointment of forensic examinations and expert studies approved by the Order of the Ministry of Justice of Ukraine 1998, 53/5, para 5.5.

a human being.[56] The latter conforms to Ukrainian copyright legislation—namely the definition of author—and confirms the interdependence of authorship and originality requirements. Therefore, the answer to whether output based on AI meets these criteria lies in assessing the *choices* made by a *human being in the course of the creative work.*

Based on this, purely AI-generated output is excluded from copyright protection, and eligibility of AI-assisted output depends on a particular case. Whereas scholarly approaches in Ukraine and other jurisdictions have generally followed the same path up to this moment—agreeing that creativity is the sole domain of humans, and that copyright is anthropocentric by its nature[57]—the way they treat AI-assisted and AI-generated output is probably the point where, mapping out the road ahead, the differences begin to emerge.

Being more cautious and aimed recently at deromanticising and demystifying modern AI systems,[58] particularly in creative industries,[59] leading foreign studies find no evidence of fully AI-generated output today.[60] By contrast, in the search for a legal framework, the doctrine in Ukraine seems to propose a broader interpretation of AI-*generated* output. While acknowledging that AI systems are still determined by humans, it does not exclude the existence of AI-generated output[61] and even refers to it in a wider context as the output generated by a computer programme with no

[56] See Grygorii Prokhorov-Lukin, 'Forensics: The Concept and Types of Intellectual Property' (2016) 6 Theory and Practice of Intellectual Property 17 (20–21).

[57] See Jane C Ginsburg, 'People Not Machines: Authorship and What It Means in the Berne Convention' (2018) 49 International Review of Intellectual Property and Competition Law 131; Hugenholtz and Quintais, 'Copyright and Artificial Creation' (n 12) 1190 (1195); Sam Ricketson, 'The 1992 Horace S. Manges Lecture—People or Machines: The Bern Convention and the Changing Concept of Authorship' (1991–1992) 16 Columbia-VLA Journal of Law & the art 1 (8, 10–11); Sean D Kelly, 'What Computers Can't Create: Why Creativity is, and Always Will Be, a Human Endeavor' *Technology Review, Inc.* (1 March 2019) https://www.thefreelibrary.com/What+computers+can%27t+create%3a+Why+creativity+is%2c+and+always+will+be%2c+a...-a0578441401 accessed 7 July 2022. See also Maidanyk, 'The Concept of Originality of the Work in Copyright Law' (n 36) 32 (35); Shtefan, 'Creativity and Artificial Intelligence' (n 13) 720(726); Zerov, 'Review of the Theoretical Approaches Regarding the Legal Protection of Objects Generated by Artificial Intelligence Systems in the Field of Copyright and Related Rights' (n 13) 25 (28).

[58] See Josef Drexl et al., 'Technical Aspects of Artificial Intelligence: An Understanding from an Intellectual Property Law Perspective', (2019) No. 19–13 Max Planck Institute for Innovation and Competition, Q6–Q9, providing an overview of AI with a special focus on machine learning and arriving at the conclusion that machine learning models are not autonomous. See also Eliza Mik, 'AI as a Legal Person' in Jyh-An Lee et al. (eds), *Artificial Intelligence and Intellectual Property* (Oxford University Press 2021) 419 (423–426) treating autonomy in technical context as an advanced form of automation.

[59] See James Grimmelmannn, 'There's No Such Thing as a Computer-Authored Work—And It's a Good Thing, Too' (2016) 39 Columbia Journal of Law & the arts 403 (407) arguing that computers have influenced the speed of operations making "some kinds of creativity practically *feasible*, but they do not make anything newly *possible*".

[60] See Drexl and others, 'Artificial Intelligence and Intellectual Property Law' (n 14), para III(21); Hugenholtz and Quintais, 'Copyright and Artificial Creation' (n 12) 1190 (1201).

[61] See Shtefan, 'Creativity and Artificial Intelligence' (n 13) 720 (727–728).

(direct) influence of human creativity.[62] It may be due to the fact that such actions as pressing the "generate in style" button or setting parameters for further autonomous work tend not to be considered "free creative choices" of an end user.[63] This leads us to conclude that it is the quality rather than the quantity of human contribution that matters. Consequently, it is very likely that such an object would be considered AI-*generated* under the Ukrainian approach even if there is human involvement, but it is not creative. The question regarding what counts as a creative contribution, remains open. However, examining various examples of AI-based applications, namely those where the process of generating objects is reduced to a few clicks, Ukrainian scholars generally treat AI-assisted (where AI is no longer a mere tool) and AI-generated output as non-copyrightable.[64]

Based on this as well as out of concern that the lack of copyright protection will lead to abuses, particularly to the concealment of AI involvement in generating output and the abuse of existing copyright presumptions of authorship and originality,[65] Ukrainian legal scholarship is searching for a regime that will adequately meet these challenges.

4 Overview of Ukrainian Scholarly Endeavours to Find a Legal Framework for Output Based on AI as Part of a Global Search

Having reached the conclusion that a considerable part of the output based on AI is not eligible for copyright protection under current law, Ukrainian scholarly circles have actively embarked on a search for a legal framework for such output. In his article, Zerov brings up the following factors against keeping the output based on AI in the public domain: (a) the absence of a human creator does not preclude providing IP protection in general; (b) social relations around the output have already emerged; (c) AI- and human-based output may have identical or similar social value,[66] which

[62] See Zerov, 'Review of the Theoretical Approaches Regarding the Legal Protection of Objects Generated by Artificial Intelligence Systems in the Field of Copyright and Related Rights' (n 13) 25 (28).

[63] Ibid 29.

[64] See Shtefan, 'Creativity and Artificial Intelligence' (n 13) 720 (727–728); Zerov, 'Review of the Theoretical Approaches Regarding the Legal Protection of Objects Generated by Artificial Intelligence Systems in the Field of Copyright and Related Rights' (n 13) 25 (29–30).

[65] See Zerov, 'Review of the Theoretical Approaches Regarding the Legal Protection of Objects Generated by Artificial Intelligence Systems in the Field of Copyright and Related Rights' (n 13) 25 (30).

[66] For an alternative view, see Kelly, *Technology Review, Inc.* (n 57) accessed 7 July 2022; Martin Senftleben, 'A Tax on Machines for the Purpose of Giving a Bounty to the Dethroned Human Author—Towards an AI Levy for the Substitution of Human Literary and Artistic Works' *SSRN*. See also Shtefan, 'Creativity and Artificial Intelligence' (n 13) 720 (720) arguing that these types of output cannot be equated with each other.

makes the decision to freely circulate the former and to grant protection to the latter somewhat arbitrary; and (d) creating even narrow AI systems requires large investments. He also cautions that providing a legal framework for the output based on AI should not hinder human creativity, and AI systems should not become a tool for the abuse of the law with its capability to generate all possible options within the set parameters.[67] This, in turn, has set the tone for the Ukrainian debate which has focused mainly on the type of protection that *can* be provided to the output based on AI, rather than on the question whether such output *should* receive protection. Thus, the ideas that are covered in Ukrainian academic circles can generally be divided into the ones that remain within IP law and those that fall outside its scope. We will start with the former group.

Ukrainian doctrine is generally unanimous in saying that the search for a legal regime should not result in undermining fundamental concepts of copyright law, which implies preserving its anthropocentric nature.[68] This may be the reason why Ukrainian doctrine covers the ideas of the computer-generated works regime under the Copyright, Designs and Patents Act 1998 in the UK[69] and the work-for-hire doctrine reinterpretation in the US,[70] but gives them more theoretical significance and doubts whether they can be an adequate solution for Ukrainian copyright law.

Contrary to the previous ideas, Ukrainian doctrine seems to be more receptive to the initiative of extending related rights to cover the output based on AI.[71] However, at present, this idea has hardly been further developed. Among all the deliberations

---

[67] See Zerov, 'Review of the Theoretical Approaches Regarding the Legal Protection of Objects Generated by Artificial Intelligence Systems in the Field of Copyright and Related Rights' (n 13) 25 (28–29). By referring to the capability of AI systems to generate all possible options within the set parameters, Zerov is likely referring to the example given by Jesus M N Zatarain, 'The Role of Automated Technology in the Creation of Copyright Works: The Challenges of Artificial Intelligence' (2017) 31(1) International Review of Law, Computers and Technology 91 (91–93). Zatarian provides the example of Qentis, a company which has generated and deployed 97.42% of all possible texts of ten to four hundred words in length.

[68] See Ibid 29–30; Maidanyk, 'The Concept of Originality of the Work in Copyright Law' (n 36) 32 (35).

[69] For the debate on the regime, see Andres Guadamuz, 'Comparative Analysis of Originality in Artificial Intelligence Generated Works' in Jyh-An Lee et al. (eds), *Artificial Intelligence and Intellectual Property* (Oxford University Press 2021) 147; Jani McCutcheon, 'The Vanishing Author in Computer-Generated Works: A Critical Analysis of Recent Australian Case Law' (2013) 36 Melbourne University Law Review 915; Jani McCutcheon, 'Curing the Authorless Void: Protecting Computer-Generated Works Following IceTV and Phone Directories' (2013) 37 Melbourne University Law Review 46; Jyh-An Lee, 'Computer-generated Works Under the CDPA 1988' in Jyh-An Lee et al. (eds), *Artificial Intelligence and Intellectual Property* (Oxford University Press 2021) 177.

[70] See Kalin Hristov, 'Artificial Intelligence and the Copyright Dilemma' (2017) 57(3) IDEA: The IP Law Review 431; Shlomit Yanisky-Ravid, 'Generating Rembrandt: Artificial Intelligence, Copyright, and Accountability in the 3A Era—The Human-Like Authors Are Already Here—A New Model' (2017) 2017 Michigan State Law Review 659.

[71] See Zerov, 'Review of the Theoretical Approaches Regarding the Legal Protection of Objects Generated by Artificial Intelligence Systems in the Field of Copyright and Related Rights' (n 13) 25 (31). See also Yuriy Kapitsa, 'Texts, Music, Images, That are Generated by Artificial Intelligence: Towards Defining a Model of Legal Protection' (2021) 36 Information and Law 45 (51).

on the IP regime for the output based on AI, the idea of introducing a new *sui generis* right has appeared to be the most popular. As it is the only option that has so far made its way to the legislative initiative level, it will be the subject of closer scrutiny in Sec. 5.

Before turning to this, we will shortly outline the ideas that go beyond copyright and IP law.

In particular, the question of AI systems' status in civil legal relations in general has gained prominence in Ukrainian academic publications in recent years, bringing up the issue of their legal personhood which, among other things, can influence the authorship requirement. Summarising existing approaches in this respect, Stefanchuk and others have identified three perspectives of treating AI in civil legal relations which are as follows: (a) AI exclusively as an object; (b) AI exclusively as a subject; and (c) the differentiated determination of AI status, according to which AI can be both a subject and an object depending on its classification, primarily conditioned on technical capabilities.[72] The practical significance of the debate around AI status in civil legal relations is enhanced by the fact that, as of 2019,[73] Ukraine has been in the process of recodifying its civil legislation.[74] Guided by the Concept of Updating the Civil Code of Ukraine presented by the Working group in 2020, one might notice that endowing AI systems with legal personhood is not currently on the agenda. On the contrary, the Concept proposes to expand the list of objects of civil rights to include AI.[75] This is indicative of adherence to the first approach, according to which AI systems are regarded exclusively as objects of civil legal relations.

Given that Ukrainian law defines information as an object of civil rights, Ukrainian doctrine also considers it possible to extend the right to information to the output based on AI, yet it disagrees on how exactly this should be done. On the one hand, there is an idea to treat the output as non-copyrightable material and to extend the publicly available information regime to it.[76] On the other hand, there is a proposal to devise special rules on the term of protection, economic rights, etc. under the right to information.[77]

There are other ideas falling beyond IP law on the regime for output based on AI, which have been raised in the doctrine of other jurisdictions but have not yet been

[72] See Mykola Stefanchuk et al., 'Prospects of Legal Regulation of Relations in the Field of Artificial Intelligence Use' (2021) 28(1) Journal of the National Academy of Legal Sciences of Ukraine 157 (164).

[73] Resolution of the Cabinet of Ministers of Ukraine on the establishment of the Working group on recodifying (updating) Ukrainian civil legislation 2019, 650.

[74] See Anatolii Dovgert et al., 'Codification of Civil Legislation: At the Turn of the Era' (2021) 10 Global Journal of Comparative Law 16 (22–27).

[75] Working Group on Recodifying (Updating) Ukrainian Civil Legislation, 'Concept of Updating the Civil Code of Ukraine' ArtEk 2020, book 1(III) (1.12) 2020.

[76] See Mariia Dubniak, 'Problems in Determining the Legal Regime for Objects Generated Using Neural Network Technologies' (2019) 31 Information and Law 45 (51–52).

[77] See Kapitsa, 'Texts, Music, Images, That are Generated by Artificial Intelligence' (n 71) 45 (52).

widely covered in Ukraine's. They lie within the realm of tax law[78] and unfair competition law,[79] and they might be of interest to Ukraine with respect to its aspiration to provide the legal framework for the output.

In the author's view, the Ukrainian legal system may also benefit if its debate takes a step back and questions again whether the output based on AI *should* receive protection. It seems that recently we have started to take a more realistic view of the issues surrounding the use of AI systems in creative industries. This has shifted the focus from incentivising their development to disincentivising concealment of AI involvement. If we take a closer look at the economic[80] and technical aspects of AI systems, the approach to seeking a regime may change even more.

5 Ukrainian Legislative Proposal of Introducing a New "*Sui Generis* Right for Non-Original Computer-Generated Objects"

5.1 Outline of Context and Main Provisions

Ukrainian IP law has been undergoing a complex legislative reform processes over the past years. The Association Agreement has proved to be one of the driving forces behind the legislative changes. Though it lacks provisions on general commitments for Ukraine to approximate its legislation with the EU IP *acquis*,[81] Ukraine's favourable and welcoming attitude towards the EU IP *acquis* has contributed to the country's proactive role in this regard.[82] In addition to the approximation objective set for carrying out the reforms,[83] this is best exemplified by the fact that implementation of the EU IP *acquis* is among the priorities established by the Ukrainian government.[84]

---

[78] See Senftleben, 'A Tax on Machines for the Purpose of Giving a Bounty to the Dethroned Human Author—Towards an AI Levy for the Substitution of Human Literary and Artistic Works' (n 66).

[79] See Scheuerer, 'Artificial Intelligence and Unfair Competition' (n 54) 834 (844).

[80] See Jan Smits and Tijn Borghuis, 'Generative AI and Intellectual Property Rights' in Bart Custers and Eduard Fosch-Villaronga (eds), *Law and Artificial Intelligence* (T.M.C. Asser Press, 2022) 323(336–337) supposing that "there is no clear economic rationale for granting copyright or related rights protection to AI outputs".

[81] See Yuriy Kapitsa, Association Agreements and Problems Approximating Intellectual Property Legislation of Third Countries with the EU Acquis: The Case of Ukraine' in this Volume.

[82] See Anastasiia Kyrylenko, 'The Reformed Design Law in Ukraine: What is Right with EU Trade Agreements?' in this Volume.

[83] See Anastasiia Kyrylenko, 'The Reformed Design Law in Ukraine: What is Right with EU Trade Agreements?' and Yuriy Kapitsa, 'Association Agreements and Problems Approximating Intellectual Property Legislation of Third Countries with the EU Acquis: The Case of Ukraine' in this Volume.

[84] Decree of the Cabinet of Ministers of Ukraine on the approval of the conceptual foundation for reforming the state system of intellectual property protection of Ukraine 2016, 402-p.

The copyright law reform process continues. In 2021, five draft laws were submitted, the examination of which led to the conclusion that they all needed to be amended and merged into one comprehensive document—which did not happen.[85] Apart from pursuing the objective of modernising existing Ukrainian copyright law and approximating it with the EU *acquis*, three out of five draft laws propose to introduce a brand new "*sui generis* right for non-original computer-generated objects" (CGOs).[86] Albeit with certain differences,[87] all three draft laws converge on the basics of such a *sui generis* right. Since on 1 July 2022 the Ukrainian parliament approved the Draft Law "On Copyright and Related Rights" 5552-1 (Principal Draft Law) *as a basis*,[88] and it is very likely that the Principal Draft Law will be adopted soon, the analysis of the proposed *sui generis* right will be primarily based on it.

The drafters' idea is to include provisions on the *sui generis* right in Art. 35 Ukrainian Law "On Copyright and Related Rights". The Article defines a non-original CGO as the one that differs from the existing similar objects[89] and is created by the functioning of computer programme(s) without the direct involvement of an individual in its creation. Article 35 explicitly excludes works created by individuals *using* computer technologies from its scope. It also makes clear that the *sui generis* rights with respect to CGOs are economic rights and that no moral rights apply to CGOs. The scope of economic rights under the *sui generis* right in question is determined by economic rights under copyright law. Such economic rights can be both licensed and assigned. The *sui generis* right is subject to the exhaustive list of exceptions that apply in case of copyright. Subjects (holders) of the right are the persons who own the economic rights or who have the licensing rights to a computer programme by which the object was generated. These can be authors of a computer programme, their heirs, persons to whom economic rights to a computer programme have been assigned, or legitimate users of a computer programme. Similar to copyright law, the Principal Draft Law provides that the *sui generis* right arises automatically when a non-original CGO is generated. The proposed term of protection is 25 years.[90]

---

[85] See Anna Shtefan, 'Copyright and Its Exceptions and Limitations in Ukraine' in this Volume.

[86] Ukrainian Draft Law on Copyright and Related Rights 2021, 5552-1; Ukrainian Draft Law on Copyright and Related Rights 2021, 5552-2; Ukrainian Draft Law on Copyright and Related Rights 2021, 5552-4.

[87] For example, the draft laws use different terms—"generation" and "creation"—to refer to the functioning of a computer programme, resulting in non-original CGOs.

[88] See Resolution of the Verkhovna Rada of Ukraine on adopting the Ukrainian Draft Law on Copyright and Related Rights as a basis 2022, 2335-IX approving the Principal Draft Law as a basis and instructing that it should be refined by the second reading, taking the suggestions and amendments into account.

[89] While Draft Law 5552-2 also uses the mentioned wording, Draft Law 5552-4 defines non-original CGOs by distinguishing them from the "existing objects" without using the term "similar".

[90] Both Draft Law 5552-1 (Principal Draft Law) and Draft Law 5552-4 envisage that the *sui generis* right is effective from the act of generation. However, they stipulate different provisions for the calculation of 25 years. According to Draft Law 5552-4, the term commences on the first of January of the year following the year when the non-original CGO was generated. The Principal Draft Law probably contains a misprint in this regard. It provides that the term expires on the last day of the

5.2 *Analysis of the Proposal*

The idea to devise a new *sui generis* right for output based on AI is not unique, belonging solely to Ukraine,[91] but Ukraine can be regarded as the country that has taken it particularly seriously. As a *sui generis* regime allows designing a new legal framework tailored to the specific needs, the Ukrainian proposal has been presented as a compromise option between ignoring the phenomenon of output based on allegedly creative AI systems and undermining fundamental concepts of copyright law.[92] Bearing in mind that the introduction of any new regime has to be justified to avoid it turning into excessive IP protection with dysfunctional effects and related deadweight loss,[93] it is important that the legislative proposal sparked a lively debate between proponents and opponents.

Discussing the introduction of the *sui generis* right for non-original CGOs, Zerov believes its benefits lie in the fact that its application will (a) not lead to significant changes in copyright law; (b) protect the interests and investments of developers of AI systems; and (c) theoretically allow to use the case-law of the Court of Justice of the European Union on legal protection of non-original databases.[94]

Among these arguments, the second one, which relates to investment, deserves special attention. Upon analysing deontological and utilitarian economic grounds, Hilty and others have singled out investment protection theory as a possible ground in terms of economic justification for granting IP protection for output based on AI systems. However, they have caveated that considerable (in particular economic) research is needed before such a decision is made. Such research is expected to consider the potential creation and innovation incentivizing function of IP rights when the chances for undertakings to recover costs are at stake, and the complex set of economic costs that such rights also entail.[95] In such a case the burden of

---

calendar year when the non-original CGO was generated. Apparently, the drafters were referring to the last day of the calendar year in 25 years. We believe this misprint will be corrected during the finalisation of the Principal Draft Law.

[91] World Intellectual Property Organization, 'WIPO Conversation on Intellectual Property and Artificial Intelligence—Summary of the First Session' WIPO 2019, WIPO/IP/AI/GE/19, 2019, para 81;

World Intellectual Property Organization, 'WIPO Conversation on Intellectual Property and Artificial Intelligence—Summary of the Second and Third Sessions' WIPO 2020, WIPO/IP/AI/3/GE/20/INF/5, 2020, para 37.

[92] See Liubov Maidanyk, 'Artificial Intelligence and Sui Generis Right: A Perspective for Copyright in Ukraine?' (2021) 3(11) Access to Justice in Eastern Europe 144 (150–151).

[93] See Reto M Hilty et al., 'Intellectual Property Justification for Artificial Intelligence' in Jyh-An Lee et al. (eds), *Artificial Intelligence and Intellectual Property* (Oxford University Press 2021) 50 (50).

[94] See Zerov, 'Review of the Theoretical Approaches Regarding the Legal Protection of Objects Generated by Artificial Intelligence Systems in the Field of Copyright and Related Rights' (n 13) 25 (32).

[95] See Reto M Hilty et al., 'Intellectual Property Justification for Artificial Intelligence' in Jyh-An Lee et al. (n 93) 50 (64–68).

justification "generally rests upon those advocating in favour of introducing the new right".[96]

Although the Explanatory Notes of the Ukrainian draft laws do not explicitly mention the investment protection argument as the basis for the *sui generis* right for non-original CGOs,[97] doctrinal sources generally attribute to it a central role in justifying the introduction of the regime.[98] Nonetheless, there is still no publicly available information about whether the research on the economic justification for the Principal Draft Law in general and Art. 35 in particular (which are likely to be adopted in the near future) was conducted.

Apart from the lack of the economic justification, the content of the proposed provisions also raises some concerns. Firstly, the Principal Draft Law leaves the nature of the new right ambiguous. It does not provide for the inclusion of objects covered by the *sui generis* rights[99] in the list of objects of IP law stipulated in Art. 420 Civil Code of Ukraine. Nonetheless, the preamble of the Draft Law, which sets out its scope, treats the *sui generis* rights enshrined in it as the regimes related to the field of copyright and/or related rights.[100] From this we can conclude that the *sui generis* rights do fall under IP law, but its relation to copyright and related rights remains unclear. Draft Law 5552-4 (Alternative Draft Law) is clearer in this respect. It explicitly includes objects that are protected by the *sui generis* regimes in the list of objects of IP law,[101] and its preamble distinguishes between relations arising from copyright and related rights and *sui generis* rights,[102] making them separate regimes.

Secondly, the definition of a non-original CGO casts some doubt. The Principal Draft Law imposes two criteria for objects that fall under its Art. 35: (a) the CGO must differ from the existing *similar* objects; and (b) it must be created as a result of the functioning of computer programme(s) without the *direct* involvement of an individual in its creation. The Principal Draft Law gives no guidance about what is meant by the term "similar" and to what extent the CGO must be different. A literal interpretation of this provision raises the question of whether the identical CGO will be excluded from the protection. It is likely that the drafters implied this, but the provision leaves a gap in this respect. Moreover, it remains uncertain what exactly the CGO is to be compared with. It appears unlikely that the drafters wanted to exclude works subject to copyright protection from the scope for comparison, but

[96] See Drexl and others, 'Artificial Intelligence and Intellectual Property (n 14), para III (22).

[97] Explanatory Note to Ukrainian Draft Law on Copyright and Related Rights 2021, 5552-1; Explanatory Note to Ukrainian Draft Law on Copyright and Related Rights 2021, 5552-2; Explanatory Note to Ukrainian Draft Law on Copyright and Related Rights 2021, 5552-4.

[98] See Maidanyk, 'Artificial Intelligence and Sui Generis Right' (n 92) 144 (151); Zerov, 'Review of the Theoretical Approaches Regarding the Legal Protection of Objects Generated by Artificial Intelligence Systems in the Field of Copyright and Related Rights' (n 13) 25 (30–32).

[99] Apart from CGOs, the Draft Law also contains provisions on the *sui generis* rights as regards databases and intangible cultural heritage.

[100] Ukrainian Draft Law on Copyright and Related Rights 2021, 5552-1, preamble.

[101] Comparative Table to Ukrainian Draft Law on Copyright and Related Rights 2021, 5552-4.

[102] Ukrainian Draft Law on Copyright and Related Rights 2021, 5552-4, preamble.

the fact that the Principal Draft Law refers to *similar* objects as a point of comparison makes this issue ambiguous.

The criterion that the CGO must be created without the direct involvement of an individual in its creation presents another matter of concern in terms of the CGO's definition. As Maidanyk notes, it seems that the definition covers fully AI-generated output.[103] We have previously discussed that generating such output does not seem plausible under the current state-of-the-art. If such interpretation of the definition holds true, then the provisions in question will not be viable at present. It is also possible that by employing this criterion the drafters refer to objects that have a human hand in their generation, but the hand's actions do not constitute creativity. This reflects the understanding of AI-generated output prevailing in the current Ukrainian doctrine outlined earlier in this chapter. Even when interpreted in this way, the Article leaves the question of its subject-matter open. It further remains unclear where the border between *indirect involvement* and the *use* of computer technologies lies. The lack of clarity may have two consequences: either Art. 35 will not be "viable" and frequently invoked in courts; or there will be plenty of lawsuits for the court to determine the issue on a case-by-case basis. Since it is unlikely that a uniform "formula" covering all types of output can be developed to distinguish between creative and non-creative human contributions, creating guidelines with criteria and examples may be a possible solution.

As far as the definition is concerned, it is worth taking note of a view that the drafters of the Alternative Draft Law have intended to remain within copyright subject-matter and to grant the *sui generis* rights only to those objects that would receive copyright protection if they were created by a human being.[104] Since the Principal Draft Law and the Alternative Draft Law provide very similar texts of Art. 35, it can be supposed that the drafters of the former share the same intention. While acknowledging the possibility of this intention, the author considers that the text of Art. 35 neither directly states this, nor contains adequate safeguards against such an expansion of the subject-matter.

Thirdly, given the impact of technologies (including AI systems) on the speed of creative industries' development, questions arise around the term of protection. Unfortunately, it is not known whether research has been conducted to justify it.

Furthermore, it can be assumed that the idea of the *sui generis* right for non-original CGOs was inspired by the EU *sui generis* database right. Since it is a question of granting protection to objects that do not meet the originality requirement, the doctrine often mentions them together.[105] As previously stated, the theoretical possibility to use the case-law of the Court of Justice of the European Union on the

---

[103] See Maidanyk, 'Artificial Intelligence and Sui Generis Right' (n 92) 144 (153).

[104] See Zerov, 'Review of the Theoretical Approaches Regarding the Legal Protection of Objects Generated by Artificial Intelligence Systems in the Field of Copyright and Related Rights' (n 13) 25 (33).

[105] See Kapitsa, 'Texts, Music, Images, That are Generated by Artificial Intelligence' (n 71) 45 (48–50); Zerov, 'Review of the Theoretical Approaches Regarding the Legal Protection of Objects Generated by Artificial Intelligence Systems in the Field of Copyright and Related Rights' (n 13) 25 (32).

sui generis database right as a reference point for the *sui generis* right for non-original CGOs is presented by Zerov as one of the arguments for introducing the new right in Ukraine. However, the author considers that, apart from the need to distinguish between input and output as objects of protection in this regard, it is essential to take a deromanticised look at the EU *sui generis* database regime in the light of recent research questioning its original basics.[106]

Finally, there are doubts about whether introducing this *sui generis* right for non-original CGOs aligns with the aforementioned objective to approximate Ukraine's legislation with the EU IP acquis. There is currently no indication that the European Union is considering introducing an identical or similar regime. On the contrary, the European Commission seems to follow the view that current EU IP framework appears "broadly suitable to address the challenges raised by AI-assisted inventions and creations".[107] Moreover, the view that "creation, research and innovation into AI solutions and the resulting AI output, as well as the business model behind it, are not hampered by the absence of protection under copyright" has not been refuted.[108] This prompts us to conclude that the legislative "race" to introduce such *sui generis* regime can make it more difficult to achieve the approximation goal.

Taking all this into account (namely the state-of-the-art of AI systems and the current version of Art. 35), the legislative proposal seems to be premature.[109] This is not to deny all the challenges that the use of AI systems in creative industries has entailed and the opportunities the *sui generis* regime can provide, among them the possibility to design a new legal framework tailored to the specific needs. However, before introducing such a legal framework, it is crucial to have a solid economic and technical basis to avoid turning the regime into excessive IP protection.

---

[106] See Drexl and others, 'Artificial Intelligence and Intellectual Property (n 14), para III (23) summarising that the database *sui generis* regime needs to be adjusted or—even better—abolished altogether. See also Josef Drexl et al., 'Position Statement of the Max Planck Institute for Innovation and Competition of 25 May 2022 on the Commission's Proposal of 23 February 2022 for a Regulation on Harmonised Rules on Fair Access to and Use of Data (Data Act)' (2022) No. 20–05 Max Planck Institute for Innovation and Competition, paras 254–266 on limiting the *sui generis* database right. The importance of conducting such a sober analysis is underscored by the fact that Ukrainian copyright reform also involves updating provisions on the *sui generis* database right via introducing rules that have been inspired by the EU *sui generis* database regime. Current Ukrainian law only mentions *sui generis* database right without providing the rules on it.

[107] European Commission, 'Making the Most of the EU's Innovative Potential—An Intellectual Property Action Plan to Support the EU's Recovery and Resilience' (Communication) COM(2020) 760 final, 7.

[108] European Commission, 'Study on Copyright and New Technologies: Copyright Data Management and Artificial Intelligence' (Study) SMART 2019/0038, 274.

[109] See Maidanyk, 'Artificial Intelligence and Sui Generis Right' (n 92) 144(153).

6 Conclusion

If we imagine the search for a legal framework for output based on AI as a maze race, which is not so much about being first to an exit, but rather about finding the right one, we will certainly see Ukraine among many countries participating in it. This is directly linked to the use of AI systems in creative industries, where developers have been increasingly seeking to make advances in automation and reduce human input to a few clicks. The success in achieving these goals seems to be directly proportional to the challenges AI systems raise for copyright law.

Though the fixation requirement is unlikely to present an obstacle to copyrightability of the output under Ukrainian copyright law, the same cannot be said for the originality and authorship criteria. The concept of originality in Ukrainian copyright law is still evolving and will probably soon undergo changes towards a more straightforward enshrinement of the subjective standard. Under any circumstances, it remains linked to the authorship requirement, which, in turn, expressly stipulates that the author is an individual, i.e. a human being. This makes output based on AI, where AI systems are no longer a tool, ineligible for copyright protection.

Having reached this point, the chapter reveals that the way the doctrines in Ukraine and other jurisdictions treat output based on AI further determines the racers' strategies. A particular feature of the Ukrainian doctrine seems to be its broader interpretation of AI-generated output as the one generated by a computer programme with no (direct) influence of human creativity. Such actions as pressing buttons or setting parameters are not considered to constitute human creativity.

The chapter identifies the ideas raised in the Ukrainian doctrine that fall within and beyond IP law and places them in international context. As among them only one—the introduction of a *sui generis* right for non-original computer-generated objects—has so far made its way to the legislative initiative level, it has become the subject of closer scrutiny in this chapter.

While recognising the general attractiveness of the *sui generis* right, based on the lack of economic research and the contentious nature of the Article's provisions, the chapter cautions against its prematurity. To avoid introducing a regime that may turn into excessive IP protection, it also invites us to take another round and return to the question of whether output based on AI should receive any protection. Careful research (and in particular economic research) should be carried out in this regard, which will assist in determining the direction and speed of travel along the path.

References

Warren E Agin, 'A History of Artificial Intelligence' in Theodore F Claypoole (ed), *The Law of Artificial Intelligence and Smart Machines: Understanding A.I. and the Legal Impact* (American Bar Association 2019) 3

Nadia Banteka, 'Artificially Intelligent Persons' (2021) 58(3) Houston Law Review 537

Anatolii Dovgert, Viktor Kalakura and Nataliia Vasylyna, 'Codification of Civil Legislation: At the Turn of the Era' (2021) 10 Global Journal of Comparative Law 16

Anatolii Dovgert, 'The Doctrine of Private International Law in Ukraine at the Turn of the Century' (2020) 6 Law of Ukraine 13 [Анатолій Довгерт, 'Доктрина Міжнародного Приватного Права в Україні на Зламі Століть' (2020) 6 Право України 13]

Josef Drexl and others, 'Position Statement of the Max Planck Institute for Innovation and Competition of 25 May 2022 on the Commission's Proposal of 23 February 2022 for a Regulation on Harmonised Rules on Fair Access to and Use of Data (Data Act)' (2022) No. 20–05 Max Planck Institute for Innovation and Competition

Josef Drexl and others, 'Artificial Intelligence and Intellectual Property Law—Christopher Rowland,Position Statement of the Max Planck Institute for Innovation and Competition of 9 April 2021 on the Current Debate', (2021) No. 21–10 Max Planck Institute for Innovation and Competition

Josef Drexl and others, 'Technical Aspects of Artificial Intelligence: An Understanding from an Intellectual Property Law Perspective', (2019) No. 19–13 Max Planck Institute for Innovation and Competition

Mariia Dubniak, 'Problems in Determining the Legal Regime for Objects Generated Using Neural Network Technologies' (2019) 31 Information and Law 45 [Марія Дубняк, 'Проблеми Визначення Правового Режиму Об'єктів, Створених за Допомогою Технологій Нейромереж' (2019) 31 Інформація і Право 45]

European Commission, 'Making the Most of the EU's Innovative Potential—An Intellectual Property Action Plan to Support the EU's Recovery and Resilience' (Communication) COM(2020) 760 final

European Commission, 'Study on Copyright and New Technologies: Copyright Data Management and Artificial Intelligence' (Study) SMART 2019/0038

Katherine B Forrest, 'Copyright Law and Artificial Intelligence: Emerging Issues' in Theodore F Claypoole (ed), *The Law of Artificial Intelligence and Smart Machines: Understanding A.I. and the Legal Impact* (American Bar Association 2019) 347

Jane C Ginsburg, 'People Not Machines: Authorship and What It Means in the Berne Convention' (2018) 49 International Review of Intellectual Property and Competition Law 131

James Grimmelmannn, 'There's No Such Thing as a Computer-Authored Work—And It's a Good Thing, Too' (2016) 39 Columbia Journal of Law & the Arts 403

Andres Guadamuz, 'Comparative Analysis of Originality in Artificial Intelligence Generated Works' in Jyh-An Lee, Reto M Hilty and Kung-Chung Liu (eds), *Artificial Intelligence and Intellectual Property* (Oxford University Press 2021) 147

Tianxiang He, 'The Sentimental Fools and the Fictitious Authors: Rethinking the Copyright Issues of AI-generated Contents in China' (2019) 27(2) Asia Pacific Law Review 218

Reto M Hilty, Jörg Hoffmann and Stefan Scheuerer, 'Intellectual Property Justification for Artificial Intelligence' in Jyh-An Lee, Reto M Hilty and Kung-Chung Liu (eds), *Artificial Intelligence and Intellectual Property* (Oxford University Press 2021) 50

Kalin Hristov, 'Artificial Intelligence and the Copyright Dilemma' (2017) 57(3) IDEA: The IP Law Review 431

P Bernt Hugenholtz and João P Quintais, 'Copyright and Artificial Creation: Does EU Copyright Law Protect AI-Assisted Output?' (2021) 52 International Review of Intellectual Property and Competition Law 1190

Oleksandra Javorska, 'Presumption of Creative Nature of the Work, Resulted in the Object of Intellectual Property Law: Theory and Practice of Application' (2017) 23 Časopis civìlìstiki 78 [Олександра Яворська, 'Презумпція Творчого Характеру Праці, Результатом якої є Об'єкт Інтелектуального Права: Теорія та Практика Застосування' (2017) 23 Часопис Цивілістики 78]

Yuriy Kapitsa, 'Texts, Music, Images, That are Generated by Artificial Intelligence: Towards Defining a Model of Legal Protection' (2021) 36 Information and Law 45 [Юрій Капіца,

'Тексти, Музика, Зображення, що Створюються Штучним Інтелектом: до Визначення Моделі Правової Охорони' (2021) 36 Інформація і Право 45]

Sean D Kelly, 'What Computers Can't Create: Why Creativity is, and Always Will Be, a Human Endeavor' *Technology Review, Inc.* (1 March 2019) https://www.thefreelibrary.com/What+computers+can%27t+create%3a+Why+creativity+is%2c+and+always+will+be%2c+a...-a0578441401

Olha Kronda, 'Application of the Association Agreement between Ukraine and the European Union in the Field of Intellectual Property' (2018) 53 Uzhhorod National University Herald. Series: Law 105 [Ольга Кронда 'Застосування Угоди про Асоціацію між Україною та Європейським Союзом у Сфері Інтелектуальної Власності' (2018) 53 Науковий Вісник Ужгородського Національного Університету. Серія: Право 105]

Anastasiia Kyrylenko, 'Direct Effect in Ukraine of IPR Provisions from the EU–Ukraine Free Trade Agreement: A Principled Approach to the Zentiva Case' (2019) 14(9) Journal of Intellectual Property Law & Practice 716

Jyh-An Lee, 'Computer-generated Works Under the CDPA 1988' in Jyh-An Lee, Reto M Hilty and Kung-Chung Liu (eds), *Artificial Intelligence and Intellectual Property* (Oxford University Press 2021) 177

Natasha Lomas, 'Reface Grabs $5.5M Seed Led by A16z to Stoke its Viral Face-Swap Video App' *TechCrunch* (8 December 2020) https://tcrn.ch/33QdRAI

Liubov Maidanyk, 'Artificial Intelligence and Sui Generis Right: A Perspective for Copyright in Ukraine?' (2021) 3(11) Access to Justice in Eastern Europe 144

Liubov Maidanyk, 'Notion and Boundaries of Objective Form of Expression of a Work: Analyze of European and Ukrainian Approaches' (2019) 1 Theory and Practice of Intellectual Property 94 [Любов Майданик, 'Поняття та Межі Об'єктивної Форми Вираження Твору: Аналіз Європейського та Українського Підходів' (2019) 1 Теорія і Практика Інтелектуальної Власності 94]

Liubov Maidanyk, 'The Concept of Originality of the Work in Copyright Law: Experience of the EU, Ukraine and Other Foreign Countries' (2018) 10 Entrepreneurship, Economy and Law 32 [Любов Майданик, 'Поняття Оригінальності Твору в Авторському Праві: Досвід ЄС, України та Інших Зарубіжних Країн' (2018) 10 Підприємництво, господарство і право 32]

Jani McCutcheon, 'Curing the Authorless Void: Protecting Computer-Generated Works Following IceTV and Phone Directories' (2013) 37 Melbourne Univeristy Law Review 46

Jani McCutcheon, 'The Vanishing Author in Computer-Generated Works: A Critical Analysis of Recent Australian Case Law' (2013) 36 Melbourne Univeristy Law Review 915

Eliza Mik, 'AI as a Legal Person' in Jyh-An Lee, Reto M Hilty and Kung-Chung Liu (eds), *Artificial Intelligence and Intellectual Property* (Oxford University Press 2021) 419

Grygorii Prokhorov-Lukin, 'Forensics: The Concept and Types of Intellectual Property' (2016) 6 Theory and Practice of Intellectual Property 17 [Григорій Прохоров-Лукін, 'Судова Експертиза: Поняття та Види Об'єктів Інтелектуальної Власності' (2016) 6 Теорія і Практика Інтелектуальної Власності 17]

Sam Ricketson, 'The 1992 Horace S. Manges Lecture – People or Machines: The Bern Convention and the Changing Concept of Authorship' (1991–1992) 16 Columbia-VLA Journal of Law & the Arts 1

Stefan Scheuerer, 'Artificial Intelligence and Unfair Competition—Unveiling an Underestimated Building Block of the AI Regulation Landscape' (2021) 70(9) GRUR International 834

Martin Senftleben, 'A Tax on Machines for the Purpose of Giving a Bounty to the Dethroned Human Author—Towards an AI Levy for the Substitution of Human Literary and Artistic Works' *SSRN* (2 Jun 2022) https://ssrn.com/abstract=4123309

Anna Shtefan, 'Creativity and Artificial Intelligence: A View from the Perspective of Copyright' (2021) 16(7) Journal of Intellectual Property Law & Practice 720

Anna Shtefan, 'Some Issues of Application of the Association Agreement as the Source of Copyright of Ukraine' (2019) 1 Theory and Practice of Intellectual Property 5 [Анна Штефан, 'Деякі

Проблеми Застосування Угоди про Асоціацію як Джерела Авторського Права України' (2019) 1 Теорія і Практика Інтелектуальної Власності 5]

Anna Shtefan, *Copyright and Related Rights: Peculiarities of Legal Protection, Enforcement and Defence* (Intellectual Property Research Institute of National Academy of Law Sciences of Ukraine, Ltd NVP Interservice 2017) [Анна Штефан, *Авторське Право і Суміжні Права: Особливості Правової Охорони, Здійснення та Захисту* (НДІ Інтелектуальної Власності НАПрНУ, ТОВ НВП Інтерсервіс 2017)]

Olena Shtefan, 'The Concept of the Object of Copyright and the Criteria for its Protection' (2006) 6 Theory and Practice of Intellectual Property 3 [Олена Штефан, 'Поняття Об'єкту Авторського Права та Критеріїв його Охороноздатності' (2006) 6 Теорія і Практика Інтелектуальної Власності 3]

Jan Smits and Tijn Borghuis, 'Generative AI and Intellectual Property Rights' in Bart Custers and Eduard Fosch-Villaronga (eds), *Law and Artificial Intelligence* (T.M.C. Asser Press, 2022) 323

Mykola Stefanchuk, Oksana Muzyka-Stefanchuk and Maryna Stefanchuk, 'Prospects of Legal Regulation of Relations in the Field of Artificial Intelligence Use' (2021) 28(1) Journal of the National Academy of Legal Sciences of Ukraine 157

Joseph Straus, 'Artificial Intelligence—Challenges and Chances for Europe' (2020) 29(1) European Review 142

The Expert Committee on the Development of Artificial Intelligence under the Ministry of Digital Transformation of Ukraine http://ai.org.ua/index.html

Ilarion Tomarov, 'Presumption of Works' Originality: is There a Need for It or Not?' *LegalShift* (22 March 2019) http://www.legalshift.com.ua/?p=1332 [Іларіон Томаров, 'Презумпція Оригінальності Твору: Потрібна чи Ні?' *LegalShift* (22 березня 2019)]

Working Group on Recodifying (Updating) Ukrainian Civil Legislation, 'Concept of Updating the Civil Code of Ukraine' (ArtEk 2020) [Робоча Група щодо Рекодифікації (Оновлення) Цивільного Законодавства України, 'Концепція Оновлення Цивільного Кодексу України' (АртЕк 2020)]

World Intellectual Property Organization, 'WIPO Conversation on Intellectual Property and Artificial Intelligence—Summary of the Second and Third Sessions' WIPO 2020, WIPO/IP/AI/3/GE/20/INF/5, 2020

World Intellectual Property Organization, 'WIPO Conversation on Intellectual Property and Artificial Intelligence—Summary of the First Session' WIPO 2019, WIPO/IP/AI/GE/19, 2019

Shlomit Yanisky-Ravid, 'Generating Rembrandt: Artificial Intelligence, Copyright, and Accountability in the 3A Era—The Human-Like Authors Are Already Here—A New Model' (2017) 2017 Michigan State Law Review 659

Jesus M N Zatarain, 'The Role of Automated Technology in the Creation of Copyright Works: The Challenges of Artificial Intelligence' (2017) 31(1) International Review of Law, Computers & Technology 91

Kostiantyn Zerov, 'Review of the Theoretical Approaches Regarding the Legal Protection of Objects Generated by Artificial Intelligence Systems in the Field of Copyright and Related Rights' (2021) 6 Theory and Practice of Intellectual Property 25 [Костянтин Зеров, 'Огляд Теоретичних Підходів щодо Правової Охорони Об'єктів, Згенерованих Системами Штучного Інтелекту у Сфері Авторського Права і Суміжних Прав' (2021) 6 Теорія і Практика Інтелектуальної Власності 25]

On the Reforms, Practice and Perspective of the Law on Collecting Societies in Ukraine

Liubov Maidanyk

Contents

Abstract This chapter explores the current state and potential of collective management of copyright and related rights in Ukraine after the adoption of the Law on Collective Management Organisations in 2018 (Law on CMOs). Despite the overall success of the collective management reform, this remains one of the most controversial areas of copyright in Ukraine. This chapter identifies and explores positive and negative processes caused by the new law and perspectives for collective rights management in Ukraine. The following positive outcomes of the reform of the Law on CMOs are considered: (1) bringing Ukrainian CMOs' standards closer to European standards; (2) elimination of state involvement; (3) introduction of new types of rights into collective management; and (4) increased transparency of CMOs. Further, the law has strengthened the obligations and rights of all subjects of the Law on CMOs, but first and foremost of CMOs with regard to transparency and accountability of their activities. The process of liquidating the state CMO, as a vestige of Soviet legal approaches, is also considered as a positive outcome of the reform. As a negative

---

L. Maidanyk (✉)
Intellectual Property and Information Law Department of the Educational and Scientific Institute of Law, Taras Shevchenko National University of Kyiv, Kyiv, Ukraine
e-mail: Liubov_maidanyk@knu.ua

H. Richter (ed.), *Competition and Intellectual Property Law in Ukraine*,
MPI Studies on Intellectual Property and Competition Law 31,
https://doi.org/10.1007/978-3-662-66101-7_23

practice, certain problems of applying the law are discussed. These are: (1) the slow implementation of the law's provisions; (2) the uncertainty surrounding the procedure of withdrawing rights from collective management; and (3) problems relevant to the tariff-setting process. Although the introduction of the rights withdrawal procedure has undoubtedly strengthened the rights of authors and rightholders, the Ukrainian practice so far has been ambiguous. Based on these findings, the chapter considers perspectives for collective management in Ukraine.

1 Introduction

Ukraine's intellectual property system has been in a gradual process of reform over the past five years. The signing of the Association Agreement between the European Union and Ukraine was a defining moment in choosing the direction of development in this area. Given the post-Soviet legacy of unjustified state involvement in legal relations and insufficient protection of private intellectual property rights, Ukraine has a long way to go in harmonising its national legislation with EU intellectual property law. Unfortunately, the pace of change is not fast enough to see an obvious result. However, significant improvements have already been made in the field of copyright, namely with regard to collective management of copyright and related rights, albeit with certain reservations. In 2018, a new Law of Ukraine "On Collective Management Organisations" was adopted—with the long title "On Effective Management of Holders' Economic Rights in the Sphere of Copyright and Related Rights (Law on CMOs)". This law has established new rules of the game for all participants in the collective management of copyright and related rights. The problems of disorder and total lack of transparency in Ukraine's system of collective management have long called out for the adoption of completely new regulation. Unfortunately, there is little fundamental academic research to evaluate the collective management innovations adopted in Ukraine since 2018. This is due to the fact that the changes themselves were highly anticipated and, as a consequence, positive expectations were initially placed on the Law on CMOs.[1] However, difficulties in practice in implementing the new law have indicated both inflated expectations and a long road ahead for effective management of copyright and related rights. Unfortunately, the rightholders themselves do not trust the CMOs and are not satisfied with their activities. According to a survey conducted by LB.UA in 2020, only 3.2% of representatives of the music industry were satisfied with royalty payments—and of artists, only 2.9%.[2]

[1] Leonid Tarasenko, 'Innovations in the Exercise of Collective Management of Copyright and Related Rights' (2019) 33 Journal of Civil Studies 55 (58ment of Copyright and Related Rights Subjects' (2016) 7 Entrepreneurship, Economy and Law 26 (30).

[2] Sergiy Kane, 'Ukrainian Music Market: 7 Key Studies' *LB.UA* https://lb.ua/culture/2020/10/20/468513_muzichniy_rinok_ukraini_7_klyuchovih.html accessed 29 September 2021.

This chapter is not aimed at proposing new approaches to collective management of copyright and related rights in Ukraine. Instead, I try to make an objective assessment of the results of the CMO reform from an academic point of view based on the analysis of the practical application of the norms of the new law by organisations and the tendencies of national court practice. Also, this chapter analyses the implementation of certain provisions of EU Intellectual Property Law in the provisions of the Law on CMOs. In terms of implementation of the EU directives the following issues will be addressed: First, the general requirements for the operation of a CMO, and second, the special case of mandatory collective rights management, focusing on the resale right and cable retransmission right. From the rightholders' perspective the right to withdraw rights from CMOs is of high relevance, and particularly for the users the tariff-setting procedure lies at the heart of the reform of the Law on CMOs. This chapter will discuss the visible positive and negative effects of the implementation of this law, as well as its shortcomings and prospects for addressing them.

The chapter is structured as follows. Section 2 gives a brief overview of the Ukrainian system of collective management of copyright and related rights and outlines the prerequisites for reform in this field. Section 3 addresses the main new provisions of the Law on CMOs and provides a legal assessment of its practical implementation. Section 4 maps the main positive and negative results of the CMO reform.

2 General Overview and Prerequisites for the Reform of Collective Management

From the very beginning, after gaining independence from the USSR in 1991, Ukraine introduced a specific copyright system in which the foundations of private law were just beginning to take root. In the USSR, collective management of authors' rights was conducted only by authorised state bodies. For this purpose, the All-Union Copyright Office was established in 1932. Until 1973, this authority collected remuneration only in the interest of Soviet authors, while legislation neglected the rights of foreign authors.[3] In addition, related rights were not protected by the intellectual property law of the Soviet Union at all. The situation changed only after the USSR joined the World Copyright Convention in 1973. In 1992, in accordance with the Resolution of the Cabinet of Ministers of the already independent Ukraine, a new state copyright and related rights management authority was established as the successor of the Ukrainian branch of the Soviet All-Union Copyright Office (now it is the non-profit state-owned organisation Ukrainian Agency on Copyright and

---

[3] Yuriy Kapitsa et al., *Copyright and Related Rights in Europe* (Logos 2012) 311.

Related Rights—UACRR).[4] As market economy approaches have been successfully introduced in the creative industries, the question of adequate protection of copyright holders' rights to royalties has become particularly acute and has resulted in the adoption of the Ukrainian Law on Copyright and Related Rights permitting non-government collective management organisations. Therefore, after 1993 the growing number of CMOs caused problems of overlapping authority and consequent competition between organisations, the absence of a mandatory reporting for royalty payments and ineffectiveness of control of CMOs by authorities, as well as the absence of a transparent, fair and predictable system for royalty distribution.[5]

The issue of the admissibility of collective management by an organisation established by a state body became particularly acute in 2013, when the Constitutional Court of Ukraine unambiguously clarified the private law nature of collective management organisations established by subjects of copyright and related rights.[6] Although subsequent national court practice has been ambiguous on the admissibility of a CMO in the form of a state-owned organisation, the inconsistency between the activities of the state-owned organisation UACRR and the essence of collective management became apparent.[7] Since the state organisation UACRR was founded by the Ministry of Economy of Ukraine, this was called into question due to the inconsistency with the private law essence of collective management. With the adoption of the new rules, the existence of such an organisation is against the law, so it is to be liquidated.[8]

Eventually, the Ukrainian Law on CMOs was adopted in 2018, and it aims to bring national legislation closer to the provisions of the EU and Ukraine Association Agreement, which contains provisions of the relevant EU directives on copyright and related rights: Directive 2014/26/EU of the European Parliament and of the Council of 26 February 2014 on collective management of copyright and related rights and multi-territorial licensing of rights in musical works for online use in the internal market (Collective Rights Management Directive) and Directive 93/83/EEC of 27 September 1993 on the coordination of certain rules concerning copyright and rights related to copyright applicable to satellite broadcasting and cable retransmission (Satellite and Cable Directive). However, apart from the fulfilment of direct international obligations, there were other internal prerequisites for a separate legal regulation of this area. At the time the draft Law on CMOs was presented in 2017, there

[4] See more at Ukrainian Agency for Copyright and Related Rights http://uacrr.org accessed 29 September 2021.

[5] Oleksandr V Dem'yanenko, *White Book–2. Intellectual Property in the Innovative Economy of Ukraine* (Parliamentary Publishing 2008) 34–39.

[6] Constitutional Court of Ukraine, Decision 12-рп/2013 (2013) 1-17/2013, para 2.2.

[7] In 2016, a private organisation called the Collective Management Organisation for Copyrights and Related Rights asked the Constitutional Court of Ukraine to interpret the law on copyrights with regard to the legality of the existence of a state-owned CMO. Although no decision has been taken on this request, one of the applicant's strong arguments was legal uncertainty due to different court practices.

[8] At the time of writing this chapter, a liquidation process of the state organisation UACRR has been initiated.

were 19 non-profit collective management organisations in Ukraine. The Ministry of Economy, which was then mandated to control CMOs, was unable to do so due to litigation over the legality of the relevant regulations.[9] In addition, the idea of an economic justification for collective management in Ukraine, which is the reduction in transaction costs and related economies of scale in administering copyrights, is not generally accepted.[10] Rather, collective management is seen as a necessity stipulated by law. These and other reasons have shaped the distrust of Ukrainian authors and users in collective management as a corrupt and dysfunctional mechanism. In addition, the need to create a legislative framework for collective management organisations was related to the inclusion of Ukraine on the Priority Watch List under the Special 301 Report[11] due to the inadequacy of the system of collective management of copyrights and related rights.[12]

3 The Law on Collective Societies: Main Aims and Novel Provisions

3.1 General Principles of Collective Management

Despite the long and complicated title of the Law on CMOs, lawmakers have pointed to the main purpose of the law as being the effectiveness of collective management in Ukraine.[13] It can be assumed that the authors of the law wanted to reflect in the

---

[9] Between 2013 and 2016, the legality of the procedure for determining the authorised collective management organisations for extended collective management was questioned: Order of the Ministry of Education and Science of Ukraine No. 1249 on approval of the procedure for determining the authorised collective management organisations that will collect and distribute the royalties for the use of phonograms and videograms published for commercial purposes' 2013. It was only at the end of 2016 that the Supreme Administrative Court of Ukraine upheld the legality of this regulation; Supreme Administrative Court of Ukraine, Decision K/800/36287/14 (2016) 826/16333/13-a.

[10] Daniel J Gervais, 'The Economics of Collective Management' in Ben Depoorter and Peter S Menell (eds), *Research Handbook on the Economics of Intellectual Property Law, Volume 1* (Edward Elgar 2019) 495.

[11] Office of the United States Trade Representative, '2017 Special 301 Report' (Report) USTR (2017), 49.

[12] Ukrainian Parliament, 'Explanatory Note to the Draft Law on Effective Management of Rights Holders' Property Rights in the Field of Copyright and Related Rights' (Explanatory Note), 2017. In 2017, the US decided to suspend some of Ukraine's benefits under the Generalized System of Preferences Program (GSP). Such actions were due to insufficient protection of intellectual property rights, not least because of the non-transparent collective management system, because foreign rightholders were not receiving full royalties from Ukrainian CMOs.

[13] Ukrainian Law on Effective Management of Holders' Economic Rights in the Sphere of Copyright and Related Rights 2018, 2415-VIII, art 5.

title the "good governance" objective declared in the Collective Rights Management Directive in order to reiterate its EU-integration aim. The essence of effectiveness is revealed through the principles stated in the Law: Acting in the interests of rightholders, equality, transparency, accountability and the effectiveness of management itself. The following section considers the practical mechanisms of implementation of these principles declared in the Law on CMOs.

A CMO in Ukraine may only be established by holders of copyright and related rights as a non-profit public association. The founders of such organisations may be only creators and rightholders—citizens of Ukraine and foreigners, as well as legal entities of private law.[14] Before the reform, legislation did not provide clear requirements for the form of operation of a CMO, which led in some cases to non-transparent distribution of royalties, e.g. in the case of the establishment of a CMO by licensees. Unlike the Collective Rights Management Directive, Ukrainian legislation does not provide for commercial collective management organisations, irrespective of whether they are founded by rightholders or not. Regarding the management of property rights of foreign rightholders, the Law on CMOs provides that collective management organisations have the right to manage them on the territory of Ukraine on a general basis or on the basis of agreements with foreign CMOs. For example, a Ukrainian CMO may conclude a reciprocal representation agreement with a foreign organisation. Also, a foreign rightholder may directly conclude a collective management agreement with a Ukrainian CMO.[15]

CMOs can also delegate the management of property rights of Ukrainian rightholders abroad on the basis of contracts with similar foreign organisations, including agreements on the representation of rights. In addition, CMOs can join together on a contractual basis for the implementation of joint tasks and conclude partnership agreements and agreements on the representation of rights.

In addition, CMOs are given the possibility to cooperate on a contractual basis for the implementation of joint tasks and to conclude partnership agreements and agreements on the representation of rights. However, extended and mandatory collective management functions cannot be transferred under a partnership agreement or an agreement on the representation of rights.

[14] Ibid.

[15] Ibid.

3.2 *Accreditation*

3.2.1 Voluntary, Extended and Mandatory Management of Rights

The new law clearly distinguishes types of collective management that were previously not specified explicitly in legislation but have only been identified and distinguished by researchers[16]: voluntary, extended and mandatory. With these new provisions on the types of collective management, legal certainty has emerged. Voluntary management of rights is conducted by CMOs only for the rights that are in their catalogue, meaning previously transferred to them under a collective management agreement. Voluntary collective management can only be conducted on the basis of an agreement with a collective management organisation and it may extend to any field of copyright and related rights (except for those rights for which extended or mandatory collective management is exercised). Extended collective management is performed by CMOs specifically accredited for this purpose exclusively, regardless of the existence of a collective management agreement with the rightholder, but individual management of the rights is also permitted. The rightholder therefore has the right to withdraw rights from extended collective management. Extended collective management of copyright and related rights is exercised only in the following areas: Public performance and public broadcasting of musical works; the right to fair remuneration that is shared between the performers and the producers of the phonograms and videograms for public performance; and broadcasting of phonograms and videograms. Mandatory collective management is exercised by an accredited CMO exclusively in the areas provided for by the Law on CMOs, regardless of the existence of a collective management agreement. Mandatory collective management covers the resale right, the right to reprographic reproduction, the private copying right and the right to cable retransmission. Withdrawal of rights (whether full or partial) from mandatory collective management is not allowed by law.

The Law on CMOs states in Art. 12 that only one collective management organisation may be accredited for each area of mandatory management, but a single CMO may be accredited for several areas of mandatory management at the same time. Therefore, until at least the beginning of 2023, only one CMO in Ukraine—the Ukrainian Authors Right Agency—is authorised in two categories of rights: The resale right and the right of reprographic reproduction of works or excerpts. Such a provision of the law is controversial and should be clarified for the purposes of legal certainty with a subsequent amendment to the Law on CMOs. Article 16 Law on CMOs introduced the notion of accreditation—special authorisation of organisations for extended and mandatory collective management based on an open tender in accordance with the explicit requirements of the law. The open competition for accreditation is organised by the Ministry of the Economy and conducted by the Standing Committee on Accreditation. The commission includes representatives

[16] Liubov Maidanyk, *Collective Management of Copyright and Related Rights under Civil Law of Ukraine*, (Alerta 2013) 135–136; Yuriy Kapitsa et al., *Copyright and Related Rights in Europe* (Logos 2012) 311 (113).

of the Ministry of Economy of Ukraine, Ukrpatent, associations of rightholders, associations of users, the National Television and Radio Council and international organisations in the field of copyright and related rights. In order to be accredited, the organisation must be representative, which means that it must have concluded contracts with Ukrainian rightholders as well as contracts with foreign CMOs. The CMOs' accreditation is valid for three years for each area of mandatory or extended management. It is difficult to assess whether such a period of CMO accreditation is sufficient for the effective collection and distribution of royalties to rightholders. However, given the large number of legal disputes in certain areas of collective management, which in itself delays the payment of royalties, it may be that the user closes the contract with one accredited CMO when the time comes to conclude a contract with a new accredited organisation.

The practical implementation of the accreditation procedure is very complex and has led to numerous conflicts between de facto competing CMOs. CISAC also drew attention to the "chaotic" situation regarding the accreditation of CMOs in Ukraine and expressed the support of its Ukrainian members, UACRR and CINEMA.[17] Due to the appeal of the tender results and the negative publicity,[18] the rights management process in several spheres was blocked.[19] The efficiency of the accreditation procedure and its implementation by the members of the Standing Committee on Accreditation is questioned and changes in the legislation are envisaged. At the end of 2020, the District Administrative Court of Kyiv ruled that the order of the Ministry of Economy of 18 February 2020 No. 268 on Accreditation of Collective Management Organisations was illegal and overturned it.[20]

Extended and mandatory collective management is conducted only by specially accredited CMOs. Extended collective management covers the following categories of rights: (1) public performance of musical non-dramatic works with or without text, including those works included in the audiovisual works; (2) public broadcasting of musical non-dramatic works with or without text, including those works included in the audiovisual works, except for cable retransmission; (3) the right to a fair remuneration combined for the performers and producers of phonograms (videograms) for the public performance of the phonograms and the performances recorded therein for commercial purposes; (4) the right to a fair remuneration for the public communication of phonograms, videograms and fixed performances published for commercial use. Categories of rights covered by extended collective management existed before

---

[17] International Confederation of Societies of Authors and Composers, '2020 Annual Report' (Report) CISAC (2020).

[18] 'The Ministry of Economy has not yet Signed a Decree on the Accreditation of Entities that Collect Copyright Fees' *Detector Media* (12 January 2021) https://detector.media/rinok/article/183937/2021-01-12-minekonomiky-shche-ne-pidpysalo-nakaz-shchodo-akredytatsii-organizatsiy-yaki-zaymayutsya-zborom-avtorskoi-vynagorody/ accessed 29 July 2021.

[19] Although the accreditation of the CMO took place in December 2020, the Ministry of Economy has not yet approved the accreditation of organisations that collect royalties for the public performance of non-dramatic musical works and the public broadcasting of non-dramatic musical works. Consequently, the tariff negotiation process cannot begin either.

[20] Kyiv District Administrative Court, Decision 93045878 (2020) 640/13375/20.

the reform and were administered by special authorised CMOs. However, there was no legal certainty in the law, so it was often judicial practice that drew the line.[21] It is clear that extended collective management is of great importance for rightholders in the music sector. Cafés, restaurants and other venues of the so-called HoReCa (Hotel, Restaurant, Café/Catering) segment, where musical works are publicly performed and/or records of musical works are played, are obliged to conclude agreements with accredited CMOs. A similar obligation to conclude agreements with the CMOs is imposed on radio stations publicly broadcasting phonograms and the performances recorded in them.

Mandatory collective management is conducted according to an exhaustive list of areas of rights, regardless of the existence of a collective management agreement with the rightholder. The legislature thus enforces the right to fair remuneration, which is partially referred to in Art. 14 ter Berne Convention for the Protection of Literary and Artistic Works. Mandatory collective management applies to the following types of rights: (1) resale right; (2) reprographic reproduction of the works and their parts; (3) reproduction at home and for personal purposes of works and performances recorded in phonograms, videograms and their copies as well as audiovisual works and their copies (private copying); 4) cable retransmission of copyright objects and/or related rights, other than the rights of broadcasting organisations to their own broadcasts. It is worth taking a closer look at each area of mandatory management.[22]

3.2.2 Resale Right

Prior to the reform, the legislation provided for payment of remuneration for resale right in three optional ways: To the author personally, through his or her representative or through collective management organisations. In practice, however, payments were minimal or not made at all in any way. Therefore, the definition of a single entity to collect the remuneration is seen as a positive change for the authors and their heirs. It is worth noting that the CMO interprets the law in its own favour with the respect to the scope of the resale right. According to the documents approved by accredited CMOs in this area, the resale right covers the sale of original works, which include sculptures, paintings, engravings and drawings, but does not include manuscripts, although Art. 448 Civil Code of Ukraine provides for this.[23] Taking into account the provisions of Art. 190 EU–Ukraine Association Agreement and Art. 2 Directive 2001/84/EC of the European Parliament and the Council of 27 September 2001 on the resale right for the benefit of the author of an original work of art, the scope of the said article of the Civil Code of Ukraine is wider and goes beyond the

---

[21] Supreme Commercial Court of Ukraine, 'On the Questions of the Practice of Application by Commercial Courts of the Legislation on the Protection of Intellectual Property Rights (on the Cases Examined by the Ukrainian Commercial Court of Cassation of the Supreme Court)' (Overview Letter) 2012.

[22] Ukrainian Law on Effective Management of Holders' Economic Rights in the Sphere of Copyright and Related Rights 2018, 2415-VIII, art 12.

[23] The Ukrainian Author's Rights Agency, 'Tariff for Resale Right' 18 February 2020.

EU understanding of resale right. It is in relation to the resale right that the tariff is set in the Civil Code of Ukraine and in the Law of Ukraine "On Copyright and Related Rights" at 5% of the sale price of the original work. Therefore, for a uniform understanding, amendments according to the *acquis communautaire* are expected to respective legal regulations of Ukraine.

3.2.3 Reprographic Reproduction and Private Copying

Ukrainian legislation defines reprographic reproduction as a facsimile reproduction in any size (including enlarged or reduced) of an original written or other graphic work or its copy by photocopying or by other similar means, except recording in electronic (including digital), optical or other forms readable by a computer.[24] Ukraine has opted for an indirect remuneration payment model for copyrights, identifying producers and importers of special equipment as users. Article 23 of the law states that fair remuneration for reprographic reproduction and private copying shall be collected from manufacturers and importers of equipment and tangible media through which such reproduction is possible. The main difficulty lies in determining the tariffs for reprographic reproduction, as this provision is new and there has been no previous practice compared to private copying.

Private copying fees were levied even before the adoption of the Law, based on the provisions of the Law of Ukraine "On Copyright and Related Rights", while types of equipment, materials and tariffs were regulated by a special Decree of the Cabinet of Ministers of Ukraine.[25] Although remuneration collected for private copying was relatively low compared to neighbouring countries such as Poland and the Slovak Republic,[26] the newly introduced Ukrainian model allowing the CMOs to independently set provisional tariffs has increasingly been criticised by representatives of large business associations such as the European Business Association and Better Regulation Delivery Office.[27] The arguments against it include: The increasing role of streaming services as compared to reproduction on any media and the consequent economic unreasonableness of the tariffs; the fee is included to the final cost of the of equipment; disregard of the practice of the European Court of Justice in relation

---

[24] Ukrainian Law on Copyright and Related Rights 1994, 3792-XII, art 1.

[25] Decree of the Cabinet of Ministers of Ukraine No. 922 'The amount of charges payable by manufacturers and importers of equipment and physical media which can be used to reproduce works and performances recorded on phonograms and/or videograms at home'.

[26] According to the CISAC Private Copying Global Study 2020, in 2017 Ukrainian CMOs collected 444,916 EUR compared to 2,339,282 EUR and 4,378,914 EUR from Poland and the Slovak Republic, respectively (International Confederation of Society of Authors and Composers, 'Private Copying Global Study' (Report) 2020).

[27] BRDO, 'Prices of Laptops and Phones May be Reduced' (21 April 2017) https://brdo.com.ua/top/tsina-na-noutbuky-telefony-mozhe-znyzytysya/ accessed 21 July 2021; EBA, 'Tax on Equipment: Business Urges to Establish an Anti-Crisis Working Group to Build a Transparent System of Copyright Fees' (19 June 2020) https://eba.com.ua/en/podatok-na-tehniku-biznes-zaklykaye-stvoryty-antykryzovu-robochu-grupu-dlya-pobudovy-prozoroyi-systemy-vidrahuvan-za-avtorskyj-kontent/ accessed 20 July 2021.

to private copying. In *Padawan v. SGAE* the European Court of Justice ruled that "fair compensation" is linked to specific compensation schemes triggered by the existence of harm to the detriment of the rightholders, which gives rise, in principle, to the obligation to "compensate" them.Thus, it follows that fair compensation must necessarily be calculated on the basis of the criterion of the harm caused to authors of protected works by the introduction of the private copying exception.[28] In *SGAE ECJ and Copydan Bandkopi v. Nokia* the court again addressed the position of no obligation for payment in case of minimal prejudice to the rightholder. Thus, for this purpose the state may provide, in certain cases covered by the private copying exception, for an exemption from payment of fair compensation, provided the prejudice caused to rightholders in such cases is minimal.[29]

3.2.4 Cable Retransmission of Works Subject to Copyright and/or Related Rights

Mandatory collective management on cable retransmission is implemented through the provisions of Art. 9 Council Directive 93/83/EEC of 27 September 1993 on the coordination of certain rules concerning copyright and rights related to copyright applicable to satellite broadcasting and cable retransmission. Cable retransmission is defined in Ukrainian legislation as simultaneous transmission and reception of programmes by a broadcaster, regardless of technical means, as well as works protected by copyright or related rights, provided that the original transmission was made by a broadcaster who is not under the jurisdiction of Ukraine.[30] This definition of "transmission" covers the activities of broadcasters, programme service providers and OTT (over-the-top media service) providers.[31] This area of governance is new to Ukrainian copyright law and broadcasters have reacted with resistance and unwillingness to pay. As a consequence a large number of legal disputes have arisen,[32] concerning the legality of the CMO's accreditation in this area, as well as the unreasonableness of the CMO's requirements to conclude contracts with consumers and to pay remuneration from the moment tariffs are approved rather than from the entry into force of the court decision.[33] The majority of the court disputes have been resolved

[28] ECJ C-467/08 *Padawan v. SGAE ECJ* (2010) EU:C:2010:620, paras 41–42.

[29] ECJ C-463/12 *SGAE ECJ and Copydan Bandkopi v. Nokia* (2012) EU:C:2015:144, para 68.

[30] Ukrainian Law on Copyright and Related Rights 1994, 3792-XII, art 1.

[31] It is worth noting that Ukrainian courts understand the term "provider" to mean only a legally licensed one, so it does not cover the activities of some online services for which a licence is not required. Although it is too early to indicate an established practice on this issue, it is likely to lead to an expansion of the list of licensors.

[32] CAMR, '100 Lawsuits, 100 Contracts – Ukrainian Providers Started Paying Royalties for Copyright and Related Rights' (16 July 2021) http://camr.org.ua/?p=292 accessed 3 September 2021.

[33] Oksana Tchaikovska, 'How Providers can Defend Themselves in Court Against CMO Lawsuits' Detector Media (6 June 2021) https://detector.media/rinok/article/188852/2021-06-06-yak-provay deram-zakhystytys-u-sudi-vid-pozoviv-oku/ accessed 20 July 2021.

in favour of the CMO, but the very fact of such a tendency indicates the resistance of the CMOs to pay remuneration under the existing conditions, but not the obligation stipulated in the law itself. It may be assumed that this is due to the broadcasters' opposition to tariffs in this area and the generally complex tariff-setting process, as will be discussed below.

Scholars generally agree that rights may be subject to mandatory collective management in cases determined by law: Either international or national.[34] In this regard the Ukrainian model of non-voluntary collective management in relation to each area of rights analysed above is quite justified both from the point of view of practical impossibility of individual exercise or voluntary collective management and permitted by national and international law. Also, in some cases Ukrainian legislation has been harmonised with the EU *acquis communautaire*, which is also a sufficient justification for certain restrictions on the exclusive rights of authors and holders of related rights.

3.3 Transparency

Article 5 Law on CMOs defines transparency as one of the principles that requires CMOs to make information on their activities freely available to rightholders, users and the public. For this purpose, the Law on CMOs stipulates mandatory reporting on the organisations' activities. The executive and supervisory bodies of collective management organisations report to the general assembly annually. The governing body shall regularly report to the general meeting on its interests in the collective management organisation, on the amount of remuneration received for its activities for the reporting year, on the amount of remuneration received by rightholders (if such rights exist) from this organisation, about existing or potential conflicts of interest between the duties of the head of the collective management organisation and his or her duties in relation to other natural or legal persons. A collective management organisation shall publish its annual report on its activities on its website and make it freely available for a period of five years from the date of publication. The information in the CMO's annual report on its activities shall be audited in accordance with the law. The mandatory reporting system introduced in the new law is a very important factor for transparent and effective collective management. In general, the Ukrainian version of the legislation in this respect can be considered as good practice. For the purposes of this chapter the author reviewed the official websites of three Ukrainian

[34] Oleksandr Bulayenko, 'Permissibility of Non-Voluntary Collective Management of Copyright under EU Law – The Case of the French Law on Out-of-Commerce Books' (2016) 7 JIPITEC 51 para 3; Mihály Ficsor, 'Collective Management of Copyright and Related Rights at a Triple Crossroads: Should it Remain Voluntary or May it Be "Extended" or Made Mandatory?' (UNESCO Copyright Bulletin 4), 2003.

accredited CMOs[35] for availability of sufficient information such as annual reports, tariffs, statutes of CMOs, rights withdrawal procedure (where it is permitted) and rules for distribution of collected remuneration. It is possible to come to a quite optimistic conclusion about improvement in this aspect, as each of the above-mentioned documents was available on the website of the respective organisation. At the same time, there is still no special electronic system for the administration of copyrights and related rights, which is mentioned in Art. 1, 12 Law on CMOs. The system could give the rightholder and the user one-stop access to information on copyright and related rights, the amounts collected and the distributed royalties.

3.4 *Tariff Setting*

The relationship between users and CMOs has always been an area for legal battles, primarily regarding the setting of tariffs. In Ukraine, tariff setting is historically linked to state participation. Before the adoption of the new law, it was the state, through Cabinet of Ministers decrees, and which provided guidance for the CMOs regarding different types of uses of copyright and related rights. Minimum remuneration rates for the use of subject matter of copyright and related rights set by the state in special decrees of the Cabinet of Ministers of Ukraine are still valid at the time of writing this chapter.[36] The rates of royalties are calculated as a percentage of the amount of the gross proceeds from the sale of tickets for public performance of one work or programme, or of income earned from the activities in the course of which the copyright was used. After the adoption of the Law on CMOs, a multi-stage system of tariff approval was set. It was assumed that this would then abolish the Cabinet of Ministers' decrees.

The original version of Art. 20 of the Law on CMOs stipulated the following procedure for setting tariffs: Tariffs were negotiated between the CMO and the user associations and, if negotiations failed, the state set interim tariffs for up to six months until the remaining tariffs were approved by the parties. If negotiations were unsuccessful after six months of interim tariffs, then the tariffs were determined by a court. There is no current court practice on this issue, nor is there any indication of the methodology for approving court tariffs. In general, the mentioned provision seems to be such that this duty is not vested in the court. At the same time, the Law on CMOs implemented to some extent the provisions of Art. 16, together with Recital 31 Collective Rights Management Directive that tariffs must be objective and

[35] The public information of the following organisations accredited for extended and mandatory management was examined: Ukrainian Music Alliance (UMA), Ukrainian League of Copyright and Related Rights (ULCRR), Ukrainian Author's Rights Agency (UARA).

[36] At the time of writing this chapter the following decrees are still valid: Cabinet of Ministers of Ukraine Decree No. 72 on approval of minimal royalty rates for the use of copyright and related rights objects and No. 71 on approval of the amount, procedure and conditions for the payment of royalties for the commercial use of phonograms, videograms, their samples and recordings published for commercial purposes.

reasonable, taking into account *inter alia* the economic viability of the exploitation of copyright objects and/or related rights in business activities, the nature and extent of use of copyright objects and/or related rights, the type of activity of the owner and the financial and economic indicators of the market in which the use of these objects is performed. Despite the fact that the law on CMOs declares that organisations must build relations with users on the basis of fairness and reasonable tariffs, this is not so easy to fulfil in practice. After another unsuccessful round of negotiations between Ukrainian user associations and CMOs, the Cabinet of Ministers of Ukraine approved the interim tariffs according to the law. However, the basis for approval was not the new system justified according to the previously mentioned criteria, but the current rates stipulated earlier by Cabinet of Ministers decrees. Ukraine's biggest users[37] disagreed with these actions and went to court demanding that the approval resolution be overturned. Subsequently, it was the lack of an economic justification and disregard for the possible negative impact on business operations that led the court to declare the Cabinet of Ministers' resolution approving the interim tariffs illegal and to overturn it.[38]

Nowadays, the current version of Art. 20 takes unsuccessful experience into account, so the provision for the approval of interim tariffs by the state has been removed. Tariffs have now been approved for the following types of use: Public performance of phonograms and sound recordings thereof or public demonstration of videograms and sound recordings thereof published for commercial use; resale right for works of art; cable retransmission of copyright objects and/or related rights, except for the rights of broadcasters to their own programs. The tariffs for the reprographic reproduction rights of works and excerpts as well as private copying have not yet been agreed and negotiations are unsuccessful.

3.5 Withdrawal Right

By holding that a rightholder may license non-commercial use and withdraw rights from collective management the new Law on CMOs echoes to some extent Art. 5 Collective Rights Management Directive. The provision on rights withdrawal is crucial for strengthening the right of rightholders to choose between individual and collective management. Initially withdrawal of rights from collective management was declared in the Ukrainian Law "On Copyright and Related Rights", but it was only after the adoption of the Law on CMOs that a clear procedure was established. The rightholder has the right to apply for the removal of his or her rights from collective rights management (other than mandatory) and the CMO is obliged to perform a number of actions related to the termination of such management within six months of receiving such an application: It has to pay remuneration, amend

[37] Radio broadcaster "Business-Radio" and one of the biggest Ukrainian Production Companies "Studio 1 + 1".

[38] Sixth Administrative Court of Appeal, Decision 90713161 (2020) 640/18952/19.

licensing agreements, post relevant information on its website and terminate the management of rights. Article 8 Law on CMOs sets out that in the application for withdrawal, the rightholders shall specify the objects and rights they want to withdraw from the CMO. Ukrainian law thus allows for a partial withdrawal of rights from collective management. This is also reflected in the procedure for withdrawal of rights set by collective management organisations, e.g. ULCRR[39] and UMA.[40] Some state-related CMOs have interpreted the procedure for withdrawal of rights referred to in the Law on CMOs to mean that it applies only to voluntary collective management, not to extended collective management.[41] The ULCRR has established additional controversial requirements (that go beyond the general legal requirements for withdrawal in Art. 8 Law on CMOs) for the withdrawal of rights from extended collective management: An indication of the grounds for the withdrawal; a copy of any transfer agreements; proof that the person is the author, performer or producer of the phonogram; proof that the person has not disposed of his rights before filing the application. Of course, a balance must be struck between the effectiveness of collective management and the free choice of the rightholder regarding the type of management, but such requirements can be seen as limitations and obstacles to the withdrawal of rights and the consequent individual management of the rights. In the Daft Punk case,[42] the European Commission deemed it unacceptable for two members of the music group Daft Punk to be denied SACEM membership on the grounds that the rightholders had chosen to manage two categories of rights individually (meaning partial withdrawal of rights). In the Commission's arguments for this decision "the fact that only a few Collecting Societies imposed limits of this kind was taken as evidence that these measures were not indispensable".[43] Following this logic, similar conclusions can be drawn regarding the rules for rights withdrawal from the extended collective management set by the Ukrainian ULCRR. Such rules may therefore be considered abusive of the rights of rightholders, as well as beyond the statutory authority of the CMO.

Also, additional legal uncertainty was created in the practice concerning the moment of rights withdrawal. The desire of the rightholder to withdraw rights from the management of the CMO may be due to a number of reasons, including lack of confidence in collective management and fair distribution of remuneration or a desire to manage the rights individually. Therefore, the rightholder wants to reach the point at which the CMO has no right to collect remuneration from users as quickly

[39] Ukrainian League of Copyright and Related Rights is a Ukrainian CMO which manages the rights of performers and producers of phonograms. For more information, see www.ulasp.com.ua accessed 21 November 2021.

[40] Ukrainian Musical Alliance is a Ukrainian CMO for related rights in music. For more information, see www.uma.in.ua accessed 21 November 2021.

[41] Ukrainian League of Copyright and Related Rights, 'Rights Withdrawal Procedure' https://drive.google.com/file/d/1MJZygJqffkEzt2-iEDMxKzPCUocGONin/view accessed 9 September 2021.

[42] European Commission, Rejection Decision COMP/C2/37.219 *Banghalter/Homem Christo (Daft Punk) v. SACEM* (2002).

[43] Torben Toft, 'Collective Rights Management in the Online World. A Review of Recent Commission Initiatives' (Speech) 8 June 2006.

as possible, while the CMO wants to delay it. The Ukrainian Commercial Court of Cassation of the Supreme Court ruled that the decision as to whether or not the works were or were not withdrawn from the management of the CMO does not depend on the CMO's subjective judgement, its willingness or desire, but on the existence of the authority to carry out such an action, which is given when the rightholder sends a notification.[44] Thus, the withdrawal of rights from the management is seen as a unilateral exercise of the rights of the rightholder, and the CMO is only the executor. However, the Supreme Court has not yet ruled on the exact moment of rights withdrawal from collective management.

3.6 Payment and Distribution of Remuneration

Before the collective management reform in Ukraine, there was a completely non-transparent system of collecting and distributing royalties: The lack of clear distribution rules led to unscrupulous activities of CMOs regarding the identification of rightholders, a lack of public reporting and the problem of undistributed remuneration.[45] While much remains to be done, the legislative basis for positive change has already been laid. In addition to the obligation to implement and communicate a clear distribution scheme (and the prohibition to pay remuneration without or under circumvention of such a distribution scheme), Arts. 21 and 22 Law on CMOs also stipulate a payment deadline of no more than nine months after the end of the financial year. Separate distribution procedures are provided for reprography, private copying and cable retransmission, due to the specificity of the mandatory management of these rights. Distributions are made on the basis of percentages to authors, performers and phonogram producers. There is also a general procedure for identifying the rightholder for payments that imposes deadlines and includes methods. In case of failure to identify a rightholder and thus to pay the royalties designated to him or her, the related royalties are considered to be unclaimed money after three years and are to be transferred to the development of Ukrainian culture in accordance with the procedure established by the Cabinet of Ministers. Also, 25% of the revenue collected by the accredited organisation for reprographic reproduction and private copying is allocated to cultural development. Unfortunately, the Cabinet of Ministers has not yet adopted the procedure for transferring the revenue to benefit Ukrainian culture and since 2019 there is only a draft decree[46] that requires CMOs

---

[44] Ukrainian Commercial Court of Cassation of the Supreme Court, Decision 84634246 (2019) 910/6793/18, para 8.11.

[45] Oleksandr V Dem'yanenko, *White Book on Intellectual Property in the Innovative Economy of Ukraine, Volume 2* (Parliamentary Publishing 2008) 53–54.

[46] Ministry of Economy of Ukraine, 'Draft Cabinet of Ministers Decree on Approval of Procedures and Conditions for Transferring Funds by Collective Management Organisations to the State Institution Performing Special Functions to Promote the National and Cultural Development of Ukraine' (2019).

to transfer a part of the remuneration to the Ukrainian Cultural Foundation,[47] which itself determines how to use the funds received. The provision on transferring remuneration for the development of culture has been criticised by Oleksandr Kostiv as a compulsory transfer of private property to the state. In addition, doubts have been raised about the efficiency and transparency of the management of such sums by the Ukrainian Cultural Fund.[48] Some other Ukrainian researchers believe that the mechanism of compensation for reprographic reproduction is inconsistent with a democratic society, because it violates the property rights of the rightholder and is considered as "hidden nationalization", so it should be abolished.[49] Although the deadline for transferring the unclaimed funds has not yet expired and the actual collection of reproduction fees is blocked by the not-yet-approved tariffs, the procedure for transferring funds for the development of Ukrainian culture would bring additional certainty to the respective participants in this area.

Ukrainian legislation has for the first time provided sufficiently clear definitions of the fees which may be deducted by the organisation for various purposes, which are prescribed by law and statute.[50] Two types of fees are allowed: First, an administrative fee to cover the needs of the CMO and second, deductions for cultural, educational and social purposes. The amounts of the administrative fees and other deductions must be shown in the organisation's annual report. Article 20 Law on CMOs provides for several cases in which the CMO may withhold a limited amount from the remuneration collected as an administrative fee. The CMO is entitled to withhold no more than 20% of the collected remuneration in the event of a subsequent direct distribution of royalties to the rightholder, as is usually the case with voluntary collective management. In the case of remuneration through several CMOs, e.g. regarding mandatory collective management of cable retransmission rights, the total limit of the administrative fee is limited to 25%. In addition to the administrative fee, the Law on CMOs allows the CMO to deduct a 15% remuneration for cultural, social and educational services for its members and other rightholders. The amounts of administrative fees and other deductions should be shown in the organisation's annual report. These provisions aim at resolving the previous negative practice where the organisation itself determined the amount of fees without notifying the rightholders.

---

[47] The Ukrainian Cultural Foundation is a state institution established in 2017 under the relevant Ukrainian law to promote the development of national culture and art in the country. The Ukrainian Cultural Foundation supports projects on a competitive basis.

[48] Oleksandr Kostiv, 'Peculiarities of Collecting and Distributing Remuneration for Reproduction and Private Copying in Ukraine and EU Countries' Actual Problems of Law 4 (2019) 180 (185).

[49] Nadiia Moscaliuk, *Theoretical and Practical Issues of State Property Law and its Implementation* (2021) 8.

[50] Ukrainian Law on Effective Management of Holders' Economic Rights in the Sphere of Copyright and Related Rights 2018, 2415-VIII, art 21.

4 Outcomes and Perspectives of the Reform

Only three years after the beginning of the reform, some short-term positive effects of the reform can be named. From an overall national perspective, there has been a fulfilment of global international obligations to raise standards in the sphere of collective management of copyright and related rights under the EU–Ukraine Association Agreement, which has been repeatedly reported as significant progress in the harmonisation of Ukrainian law with European Union law.[51] At this point, it could be concluded that the reform of CMOs in Ukraine has brought general legislative framing solutions to various long-term internal problems in the field of collective management: In general the reform filled the lack of adequate legislative regulation, defined the principles of collective management consistent with EU approaches and increased transparency of collective management through the reporting obligation. Further, the reform led to a distinction between voluntary, mandatory and extended management in line with the general provisions of the corresponding EU directives, it introduced a withdrawal procedure of exclusive rights from collective management, fostered control over CMO activities through public reporting and an increase of the internal control by the rightholders as CMO members, established a negotiation procedure for tariff setting between users and CMOs and, finally, regulated the liquidation of the state CMO.

4.1 Implications of Implementation of the Law on CMOs

One outcome that is a problem is the very slow implementation of the Law on CMOs, which resulted in a failure to fulfil the obligation of users to pay royalties (for example, for the right to cable retransmission) and delayed the process of setting tariffs. Also, the use of modern technology in collective management, which is indicated in the legislation, would greatly simplify interaction processes and increase transparency. For instance, the Law on CMOs provides for the declaration of rights by the rightholder for the purpose of identifying works and objects of related rights. Such a procedure may be in the traditional written form, or it may be done electronically, through an electronic system of administration stipulated by Law. On the one hand, according to Art. 13 of the Law, declaration is made in accordance with the procedure established by the organisation itself; on the other hand, the Law on CMOs also envisages the creation of an electronic system of administration, which would allow rightholders and users to identify individual copyrights and related rights as

---

[51] In January 2020 the European Commission published a report on intellectual property rights that highlights developments in Ukraine, where it acknowledges as a positive development the adoption of the Law on CMOs. EU Neighbours East, 'EU Report on Intellectual Property Rights Highlights Developments in Ukraine' (13 January 2020) https://www.euneighbours.eu/en/east/stay-informed/news/eu-report-intellectual-property-rights-highlights-developments-ukraine accessed 11 September 2021.

well as to collect and distribute royalties in an automatic mode. However, at the time of writing this chapter, the practical implementation of this provision has not been carried out. It is reasonable to argue that an electronic administration system could solve the problems of non-transparent distribution and payment of remuneration and the representativeness of organisations for accreditation and simplify the identification of the amount of remuneration for a particular rightholder. All this extremely hinders the enhancement of protection and enforcement of copyright and related rights both from the national and the international point of view.[52]

Despite the generally positive role of the norms regarding the accreditation of CMOs for mandatory and extended collective management, the practice of application has (unfortunately) shown weaknesses in the new legislation: Evidence of this is the litigation concerning CMOs' accreditation and tariff-setting procedures. It has led to numerous proposals by Ukrainian Members of Parliament to amend the Law on CMOs. For the period of May–June 2021 only, six draft laws were submitted to the Ukrainian Parliament with proposals to change partially or almost completely certain provisions of the law on collective management.[53] Almost every one of them reflects different approaches in i.a. defining a monitoring body for CMOs, changing the accreditation procedure, or introducing the concept of cable retransmission. Some of these proposals are at least in part noteworthy as they could have a positive impact on collective management. Draft Law 5552, for example, proposes beneficial changes to the Law on CMOs by introducing an electronic system of registration of copyright and related rights, which would undoubtedly ensure transparency and efficiency of collective management.[54] Another draft law (5552-2) proposes to supplement the existing provisions on extended collective management with the right to remuneration for public demonstration and public broadcasting of music videos. Such an amendment appears excessive, as compensation to rightholders is already provided for within other spheres of extended collective management. A different payment procedure is also proposed for private copying and reprographical reproduction. It aims at circumventing traditional collective management organisations by directly authorising the Ukrainian Cultural Foundation to collect and distribute those royalties. However, under the provisions of Arts. 12 and 24, the Ukrainian Cultural Foundation will actually perform the functions of CMOs for collecting and distributing remuneration. Therefore, this provision requires further analysis and

[52] In April 2021 the European Commission published its Report on the protection and enforcement of intellectual property rights in third countries, in which Ukraine remains in Priority 2 along with Turkey, Russia and India Among other things, the Report points to the numerous problems in the field of collective management of copyright and related rights as a barrier to European investment.

[53] Six draft laws were submitted to the Parliament of Ukraine proposing changes to the collective management system: Ukrainian Draft Law on Effective Management of Property Rights of Copyright Holders in the Field of Copyright and Related Rights 2021, 5572; Ukrainian Draft Law on Copyright and Related Rights 2021, 5552; Ukrainian Alternative Draft law on Copyright and Related Rights 2021, 5552–1; Ukrainian Alternative Draft Law on Copyright and Related Rights 2021, 5552–2; Ukrainian Alternative Draft Law on Copyright and Related Rights 2021, 5552–3; and Ukrainian Alternative Draft Law on Copyright and Related Rights 2021, 5552–4.

[54] Ukrainian Draft Law on Copyright and Related Right 5552 of 24 May 2021, arts 12, 21.

revision.[55] Some of the proposals concern greater control of CMOs through various means, which could certainly benefit rightholders. Article 54 draft law on Copyright and Related Rights introduced by the Ministry of Economy proposes to recognise abusive behaviour of CMO officials that results in non-payment and improper distribution of royalties as a violation of copyright.[56] Such a diverse vision of collective management once again confirms the existence of gaps in the Law on CMOs and the great desire of the community to enact changes. At the same time, without a common compromise approach between CMOs, users and rightholders, this process will be endless, so any actions in the form of round tables and public discussions will be beneficial. On 15 December 2021, the Ukrainian Parliament adopted the Law "On Amendments to the Law of Ukraine on Effective Management of Property Rights of Copyright Holders and (or) Related Rights" registered under number 5572. This suggests the restart of CMO accreditation concerning the extended collective management in order to remove the situation from the long deadlock.

4.2 *Lack of a Common Perception of the Role of CMOs*

Sometimes the completely opposite perception of the role of CMOs by organisations and rightholders leads to disputes regarding the limits of protection of exclusive rights by the organisation in court. As previously mentioned, Art. 5 Law on CMOs defines good governance as the main principle, which primarily means the collection, distribution and payment of income arising from the rights of rightholders in the most expeditious, efficient and accurate manner. In essence, this constitutes the entire activity of the organisations in relation to the managed rights. However, CMOs often exceed the law by overstepping the rightholder's authority. An example of such practice can be seen in various attempts of some CMOs to claim payments in the form of damages for lost income based on rights that have never been transferred to them. The Ukrainian Commercial Court of Cassation of the Supreme Court commented negatively on this matter, stating that, in fact, CMOs are collectors of royalties and this money should not be considered as income of CMOs and therefore should not be considered as lost profits.[57]

For the purposes of balancing the interests of rightholders, represented by CMOs, and society, represented by producers and importers of equipment, it would be worthwhile to further analyse the concept of fair compensation in relation to private copying, taking into account the particularities of Ukrainian society. As a result, changes could be introduced to the list of exceptions to private copying, as well as in

---

[55] Ukrainian Draft Law on Copyright and Related Rights 5552–2 of 9 June 2021.

[56] Ministry of Economy of Ukraine, Draft Law on Copyright and Related Rights (10 March 2020) https://www.me.gov.ua/Documents/Detail?title=ProktZakonuUkrainiproAvtorskePravoISumizhniPrava accessed 27 September 2021.

[57] Ukrainian Commercial Court of Cassation of the Supreme Court, Decision 94393897 (2021) 904/951/20, para 6.

the approaches to the formation of tariffs for this category of rights. In this context, it would be possible to link the obligation of compensation for private copying to the potential harm to rightholders, taking into account the practice of the European Court of Justice discussed above. Moreover, recent proposed amendments to the Law on CMOs on the procedure for payment for private copying and reprography that would avoid CMOs support the need to rethink the role of the CMO in this matter for Ukraine.[58]

4.3 Perspectives for Dispute Resolution

The reform of the Law on CMOs has not been sufficiently communicated to the public and those affected by it. Thus, it is only known to a small circle of stakeholders, which has led in some cases to non-acceptance by users of the CMOs' remuneration claims provided for by the new law. The responsibility for insufficient information and public awareness-raising activities on the importance of collective management of copyright and related rights also rests with the CMOs themselves. After all, the role of CMOs is not only to collect and pay royalties, but also to enhance the role and value of the outcome of intellectual activity and exclusive rights to its rewards. The lack of understanding of the collective management mechanism and the non-acceptance of high tariffs for certain categories of rights (e.g. cable retransmission) is reflected in an increasing number of lawsuits (more than 150) by accredited CMOs against users, and counterclaims from users asking that the CMO's demand for payment of royalties be declared unlawful.[59] The current situation is not conducive to successful tariff-setting negotiations or to raising the value of the CMO for the industry as a whole. The problem of opposition to tariffs by users can be solved through the formation of tariffs, including temporary tariffs, in terms of economic reasonableness and compliance with economic indicators for a certain period, as well as in terms of the impact of such temporary tariffs on the economic activities of enterprises. This is actually what the Law on CMOs provides for in Art. 20. However, there is a question about the mechanism for forming such tariffs. The said law establishes only general eligibility criteria, as well as the procedure for setting tariffs through a negotiation procedure. The CMOs, when submitting tariffs for approval by the general assembly, could submit an independent economic justification with a transparent indication of the criteria that have been used. In addition, in the case of tariff setting by the court under Art. 20 Law on CMOs, the indicators in the economic study may help the court in its decision making, especially if the opposite party has submitted its own economic studies. However, it is more productive to set tariffs through negotiations,

[58] Ukrainian Draft Law on Copyright and Related Rights No. 5552–2 proposes to authorise the Ukrainian Cultural Foundation to collect and distribute royalties for private copying.

[59] Oksana Tchaikovska, 'How Providers Can Defend Themselves in Court Against CMO Lawsuits' *Detektor Media* (6 June 2021) https://detector.media/rinok/article/188852/2021-06-06-yak-provaynderam-zakhystytys-u-sudi-vid-pozoviv-oku/ accessed 20 July 2021.

even if it takes many rounds until the parties come to a compromise. Given the number of tariff disputes that currently block royalty payments, it is worth thinking about the ineffectiveness of the dispute resolution mechanism in this regard. In fact, if negotiations fail, the parties can only go to court. No other, e.g. alternative dispute resolution, procedures are provided for under Ukrainian law. Article 35 Collective Rights Management Directive provides for alternative dispute resolution between users and CMOs on proposed or existing contract conditions, meaning that parties involved in a dispute should have the possibility of easily accessible, efficient and impartial out-of-court procedures, such as mediation or arbitration, for resolving conflicts.[60] The experience of implementation of the Collective Rights Management Directive by EU countries could be useful in this respect. For example, in Germany the Arbitration Board of the German Patent and Trade Mark Office is authorised to solve tariff disputes under the Law on Collective Management Organisations.[61] This body mediates disputes, which may be followed by settlement agreement, which is binding for the parties if not contested. If no agreement can be reached through the Arbitration Board, the parties can go to court. This experience could also be taken into account in the development of the Ukrainian alternative dispute resolution model for disputes between CMOs, CMOs and users, and CMOs and rightholders.

Much remains to be done, but one thing is certain—at the end of the day, Ukraine will have an effective system of collective management for the benefit of creators and rightholders.

References

Better Regulation Delivery Office, 'Prices of Laptops and Phones May be Reduced' (21 April 2017) https://brdo.com.ua/top/tsina-na-noutbuky-telefony-mozhe-znyzytysya

Oleksandr Bulayenko, 'Permissibility of Non-Voluntary Collective Management of Copyright under EU Law—The Case of the French Law on Out-of-Commerce Books', (2016) 7 JIPITEC 51

CAMR, '100 Lawsuits, 100 Contracts—Ukrainian Providers Started Paying Royalties for Copyright and Related Rights' (16 July 2021) http://camr.org.ua/?p=292

Oleksandr Dem'yanenko, *White Book-2, Intellectual Property in the Innovative Economy of Ukraine (Parliament Publications 2008) [Олександр Дем'яненко, 'Біла Книга-2, Інтелектуальна Власність в Інноваційній Економіці України* (Парламентське Видавництво 2008)]

European Banking Authority, 'Tax on Equipment: Business Urges to Establish an Anti-Crisis Working Group to Build a Transparent System of Copyright Fees' (19 June 2020) https://eba.com.ua/en/podatok-na-tehniku-biznes-zaklykaye-stvoryty-antykryzovu-robochu-grupu-dlya-pobudovy-prozoroyi-systemy-vidrahuvan-za-avtorskyj-kontent/

Mihály Ficsor, *Collective Management of Copyright and Related Rights at a Triple Crossroads: Should it Remain Voluntary or May it Be "Extended" or Made Mandatory?* (UNESCO Copyright Bulletin 2003)

---

[60] Daniel Gervais, *Collective Management of Copyright and Related Rights* (Wolters Kluwer 2015) 536 (157).

[61] German Law on Collective Management Organisations 2016, sec 92.

Daniel J Gervais, 'The Economics of Collective Management' in Ben Depoorter & Peter S Menell (eds), *Research Handbook on the Economics of Intellectual Property Law, volume 1* (Edward Elgar 2019), 495

Daniel Gervais, *Collective Management of Copyright and Related Rights* (Wolters Kluwer 2015)

Sergiy Kane, 'Ukrainian Music Market: 7 Key Studies' *LB.UA* https://lb.ua/culture/2020/10/20/468513_muzichniy_rinok_ukraini_7_klyuchovih.html

Yuriy Kapitsa, Sergiy Stupak and Oleksandr Juvaka, *Copyright and Related Rights in Europe* (Logos 2012) 311 [Юрій Капіца, Сергій Ступак, Олександр Жувака, *Авторське Право і Суміжні Права в Європі* (Логос 2012)]

Oleksandr Kostiv, 'Peculiarities of Collecting and Distributing of Remuneration for Reproduction and Private Copying in Ukraine and EU countries' (2019) 4 Actual Problems of Law 180 [Олександр Костів, 'Особливості Збору та Розподілу Винагороди за Репрографічне Відтворення Творів і Приватне Копіювання в Україні та Країнах ЄС' (2019) 4 Актуальні Проблеми Права 180]

Liubov Maidanyk, *Collective Management of Copyright and Related Rights under Civil Law of Ukraine* (Alerta 2013) [Любов Майданик, *Колективне Управління Майновими Авторськими і Суміжними Правами за Цивільним Законодавством України* (Алерта, 2013)]

Nadiia Moscaliuk, *Theoretical and Practical Issues of State Property Law and its Implementation* (2021) [Надія Москалюк, *Теоретичні та Практичні Проблеми Права Державної Власності та його Реалізації* (2021)]

Office of the United States Trade Representative, '2017 Special 301 Report' (Report) USTR (2017)

Leonid Tarasenko, 'Innovations in the Exercise of Collective Management of Copyright and Related Rights' (2019) 33 Journal of Civil Studies 55 [Леонід Тарасенко 'Новації Щодо Здійснення Колективного Управління Майновими Авторськими та Суміжними Правами' (2019) 33 Часопис цивілістики, 55]

Oksana Tchaikovska, 'How Providers can Defend Themselves in Court Against CMO Lawsuits' *Detektormedia* (6 June 2021) https://detector.media/rinok/art/188852/2021-06-06-yak-provayderam-zakhystytys-u-sudi-vid-pozoviv-oku/ [Оксана Чайковська 'Як Провайдерам Захиститись у Суді від Позовів ОКУ' *Detektormedia* (6 червня 2021)]

Oleksandra Yavorska, 'Management of Copyright and Related Rights Subjects' (2016) 7 Entrepreneurship, Economy and Law 26 [Олександра Яворська, 'Управління Майновими Правами Суб'єктів Авторського Права і Суміжних Прав' (2016) 7 Підприємництво, Господарство і Право 26]